THE SOUTHWEST:
Old and New

THE Southwest:
OLD AND NEW

by W. Eugene Hollon

A BISON BOOK

University of Nebraska Press · Lincoln

Copyright © 1961 by W. Eugene Hollon
All rights reserved
Library of Congress Catalog Card Number 61-9232
Manufactured in the United States of America

First Bison Book printing: 1968

Bison Book edition reproduced from the first edition by arrangement with Alfred A. Knopf, Inc.

To Walter Prescott Webb

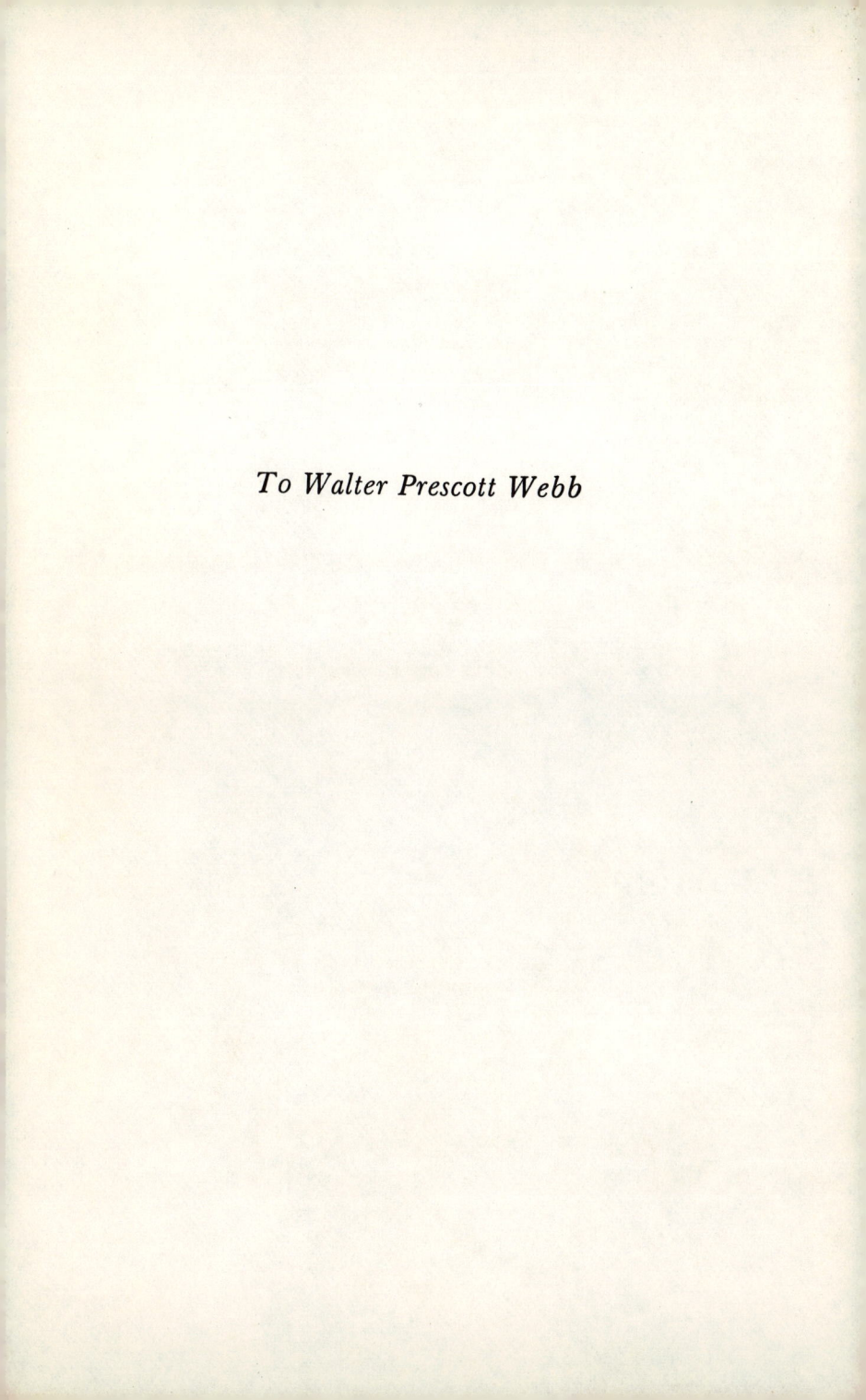

FOREWORD

When *The Southwest: Old and New* first appeared in 1961, its dust jacket had a Terry Hill photograph of author W. Eugene Hollon that was dramatic and thoughtful. Semiprofile, it showed Hollon, chin on fist, looking meditatively into that blankness lying beyond the limits of the photographer's space. What particularly struck me about the photograph was, and still is, the fact that though I had known Gene Hollon for a score of years and we had supped and traveled and complained and politicked together all those years, I suddenly realized that I had underestimated him all this time. I had seen him so long as one of the rare men of action in the historical profession and at the same time as an almost typical Southwesterner, if there is such a creature, that I had not perceived how deeply he had probed into the problems of his region and how profoundly he understood so many of them.

The Southwest: Old and New was Hollon's first really thoughtful, suggestive book. The others had been biographies, with an overlay of regional geography and travel. They were good books, destined to find their way into the continuing bibliographies of authors working in the materials of the West and Southwest, but in none of them did Hollon have to stick out his neck.

With *The Southwest: Old and New*, however, Hollon indeed placed his opinions and perceptions on a line where men of strong opinion could get at him. Naturally he got his neck chopped, but never severed. And having lived with danger, he has come back with still another undertaking entitled *The Great American Desert:*

The Southwest: *Old and New*

Then and Now. Like James Bond, he seems to be stimulated by danger.

A good portion of *The Southwest: Old and New* is hung on a frame of reasonably narrative history. No one faulted him here, although even in the straightforward chapters he injected enough of his liberal views to annoy some local readers and reviewers. He is dead right when he writes "As long as one avoids the subject of the 'New Deal' the Southwestern rancher is a pleasant individual to know," but many Southwesterners would argue that Hollon must be soft if he suggests that one can be pleasant in the presence of a New Deal that apparently has come to stay. To their way of thinking, God deserted the Southwest not when barbed wire came in but rather when he let "That Man" into the White House.

It is in the later chapters, however, that Hollon goes to work with sympathetic incision on his patient. If he plays rough, it is because he has grown up with the problems and has spent his adult life fighting and inveighing against what he calls "the public's apathy." He feels strongly that too many progressive measures aimed at ameliorating the problems of the region "are stymied by fights between politicians and special interests," and then he goes on to specify "the politicians and the special interests." Such hard-hitting strictures, though they may draw praise from political and economic nondescripts like me, are hardly calculated to bring a warm surge of pride in the breasts of his more concerned readers. Hollon is forthright in expressing his regret that the Southwest, with a liberal tradition which had "eagerly embraced most reforms advocated by Populists, Progressives, and New Dealers," should see its burgeoning growth and wealth lead it into

> an abrupt turn to the political right, marked by a violent reaction against the New Deal and increased conservatism on the part of metropolitan newspapers. Opposition to various liberal ideas came chiefly from farmers and ranchers who desired government handouts without federal control, manufacturers who objected to the forty-hour week and so-called "coddling of labor unions," exploiters of natural resources who

Foreword

opposed federal conservation practices, racial bigots who considered Mrs. Roosevelt a "nigger lover," anti-intellectuals who distrusted government experts, and the *nouveaux riches* who complained with increasing bitterness as they moved into higher income-tax brackets.

He shows the fallibility of Arizonans who want federally financed dams but who reject the principle of federal subsidies, as well as of San Antonians who preen themselves on the beauties of La Villita and the San Antonio River at the same time they throw out the mayor, Maury Maverick, who made possible the modern look of such beauties, because he seems to approve of government spending.

But Hollon is optimistic. Like a good liberal he believes that people can improve, and he thinks the Southwest has a real future if it will only face up to it. On the other hand, he is gloomy about the dimming of the distinctive qualities of the Southwest as it moves into the mainstream of the nation. My guess is that he liked it better when it was ornery and apart, and when he had even more to fight about than he does today.

Now all that is left for W. Eugene Hollon is to live up to that Terry Hill photograph, quit being so everlastingly active in trying to upgrade his region, and become the thoughtful philosopher-sage who keeps a vigilant, critical, and avuncular eye on the Southwest, both old and new, that he knows so intimately.

JOE B. FRANTZ

University of Texas

PREFACE

THIS BOOK attempts to cover various aspects of the social, political, and cultural history of the American Southwest from the early cliff dwellers to the present. In limiting the region to the four states of Texas, Oklahoma, New Mexico, and Arizona, I have labored at times under considerable handicaps. Even though people tend to think in terms of artificial boundaries, no combination of states has an extensive set of characteristics peculiarly its own.

The absence of bordering states, especially California, from the study necessarily leaves some obvious gaps. Yet certain arbitrary limits have to be imposed on any regional study; otherwise its history might never be completed.

Few agree on the boundaries of the Southwest, for the term means different geographic areas to different people. Some even deny that a Southwest exists, yet they accept the actuality of a South, a Northeast, a Pacific Northwest, or a Middle West. But the Southwest is just as real as any of the above regions, and it is no mere state of mind. Also, its history is no more relative nor less relative to its surroundings than that of any other region, state, or nation.

While emphasizing the common characteristics, problems, and traditions of the Southwest, I have not been oblivious to the fact that many of these are apropos to the rest of the United States. Whatever its shortcomings, therefore, this book is forced to stand on my own acceptance of the Southwest. Regardless of what states I failed to include, incongruities would still exist.

The Southwest: *Old and New*

Some readers will find the early chapters on geography and Indians a bit tedious. But both subjects are complex and diverse and so much a part of some larger things that a certain amount of encyclopedic treatment and cataloguing of data is almost inevitable. The alternative is superficiality.

Perhaps more attention should have been given to certain elements of consequence to the Southwest. The railroads, the tourists, and the health seekers, for example, have been and are extremely important in the political, social, and economic history of the area, and each is worthy of a separate chapter. But it is obviously impossible to present in a single volume a detailed account of every important facet of several hundred years of regional history.

I have spent all my life in the Southwest, taught at colleges and universities in Texas, Oklahoma, and New Mexico for twenty years, and traveled extensively in Arizona. For the past fifteen years I have taught a graduate course on Southwestern history at the University of Oklahoma. The writing of this book was begun in 1955, and would have been completed earlier except for heavy teaching duties and a year's interlude in Peru.

The Graduate Research Council at the University of Oklahoma provided funds for special travel and for typing the final draft of the manuscript. I wish especially to thank Dr. Duane Roller, Chairman of the above committee, and his efficient secretary, Mrs. Joyce Ospovat. Mrs. Jo Soukup typed the preliminary drafts of the manuscript, while Mrs. Ospovat did the publisher's copy.

Miss Jane Howe of Norman, Oklahoma, checked the citations, corrected many errors of spelling, and eliminated some of the obvious faults in syntax. Dr. John Caughey, an authority on the Southwest and editor of the *Pacific Coast Historical Review*, also read the entire manuscript and offered expert criticism that proved most beneficial. In addition, I am deeply appreciative of the advice and help given by Dr. Walter Johnson, Chairman of the Department of History, University of Chicago, who read the first fifteen chapters. Dr. Johnson helped launch the project and offered valuable suggestions as to its scope and content.

Preface

Dr. Nelson Peach, Chairman of the Department of Economics, University of Oklahoma, read the chapter on the industrial boom in the Southwest and evaluated my observations and conclusions. He also prepared the charts and graphs that supplement the narrative of this chapter. Dr. Gilbert Fite, Research Professor of History at the University of Oklahoma, checked the material on agriculture and water, and also offered suggestions on the chapters dealing with politics and politicians. Dr. Walter Prescott Webb, Emeritus Professor of History at the University of Texas, rendered a critique on the "Desert and Oasis" chapter.

Members of the University of Oklahoma Library staff who assisted beyond the call of duty are Dr. Arrell M. Gibson, Jack Haley, Arthur Long, Mrs. Sandra Stewart, and Miss Opal Carr. I am especially grateful to the Manuscripts Division for collecting many of the photographs used for illustrations. Others who co-operated in this respect are Mr. Raymond Carlson, Editor, *Arizona Highways*, Phoenix; Mr. Fred W. Phelps, Director of New Mexico Department of Development; Dr. Joe Frantz, Chairman, History Department, University of Texas; Mr. Wayne Mauzy, Museum of New Mexico; Mrs. J. P. Moore, Arizona Pioneers' Historical Society; Dr. Seymour Connor, Texas Technological College; and Dr. Elmer Fraker, Director, Oklahoma Historical Society.

The secretaries and research directors of the chambers of commerce of all the important Southwestern cities were generous in supplying statistical information and excellent photographs. Southwesterners who submitted to interviews and answered specific questions are numerous, but special notice should be given to Mr. Orme Lewis and Mr. Herbert Leggett of Phoenix, Mayor Don Hummel and Dr. John Alexander Carroll of Tucson, Mr. Everett Grantham of Albuquerque, and Mr. Will Harrison of Santa Fe, and Mr. Carl Hertzog, Dr. C. L. Sonnichsen, and Dr. Rex Strickland of El Paso. No one could have asked for more co-operation, patience, and personal interest than I have received from my publisher, Alfred A. Knopf. Errors that inadvertently appear are my own responsibility.

W. Eugene Hollon

Norman, Oklahoma

CONTENTS

I ·	THE LAND OF CONTRAST	3
II ·	BEFORE THE WHITE MAN	22
III ·	FIRST CAME THE SPANIARDS	44
IV ·	APPROACH AND RETREAT OF THE FRENCH	67
V ·	ANGLO-AMERICANS COME TO STAY	86
VI ·	THE CLASH OF CIVILIZATIONS	107
VII ·	LIFE AND CULTURE IN THE TEXAS REPUBLIC	131
VIII ·	THE MEXICAN CESSION	152
IX ·	THE IMPACT OF GOLD ON THE SOUTHWEST	175
X ·	COACHES AND CAMELS	196
XI ·	THE SOUTHWEST AND THE CIVIL WAR	218
XII ·	LONGHORNS AND WOOLLIES	242
XIII ·	COMPLETION OF STATEHOOD	268
XIV ·	THE CHANGING INDIAN	290
XV ·	DESERT AND OASIS	312
XVI ·	THE BIG INDUSTRIAL BOOM	334
XVII ·	POLITICS AND POLITICIANS: TEXAS AND OKLAHOMA	360
XVIII ·	POLITICS AND POLITICIANS: NEW MEXICO AND ARIZONA	390
XIX ·	MONEY AND BRAINS	413
XX ·	CITIES AND CULTURE	438
·	*Bibliographical Notes*	465
·	*Index*	*follows page* 487

ILLUSTRATIONS

		FOLLOWING PAGE
1a ·	Kit Carson home, Taos, New Mexico. (*Courtesy Museum of New Mexico*)	142
1b ·	Zebulon Montgomery Pike. (*Courtesy University of Oklahoma Press*)	142
2a ·	The Battle of Resaca de la Palma. (*Courtesy National Archives*)	142
2b ·	The Battle of Palo Alto. (*Courtesy National Archives*)	142
3a ·	Stephen F. Austin. (*Courtesy The University of Texas Library*)	142
3b ·	Sam Houston. (*Courtesy University of Oklahoma Press*)	142
4 ·	The Alamo. (*Courtesy San Antonio Chamber of Commerce*)	142
5a ·	Santa Fe, New Mexico, in the late 1860's. (*Courtesy Museum of New Mexico*)	142
5b ·	Albuquerque, New Mexico, approximately 1890. (*Courtesy Museum of New Mexico*)	142
6a ·	Guthrie, Oklahoma, three weeks after first opening in 1889. (*From the A. P. Swearington Collection, University of Oklahoma Library*)	142
6b ·	Oklahoma City—one month after the opening in 1889. (*Courtesy University of Oklahoma Library*)	142
7 ·	The great Silver King mine. (*Courtesy Pioneers' Historical Society of Arizona*)	142
8 ·	Old City Hall in Tombstone, Arizona. (*Courtesy Arizona Highways*)	142

Illustrations

9a ·	Roundup on the open range. (*From the A. A. Forbes Collection, University of Oklahoma Library*)	270
9b ·	Waiting for the Cherokee Strip opening. (*From the Frank Phillips Collection, University of Oklahoma Library*)	270
10a ·	Early settler in the Cherokee Strip. (*From the Fred Wenner Collection, University of Oklahoma Library*)	270
10b ·	Arapaho Indian camp. (*Courtesy University of Oklahoma Library*)	270
11 ·	South rim of the Grand Canyon. (*Courtesy* Arizona Highways)	270
12a ·	Giant Saguaros. (*Courtesy* Arizona Highways)	270
12b ·	Montezuma Castle. (*Courtesy* Arizona Highways)	270
13 ·	San Xavier del Bac Mission. (*Courtesy* Arizona Highways)	270
14 ·	The Enchanted Mesa. (*Courtesy New Mexico State Tourist Bureau*)	270
15a ·	Petrified Forest. (*Courtesy* Arizona Highways)	270
15b ·	Canyon de Chelly. (*Courtesy* Arizona Highways)	270
16a ·	In the heart of the Dust Bowl. (*Courtesy University of Oklahoma Library*)	270
16b ·	Oil derrick and pump. (*Courtesy Standard Oil Company*)	270
17 ·	Laying an 18-inch pipeline. (*Courtesy Standard Oil Company*)	366
18a ·	Refinery at Baytown, Texas. (*Courtesy Humble Oil and Refining Company*)	366
18b ·	Open-pit Jackpile uranium mine. (*Courtesy The Anaconda Company*)	366
19 ·	Roosevelt Dam. (*Courtesy* Arizona Highways)	366
20a ·	Navajo Indian sand painters. (*Courtesy* Arizona Highways)	366
20b ·	Navajo Indian rug weaver. (*Courtesy* Arizona Highways)	366
21a ·	Cattle branding. (*Courtesy* The Cattleman)	366

Illustrations

21*b* · Sheep ranch. (*Courtesy* Arizona Highways) 366
22 · Modern Phoenix. (*Courtesy Phoenix Chamber of Commerce*) 366
23*a* · Houston. (*Courtesy Houston Chamber of Commerce*) 366
23*b* · Dallas. (*Courtesy Dallas Chamber of Commerce*) 366
24 · Oklahoma's State Capitol. (*Courtesy Oklahoma City Chamber of Commerce*) 366

MAPS

1 · Physiographic Regions of the Southwest xx
2 · Principal Rivers and Cities of the Southwest xxi

PHYSIOGRAPHIC REGIONS
OF
THE SOUTHWEST

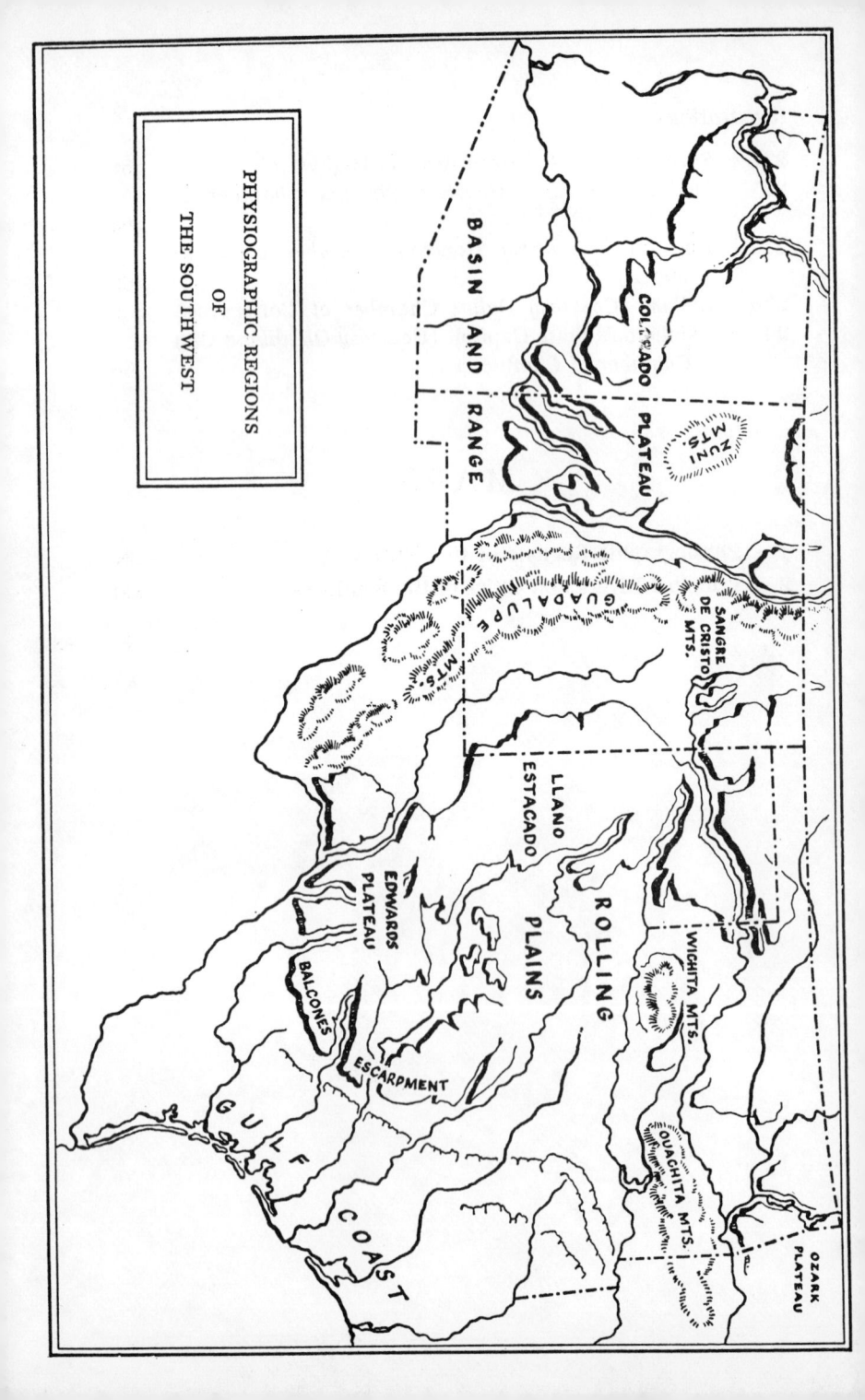

PRINCIPAL RIVERS
AND CITIES
OF THE SOUTHWEST

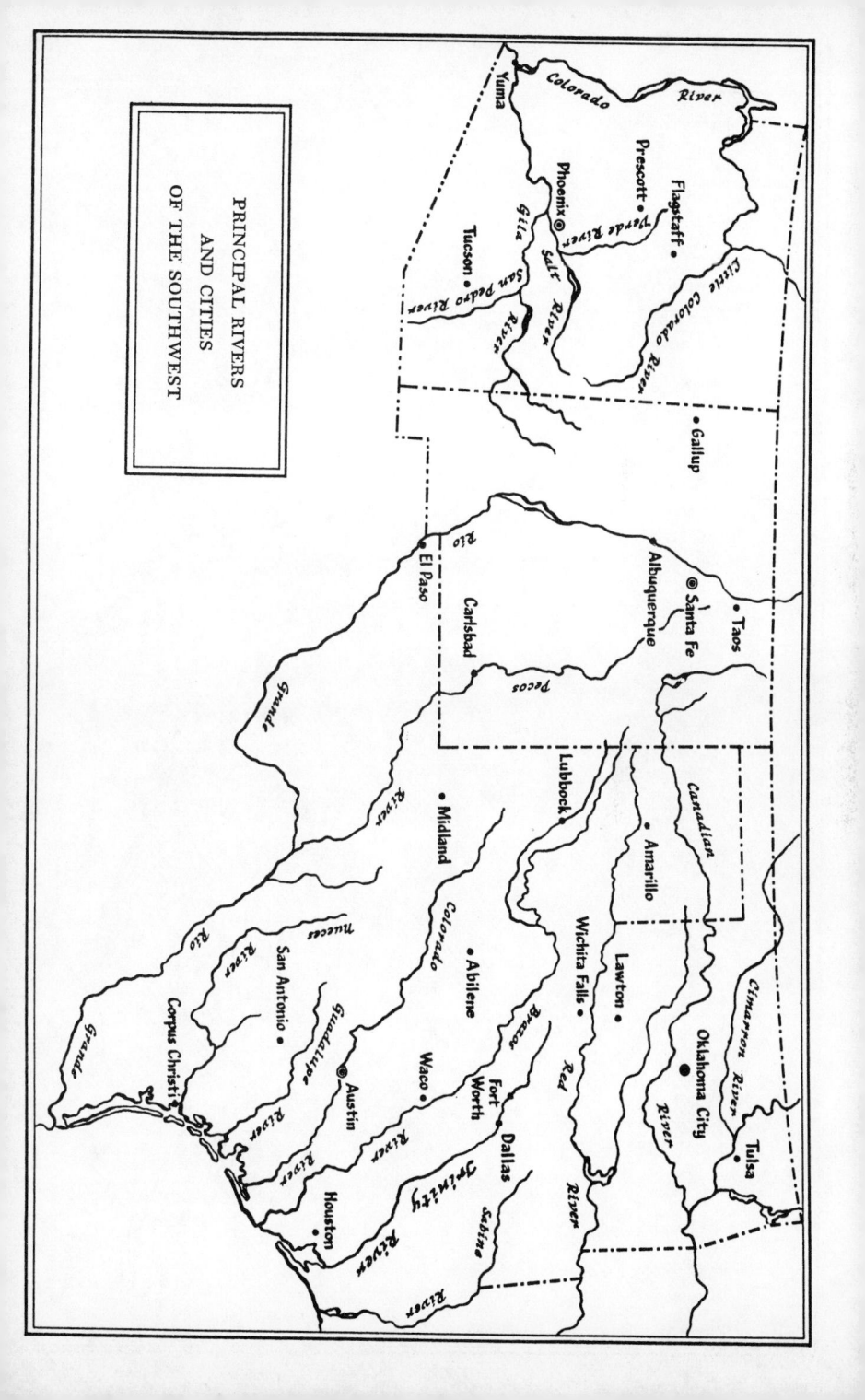

THE SOUTHWEST:
Old and New

I

LAND OF CONTRAST

Everyone has his own definition of the Southwest. The more one tries to limit and define it, the more elusive the area becomes. For every common characteristic, two or three very uncommon ones crop up to make the exceptions overshadow the general rule. History does not help much either.

Before 1803 "the Southwest" meant the region south of the Ohio River, east of the Mississippi River, and west of the Appalachian Mountains. In other words, the present states of Kentucky, Tennessee, Mississippi, and Alabama.

The purchase of the Louisiana Territory shifted the center of

THE SOUTHWEST: *Old and New*

the Southwest to New Orleans and added the present states of Louisiana, Arkansas, Missouri, and parts of Oklahoma, Kansas, and Colorado. The annexation of Texas in 1845 altered the concept of the Southwest still further, and the Mexican Cession three years later changed the meaning of the term completely. Geometrically, the Southwest today is that area of the United States where South and West overlap, or the lower left-hand quarter of the nation. This is the region below the 40th parallel and west of the 98th meridian, or most of the present states of Texas, Oklahoma, Kansas, Colorado, New Mexico, Utah, Arizona, Nevada, and California.

Although the historian refers to this area as the Greater Southwest, the geographer recognizes no strict artificial boundaries. Indeed, he refuses to identify the Southwest as a region at all. A geographic region must possess common economic and physical characteristics. Since the Southwestern portion of the United States contains a great diversity of both, one has to look elsewhere to establish it as a region that merits examination and analysis.

The broadest concept of the Southwest is the geometric one which Richardson and Rister use in their work *The Greater Southwest*. They extend the area to that part of the United States west of the eastern border of the Great Plains, about the 98th meridian, and south of the northern boundaries of states extending from Kansas to California. Walter Campbell, the Southwestern author who wrote under the pen name Stanley Vestal, restricted the Southwest to western Texas, the western half of Oklahoma, New Mexico, and those parts of Colorado "which are definitely Southwestern in background and outlook." J. Frank Dobie rarely ranges beyond Texas and New Mexico in his writings and references to the Southwest. E. E. Dale, another well-known authority associated with the Southwest, confines his study of *Indians of the Southwest* to the aborigines of New Mexico, Arizona, Utah, and Nevada.

Still another concept of the Southwest is that used by Erna Fergusson. In her book *Our Southwest* she uniquely bounds the area in this manner: the land lying north of a route from San An-

I · *Land of Contrast*

tonio to Los Angeles, "the highways best suited to winter travel," and south of a line extending east from Los Angeles to Fort Worth, "the highways best suited for summer travel." And according to the editors of *Look,* in their regional volumes on America, the Southwest consists of the states of Texas, Oklahoma, New Mexico, and Arizona.[1]

Is it a political area? The Southwestern historian John Caughey says "No." There is no intermediate between the Southwestern states and the nation, he points out, "nor has there been such a unit since the brief appearance of the Comandancia General de las Provincias Internas of the seventeen-seventies and eighties." Furthermore, Caughey observes, it has produced no political spokesman in behalf of its peculiar interests. No single newspaper speaks for the entire area, nor does it have a common literature. It is neither South nor West, yet it partakes of both. Most important, it has never been embattled as was the South. The Indian, Spanish-American, or Anglo-American of New Mexico feels no instinctive rapport with the sandy-land farmers east of the Cross Timbers or with the sheepherders in the Arizona desert. The transplanted Yankee who raises citrus fruit in the Lower Rio Grande Valley in Texas has as much in common with the lead and zinc miner of Northeastern Oklahoma, or the uranium prospector of northern New Mexico and Arizona, as an Indian medicine man has with a Fifth Avenue debutante.

What, then, is the Southwest? Is it merely a state of mind? Or is it a region set apart by characteristics uniquely its own? Before attempting an answer, perhaps it would be well to establish the boundaries of the Southwest in respect to this particular study. A history of any region must restrict its geographic scope or else risk being out of focus. Yet any grouping of states into a rigidly bounded section immediately reveals all sorts of geographic, historic, intellectual, and economic incongruities. Be that as it may,

---

[1] On the other hand, the *Southwestern Historical Quarterly,* published at Austin, Texas, has for sixty years devoted most of its space to articles almost exclusively relating to Texas history.

The Southwest: *Old and New*

the term "Southwest" as hereinafter used refers only to the four large states of Texas, Oklahoma, New Mexico, and Arizona.

The region—to a degree—is a state of mind. One frequently hears the expression "I'm a Texan" or "I'm an Oklahoman." But "I'm a Southwesterner" is rare. Yet what Texan, Oklahoman, New Mexican, or Arizonan would not stoutly defend his right to be called a Southwesterner?

Perhaps no single word can describe the Southwest better than "contrast." Indeed, its great variety of climate, topography, industry, language, and people constitutes one of its most characteristic qualities. For the most part the climate is sub-humid, although every type may be found between the sea-level coastal region of Texas and the towering mountain ranges of New Mexico and Arizona. Flora and fauna vary from subtropical to subarctic. At least three fourths of the Indians surviving in the United States reside in present-day Oklahoma, New Mexico, and Arizona. An even larger proportion of Spanish-Americans is scattered through southern Texas, New Mexico, and Arizona. Oklahoma was settled by people from almost every state in the Union, and Texas attracted emigrants from the United States and practically every country of western Europe. In Taos, Santa Fe, Albuquerque, Phoenix, and every other large city in the Southwest the natives have long since become a minority. Tourists, prospectors, artists, health seekers, and company men have swarmed from all directions to make these places veritable melting pots.

The blood of Anglo-Saxons courses through the veins of more than two thirds of the population, yet practically all Southwestern rivers and mountains, except in Oklahoma, bear Spanish names. The architecture still retains a strong Spanish flavor in the ranch-style house that continues to be more popular than the conventional "Cape Cod" or even the modern "outside-inside" structure of the Frank Lloyd Wright school. All of the Southwest was once owned and ruled by the Spaniards and, except for Oklahoma, by the Mexicans. Laws pertaining to landholdings, marital relations, property rights of married women, and the system of pleading and procedure are more Spanish than English. And land surveys

I · *Land of Contrast*

throughout Texas, New Mexico, and Arizona were originally based on the league (4,439 acres) and labor (177 acres), rather than on the section and township.

Likewise, the Southwest can claim to be America's last frontier as well as the seat of its oldest settlements. The Pueblo Indians of the Upper Rio Grande Valley were living in villages and irrigating fields of corn, beans, melons, and squash long before 1492. The name "New Mexico" is older than that of any other state except Florida, though it, like Arizona and Oklahoma, was among the last to be admitted to the Union. Nowhere is the "spirit of the frontier" more apparent today than in the Southwest. And perhaps it is this paradoxical combination of youthful exuberance and age which sets the Southwest apart. Centuries of sedentary life overlay the region with a certain dignity and refinement, while its newness sometimes makes it crude and overly aggressive.

To some, the Southwest is the place where "you get that first clear breath of high, dry air." To others it is a region that you drive through as quickly as possible. A tourist recently commented that he always knew he had reached the Southwest whenever the bugs obliterated his windshield. One writer facetiously described the region as a "geographic hemorrhage." And, of course, who has not heard the old saw about the Southwest having "more rivers and less water, more cows and less milk, where one can travel farther and see less than in any other part of the world." Practically all agree that it is a land of extremes—of tall men and taller tales, of wide open spaces and plenty of sunshine and cactus but little rain, and of extremes of wealth and poverty—all as obvious as those found in the climate and geography.

The relentless hand of nature has fashioned the people of the Southwest into a special breed that, despite droughts, floods, dust, storms, tornadoes, and crop-killing freezes, has managed to retain unlimited optimism and enterprise. Erna Fergusson described the phenomenon in these words: "The arid Southwest has always been too strong, too indomitable for most people. Those who can stand it have had to learn that man does not modify this country; it transforms him, deeply. Perhaps our generation will come to appreciate it as the country God remembered and saved for man's delight when he could mature enough to understand it. God armored it, as the migrating Easterner learned in his anguish, with thorns on the trees, stings and horns on the bugs and beasts. He fortified it with mountain ranges and trackless deserts. He filled it with such hazards as no legendary hero ever had to surmount. The Southwest can never be remade into a landscape that produces bread and butter. But it is infinitely productive of the imponderables so much needed by a world weary of getting and spending. It is a wilderness where a man may get back to the essentials of being a man. It is magnificence forever rewarding to a man courageous enough to seek to renew his soul." [2]

Except in the wooded area of eastern Oklahoma and Texas, the Anglo-American pioneer found the Southwest a perplexing country to which he could not easily adapt his former institutions and cultural complexities. Walter Prescott Webb convincingly demonstrated in *The Great Plains* that the climate and geography of the region beyond the 98th meridian, wherein lies much of our Southwest, have influenced institutions in a most singular manner and modified them to fit the local environment. An examination of the climate and geography is necessary, therefore, before the institutions can be adequately understood.

It would be easier to describe the geography of the Southwest and make generalizations about its topography, climate, and plant life if it included a north-south rather than an east-west collection of states. Combinations of states limited on east and west by mountain ranges or great rivers show more uniform characteristics. The subject of Webb's monumental study was bounded not by rigid state lines but by natural geographic features. Thus, what he said about any segment of the Great Plains applied to all of the region. Not so in our four Southwestern states, where five general geographic provinces meet.

The first of these, the Coastal Plains, extends from the Atlantic Coast through the Southern states into Texas and the south-

---

[2] Erna Fergusson: *Our Southwest* (New York: Alfred A. Knopf; 1952), pp. 18–19.

I · *Land of Contrast*

east corner of Oklahoma as far west as Balcones scarp and the Cross Timbers. The Great Plains sweep down from Canada to engulf most of Oklahoma, western Texas, and eastern New Mexico. The Southern Rockies lap over into north-central New Mexico, then disappear into the desert around Albuquerque. All of Arizona, the southern half of New Mexico, and a corner of southwestern Texas lie within the great Intermontaine Province, more commonly called the Basin and Range Province. The fifth geographic region that protrudes into the Southwest is the small Interior Highlands Province of southern Missouri, northwestern Arkansas, and eastern Oklahoma. This woody, hilly region barely overlaps into Oklahoma and is the least southwestern of the five.

Although similarities can easily be found among all these regions, each is distinctive—either because of or in spite of climate and geography. The Coastal Plains area, for example, is low and flat, containing more vegetation, people, water, industry, and agricultural productivity than any single section of the Southwest, possibly more than all sections taken together. Its western boundary is marked by the Balcones fault scarp and the Eastern Cross Timbers of northeastern Texas. This scarp, which rises several hundred feet above the Coastal Plains, is the dividing line between the sub-humid east and the semi-arid plains of western Texas and Oklahoma and eastern New Mexico. It follows a course in Texas extending east of Del Rio to San Antonio and north through Austin to the vicinity of Waco. From there into southern Oklahoma the fault line becomes faint, and the Eastern Cross Timbers—formerly a strip of scrub oak and dwarf timber extending from the Brazos River north through the center of Oklahoma into southern Kansas—round out the northwestern corner of the Coastal Plains area. The extreme southeastern portion of Oklahoma along Red River is also a part of the region.

From the Balcones scarp at the western tip of the Coastal Plains the land slopes toward the Gulf of Mexico at an average rate of two to three feet per mile. This is the section of the Southwest most recently under the sea; thus, the sedimentary rocks near its surface are among the youngest in North America. Large rivers such as the Red, Trinity, Brazos, Colorado, and Rio Grande have cut wide valleys across the vast slope and inadvertently brought down rich sediments from the High Plains into the bottom lands. Because of this the Coastal Plains contain many types of soil: black waxy in the northwest, gray, sandy soils with red or yellow clay beneath in the timber country of northeastern Texas and southwestern Oklahoma, clay or gray sand along the Gulf Coast, and fertile sandy and loamy soils in the Rio Grande Plains of southern Texas.

Rainfall in the Coastal Plains also varies. It is heaviest along the eastern part of the coast, ranging from approximately fifty inches annually at Houston to twenty-five inches at Corpus Christi. Since the coastal land is only a few feet above sea level, drainage is frequently poor and swamps are common. Farther north in eastern Texas and southeastern Oklahoma the rainfall continues heavy, averaging about forty-five to thirty inches from east to west. There is less rain in the southern portion of the Coastal Plains, the section lying south of a line drawn from Corpus Christi through San Antonio to Del Rio. Only fifteen or twenty inches fall here during an average year. But irrigation in the Winter Garden section of southern Texas and the Lower Rio Grande Valley corrects this deficiency. Parts of the semi-desert region have been converted into some of the most valuable agricultural land in the world.

Much of the Coastal Plains suffers from too much rainfall rather than from too little. Paradoxically, the same region may experience droughts of several weeks or even months. But whether there is too much moisture or none at all, crops often become victims of nature's erratic behavior. Snow is rare, but killing frosts sometimes reach as far south as the Lower Rio Grande Valley. In the late summer and early autumn the coastal area is subject to the hazard of infrequent hurricanes. Fortunately for this heavily populated section of the Southwest, spring tornadoes are not so common as in the Great Plains region.

The warmest part of the Coastal Plains is the Lower Rio Grande Valley, with an annual mean temperature of 74 degrees

I · *Land of Contrast*

Fahrenheit. Temperatures above 100 degrees, with a relatively high humidity, are common throughout the area during July and August. However, the long growing season—varying from ten months in the extreme south to seven months in the Red River Valley—compensates somewhat for the uncomfortable summer climate.

The heavy rainfall and the level-to-undulating surface produce lush vegetation throughout most of the Coastal Plains. Tall grasses and wild cane once grew abundantly in the scattered prairies between the Nueces and Sabine rivers, and the banks of the streams were shrouded with cypress, cottonwood, and elm. Farther north and away from the river bottoms a great natural forest covered the surface. Much of this longleaf, shortleaf, and loblolly pine, plus post oaks, hickories, pecans, and numerous hardwoods are still extant in the Piney Woods of eastern Texas.

In the extreme southern portion of the Coastal Plains, where the rainfall is less than half as much as in the east, a dense chaparral formerly blanketed the whole of southern Texas. This is still known as the "brush country," although millions of acres of mesquite and cactus lands have recently been cleared for farming. Prior to the opening of the High Plains to the northwest, the "brush country" was the nation's chief beef- and cattle-producing area; it still contains one of the largest and most famous landholdings in the world, the King Ranch.

North of the Coastal Plains Province in the extreme northeastern portion of the Southwest are the Interior Highlands, which include less than one fifth of Oklahoma. Culturally this heavily forested, mountainous region does not belong to the Southwest, but nevertheless a corner of it lies within the artificial boundaries that have been imposed. Elevation of the area ranges from 2,800 feet near the Arkansas line to approximately 1,000 feet above sea level where it merges with the Great Plains to the west. Originally the whole area was covered with timber, and lumbering is still important in the Ouachita Mountain section. The topography is rough and the soil thin. Swift-flowing streams, especially in the northern part of the Interior Highlands, have cut steep slopes and

The Southwest: *Old and New*

narrow ridges throughout the occasional valleys and open patches of prairie land.

Rainfall is heavy in the portion of the Southwest that lies within the Interior Highlands, varying from forty to fifty inches annually. Although the winters are longer and more severe than in the Coastal Plains to the south, they still are milder than those experienced on the Great Plains. Because of its topography and forests, this region has remained rather isolated, and traditionally it is associated with the "hillbilly" country of Arkansas and southern Missouri. It is mostly a region of small farms and livestock raising, but its many artificial lakes and rugged scenery are appreciated for their recreational values.

Bordering the Interior Highlands and Coastal Plains to the west are the Interior Plains—Great Plains and Central Plains—which extend as far south as the Rio Grande, encompassing more than four fifths of Oklahoma, half of Texas, and the eastern third of New Mexico. This region is sometimes called the South Plains, to distinguish it from the major province that extends into Canada. The dividing line between the South Plains and the Coastal Plains in Texas is abrupt, because of the Balcones fault and the Eastern Cross Timbers. But no such exact limit is evident farther north between the plains and highland region of eastern Oklahoma. Here the two provinces gradually merge and overlap.

The South Plains are divided into two physiographic provinces—the High Plains, or Great Plains, and the Low Plains, or Rolling Plains.[3] The High Plains lie next to the Southern Rockies and the Pecos Valley at an elevation of 3,000 to 5,000 feet, while the Rolling Plains are farther east. They slope gently from approximately 3,000 feet to 1,000 feet from west to east, and are bounded on the west by the Llano Estacado, or Staked Plains, on the south by the Edwards Plateau, and on the east by the Coastal Plains and Interior Highlands. Much of Oklahoma and a large rectangular segment of north-central Texas are within the Rolling Plains.

---

[3] To add to the confusion of terms, the Rolling Plains are also referred to as part of the Central Lowlands.

I · *Land of Contrast*

Unlike the High Plains, the Rolling Plains are not treeless. Mesquite, live oak, cedar, stunted post oak, cottonwood, hackberry, elm, and pecan grow along the creek and river valleys, especially in the southern portion and near the eastern fringes. North of Red River and west of the 98th meridian the country is more aptly described as prairie. Formerly it was carpeted with native blue stem, mesquite, buffalo, and grama grasses that centuries of buffalo and Indian occupation failed to deplete. Many explorers, travelers, hunters, and cattlemen, coming upon the great natural prairie of the Rolling Plains for the first time, were moved to describe it as a "sea of grass."

When the military expedition commanded by Randolph B. Marcy reached the edge of the Rolling Plains in 1849 en route to Santa Fe, Marcy wrote to his wife: "We are now launched upon the broad Prairie of the West and feel as if we are upon the wide ocean, nothing intercepts the view to the West. As far as the eye can extend it is one uninterrupted expanse of prairie, with occasional skirts of small trees along the water courses." [4] Marcy's impression was typical of those who came before and those who followed, until the grass eventually was gone. Once crops were grown successfully on the prairie, newcomers arrived in large numbers and rapidly conquered the region for agriculture. Clearing the land was unnecessary; all one needed was a steel plow and a team of horses. In time the pristine "big pasture" would become an ugly "dust bowl."

Winters on the Rolling Plains are cold and dry, although less so than those experienced farther west on the High Plains. Average annual precipitation is twenty-five to thirty inches, while temperatures in the summer months, aggravated by the hot winds from the south, frequently exceed 100 degrees Fahrenheit. Also the sub-humid Rolling Plains lie directly in the path of the tornadoes that visit the region throughout the spring months. Furthermore, all of the plains people must learn to live with the frequent "north-

---

[4] Quoted in W. Eugene Hollon: *Beyond the Cross Timbers* (Norman: University of Oklahoma Press; 1955), p. 64.

ers" that sweep down on them. These cold blankets of air, sometimes accompanied by black clouds and solid sheets of sand, drop the temperature with incredible speed and bring discomfort to range stock and people and ruination to crops and plant life. Only hearty and determined men, animals, and plants can endure what nature has wrought upon this region.

The portion of the Rolling Plains which extends below Red River and along the fringe of the Cross Timbers is severely eroded in places and can hardly be called prairie country. Not only have the southwestern rivers in the area cut sharp entrenchments across the landscape, but numerous escarpments and steep-sided buttes and mesas make it a rugged and thinly settled land. There are extensive areas that have excellent soils for farming, but in general the southern section of the Rolling Plains is more suited to cattle, goat, and sheep ranching because of the terrain, the vast stretches of cedar breaks and mesquites, and the inadequate rainfall.

Rising suddenly above the Rolling Plains toward the west is the major subdivision of the South Plains—the High Plains of Texas and New Mexico. These may be described as perfect plains, level, wholly treeless, and semi-arid. All the vicissitudes of nature found elsewhere in the Great Plains area are present here in an extreme form: the wind is of greater velocity, for there are no hills and trees to check it; the dust and sand often blow incessantly during the spring and early summer months; the winters are more severe; the annual rainfall is five to ten inches less and evaporation is greater; and damaging hailstorms provide still another curse to human, plant, and animal life.

The South Plains reach into Texas on the high ridge between the headwaters of the Canadian, Red, Brazos, and Colorado rivers on the east and the Pecos Valley in New Mexico on the west and extend southward to the Balcones escarpment. There are two subdivisions: the Llano Estacado of the Panhandle and the Edwards Plateau of southwestern Texas. The Llano Estacado, or Staked Plains, was first visited by a white man in 1541, when Coronado in his search for Quivira approached this strange land of boundless

I · Land of Contrast

space and awful silence. His chronicler wrote that the surface of the earth was so flat that if one looked at the buffaloes "the sky could be seen between their legs," and if a man lay down on his back "he lost sight of the ground." Even today the Llano Estacado has retained its character, for the horizon is unbroken, no matter where one looks. As far as the eye can see, the earth seems to rise in great swells so that one has the feeling of standing on a tremendous, suspended carpet that is sagging slightly in the middle from his own weight.

The Llano Estacado has remained practically untouched by erosion, doubtless because it rests upon a caprock base that rises approximately a thousand feet above its surroundings. Around the fringes, however, are some deep erosions, the most conspicuous being the Palo Duro and Tule canyons of the Texas Panhandle. It did not occur to the Spaniards and early Anglo-American explorers that the great geographic phenomenon, the Llano Estacado, was worth settling, nor did it seem possible to them that it could ever be inhabited by white men. This short-grass country seemed intended by nature to remain a place for antelope and buffalo and untamed Indian.

Today a considerable part of the lime-base soil is being cultivated, and Lubbock is the center of one of the greatest cotton-producing areas in the world, while Amarillo is equally noted for its production of wheat. Here on the Llano Estacado, man has conquered nature by tapping the underground supply of water for irrigation. But he has also sowed seeds of ultimate destruction of this region as a great agricultural center. For several years water has been taken from the subsurface at an alarming rate, and the newly created oasis may soon become a desert unless conservation is practiced and adequate facilities for storage of ground water are constructed. Much of the High Plains area of the Southwest remains ranch land, since the blue-stem grama grass continues to be the region's greatest natural resource.

The Edwards Plateau occupies the extreme southern end of the High Plains. It is considered a physiographic and geographic sub-region separate from the Llano Estacado because it does not have a stream-deposited top soil. Furthermore, its dominant activity was and is ranching, primarily the raising of sheep and goats. In fact, this is the greatest mohair- and wool-producing section of the continent. Its chief cities, Del Rio, San Angelo, and Kerrville, reflect these ranching activities. The area is quite dry, with a few acres under irrigation and with little cultivated land. Much of the soil is thin and rocky, and in parts it is severely broken by hills and escarpments. Brush cedar, cactus, and Spanish dagger (yucca) are the most common plants. However, large cypress, pecan, and scrubby hardwood grow in some of the canyons. In all directions toward the edges of the Edwards Plateau the land becomes rougher, especially where the Pecos, Devils, Guadalupe, Frio, Medina, and Nueces rivers have cut steep cliffs.

The Edwards Plateau country contains some of the most beautiful scenery in the Southwest. Much of its elevation is between 2,000 and 3,000 feet, and its climate is milder in both winter and summer than in any other part of the plains area.

The fourth major geographic province in the Southwest is the Southern Rockies of northern New Mexico. These mountains are really the end of the great Rocky chain that starts in the Bering Sea and sweeps down through the western portion of North America in a southeasterly direction before its ultimate disappearance some distance below Santa Fe. Like the Interior Highlands that lap over into eastern Oklahoma, the mountain province of New Mexico constitutes a relatively small area of the Southwest, but it provides awe-inspiring scenery and superb climate. Civilizations developed and flourished here centuries before Columbus reached the Western Hemisphere.

The Southern Rockies run between the Great Plains on the east and the Colorado Plateau on the west. The southern tip disappears in central New Mexico, only to emerge again as isolated ranges farther south. These include the Sandias, east of Albuquerque; the Manzano and Guadalupe Ranges to the south; and the Davis Mountains in the Big Bend, which actually belong to the Basin and Range Province.

One of the distinctive features of the mountain region of

I · *Land of Contrast*

northern New Mexico is the Rio Grande River, which enters the Southwest from Colorado by way of a broad fertile valley. The bed of the river wanders from the slope of the Sangre de Cristo Mountains on the east to the San Juan and Jemez Mountains on the west until it becomes a narrow gorge. Then it alternately meanders across green valleys and cuts through canyons as it continues its route to El Paso, where it turns southeast to become an international boundary between the United States and Mexico.

The parallel ranges of mountains which flank the northern portion of the stream break off into rugged fingers on both sides of the trough through which the river makes its way toward Mexico. Varying in width from five to fifty miles, this valley possesses some of the best farming and ranching lands in New Mexico. The Sangre de Cristo (Blood of Christ) Range boasts a few high points, the highest Wheeler Peak near Taos Pueblo with an altitude of 13,151 feet. The Jemez Mountains west of Santa Fe reach a height of 11,000 feet.

Along the eastern slope of the Sangre de Cristo Mountains, near the southern boundary of Colorado, are the headwaters of the Pecos and Canadian rivers. The Pecos flows toward the south, almost parallel to the Rio Grande, to outline the western border of the High Plains, while the Canadian flows from west to east along the northern rim of the Llano Estacado. The ranges of mountains west of the Rio Grande which form the Continental Divide merge into the Colorado Plateau, a subregion of the Basin and Range Province. Their rugged scenery represents a great financial asset to the Southwest, particularly New Mexico.

Pine, spruce, and aspen grow in the higher altitudes of the Southern Rockies, while piñon and dwarf cedars are found along the slopes. Cottonwood predominates in the river bottoms, and there are patches of what was once a valley carpet of succulent grasses that supported thousands of antelope and elk. Herds of cattle and sheep find forage here today, but much of the land produces wheat, alfalfa, barley, peppers, potatoes, and melons in large quantities during the short growing season on the irrigated farms. Although this mountain region of New Mexico is semi-arid,

THE SOUTHWEST: *Old and New*

fierce downpours come with little warning, especially in July and August, and turn the Rio Grande into a raging torrent of mud and water. During the winter months as much as 300 inches of snow may fall in the Sangre de Cristo Mountains, but the average annual rainfall for the entire state rarely exceeds fifteen inches.

Because of the low humidity and the high altitude, the daily range in temperature in the Southern Rockies is very wide: forty degrees or more. January is the coldest month, with an average daily temperature of approximately twenty to twenty-five degrees. The warmest month is July, with an average of about sixty degrees. Thus, this portion of the Southwest possesses a delightful climate, which, combined with the scenery, constitutes the area's outstanding asset. Thousands of people visit the region each year.[5]

The fifth major geographic region in the Southwest, and by far the largest, is the Basin and Range Province. Geographers and historians differ considerably as to the boundaries of this region, for it is by no means uniform. Nevertheless, the subdivisions that compose it have several common characteristics. In general, it is the southern fringe of the Southwest and extends from the vicinity of Los Angeles to the tip of the Great Plains in Texas. It includes all of Arizona, the western half of New Mexico, and the corner of Texas which lies west of the Pecos River. The northern half of Arizona and the northwest corner of New Mexico are actually within the great Colorado Plateau, but this area is commonly considered a subdivision of the Basin and Range country.

The Colorado Plateau, situated west and slightly south of the Southern Rockies, includes the Four Corners, where New Mexico, Arizona, Colorado, and Utah meet. It is a region of great elevation: all but the bottoms of the canyons and the highest peak (12,600 feet) lie between 4,000 and 8,000 feet. Only the fame of the Grand Canyon draws visitors here; the rest of this area is less visited than

---

[5] Bandelier National Monument, forty-two miles northwest of Santa Fe in the heart of the Jemez Mountains, attracts approximately 100,000 visitors each summer.

I · Land of Contrast

almost any other part of the United States, for it is eroded and difficult to traverse. Numerous arroyos have cut it into a maze of steep-sided chasms, flat-topped islands of resistant rock, or mesas, and remarkable canyons. Much of the Colorado Plateau is devoid of soils; where present, they are limy, light grayish-brown or gray in color, and contain little organic material. But when water is available for irrigation, the land that is free from an excess of salts becomes highly productive and is capable of growing a wide variety of crops, including alfalfa, barley, corn, cotton, grain sorghums, and wheat.

Surprisingly, more than half of the Colorado Plateau is clothed with trees of some kind, though there is little commercial lumbering. Where the altitude varies from 6,000 to 7,500 feet, western yellow pine contributes most of the saw timber. Douglas firs likewise grow in the higher elevations, since rainfall is relatively heavy in places, but where the moisture is inadequate, piñon, juniper, scrub oak, and chaparral predominate. Bunch grasses are also found on the Plateau, and vast herds of deer, elk, and antelope graze here, furnishing food for the Navajo, Ute, and Zuñi Indians, who still claim the region as their home. Except for its tourist attraction, this area seemed destined to remain a grazing country until the recent discoveries of oil, gas, and uranium.

A mountain barrier rims the Plateau on the south, separating it from the desert region of Arizona and New Mexico. Three streams, the Gila, Colorado, and Little Colorado, have each carved at least one gorge or canyon through the region. These rivers, particularly the Gila and Colorado, have also built a giant delta into one of the great deserts of the Southwest. The desert-like region extends from southern California as far east as the Pecos River in Texas and south across the International boundary to include the Sonoran Desert of Mexico. Its northern boundary skirts the southern limits of the Sierra Nevada Mountains and the Colorado Plateau, protruding as far north in New Mexico as the end of the Southern Rockies near Santa Fe.

The desert region differs from the rest of the Basin and

Range Province in several aspects. It has a negligible annual rainfall, and the elevation is slight. The result is a land of baking heat which does not support enough vegetation for extensive grazing. Truck and subtropical fruits are grown, however, in certain irrigated districts of Arizona and in the Pecos Valley of New Mexico. Some nutritious mesquite grass is scattered through the area, but for the most part the native plants are cactus, yucca, juniper, and bush cedar, which have learned to survive with little moisture.

Not all of the region outside the Colorado Plateau should be considered as desert, for the surface of the Basin and Range country consists of great and small mountain ranges with intervening basins. The mountains do not have much vegetation, and when rains come, they come all at once and carry an immense amount of soil and debris with them. Water, even for stock and domestic use, is scarce, but in a few favored localities grasses can support a ranching industry of considerable proportions, especially in the southwestern tip of Texas. In New Mexico, near Carlsbad, Roswell, and Artesia, artesian wells have transformed the desert into a small and highly productive oasis. The same is true in the Phoenix area, where water from the great Arizona reservoirs has turned soil formerly considered worthless into farms that sell for more than $1,000 an acre.

In a sub-humid, semi-arid, or arid region such as the Basin and Range country, there is, especially at the higher altitudes, a great variation of temperature between day and night. Readings in excess of 100 degrees Fahrenheit are the rule during the summer months, but the dry atmosphere makes living bearable. The short winter, on the other hand, has a climate so attractive that much of the region of southern Arizona, New Mexico, and the area around El Paso is a mecca for winter tourists and health seekers. Annual precipitation varies directly with elevation above sea level. Yuma, Arizona, gets less than five inches, while parts of the region farther east ordinarily receive as much as fifteen inches. Snowfall is rare, although a hundred inches frequently falls each year in the mountains that divide the Colorado Plateau from the desert in Arizona.

I · *Land of Contrast*

THE NATURAL environment afforded by the Basin and Range Province is similar to that of Spain and northern Mexico. Not only did the Spaniards reach the region before the Anglo-Americans, but they planted their institutions so firmly that these have endured. Today the adobe buildings, the broad sombreros, the ornate saddles, the Mexican sheepherders, and the Spanish-speaking Indians in this area still resist most of the ways of the "Yankee." More than any other part, this sectional belt has remained typically Southwestern. It is the Southwest portrayed by Hollywood, where cattle are still worked on horseback and the pristine landscape is not marred by factories or crowded cities.

In the four states of the Southwest there are more than 567,000 square miles of land with approximately thirteen million inhabitants—people of diverse blood and culture who have borrowed no small amount from one another while still retaining much of their original customs and ways of life. More than half of the population lives in large cities in the Coastal Plains of Texas and in eastern Oklahoma. The remainder is thinly scattered over the plains, mountains, plateaus, basins, river valleys, and deserts beyond the 98th meridian, a region where the land lies open and the horizons stretch wide apart. Southwesterners are as conscious of the past as of the rapid changes taking place all around them. A closer examination of those who discovered and conquered this first and last frontier and those who were discovered and conquered by it is necessary for a full understanding and appreciation of the Southwest.

II

BEFORE THE WHITE MAN

THE FIRST white man entered the Southwest more than four centuries ago, but even today one cannot cross the region without seeing evidence of peoples who occupied it long before that event. Who these first inhabitants were and whence they came still remains in the realm of speculation, but anthropologists have diligently woven the scattered archaeological remains into a general pattern that tells us much. For example, the pioneer work of Professor A. E. Douglas of the University of Arizona in tree-ring research in the Southwest established chronological data on

II · Before the White Man

climatic conditions for several centuries past. Consequently, many of the prehistoric ruins scattered throughout the Southwest can be dated from pieces of wood found in them.

Dr. Douglas discovered, after much painstaking effort, that all trees in a given region carried the same pattern of annual rings, wider for wet years than for years of drought. By studying the oldest living trees, he was able to devise a chart that showed which periods were wet and which were dry. He then compared these ring patterns with trees cut by the ancient builders for use as beams. By matching patterns from various sites, he was able to date sites and determine which ones were contemporary. Thus, the pine trees of the dry Southwest silently keep the records of the early inhabitants and are helping archaeologists determine the evolution of permanent residential construction and habitation. More than a thousand years of human development are chronicled in the artifacts of New Mexico and Arizona.

The people who lived in the Four Corners (New Mexico, Colorado, Arizona, and Utah) were among the first sedentary human inhabitants of the Southwest. Evidence indicates that they were there as early as the first quarter of the Christian Era. A brief examination of the pre-Columbian natives of the Southwest must begin, therefore, with the cliff dwellers of the Mesa Verde National Park area. The Navajos call them Anasazi, or "Old People." At Mesa Verde and at the nearby Aztec and Chaco Canyon national monuments, archaeologists have traced the progress of the Anasazi from pit houses to great apartment dwellings, from nomadic clans to urban dwellers. These three great centers were occupied concurrently before they were abandoned late in the thirteenth century.

At first the Anasazi lived in simple shelters and subsisted by hunting, gathering wild berries and seeds, and perhaps raising maize and pumpkins. For weapons they possessed spears, and for farming equipment no more than sticks. Their shelters were "pit houses," one-room affairs that were partial excavations. Each house had a storage bin and a fire pit and was covered by a flat roof of mud and twigs supported by upright poles—an early

THE SOUTHWEST: *Old and New*

version of the nineteenth-century sod houses on the Western plains.

From pit houses the early inhabitants graduated to more substanial dwellings walled with slabs of stone and built in groups of ten or twenty. Beans were now added to the diet, bows and arrows replaced the short-range spears, and pottery took the place of baskets. By 1000 A.D. the apartment dwellings were larger and the pit houses had evolved into circular or square subterranean chambers called kivas. The kiva is a distinctive feature of Indian pueblos even today; but now it is used almost exclusively for religious ceremonies or as a communal lodge, rather than as a dwelling. It varies in diameter from ten to forty or, in some rare cases, as much as sixty feet. The great number of kivas found at all ancient Indian sites, as well as their presence in modern pueblos, is evidence of their extreme importance.

The third step in the evolutionary process of ancient living falls in the period from approximately 1050 to 1300. During this era Indians of the Southwest lived in villages capable of housing more than 5,000 persons. Most of the dwellings were now built in caverns in steep cliff faces. Others were situated on high mesas, while some were located in well-protected river valleys. Mesa Verde remains the outstanding example of cliff-dwelling culture to be found in North America. This great tableland is slashed by deep canyons, most of which contain water, natural caves, forests of piñon, juniper, pine, and Douglas fir. Thousands of people lived here before the first white man arrived on the continent.

Some of the "ghost cities" abandoned by their early builders contain structures four stories high, with watch towers, retaining walls, and dozens of round kivas. The setbacks on the dwellings provided a series of ledges against which ladders could be placed and easily drawn up in times of attack. Access to the first story was through a trap door in the roof. Overhanging cliffs made approach from above virtually impossible. Just before the Mesa Verde people left these habitations in the late thirteenth century, they probably reached their peak in culture and security. Corn

II · Before the White Man

was added to the staple crops, pottery and jewelry became more elaborate, and dyed cotton garments made their appearance. As long as water flowed on the nearby canyon floor there was little fear of starvation, for the people adapted themselves to their environment.

We know from tree rings that persons who occupied Chaco Canyon and Aztec in northwestern New Mexico were contemporaries of those who lived at Mesa Verde. The Chaco people built small houses along the sides of the canyon for thirty miles, while on the bottom slopes they constructed splendid communal dwellings capable of housing more than 5,000 souls. The largest settlement, Pueblo Bonito, contained 1,800 rooms and thirty kivas, the largest apartment house in the United States until 1882. Here the stonework reveals a high degree of artistry, and ashes from the floors of the rooms yield pieces of dyed cotton cloth, pottery, basketry, and jewelry that is superior to similar artifacts uncovered in any other ancient center of the Southwest.

The settlements at Aztec were never so large as those at Mesa Verde and Chaco Canyon, nor did the settlers ever reach so high a level of culture. Ruins at Aztec indicate an apartment house with stone walls and wooden beams which formerly contained 500 rooms. It was well planned, and its builders were first-rate masons and decorators who must have stepped back from time to time to take a look at their handiwork. But the quality of weaving and pottery found at Aztec is inferior.

During the so-called "golden age of cliff dwelling," 1000–1300 A.D., agriculture and hunting produced food enough for all, and well-filled storage bins allowed leisure during the winter months for artistic expression and increasingly complicated religious celebrations. Government was more centralized, and priests probably exercised their maximum influence. But, if we may use the modern New Mexico pueblo as a pattern, society remained basically democratic and every adult male had a voice in important matters affecting the whole community. There is no evidence of major warfare, and perhaps these ancient peoples enjoyed life to the full.

Good or bad, the situation could not last forever. Where human enemies failed for centuries to dislodge the cliff dwellers from their homes, nature accomplished the task in a little more than two decades. Again the pattern of tree rings furnishes a clue to what happened. A drought began in 1276 and lasted twenty-four years. No modern farmer could survive such conditions. The people of Mesa Verde evacuated their homes and migrated elsewhere—probably gradually at first, but by 1300 the exodus was complete. Some archaeologists maintain that Chaco Canyon and Aztec were abandoned at the same time, but others declare that the people of Chaco Canyon sealed up their doors with stones and departed a hundred years before the great migration from the other centers. At any rate, they left, and the theory that most of them moved eastward to the valley of the Rio Grande seems logical. Quite probably some of the refugees migrated westward into present Arizona.

Dr. Edgar L. Hewitt believes that part of the Chaco people stopped temporarily in the forested plateau of Pajarito, on the east flank of the Jemez Mountains. The altitude of this plateau is approximately 8,000 feet, and during the fourteenth and fifteenth centuries it was the most densely populated area in the Southwest. It contained many natural caves, deep canyons, steep mesas, and clear-flowing streams. All around the Jemez range hundreds of ruins have been located, the most famous at Rito de los Frijoles ("Creek of the Beans"), now a part of Bandelier National Monument. The walls of the canyon cut by the creek are lined with cliff-house ruins, the longest extending 700 feet and varying in height from one to four stories.

For a long time excellent living was offered on the floor of the canyon, by wild game, an abundance of water for irrigation, aspen and pines for building, and the ease of hollowing out rooms in the friable volcanic tuff. The many kivas indicate elaborate religious ceremonies. At its peak, probably no less than 5,000 people occupied the narrow canyon. But droughts, progressive desiccation, and raids by warlike nomads combined to drive the cliff dwellers onward again. Most likely the next and last area of

II · Before the White Man

settlement was along the Rio Grande to the east. No reasons are found for the general decline in cultural standards which coincided with the exodus into the Rio Grande Valley, but buildings became poorer and pottery less distinguished in form and design.

By the sixteenth century there were at least sixty or seventy villages extending from Isleta Pueblo, southwest of present-day Albuquerque, to as far north as Taos Pueblo. Not all of the settlements were along the river's course. There was one extension westward through Acoma and Zuñi to the Hopi pueblos in Arizona, and another thirty miles east of Santa Fe to the important village of Pecos. By the time the Spaniards arrived in 1540, some of the New Mexico pueblos had been abandoned. Paul A. F. Walter states in *The Cities That Died of Fear* that the villages east of the Rio Grande were probably deserted because of their vulnerability to attacks by the Plains Indians. Whatever the reason, the occupied area of New Mexico was narrowed to the Rio Grande drainage, except for the previously mentioned western offshoots to the Hopi country. Evidence shows that the Indians along the river became very numerous for a few generations, but by 1848 their population had declined to an estimated 10,000 or less. This figure, incidentally, is about half the present number of Pueblo Indians —scattered among eighteen villages that have changed little during the past century.

All of the Pueblos in the Rio Grande area speak a basic tongue, although, like Latin, it has been diversified into several languages and dialects. Tewa is the language spoken by Pueblos north of Santa Fe, Keres by those living south of it along the Jemez River and in distant Acoma and Laguna. Curiously, the extreme southern and northern pueblos, Isleta and Taos, have the same dialect: Tewa. The Hopis, on the other hand, speak the Shoshonean language, as did the warlike Comanches of the Plains, while the Zuñi have a tongue of their own. The odd relationship of all Pueblo languages and dialects supports the belief that these people have a common ancestry.

Except for periodic raids by Navajo and Apache, the Pueblos would have been quite prosperous. They were, and are, a clean, industrious, and thrifty people. Both Spain and Mexico allowed each village to continue its traditional self-government, with an annually chosen governor and council administering local community affairs. Of all Southwestern Indians, the Pueblos were probably best known to the Anglo-Americans prior to the Mexican War. The mountain men and Santa Fe traders came in contact with them as early as 1820, but, despite long association with the whites, native customs and culture prevailed among these Indians; and the twentieth-century Pueblos in many ways live and think and worship as did their ancestors.

The only Pueblo Indians in Arizona today are the Hopi ("Peaceful Ones"). They were first visited by a white man in 1540, when Coronado, en route to Quivira, passed through their villages situated at the tops of slopes and on high, sun-drenched mesas. The Hopi are a short, olive-skinned, Oriental-looking people whose homes and culture are not unlike those of the Rio Grande Pueblos. They are descendants of the Anasazi, and probably moved into the heart of the Enchanted Desert of northern Arizona from the Mesa Verde area even before the ancestors of the modern New Mexico Pueblos began their migration. Originally they were peaceful and industrious farmers who lived in pit houses and later in caves. Eventually the Hopi learned to close up the openings of the larger caves and build mud-walled rooms behind the outer walls. Montezuma's Castle and the Tonto and Walnut Canyon cliff houses, located within convenient reach of lands fit for cultivation, are outstanding examples of their work. Artifacts discovered at these sites show that the ancient Hopi were expert basket weavers and potters. Their great days appear to have been between the eleventh and fourteenth centuries.

Archaeologists have uncovered in the Salt River Valley of southern Arizona more than 150 miles of well-platted canals. They were dug around the twelfth century to divert the waters of the river into a complex network of irrigation ditches and were so well constructed that some of them are still in use. The canal builders appear to have descended from the Anasazi of northern Arizona, migrating in small groups from their cliff houses in

II · Before the White Man

much the same manner as did the ancestors of the New Mexico Pueblos. Overpopulation probably was the reason they left their relatives and friends to seek a better life to the south. The Pimas, who came into possession of much of their irrigated land, called them Hohokan ("Those Who Have Vanished"). Obviously, the Hohokan were superior to most primitive peoples; they made a practice of storing surplus food, and in addition to their impressive network of canals they erected sturdy mud-walled dwellings and community buildings.

Three castle-like structures, Chichitecalli near modern Fort Grant, Pueblo de los Muertos near Phoenix, and the famous Casa Grande on the Middle Gila, are outstanding examples of their skill and artistry. Casa Grande ("Big House") was visited by Father Kino in the early eighteenth century, and even today its four-storied bulk looms out of the desert. Some have speculated that it formerly was the center of a civilization equal to that of the Aztecs and Mayas.

The Hohokan may have merged with the Pimas, or else disappeared altogether. The great drought of the late thirteenth century certainly affected them, as it did all Indians of the Southwest, causing various families to wander far away. A kiva uncovered near Galisteo, New Mexico, is remarkably similar to those left by the Hohokan, and tends to support the theory that a segment of the population drifted eastward. Another theory is that attacks from unfriendly tribes decimated the canal builders. Any one of these circumstances, plus possible water-logged soils caused by excessive irrigation, could have destroyed the Hohokan civilization.

Although the modern Hopi are the only Pueblo Indians in Arizona today, many other tribes share their ancestry. All Arizona Indians belong to three great linguistic families: Yuman, Athapascan, and Uto-Aztecan. The last of these formerly constituted one of the most widely extended language families in America, ranging from western Wyoming through the Great Basin and down into Mexico. In addition to the Hopi, who presently number fewer than 4,000, other members of the Uto-Aztecan family are the Paiutes and the Pima. Although the Paiutes originally lived in Utah and Nevada, approximately a hundred members of this tribe now occupy a small reservation west of Fredonia, Arizona, where they subsist principally by raising cattle. The Pimas, together with their close relatives the Papago ("Bean People"), live on the Salt River Reservation and the San Xavier Reservation in the Gila Valley of southern Arizona. Both are excellent farmers and stock raisers and have acquired a considerable degree of civilization.

At the time of the American conquest of the Southwest, the Pimas numbered fewer than 6,000. Today there are more than 9,000 of them. Originally their homes were built of cacti or from the material of other desert plants and shrubs, rather than stone or adobe. For centuries they have continued to practice irrigation and raise corn, wheat, vegetables, and, more recently, tobacco and fruit. When the Spaniards first came among the Pimas, these Indians were making excellent pottery and blankets and possessed domestic animals and poultry. Like all peaceful peoples of the Southwest, they habitually suffered from raids by the outlaw Apache.

The Athapascan family is represented by the Navajos and Apaches. These tribes were formerly closely related but became more differentiated with the arrival of the Anglo-Americans in the nineteenth century. The Navajo originally occupied a continuous territory in northern Arizona, northwestern Colorado, and southeastern Utah. They have never been a pueblo people, never lived in towns, and never farmed extensively. It is believed that they did not reach the Southwest until 500 or 600 years ago, and until the arrival of the white men they were a relatively unimportant tribe. Even after acquiring sheep and cattle and developing into a pastoral people, they continued to attack the Pueblos and Spaniards. In turn they suffered at the hands of their neighbors, so that their predatory raids were not always unjustified. In 1863 Kit Carson led an expedition of New Mexico militia against the Navajo, killed most of their livestock, and imprisoned several thousand men, women, and children at Fort Sumner, New Mexico.

II · *Before the White Man*

So complete was the defeat that the Navajos never again took to the warpath.

Navajo culture is a blending of native customs with those borrowed from their neighbors. Even today they remain basically a nomadic people, moving with their herds about the vast reservation in northeastern Arizona and northwestern New Mexico wherever grass and water can be found. Their principal historical stronghold in the Southwest is Canyon de Chelly, which they still occupy. When the Anglo-Americans first came among them in the early nineteenth century, the Navajos probably numbered 15,000, but by 1867 droughts and wars had reduced this figure to fewer than 8,000. In recent years higher standards of hygiene and a declining death rate have caused the Navajos to increase to approximately 88,000, far more than their reservation can adequately support. No other Southwestern Indians have survived so well, yet few have known more abject poverty.

A traditionally distinctive feature of Navajo culture is the well-adapted home—the timber-framed hogan or the round beehive-shaped earthen structure. The latter type possesses no windows and is approximately fifteen feet in diameter. It has a hole in the roof to enable the smoke to escape easily and is dry and warm in winter. The earthen lodges are abandoned during the summer months while the Navajo seek the ventilation afforded by hastily constructed arbors. These structures, whether brush arbors or hogans, are difficult to see at a distance, for both types blend into the surrounding terrain. And rarely does one observe two or three dwellings close together, for although most of the old traditions and religious ceremonies are still practiced, pastoral society does not encourage concentrations of population.

Navajos are skillful workers in silver, but they do not make pottery. Their attractive blankets are woven from the wool of their own sheep and constitute a principal source of income. In addition to tending herds and selling the products of their handiwork, the Navajos still hunt and fish and gather piñon nuts. But the 25,000 square miles of sand, mesas, sagebrush, canyons, and forest which consitute their reservation are proving less and less adequate to support a constantly increasing population, and many Navajos are forced either to look for work off the reservation or become public charges.

The other member of the Athapascan family in the Southwest is the Apache, traditionally among the most warlike of all North American Indians. General George Crook labeled him "the tiger of the human specie," and doubtless most Anglo-Americans who came in contact with the Apache during the nineteenth century concurred. Despite their close linguistic relationship with the Navajos, the Apaches differ greatly in customs, manners, and way of life. They are not easily classified, for originally they were broken into numerous tribes, which in turn were subdivided into bands. Among the best known were the Lipans and Mescaleros of western Texas and southeastern New Mexico; the Mimbres, Mogollon, Chiricahua, and Coyotero bands of New Mexico and Arizona; and the Jicarillas of northeastern New Mexico. At the time of the Mexican conquest in 1848 there were probably fewer than 12,000 of them. They formerly roamed the vast trackless region between the Pecos on the east and the Colorado River on the west, as far north as present Utah, and below the Mexican border to the south.

The "Eastern Apache," as the Spaniards called the Lipans and Mescaleros, were really Plains Indians—not unlike the Comanches. Herbert E. Bolton says they originally resided in northern Texas and were driven south by the Comanches in the eighteenth century. The Lipans frequently raided and hunted as far eastward as the Texas Gulf Coast and were a source of much trouble during the entire period of the Texas Republic. Both they and the Mescaleros fought on horseback and used bows and arrows and spears. Long after they were brought under control by Texas Rangers they continued their forays into northern Mexico and frequently caused dozens of towns and hundreds of haciendas to be abandoned for long periods.

Throughout the middle of the nineteenth century the fiercest of all Apaches were the Chiricahuas of southeastern Arizona— "Cherry Cows" to the early settlers. This group dressed in buck-

II · *Before the White Man*

skins and lived in crude brush huts or rough wickiups made of grass. Although they learned farming from the Spaniards, they grew few crops and refused to tend sheep and goats as their kinsmen the Navajo did. They found it easier to drive off livestock and confiscate the corn and beans produced by their more peaceful neighbors to the north and south. In addition to the spoils of war, the fearful Chiricahuas subsisted on piñon nuts, mesquite beans, cactus fruit, and game from nature's scanty storehouse. They made skillful use of the bow and arrow and long spear in both warfare and hunting. Their weapons were sometimes rendered more deadly by being plunged into decomposed liver that had been freely exposed to the bite of rattlesnakes. After the arrival of the Anglo-Americans the Chiricahuas acquired firearms, but they did not completely abandon the bow and arrow until several decades later.

The Apaches' best ally was their rough and inaccessible country, which made it difficult for Spaniards or Anglo-Americans to control them, and they continued to be a chronic problem long after the Mexican War. Geronimo, Victorio, and Cochise were Apache chiefs whose very names became synonyms for terror. Travelers and settlers in the Southwest throughout most of the nineteenth century lived in constant fear of ambush, and all too frequently mounted troops were unable to track the Apaches. The Indians' best defensive strategy was to retreat and let the terrain of southern Arizona and New Mexico do their fighting.

When various bands were brought into reservations from time to time, escape was relatively easy. In the wars that followed their inevitable raids, outlaw groups under the leadership of Cochise, Geronimo, and Victorio were ultimately subdued. Except for a minor foray against the Mormon settlements in Utah in 1900, the Apaches caused the federal government little trouble after the imprisonment of Geronimo at Fort Pickens, Florida, in 1886. Eventually they learned the ranching business from those who leased their lands for grazing purposes and thereby improved their standard of living.

The third major linguistic family in the New Mexico–Arizona

THE SOUTHWEST: *Old and New*

region, the Yuma, occupy the area along the Colorado River and the lower reaches of the Gila. Like other Southwestern tribes, this group is divided into several related subdivisions.[1] The Yumas probably descended from the Hohokans who occupied the area of the Gila Valley before the great drought in the latter part of the thirteenth century. Spaniards came in contact with these tall, powerful, warlike people during the sixteenth century, but had little success in imposing Spanish culture upon them. However, contact with the whites soon reduced their numbers: by 1848 there were fewer than 2,500 Yumas in the Southwest, approximately what there are today. H. H. Bancroft characterized them as "worthless and harmless vagabonds" given to drunkenness, gambling, and plundering. Many of their women were prostitutes and consequently ridden with venereal diseases.

By far the largest and most important division of the Yumas was, and still is, the Mohave tribe. Anglo-American travelers in the nineteenth century found them living in flat-topped dirt houses. They were true vegetarians, living almost exclusively on beans, corn, watermelons, and pumpkins. Edward Fitzgerald Beale, an army officer who commanded a camel caravan that crossed Arizona in 1856, was favorably impressed by the Mohaves. "They were a fine looking, comfortable, fat, and merry set," he wrote, "naked excepting a very small piece of cotton cloth around the waist, and though barefooted, ran over sharp rocks and pebbles as easily as if shod with iron. We were soon surrounded on all sides by them. Some had learned a few words of English from trafficking with the military post two hundred and fifty miles off, and one of them saluted me with 'God damn my soul eyes. How de do! How de do!' "[2]

At present the Mohave are scattered on three reservations in Arizona and number about 1,200 intelligent and friendly people. They engage in small farming activities, fishing, railroad work, and in making beaded objects that they sell to tourists.

---

[1] The Havasupai, Hualpai ("Pine Tree Folk"), Mohave, Yuma, Cocpah, Maricopa, and Yavapai ("Sun People").

[2] Edward S. Wallace: *The Great Reconnaissance* (Boston: Little, Brown & Company; 1955), p. 262.

II · Before the White Man

Next to the Mohave, the largest group of Yumas is the Hualpai, who live on a reservation south of the Grand Canyon. This tribe numbers some 400 and still clings to its ancient customs and superstitions. In addition to stock raising, the Hualpai subsist by hunting, fishing, and gathering berries and nuts. The Havasupai, who live in a village at the bottom of Cataract Canyon, are celebrated for their almost complete self-sufficiency. They have changed little since they were first visited by a white man, Father Francisco Garces, in 1776. When Lieutenant Joseph Christmas Ives encountered this small band eighty-one years later, during his Grand Canyon expedition, he was singularly unimpressed. To him they seemed "squalid, wretched-looking creatures, with splay feet, large joints, and diminutive figures."

Because of the nature of the country that the New Mexico and Arizona Indians originally occupied, it was little coveted by white men for farming purposes. Hence, the various tribes were allowed to remain on their land or in their pueblos relatively undisturbed after the end of the Indian wars. Most of the old traditions and customs were retained, and there has been little intermarriage with other races. But the story of the natives who formerly owned the plains and woodland areas of Oklahoma and Texas is quite different. The original possessors of these lands have practically vanished, and even the descendants of the Five Civilized Tribes [3] and other transplanted Indians retain few of their tribal manners. Here the barrier of the reservation system was not retained as a permanent institution—apart from one minor exception in Texas—and thus the Indians and whites are gradually fusing into one people through constant intermarriage.

The native Indians of the Great Plains, Walter Prescott Webb points out, formed the connecting link between the natural environment and the civilization that has been imposed on the region during the last century. These Indians, he continues, profoundly influenced the white man's institutions and at the same time offered peculiar problems to those who invaded their in-

---

[3] Cherokee, Choctaw, Chickasaw, Creek, and Seminole.

The Southwest: *Old and New*

hospitable land. Few in number, they nevertheless played a much more important role in the history of the area than the relatively unknown tribes that originally occupied the eastern woodlands of Texas and Oklahoma. It is difficult to realize, for example, that the Comanches probably never numbered more than 5,000, yet they controlled a territory as large as the state of Iowa. A nomadic people, they were almost constantly on the move, and it was virtually impossible for early travelers crossing their domain to avoid detection by one or more of their parties.

The daring, ferocity, and horsemanship of the Comanches caused them to be remembered while some more numerous tribes are all but forgotten. Indeed, they generally are placed in a class by themselves because of their superb horsemanship. It is doubtful whether any people surpassed them in this skill except the Tatars on the steppes of Asia, whom they closely resembled.

Although the Comanches were the best known of the Southwestern Indians, they were only one of more than twenty tribes living in the Great Plains region at the time the first white men arrived. All of these groups possessed common characteristics even though they rarely came in contact with one another. The Comanches, Kiowas, Kiowa-Apaches, Wichitas, and Mescalero-Apaches occupied the southwest portion of the Plains. The area of the Llano Estacado and the headwaters of the Canadian, Red, Brazos, and Colorado rivers constituted the Comanche range. The Kiowa-Apaches and Kiowas, who never numbered more than a few hundred, occupied the Texas and Oklahoma panhandles, while the Wichitas claimed the remainder of Oklahoma, except the extreme southeastern corner, and Texas as far south as Waco. When these various Plains Indians arrived in the Southwest is a matter of conjecture. The Spaniards became acquainted with them in 1541; their history before that time is virtually unknown.

Since the Comanches were the most numerous and played the most significant role in the history of the Southern Plains portion of the Southwest, they deserve more attention. Anthropologists have divided them into several bands, the most important being Yamparikas ("Root-eaters"), who generally remained in the

II · *Before the White Man*

vicinity of the Arkansas Valley; the Kotsotekas ("Buffalo-eaters") of the Canadian Valley; the Kwaharies ("Antelopes") of the Llano Estacado; and the Penatekas ("Honey-eaters"), who lived in the southernmost tip of the Great Plains.

Each band maintained an independent status, but was free to move at will over the vast Comanche domain. No one chief was ever powerful enough to speak for the whole tribe; frequently a chief found it impossible to control his own band. The Comanches, like other Plains Indians, were nomadic, non-agricultural, and subsisted chiefly upon the countless herds of buffalo, from which they also obtained materials to make their domestic and war implements, clothing, and housing. Dependent upon the animal for existence, the Comanche, through religious ceremonies and customs, sought to gain the favor of its spirit. Not until the eighteenth century did these Indians evolve from a dog to a horse culture. Once they were mounted, and as long as the buffalo existed, they remained virtually unconquerable. The horse altered their civilization as the automobile later affected the white man's way of life.

It is generally believed that the Plains Indians acquired horses from Spanish herds in the Southwest. Whether the first such animal was stolen, or whether it was captured from wild herds that flourished on the Plains, is unimportant. This much is known: within a few generations after horses were brought to the New World they had so multiplied that the Comanches reckoned wealth in terms of them. The horse made the Comanches superb hunters and faster, bolder warriors than any other Indians on the North American continent. It fitted into their way of life perfectly and lifted them to a previously unknown eminence. George Catlin, the artist, wrote in the nineteenth century that a Comanche on his feet was one of the most unattractive and slovenly-looking Indians he had ever seen, "but the moment they mount their horses, they seem at once metamorphosed, and surprise the spectator with the ease and elegance of their movements. A Comanche on his feet is out of his element, and comparatively almost as awkward as a monkey on the ground, without a limb or a branch to cling to; but the moment he lays his hand upon his horse, his *face* even becomes handsome, and he gracefully flies away like a different being."

The Comanche's skill with the bow and arrow and lance, his endurance and ability to withstand hardship, his refusal to surrender, plus his magnificent horsemanship, made him as difficult to subdue as the intractable Apache. In 1855 the federal government tried unsuccessfully to restrict some of them to a small reservation on the Brazos River in Texas. Later they were moved into southwestern Oklahoma, but they still refused to abandon their traditional way of life. As long as there were buffalo to hunt and settlements on the Texas frontier to pillage, Comanches would not tolerate confinement. Various Comanche groups joined with the Kiowas, and occasionally the Southern Cheyennes, to capture or kill settlers and steal their property throughout northern Texas.

The disappearance of the buffalo ended the Indians' main source of food and supplies and forced him to seek his livelihood from other sources. As white settlers became more numerous and land and game more scarce, the Southwestern frontier became a safer place to live. By 1875 approximately 1,600 Comanches remained, and two centuries of warfare against Spaniards, Mexicans, and Anglo-Americans had at last come to an end. The Comanches, who never asked quarter and rarely gave any, now had no alternative but to accept the "white man's road."

The Kiowas were not so numerous as the Comanches, but in many ways the two were similar, and Texas settlers soon learned to fear one almost as much as the other. Kiowas were divided into six or seven divisions, including the Kiowa-Apache Indians, and roamed the area just north and northeast of the region claimed by the Comanches, with whom they were sometimes allied and frequently confused. Both tribes spoke a Shoshoni dialect, which supports the theory that both once lived northwest of the Yellowstone area and migrated to the Southwestern plains at about the same time. Kiowa culture reached its climax in the mid-nineteenth century and then rapidly disintegrated with the

II · Before the White Man

near-extinction of the buffalo. Anglo-Americans had a low opinion of the Kiowas and invariably described them as dirty and thieving, often charging them with cannibalism.

Captain Randolph B. Marcy knew the Kiowas well and tells an amusing story about them in one of his early books on the Southwest. In 1850, when he was in command of Camp Arbuckle in what is now Oklahoma, Marcy and his wife were honored with a visit by a Kiowa chief and a company of his braves. The scantily clad Indians came to see the "white squaw," and the Captain graciously invited them into his quarters. The chief and his followers entered most cautiously. Every object in the white man's lodge fascinated the red brethren, particularly a bright-colored oilcloth rug, which the chief carefully examined. He first scraped it with his nails and then wet his fingers in a vain effort to cut off the design. After a few moments of silence he looked up at the Captain and inquired if the object was a gift from the president of the United States. Marcy assured him that it was not. The chief was next attracted by a piece of delicate embroidery, which Mrs. Marcy let him fondle with his fingers. Upon learning that this was the work of the "white squaw," the old Kiowa immediately proposed to Marcy that they exchange wives. Marcy replied, with a straight face, that such a matter would have to be discussed with his wife and that the decision would be hers.

Another few moments of silence, and then the chief indignantly replied that he did not make trades with squaws, but if the "Big Captain" would only say the word, he would "swap" at once. To Mrs. Marcy's relief, no doubt, the honor was respectfully declined.

Not all social intercourse with the Kiowas was so pleasant. As early as 1835 the federal government signed a peace treaty with them, but this hardly deterred the Kiowas from raiding, especially against the Texans. In 1864 there was a general uprising of all the Plains Indians, and one result was the restriction of the Kiowas to a small reservation in Oklahoma, where they were subjected to constant military and civilian supervision. Their problems were still far from settled, however, as lawless white men were destroying the buffalo and government-promised rations were delayed or not delivered. From time to time Indian outbreaks occurred along the frontier, for which the red man was not always to blame. By 1875 most of the Kiowas were permanently settled on their reservation near Fort Sill, patiently resigned to watching their war and buffalo dances as mere entertainment and not as preludes to action.

Other major Plains Indians were the Wichita, who belonged to a group of linguistically related Caddoan bands: the Taovaya, Tawakoni, Yscani, Waco, and Kichai. The Wichita probably were forced into the Southwest, with the Comanches and Apaches, by pressure from the Sioux. Coronado encountered them in Kansas in the sixteenth century; at least, it is believed that the "Quiviras" he met in 1541 were Wichita. Later the Osage pushed them into what is now Oklahoma and Texas, where pressure from the Comanche and Apache confined them to an area on the eastern edge of the Great Plains. During the early nineteenth century the Wichita proper lived in the region of the upper Brazos and Trinity rivers in Texas and along the Arkansas and Red rivers in Oklahoma. Primarily agriculturists, the Wichita were frequently described as hospitable and reliable. Their villages were distinguished by large dome-shaped houses covered with grass thatch, long arbors, and drying platforms. In 1810 their total population was estimated by one authority at 2,800.

Forty years later the Wichita were concentrated in the Wichita Mountains area in semi-permanent homes. However, they periodically abandoned their village during the hunting seasons. Part of the tribe was placed on the Brazos River Reservation in 1855, but this experiment soon failed. As their number and strength rapidly diminished, the remnants were gathered into a reservation at Caddo, Oklahoma. Today their total population does not exceed 250. The fame of the once widely scattered Wichitas rests in geographic place names: Wichita, Kansas; Wichita Falls, Texas; the Big and Little Wichita rivers; and the Wichita Mountains.

II · *Before the White Man*

Long before the Plains Indians moved into the Southwest, the woodland areas of eastern Oklahoma and Texas were occupied by sedentary tribes called Caddo, or Kadodacho. The Moscoso Expedition in 1541 found several villages of these agricultural people in the vicinity of the Great Bend of the Red River—the adjacent corners of present-day Texas, Arkansas, Oklahoma, and Louisiana. La Salle encountered them in 1686 during his efforts to reach the Mississippi River from his ill-fated French colony at Fort St. Louis near the Texas Gulf Coast. Subsequent contacts were made by Spanish, French, and Anglo-American travelers with various eastern tribes, but endless confusion persisted as to who they were. Ultimately "Caddoan" became the official name for a whole family of languages spoken by tribes inhabiting vast areas of the Southern Plains, Central Plains, and the eastern Coastal Plains.

Linguistically and economically the woodland tribes were far removed from those who dwelt on the western Plains, and their loose confederations did not include the nomadic tribes. Early visitors described them as industrious, intelligent, exceedingly friendly, and possessed of much integrity. By 1781 the many related Caddoan tribes, such as the Hainai, Nebedache, Nacogdoche, and Nasoni, were commonly called Tejas Indians, a Spanish rendition of the Hasinai word for "friend," from which the word "Texas" may be derived.

During the early part of the eighteenth century the French in Louisiana exerted much influence on the eastern tribes of Caddos. Later the Spaniards built missions among them, but made few permanent converts to Christianity because of the bad example set by Spanish garrisoned soldiers.

Many of the Caddos fell under the jurisdiction of the United States following the Louisiana Purchase in 1803, and Dr. John Sibley, newly appointed Indian agent for the Territory of Orleans, soon reported that their numbers had been greatly reduced by war with the Choctaws and by epidemics. The Caddos also suffered as a result of tension on the Southwestern border between Spain and the United States, and their attrition continued at a more rapid rate during the period of the Texas Republic. Meanwhile, some moved from their old haunts along the Texas-Louisiana border into present-day Oklahoma.

The few remaining members of the once extensive Caddoan population in eastern Texas eventually were placed on the Brazos River Reservation. This band of approximately 300 were transferred to a small reservation near Fort Cobb in Indian Territory in 1859 after Texas settlers charged them with theft and threatened their annihilation. Today they number approximately 500 Americanized rural people and are chiefly engaged in farming and stock raising.

Another group of Texas Indians which La Salle met during his wanderings was the Karankawas, undoubtedly possessors of the most primitive of all native Southwestern cultures. These nomadic tribes lived on the strip of islands along the Texas coast and on the nearby mainland. Whether they practiced cannibalism before they came in contact with the Spaniards is not known, but certainly by the eighteenth century they used it as a means of dealing with prisoners of war. Spanish efforts to Christianize these natives produced few converts and resulted in their near-extermination; nor did the Texans treat them any better. By 1844 the few remaining members of the tribe fled to Mexico, leaving little or no trace of their culture behind.

In addition to those tribes which were natives of the Southwest, many scattered groups of woodland Indians later were forced into the area of eastern Texas and eastern Oklahoma because of western expansion following the American Revolution and the War of 1812. These were small segments of Choctaws, Chickasaws, Coushatta, Kickapoo, Delaware, Shawnee, Quapaw, Creek, and Cherokee. Like those who had previously arrived as a result of pressure from hostile Indians elsewhere, the more civilized immigrants rapidly adapted themselves to the physical environment. Those who settled in Texas, however, soon discovered that they had chosen unwisely, for the Texans showed little regard for their welfare. Eventually they were forced to resume their wandering, and all but the Alabama-Coushatta were

II · *Before the White Man*

driven north into Indian Territory or south into Mexico. Descendants of the latter group remain today on a small reservation in southeastern Texas, the only land ever returned to the Indians by that state.

Although the Spaniards adapted themselves to and built upon the Indian culture in New Mexico and Arizona, they did not do so in Texas. The obvious reason is that Texas never possessed stable Indian civilizations to the extent that New Mexico and Arizona did. Oklahoma likewise had no firm Indian culture, for the Comanches, Kiowas, Wichitas, Southern Cheyennes, and Arapahos who roamed its western plains for centuries did not remain in one place for long. Also, the Spaniards never infiltrated the land of the "Oklahoma"—the Choctaw word for "red people"—except to pass through it on rare occasions.

Centuries of human development had shaped the Southwest before the arrival of the Spaniards in the sixteenth century. The Pueblos of the steep mesas and narrow valleys, the nomadic tribes of the arid Plains, and the woodland Indians of the eastern region had evolved civilizations that fitted their simple needs. When the white man arrived with his "superior" culture, religion, and power, an inexorable change began, and life would never be the same again.

Beginning in 1830, the Five Civilized Tribes were forced to migrate from their homelands in the Old Southwest under the escort of United States troops. It was an old and sordid story. Land-hungry whites coveted the Indians' lands in Georgia, Florida, Alabama, and Mississippi. The Cherokees, Creeks, Chickasaws, Choctaws, and Seminoles were given the unwanted Indian Territory for "as long as grass grows and the waters run." After their sacrificial trek westward the civilized tribes did well for a while in their new homeland. But the Civil War took its toll of these nations and the federal government held them guilty of bad faith and confiscated much of their holdings. Thus the way was paved for eventual white settlement in Oklahoma. But that story, together with the later history of the other Southwestern Indians, belongs elsewhere.

III
FIRST CAME THE SPANIARDS

IT WAS NATURAL that the Spaniards should be the first white men to explore and colonize the Southwest, for they were closest to it during the sixteenth and seventeenth centuries. Twenty-one years after Columbus's first voyage to America, Juan Ponce de León landed on the coast of Florida, and six years later Hernán Cortés marched into Mexico City. Cortés stayed in Mexico and soon extended Spain's power and prestige over most of the country, but Ponce de León, like so many who followed him into Florida, retreated in the face of disaster; when he returned several years later, he was killed. Nevertheless, the stage was set for an

III · *First Came the Spaniards*

early penetration of the Southwest from two directions. While Cortés was pushing his conquest northward from Vera Cruz, other Spaniards were approaching the Southwest from the east.

By 1519 the entire coast of the Gulf of Mexico between Yucatán and Florida had been explored and charted in an effort to locate a strait that would lead the Spaniards toward India. This futile search was continued on land and sea for two centuries.

Chief among the early explorers in the Gulf was Captain Alonso Alvarez de Pineda, agent for the governor of Jamaica, Francisco de Garay. Pineda left Jamaica in the spring of 1519, his four ships loaded with 270 sailors, soldiers, civil servants, and friars. His orders were to cruise along the coast of Florida (which was then the name for the entire crescent of the Gulf, log the rivers and bays, and seek the legendary strait. The little fleet eventually reached Apalachee Bay and then turned westward. The mouth of the Mississippi River, which Pineda named the Espíritu Santo, was passed, and soon the coast of Texas hove into sight.

The land of Texas, referred to as Amichel by Pineda, was described as a wondrous region. Although he did not put ashore until he reached the mouth of the Rio Grande, Pineda hugged the coast from present Galveston to Brownsville as close as he dared. His tiny fleet eventually dropped anchor in the muddy brown waters of the Rio Grande, previously named the Río de las Palmas. The time was the autumn of 1519, six months after Pineda's departure from Jamaica. Doubtless the curious Spaniards marched ashore to examine the country and replenish their water and food supply; however, the records of the expedition indicate that they did not tarry long. Hopes of finding a strait were still alive, and a further examination of the coastline was necessary.

Pineda pushed on toward the south and dropped anchor off the coast of Vera Cruz, where a strange drama unfolded. Cortés was already master of these shores, and he did not welcome visitors, even fellow Spaniards. A landing party was sent ashore, not knowing that fifty of Cortés's soldiers were lying in ambush near the beach. When three members of the small party advanced from the water's edge to claim the land of Mexico for Governor Garay of Jamaica, they were promptly seized and arrested. The others beat a hasty retreat and rejoined the fleet just as it raised sails. The commander chose to abandon the three men who had been taken captive, rather than risk the entire expedition's fate in the hands of a ruthless compatriot.

Pineda did not turn back immediately toward Jamaica, for his ships were heavily swollen with barnacles and their bottoms had to be scraped if they were to remain afloat. The squadron returned to the mouth of the Rio Grande. Here Pineda and part of his crew went ashore, while the rest stayed with the careened ships. The visitors spent forty days about the mouth of the river, where they found the Indians friendly. Some eighteen miles upstream they discovered forty mud villages where the natives came for seafood when the roots and berries inland were not yet ripe enough to eat. These Indians raised no crops, but they had objects to trade to the swarthy Spaniards. Pineda observed that the land was good and the region healthful. As far as the eye could see, the terrain appeared flat: an excellent spot for a colony. The commander also saw Indians with gold ornaments, but he failed to record particulars about how much and where they had found the gold.

At last the ships were in good repair, and the visitors made ready to depart for Jamaica. They had not found the strait pointing to Cathay, but they sailed away with knowledge that no other Europeans had acquired. They were the first white men to see any part of the Southwest.

When Pineda returned to Jamaica and reported to Governor Garay his observations regarding the establishment of a colony near the mouth of the Rio Grande, Garay made haste to send another expedition there, this time under Diego de Camargo. Taking a company of 150 foot soldiers, seven cavalrymen and horses, some brass cannon, several masons, and a supply of bricks and lime, Camargo set out in the spring of 1520. Garay wanted a permanent fort built in Texas to hold his newly claimed empire against the greedy Cortés. Colonists would arrive after the fort

III · *First Came the Spaniards*

was completed. But Camargo made a mistake that Pineda had been careful to avoid. When his ships had been brought some twenty miles up the river and anchored, the commander aroused the anger of the natives. Realizing that their property, freedom, and women were in jeopardy, the Indians turned against their unwelcome visitors, and before the main party could escape down the river, eighteen men and seven cavalry horses were killed.

Camargo was forced to abandon one ship, and as food supplies were precariously low, he had no alternative but to send the strongest members of his party overland toward Vera Cruz while he tried to make that port by water. Another vessel eventually was abandoned, and the third sank a few days after reaching its destination. Thus, the survivors of the expedition were irresistibly drawn into the web of Cortés's power. Meanwhile, colonists from Jamaica arrived at the mouth of the Rio Grande to find the region abandoned. They too continued southward and soon swelled the forces under the control of the Conqueror.

On July 25, 1523, Governor Garay arrived in person at the Rio Grande, determined to plant a colony on the outermost fringe of the Southwest. This third effort should have succeeded, for Garay had sixteen ships, 700 soldiers, and fifty officers. His men were well armed with guns, crossbows, and cannon, and there were enough supplies and building materials to sustain a permanent settlement. But Garay was not destined for triumph. For some reason, soon after his arrival he abandoned his plan to lay out a settlement. Perhaps he was disappointed by what he found in Texas, for he quickly sailed away to the south, intending to locate his colony closer to the mouth of the Pánuco River, above Vera Cruz. Inevitably, he too fell into Cortés's tenacious trap and became a prisoner of the man who seemingly could not be checked. His men soon deserted him for the more powerful enemy, and within a year the "Governor of Texas" was dead.

The next Europeans arrived in the Southwest by accident. These travelers had planned to establish a colony in Florida, only to experience one of the most disastrous failures in the annals of Spanish enterprise in the Western Hemisphere. The leader of this ill-fated venture was Pánfilo de Narváez, who sailed from Spain in June 1527 with 600 colonists and a number of Franciscan friars. Narváez had received a patent from the Spanish government to command the lands once granted to Garay—the region stretching from the mouth of the Rio Grande to the Cape of Floridas. Like all Spanish encomenderos, Narváez hungered for riches, and the vague rumor that some of the natives visited by Pineda wore gold ornaments had spurred him into action. His expedition eventually reached Santo Domingo, where one-third of his colonists deserted and two of his ships were destroyed by a hurricane. With the remaining 400 he sailed north to Tampa Bay in the spring of 1528. The natives fled at the sight of his ships in the harbor, leaving nothing to deter Narváez from landing and taking possession of their deserted villages.

Eventually the frightened Indians returned and the commander learned that the land to the north, Appalachen, teemed with "yellow metal." The gullible Spaniards never perceived that it was an Indian characteristic to tell strangers exactly what they wanted to believe. Also, the Indians learned quickly that the surest way to get rid of undesirable company was to reveal that great treasures could be found to the north, east, south, or west. Narváez promptly set off overland for Appalachen; the wives of the colonists remained on board the ships, which were ordered to effect a rendezvous with him somewhere to the north. But the meeting of the land and sea parties never took place, and after a year of fruitless sailing back and forth along the Florida coast the fleet departed for Cuba. When Narváez discovered that his vessels were gone and that there was no gold to be found inland, he decided to slay his horses for food and build a fleet of horsehide boats in which to escape to Mexico. The latter was believed to be only a short distance away.

Five crude boats were constructed, and on September 28, 1528, crowded with 242 men, they put out from the Florida coast. When they reached the mouth of the Mississippi River, the current carried them far out to sea and separated them. Three of the makeshift vessels eventually regrouped and managed to draw

III · *First Came the Spaniards*

within sight of the coast once again. They continued their journey westward until November 6, when a severe storm drove two of the boats ashore. The place is generally believed to have been Galveston Island, but the Spaniards appropriately called it Malhado ("Misfortune"). Among the eighty survivors stranded on the island was Álvar Núñez Cabeza de Vaca, treasurer of the Narváez expedition. The commander himself, aboard the only vessel that survived the storm, was determined to go on, even though most of the passengers had to be put ashore to keep the frail craft from sinking. But it too was eventually destroyed, and Narváez disappeared forever.

Only fifteen of the eighty who survived the Galveston Island shipwreck remained alive after the severe winter of 1528. The men were virtually held prisoner by the Indians until all but three escaped to the mainland and fled westward along the coast. Cabeza de Vaca and two others were too ill to join them and thus had to remain on the island. When one of his companions did leave, Cabeza de Vaca remained to care for the other, Oviedo, still too weak to travel. Oviedo ultimately regained his strength, but he lacked courage to leave the island except for brief excursions to the mainland. Cabeza de Vaca remained with his companion for six long years, during which time he became a successful trader and medicine man among the coastal Indians. Sometimes he starved for days and generally led the life of a slave, but ordinary perils and hardship lost their terrors for him. His captors allowed him to come and go at will, for they believed that his prayers for their sick had miraculous powers of healing. He himself was surprised by his occasional successes in a profession for which, he subtly observed, he had taken no examinations and possessed no diplomas.

At length this hardy Spaniard fled, striking out overland for Mexico. From various Indians along the coast of Texas he learned that Spaniards were held captive by other tribes. In 1534 he came upon three of his former companions, Andrés Dorantes, Alonso de Castillo, and a Christianized Moor named Estevanico. "We gave many thanks at seeing ourselves together, and this was a day to us of the greatest pleasure we had enjoyed in life," Cabeza de Vaca wrote after his return to Spain. The meeting place of the four Europeans was somewhere on the lower Colorado or Guadalupe River. Dorantes, Castillo, and Estevanico, the only survivors of the twelve who had escaped six years before, had accompanied their Indian captors to gather nuts. The four immediately made plans to escape when the separate tribes of Indians returned during the fall season to feast on the fruit of prickly pears.

Cabeza de Vaca and his three companions were the first Europeans to enter the vast interior of the Southwest. Their exact route is not known, but they approached the edge of the Great Plains. The proof is Cabeza de Vaca's comment on the buffalo herds: "I have seen them thrice and have eaten their meat." But he apparently did not penetrate very far into the buffalo lands, for he makes no mention of skin tipis or the dog travois of the Plains Indians to which subsequent explorers devoted so much space.

As the Spaniards moved through the interior of Texas and New Mexico, they subsisted on rabbits, deer, opossums, roots, nuts, and fruits. The Indians they encountered beyond the point of escape proved much more friendly than those of the coastal region. Cabeza de Vaca says that "they even accompanied us until they delivered us to others, and all held faith in our coming from heaven." Somewhere along the way the natives outlined two routes, one leading to the "maize" and the other to the "cows."[1] The Spaniards wisely determined to go in search of maize, for the road of the cows would have carried them to the north. "We held it always certain that by going towards the sunset we would reach the goal of our wishes. . . . Thus we . . . traversed all the country until coming out at the South Sea."

Eight years after the shipwreck off the Texas coast, the four survivors encountered Spaniards on a slave-hunting foray on the frontier of New Galicia, in upper Sonora. From here they were escorted to Culiacán, arriving on April 1, 1536. Later they jour-

---

[1] Bolton believes that Cabeza de Vaca was now in the region of the Big Bend of the Rio Grande.

III · *First Came the Spaniards*

neyed to Mexico City and reported to Viceroy Antonio de Mendoza. Shortly afterward Cabeza de Vaca returned to Spain, where he wrote an account of his adventures. His legacy was passed on to the greatest of all sixteenth-century Spanish explorers of the Southwest, Hernando de Soto and Francisco Vásquez de Coronado. Both entered the region in search of gold—Coronado from the west and De Soto from the east—about the same time, and their magnificent failures caused the Spaniards to abandon the Southwest until the following century.

Cabeza de Vaca's return to Spain caused much excitement.[2] Although he carefully reported that he saw no gold, he stated that he and his companions observed signs of it throughout the Southwest. In 1538 Hernando de Soto, former Peruvian conquistador, was made governor of Cuba and *adelantado* of Florida. He tried to persuade Cabeza de Vaca to accompany him to America, where he hoped that a new Peru could be found somewhere in Florida, but Cabeza de Vaca was unwilling to take part in an expedition not commanded by himself. Nevertheless, De Soto had no difficulty in obtaining the services of more noblemen than he needed, and with 600 men tightly packed in nine small vessels he arrived at Santiago de Cuba in April 1538. One year later the Spanish Commander left Havana for the coast of Florida with the largest and best-equipped force yet assembled in North America. In his train were some 550 lancers, crossbowmen, and arquebusiers, 200 horses, and a number of Dominican friars.

The expedition landed near Tampa Bay on May 30, 1539. For the next three years De Soto was engaged in restless wandering through Florida, Georgia, Carolina, Tennessee, Alabama, Mississippi, Arkansas, Oklahoma, Louisiana, and part of Texas. Indians told them that beyond their country, Cale, and "toward the sunset" there lay a land of perpetual summer. Here there was so much gold that when its people warred with tribes of Cale "they wore golden hats like casques." The search for these "golden hats" drove

---

[2] Cabeza de Vaca was the only survivor of Narváez's expedition who left the New World.

THE SOUTHWEST: *Old and New*

De Soto on and on and resulted in the slaughter of many Indians. At length he reached the Mississippi River, where he met his death. The command of the now greatly depleted force fell to Luís de Moscoso de Alvarado, who had already grown weary of the fruitless search for gold and was ready to try to reach Mexico.

On June 5, 1542, the Spaniards moved westward from the bank of the Mississippi. They crossed present-day Arkansas and reached the Red River near where Texarkana now stands. Here they turned south and entered the Caddo villages of eastern Texas. Eventually they advanced as far as the Brazos River before turning back along their trail to the mouth of the Arkansas on the Mississippi, where De Soto had died several months before. While on the edge of the Southwest, Moscoso learned from various Indians that the "buffalo plains" were nearby, but he did not see them.

This expedition, which reached the eastern portion of the Southwest, marked another milestone in the Spanish failure to find gold. On July 3, 1543, Moscoso and his 320 men pushed down the Mississippi River in seven improvised boats. Two months and seven days later they entered the mouth of the Pánuco River, 150 miles north of Vera Cruz, where they received a warm reception from their countrymen. But news of their ill luck had come too late to prevent the launching of Coronado's great overland venture from the Pacific coast. It probably would have made no difference anyway, for the Spanish officials were determined to learn the truth about the Southwest at any cost.

Coronado's journey was the first extensive excursion into our four Southwestern states. Two fragmentary bits of information had been sufficient to effect action. One was based upon Cabeza de Vaca's report that he had heard of great cities on the Rio Grande with many-storied houses and great riches. He also stated that an Indian had given him "a copper-hawks-bell, thick and large and figured with a face," which came from the north. The second fragment about the Southwest was based on an earlier report to the viceregal government by an Indian belonging to Governor Nuño de Guzmán. The slave told the credulous governor of New

III · *First Came the Spaniards*

Galicia that as a child he had gone on a trading journey with his father to the northern Rio Grande and that he well remembered visiting "seven cities" near the river where the streets contained many shops for gold- and silver-smiths. This story caused much excitement when it was forwarded to the Spanish crown; combined with Cabeza de Vaca's report, it seemed to confirm that the so-called Seven Cities of Gold did exist.

Meanwhile, Antonio de Mendoza became the first viceroy of New Spain. A short time later, in 1539, Francisco Vásquez de Coronado was made governor of New Galicia. The viceroy eventually designated Coronado to command an expedition that would spread the power of Spain northward and search out the Seven Cities.

Before the full expedition departed from Culiacán, the capital of New Galicia, Viceroy Mendoza and Coronado planned a preliminary investigation of the Southwest. The Bishop of Mexico had a remarkable guest, Fray Marcos de Niza, a Franciscan friar who had experienced many adventures in Peru and Guatemala as an explorer and missionary. He would make an excellent addition to the Coronado company. Consequently, it was agreed that Fray Marcos (or Marcus) would journey north in advance of the main guard, pacify the Indians along the way, and send back information regarding gold and silver in the region. This role, incidentally, had first been offered to Cabeza de Vaca, but he had declined it before sailing for Spain. The three other survivors of his party, including Estevanico, the Moorish slave belonging to Dorantes, had settled in Mexico. Coronado obtained the Moor as a guide and ordered him to accompany Fray Marcos; also in the party were most of the Indians who had followed Cabeza de Vaca's party to Mexico and been held as prisoners.

Fray Marcos, clad in a gray zaragoza-cloth habit, and Estevanico, dressed in bright clothes trimmed with jingle bells, left Culiacán afoot on March 7, 1539. With them marched a large company of Indians who were to serve as guides for the main expedition, which would follow later. At Vacapa, Fray Marcos sent Estevanico and a small party ahead with instructions to establish friendly relations with the natives and send back periodic reports of the country. Cabeza de Vaca had previously used the Moor very successfully in this capacity; also, Estevanico's fondness for Indian women undoubtedly had something to do with Marcos's desire to get him out of his sight temporarily.

Estevanico advanced into the northern part of Sonora and ultimately into what is now Arizona. Here he found many Indians, who told him of seven rich cities thirty days' journey to the east, which they called Cibola. And beyond Cibola were even richer provinces. This was the kind of news Estevanico desired, and he promptly sent word back to Marcos before pushing on.

Fray Marcos wasted little time in following his agent's trail across the desert. As he passed from village to village, the stories of the fabulous land of Cibola grew more and more impressive. Meanwhile, Estevanico reached the first of the Seven Cities, but the local chief refused him entrance, and he had to sleep in a lodge outside the village, without food or drink. The Moor did not know that inadvertently he had sealed his fate by displaying various ceremonial charms formerly belonging to tribes that were enemies of the local inhabitants. The next morning they fell upon him and his Indian companions. Most of the company was destroyed, and the few who escaped fled westward to warn Fray Marcos.

Fray Marcos was crossing the Apache Plains of Arizona when he met the survivors of his advance party and learned of Estevanico's death. The Indians with him were immediately struck with terror and wanted to desert, but two finally agreed to accompany the friar to Cibola, provided he would not attempt to enter the city. Some fifteen days' journey brought them within sight of a large Indian settlement, which was probably the Zuñi pueblo of Hawikuh, one of the Seven Cities that is in ruins today. Marcos was true to his word, for he only viewed the terraced buildings of the village from a nearby hill. "Judging by what I could see from the height where I placed myself to observe it," he wrote, "the settlement is larger than the City of Mexico."

From Indians encountered nearby, the friar subsequently learned that many days' journey east of this place was a valley of

III · First Came the Spaniards

well-populated towns whose people grew corn, wore mantles of cotton, and used vessels of gold. Marcos decided against a personal investigation. Instead, he gave thanks to God that he had found Cibola, which he solemnly claimed for the King of Spain and the viceroy as the new kingdom of San Francisco. Feeling that his mission was completed, he hastened homeward "with more fear than food" over a route that is believed to have led southwestward through the mountains of eastern Arizona, up the San Pedro River, and then south into Sonora. His report convinced the Spanish officials that another Peru or Mexico awaited them.

On January 6, 1540, the Viceroy ordered Coronado to advance without delay to the Seven Cities of Cibola, promising him all the assistance "that you may need in the performance of the duties of your office." Accordingly, Coronado assembled his army of 300 soldiers, mostly gentry, and 700 Indians at Compostela on the Pacific coast in time to depart on February 23, 1540. The presence of Viceroy Mendoza lent additional pomp and ceremony to the occasion. It must have been a spectacular sight, and certainly it was the most brilliant review ever held in the New World. The cavaliers wore shining armor and were mounted on splendid horses equipped with colored blankets, leather armor, and silver-mounted harness; each foot soldier was armed with crossbow and arquebus, sword and shield; and the Indians were splashed with warpaint and decked in multicolored plumage.

The soldiers, horses, friars, and pack mules were intended to be the best-fed party that had so far entered the Southwest. Droves of cattle, sheep, goats, and swine were their walking commissary, and additional supplies were to be carried by water. Unfortunately Alarcón, the captain of the three vessels that sailed along the coast to the mouth of the Colorado River, was never able to effect a rendezvous.

At Culiacán, Coronado divided his land forces, leaving the main body to follow while he and Fray Marcos pushed ahead with twenty-five foot soldiers, several friars, some Indians and Negroes, and part of the artillery. This was on April 22, 1540. One month later the Spanish officer was crossing the divide into San Pedro

THE SOUTHWEST: *Old and New*

Valley, and a short time thereafter he was about where Fort Grant now stands. Now his course veered from east to northwest, and soon the advance party glimpsed the first of the Seven Cities, Hawikuh, fifteen miles southwest of present-day Zuñi. "It is a little, crowded village, looking as if it had been crumbled together," wrote Castañeda, historian of the expedition. The sight was a great disappointment to Coronado and his men, and bitter were the epithets they hurled at Fray Marcos now that his report proved so utterly false.

The people of Hawikuh and other nearby villages resisted Coronado's entrance into their settlements, and much fighting ensued before the Spaniards were able to take possession. At least the Spaniards found a little food, something needed more than gold or silver at the moment. The commander remained at Granada, the name he gave to the Zuñi settlements, for several weeks while small parties explored the surrounding country. One group discovered the Grand Canyon during these forays and made an unsuccessful attempt to descend to its bottom.

In the meantime Coronado sent a message in the direction of Culiacán ordering the main army to hasten forward. He also prepared to dispatch some of his men toward the Rio Grande, for an Indian had arrived at Zuñi with word that great cities stood along the riverbank and the country beyond teemed with "humpback cows." On Sunday, August 29, 1540, a small party of Spaniards under the command of Captain Hernando de Alvarado, started eastward to reconnoiter the country, locate the river cities, and report back to the general if gold existed there in the quantities that the Spaniards hoped for.

Approximately fifty miles east of Zuñi, Alvarado skirted the "sky city" of Acoma, situated on a plateau that rose straight out of the plains as high as a good musket could throw a ball. From Acoma the advance party moved almost due eastward across the desert, and one week after leaving Granada it reached the banks of the Rio Grande, which Alvarado named Río de Nuestra Señora. Here the Spaniards met Indians from some twelve pueblos, who

III · *First Came the Spaniards*

proved friendly and who told them of other settlements to the north.

Alvarado moved from pueblo to pueblo, planting crosses along his course and instructing the natives in their veneration. He also sent word to Coronado, informing him of the pueblos and of the good pasture land for the horses and advising him to bring the army to the river for the winter. By the end of autumn 1540 the various companies were assembled in the village of Tiguex, near present-day Bernalillo, New Mexico. Perhaps it is unnecessary to add that the Spaniards were not welcome.

Ultimately, the Coronado expedition left the Rio Grande for the Great Plains. Once again the credulous Spaniards were lured on by tales from a hapless Indian. This man had been rescued by Alvarado from one of the pueblo tribes who held him prisoner. He is believed to have been a Pawnee, but the Spaniards called him El Turko because of his looks. The Turk described a place in his native country called Quivira, far to the east, where the people ate from dishes of "wrought plate" and used pitchers and bowls of solid gold. When he willingly agreed to lead the Spaniards to this fabulous place, the expedition advanced across the plains toward the rising sun on April 23, 1541. Upon reaching the Pecos River it veered southward for some distance, then crossed to the opposite bank and soon emerged on the Llano Estacado. But after a month or more of marching across the flat Texas Panhandle it became clear that the guide was taking the party on a wild goose chase. By now all of the men were suffering from heat and exhaustion and their horses were tired from chasing buffalo. Also, the supply of grain was low. Coronado promptly put the Turk in irons.

A council was called near the upper waters of the Brazos River and the Turk was made to admit that he had been lying about the gold; but he insisted that Quivira really did exist. The stubborn Coronado decided to march on until he found the place—even though the prospects of gold seemed slight. He further decided that all but thirty-six of the best men and horses should return to the Rio Grande. In vain his officers tried to persuade him to

The Southwest: *Old and New*

abandon the idea of continuing across the plains; his zeal had not yet been completely destroyed by reality.

At last the demoralized army split. The main force turned back on the trackless trail, while the commander and a small band struck off in a northeasterly direction. At length they crossed the Arkansas River into Kansas, and forty-two days after leaving the Brazos River in Texas they arrived at Quivira, probably in the vicinity of Great Bend, Kansas. "Neither gold or silver nor any trace of either was found among these people." The Turk, still in chains, was tortured into making another confession: he had been detailed by the Pueblo tribesmen to lead the strangers out on the plains and lose them. Coronado promptly ordered him strung up and garroted.

So far the Spaniards had found the Southwest an inhospitable place, completely lacking in rich inhabitants and precious metals. Bad feeling spread among the men, and soon there was much grumbling and blaming of their once-respected commander. Coronado had no alternative but to return to New Mexico, where he rejoined his main army at Tiguex on October 20, 1541.

One would think that the Spaniards had suffered enough disappointment and frustration, but the commander's insatiable appetite for wealth, prestige, and honor forced him to continue the search. Parties were dispatched to the northern reaches of the Rio Grande, but, except for the discovery of well-stocked granaries at Taos Pueblo, their reports merely added new pain to old sores not yet healed. With the arrival of winter, dissension increased as rations diminished and clothing rotted. In December 1541 Coronado suffered a severe head injury as a result of a fall from his horse. As he lay ill, he faced the obvious truth of his failure and resolved to return to his wife in Mexico as soon as warm weather arrived the following spring.

Despite the fact that some of his men feared to return home and wanted to establish a permanent colony in New Mexico, in April 1542 Coronado ordered the broken command to leave for Mexico. Several hundred miles to the east, Hernando de Soto also

III · *First Came the Spaniards*

was abandoning his search for a new El Dorado and would soon die from wounds and a broken spirit.

As Coronado painfully crossed the Southwest to Mexico, he contemplated the humiliating task before him: namely, to report his failure to Viceroy Mendoza. His reputation would be gone, and shortly his office as governor of New Galicia as well, for the Spanish government showed no tolerance of failure.

It would be a long time before Spaniards again expressed interest in the interior of the Southwest.

Four decades passed after Coronado's visit before the Pueblo Indians of New Mexico were revisited by Spaniards. During the interval the frontier of Mexico was gradually pushed northward as far as Santa Barbara, in the present state of Chihuahua. From this outpost near the headwaters of the Conchos River, a tributary of the Rio Grande, the pueblos of New Mexico could be reached by an almost direct route. Its location naturally tempted the Spaniards' thirst for wealth and adventure once again, but a royal ordinance forbade military expeditions into the region where Coronado had experienced such miserable failure.

Interest in the Cibola country was revived by the appearance at Santa Barbara of a copy of Cabeza de Vaca's *Narrative*. Suddenly soldiers and miners were excited by the desire to visit the cities mentioned by the adventurer, and in 1581 they organized an expedition under the guise of a missionary venture. Among the members were three Franciscan priests, Fray Agustín Rodríguez, Fray Francisco López, and Fray Juan de Santa María, who dreamed of a virgin land in which to convert "lost souls" to Christianity. With them went a small company of soldiers and civilians.

The route of the party later became a well-traveled highway for expeditions in search of spiritual and physical conquest. It followed the Conchos to its juncture with the Rio Grande, opposite present-day Presidio, Texas, thence up that stream as far north as Taos Pueblo, New Mexico.

Fray Santa María turned back after a few hundred miles to carry reports to Mexico, and was killed by Indians near Isleta

The Southwest: *Old and New*

Pueblo. The Friars Rodríguez and López placed their trust in God and in their soldier companions, and from Taos Pueblo they eventually set out to examine the empty highlands. In their wanderings they visited the "buffalo plains" in the east and Acoma and Zuñi to the west. Here they found three members of Coronado's original party who had almost forgotten their native language. Later the soldiers abandoned the project and started southward, leaving the two friars and a few servants to establish a mission at Puaray, a short distance above modern Albuquerque. By remaining in New Mexico the brave friars showed more zeal than judgment, for shortly after the soldiers departed the Indians killed them.

Rumors of the disaster soon filtered down to Santa Barbara, but a faint hope existed that one of the missionaries, Fray Rodríguez, might still be alive. Antonio de Espejo, a soldier-trader of the region, hastened off on a mission of rescue or revenge. Espejo commanded a company of a dozen or more soldiers, one Franciscan friar, and various Indian servants. He departed from Santa Barbara near the end of 1582 and reached the mission of Puaray, not far from Coronado's old headquarters near Bernalillo, late in December.

The deaths of the two friars were soon verified, but Espejo either could not discover the guilty parties, or else he decided to forgo revenge in order to explore the country in peace. Like his predecessors, he found the temptation to search for precious metals irresistible. Leaving the Franciscan, Fray Bernardino, to his missionary work among the Pueblos, the commander struck out in search of a legendary lake of gold. His travels carried him as far as present-day Prescott, Arizona, where he did find deposits of gold and silver. This discovery led eventually to the opening of mines of considerable wealth, but at this time the Spaniards were unable to stay and develop them. Espejo retraced his steps to the Rio Grande and found that the Franciscan missionary had returned to Mexico. Espejo's arrival at Santa Barbara with samples of gold and silver ore set the Spanish frontier on fire.

Espejo hoped for a contract from the Spanish government to colonize New Mexico, which would afford him an opportunity to

III · *First Came the Spaniards*

work the metal deposits in Arizona. But governmental red tape, plus the King's preoccupation with England, caused a long delay in determining the status of the northern province. Eventually the contract went to one Juan de Oñate, a member of a distinguished family in the province of Zacatecas. In the interim, some unauthorized expeditions made attempts to colonize New Mexico, but all ended in failure.

Oñate's venture not only had royal sanction, but was prepared in feudal style so as to grant the colonists the rank of *hidalgo* for themselves and their heirs. A party of more than a hundred soldier-settlers left Santa Barbara in the spring of 1598. The departure, like Coronado's almost sixty years before, was an impressive sight. One captain required twenty-two wagons to carry his chain mail and armor, imported satin and velvet clothes, plumed and tasseled hats, leather boots and gloves, hand-carved bedstead, linen bedding, mattresses, and fancy equipment for his horses.

The journey to the Rio Grande pueblos followed a previously unused trail straight north from Santa Barbara and across the arid province of Chihuahua. Oñate reached the Rio Grande in the vicinity of El Paso, where he took formal possession "of all the kingdom and province of New Mexico on the Río del Norte, in the name of our Lord King Philip." Two months later his expedition arrived at Santo Domingo Pueblo, west of Sante Fe, and subdued all the chiefs in the region without serious difficulty. It then moved toward the north and stopped at San Gabriel, present-day Chamita.

Here, on July 11, 1598, Oñate established his headquarters, nine years before the first English colony was planted at Jamestown some 2,000 miles to the east. At San Gabriel the Spaniards erected the first church in New Mexico, and with the aid of several hundred natives began the construction of irrigation ditches. Some colonists who had left Santa Barbara with the main expedition and had stopped temporarily at the Rio Grande crossing arrived to establish homes and cultivate the land. Additional missionaries and settlers were sent for after the Indian chiefs throughout the area promised to accept the intruders and leave them in peace.

The Southwest: *Old and New*

Oñate now turned his mind to an exploration of the plains to the east and a visit to the country around Quivira. He and a few followers reached central Kansas, but gold was as scarce there as Coronado had reported. Disappointed but undaunted, the Spanish party returned to its settlement in New Mexico only to find that disaster had befallen the colony on the Rio Grande. All but a few friars had abandoned the region and returned to northern Mexico. Oñate blamed the Pueblo Indians, for driving his settlers away, and as a punishment he confiscated their food and left them destitute. "I pray that God may grant him the grace to do penance for all his deed," wrote one of the friars. But for the moment Oñate was concerned with other matters, principally his determination to hold the country. Soldiers were dispatched to Mexico to force the faint-hearted settlers to come back.

Some of the refugees did return, with seven new friars, and by 1604 Oñate was free to explore the country once again, this time toward the west. He reasoned that he could perhaps open an overland road from the Rio Grande to the South Sea, that he might obtain gold in Arizona from the site earlier visited by Espejo, or that he might find the legendary Strait of Anian. This would ensure the Spanish hold on the North American continent. Surely any one of these accomplishments would compensate for all his disappointments.

But Oñate dreamed in vain. His journey brought him to the area in Arizona visited by Espejo, thence to the Colorado River, and down its course to the Gulf of California. In April 1605 the expedition returned to the upper Rio Grande, and, like previous ones, it proved a resounding failure. Not only did Oñate fail to find the strait, but the Arizona mineral ore proved unworkable without thousands of Indian laborers and costly military forces to control them. With his wealth and energy expended, Oñate could only ask for a release from the governorship and return to Mexico in disgrace.

The Spaniards were not ready to abandon New Mexico, and early in 1609 Pedro de Peralta arrived as the new governor of the province with instructions to find a better site for the colony. Ac-

III · *First Came the Spaniards*

cordingly, he founded the town of Santa Fe a few months later and thereby assured the permanence of the Spanish outpost.

Despite superhuman efforts, neither Peralta nor his immediate successors could find any precious metals. The New Mexico province therefore reverted to a missionary field; by 1630 it supported twenty-five missions, which administered to the spiritual needs of 60,000 "converts" scattered among some ninety pueblos. For several decades the country remained at peace, and the Spanish population along the upper Rio Grande valley gradually increased to some 3,000 settlers. Even though the Indians gave partial acceptance to the Catholic religion, they grew sullen and rebellious at the friars' insistence that they abandon their own. Their conquerors also forced them to labor under intolerable conditions, and in 1680 they threw off their shackles and rebelled.

The revolt resulted in the slaughter of over 400 men, women, and children, and the complete expulsion of the foreigners. Those who survived fled south to the settlements that had sprung up around the El Paso area on the Rio Grande. There they remained until Governor Diego de Vargas ruthlessly reconquered the country of the upper Rio Grande in 1694 and paved the way for those who desired to return. Approximately 800 came back, this time to stay. For the next fifty years the colony experienced a slow but constant growth until it numbered some 10,000 inhabitants of Spanish descent. The principal settlements were El Paso, Santa Fe, Santa Cruz, and Albuquerque.

GRADUALLY the Spaniards accepted the fact that, from a material standpoint, the interior of the Southwest was of little value. By the eighteenth century the era of exploration had ended except for a few military reconnaissances and the work of the redoubtable missionaries. Meanwhile, officials in Mexico from time to time showed passing interest in Texas and Arizona.

The Southwest: *Old and New*

Between 1686 and 1690 Alonso de León conducted five separate expeditions into southern and eastern Texas to investigate French intrusion into the Spanish territory. As a result of these excursions, Spanish friars established the mission of San Francisco among the Asinai Indians near the Neches River. Father Domian Massanet and a small company of priests and soldiers occupied it until in 1693 they were forced to flee for their lives when the natives revolted.

The Spaniards did not again show interest in Texas for more than two decades. Meanwhile, French traders along the Louisiana frontier founded a post at Natchitoches on the Red River. From this point Louis Juchereau de St. Denis and a small company of Indians and Frenchmen, two of whom had survived La Salle's ill-fated Texas expedition in 1684, crossed the hot grasslands of Texas to Mexico. St. Denis's arrival on July 8, 1714, at the Mission San Juan in Coahuila, forty miles south of the Rio Grande, so alarmed the Spaniards that they decided to reoccupy eastern Texas. Although the Frenchman said that the purpose of his journey was to open up trade with Mexico, his hosts viewed the excursion as a threat to their northern province.

As a consequence, Spain founded four new missions and a garrison near the Angelina and Neches rivers in eastern Texas. Settlers came a short time later to give the region a permanent white population. In 1718 the town of San Antonio de Bejar was laid out at the site of the beautiful San Pedro Springs, on the San Antonio River. It served as a halfway point on the direct route between eastern Texas and Mission San Juan Bautista near present-day Eagle Pass. But Spain's hold on Texas would remain a precarious one for several decades. Much maneuvering with the French and fighting against the Apaches and Comanches occurred before it became secure in the middle of the eighteenth century.[3]

---

[3] By January 1722 there were ten Texas missions, four presidios, and four centers of settlement: Los Adaes (near present Natchitoches, Louisiana), Nacogdoches, San Antonio, and La Bahía (Goliad). Other sites were occupied and scattered missions built before the Mexican Revolution in 1821, but, excepting El Paso, these were either temporary or relatively insignificant.

III · *First Came the Spaniards*

In the early history of Arizona two Spanish friars stand out: Father Eusebio Francisco Kino, an Italian-born Jesuit scholar, and Fray Francisco Garcés, a Franciscan. Father Kino first entered the present Southwestern states in 1691 with a few companions in order to work among the northern Pima tribes. The party approached the region from the mission of Dolores in Sonora, and proceeded along the Santa Cruz River as far north as modern Tucson. Father Kino came back three years later and followed the Gila River to its junction with the Salt River, near present-day Tempe. It was on this trip that the Jesuit priest visited the ruins of Casa Grande, the first white man to view this ancient city. For more than two decades he continued his explorations of southern Arizona until he had examined thoroughly every part of the Gila River region.[4]

Father Kino is remembered not merely as a tireless explorer and founder of several missions, but also as the man who introduced ranching into Arizona and many varieties of fruits, vegetables, grain, and sugar cane. But for several years after his death the Spaniards neglected the northern province. Meanwhile, the missions continued their work until 1736, when explorations by Fathers Ignacio Keller and Jacob Sedlmayr aroused new interest in the region. The discovery of silver near Guevavi the next year greatly stimulated settlement and led to further conquest and settlement of the province.

Fray Garcés is associated with the last period of extensive exploration of Arizona. In 1768 he took charge of Mission San Xavier del Bac, and within six months had already visited most of southwestern Arizona. In 1771 he journeyed down the Gila River to the mouth of the Colorado River, where he met the Yuma Indians who lived in the vicinity of the river crossing that bears their name. This experience equipped him for the task of accompanying Captain Juan Bautista de Anza, who set out from Sonora in

---

[4] In 1700 Father Kino laid the foundation for the state's first ecclesiastic building, near Tucson, which he named Mission San Xavier del Bac. Later he established the missions San Cayetano (now San José), del Tumacacori, and San Gabriel de Guevavi, in addition to a number of visitas at various Indian villages.

1774 to mark a road to the Spanish missions in southern California. The expedition proceeded from Presidio Tubac along the Camino del Diablo of northern Sonora to Yuma, thence to what is now the city of Los Angeles. Fray Garcés then left the party to return alone to Mission San Xavier. On the way he journeyed through northern Arizona and visited the land of the Yavapai Indians, thus becoming the first white man to venture into this portion of the Southwest.

The next year Fray Garcés again served as a guide for Anza, this time starting at Presidio Tubac and continuing down the Gila River to the Yuma Crossing. Here he left the party bound for northern California and made a second excursion through northern Arizona, visiting the Hopi town of Oraibi before returning to Mission San Xavier by way of the Colorado River and Yuma. In 1776 he moved the presidio at Tubac a few miles north to the little village of San Agustín del Tucson, where he remained for the next three or four years, busily engaged in missionary work.

Fray Garcés finally received permission from Spanish officials to establish a number of missions on the Colorado River at the mouth of the Gila River near the crossing. This was a project dear to his heart, for since his first visit several years before he had recognized the desirability of Spanish occupation of the crossing in order to protect the emigrants going to California and to bring the Indians under spiritual control. Consequently, a fort and two missions were built and occupied, and some forty settlers were brought in by 1780. The venture was short-lived, for within a few months the Yumas had revolted and killed most of the settlers, along with Father Garcés and one other missionary.

A distinct break in the history of the Southwest, and especially of Arizona, now began. For many years there was little traffic between New Mexico and California via the Gila Valley. Meanwhile, missionary settlements were abandoned as Spain attempted to turn back various thrusts at her crumbling empire in North America, first by the French and then by the Anglo-Americans.

IV

APPROACH AND RETREAT OF THE FRENCH

WHILE THE SPANIARDS were exhausting their energy in search of gold and silver in the Southwest, the French approached the region from the north and east, but for different purposes. Not until almost a century after the De Soto and Coronado expeditions did the French adventurers reach a tributary of the great river that ultimately brought them in contact with the Spaniards. In 1634 Jean Nicollet journeyed from Quebec as far west as the Wisconsin River, where Indians told him tales of the "Mesipi." Nicollet did not know where this mighty stream led, but he and other Frenchmen were intrigued by its mysteries. Perhaps

THE SOUTHWEST: *Old and New*

it would guide them to the South Sea or the so-called Sea of Virginia, maybe to Mexico or even Japan and China.

The riddle was solved a few decades later. In 1673, sixty-five years after the founding of Quebec by Samuel de Champlain, a young Jesuit missionary, Father Jacques Marquette, and a French trader, Louis Jolliet, reached the Mississippi River via Lake Michigan and the Fox-Wisconsin waterway. From Prairie du Chien they descended the "Father of Waters" in bark canoes, committing themselves to the current. They passed the mouth of the Missouri River, beyond the spot where De Soto once crossed the Mississippi, and went near the mouth of the Arkansas River. On the site of present-day Arkansas City the travelers enjoyed a sumptuous feast at an Indian village and received a disconcerting warning that hostile natives farther on would surely kill them if they proceeded. They were now only 700 miles from the Gulf, but on July 17, 1673, they turned back and began the arduous task of ascending the river.

Before departing, Father Marquette and Jolliet learned from various tribesmen near the periphery of the Southwest that the great river poured into the Gulf of Mexico and not into the South Sea (Pacific) or the Sea of Virginia (Atlantic). New France was thus in a most favorable position, for it was now possible to pursue a continuous course by water from the Gulf of St. Lawrence, through the heart of the continent, to the Gulf of Mexico. By erecting a chain of log forts along the banks of the Mississippi, France could monopolize the fur trade of the vast interior. Meanwhile, the English would be confined to the Atlantic Coast and the Spaniards to Mexico and the Southwest.

Verbal reports of the discovery by Father Marquette and Jolliet soon reached Quebec and excited the governor, Louis de Buade, Comte de Frontenac, with dreams of extending the boundary of New France and establishment of an ice-free port on the Gulf of Mexico. The man chosen to direct the work was the famous René Robert Cavelier, Sieur de La Salle.

Not till nine years after the return of Father Marquette and Jolliet did La Salle reach the Mississippi. Meanwhile, he was busy

IV · *Approach and Retreat of the French*

developing trading stations along the Great Lakes and securing a patent from the king of France for a monopoly of the fur trade in the new region. Finally, in 1683, this greatest of all French explorers in North America started for the West at the head of a party of fifty-four men. On February 6 they approached the "Father of Waters" via the Illinois, and proceeded down it in bark canoes. One month later they reached the site near the mouth of the Arkansas where Father Marquette and Jolliet had landed. La Salle planted a cross and took "possession" of the country for the French king before drifting down to the Gulf. He repeated the ceremony at one of the mouths of the Mississippi on April 2, 1682, undisturbed by the realization that De Soto had claimed the valley of the great river for Spain 141 years earlier. But he could not linger long. The country was unhealthy, food was scarce, and the Indians were sullen and treacherous. The French *voyageurs* returned to the Mackinac River by the route along which they had come, knowing that other Frenchmen would contest the Spaniards' control of the Southwest.

Three years later La Salle came back to the Gulf, this time with 400 men in a fleet of four ships that sailed directly from France. The commander had secured permission to found colonies in Louisiana, construct a series of posts from the Gulf to the Lakes, and govern the country. In the meantime, the French had established a permanent outpost at Starved Rock on the Illinois River, and the future promised much, both for the enterprising explorer and for New France.

Now began a series of disasters that altered the course of Southwestern history. First, a storm scattered the fleet, and the expedition sailed past the mouth of the Mississippi. Then the Spaniards captured one ship. In January 1685 the other members of the party rendezvoused in Matagorda Bay, some 400 miles west of their destination. One of the ships, the *Amiable*, ran aground, barely 100 miles from the spot where Cabeza de Vaca had been shipwrecked a century and a half before. Another vessel was lost some time later, and the fourth eventually returned to France.

La Salle and most of his soldiers and colonists went ashore

to establish temporary headquarters. A stockade was constructed, enclosing six crude huts, and the place was appropriately named Fort St. Louis.[1] Disease soon decimated the pioneers, the Indians proved hostile, and the morale of the ill-equipped colony began to waver. For a while supplies from the wrecked vessels sustained the Frenchmen. Meanwhile, exploring parties attempted to reconnoiter the country and find the Mississippi. Dissensions became more frequent. After two years of fruitless wandering and with supplies almost exhausted, La Salle decided to march overland to Canada. Early in January 1687 the commander and sixteen half-starved companions set out on the desperate journey. Twenty men were left behind as a garrison force.

Sixty-eight days later and 250 miles from Fort St. Louis, La Salle met his death at the hands of three disgruntled followers. The command of the expedition now fell to Joutel, the chronicler of the colony. Eventually he and a handful of comrades arrived at the mouth of the Arkansas River, where they found two members of a searching party from the French post at Starved Rock. Joutel went on to Canada and later to France.

As for the small, miserable garrison force that La Salle had left behind on the Texas coast, the French made no effort to rescue it. In 1689, Spanish marines from Vera Cruz sighted the wrecked French ships off Matagorda Bay. This discovery thoroughly upset the Spaniards and resulted in several expeditions across Texas to find and destroy the French settlement. Captain Alonso de León eventually reached the fort, but disease, starvation, and Indians had already disposed of its occupants. Subsequently it was learned that Indians in the region held as prisoners a few survivors, who were eventually ransomed. Thus the book was closed on an exploring venture into the Southwest that was as tragic as any of the Spaniards' own grand failures.

La Salle's dream of colonizing the country near the mouth of

---

[1] The site of this post was fixed by E. W. Cole, who spent some fifteen years of research on La Salle's experiences in Texas, as Demmit's Point, about five miles above the mouth of the Lavaca River in Jackson County, Texas.

IV · Approach and Retreat of the French

the Mississippi was allowed to rest for several years, but it was not forgotten. In 1699 two shiploads of colonists from France arrived in the Gulf and prepared to establish a permanent foothold where La Salle had failed. This time, after first erecting a stout fortification near present-day Biloxi, they found the Mississippi River. The enterprise was commanded by Pierre le Moyne, Sieur d'Iberville, who, with his younger brother, Jean le Moyne, Sieur de Bienville, later played a dominant role in the early history of Louisiana. The brothers, together with Douay, a survivor of La Salle's last expedition, and forty-eight soldiers, departed in canoes and rowboats from the well-garrisoned post near Biloxi and proceeded westward along the coast. On March 2, 1699, they reached the mouth of the elusive river—"the water all muddy and very white"—and turned upstream. At the site where New Orleans was established nineteen years later, the Frenchmen stopped to plant a cross and partake of a freshly killed buffalo. Another few hundred miles brought them to the mouth of the Arkansas River, where other French parties had previously camped. Here they discovered indisputable evidence that they were in the heart of the country which had intrigued La Salle and to which he had drawn the attention of France.

Iberville soon returned to Biloxi, and in succeeding years several parties from his settlement explored the interior, prospected for gold, and traded with the Indians. Some of his men struggled as far north as the Illinois country, while French fur traders from that region made the journey down to the lower Mississippi valley. Despite its isolated position, the French settlement on the Gulf managed to survive. Iberville died in 1706, and Bienville became governor of the colony. Subsequent settlements were made at Mobile (1710), Natchitoches (1714), and New Orleans (1718).

During the eighteenth century the French in Louisiana were more interested in widening their commercial trade than in establishing a rival to Spain's Southwestern empire. It was primarily for this purpose that St. Denis, in 1714, built the fort at the head of navigation on Red River, 125 miles upstream from the Mississippi.

THE SOUTHWEST: *Old and New*

In time the settlement became the town of Natchitoches, the first French outpost on the edge of the Southwest. As soon as it neared completion, St. Denis set off across the interior of Texas, traveling over much of the route covered by Cabeza de Vaca two centuries earlier. It has already been observed that his appearance in northern Mexico excited the Spaniards. St. Denis was arrested, but he demonstrated his honorable intentions by falling in love with the pretty niece of a Spanish officer, Captain Domingo Ramón. The Spanish Viceroy at Mexico City became suspicious of the Frenchman's proposal for trade between the two countries, and he decided to send an expedition to establish a series of towns and missions along the eastern frontier. These, he hoped, while trading with the French, would also close off French expansion across Texas. St. Denis agreed to guide the expedition, which left the Rio Grande in 1716 and followed a route that later became the Old San Antonio Road, or the Camino Real.

The Spaniards founded several missions in eastern Texas in the neighborhood of what is now Nacogdoches, and about seventy-five miles farther east the mission of Nuestra Señora del Pilar de los Adaes was constructed. This settlement was only fourteen miles west of St. Denis's fort at Natchitoches, and for fifty-six years it remained the official capital of Spanish Texas.[2] Thus, the Spaniards and French moved closer to one another—close enough to observe one another's actions. And while the former continued to be suspicious and lethargic, the enterprising French expanded their fur trade with the Indians. One of their objectives was to reach the Spanish settlement of New Mexico and tap the rich reservoir of trade offered by that Spanish province.

In 1719 a European war between Spain and France furnished an opportunity for some of the more aggressive French traders in Louisiana to expand operations. The commander of the post at Natchitoches invaded eastern Texas with a small force, whereupon the Spaniards abandoned their settlements and fled to San

---

[2] The Sabine River was not recognized as the boundary between Texas and Louisiana until several decades later.

IV · *Approach and Retreat of the French*

Antonio. A plan to follow this raid with another to seize San Antonio was now proposed. St. Denis, who had been arrested by the Spaniards in 1714 and again in 1717 on his second visit to the Rio Grande, was ready to lead the expedition. But the venture was halted at the last moment. Hostilities between France and Spain ended, and on July 16, 1721, Governor Bienville of Louisiana received orders from France to stop the war in America. Fortunately, St. Denis was informed before he departed for San Antonio.

Meanwhile, news of the disturbance in eastern Texas reached officials in Mexico. On the scene was the renowned second Marquis de San Miguel de Aguayo, a wealthy citizen of Coahuila, who quickly offered his services to restore Spanish dominion over Texas. Aguayo feared that the whole northern frontier, New Mexico as well as Texas, was greatly endangered by the French assault and he was moved by "insatiable zeal" to drive back the enemy. The Viceroy accepted his offer and conferred upon him the governorship of the provinces of Coahuila and Texas.

Aguayo raised a company of soldiers, but ill luck prevented his departure across the Rio Grande until March 20, 1721. At Mission San Juan Bautista he divided his forces, sending forty soldiers under Captain Domingo Ramón down the Rio Grande and ultimately to La Bahía, the site of La Salle's old colony. The Marquis expected that the French would attempt to reoccupy the region, and he wished to thwart their efforts. The main expedition later proceeded to San Antonio by way of the Old San Antonio Road. After a series of forced marches through intense heat, it arrived there on April 4, 1721. The same day Ramón took possession of La Bahía, near Matagorda Bay.

From San Antonio, Aguayo continued toward eastern Texas, following a northward route along the slope of the Balcones Fault to the vicinity of present-day Temple. Then he veered due eastward to meet the San Antonio Road. Before he reached the former Spanish settlements and missions in eastern Texas, the Spanish commander was intercepted by a Frenchman sent by St. Denis, now commandant of French forces on the southwestern frontier. The Marquis was informed that he was to be given safe conduct to St. Denis in order that matters of interest between their respective crowns could be discussed. The two officials eventually met on the east bank of the Neches River, and St. Denis told Aguayo that a truce had been declared in Europe. He also explained that the French invasion of Spanish settlements in Texas two years before had been a "personal action"; the officer responsible had been declared a delinquent by the French Governor at Mobile and probably by now was dead.

Aguayo accepted St. Denis's explanation and was further assured of French sincerity by his promise to abandon France's holdings in Texas and withdraw to Natchitoches. Obviously, the new attitude of the French was dictated by their desire to renew trade with the Spaniards and to extend intercourse with the Indians with a minimum of difficulty. Besides, their hold on Texas was too tenuous to withstand any Spanish offensive action.

Relieved by the exodus of the French, the Marquis turned to winning the loyalty of the local Indians for Spain. He also rebuilt and fortified the five missions and presidio in eastern Texas and the mission and presidio at Los Adaes in what is now Louisiana. On October 17, 1721, Aguayo commenced his return to San Antonio. All of the establishments had been reoccupied, and eastern Texas was restored to Spanish control. Only one important task remained before the Marquis could feel free to return to Coahuila. This was a brief visit to Presidio La Bahía.

A force of forty men had arrived there the previous spring, but the Marquis thought it advisable to augment it with an additional forty soldiers from his own contingent. Although the French appeared sincere in their desire for good relations, Aguayo felt that fortifications should be constructed and manned in the region of La Salle's old colony in case the French changed their intentions regarding Texas. The post was eventually completed and supplied with artillery pieces, and two new missions were erected by the end of May 1722. Aguayo again withdrew to San Antonio, confident that he had removed permanently the French threat to Texas. Later he inaugurated a colonization scheme that strengthened the Spanish hold on the province for a full century.

IV · *Approach and Retreat of the French*

Two weeks after the Marquis had disbanded his forces in Coahuila, he recommended to the king that 200 families from Coahuila, the Canary Islands, or Havana, and an equal number of loyal Tlascaltecan Indians be moved to Texas. According to Aguayo, these settlers should be distributed among San Antonio, Presidio La Bahía, and the various missions in eastern Texas. "Without these families it will be most difficult, if not impossible, for that province to be self-supporting. By so-doing Your Majesty will have one of the best provinces in America from the standpoint of fertility and delightfulness of the country. . . . It is suitable for the cultivation of crops and for the raising of cattle." The King of Spain approved Aguayo's recommendation, and a few years later some Canary Islanders colonized the Southwestern province. They, together with the 269 soldiers that the Marquis had left in 1721–2, held the region for Spain so firmly that title to it was never again in dispute until the Anglo-Americans arrived in the nineteenth century.

At the time when the French were trying to establish trade with the Spaniards in Texas, including the brief military occupation of eastern Texas, 1719–21, they also strove mightily to penetrate the Southwest via New Mexico. In the same year in which rumors first reached Mexico that French plans were afoot to reoccupy the site of La Salle's ill-fated colony near Matagorda Bay, the Viceroy also learned that a number of Frenchmen had departed for the "mines of Santa Fe." Aguayo's subsequent occupation of Presidio La Bahía dispelled the first rumor, but New Mexico posed a much more complicated threat.

The mines of New Mexico had early fascinated and excited the French colonists in America.[3] News soon reached Santa Fe that the intruders were forming alliances with various Indian tribes and supplying them with firearms, gradually preparing the way for an advance on the Spanish settlements. That the French

---

[3] An original manuscript in the Library of the Museum of the American Indian, Heye Foundation, New York City, reveals that Frenchmen were on the plains northeast of New Mexico by 1695.

had an interest in New Mexico there is little doubt. The valleys of the Missouri, Arkansas, Red, and Platte rivers afforded an inviting field for the activities of the energetic and enterprising Gallic *voyageurs*. But before they could reach Santa Fe from the northwest and tap the lucrative trade that the province appeared to offer, they first must establish alliances with the Indians. This meant settling ancient enmities among the various tribes and then using those tribes as intermediaries with the Spaniards. Thus, the French reasoned, they not only would be able to enter New Mexico, but also could carry on a profitable business with the Indians on the way.

The French plan was a long-range one and thus was slow to develop. As early as 1704, Canadians in substantial numbers reached the headwaters of the Missouri River. During succeeding years the traders Lourain, Bourgmond, and DuTisne were active among the Pawnee, Osage, and Arapaho tribes. Their movements did not go unnoticed by the suspicious Spaniards, but there was no cause for great alarm while Louis XIV remained alive to perpetuate the intimate relations between the French and Spanish crowns.

The death of the Sun King in 1715 brought a change in the attitude of the officials of New Spain toward the French. The activities of the *voyageurs* would be disregarded no longer. Especially did this become apparent after Bernard de La Harpe left Natchitoches in 1719 and established an alliance with the Wichita Indians camped near the mouth of the Canadian River in present-day Oklahoma. Later in that same year he erected a trading post in the vicinity of Texarkana. The settlement proved a temporary one, but the Spaniards looked upon it as part of a grand scheme to encircle their northern provinces. Knowledge of La Harpe's activities on the northeastern fringe of the Spanish Southwest, together with the occupation of the eastern Texas settlements that same year, galvanized the lethargic Latins into action. Accordingly, the Viceroy of New Spain ordered Don Antonio de Valverde, Governor of New Mexico, to investigate the activities of the French on the northern frontier.

The command reached Valverde too late in 1719 for an ex-

IV · *Approach and Retreat of the French*

tensive reconnaissance to be undertaken that year. He promised, however, to send out an expedition from Santa Fe the following spring. In the meantime, Comanche and Ute depredations against the province constituted problems more pressing than a rumored French invasion. In September Valverde left the capital of the province with a force of 100 Spaniards and twice as many Indians and proceeded northward to the region beyond the Arkansas River. No enemy Indians were sighted, but on the return trip Valverde encountered a band of friendly Apaches.

These Indians reported that they had recently fought a battle with some Kansas tribes and that their enemies were aided by white men who carried long muskets, traveled on foot, and wore red hunting caps. They further revealed that white men had built several villages along the Platte River and had entered into alliances with the Pawnee and other plains tribes of the region. This information left no doubt that the French had taken possession of the territory to the north and were advancing toward the Spanish frontier. Valverde hastened to Santa Fe to prepare a detailed report for the Viceroy in Mexico and to make preparations for another expedition as soon as he could get reinforcements of men and arms. His dispatch to the Viceroy was followed by others, each more exaggerated than the previous one. Eventually Valverde tried to convince his superiors that the French had a force of more than 6,000 men only seventy leagues from Santa Fe and were pushing the whole Apache nation before them.

Spanish officials in Mexico studied Valverde's communications with some care. Although they believed his story of the French invasion was considerably exaggerated, in January 1720 they decided upon a course of action. An Indian buffer state would be set up between the French villages on the Platte and the New Mexican settlements in the Rio Grande Valley; the northern frontier of New Spain would be extended as far as the present state of Kansas; a military post would be erected as close to the Platte River as was practicable, and would thus place a definite limit to the French advance.

The plan was forwarded to Governor Valverde with orders to

expedite it, but the Governor had misgivings. In his opinion, a post near the Platte River would be too far away for adequate communications and maintenance. After considerable delay he suggested to the Viceroy that a better site would be La Jicarilla, 110 miles north of Santa Fe, and said he would await a final decision before constructing the frontier post. Meanwhile, a reconnaissance party of 100 men would be sent forward to investigate the French settlements.

Captain Don Pedro Villasur was chosen to head the expedition into the north, with Jean de l'Archeveque, one of the assassins of La Salle and now a resident of Santa Fe, acting as guide. The party of forty soldiers and sixty Pueblo Indians left Santa Fe on June 16, 1720, and with little difficulty proceeded via Taos Pueblo to the vicinity of the Platte River. Here, some 500 miles north of Santa Fe, the Spaniards camped on the south side of the river in sight of a Pawnee village. Messengers were sent to contact the "other white men," but no answer was forthcoming. It was evident that the Indians were hostile, and a council was promptly called to discuss the feasibility of an immediate return to Santa Fe. On the morning of August 13, just as the expedition was breaking camp, it suffered a surprise attack. Most of the soldiers were slain, including Captain Villasur, a chaplain, and Archeveque. Not until twenty-four days later did the thirteen survivors reach Santa Fe with news of the disaster, and Governor Valverde, who was never known for his courage, doubtless thanked his patron saint that he had not led the expedition in person.

The Spaniards were thrown into a panic because they feared an immediate invasion of New Mexican settlements by the Indians and French responsible for the massacre. Valverde hastened to relay the bad news to Mexico, with an urgent appeal for reinforcements. The Viceroy prepared to take prompt measures. Orders were to be relayed to Aguayo in Texas to resume aggressive warfare, in spite of previous instructions to the contrary. Additional troops were to be dispatched to New Mexico, the garrison of Santa Fe was to be restored to its full strength, and the proposed fort would be established at La Jicarilla in accordance with Valverde's previous

IV · Approach and Retreat of the French

recommendations. But before these forceful steps could be put into effect, a treaty of peace was signed by France and Spain and danger of further hostilities evaporated. In 1722 Valverde was removed because of his failure to lead the expedition to the Platte River in person.

For the next few years the Spaniards felt secure in regard to the French. Occasionally the Viceroy's office in Mexico City received warnings from New Mexico officials that French traders were still active on the plains, forming alliances with various tribes. These alarms usually were explained away by the Viceroy with the argument that the close relationship now existing between France and Spain precluded any fear of an invasion and that the aims of the French north of New Mexico were doubtless peaceful. This was not entirely true, for, even though a treaty had been signed, the French were as thoroughly alarmed by Captain Villasur's expedition to the Platte country in 1720 as the Spaniards were chagrined by his total defeat. And while professing peace, they secretly resolved to stop any future efforts of the Viceroy to win over the Indians.

In November 1723 Etienne Venyard de Bourgmond, former commander of Detroit and a French trader of much renown, proceeded up the Missouri River from its mouth. With him were forty Frenchmen, and their object was to construct a fort on the river and ultimately make peace with the Comanches so that a buffer against the Spaniards could be established in the northern provinces. On the north bank of the Missouri River in present-day Carroll County, Missouri, Bourgmond built Fort Orléans and left part of his company in permanent quarters. He and the remainder of his party continued their journey in July 1724 to the vicinity of what is now Kansas City. There they purchased several Comanche slaves from a tribe of Kansas Indians and sent them farther westward to their people as a peace offering. Some months later the Frenchmen and a delegation of Missouris, Osages, Otoes, and other Indians pushed on up to the Comanche camp in central Kansas. The party was received with an outward show of much enthusiasm, since the freed slaves had already preceded them.

THE SOUTHWEST: *Old and New*

After distributing generous gifts of guns, knives, cloth, axes, and hand tools, Bourgmond explained to the Comanches that he wanted them to make peace with the tribes represented in his party and to allow the French to return in the future for friendly trading. Also, he impressed upon them his desire to be allowed to pass through their country in order to reach the Spaniards to the southwest. The Indians, with visions of additional gifts in later meetings, replied that Frenchmen would always be welcome to trade among them and to journey through their country without fear of attack.

Thus, Bourgmond's visit appeared to be a huge success and to remove a major obstacle on the road to Santa Fe. But the French were not able immediately to follow up their *coup*. A widespread Indian uprising in the Great Lakes region threatened their far-flung trade empire. At the same time, trouble with the Natchez along the lower Mississippi forced a temporary retrenchment on that front. Consequently, Fort Orléans on the Missouri had to be abandoned in 1728, and New Mexico was once again beyond the reach of the French.

Gradually the Indian troubles in the far north and south abated, and throughout the decade of the 1730's the persistent *voyageurs* edged closer to the "promised land." Traders worked their way from Natchitoches up the Red River to barter with tribes of eastern and northern Texas. Along the Arkansas River they penetrated into the Southwest as far as eastern Oklahoma, and from the Missouri River they once again established contact with the Kansas and Pawnee tribes on the plains.

Finally, in 1739 a party of eight Frenchmen led by Pierre and Paul Mallet ascended the Platte River, starting from its mouth some distance below Council Bluffs. They eventually turned toward the southwest and continued across the "barren prairies" of Kansas and southeastern Colorado into Comanche and Apache country. Somewhere on the Arkansas River in Colorado they found an Aricara Indian who had formerly belonged to a Spaniard in New Mexico and was now living with a tribe of Comanches.

The Aricara was engaged as a guide and led them to Santa

IV · *Approach and Retreat of the French*

Fe, where they arrived on July 22. New Mexican officials, surprisingly, were not alarmed by the appearance of the French traders, who made it clear that they sought only the privilege of peaceful trade. Such permission would have to receive the approval of the Viceroy in Mexico City, so the Mallet party settled down in Santa Fe to await the answer. After several months, word arrived that they were welcome to remain in New Mexico and that they were invited to explore the region to the west. But the Frenchmen were interested only in commerce, and they hastened to depart for French territory to relay the news that traders were at last free to enter New Mexico.

On May 1, 1740, the Mallet party left Santa Fe to open a southern trail to lower Louisiana. Their course took them to the Canadian River, where half the company turned northeast to Illinois. The other four built canoes and floated down the stream, eventually reaching New Orleans via the Arkansas and Mississippi rivers. The report of their successful entry into Santa Fe caused considerable excitement, and Governor Bienville decided to send out another expedition. Accordingly, with the Mallet brothers serving as guides, a party of traders led by Fabry de la Bruyère left New Orleans the next year. Their immediate objective was to visit the Indians living in the valley of the Arkansas in what is now Oklahoma. The Mallets had suggested that these people would have to be won over if the French expected to travel to and from New Mexico in safety. Bruyère planned, therefore, to assemble the principal chiefs of the area and persuade them to cease their attacks on the New Mexican settlements, explaining that the French and Spaniards were now friends and that commerce between the two countries on the frontier would benefit the Indians too.

But the expedition ran into all sorts of difficulty and accomplished little. The Canadian River proved so shallow that boats could not be floated on it. Also, the Indians in the region were engaged in a full-scale war among themselves, and the efforts of the French to establish peace required much time and patience. The Mallets tried to persuade Bruyère to transfer the expedition to horses in an attempt to reach Santa Fe, but the commander rejected their advice. The guides eventually quit the expedition in 1742, and Bruyère later abandoned the project and turned south to the Red River.

Frenchmen still remained obsessed with the idea of reaching New Mexico. By the end of the decade they had succeeded in making friends with the Comanches and Wichitas and establishing peace between them and their neighbors. Thus the Arkansas route to New Mexico was at last made safe and the road to Santa Fe was opened for extensive trade. In 1749 a party of French traders with Comanche guides reached Taos in time for the annual mercantile fair, but Spanish officials promptly placed them under arrest. Another party received the same treatment when it arrived in Santa Fe three years later. The sudden change in policy was the result of Spanish alarm over the increasing traffic in firearms on the plains. Ironically, the only way the French could make their route to New Mexico via the Arkansas River safe was to bring guns and ammunition to the tribes along the way, and for this very reason the Spaniards closed the door to them.

The French were also active along the Louisiana-Texas border. Even after Aguayo re-established the Spanish hold on Texas in 1722, rivalry between the French and Spanish colonials on the eastern Texas frontier continued. However, there was never any open conflict such as occurred on the northern New Mexico frontier. In 1729 the Spaniards abandoned their presidio on the Angelina River in eastern Texas and moved three of the missions to the vicinity of San Antonio. This action practically isolated the Spanish outpost near the Louisiana border and consequently forced the settlers to depend upon their neighbors the French at Natchitoches.

Some time prior to 1734 the French moved their post at Natchitoches from the east side to the west side of the Red River. The Spanish Governor of Texas did not protest the move, and for this apparent negligence he was seriously reprimanded by the King's Attorney. No effort was made to dislodge the French from any territory claimed by the Spaniards, but for several years the question of whether or not they were actually trespassing on Span-

IV · *Approach and Retreat of the French*

ish soil continued to arise. On three occasions between 1740 and 1751 Spanish governors were ordered to investigate the matter but failed to decide the exact boundary between Texas and Louisiana. Finally, in 1753 the Governor of Texas, Don Jacinto de Barrior y Jauregui, informed the Spanish Attorney General that, in his opinion, the French were trespassing on Spanish territory. The official studied Jauregui's report very carefully and, strangely enough, did not agree with it. Instead, he stated that the new site of Natchitoches was two and a half leagues east of the Spanish border, which he claimed was the Arroyo Hondo and not the Red River.

As a result of the position taken by the Attorney General, the Spaniards made no effort to disturb their French neighbors on the Texas-Louisiana frontier. Indeed, they persistently maintained that the Arroyo Hondo constituted the eastern boundary of the Province of Texas—long after the transfer of Louisiana to the United States in 1803. They did not alter this position until the Adams-Oñis Treaty in 1819, when they retreated to the Sabine River. At the same time, the United States had to pay cash to the Spaniards to persuade them to withdraw a few miles west of the Arroyo Hondo and accept the small loss of territory.

In 1754 other developments in North America overshadowed the Franco-Spanish tension along the Southwestern frontier. Far to the northeast, in the Ohio Valley, a contest between England and France for domination of most of the American continent began. The French bent every effort to win Spain as an ally, but not until a new king came to the Spanish throne in 1759 did they make any progress. Charles III was anxious to acquire Louisiana, and the French position by now was so desperate that they offered the territory as the price of collaboration. In August 1761 an alliance known as the Family Compact was signed, but it came too late to be of any help to France. The English declared war on Spain a few months later, and before the end of 1762 both Spain and France were virtually at the mercy of the English fleet. France was now ready to call a halt.

By the terms of the Peace of Paris in 1763 France relinquished all her possessions in the New World except two small islands in the Caribbean and two others off the coast of Nova Scotia. In the exchange Spain received the vast Louisiana territory as compensation for Florida and other losses to England. Now the international boundary became the Mississippi River, and the Franco-Spanish rivalry for the Southwest ended for all time. But Spain had gained only temporary possession of a large province. She would lose it to France in 1802, and later most of her empire would fall to revolutionary forces. Meanwhile, France was no longer to be feared as a rival, but this security was costly: Spain's new neighbors in the Southwest, the Anglo-American pioneers, were a different breed entirely.

ALMOST THREE centuries of Spanish colonization and one century of contact with the French preceded the Anglo-American invasion of the Southwest. During this long span the Spaniards and the Indians, and even more so the French and the Indians, came to understand each other and grew more alike. Indeed, by the nineteenth century the Europeans in the Southwest could scarcely be distinguished from the original owners of the land except by their dress. The Plains Indians acquired the horse and gun and became wilder than before and more aggressive than the soldiers of the early conquistadores or the French traders from Louisiana and Canada. The Pueblo Indians adopted a veneer of things Spanish: dress, crafts, and even the Spanish God.

The French eventually withdrew, leaving little evidence of their activities except in Louisiana. Though many Spanish institutions proved well suited to the Southwest, the Spaniards, in time, acquired a little of the temperate and stoic nature of the Indian. Green Peyton writes in *America's Heartland: The Southwest* that the two peoples came to have "the same dignity and aloofness, the same practicality and mysticism, and the same habit of regarding

IV · *Approach and Retreat of the French*

the basic facts of life and death." In many ways the Europeans were better suited to the arid soil of the Southwest than the American pioneers who followed. It required more time for the latter to adjust to the new environment, but in the end they too adopted some of the qualities of the land and the people whom they conquered.

V

THE ANGLO-AMERICANS COME TO STAY

ALMOST TWO CENTURIES elapsed between the founding of Jamestown and Anglo-American penetration of the Spanish Southwest. There were valid reasons. The Southwest was a *"tierra incógnita,"* and the Spaniards, like the ancient Chinese and the modern Russians, did not welcome visitors. Besides, before 1800 the Anglo-Americans had little curiosity about the region beyond the Mississippi. The population of the United States was not yet six million, and to travel from New England to New Orleans took four difficult weeks.

By the time the Spaniards' frontier venture was reaching its

V · *The Anglo-Americans Come to Stay*

peak, the Americans were beginning theirs. The latter's approach to the Southwest was slow and cautious but relentless, and when they reached the edge of Spanish territory they had already evolved a culture that well suited their needs. As the buffalo was to the Plains Indians, the forest was to the Anglo-Saxon pioneers: for from it they obtained food and shelter. It was natural, therefore, that the Anglo-Americans should first settle the corner of the Southwest which constitutes a peninsula of the great eastern forest—the wooded area of eastern Texas. Here survival depended on a mere extension of time-tested institutions, not on the hazardous development of new ones.

Migration into eastern Texas, a small trickle in the first two decades of the nineteenth century, turned into a virtual flood during the next three. Thus, as settlers left the woods to push forward over the plains and deserts of the Southwest, ample numbers sustained their momentum. Once the tide began to roll, nothing could stop a restless and determined people from reaching the Pacific Coast.

When the first Anglo-American entered the Southwest is unknown. In 1791, one Edward Murphy of Pennsylvania acquired a land grant on the Arroyo Hondo, a few miles east of the present Texas-Louisiana boundary. The 140-acre tract lay astride the road between Natchitoches and Nacogdoches in what was recognized as Spanish territory. Three other Americans had settled in the same area by 1798: Luther Smith, William Barr, and Samuel Davenport. Their activities frequently carried them into the interior of Texas to trade with Spaniards and Indians. These men, like Murphy and other Anglo-Americans in the Southwest, combined trading in wild horses with farming and other operations.

The principal attraction that brought adventurous Americans to the region at this period was the wild mustang, found in vast herds immediately beyond the Texas Cross Timbers. When captured alive, these Spanish "barb" horses were valuable as beasts of burden. Dead, their manes and tails made excellent rope, and the hides were easily tanned for leather.

If it is true that he arrived in San Antonio from Natchez in

The Southwest: *Old and New*

1785, then the distinction of being the first Anglo-American to cross a large portion of the Southwest probably belongs to Philip Nolan. A letter written by Thomas Jefferson on June 24, 1798, implies that Nolan was the first Anglo-American to engage in wild-horse trading in Texas.

Nolan's Southwestern adventures appear to have covered approximately fifteen years. In October 1800 he and twenty companions set out for the interior of Texas. On the Brazos River, not far from modern Waco, the party built a stockade and soon had three hundred mustangs corralled. During the following spring a large Spanish force attacked the camp and killed Nolan and several of his followers. The others were taken to San Luis Potosí and later to Chihuahua. Ultimately, all but one member of the original party faced a firing squad or succumbed to the wretched conditions of prison life. The survivor was Ellis P. Bean, an ancestor of Roy Bean, "The Law West of the Pecos." Ellis Bean later described his many years in Mexico in his *Memoirs,* which constitute one of the most adventurous narratives ever published; no other American of his generation acquired so much firsthand knowledge of Mexico and the Southwest.[1]

Among the early Americans who followed Bean into the Southwest, none is more significant than Zebulon Montgomery Pike, the young explorer who arrived in Santa Fe in 1806 as a prisoner of the Spaniards. Pike had been captured in present-day southern Colorado and charged with trespassing on Spanish territory. He was eventually escorted to Chihuahua and later back to the United States via San Antonio and Nacogdoches. During the year he spent in the Spanish Southwest he talked extensively with local officials and collected voluminous and valuable notes on the geography, soil, climate, resources, people, and military strength of New Spain.

---

[1] Bean is supposed to have been living in Chihuahua City at the time Zebulon Pike was brought there as a prisoner from New Mexico. Both men later wrote of their experiences, but, surprisingly, neither man mentioned the presence of the other.

V · *The Anglo-Americans Come to Stay*

Pike arrived in the Southwest during a tense period in the relations between Spain and the United States. The purchase of Louisiana in 1803 from France had brought the young republic close to her older but still suspicious neighbor. The earlier border struggle for domination between Spain and France broke out anew, with the United States replacing the French. Threat of war between the two powers was not arrested until 1819, when the Adams-Onís Treaty was signed and the boundary between the Spanish Southwest and Louisiana was finally settled.

Pike was the first Anglo-American to enter the vast territory beyond Louisiana and return to the United States with extensive knowledge about the country. The official report of his expedition was published in 1810, and for more than a decade it remained the only printed source of information about a region generally unknown to his countrymen.

The "Lost Pathfinder's" journey to the source of the Arkansas River in what is now Colorado and his travels as a prisoner of the Spaniards through New Mexico, south to Chihuahua, and thence across the broad expanse of Texas were only slightly overshadowed by the Lewis-and-Clark expedition of the same period. Unfortunately, his reputation suffered because of his direct connections with the notorious James Wilkinson and an alleged indirect connection with Aaron Burr. But, regardless of the motives behind the Pike expedition, his observations about the mysterious Southwest deserve close attention.

One statement that proved prophetic in a curious way concerned the natural advantages that might arise from the immense prairies of the West and Southwest. Like many Americans of his day, Pike viewed with alarm the ever extending frontier and the scattering of the population over so vast a territory. The prairies, he thought, would confine the population within definite limits and thereby preserve the Union. "Our citizens . . . [should] leave the prairies to the wandering and uncivilized aborigines of the country," he concluded. The American people were indeed restricted and their movement into the West and Southwest temporarily averted when the cotton kingdom halted at the Balcones

The Southwest: *Old and New*

Escarpment. And following the war that preserved the Union, the federal government toyed with the idea of leaving the Southwest prairies to the Indians.

WHEN PIKE RETURNED to the United States in 1807, the country's attention was focused on the Burr conspiracy and on the trial of Burr at Richmond, Virginia. His expedition, at a time when Burr's scheme to seize the Southwest and Mexico was under investigation, plus the duplicity of General James Wilkinson, who was in the pay of the Spaniards,[2] caused the anxious Latins to guard their frontier with renewed determination.

The excitement caused by the conspiracy and Jefferson's embarrassment over the revelation of Wilkinson's connection with it delayed immediate efforts by the federal government to explore the Southwest. Also, there were more pressing matters facing the young republic: a gradual drift toward war with England was beginning.

Meanwhile, there had been other official explorations by Anglo-Americans in the Southwest. Soon after Jefferson launched the Lewis-and-Clark expedition to the Pacific Northwest in 1804, he made plans for another party to ascend the Red and Arkansas rivers. He chose Sir William Dunbar, a well-known English scientist, and Dr. George Hunter, a chemist from Philadelphia, to direct the examination of the Southwestern frontier. The Spaniards had

---

[2] General James Wilkinson, military governor of Upper Louisiana in 1806, ordered Pike to explore the Southwest. President Jefferson was later informed of the action and approved it. Subsequent events revealed that Wilkinson was involved in Burr's attempted invasion of the Southwest and at the same time was selling military information to the Spaniards.

V · *The Anglo-Americans Come to Stay*

not yet recognized the Red and Sabine rivers as international boundaries and were prepared to turn back any Anglo-Americans. Even so, Jefferson was boldly proclaiming that much of the Southwest lying east of the Rio Grande River rightfully belonged to the United States by virtue of the Louisiana Purchase, and he was determined to explore it.

Dunbar and Hunter were thwarted by the Spaniards, and another expedition in 1806 led by Thomas Freeman failed to go beyond present-day Shreveport, Louisiana. More than a decade elapsed before the United States again turned its attention to the region. This time military expeditions were sent into the plains country to establish posts that would hold the Indians in check, open the way for fur traders, and clear the path for settlers. Major Stephen H. Long built two log blockhouses between 1817 and 1819, one at Fort Smith near the Southwestern frontier and the other at the junction of the Mississippi and Minnesota rivers. On July 4, 1819, he and Colonel David Atkinson set out from St. Louis at the head of a large party bound for the Mandan village near the source of the Missouri River. They planned to construct a fort there, but delays and mismanagement prevented this. When Congress finally withdrew the appropriation for the fort, army officials decided to salvage as much from the venture as possible by ordering Long to continue westward to the Rockies and descend the Red River to its mouth.

A company of twenty men pushed on to the edge of the Rockies, thence southward along the Front Range until they encountered the Arkansas River. Part of the group left to descend the stream, while Long and the main force continued on in search of the Red River. At last they came to a ravine leading out of the mountains and cutting across the plains. Major Long was happy indeed to turn his men along its banks, for he believed that he had found the river. Not until he reached its mouth a few miles west of Fort Smith did he realize that he had followed the course of the Canadian. By midsummer 1820 his two parties had joined forces, having accomplished almost nothing except the most extensive

THE SOUTHWEST: *Old and New*

exploration of present-day Oklahoma by American travelers up to that time.[3]

Long wrote that the region he had traversed "is almost unfit for cultivation, and of course uninhabitable by a people depending upon agriculture for their subsistence." This statement strengthened the psychological barrier that Pike had already erected in respect to the settlement of the Southwestern plains. During the next two decades the only parts of the Southwest that interested Anglo-Americans—except for the lower river-bottom areas of Texas—were the mountains and valleys of New Mexico and Arizona. The latter regions were first visited by traders and trappers, who gradually disproved the myths left by Long and others, and in the 1840's the federal government renewed its efforts toward extensive scientific exploration of the Southwest.

Meanwhile, in 1826 Jedediah S. Smith of the Rocky Mountain Fur Company explored a portion of the Southwest never before visited by Anglo-Americans. On August 22 he left the company rendezvous at Great Salt Lake with a small party of trappers en route to the California coast. His journeys took him southwestward along the banks of the Sevier and across a mountain range to the Virgin River. Following that stream, the trappers crossed the northwest corner of present-day Arizona, continued on to the Colorado River and thence to the Mohave villages. There they turned westward along a route similar to that of the Santa Fe Railroad today. The Smith party eventually reached San Gabriel, California, and thus became the first Americans to have blazed an overland trail across the continent via the Southwest. The next year Smith retraced his journey from Great Salt Lake to San Gabriel and crossed the northwest corner of Arizona once again. Unfortunately, this Puritan from New England did not live long enough to publish his journals and maps.

---

[3] Major Long was not the first American explorer in Oklahoma. In 1806 Lieutenant James B. Wilkinson, son of General James Wilkinson, descended the Arkansas River from the region of Larned, Kansas, diagonally across Oklahoma to Fort Smith. Wilkinson later wrote a report describing the country through which he passed.

V · *The Anglo-Americans Come to Stay*

Another American party visited Arizona a short time after Smith, and its adventures form one of the most notable examples of travel and exploration in the annals of western frontier history. Sylvester Pattie, his son James Ohio, and three companions arrived in Santa Fe in November 1824, which marked the beginning of their fur-trading career in the Southwest. From then until March 1828, when they reached Santa Catalina Mission in lower California, they trapped along the banks of the Arkansas and Rio Grande rivers in New Mexico, explored much of the Colorado River, including the Grand Canyon, in Arizona, and examined the entire course of the Gila River from its source to its mouth. The trail-blazing by fur traders such as the Patties and Smith in the 1830's inexorably paved the way for Saxon conquest.

Meanwhile, regular commercial intercourse was established between St. Louis and Santa Fe. The New Mexican capital not only became the destination of yearly caravans that moved overland from Missouri, but also developed quickly into a hub for trade extending westward to California and southward to Chihuahua and Sonora. It became the equipping center for American trappers on the Arkansas, Rio Grande, Gila, and Colorado rivers and the point of departure for an ever increasing flow of immigrants venturing west to California.

As early as September 1821 a party of traders, trappers, and merchants, led by Jacob Fowler of Covington, Kentucky, and Colonel Hugh Glenn of Cincinnati, left Fort Smith, Arkansas on an expedition that played a vital role in the opening of the Santa Fe trade. They reached the capital of New Mexico after following the Arkansas River to the Rocky Mountains. The local authorities not only welcomed them, but, surprisingly, granted permission to trap the region for beaver. Before their return to St. Louis another party had departed for Santa Fe over a route that later became the Santa Fe Trail. William Becknell organized this venture "for the purpose of trading for horses and mules, and catching wild animals of every description." At Taos he disposed of his merchandise of coarse cotton goods in profitable exchange for specie, burros, Spanish coverlids, and blankets.

THE SOUTHWEST: *Old and New*

The success of Fowler, Glenn, and Becknell opened a new and dramatic chapter in the history of the Southwest. New Mexico and Arizona soon witnessed a steady flow of trappers and traders from the north and east. Taos quickly developed into a favorite rendezvous for mountain men such as Kit Carson who brought pelts to exchange for whisky, supplies, and the pleasures of the senses. James Baird, a former resident of Missouri who was living in New Mexico in 1826, estimated that more than $100,000 in beaver skins alone had been taken from the mountain streams of New Mexico and Arizona during the previous five years.

The trade in skins was interwoven inseparably with the demand for manufactured goods from St. Louis. Merchants at Taos and Santa Fe tolerated the "foreigners" because of the profits their activities brought. After 1824 great wagon caravans stretched across the 780 dusty miles between Independence, Missouri, and Santa Fe. Six or eight oxen pulled each heavy wagon, which carried from 2,400 to 7,000 pounds of merchandise ranging from glass beads to rifles, from jew's-harps to silk stockings, and from brightly colored ribbons to calicoes and coarse domestic cotton. Much of the material eventually found its way far beyond the New Mexican settlements of Taos and Santa Fe to northern Mexico and southern California. On the return trips to St. Louis the caravans carried furs, silver, gold, and mules.

The Santa Fe trade grew steadily in volume and value despite hazards from the Indians on the trail and the ever increasing Mexican custom rates. In time many of the shops around the plazas at Taos and Santa Fe were owned and managed by Americans, who gradually came to dominate the economic life of the province. Mutual contempt existed between the natives and the "gringos" from the very beginning, but neither could do without the other.

New Mexican officials sometimes grew suspicious of the traders' efforts to avoid custom duties and seized their goods or levied excessive fines or taxes. The Americans, on the other hand, often traded guns and ammunition to the Indians, hunted beaver without permits, and sometimes engaged in drunken brawls on the streets and in the taverns. When racial and political tensions be-

V · *The Anglo-Americans Come to Stay*

came too strained, the Anglo-Americans retired beyond the reach of the New Mexican officials and established fortified posts, from which they continued their trapping and trading operations to the great financial loss of Taos and Santa Fe. Bent's Fort, on the Arkansas River near where La Junta, Colorado, now stands, was the most famous of these trading posts. Built and operated by Charles and William Bent and Ceran St. Vrain, it was more than an ordinary post: it was a feudal institution. Standing alone, like a medieval castle, it represented a constant menace to the independence of New Mexico.

The Santa Fe trade laid the basis for many private fortunes, both in the United States and in the Southwest. It served as an outlet for manufactured goods from the East and as a source of needed specie at a time when little gold or silver was being mined in Georgia. It helped dispel the myth that the Southwestern plains were a desert, for Missouri farmers who followed the trail recognized good farm land. And it contributed an exciting chapter to the rambunctious history of the Southwest. More significantly, the Santa Fe trade furnished the means by which aggressive pioneers infiltrated the Southwest. When the war for possession of the region came, the United States had an effective "fifth column" planted firmly in the enemy's camp.

AT THE SAME TIME that New Mexico was being infiltrated by foreigners from the United States, Mexico's hold on her northern province of Texas was loosening even more rapidly. Before 1800, as we have already seen, Anglo-Americans began slipping beyond Spain's thin military barrier to steal glimpses of the vast underdeveloped region beyond the Sabine River. In the end, they and their successors stole more than a mere view of spacious scenery. Unlike the venturers in New Mexico and Arizona, these interlopers were not after beaver skins or silver and gold; they wanted land and political power.

Because this Spanish province was all but unknown to the general public, it offered an especially fertile field for conquest by the restless frontiersmen along the Southwestern border. Men such as Philip Nolan and Ellis P. Bean fared badly against the austere Spaniards, and Aaron Burr with his fuzzy dream of a Southwestern empire became entangled in his own machinations. Some of Burr's men fled to the region between the Sabine River and the Arroyo Hondo (Neutral Ground), and more than once they and other squatters joined filibustering expeditions across Texas. In lower Louisiana lived some Spanish exiles and some disgruntled Americans who stoutly proclaimed that Texas was part of the purchase of 1803. From these groups came the capital and leadership for the attempted conquests of Texas, while Natchez, Baton Rouge, Natchitoches, and the Neutral Ground had a supply of men who thirsted for spoils and adventure.

José Bernardo Maximiliano Gutiérrez de Lara, a revolutionist agent who fled Mexico in 1812, and a former American army officer named Augustus Magee led the expedition that almost succeeded in wresting Texas from permanent Spanish control. The two became acquainted at Natchitoches and quickly formed a conspiracy to invade Texas. Gutiérrez was to be nominal commander of a volunteer army in order to attract the Spanish population of Texas, but Magee would direct actual operations. They promised each recruit forty dollars a month and a league of land. A force of more than a hundred men was quickly assembled under the banner of the Army of the North, and in August 1812 it reached the outskirts of Nacogdoches on the Texas frontier. The conquest of that lethargic community remains one of the quickest on record, for the Spanish commander of the post, Bernardino Montero, witnessed the "evaporation" of his military forces within a matter of minutes. He hastily departed on the road to San Antonio and left the post open to the invaders.

The bloodless capture of Nacogdoches and the booty it supplied brought several hundred volunteers to the banner of Magee and Gutiérrez. About the middle of September the Army of the

V · *The Anglo-Americans Come to Stay*

North started inland toward its destination, San Antonio de Bejar. At Robbins' Ferry on the Trinity River, Magee's forces captured a Spanish spy who revealed that La Bahía Presidio, near present-day Goliad, was manned by only a small company of soldiers and could be taken easily. The invaders altered their line of march and turned toward the southwest. When they appeared outside the walls of the stone fort, the Spanish troops again demonstrated that they had no stomach for a fight. The Americans won another victory without the discharge of a single musket. But their incredible luck could not last indefinitely.

Three days later a Spanish force of more than a thousand men arrived from San Antonio to attack the fortress of La Bahía. The siege lasted for three or four months, during which time Magee died in mysterious circumstances. The American command fell to Samuel Kemper a few days before the Spaniards withdrew on February 16, 1813. The road to San Antonio now lay open. Within a week after the enemy departed, the Army of the North, now numbering some 800 men, pushed across the mesquite flats of southern Texas.

This time the Spaniards did not panic when the invaders arrived. Twenty-five hundred regulars and militia met the "troops" under Kemper's command on the Salado River a few miles below San Antonio. But the so-called "battle" of Rosalis ended in another rout of the demoralized Spaniards, and the filibusters took over their third town and most important population center of Texas. The ease with which this mob of ill-equipped and disorganized American adventurers could capture a province almost as large as the thirteen original states reflects the decadent condition of the Spanish empire during the early part of the nineteenth century.

Such a crew of cutthroats could not long be held together. In disgust Kemper abandoned the cause of establishing an Anglo-American republic in Texas when his sadistic "front man," Gutiérrez, ordered twelve Spanish officials butchered in cold blood. The command now fell to José Alvarez de Toledo, but discipline was not improved. A Spanish army of 3,000 men from Mexico had little difficulty, in August 1813, in killing or capturing most of the force that held San Antonio. Only a handful of Americans escaped.

Texas was swept clean now of disaffected Spaniards and outside meddlers, but the spirit of the filibusters was not crushed. The stubborn and unruly frontiersmen along the Southwestern border resolved to take the province from the crumbling Spanish empire. Between 1813 and 1819 they made numerous attempts to launch expeditions from Natchez and Natchitoches. None proved a serious threat, however, until news reached lower Louisiana that John Quincy Adams and Don Luis de Onís had negotiated a treaty fixing the Sabine River as the permanent boundary between Texas and Louisiana. Dr. James Long of Natchez now agreed to assume command of an American expedition that had the backing of several prominent citizens of Louisiana and a few men in high places in the federal government, including Senator Thomas Hart Benton. Long crossed the Neutral Ground without difficulty and established headquarters at Nacogdoches. He promptly organized a government, solicited additional recruits, and proclaimed Texas an independent republic.

The Americans realized that a force of three hundred men camped on the edge of the wilderness province could not hope to maintain its independence. During the late summer of 1819, therefore, Dr. Long journeyed to Galveston Island to urge the pirate Jean Lafitte and his band to join the cause. But buccaneering in the Gulf was lucrative, and Lafitte saw no reason to diversify his interests. Long returned to Nacogdoches only to learn that Spanish troops from San Antonio had arrived during his absence and chased his followers across the Sabine River.

The self-styled President of the so-called Republic of Texas gradually reassembled his army and transferred his headquarters to Galveston Island, which Lafitte had abandoned. Here he allied himself with a group of Spanish revolutionists who were seeking Mexican independence. In October 1821 Long and a few score of men took La Bahía Presidio at Goliad by surprise and hoped to march on to San Antonio unopposed. But victory was short-lived,

V · The Anglo-Americans Come to Stay

for the Spaniards quickly retaliated and captured the entire command. General Long was taken to Mexico City as a prisoner of war. His death at the hands of an assassin a short time later ended all hopes of the filibusters in the Southwest. An era came to an end. Had Long's ill-fated army been in control of San Antonio and Goliad when Mexican independence came, Texas might well have become a part of the United States several years earlier than it did.

EVEN BEFORE Mexico separated from the mother country, Spain relieved tension on the Southwestern frontier by reversing her long-standing policy of exclusion. The signing of the Adams-Onís Treaty on February 22, 1819, by which the United States renounced future claims to the province of Texas, made this unprecedented action possible. And nineteen months later the Spanish government enacted one of the most liberal land laws in history. Under its provisions, Anglo-Americans could obtain legal title to grants in Texas. Already one Moses Austin of Missouri, aware of the resources of the Spanish province, had conceived a systematic plan for the colonization of Texas by Americans. With the assistance of Baron de Bastrop, whom Austin had known in Missouri, he applied to the Spanish governor at San Antonio for the right to settle 300 families in Texas. The recently enacted land law assured that his request would be granted.

Soon afterward the fifty-seven-year-old Austin returned to his home in Missouri, where he died of tuberculosis in June 1821. His son, Stephen F. Austin, founder of the city of Little Rock, Arkansas, received the news of his father's death in New Orleans, where he was soliciting support and supplies for the proposed Texas colony. Young Austin and a few companions hastened overland to San Antonio to petition the Governor for permission to carry out the colonization scheme. The travelers had an audience with the Spanish official on August 10, 1821. The Governor not only recog-

The Southwest: *Old and New*

nized Austin as heir to his father's grant, but also encouraged him to examine the region of Texas between the lower Colorado and Brazos rivers and select the choicest farm land available.

Austin painstakingly carried out the mission and returned to New Orleans to complete arrangements for supplies and recruits. He then published his scheme for colonization in the local newspapers: each settler would get 640 acres of land, plus 320 acres if he was married, 100 for each child, and 80 acres for each slave. As the panic of 1819 was still being felt in the United States and an eighty-acre homestead cost $100 cash, Austin had little trouble in attracting the desired number of settlers.

Before leaving New Orleans with a party of colonists to proceed overland to Texas, Austin bought a small ship, the *Lively*, which was to bring additional settlers, farming tools, and seed, sound out the coast of Texas, and land at the mouth of the Colorado River. There its passengers would built a fort, plant a crop, and await the arrival of the main party. But the ship failed to keep the rendezvous. Instead, it landed at the mouth of the Brazos River, and when Austin arrived on the lower Colorado late in December, he and his followers faced the bleak prospects characteristic of all new frontiers. Nevertheless, the vanguard of settlers was permanently anchored.

When Austin went to San Antonio in March 1822 and received the disconcerting news of the change in the political affairs in Mexico as a result of independence, he thought it advisable to go to the capital. The 1,200-mile journey to Mexico City exhausted his already overworked body. Nine boring months elapsed before the Mexican government enacted legislation relative to the Texas colony. Finally, in January 1823, it passed a law that provided even more generous terms: each settler would receive one league of land—one *labor*, or 177 acres, for farming and the rest for ranching, the total equivalent to 4,428 acres. One provision of the measure which caused future misunderstanding stipulated that each immigrant must be of the Roman Catholic faith. Another required each contractor to establish a town in relation to the settlement he organized.

V · *The Anglo-Americans Come to Stay*

Austin, of course, did not enter the colonization business for humanitarian reasons. For each hundred families he brought to Texas, he was to be given five leagues of grazing land and five *labors* of farming land. Also, for each acre assigned to settlers the *empresario* (the Spanish term for colonizer or contractor) hoped to collect twelve and a half cents cash from the settlers to cover his survey and administrative expenses.[4] By September 1824 he had issued land titles to 272 men, some of whose families had not yet arrived. One year later the settlement had a population of 1,800 persons, 443 of whom were slaves. A short time later Austin inaugurated a democratic system of government to meet the needs of his growing colony.

In March 1825 the legislature of Coahuila provided for additional colonization grants. Eventually it approved a total of fifteen additional permits, including three for Austin and generous grants for Lorenzo de Zavala, Joseph Vehlein, David G. Burnet, and others. Although these latter *empresarios* undoubtedly entered into contracts with the Coahuila-Texas government in good faith, not a single one of their agreements was carried out to the letter. Thus they added substantial fuel to the Mexican distrust of American intentions in Texas.

At the end of a decade of colonization at least 20,000 American pioneers from Missouri, Ohio, Kentucky, Tennessee, and the Old South had migrated into Texas. They claimed all of the land between the Nueces River on the south and the Sabine River on the east for more than two hundred miles inland from the Gulf. To the old towns of San Antonio, Goliad, and Nacogdoches the settlers added a few of their own, including the capital of Austin's colony, San Felipe de Austin, and the port of Anahuac on Galveston Bay. This tide of immigration gave new momentum to the conquest of the wilderness and the extension of the culture of cotton into Texas.

Inadvertently, the Spanish created and the Mexican govern-

---

[4] This nominal fee proved all but impossible to collect. It was later reduced to $30 per league, payable in three installments.

THE SOUTHWEST: *Old and New*

ment nurtured a veritable Frankenstein's monster. Once they opened the door to colonization, they could not check the aggressive and unruly Anglo-Saxon frontiersmen. It was a lesson learned the hard way, and—as is often the case—it was learned too late for the Mexican government to profit by the experience.

WHILE THE surplus population of the trans-Mississippi West was settling Texas and the trappers and traders were occupying New Mexico and Arizona, the northeastern corner of the Southwest—the present state of Oklahoma—was virtually ignored. This region belonged to the United States for more than forty years before the remainder of the Southwest was acquired, yet it was the last section to be occupied by white men.

The barrier to the settlement of Oklahoma was not Spanish or Mexican laws, as with Texas and New Mexico, but nature itself. Oklahoma had no Santa Fe or Taos through which the resources of the mountains and streams flowed. It had no great navigable rivers, nor did it border any body of water whereby the products of its soil and scrubby forest could be carried to nearby markets. It did have on its western plains, however, Indians as wild and savage as any who ever inhabited the American continent. And as long as land was available elsewhere, adventurous pioneers had no burning desire to intrude here. Moreover, Pike's and Long's descriptions had established a legend that this region was part of a great desert, unusable except by nomadic Indians.

Except for a mere handful of government explorers, only a few white men ventured into Oklahoma during the first quarter of the nineteenth century. In 1817 Auguste Pierre Chouteau established a trading post among the Osage on Grand River in what is now eastern Mayes County. Here he lived for many years in grand style in a "two-story log palace." Other white traders entered the wooded area of eastern Oklahoma during the next few years, and

V · *The Anglo-Americans Come to Stay*

they, together with various peaceful tribes of the region, brought furs and hides to Chouteau's establishment to exchange for supplies. The trader later shipped these items to markets in St. Louis and New Orleans. Thus the region that constituted the western portion of Arkansas Territory gradually became less a wilderness.

At about the time that Chouteau settled in Oklahoma, other events were shaping the future of this corner of the Southwest. The expansion of the cotton kingdom beyond the Atlantic seaboard stirred anew the racial tension between the red men and the whites who coveted their land. In 1816 and 1817 treaties were signed with the Choctaws and Cherokees by which both tribes agreed to cede a portion of their holdings east of the Mississippi River in exchange for tracts in Arkansas Territory. Various bands of Cherokees residing in Tennessee moved to the new region in 1817. They were allotted land lying north of the Arkansas River, while the territory south of the river was given to the Choctaws. Thus the demands of white men for valuable properties in Tennessee and Mississippi were satisfied—but not for long.

By 1825 the demands for additional Indian lands had increased and the age-old racial problem became more vexing. John C. Calhoun, Monroe's Secretary of War, estimated the Southern tribes that year at 79,000. He proposed the removal of all natives to a permanent home in the Great American Desert. (The estimated 14,000 Indians living in the Old Northwest could be shifted to Wisconsin.) Gifts and annuities totaling $30,000 would be an added inducement for the red men to accept western land for their present holdings, a cheap price indeed for solving the Indian problem for all time. Congress concurred with Calhoun's plans in February 1825.

The Five Civilized Tribes that resided in western Georgia, Alabama, Mississippi, and Florida did not wish to abandon their homes and migrate to the West. Though the new holdings would be larger than their present ones, they feared the wild tribes of Oklahoma even more than their greedy neighbors in the Southeast. Contacts with missionaries and proximity to democratic forms of government had enabled them to absorb some of the better aspects of white civilization. This was particularly true of the Cherokees, who soon developed their own unique alphabet and rapidly became literate. The Choctaws also had reached a high state of civilization, but, like all other tribes, they had to accept the removal plan or face annihilation. Only a few die-hard Seminoles remained. The prolonged war that followed in the swamps of Florida decimated their numbers and ended the careers of many promising United States Army officers.

Before the removal of the Civilized Tribes to large reservations in what is now eastern Oklahoma, the native Indians and migratory whites in the region first had to be moved. Also, the lands in western Arkansas which had been assigned earlier to various Choctaws and Cherokees were now considered too valuable for Indians to own. These groups were "persuaded" to exchange their recent holdings for property farther west. The Choctaws eventually accepted a large tract between the Canadian and Red rivers in the southeast corner of present-day Oklahoma. In 1828 the Arkansas Cherokees moved to an equally large reservation immediately north of the Choctaw Nation and thus cleared the way for the great migration of the eastern tribes.[5]

Fifteen grim years elapsed before most of the Civilized Tribes abandoned their property and accepted homes along the Indian frontier. Bribery, corruption, and cruelty accompanied the signing of various removal treaties, but these injustices were insignificant in comparison with the hardship and deaths that characterized the actual removals. As various groups reached the new country, they were assigned land west of the Choctaws and Cherokees. Smaller tribes [6] that formerly resided in the Old Northwest were later squeezed into crowded reserves in territory not already occupied.

The federal government foresaw that attempts to solve the

---

[5] The Cherokees received the added inducement of an "outlet," fifty-eight miles wide, across northern Oklahoma to the western buffalo country.

[6] The tribes from the old Northwest which were eventually moved to Oklahoma were the Kickapoo, Sauk, Fox, Chippewa, Iowa, Potawatomi, Ottawa, Peoria, and Miami.

V · *The Anglo-Americans Come to Stay*

racial strife between white and red would result in a serious conflict among the Indians unless the eastern tribes received protection from their wandering brethren of the plains. Naturally, the newcomers would not be popular with Osage, Comanche, Kiowa, and Wichita tribes who lost their hunting grounds. To forestall attacks on the Civilized Tribes, several military forts were built in the new Indian Nations and occupied by United States infantry troops and dragoons. Fort Smith on the Arkansas River had been laid out near the present Oklahoma line in 1817, when the first Cherokees and Choctaws moved to the West. As more immigrants arrived, the post proved inadequate to guard the far-flung Indian frontier. Fort Towson, near the Red River, and Fort Gibson, up the Arkansas River from Fort Smith, were built in 1824. For several years these log outposts acted as effective deterrents, keeping the hostile forces apart.

As time passed and the Indian population of eastern Oklahoma continued to swell, the wild tribes became more aggressive. Commissioners hurried to the West between 1834 and 1837 and negotiated a number of treaties among the Plains Indians and the Osage of southern Kansas and northern Oklahoma and the Five Civilized Tribes. Unfortunately, the agreements proved easier to make than to keep, and for the next dozen years threats of a major intraracial war remained constant. The eastern tribes soon learned not to venture into the hunting grounds of the Plains Indians west of the Cross Timbers. And the latter were reluctant to intrude across this thirty-mile-wide belt of scrub oak and underbrush separating the woodland area from the grassy regions of the West. Ultimately the line of military posts was moved westward to be nearer the wild tribes of the plains, and they maintained a precarious peace on the frontier for a full decade before the Civil War.

UNWITTINGLY, the federal government created a barrier to pioneer settlement by establishing the large reservations in Oklahoma. For more than two generations the western movement either passed through or around this corner of the Southwest, and the only white men who had an excuse to settle were the licensed traders, missionaries, soldiers, half-breeds, and outlaws.

Between the 95th meridian on the east, near the present Arkansas boundary, to the Cross Timbers on the west, the Civilized Tribes were again free to live and run their own affairs. The Indian Intercourse Act of 1834 forbade all whites except licensed traders to settle in the region. Two years earlier Congress had created the Bureau of Indian Affairs and assigned it the task of establishing schools and teaching farming skills to the Indians. These measures, together with the presence of great buffalo herds to the west, were designed to keep the red man completely independent "as long as the grass grows and waters run."

While the displaced Indians struggled to adjust themselves to their new environment in eastern Oklahoma and the wild tribes beyond the Cross Timbers fought valiantly to keep their culture intact, the remainder of the Southwest was entering a new era. The phrase "Manifest Destiny" was not coined until 1846, but groundwork for it was laid much earlier. At least 80,000 Anglo-Americans had pushed into the Southwest within the previous two and a half decades. Texas received most of these frontiersmen and won its independence in 1836. By 1845 the republic stood one step from annexation to the United States. Meanwhile, New Mexico—including the area that later became Arizona—had lost most of its respect for the federal overlords in Mexico. Also, its local officials were corrupt, unable to govern, and dependent almost completely upon the precarious Santa Fe trade for revenue.

Such was the picture in the Southwest as mid-century approached. The acquisition of the entire territory by the United States was inevitable—regardless of the pious explanations that it was God's will. And Texas was the first plum snatched from the vast but sparsely cultivated Spanish orchard.

VI

THE CLASH OF CIVILIZATIONS

THE ANGLO-AMERICAN SETTLERS who flocked into Texas after 1820 were not content with existence under a foreign government. Mexican residents quickly discovered that many of the new arrivals were aggressive, opinionated, domineering, and intolerant. They made little effort to disguise their feeling of racial superiority and their belief that their democratic institutions and traditions were God's bequest to the select few. The frontier spirit of equality was admirable, but it applied only to the white race. The great majority of Mexican settlers were placid, illiterate, and superstitious. And the immigrant pioneers from the United States

The Southwest: *Old and New*

tended to look upon them with the same disdain that they accorded to Negroes and Indians.

Most of the early settlers in Austin's colony had little contact with the old Mexican residents of Texas or with government officials. Austin chose these immigrants with care, and only a few who arrived before 1830 were ruffians or criminals or fugitives from creditors. There is ample evidence that these Anglo-American pioneers were grateful for the generous land bounties, as opportunities to acquire such vast holdings did not exist in the United States. The mere fact that almost twenty thousand Anglo-Americans rushed to Texas within a decade reflects the liberality of the Mexican government. Why more did not take advantage of the opportunity is a mystery.

Some of the later *empresarios* operating under state permits became so anxious to acquire land that they fulfilled their contracts by accepting all settlers without question, even the uninvited drifters. As closer contact developed between the Americans and Mexicans, cultural conflicts became unavoidable. For the most part, the immigrants who arrived after 1830 constituted the less desirable element of the population, and they frequently precipitated racial conflicts.

These people considered themselves as "rugged individuals" and were contemptuous of any authority other than their own. Previous experience had imbued them with the ideals of complete political and religious freedom, whereas the sensitive Mexicans generally observed tradition and paternal authority. The Anglo-Americans never hesitated to discharge unpopular ministers of their Protestant churches or officials of government, and they openly ignored laws that did not suit them. It was natural, therefore, that criticism of both the Catholic Church and the Mexican government steadily increased as more immigrants arrived. Much of the criticism was justified. A strong effort to administer to the spiritual needs of the settlers was not always made, and the central government remained in a perpetual state of chaos, confusion, contradiction, and revolution.

Slavery was one of the first matters to cause friction between

VI · *The Clash of Civilizations*

the Texans and their new government. Even though the Mexican constitution outlawed this institution, some former residents of Kentucky, Tennessee, Missouri, and the Old South brought human chattels with them in open violation of the law. From the beginning the majority of Texans were sympathetic to slavery, though few actually owned more than a handful of household servants and a large part of the population owned none at all. There were exceptions, of course—one man claimed almost a hundred Negro slaves.

At first the Mexican government did not attempt a serious enforcement of the anti-slavery legislation. Nevertheless, the settlers faced the constant threat of losing their slaves until in 1828 Stephen F. Austin secured the passage of a new law. The measure provided for the liberation of all slaves, but it could hardly be considered an enlightened piece of legislation, for it left the Anglo-Americans free to sign labor contracts with the so-called freedmen. Thus the former Negro slaves merely became indentured servants for life. Later, when the new law was repealed, abolition could not be enforced.

Religion soon replaced slavery as a source of friction. During the three hundred years that Mexico remained a province of Spain, the king tolerated no other form of worship than Catholicism. This union of church and state continued after independence, for all Mexican colonization laws stipulated that immigrants to Texas must become converts before receiving title to land. Most of the settlers in Austin's colony tactfully accepted the restriction, doubtless telling themselves that there were worse vices than hypocrisy.

Mexico unwisely failed to take full advantage of the situation. She did not erect enough churches; her government officials were often personally corrupt; and priests were so few in number that most communities were visited by a priest only once or twice each year. Between visits, weddings and funerals usually were conducted without formal religious ceremonies and baptisms were neglected.

Austin complained, but he dared not ask for complete religious freedom for fear of jeopardizing his position and antagonizing the Mexican officials. An arrangement was eventually carried through similar to that regarding slavery. Protestants were not required to attend Catholic services and were excused from taking an oath that they were converts, but they were still prohibited from building churches of their own faith. Though services in private homes were legalized, the Anglo-Americans felt that their fundamental right of religious freedom was denied. This idea was of special concern to many would-be settlers, and Texans later used it as a convincing argument against the Mexican government. A short time before the outbreak of the Texas revolution in 1836 the legislature of Coahuila-Texas passed a law guaranteeing complete religious toleration, but the reform came too late.

MOST OF THE immigrants to Texas after 1821 preferred Austin's colony, since the bottom lands along the lower Brazos River were among the most fertile in North America. Also, the *empresario* was a tireless worker, and his determination to abide by the terms of federal and state contracts impressed the authorities and enhanced his prestige. Thus he was able to extract concessions from Mexican officials which other contractors could not obtain. By the close of 1833 Austin had issued land titles to 1,065 families, far more than any other *empresario* in Texas.

The early colonists were too busy building cabins, clearing land, and protecting themselves against Indian attacks to become excited about political and religious matters. Gradually the wilderness receded before the ax and the plow, a development that impressed the stream of visitors who came to observe. Upon their return to the United States or Europe they invariably spoke of the opportunities that existed in Texas, of its excellent climate, natural waterways, fertile soil, verdant forests, and grassy prairies. No other type of advertisement could have been more effective,

VI · *The Clash of Civilizations*

and the number of families which followed muddy trails across present-day Oklahoma and Louisiana into Texas quickly swelled. Many more arrived by boat via New Orleans and pushed into the interior from various points along the Gulf.

Mexico welcomed new citizens at first and tolerated their complaints and their attitude of superiority. But as the flood of immigration reached the proportions of a tidal wave, complacency changed to alarm. In various newspapers in the United States, advertisements of Texas lands appeared for which the proposed sellers had no title or claim. Even more disconcerting was the behavior of various *empresarios* who flagrantly violated agreements and claimed unsettled portions of their grants as personal property. A special Mexican law had previously set aside such lands as part of the national domain. In addition, hundreds of uninvited home-seekers arrived in Texas and pre-empted tracts without bothering about titles. Worse yet, some Mexican families who had lived in the eastern part of the province for generations were dispossessed of their property by Anglo-Americans using force or intimidation.

This aggressive activity in eastern Texas started a long chain of events that led ultimately to revolution. The trouble began when the state of Coahuila-Texas granted Haden Edwards permission to settle eight hundred families in the vicinity of the old Spanish town of Nacogdoches. His vast holdings extended as far westward as the edge of Austin's colony and eastward to the "Neutral Ground," where squatters were already in illegal possession of choice sites. Edwards's contract stipulated that he must respect the holdings of former settlers who could show proper evidence of ownership of their lands. Soon after his arrival in Nacogdoches in September 1825 he issued a proclamation calling on all people to produce their titles. Those who could not were given the alternative of purchasing their old claims or leaving the region.

Though many of the Mexican settlers could prove that their family holdings had been continuously occupied for a full century, few of them possessed title abstracts. They, like the squatters in the Neutral Ground and assorted Cherokee families who resided in the region, bitterly resented Edwards's high-handed behavior.

When it became obvious to the *empresario* that his proclamation would not be honored, he threatened to drive out the recalcitrant settlers by force. The Mexicans retaliated by sending petitions to the state legislature stating their grievances against Edwards and pleading for secure titles. Edwards also wrote the authorities at San Antonio and Saltillo and presented his side of the case. His manner and attitude were anything but discreet. No immediate action was taken, but an endless stream of complaints finally caused the Mexican officials to cancel the *empresario*'s contract.

The news stunned Edwards, but he refused to be frightened or to concede defeat. First, he and his brother Benjamin hurriedly made an agreement with the Cherokees for part of their lands. Then a score of men followed Benjamin Edwards into Nacogdoches behind an unfurled red-and-white banner bearing the words INDEPENDENCE, LIBERTY, AND JUSTICE.

This incident occurred in 1826 and has been dignified with the name "Fredonian Rebellion," but it never involved more than thirty Americans and had little support among Texas settlers or individuals outside the eastern area of the province. Practically all actual participants were former criminals from the Neutral Ground who thrived on excitement and trouble. Nevertheless, they surprised the residents of Nacogdoches, barricaded themselves in an old stone house, and proclaimed the new Republic of Fredonia. Many of the Mexicans who had signed the petition against Edwards promptly fled across the Sabine River into Louisiana.

Garbled accounts of the uprising reached Austin's colony a short time later. Reaction was both prompt and vocal, and only the *empresario*'s wise counseling prevented his settlers from rushing to the aid of their fellow Americans. Austin next tried to intercede personally and arrange a peaceful settlement of the controversy, but Edwards replied that he would be satisfied with nothing less then complete "independence from the Sabine to the Rio

VI · *The Clash of Civilizations*

Grande." Soon afterward a Mexican force reached Nacogdoches from San Antonio, supported by a few companies of militia from the Austin colony. The Fredonians fled across the Sabine River, their "republic" collapsed with scarcely a shot fired, and the old residents of the area returned safely to their homes.

The insurrection was hardly more than a futile and insignificant defiance of authority, but the Mexican officials later attempted to inflate its importance. They loudly proclaimed that the revolt proved that Americans in and out of Texas had aggressive designs on the Republic of Mexico.

Mexico's fears were substantiated in 1827 when President Adams sought a modification of the boundary line between Louisiana and the Spanish Southwest. Two years later President Jackson, whose public remarks about the neighboring republic had never been flattering, instructed his minister to Mexico to offer five million dollars for the province of Texas. Mexico declined in no uncertain terms, considering the proposition additional proof of expansionist tendencies on the part of the United States. And when news reached the Mexican capital that the leading newspaper in Washington, *The National Intelligencer,* carried an advertisement for the sale of forty-eight million acres of Texas-Coahuila land by an Anglo-American land company, Mexican suspicions were suddenly compounded.

Meanwhile, General Manuel de Mier y Terán, Commandant-General of the Eastern Interior Provinces of Mexico, made an extensive tour of the Texas frontier. His carefully drawn report to his superiors contained a forceful plan for saving the province from American absorption. One result was the colonization law of April 6, 1830, whereby "citizens of foreign countries lying adjacent to the Mexican territory" were forbidden to settle in Texas. This measure also prohibited the further introduction of slavery into the province and required all travelers from the United States to obtain passports from Mexican officials.

Mexico also planned to force the Texans into closer economic ties with the central government by levying a tariff on goods from the United States. And a policy of encouraging Mexican nationals to migrate to the northern province was adopted in the hope that the Anglo-American settlers would ultimately be reduced to a minority.

To enforce the various tariff and immigration restrictions and to prevent discrimination against the rights of the Mexican nationals required that several companies of troops be scattered at strategic points throughout Texas. At this stage the Mexicans might well have profited by previous experiences of the British. For without the presence of garrison troops, the leaders of the American Revolution might have had considerable difficulty in igniting the sparks of resistance. The British learned in the 1770's that occupation troops forced upon unwilling subjects inevitably resulted in conflict. The Mexicans learned the same lesson half a century later.

In spite of the law of April 6, 1830, immigration from the United States did not cease. In fact, "irresponsible and undesirable squatters" seemed to be attracted to Texas all the more. Among this reckless breed was Sam Houston, who, like some other late arrivees, became a leader in the struggle for independence. Mexican efforts to force the Texans to trade with her were no more successful than those to restrict immigration. Furthermore, the government was never able to persuade her nationals to migrate to the region north of the Rio Grande. The decision to garrison the province was the only part of Terán's plan that was carried out—and it proved the worst mistake of all.

By 1832 the stage was set, and the preliminaries to an exciting drama began. Ironically, the first Mexican official to precipitate the controversy was an American: Colonel John Davis Bradburn, an overbearing soldier of fortune from Kentucky. Bradburn arrived at Anahuac in the spring of 1832 as commander of a garrison force. His duties were to check the wave of unauthorized

VI · *The Clash of Civilizations*

settlers pouring into Texas and to collect tariffs on imports from the United States. The commander began his tour of duty in high-handed fashion and ignored orders from General Terán not to antagonize the local inhabitants. He first procured slaves without compensation to build a fortification and then further insulted their owners by encouraging the Negroes to revolt. When several prominent citizens of the area were imprisoned without benefit of civil trial, the reaction was immediate. In June 1832 a small Texas force from Brazoria attacked the fort on Galveston Bay and soundly whipped the Mexican troops under Bradburn's command. This was the first demonstration against federal authority since the Fredonian uprising six years before.

The Texans knew the seriousness of this action and hastened to clear themselves with the Mexican government in the hope of avoiding retribution. At this very time Mexico experienced one of its periodic revolutions and Antonio López de Santa Anna, so-called "champion of civil liberty and enemy of autocratic government," appeared ready to assume power. Those who had marched against Anahuac affixed their signatures to a petition and forwarded it to the "distinguished leader of democracy." They pledged their lives and fortunes to his cause and assured him that their quarrel with Bradburn was a personal affair. Even Austin, who abhorred the thought of people taking the law into their own hands, assured Santa Anna that the action at Anahuac was directed solely against the commander and not the Mexican government. He added that the people of Texas supported Santa Anna's Liberty Party with all the sincerity and patriotism they could command. When Santa Anna finally won control of Mexico, the Texans breathed more freely, confident that their timely gesture of good will had put them in a favorable position for obtaining reforms.

In April 1833 delegates from various Texas settlements assembled at the small town of San Felipe. This was the second time they had called a convention. In their first one, several months previous, they had petitioned for a redress of certain grievances, but the request had been ignored by Mexican officials at San Antonio. Now the delegates voted to send a representative to Mexico City to plead their case more forcefully. Austin reluctantly agreed to make the long journey through the heat and dust of summer, realizing that his rapport with the Mexican government was Texas's only hope.

Then Anglo-American settlers' major goal was a separation of the Texas province from the state of Coahuila. Their principal argument was that seven hundred miles of desert and brush land isolated them from the capital at Saltillo, making it almost impossible for Texas to be governed as a "crown colony" of that state. Also, the Anglo-Americans maintained that they were not properly represented in the one-house Coahuila legislature.[1] They further pointed out that the Spanish laws could not be understood by more than one tenth of the settlers, and asked that legislation pertaining to Texas be published in English. In addition, they requested a revocation of the tariff of 1830 and a repeal of the measure prohibiting immigration from the United States. And they found even more objectionable the judicial system, in which juries did not exist and the accused did not face a judge. Decisions were rendered on the basis of written testimony, costs were high, and delays were unnecessarily long. A complete reorganization of the courts, therefore, was desired.

Austin reached the Mexican capital in July 1833 and almost immediately sensed the enormity of his task. Santa Anna was in power, but confusion and instability characterized his government. Months of frustration and doubt passed before the dictator granted an audience to Austin. When the day came at last, the mild-mannered Austin prepared for the worst, but, to his surprise, he found Santa Anna a man of great charm and magnanimity. As he laid the various requests before *El Presidente,* Santa Anna generously agreed to everything except separate statehood for

---

[1] Texas at first had only one representative in the legislative body of twelve men. This was increased to two and later to three, but the complex process by which the governor was chosen gave the Texans little voice in their own affairs.

VI · *The Clash of Civilizations*

Texas—far more than the Texas representative had expected. Elated, Austin hastened toward home with the good news. But before he reached the Rio Grande, a previous act of indiscretion overtook him and brought about his arrest.

During his long wait in Mexico, when his enthusiasm for Santa Anna's new government was declining, Austin had committed a tactical error. In a rare moment of extreme anger he had written to friends in his colony that a separate state government should be formed in Texas even if Mexico withheld consent. When Santa Anna granted unexpected concessions, Austin undoubtedly regretted the statement. But regrets were of no avail after the police opened his letter and discovered its contents. By this time Austin was en route to Texas. Mexican officials issued orders for his arrest, and he was taken into custody at Saltillo. When finally he was released in July 1835, he returned home and found conditions north of the Rio Grande approaching a climax.

During the two years that Austin remained in Mexico a full cycle of events had transpired in Texas. First, the Coahuila legislature enacted a number of reforms: they granted trial by jury; they increased Texas representation in the legislature to three members; and they abolished the law that required the Texans to trade only with Mexico. Business suddenly boomed, and talk of separation from Coahuila subsided. But a complete reversal came in April 1834, when Santa Anna proclaimed himself dictator of Mexico and repudiated his program of liberal reforms. Rumors raced across the Texas settlements like a prairie fire: federalism would be abolished, Anglo-Americans disenfranchised, and garrisons re-established at Presidio Anahuac and at the mouth of the Brazos River.

Fears became grim reality in January 1835, when Mexican troops returned to the province. Texans viewed the action as one of tyranny. Many who heretofore had remained tolerant and calm now agreed that Mexicans were degraded cowards and treacherous rascals who could never be trusted. Conflict appeared inevitable, with only a single incident needed to start a conflagration. It came quickly. A group of hotheads under William Barrett

Travis and other leaders marched against the garrison at Presidio Anahuac on June 30, 1835, with the idea of forestalling the arrival of reinforcements from Mexico. They captured the fort with almost as much ease as in 1832, and though some moderates condemned the action, the spirit of revolution continued unchecked. In the midst of this excitement and confusion Austin arrived from his long imprisonment in Mexico.

Stephen F. Austin is generally pictured as a man of delicate features and a relatively weak constitution. During his early years of struggle to establish the colony he tempered his actions with calmness and deliberation. He preferred compromise to strife. He could be stern with his colonists when the situation demanded, and he did not hesitate to defend Mexican policy when he thought it just, but always he tried to be judicial and co-operative, and both the Mexicans and the Anglo-Americans respected him. Long months in a Mexican prison weakened his already frail body but sharpened his spirits, and when he returned to Texas in the summer of 1835 he was not the same individual his friends and associates had known. His tolerance had been shattered and his patience exhausted. The compromiser no longer advocated peace, but realistically accepted the certainty that Texas would never know order and freedom without a fight.

Events in the Mexican province throughout the remainder of 1835 and early 1836 were not unlike those in the English colonies in North America at the dawn of the American Revolution. Committees of Safety and Correspondence sprang up in every community, like those which had preceded the skirmishes at Lexington and Concord. Meanwhile, General Santa Anna left the Mexican capital with a large army to stamp out rebellious movements throughout the nation—particularly in Texas. He designed his action as a mere show of force, for he expected that opposition to authority would evaporate in the face of overwhelming military might. The "Napoleon of the West," as the egotistical dictator sometimes referred to himself, planned to teach the Anglo-Americans a lesson. But, like others of his type, he made the fatal error of believing his subjects to be contemptible cowards.

VI · *The Clash of Civilizations*

Late in the summer of 1835 an advance cavalry detachment reached San Antonio. Its commander, Domingo de Ugartechea, learned that the citizens of nearby Gonzales had organized a militia company and acquired a small cannon. A lieutenant led a column of a hundred dragoons to Gonzales to confiscate the weapon and order the Texans to disband. When the Mexicans reached the outskirts of town, they found a band of angry and determined farmers awaiting them. The reception committee had its artillery piece primed with powder and loaded with chains and scrap iron. When ordered to surrender the weapon, they answered by unfurling a white flag bearing the words COME AND TAKE IT. A challenge of this sort could not be ignored, but when the cavalry attacked they met such a furious defense that discretion suddenly seemed the better part of valor and the Mexicans scurried back to San Antonio.

The victory at Gonzales on October 2, 1835, convinced the Texas rebels that San Antonio could be regained with equal ease, and within a few days volunteers swelled the original force of less than 200 to more than 500 men. Stephen F. Austin now took personal command. The forty miles from Gonzales to San Antonio were covered without opposition, and after a siege of six weeks the Mexicans surrendered the town. Texas soil was free of Mexican troops. But everyone knew that Santa Anna would march on San Antonio with an overwhelming force in order to save face at home.

Developments in other areas also moved swiftly. Two weeks after the skirmish at Gonzales, delegates from twelve Texas communities assembled once again at San Felipe to chart a course for the future. Moderates got control of the convention and defeated an outright vote for independence. A "declaration of causes" for taking up arms against Mexico and an expression in support of the Mexican constitution of 1824 were drafted instead. The body also decided that three commissioners should be sent to the United States to solicit aid and sympathy for the Anglo-American cause. Stephen F. Austin, still with the volunteer army before San Antonio, became one of the commissioners, and Sam Houston, delegate from Nacogdoches, accepted command of the Texas forces. Following the American tradition of the Second Continental Congress, the Texas convention formed a provisional government to operate until a permanent one could be created.

The convention adjourned on November 3, 1835, but not before it had elected Henry Smith provisional governor of the interim state. Confusion, fear, and mismanagement characterized the months that followed. Smith's duties were poorly defined, and the council of twelve appointed to assist the Governor spent its time quarreling and fighting for control. Equally serious was the situation among the military officials. Only a crisis worse than anything the Texans had yet faced could unite them against a common enemy. The Mexicans soon supplied it.

On February 12, 1836, General Santa Anna reached the Rio Grande with an army of over 4,000 men; eleven days later his advance guard came in sight of San Antonio. The Texas force that had taken the city a few months before had dwindled to approximately 150 men under the leadership of William Barrett Travis and James Bowie. Austin had departed for the United States, and Houston was trying desperately to assemble and train an army at nearby Gonzales. Taking San Antonio appeared to present only minor difficulties for the Mexicans, but the small band of Texans there resolved to make the effort a costly one. Rather than flee to the east, they took refuge in the old Mission San Antonio and converted it into a fort known as the "Alamo." And when the main Mexican army arrived a few days later, the Texans knew that all avenues of escape had disappeared.

When word reached the communities of the interior of Texas that a death struggle was about to take place at San Antonio, the fog of bickering and confusion lifted. Some men fled with their families toward the Sabine River, while others assembled guns and knives and hastened to defend the frontier. They had at last come to the hour that all had feared so long. On February 24, 1836, Travis sent a message "to the people of Texas and all Americans in the world" pleading for help. His memorable words could have been written only during a moment of desperation by a man who

VI · *The Clash of Civilizations*

faced certain death. Perhaps he knew that time had already run out and that appeals for military aid were hopeless. Yet a small column of Texans did slip through the Mexican lines during the final hours of the struggle, increasing the beleaguered force by approximately thirty men.

The fall of the Alamo came on the morning of March 6, when Mexican hordes stormed the walls of the mission church to give no quarter and to receive none. All the defenders were killed, but it was a costly victory for Santa Anna. Not only did he lose a third of his army, but he inadvertently supplied the enemy with 187 martyrs, including David Crockett, William Travis, and James Bowie. "Remember the Alamo" became the rallying cry for all Texans, and their distrust and hatred of Mexicans reached a feverish pitch. When Mexican troops captured and killed 350 men under James W. Fannin, Jr., at Goliad three weeks after the fall of the Alamo, public indignation was unanimous. Volunteers flocked to Houston's little army at Gonzales, the only force that stood between the people and ultimate destruction. This unruly mob soon earned the dignified title of "the Texas Army."

Five days before the massacre at the Alamo, delegates from a dozen Texas towns assembled in another convention, their fourth and most important. The site was the small community of Washington-on-the-Brazos, which long since has become a ghost town. It was here on March 2, 1836, that fifty-nine grim-faced Texans affixed their signatures to a document modeled on the Declaration of Independence adopted seventy years before at Philadelphia. A few days later they created a framework of government. Though both the Texas declaration of independence and the constitution appeared no more durable than papier-mâché buildings, they provided the people with something more positive than slogans and revenge.

Before the convention adjourned early in March 1836, it also appointed David G. Burnet as temporary president and confirmed Sam Houston as commander-in-chief of the army. Burnett and his cabinet left Washington soon afterward and took refuge at Harrisburg. Later this ineffective government fled to Galveston

THE SOUTHWEST: *Old and New*

Island while the people panicked and Houston's army desperately retreated before Santa Anna's forces.

When word of the Alamo disaster reached the Texas army at Gonzales, its commander had no alternative but to turn eastward. Previously he had ordered Travis to blow up the fortress at San Antonio and join him, but the instructions had been flagrantly disobeyed. Ironically, the dead men now were worth more to the cause than if they had been alive. Houston's immediate problem, meanwhile, was to delay Santa Anna's advance until the settlers could reach the Louisiana boundary. This decision was not popular with the rank and file of his army, who fervently wanted revenge for the men slain at San Antonio and Goliad. But the commander consulted neither his troops nor his officers. He alone took the responsibility.

As the ragged army slushed through the quagmire that engulfed the river bottoms of eastern Texas, Santa Anna confidently followed. The much maligned Texas commander did not choose to stand and fight until his force had retreated more than a hundred miles. By now his army had swelled to 783 recruits, many of whom had flocked in from the United States. On April 20 the Texans camped in an open prairie near the banks of the San Jacinto River. Less than a mile away "the flower of the Mexican army" bided its time and prepared for another battle of extermination. At noon on April 21, just as the Mexicans settled down to their siesta and Santa Anna retired to his tent with his mulatto mistress, Houston reached the hour of decision. He moved his Texans forward and, by an incredible stroke of luck, escaped detection until they were within two hundred yards of the enemy's defenses. As the commander rode in front of his infantry, he shouted frantically: "Hold your fire! God damn you, hold your fire!" When his men came within firing range, a great cloud of smoke suddenly rose above the field as hundreds of muskets spoke in unison. "Remember the Alamo" took on grim meaning for the hapless Mexicans, who ran pell-mell in all directions. Santa Anna was literally caught napping; his army was routed and hundreds were slaughtered.

VI · *The Clash of Civilizations*

The Battle of San Jacinto lasted almost fifteen minutes. More than six hundred Mexicans died, and nine Texans. Houston's forces captured more than seven hundred prisoners, including Santa Anna himself, while those who escaped lost little time in their hasty retreat to the Rio Grande. The Texans' revenge had come suddenly and dramatically, but the road ahead was still far from smooth.

The Mexican General remained a prisoner for two months, during which time many veterans of the battle and refugees who had returned to their homes urged that he be hanged. The few who kept their heads, including Sam Houston, argued convincingly that a dead Mexican would be of little benefit in maintaining independence. This point proved correct—temporarily, at least; before Santa Anna was released he agreed to a formal treaty of peace and pledged support for an independent republic with the Rio Grande as its southern boundary. Although the Mexican government rejected the Treaty of Velasco and the wily Santa Anna repudiated his pledge after his return to power in 1839, the Texans received a needed breathing spell.

THE SEPARATION of Texas from Mexico and its ultimate annexation to the United States awakened the American people to their "manifest destiny" and altered the course of American history. The Texas question precipitated the Mexican War, and it can be argued with good evidence that it likewise made the Civil War inevitable. Certainly no issue commanded more national attention between 1836 and 1846 than that of the republic which had been carved out of the muddy wilderness by the hardy hands of Anglo-Saxon frontiersmen.

Myths are the natural products of such events. One that persisted in American history and was perpetuated by Marquis James in his biography of Sam Houston, *The Raven,* established

President Jackson as the mastermind behind a carefully drawn plan to acquire Texas from Mexico. According to this, Jackson entered into a plot with his protégé Sam Houston whereby the latter was to go to Texas, foment trouble with Mexico, establish an independent republic, and eventually annex it to the United States. Many of the happenings in Texas fit neatly into this pattern, but careful research reveals that this thesis was manufactured after the events. Jackson's interest in the province is beyond question, and he made efforts to acquire it soon after coming to office. But once the defeat of Santa Anna was complete, he adopted a course of "watchful waiting" and did not even recognize the independence of the republic until March 3, 1837, when he felt reasonably sure that Texas could maintain itself.[2]

Independence was one thing, but a stable government proved a different matter entirely. Soon after the Battle of San Jacinto Sam Houston departed for New Orleans to receive treatment for a severe wound acquired in action, while Thomas J. Rusk took command of the Texas forces. The peacetime army quickly swelled to more than 2,500 men, who proved about as troublesome as the former enemy. When a plan for a punitive expedition across the Rio Grande aborted, the disgruntled commander and his ill-tempered, unpaid troops plotted a mutiny against their own government for having released Santa Anna. Some order came out of the confused situation in October 1836 at a general election: the Texans accepted a proposed constitution by a nearly unanimous vote; Houston easily defeated Stephen F. Austin for the presidency; and some 6,000 people voted for annexation to the United States, while less than 100 disapproved. Houston's inauguration at Columbia a short time later launched a new political career that dominated Texas politics for the next two and a half decades.

The new President's policy was simple and direct. He fa-

---

[2] Doubtless Jackson would have liked to recognize Texas's independence immediately following the Battle of San Jacinto, but he did not want to jeopardize Van Buren's chances for election to the presidency. Later he was an avid supporter of annexation and took a strong stand on this position during the presidential campaign in 1844.

VI · *The Clash of Civilizations*

vored a program of rigid economy, friendly relations with the Indians, a conciliatory attitude toward Mexico, encouragement of immigration, and annexation to the United States. Even a giant such as Houston could not accomplish so much in one brief term, but he made great strides. In spite of his spartan efforts, a heavy public indebtedness could not be avoided because of the shortage of money and the inability of citizens to pay taxes. Import duties and the issuance of scrip provided some circulating funds, but income never approached public expenses.

One of the largest problems was the army, which by 1837 had increased to more than 3,000 men. Salaries were always in arrears, and irresponsibles in command of the troops continued to advocate an invasion of Mexico. Such action would only have united the Mexicans and goaded them into retaliating at a time when the Anglo-American republic could least afford another war. "Old Sam" finally solved the question by furloughing all but 600 troops. Fortunately, the instability of the government in Mexico prevented an invasion from the south, and a conciliatory policy toward the Indians made it unnecessary for Houston to recall the men from their involuntary leave of absence.

The new republic had one great asset: its land. In December 1836 the Texas Congress passed a law granting 1,280 acres to all newcomers with families and 640 acres to single men, with the right to pre-empt additional lands at fifty cents per acre. Within ten years the population increased from 30,000 to 140,000. Few other American frontiers attracted so many in such a brief span. People arrived by wagon, on horseback, and on foot from the Old South and the Mississippi Valley, while thousands came from the Atlantic Coast and various parts of the East. After Texas revived the *empresario* system in 1841, group migration from Germany, England, France, and the United States helped sustain the tide of immigration for several years.

But the most important plank in Houston's plan—annexation to the United States—had the least chance of immediate fulfillment. Soon after the hero of San Jacinto assumed the office of chief executive, he dispatched William H. Wharton to Washington with instructions to make every effort to achieve this goal. In spite of the close friendship between Houston and Jackson, the President of the United States unequivocally informed the Texas agent that prompt annexation was out of the question. There was strong and bitter opposition to the idea throughout the North, and most Southern Congressmen were only lukewarm to the idea. Moreover, such action would almost certainly bring on an unpopular war with Mexico. Jackson's rebuff left Wharton no alternative but to work for recognition of the republic, which he achieved only just before Jackson left office. After Van Buren's inauguration in 1837 the Texas offer for annexation was withdrawn completely.

When Houston's first term expired in October 1838, he was succeeded by Mirabeau B. Lamar. The second president already had become one of Old Sam's bitterest antagonists, and he quickly reversed many of his policies. An unrelenting war against the Indians was a typical example, and it, like other Lamar schemes, helped push the republic to the brink of economic chaos. Lamar made some progress between 1838 and 1841 toward establishing an educational system for Texas. Also, England, France, the Netherlands, and Belgium extended recognition during this period, but efforts to secure Mexico's acknowledgment of Texas's independence failed miserably. The Mexicans' refusal even to discuss the matter caused the flamboyant Lamar to turn his attention to New Mexico in the hope of bringing that province into the republic.

A handful of soldiers and some three hundred traders and adventurers, including George Wilkins Kendall of the *New Orleans Picayune* left the small settlement of Austin for Santa Fe on June 2, 1841. The expedition had all the trappings of a commercial caravan, but its real objective was to persuade the New Mexicans that they would be happier under the flag of the Republic of Texas. Since the people along the Río Grande del Norte had recently shown signs of revolt against the federal government of Mexico, Lamar believed that they would gladly join the Anglo-

VI · *The Clash of Civilizations*

Americans. At least, he argued, they would welcome the opportunity for regular trade with Texas.

The long trek across the flat Indian lands of western Texas and eastern New Mexico all but decimated the party. And when they arrived at Santa Fe, Governor Armijo, instead of receiving them with open arms, ordered their arrest. Armijo rushed news of the "great victory over the Texas invaders" to Mexico City, confident that his decisive action would put him in good grace with his superiors. He was correct. Eventually the Texans were marched to southern Mexico and thrown into dungeons. Some failed to survive the long death march, and many others perished from barbaric treatment in prison.[3]

This ill-fated venture doomed Lamar's administration. In 1841 Sam Houston came to power for a second term after winning a decisive victory over David G. Burnet, Lamar's handpicked candidate. The three years that followed were the most difficult of all for the struggling republic, and it was well for Texas that she had a man of Houston's caliber in charge. He inherited a bankrupt government; trade was at a standstill, credit practically nonexistent, and the morale and equipment of the army and navy in complete disintegration. Despite his many picayunish faults and his ability to make acrimonious enemies by the dozen, Houston almost single-handedly kept the government intact and the heterogeneous population together.

To complicate Texas's many problems, in 1842 the Mexicans ceased fighting at home long enough to send raiding parties across the Rio Grande on two separate occasions. Several towns, including San Antonio, were surprised and prominent leaders were captured and carted off to Perote prison. Although the invaders

---

[3] The prisoners surviving the Santa Fe expedition along with other Texans captured by the Mexicans on the second venture a short time later, plus several prisoners taken during Mexican and Texan forays across the Rio Grande in 1842, were not released until late in 1843. Almost half of the seven or eight hundred prisoners were executed or died of starvation and disease in Mexico.

withdrew from Texas soil after only a few weeks, the action kept the settlers throughout the entire republic in constant anxiety for more than a year. Farmers neglected their crops to protect the frontier. It took all the cunning and subtlety that the President could muster to prevent a large-scale retaliatory invasion of Mexico, something which he knew the government could not afford. Houston's enemies ranted and threatened, but, in spite of slander and intimidation, he refused to be drawn into a full-scale war, maintaining that the raids were only meant to have a psychological effect. His insistence on turning the other cheek proved a wise course. Near the end of 1843, thanks to the help of British and French diplomats, he made a truce with Santa Anna, and hostilities ended. But other problems remained.

At the end of the inept and extravagant Lamar administration the public debt was the equivalent of seven million United States dollars, while Texas scrip was worth only fifteen cents per dollar. All Houston's efforts to reverse the trend in deficit spending failed, and the debt mounted. New exchequer bills issued by the congress commanded little prestige, money could not be borrowed from abroad, and revenues from imports declined. It became increasingly clear that annexation to the United States was the only alternative to financial chaos.

Houston devoted much of his skill and energy between 1841 and 1844 to annexation, the question having lain dormant during Lamar's three years in office. Meanwhile, events in Washington and Europe gradually brought about a more favorable climate. John Tyler had scarcely succeeded to the presidency in 1841 when his close political friend Henry Wise, of Virginia, suggested that he acquire Texas. Other matters before the Senate of the United States caused Tyler to hesitate in making known his desire to annex the Southwestern republic. Houston probably had no inkling of the President's personal attitude, but he recognized the growing spirit of expansion in the United States and cleverly capitalized on it. By playing a cunning game of "studied indifference" and at the time exaggerating the extent of British interest in Texas, he balanced the suspicions of one country against the

VI · *The Clash of Civilizations*

"designs" of the other.[4] When Tyler learned in March 1843 that England was anxious to see Texas free her slaves, he felt that England was plotting against slavery in the United States. So did Southern senators and congressmen. As they became aware that Texas held the key to the security of their cherished institution, their concern mounted.

Houston made it appear that the British had been responsible for establishing peaceful relations between Texas and Mexico and that the infant republic now looked to the British rather than the Americans for guidance. Even Andrew Jackson was convinced by this sly game, and he immediately came out of retirement with a strong statement recommending annexation in order "to forestall a British foothold in the Southwest."

A few days later, on October 16, 1843, Tyler's Secretary of State, Abel Upshur, advised Isaac Van Zandt, the Texas representative in Washington, that the chances for annexation looked very good. Van Zandt forwarded the information to Houston, but the latter remained cagey. Finally, he replied that Texas must be assured of statehood in advance of negotiations; otherwise, it could not afford to compromise its good relations with England and France. And thus the matter stood.

In January 1844 Andrew Jackson wrote his personal friend and former protégé in an attempt to overcome his apparent objections to annexation. One month later Secretary Upshur sent a long communication to the Texas government in which he too urged annexation; there was not, he said, the "slightest doubt of the ratification of the treaty of annexation, should Texas agree to make one." Houston expressed his willingness to accept, but fate stepped in before the Senate voted on the treaty. Upshur was killed in an accident, and John C. Calhoun became Secretary of State. In his first official act he urged the admission of Texas

---

[4] England did not disguise the fact that she wanted Texas as a potential market for British goods, free from protective tariffs. She doubtless entertained hopes that emancipation of the slaves in Texas might serve as a base to undermine slavery throughout the South.

The Southwest: *Old and New*

into the Union as a means of preserving the institution of slavery in the United States, and thus guaranteed the defeat of the treaty. On June 8, 1844, the Senate voted thirty-five to sixteen against ratification.

This setback proved a temporary one. In the presidential election of 1844, James K. Polk became the Democratic standard-bearer with the slogan of "Reannexation of Texas and reoccupation of Oregon." The Texas question had been dramatically revived and placed on a national instead of a sectional basis: a vote for Polk was a specific endorsement of annexation. When Henry Clay, the Whig candidate, half agreed with the idea, he assured his own defeat. Polk won by a very narrow margin, but a majority of the people indicated that they favored rampant expansion in general and the annexation of Texas in particular. Only the formalities of admission into the Union remained, but Texas now had greater bargaining power than before: it could demand and receive admission as a state rather than a territory.

The former Mexican province officially entered the Union as the twenty-eighth state on December 31, 1845. By now Houston had completed his second term, and the fourth President of the republic, Anson Jones, held the office. In addition to the unqiue privilege of keeping possession of its public lands, Texas also retained the right to divide itself into as many as five states. This privilege was never exercised, although Texas lost part of its claimed domain in the Compromise of 1850. "This state will never divide itself into separate parts," Texans frequently explain, "for who will ever relinquish his individual claim to the Alamo?"

Somehow Texas had managed to survive one financial, political, and military crisis after another until it achieved annexation. The natural optimism of its pioneer people had been its one great source of strength. Without it the Texas Republic doubtless would have experienced an even more turbulent course of events.

VII

LIFE AND CULTURE IN THE TEXAS REPUBLIC

WHEN TEXAS won independence from Mexico in 1836, its population numbered less than half that of the smallest state in the Union. In theory the Republic took in all lands north and east of the Rio Grande, south of the Red River, and west of the Sabine River. In less than one tenth of this vast area dwelt some 30,000 people, most of them living within an inland arc of 100 miles from Galveston Island. Mexican-populated San Antonio lay on the western fringe of the frontier, Austin and Dallas were mere crossings on the Colorado and Trinity rivers, and there was a cluster of settlements in the vicinity of Nacogdoches. Only a dozen or more of these deserved to be called towns. After independence this situation changed rapidly.

Although political, military, and diplomatic struggles overshadowed all other activities in the Republic of Texas, the everyday affairs of the inhabitants were nonetheless significant. Their personal problems were as trying to them as those experienced by the government, and perhaps played equally important roles in shaping the pattern of the future. Acutely aware that history watched, these fiercely proud and stubborn frontier folk were anxious to present a respectable front to the world. Their determination in the face of adversities must be remembered if one is to understand modern Texas.

Whether they came from high or low stratas of society in the United States, France, or Germany, Texas immigrants blended readily into a typical frontier society once they reached the "promised land." The new citizens did not find it the land of milk and honey pictured by overzealous boosters, although one observer remarked that it was literally true that honey could easily be found in the woods and wild cattle thrived on the prairie. Survival demanded hard physical work, and most of the settlers turned quickly to the business of raising cotton and corn. One was marketed in Galveston and New Orleans, while the other supplied the standard dull fare of corn meal and mush upon which pioneer families relied.

Cotton grew well in the virgin land of the river bottoms, and some tracts yielded as much as 2,000 pounds an acre during the first two or three years. Indeed, it was the universal practice to plant more than one family could gather in a single season. Even planters who possessed slaves were not always able to harvest and gin their entire crop before severe weather set in. Some, in desperation, offered prospective laborers half of what they picked as compensation, but the unstable price of cotton and the high United States tariffs frequently caused such generous proposals to be refused. Nevertheless, Texas continued to depend on cotton as its chief money crop, a practice that prolonged acute poverty until admission into the Union brought the removal of the tariffs.

VII · *Life and Culture in the Texas Republic*

Adequate records of the total production of cotton during the decade of 1836–46 do not exist. Much of it was smuggled down the Red River into Louisiana on rafts and steamers. Approximately 30,000 bales were cleared through the customhouses at Galveston and Matagorda in 1845. But the high cost of freight and the extraordinary duties imposed made shipping to New Orleans rarely worth the effort. Some planters shipped directly to England, but this seldom, if ever, proved wise. One farmer in Huntsville sent ten bales to Liverpool in 1842, only to find that freight charges, import duties, and other costs reduced his net to less then eighteen dollars a bale. This scarcely paid the cost of harvesting.

During the early years of the Republic, Texas farmers consumed most of their locally produced livestock and crops, except cotton. Corn became the "staff of life." The pitch of the stalk produced a "corn-stalk molasses," while a variety of foods could be prepared from the kernels. The green ears were cooked in boiling water or roasted in hot ashes while still in the shuck. Mature corn was either made into hominy or ground into a coarse meal and boiled as mush. More often the housewife mixed the meal in a batter and roasted it on live coals as "johnny cake" or placed it in an oven and converted it into "corn pone." The addition of eggs, honey, molasses, soda, or spices made the product considerably more palatable, but these ingredients were difficult to secure.

During the spring and summer months Texas pioneers enjoyed a variety of vegetables and fruits. Sweet potatoes grew well in the sandy soil and could be boiled, baked, fried, made into bread, brewed into beer, or eaten raw. Pumpkins, melons, cabbages, peas, and okra likewise were grown with ease. Wild fruit, such as peaches, berries, plums, persimmons, and grapes, usually abounded in the nearby woods, but the settlers did not always reach them before the bears, coons, and opossums. A few enterprising farmers planted their own orchards, but rarely gave their trees proper care.

The abundance of wild game supplied most farm families

with large quantities of fresh meat. Deer, turkeys, swine, bear, grouse, ducks, geese, and buffalo added variety to an otherwise dull diet during the winter months. Settlers along the coast also enjoyed fish and oysters, and those in the interior sometimes ate the coarse flesh of mustang or small game. Even city dwellers regarded white bread, sugar, and coffee as luxuries. A substance called "coffee" could be brewed from the seed of dried okra. Sassafras tea was a more common beverage and was believed to have certain medicinal virtues. Some Texans, particularly the Mexicans and those living in the former Spanish settlements, consumed large quantities of chili peppers, beans, and tortillas.

The tables of the more prosperous planters and merchants were laden, on special occasions, with a great variety of meats, vegetables, fruits, pies, cakes, and even imported wines and liquors. In the taverns and hotels of Galveston and other coastal cities the traveler usually found superior accommodations. William Bollaert, an English observer of the Texas scene between 1842 and 1844, wrote that a night's lodging cost two dollars at Galveston's finest hotel, the Tremont. This included a "petite" supper and breakfast. Drinks were extra, but tipples from "gin sling" to "peach punch" cost only twenty-five cents.

"All through Texas," the Englishman continued, "the traveller can be accom[m]odated at the Farm Houses and 'entertainment' for man and beast for a dollar a night—that is, supper on arrival in the evening—bed—and breakfast the following morning, but the majority of farmers will not receive payment." [1]

If one wished to remain several days or weeks in a particular locality, most farmhouse or plantation owners charged very reasonable rates—about half the fifteen or twenty dollars per month charged by the hotels and taverns. "Under no circumstances," Bollaert observed, "is a traveller, rich or poor, turned from the door. Two families from Alabama, about fifteen in number, with three wagons, fifty Negroes, oxen, horses, and mules—

---

[1] W. Eugene Hollon and Ruth Lapham Butler (eds.): *William Bollaert's Texas* (Norman: University of Oklahoma Press; 1956), p. 111.

VII · *Life and Culture in the Texas Republic*

their expenses on the road about 120 dollars, a considerable portion of this paid for ferries and repairing wagons." Many travelers preferred camping out if they could find good pasture for their horses and the weather was not too severe.

The average immigrant reached Texas by way of Preston Crossing on Red River, northeast of present-day Dallas, or by the road from Natchitoches to Nacogdoches, crossing the Sabine River at Gaines Ferry. His party might be composed of himself, wife, sons, and daughters. The elder children usually walked while the younger ones rode in the "Jersey" wagon with the mother, household furniture, farming equipment, carpentering tools, garden seed, a pig or two, and a few chickens. The settlements through which the immigrants passed proved friendly and helpful. Advice about good farm sites was eagerly sought and freely given. If the immigrant was a farmer, as most of the new settlers were, he frequently homesteaded the first unclaimed land that suited him, or else purchased surveyed land for as little as twenty-five cents an acre.

Newcomers made their wagons serve as houses until log cabins could be erected. After the one- or two-room domicile, a cookhouse, a stable, a granary, and a "lot" or small enclosure for the cattle were completed before the first crop was harvested. If the farmer had several sons old enough to work, owned a few slaves, or had the help of neighbors, he enclosed his new cotton and corn lands with a Virginia fence as a protection against deer and stray cattle. The surplus timber on the farm land was cleared by girdling each tree. In a short time the leaves dropped and the tree died. A year or two hence it was burned or cut up for firewood. Thus the land could be reclaimed with little capital, a sharp ax, and a minimum of labor.

Most of the Texas houses were one- or two-room cabins that served "more for utility than ornament." A lean-to shed was added in time, or a duplicate structure was placed beside the original cabin and the two buildings were joined by a common roof. The open passage caught the summer breezes and provided a comfortable sitting or lounging place during the torrid summer months. A long porch gave the complete structure a more pretentious appearance.

Texas cabins were constructed of rough pine, gum, or oak logs, and the chinks were filled with clay and grass or moss and sticks. Handmade boards or "shakes" served for roofing, held down by rocks or poles when nails were unavailable. Floors were either dirt or split logs laid with the dressed side up. One to three openings were made in the front wall for door and windows. Wooden shutters were opened and closed from the inside, and a thin piece of rawhide served as an inadequate substitute for glass to admit light and keep out flies and mosquitoes. Among the poorer settlers the rawhide covering, like the log-and-clay chimney and dirt floor, remained a permanent feature of the cabins. Glass windows, wooden floors, rock chimneys, and stone hearths were marks of prestige, but they were found only in large, elaborate cabins.

If the settler became moderately prosperous, he either weatherboarded and enlarged his cabin or else built a new dwelling of lumber, stone, or brick. One successful planter constructed a mansion in Colorado County in the 1840's known as "Robson's Castle," the showplace of the entire area. The homemade lime-and-gravel "castle" covered a fifty-acre plot along the banks of the Colorado River. This was probably the first residence in Texas with a roof garden, running water, and a moat with a drawbridge.

Some large plantations contained as many as two dozen outhouses, barns, and cabins for slaves, two or three deep wells for water, and its own cotton gin, syrup mill, and grist mills. The main house might contain mahogany or cherry furniture, horsehair sofas, a piano, a Franklin stove, silverware, china, fine linens, woolen-damask curtains, and beautifully bound books.

The poorer settlers furnished their cabins with homemade chairs and tables. Beds were built in a corner of the room by anchoring hand-hewn boards to notches cut in the walls and to a single post driven into the ground. The frame was covered by a lattice of rawhide strings or hemp rope. A featherbed brought from the States or else a thick layer of dried moss probably served

VII · *Life and Culture in the Texas Republic*

as a mattress. Food was boiled over the fireplace or baked or fried on a pile of coals on the edge of the hearth, with a few pans or iron pots constituting all the cooking utensils. A flat board or shingle sometimes provided the dinner plate, while a bowie knife and a few wooden spoons sufficed for silverware. In time these household furnishings underwent considerable refinement, usually by the end of the first decade and certainly with the second generation of settlers.

Living conditions in the towns did not always offer a great improvement over life in the country. Here one would find a mixture of log cabins, sod houses, shanties, and crudely constructed frame houses covered with unpainted siding or split-pine boards. San Antonio, Nacogdoches, and Goliad possessed several stone and adobe buildings even before the revolution and thus presented a more respectable appearance than most places. Houses in these towns were one-story and flat-roofed, with a well-shaded patio in the rear and a covered portico in front.

It was the architecture of the newer settlements which least impressed visitors to Texas. Bollaert noted that the flimsily built houses in Galveston in the 1840's were "so constructed that even a three-story dwelling can be moved from one end of town to the other at pleasure. . . . It is not a question of moving one's furniture, but one's house in the bargain." The Englishman showed even more surprise when he visited Austin a few months later and found it a town of dreariness and desolation. "The President's home looked gloomy, the streets filled with grass and weeds. . . . The capital is the abode of bats, lizards and stray cattle. [Some people in Texas today make similar charges.] These buildings having been built of green wood and run up with great expedition, the timbers have dried and become loose, the plaster peeling off, and the Austin soft stone cracking. If these buildings and others in the city are not repaired in a short time Austin will be in a heap of ruin." [2]

While the majority of the newer towns in Texas appeared

---

[2] Ibid., p. 198.

as gloomy as Austin, there were a few exceptions. San Augustine, for example, expressed itself in the form of several two-story dwellings with large classical columns, glass windows, and neatly painted paling fences. Galveston and Houston also boasted a few pretentious homes plus several brick buildings by 1845 that broke the monotony of shanties and outhouses along the main street.

Even more primitive than the houses and public buildings were the streets. Except in the older towns such as San Antonio, the principal "avenues" contained a sufficient number of tree stumps strategically located to hamper traffic and "just high enough to bark a man's knees at night." Indeed, a stranger dared not venture down main street after dark without a lantern or an experienced guide.

After a settlement became fairly civilized and the stumps were removed, the streets remained veritable "pig styes" during the rainy season—cut by deep ruts from wagons and carriages and filled with puddles of water. Still, this condition was better than the choking dust that permeated the atmosphere during the summer months. City councils made feeble efforts to water the streets and keep them in repair. Crossing from one side to the other frequently became a minor adventure for the pedestrian. A citizen of Matagorda complained in the local paper in 1841 that some of the ditches had already reached a depth of ten or fifteen feet and thereby constituted a hazard to "life and limb."

Roads between towns were not much better. During dry weather they resembled dusty trails, and in the wet season they were quagmires of mud and slush. One foreign critic, Nicholas Doran P. Maillard, who returned to England in 1842 to publish a *History of the Republic of Texas,* covered the entire subject with the curt statement that "there are no roads in Texas except natural ones." This was not altogether true, for the Spaniards and Mexicans cut several roads across Texas before the Anglo-Americans arrived. Some of these in the beginning, however, were little more than trails marked by "blazes" on trees, with the intermediate brush and undergrowth removed. Yet, it was possible to travel

VII · *Life and Culture in the Texas Republic*

by carriage from Mission San Juan Bautista on the Rio Grande to Nacogdoches, a distance of some 600 miles. Other roads extended westward from Houston to Austin and San Antonio and from the latter point to Corpus Christi, Laredo, and Goliad.

Few visitors to the Republic traveled as extensively as William Bollaert, and he doubtless spoke with firsthand knowledge when he reported in 1842 that "with few exceptions the greater portion of the country can be traversed in pretty direct lines by waggons at least, or how could the settlers move onward." Even an apologist such as Bollaert had to admit, however, that travel by carriage during wet weather was exceedingly difficult and slow. The absence of bridges over streams sometimes caused delays of several days. For one traveling on horseback, the only alternative, in the absence of ferries, was to swim the animal across. If afoot, a man could simply strap his clothes to his back and chance the stream alone.

Most long-distance travel in Texas was by small parties of men on horseback, with their baggage, if any, brought in wagons pulled by oxen or mules. When wagons or carriages were not available, each member of the party carried provisions in his saddle bag and was equipped with at least a blanket or two, rifle, pistol, bowie knife, frying pan, and coffeepot. At night the party pitched camp and cooked over open fires. Later each took out his pipe and all sat back to tell stories, sing songs, or play cards while the inevitable bottle made the rounds. Then, one by one the men retreated from the circle and rolled up in blankets at the foot of a nearby tree. A night watch guarded the hobbled animals, kept the fire from burning out, and sounded a warning in case of a visit by a curious bear or hungry panther.

Except on the extreme western frontier beyond San Antonio and Austin there was little to fear at night from Indians. Even so, the experienced traveler dared not proceed except in an emergency, for the poorly marked roads made it easy to lose one's way even in familiar country.

There was considerable water travel by small barge, especially downstream, with little danger of running aground. Keel boats also carried both passengers and freight, for they drew no more than a foot of water and could be "poled" across the shallow passes without much delay.

Wagons transported most of the freight, but several steamboats plied the rivers, hauling cotton from the various plantations and settlements to Houston, Galveston, and Matagorda. Their greatest difficulties were encountered at the mouths of rivers, which were usually blocked by sand bars except when rain had swelled the streams. Often the cargo had to be unloaded before the vessel could pass, and such delays became costly. For sidewheelers going upstream the course increased in danger with each mile because of numerous "rafts" and sand bars. Ships aground or with holes knocked in their bottoms and partly sunk were not uncommon sights. One stranger remarked facetiously that the steamboat on which he journeyed up the Trinity River in the 1840's spent so much time on bars that it would have made greater speed if it had started overland in the first place.

Numerous attempts to construct railroads before 1845 failed because of the financial stringencies and the renewal of war with Mexico. Merchants and promoters in the more heavily populated cities near the Gulf financed most of the projects. Not until a decade later, after Texas became a state, did railroad construction begin in earnest. Meanwhile, the establishment of a number of stage routes alleviated the problem of transportation. Several small lines operated between two or three towns—such as Houston and Harrisburg, and Houston and Richmond—as early as 1837. The fares varied from one to seven dollars per person, depending upon the total distance traveled.

Stage service between Houston and the new capital at Austin was inaugurated in 1839, with a regular schedule of two trips each week. The distance was negotiated in three days during good weather. The fare was twenty-five cents a mile, which greatly limited the number of customers. After the government began to subsidize the stage, the line reduced its rate considerably. By 1845 the roads were greatly improved and connected practically all of the principal cities. A few years before the Civil War

VII · *Life and Culture in the Texas Republic*

regular passenger service was started between San Antonio and San Diego, California. A still longer route, the Butterfield Overland Stage, went into operation across Texas in 1858. Coaches departed from Missouri and California twice weekly, entering Texas at Preston Crossing near present-day Sherman at one end of the state and at El Paso at the other.

In spite of the progress made between 1836 and 1846, frontier conditions disappeared slowly. This was especially true of wearing apparel, for the average pioneer either could not afford "store-boughten clothes" or else found them impracticable in a society where rough outdoor work remained the rule. Buckskin, though far from comfortable, was still the most common garb for rural people. As it was both durable and plentiful, whole families outfitted themselves in it, including pantaloons, shirt, coat, shoes, and hat. Among the "uninitiated," cotton drawers were virtually unknown.

The rural people gradually expanded their wardrobes by the addition of linsey shirts and dresses, as cotton and wool became plentiful and the women found time to card, spin, and weave. On Sundays and special occasions the more prosperous planters and merchants wore broadcloth, woolen suits, linen shirts, beaver hats, and patent-leather shoes. Their wives and daughters might possess several silk dresses, usually black, a fancy bonnet or two, white silk stockings, and black slippers. For everyday use they wore gingham or calico dresses, walking shoes, and hand-knit stockings—apparel that country women cherished as "Sunday best."

The frock coat remained a mark of distinction for several decades. It was worn by gentlemen in parlors and in public places, usually with an ornate vest, false collar, ruffled shirt, string tie, and perhaps a stovepipe hat. An overcoat or cape would be added for colder weather. With the backwoodsman or hunter the overcoat took the form of a heavy horse blanket with a slit in the middle so that it could be worn poncho fashion. Frequently a bearskin or buffalo hide had to suffice, but a decorative Mexican blanket was considered the height of rural fashion. The coonskin cap did not disappear from the frontier for a full generation after the

Republic ended, although it never became the exclusive headgear of the Texas pioneer.

Texans manufactured their own brand of entertainment, and inhibitions rarely handicapped them in their own surroundings. For country people no social event called for a more boisterous celebration than a wedding, and some people rode forty or fifty miles to attend one. Formal invitations were not necessary, unless, of course, the ceremony was performed in haste because the girl's parents refused permission or as a result of a premarital indiscretion.

A liberal consumption of corn whisky generally preceded the ceremony, while the women prepared food, gossiped among themselves, and fussed over the bride. After the reading of the marital rites, a "supper consisting of all the good things of life" was made ready for the assembled company. With the fiddles well tuned, the cotillions and contradance commenced. "Rcsin the Bow," "Jim Along Josey," "Zip Coon," "Old Dan Tucker," and "Roaring River," were the favorites. The "more venerable" part of the group usually departed in buggies, wagons, or on horseback by midnight, but the younger people frequently danced and sang until the following morning.

Horse racing attracted large crowds in the country and even larger ones in the cities. Such contests, generally run on a straight 400-yard track, were free, and nearly everyone in attendance placed a wager or two. Races usually were run between two horses, whose owners sometimes bet their slaves, livestock, and even their farms. Several circular race tracks appeared in such coastal cities as Velasco, Galveston, and Houston before 1840, accompanied by organized jockey clubs and purses comparable to those at New Orleans and St. Louis tracks. Sometimes the manager of the race arranged a "fancy ball" as a climax to the day's events, but only the "elegant" ladies and "high-bred" gentlemen attended.

Religion offered other opportunities for social intercourse as well as spiritual fulfillment. Although less than twenty per cent of the people claimed to be active church members, turnouts at

1a (above) *Kit Carson home, Taos, New Mexico, before restoration.*
1b (below) *Zebulon Montgomery Pike (1779–1813). The first Anglo-American to explore and describe extensively the Southwest. From an original painting owned by The American Philosophical Society.*

2a (above) *The Battle of Resaca de la Palma, May 9, 1846.* From a contemporary lithograph published by Kellogs & Thayer.
2b (below) *The Battle of Palo Alto, May 8, 1846.* From a contemporary lithograph published by Kellogs & Thayer.

3a (*above*) Stephen F. Austin (1793–1836). American colonizer in Texas. Secretary of State, Republic of Texas (1836). From a painting believed to have been done by George Catlin.
3b (*below*) Sam Houston (1793–1863). Commander-in-Chief of the Texas Army, twice President of the Texas Republic, United States Senator, Governor of Texas, and strong believer in the Union. From an original photograph made in 1857 and now in the possession of the San Jacinto Memorial Museum.

4 *The Alamo—shrine of Texas liberty.*

5a (above) Looking east from Plaza at a Santa Fe wagon caravan, Santa Fe, New Mexico, in the late 1860's.
5b (below) Main Street in Albuquerque, New Mexico, approximately 1890. Area now restored and called Old Town Plaza.

6a (above) Bank and outdoor saloon, Guthrie, Oklahoma, three weeks after first opening in 1889.
6b (below) Oklahoma City—one month after the opening in 1889.

7 *The great Silver King mine near Superior, Arizona, in the 1870's.*

8 Old City Hall in Tombstone, Arizona—now a museum.

VII · Life and Culture in the Texas Republic

frequent revival meetings sometimes included more than half of the entire community. After Texas became independent in 1836 the Protestant churches dominated the religious scene, with the Methodists boasting more than half of the registered members. Below them in numbers ranked the Baptist, Presbyterian, Roman Catholic, and Episcopal churches. The Methodist system of circuit riders gave this denomination a tremendous advantage, for it filled the need of the isolated settlers and did not depend on an established congregation nor a special church building.

The most dramatic feature of frontier religious life was the camp meeting. Usually conducted by the Methodists or the Cumberland Presbyterians, these affairs lasted from one to two weeks and attracted hundreds of people, who arrived in wagons or on horseback prepared to camp out for part or all of the time the meeting lasted. The campgrounds most often were located in forest clearings near streams or springs. A brush arbor served as a church building, with log benches in place of chairs. The long-winded sermons of the evangelists, the melodious singing and shouting of the worshippers, and the loud ejaculations and testifying of the "sinners" reverberated through the forest from sunset until late at night.

Not all the people who attended camp meetings were poor and uneducated. Undoubtedly a thirst for companionship and a desire to escape the monotony of everyday living motivated many. Some appeared because of social pressure from their neighbors and friends, some as a result of curiosity, and others for political reasons. One contemporary writer observed that the preacher exercised a tremendous power over his flock, as demonstrated in the following conversation that he overheard:

" 'Friend—we never see you at the meeting.'

" 'I read my Bible at home.'

" 'That's well, but, but, but, it would be better to attend meetings and if it is true what I hear that you intend running for Congress next year, if you do not mix with your Methodist friends, you will not be elected . . . they will oppose your election, and probably someone will get the votes over you who may do us great harm in Congress. My Christian friend, consider this, and I'll do much for you with the brethren and ministers.'

"'I will take your views into consideration and will attend meeting next Sunday.'"[3]

William Bollaert, like many other observers from abroad, expressed astonishment at the emphasis placed on religion in Texas. During a prolonged siege of the ague he stayed at a farmhouse near Columbia and for several days was unable to secure the help of a physician because all the local medics were attending a revival meeting in a nearby community. "Camp meetings are a disgrace to society," he wrote scornfully in his journal.

In the towns and cities the Protestant revival replaced the camp meeting and was different only in that the minister and the congregation displayed more decorum and sophistication. Yet, in spite of the unceasing battle against intemperance, gambling, and non-attendance at church services, a clear-cut victory over the devil never quite emerged.

Houston and Matagorda had theaters long before either had a church, and the frontier town of Austin did not support a regular church until 1841, three years after its first permanent settlement. Galveston boasted four church buildings in 1845, more than any other Texas city. At San Antonio and the two or three centers of Mexican population several impressive missions constructed of stone and featuring stained-glass windows, spires, and bell towers dominated the landscape. Many of these old Spanish missions have remained in continuous use for the past two centuries and give a distinctive flavor to Southwestern architecture.

Early Texans showed only slightly more concern with religion than with education. Some of the town churches conducted regular Sunday schools—about the closest that most children came to formal education. The Sunday school, however, frequently proved the first step in a community's effort to establish a public school, and the transition from preacher to teacher, or a combination of the two positions, proved a natural development.

---

[3] Ibid., pp. 294–5.

VII · *Life and Culture in the Texas Republic*

Except for some poverty-stricken schools in the old Spanish towns, public education was almost nonexistent before the Texas Revolution. Such institutions as were in operation were little better than none at all, a fact that Texas did not overlook in its list of charges against Mexico. Two years after the founding of the Republic, President Lamar initiated a public-school program. Each county was granted four leagues of land for the creation of common schools and academies, but the counties responded slowly.[4]

The town fathers of Houston opened a public school in 1839 under the direction of the local Protestant Episcopal minister. It eventually attracted a few qualified "professors," but the absence of regular financial support during the next decade made its existence tenuous. While other towns showed little interest in following Houston's pioneering example, a few supported private academies that offered reading, writing, orthography, arithmetic, grammar, and geography. Tuition fees were two or three dollars a month. An advanced curriculum featuring Latin, Greek, philosophy, and "higher matter" was sometimes available for the ambitious.

Inadequate as these academies were, Texas newspapers of the period praised them generously and frequently assured the public that children below the age of twelve would not suffer corporal punishment or be exposed to "vulgar or profane language." One academy posted a warning that "there shall be no intercourse between male and female students except at the pleasure of the faculty."

Children in the rural areas and inland villages had little opportunity for formal schooling unless their families could afford private tutors. Textbooks, other than the Bible and a *Blue Back Speller*, or *McGuffey's Reader* brought from the States, were scarce. Where schools and private tutoring existed, lessons in spelling, arithmetic, and writing were of necessity conducted as memory exercises. Terms rarely extended beyond two or three

---

[4] The present county-school system in Texas was begun in 1854.

months each year, depending on the weather, the condition of the crops, Indians, and how long the itinerant teacher remained in the neighborhood. Sometimes the terms were staggered so that girls and boys could attend separately.

Planters and merchants often sent their daughters to "female seminaries" to be transformed into "ladies." For two or three dollars per month a girl could be exposed to philosophy, chemistry, botany, music (piano, guitar, and voice), drawing, needlework, and even French and Italian. The daughters of the prosperous and proud attended academies or seminaries in the States for a year or two, but by 1845 there were at least a dozen girls' schools in Texas.

Although there was much talk about "higher education" after Congress set aside fifty leagues of land for "two colleges or universities," no such public-supported institutions materialized until decades later. Some towns in the 1840's boasted of universities that never existed except in the fertile imagination of local promoters. Three or four academies dignified their names by the word "college" or "university," but their faculties and curricula fell far short of such liberal classification.

Perhaps Rutersville College, a Methodist school opened early in 1840, made the closest approach to an institution of higher learning, judging from the impressive list of courses and degrees offered. But one visitor in 1841 stated that it was no more than an American elementary school and that the catalogue of courses was "more ornamental than solid." During its sixteen years of existence, the student body averaged a hundred students a year—about the same as the present population of the town of Rutersville itself.

Other so-called colleges or universities supported by various religious denominations opened their doors during the 1840's: Galveston University, the University of San Augustine, the San Augustine Wesleyan Male and Female College, Marshall College, Nacogdoches University, and Baylor University. All these institutions made extravagant academic claims that could not be fulfilled, and of the group only Baylor University, later moved from

VII · Life and Culture in the Texas Republic

Independence to Waco, survived. The failure of the Republic to establish a public-school system worthy of the name, create a state college, or support the private institutions already in existence reflects the people's poverty and their indifference to learning. In the latter respect Texas progressed less rapidly than any other American frontier community of the nineteenth century.

Even now its expenditures on public education are not commensurate with its population and wealth. Texas leads the nation in oil and gas production, but, the 1954–5 issue of *The Book of States* ranked it in the lowest quarter in most important social categories. In education, for example, Texas stood thirty-second in expenditure per pupil and twenty-sixth in teacher salaries. This despite the fact that the state received more federal grants in aid than any other except California and New York.[5]

No COMMODITY remained scarcer during the decade of the Republic's existence than money. The few people who possessed cash could buy valuable property at phenomenally low prices. In 1843, because of diplomatic uncertainties, unusually poor crops, and the near-bankruptcy of the government, an 800-acre farm sold for one Negro slave and a $200 long-term note. The price included good outhouses, enclosed stables, 40 head of stock, 600 bushels of corn, several cartloads of potatoes, 200 pigs, and titles to a league of unsurveyed land and 500 acres of surveyed land.

As most of the people in Texas depended on farming, barter was substituted for money. While professional men no doubt found the system awkward, they had no alternative but to accept livestock, corn, wheat, oats, cotton, poultry, or vegetables in lieu of fees. Few were encumbered by formal study, but this in no way deterred them from charging all that the market would bear. "Had

---
[5] *The Texas Observer* (Austin, Texas), April 25, 1956.

their bills been promptly paid," an observer wrote, "they would all soon be rich."

Many professional people combined their work with politics or on the side taught school, preached, edited newspapers, and operated taverns and bars. Both Sam Houston and Mirabeau B. Lamar engaged in the overcrowded profession of law before getting into Texas politics. Lawyer Thomas J. Rusk in 1845 complained of the poverty of the people and the surplus of lawyers. In San Antonio more than fifteen lawyers tried to live on barely enough business to support one third that number.

Unquestionably the ease with which one could be admitted to the bar or licensed to practice medicine in the Republic contributed to the surplus of professional people. Almost any young man with the ability to read, write, and speak coherently could pass the bar examination with a minimum of preparation. And there was no law to prevent anyone from putting the letters M.D. after his name, acquiring a small stock of quinine, calomel, ipecacuhana, tartar emetic, rhubarb, and Dover's powder, and opening his own "clinic." A few of the physicians, of course, had attended medical lectures in the States before moving to Texas, and some were competent surgeons. Anson Jones, the fourth president of the Republic, was a legitimate physician, and so was Ashbel Smith, the Texas minister to England. But the great majority were even then considered to be quacks.

Because of the remoteness of certain areas, doctors often treated patients by correspondence. Minor ailments, however, were treated with home remedies such as poultices made from bark roots, tobacco juice, gunpowder, salt, or lard. The ague, now known to have been malaria, was in the 1830's and 1840's the most common disease, and many remedies were prescribed for it. Everyone believed that exposure to the sun caused this illness. The best treatment included a starvation diet, bleeding, and the consumption of a vile assortment of calomel, pills, tonics, and other patent medicines. An attending physician could not have done any better.

In 1838 Dr. Theodore Leger of Brazoria wrote an essay on the

VII · *Life and Culture in the Texas Republic*

treatment of ague, which concluded with the following: "How often do we not see our self-styled Doctors hurry to pour down their incendiary drugs, to administer purgatives, vomatives, bleeding and cupping, and bring into play all the resources of their pharmaceutic arsenal? Calomel and Blue-pills form their heavy artillery; then advance in second rank, Jalap and Rhubarb; Epsom-salts and Castor Oil bring up the rear."

LIKE EVERYTHING ELSE on a new frontier, Texas culture was crude and simple. Music was the most universal expression of the aesthetic impulse. Brought from Kentucky, Tennessee, and the Old South, it was played mostly at dances and "meetings." It was a rare Texan who could not perform on the fiddle, guitar, harmonica, flute, jew's-harp, or at least a comb and paper. The musician's repertoire might not range far, but it made up in volume of sound for what it lacked in quality of tone. William R. Hogan, the Texas social historian, unqualifyingly characterized the Republic as "a singing country," an observation that is well supported by travelers of the period. Wherever a group of people gathered, in homes, taverns, churches, theaters, or around a campfire, singing invariably resulted.

The interest in music is further reflected in the emphasis placed on it by the schools, particularly the female academies. Both Rutersville and Wesleyan colleges offered instruction in piano, while all the others at least taught voice. Many families hauled pianos or organs with them when they migrated to their new homes on the frontier; and when visitors came for dinner, the performance by one or more daughters of the host was a common ritual. German immigrants were especially adept at singing and playing classical and folk music. And music remained very much a part of the lives of the Mexican inhabitants, judging from visitors' inevitable references to concerts and fandangos in the plazas of the old Spanish towns.

Concerts by professional musicians were not uncommon in Galveston, Houston, and Matagorda. Local amateur companies also presented public programs to large and appreciative audiences—even though the artists rarely stayed on key and "the collection of kettles" that passed for a piano was seldom in tune. But some, at least, took their culture seriously. In announcing a forthcoming concert, the editor of the *Civilian and Galveston Gazette* in 1842 concluded with this blunt remark: "We need not remind our readers of what Shakespeare said of the individual who was so unfortunate as to have no music in his soul. They will all recollect that that close observer of human character pronounced such fit only for the vilest uses."

Occasionally a troupe of professional actors and actresses would arrive to put on plays, with local talent in the minor roles. Almost every town of 500 or more people supported a "thespian society" that produced such standard dramas of the day as *The Two Thompsons* and *When Shall I Dine*. Between acts the audience engaged in group singing or listened to an original song by a member of the audience who had been called to the stage by popular demand. Poems or brief patriotic speeches might also be recited while the curtain was drawn and the scenery rearranged.

The Texas frontier gave birth to a host of poets, most of whom were of doubtful literary merit. The Alamo, Sam Houston, David Crockett, and Stephen F. Austin were favorite subjects, and there were many attempts at humor with such titles as "Tobacco in Church" and "To an Aching Tooth." Much verse written by Texans was of a grandiloquent nature, warlike and anti-Mexican, but most of it did not rise to a very high intellectual level.

But, for all its uncouth and primitive society, its frustrations, poverty, and lack of services and conveniences, pioneer Texas retained an optimistic faith in its future. Professor Hogan maintains that raw courage, humor, and kindness are silhouetted against the drabness of frontier life and that bitter experiences worked a curious alchemy upon the people. "The Republic took the sons and

VII · *Life and Culture in the Texas Republic*

daughters of Tennessee, the Carolinas, Georgia, Mississippi, New York, France and Germany," he wrote, "and set its own ineffaceable stamp on their souls. The same process is still working today."[6]

This process has not changed Texans into a separate race of Americans, as some like to claim, but somehow it has made them different. The immense urge to do things, the braggadocio of many of its citizens, and the furious local patriotism of all its people are frontier characteristics more apparent in mid-twentieth-century Texas than in any other part of the nation.

---

[6] William R. Hogan: *The Texas Republic: A Social and Economic History* (Norman: University of Oklahoma Press; 1946), p. 298.

VIII

THE MEXICAN CESSION

SAMUEL FLAGG BEMIS wrote that the acquisition of Texas was "orderly, proper, [and] desired by the people of both nations." Mexico could not deny that it was "desired," but she could question whether it was "orderly" and she could never accept the *ex post facto* argument that it was "proper."

Bemis's views probably are shared by a majority of Americans today. A generation or so ago, however, there was wide support among historians for the belief that greedy slaveholders seeking more territory for their peculiar institution had goaded the United States into an imperialistic war. This, incidentally, was the

VIII · *The Mexican Cession*

viewpoint held by Mexico in the 1840's, thanks chiefly to John C. Calhoun's ill-timed remark that the annexation of Texas was essential to the preservation of slavery.

"Those who held this view," writes Ray Billington, "ignored both the psychology of the American people and the attitude of their government." Indeed, in the 1840's few Americans outside of New England disputed the idea that "expansion was a divinely ordered means of extending enlightenment to despot-ridden masses in nearby countries." Such an attitude made the annexation of Texas and the subsequent acquisition of the Spanish Southwest inevitable.

Mexico had reason to believe that the acquisition of Texas was intended by the United States as the first giant step in its march to the Pacific Coast. She could point to the frequent attempts to purchase the province soon after she gained her independence from Spain in 1821. Anglo-Americans who had infiltrated New Mexico and California were provoking the same sort of trouble that had occurred in Texas. And Commodore Thomas A. C. Jones's abortive seizure of the port of Monterey, California, in October 1842 furnished overwhelming proof of the United States government's intentions.

Regardless of how often the administration proclaimed its peaceful intentions during this period, the Mexican people were not convinced. Mexico had never recognized the independence of Texas, and her leaders were determined to fight rather than admit its final loss. When Santa Anna sent a trumpeting warning to the United States during the election campaign of 1844, the Mexican people applauded. To most political leaders in Washington the warning that annexation meant immediate war seemed so much Latin bombast. But subsequent events proved that the Mexicans were determined not to be "raped" without resisting. When Congress moved toward the passage of an act that provided for the annexation of Texas, the Mexican minister in Washington called for his passport and made immediate preparations to return home.

The war that soon followed lasted two years before Mexico capitulated and the United States fell heir to more than half of her

THE SOUTHWEST: *Old and New*

present territory. Fighting ranged over a vast land front—2,000 miles wide and more than 1,500 miles in length. It consisted of four principal movements: General Zachary Taylor's push into northern Mexico from the lower Rio Grande, General John E. Wool's advance from San Antonio toward Parras, General Stephen W. Kearny's march to California by way of New Mexico and Arizona, and, later, General Winfield Scott's expedition to Vera Cruz and subsequent invasion of Mexico City. Much of the fighting took place outside the four Southwestern states with which we are particularly concerned. However, several campaigns involved the soil as well as many native sons of Texas and New Mexico. Perhaps these campaigns were not decisive ones, but they did give the United States possession of territory that it was able to hold on to after the fighting in Mexico ended.

A few weeks after his inauguration as our eleventh president, James K. Polk dispatched federal troops to Texas to protect that republic from possible invasion. Although war with Mexico appeared certain, the Latins did not attack as they had promised. As General Zachary Taylor settled near the mouth of the Nueces River in Texas, a Mexican army assembled on the Rio Grande more than 150 miles southward. A level plain of alluvial soil covered with mesquite, cactus, and dense chaparral separated the two forces. (Most of this vast domain, then known as the Wild Horse Desert, eventually became the property of Captain Richard King. In 1845, however, the future owner of the fabulous Texas ranch was still gaining experience in steamboating on the Alabama River; he did not come to Texas until the next year.)

With the two armies in position to move against each other, President Polk resorted to diplomacy in the hope that he could arrange a settlement without war. There can be no question that he coveted more than Texas. Like Andrew Jackson, he realized the enormous potential of California and the advantages that the fine harbor of San Francisco Bay would offer American commerce. If Mexico could be persuaded to sell this Pacific Coast province, Polk stood ready to pay a handsome price for it as well as for the remainder of the Spanish Southwest. Accordingly, the President dis-

VIII · *The Mexican Cession*

patched a confidential agent, William S. Parrot, on the same ship that took the Mexican minister home. Parrot was to ascertain if the Mexican government would receive an American minister empowered to settle all outstanding issues between the two countries.

These issues included some matters of ancient origin, new ones created by the occupation of Texas by Taylor's troops, and others in respect to the United States claim to all of the land north and east of the Rio Grande. This claim was based upon the Treaty of Velasco, which the captured Santa Anna and the representatives of Texas had signed soon after the Battle of San Jacinto. The Mexican Senate had naturally rejected the treaty, which Santa Anna had signed only because it was a condition of his release. Subsequently Mexico had produced ample evidence that the Nueces–Rio Grande strip had never belonged to the Texas province, and was considered a part of the state of Tamaulipas. Polk insisted that Texas's claims to the disputed area were legitimate; but at the same time he was willing to arbitrate.

The President was on stronger grounds in emphasizing the older issues, for they involved claims against Mexico which dated back for two decades or more. These were mostly clear-cut cases of the seizure of American property without compensation, and Mexico, as early as 1839, had recognized their legitimacy; her efforts to make retribution had quickly faltered, however. Polk intended now to revive the claims and use them as a means of reaching a settlement with Mexico. When his special agent reported that the Mexican government, under the precarious leadership of General José J. Herrera, had agreed to receive an envoy, the President immediately dispatched a minister plenipotentiary, John Slidell of Louisiana.

Slidell's instructions certainly indicated Polk's willingness to give Mexico ample opportunity to settle her accounts short of war and without relinquishing any territory south of the Rio Grande. In return for recognition of this river as the international boundary between the two countries, the United States would forgo its claims of slightly more than two million dollars. With this point settled, Slidell was to negotiate for the purchase of California and the intervening region. The price "would be of no object"; the President believed that fifteen to twenty million dollars was fair, but he was prepared to pay as much as forty million if necessary. In case Mexico refused to relinquish California, Slidell was to try to purchase the drainage basin of the Río del Norte—present-day New Mexico—for five million dollars.

So far Polk's intentions seem honorable and proper, but he misjudged the temper of the Mexican people. In the end, the government refused to deal with Slidell on the ground that it had agreed to receive a "commissioner" and not a regular minister plenipotentiary. Slidell waited anxiously in Mexico for several weeks before returning to the United States. In Washington he reported that Mexico was determined to fight over the annexation of Texas, and that troops were being massed near the Mexican frontier.

Polk does not seem to have been greatly distressed by the failure of Slidell's mission. If the Latins wanted war, then their wishes would not be denied. Perhaps the President already realized that a peaceful settlement of the Rio Grande boundary would delay the ultimate annexation of the Southwest.

Meanwhile, General Taylor and his force of approximately 3,000 men remained camped on the banks of the Nueces River near the Mexican hamlet of Corpus Christi. Bernard De Voto has described the general as a leader who was "totally ignorant of the art of War." He could have added that Taylor was equally deficient in the science of sanitation, judging from the hundreds of men who died in camp of dysentery and the hundreds more who remained on the sick rolls throughout the period of encampment.

Until it became obvious that the war was to be carried to the Mexicans, little effort was made to prepare the troops for action other than to acquire a few wagons and to break mules and wild mustangs to harness.

Fortunately, a large herd of wild horses roamed the mesquite prairies in the vicinity of Corpus Christi and good mounts could be purchased from the Mexican mustangers for as little as six or eight dollars each. The army, therefore, had plenty of livestock to

VIII · *The Mexican Cession*

pull its supply wagons and serve its officers and men. After the soldiers mastered the technique of "mule-skinning," most of them idled away their time in gambling, drinking, and fraternizing with the women of the village and the inevitable horde of camp followers.

Orders to shift the encampment to the north bank of the Rio Grande reached Taylor on March 8, 1846. President Polk had decided, after Slidell's mission failed, that a little pressure should be put on the Mexicans. Already a large force under the command of General Mariano Arista was stationed at Matamoros on the south bank of the river, considerably beyond shooting range of the troops at Corpus Christi. Taylor's army traversed the strip of semi-desert plains separating the two armies in a little more than a week. Some 2,500 men marched overland, while another 500 not yet recovered from dysentery were transferred by boat to Point Isabel, near the mouth of the Rio Grande. Most of the heavy siege guns and other bulky equipment and supplies were also shipped by water.

Taylor divided his main force into four columns, each separated from the others by a day's march. Except for the mesquite, cactus, and dust, there was nothing to impede his advance. Not a single living inhabitant was encountered other than the comical-looking chaparral cocks, armadillos, deer, antelopes, and wild horses. Indeed, the army was rarely out of sight of mustangs during the entire journey. "As far as the eye could reach to our right, the herd extended," wrote Lieutenant U. S. Grant. "To the left it extended equally. There is no estimating the number of animals in it. I have no idea that they could have been corralled in the State of Rhode Island, or Delaware at one time. If they had been, they would have been so thick that the pasturage would have given out the first day."

When the Americans arrived on the north bank of the Rio Grande, they constructed a small fort not more than 400 yards from the river and within sight of General Arista's army encamped at Matamoros. If the Mexicans' previous threats of war meant anything at all, they now had the opportunity to carry them out.

The Southwest: *Old and New*

Their chance came on April 24, 1846. A large scouting party ambushed a company of United States dragoons reconnoitering the area. Sixteen Americans were killed or wounded. Captain S. B. Thornton, their commander, managed to escape by a tremendous leap of his horse over a high hedge amid a shower of Mexican bullets, but the remainder of his company fell into the hands of the enemy. Blood had been shed at last. The Mexicans claimed that Taylor's troops had trespassed, but Polk later made a tremendous point out of the charge that American soil and lives had been violated.

Meanwhile, "Old Rough and Ready" Taylor found himself in a precarious spot; not only was he outnumbered, but most of his heavy artillery was on board the supply ships lying off Point Isabel. Major Jacob Brown and a hundred men were left in charge of the new fort [1] while Taylor and the main force rushed across the salt-grass flats toward the coast to secure the supplies. General Arista was quick to take advantage of the situation. On May 3, 1846, he moved across the river to attack the fort. Brown was among those killed during the early hours of fighting, but, in spite of continuous bombardment, the beleaguered Americans refused to surrender.

The supply ships were not completely unloaded until May 7. By then Taylor and his men were extremely concerned about their comrades, for the ominous sounds of firing in the distance had rarely ceased during their absence from the fort. Fortunately, the twenty-five miles between Point Isabel and the Rio Grande was level country and the possibilities of an ambush by the Mexicans were remote. Even so, the enemy determined to intercept the Americans. A force of more than 5,700 men took a position at a spot called Palo Alto, nine miles northeast of the river and near the road that Taylor would travel. It was not long before the two armies faced each other across an 800-yard plain of marsh land and stiff salt grass as high as a man's shoulders.

---

[1] This log stockade surrounded by dirt embankments was first named Fort Taylor. A short time later it was renamed Fort Brown and constituted the beginnings of what is now Brownsville, Texas.

VIII · *The Mexican Cession*

At half past two o'clock on the afternoon of May 8, 1846, a Mexican band started to play, and a few minutes later an artillery barrage was begun. The solid shots from the enemy cannon fell far short of the mark, ricocheting off the ground and tearing through the grass like bowling balls. Taylor's lines, spread out over approximately half a mile, opened here and there to allow the projectiles to pass without harm. The right flank of Arista's army then began an advance on the Americans' left like a giant swinging gate, but the defending infantry held fast while the ammunition wagons drawn by oxen were wheeled into place and several eighteen-pound cannon were brought into position.

Soon a withering shower of grape and canister greeted the Mexicans. Sometimes a single discharge mowed down a whole platoon of mounted men, but the gaps were quickly closed. In spite of the shouts of *"viva"* and the bravery and dash displayed by the onrushing cavalry and infantry, the American small arms outshot Mexican muskets. Arista lost more than 600 killed and wounded, compared to a mere handful of Americans. Among the young West Point officers who took part in the first engagement were Lieutenants Ulysses S. Grant, James Longstreet, and George Gordon Meade.

As the Mexicans retreated through the thick grass and chaparral to the low eminence behind their right flank, Taylor's men bivouacked where they stood. Some gave attention to their fallen comrades by the fitful glare of the burning grass. Others prepared a hasty meal before they lay down to rest, certain that a battle was over but that the war was still to be fought. Soon the prairie fire burned out, the smoke drifted away, and a full moon appeared.

When the morning mist lifted on May 9, the Americans saw that the Mexicans were in full retreat. Taylor hesitated and then decided to pursue. The delay gave Arista time to occupy a heavily wooded ravine surrounded by thick chaparral, a better position by far than the one of the previous day. The place, known as Resaca de la Guerrero, was an ancient channel of the river several hundred feet wide and three or four feet deep at the banks. As the Americans advanced the five or six miles that separated their camp from the *resaca*, they discovered that the Mexicans were well entrenched behind the natural embankment, their artillery turned upon the road that led to the American fort. Taylor halted and established temporary headquarters at Resaca de la Palma, on the edge of the woods that shielded the enemy. The skirmish that followed took its name from this place rather than the site of the actual battle.[2]

The Americans did not come in contact with Arista's muskets and cannon until nearly three o'clock in the afternoon, at which time both armies were so well concealed by the dense foliage that the action was almost a game of hide-and-seek. Frequently the officers of both sides were unable to see their own men, let alone the enemy. At times the confusion was so great that it was difficult to tell who was fighting whom, but eventually the "Gringos" carried the field and soon the better-uniformed Mexicans were in full retreat toward the Rio Grande. The Mexicans had given a good account of themselves, but their numbers were too few. Also, most of them had not eaten or slept for twenty-four hours and had lost confidence in their commanding officers because of cowardly behavior on the previous day. But even if the leaders had been competent, brave, and imaginative, the murderous fire from the American artillery would have overwhelmed them.

The retreat degenerated into a rout. Before the end of the day all Mexican troops except the dead and injured crossed the Rio Grande at Matamoras. The slow and unskilled Taylor allowed them to escape without showing much concern. This did not endear him to his subordinates—one lieutenant observed that he was "utterly, absurdly incompetent to wield a large army." But the general public in the States knew only that Taylor had won two complete victories against heavy odds.

Even before the news of Palo Alto and Resaca de la Palma reached Washington, Polk, informed of the skirmish between American troops and Mexican cavalry on April 24, had reported to Congress that "hostilities have commenced." Congress responded

---

[2] Resaca de la Palma extends to within a few feet of the terminus of present United States Highway 77 on the northwestern edge of Brownsville.

VIII · *The Mexican Cession*

on May 13 with a declaration that a state of war existed by the "act of the Republic of Mexico."

WITHIN LESS than one month after Palo Alto Taylor's army increased to more than 8,000 men, many of them short-term volunteers from the East who barely arrived in camp before their period of enlistment expired. Before the army left the area, no less than 20,000 soldiers and the inevitable host of civilian followers were camped on the Rio Grande in the vicinity of Point Isabel and Brownsville.

The volunteers soon became disillusioned. Dysentery, mosquitoes, maggots, land crabs, snakes, brackish water, and the torrid summer sun made life miserable. Most of the troops, including the regulars, had no protection from the heat, dust, and rain except hastily built brush arbors or woolen blankets thrown over bushes. An epidemic of measles made day-by-day existence even more intolerable. Those who came for glory and adventure and to "revel in the halls of Montezuma," as the recruiting posters had invited them to do, were sadly disappointed. Military orders were openly flouted, and volunteers resisted attempts to discipline or train them. Some discharged their rifles at will, and it was dangerous to venture through the camp.

"Old Rough and Ready" Taylor eventually crossed the Rio Grande and occupied previously abandoned Matamoros. From here he moved sluggishly by water to Camargo, some 400 miles from the Gulf. Near the end of August his 15,000 troops camped along the San Juan River, a Mexican tributary of the Rio Grande. The road to Monterrey extended 125 miles to the southwest across a hot desert of sand, sagebrush, and sotol. By the fourth week of September, American troops had reached the outskirts of the city, preceded by a band of Texas Rangers serving as scouts.

Ben McCulloch and Jack Hays led the outlandish-looking

Texans, whose unshaved faces and buckskin garb marked them as unique. The rangers carried heavy rifles and Colt five-shooters, with which they later mowed down Santa Anna's lancers at every charge. The uncouth manners and individualistic dress of the rugged frontiersmen alarmed the civilians, and their blood-curdling yells, later to become famous as the rebel yell of Confederate troops, chilled the Mexican troops even more. Some of the rangers who spearheaded Taylor's encirclement of Monterrey were on familiar ground. Among them was William Alexander ("Big Foot") Wallace, a member of the ill-fated Mier expedition of 1841, which had been captured and marched in chains to Perote prison in southern Mexico. Wallace now had the satisfaction of seeing the city "pretty well battered by our artillery."

After three days of desperate fighting, September 21–3, 1846, the Americans were in full control of Monterrey. Now they paused for two months before advancing southwest to Saltillo, where they were joined by a small force under General John E. Wool, who had moved from San Antonio by way of Monclova and Parras. Another column under the command of Colonel A. W. Doniphan meanwhile moved south from Santa Fe to Chihuahua City and then eastward through the desert of northern Mexico. This undisciplined army of volunteers, who styled themselves the "ringtailed roarers" (but whom the New Mexicans more appropriately named "Los Goddammies), arrived before the battle of Buena Vista. Doniphan's men performed outstanding service, capturing both El Paso and Chihuahua against odds of three to one.

WOOL'S MARCH from San Antonio to Parras covered approximately 900 miles, less than half the distance traversed by Doniphan. Although his men never fired a shot or spilled a drop of Mexican blood during their journey, they had to overcome hardships all the way. Indeed, from the time they assembled in San An-

VIII · *The Mexican Cession*

tonio for an expedition against Chihuahua City, the men suffered from epidemics of mumps, measles, yellow fever, and dysentery. Also they managed to excel in debauchery and drunkenness.

Aside from the few companies of regulars, Wool's followers were largely composed of the floating population of Mississippi River towns and volunteers from Texas. In addition, a company of Texas Rangers were enlisted as scouts. By the time they all arrived at Monclova this heterogeneous mob was forged into a "keen, tough, and highly tempered blade" that would soon prove its value. Samuel E. Chamberlain, a young volunteer from Boston, described the ranger company. "A more reckless, devil-may-care looking set it would be impossible to find this side of the Infernal Region," he wrote in his memoirs. "Some wore buckskin shirts, black with grease and blood; some wore red shirts, their trousers thrust into high boots; all were armed with Revolvers and huge Bowie Knives. Take them altogether, with their uncouth costumes, bearded faces, lean and brawny forms, fierce wild eyes, and swaggering manners, they were fit representatives of the outlaws who made up the population of the Lone Star State."

By the time the three armies under Doniphan, Wool, and Taylor had marched across the country, frightening civilians, defeating various armies, and occupying towns in northern Mexico, Taylor had received orders that deprived him of most of his best soldiers. Meanwhile, the term of enlistment for Doniphan's forces had expired, and the commander and his men returned to the United States to be received as heroes in every town, hamlet, and city through which they passed.

Responsibility for the transfer of the seasoned infantry and cavalry under Taylor's command belonged to the President himself. Some of Polk's enemies maintained that he had deliberately tried to eliminate a possible political rival from the next presidential campaign. Others shared the President's opinion that Taylor had erred in not insisting on the unconditional surrender of the Mexican army. But the public as a whole now considered "Old Rough and Ready" not only a hero but also a martyr.

Polk's decision to reduce Taylor's command and shift the offensive from the north to the south proved militarily sound, but if his purpose was to end Taylor's prominence, he could not have acted more unwisely. As soon as Santa Anna learned of the reduction of the American forces, he assembled an army of some 20,000 troops and marched rapidly northward. Taylor, who now had less than 6,000 men, mostly unseasoned, met the advance at Buena Vista, February 22, 1847. A fierce battle raged for two days and at times the Americans appeared hopelessly beaten, but somehow their lines held until the Mexicans wavered.

Captain Braxton Bragg and Colonel Jefferson Davis distinguished themselves in the fighting at Buena Vista, and the General compensated for military ineptness by his personal display of courage and the cool manner in which he sat on his horse throughout the fury of the contest. His only direct order was to Bragg: "Give 'em a little more grape, Captain." This, the bloodiest victory of the war, assured the General's future residence on Pennsylvania Avenue, Washington, D.C. Shortly after Buena Vista he returned to the United States to campaign for the presidency.

The Mexicans lost 2,000 men at Buena Visita, while less than half that number of Americans were killed. Once again a defeated army managed to escape, thanks to Taylor's blundering, but all of northeastern Mexico remained in undisputed control of the "Gringos."

By the time Santa Anna arrived in Mexico City with his battered army, General Winfield Scott had landed at Vera Cruz and was marching toward the capital. The subsequent battles of Cerro Gordo, Contreras, Churubusco, Molino del Rey and Chapultepec were fought far from the Southwestern borders, but the rambunctious Texans were present in large numbers and naturally did not go without notice—from either their fellow Americans or the Mexican soldiers and civilians. Many of the Texas troops and rangers saw service with Taylor in the north. Their memories of the Texas revolution and the events of the subsequent decade had transformed them into professional Mexican-haters. They looked on the war, therefore, as an opportunity for personal vengeance.

Before the battles in the south ended the Mexican conflict,

VIII · *The Mexican Cession*

there was activity on other fronts which profoundly affected the history of the Southwest: the "conquest" of New Mexico, Arizona, and California. Here the fighting was less bloody, but the results were just as far-reaching. Fortunately, Taylor's failure to capture the Mexican army after Palo Alto and Resaca de la Palma had given Polk time to dispatch troops into this vast section of the continent before the Mexican government collapsed. Consequently, the military occupation of the area by the United States forced the Latin republic to recognize a *fait accompli* at the Treaty of Guadalupe Hidalgo.[3]

ON THE DAY that war was declared against Mexico, May 11, 1846, Polk remarked to his cabinet that "we shall acquire California and New Mexico, and other further territory, as an indemnity for this war, if we can." To secure this territory it was necessary to send an army "large enough to conquer but small enough not to alarm the conquered." Colonel Stephen W. Kearny was assigned the task of organizing the so-called "Army of the West," which was to march from Fort Leavenworth, Kansas, to Santa Fe and thence to California. Here it would join a sea-borne force in the conquest of the Pacific Coast territory.

Kearny proved an able organizer. To his 300 regular dragoons, he added 856 men of the First Missouri Mounted Volunteers, plus an assortment of backwoods recruits to man the sixteen cannon that constituted his light artillery. Certainly this was one of the most heterogeneous forces in the military history of the frontier, including even the one assembled by General Wool at San Antonio.

---

[3] At the conclusion of hostilities, the United States occupied northern Mexico and the region of Mexico City. It could just as easily have annexed the whole of Mexico, but that had not been Polk's original objective, and criticism of the war by his political opponents, plus the force of world opinion, prevented him from taking more Mexican territory than he did.

The Southwest: *Old and New*

No sooner was the army recruited than it was on its way to New Mexico, following the route of the Old Santa Fe Trail via Bent's Fort in southeastern Colorado. Behind this conglomerate mob of regulars, volunteers, traders, and camp followers came an even more remarkable frontier gathering of some 550 Mormon volunteers led by Colonel Sterling Price. The latter group was more shepherded than commanded, having been gathered from the ranks of Brigham Young's colonists bound for present Utah. They did no fighting, but they did perform the remarkable feat of crossing almost 2,000 miles of desert, mountains, and plains without adequate food or water. At Santa Fe the Mormons were placed under the command of Colonel Philip St. George Cooke and continued toward California along a route that today is roughly paralleled by the Southern Pacific line from El Paso to San Diego. Their trail across New Mexico and Arizona is now marked by obelisk-like monuments of field stone, solid reminders of the first large-scale migration of American settlers across the Southwest.

Kearny marched the 650 miles from Fort Leavenworth to Bent's Fort in less than two months. The "Army of the West" and the large caravan of Santa Fe traders that accompanied it from Missouri camped some nine miles below the old fort. The remainder of the journey was more difficult, but at least the discomfort of the stagnant waters of the plains was behind. The road that turned south toward Santa Fe afforded the New Mexicans ample opportunities for defensive action, for it wound through two or three narrow passes in the Southern Rockies. Kearny hoped that the natives could be persuaded not to resist, although by now his men had been toughened by the trail.

Fortunately for the Anglo-Americans, the New Mexicans had little interest in fighting. No doubt their acquaintance with the boisterous Santa Fe traders and wild mountain men had discouraged them. But, aside from this, a people long oppressed by disreputable Mexican officials could hardly be expected to lay down their lives in order that their descendants might continue to be robbed. All civil and military power was vested in Manuel Armijo, as cunning, cowardly, and immoral a mountain of flesh as ever

VIII · *The Mexican Cession*

swaggered around the Santa Fe plaza. Even before the Americans arrived, some of the New Mexican representatives in the national Congress had openly supported a move to separate from Mexico and join the United States. Thus, the situation was ready-made for a bloodless conquest.

When Armijo learned that Kearny was poised on the northern frontier ready for an *"entrada"* into his province, he made a desperate effort to collect an army. Some 4,000 poorly armed Indians and peons unenthusiastically responded to the call and prepared to defend the capital at Apache Canyon, a few miles east of Santa Fe. Meanwhile, at Bent's Fort, Kearny had already dispatched Colonel Philip St. George Cooke and twelve picked men to escort his personal "ambassador," James Magoffin, to the New Mexican capital. Magoffin, a jovial and bluff Kentucky Irishman and trader, had many friends among his former customers in Santa Fe. He knew the character of the natives and had often shared a bottle with the bulbous Governor.

The details of the subsequent meeting between the American trader and Armijo are still clouded in secrecy, but they can be imagined. Armijo halted the defense of Santa Fe, paused long enough to gather up his valuables, which included the public treasury but not his portly wife, and announced his "retirement" from the scene. Later, when Congress appropriated $25,000 to cover Magoffin's expenses, the administration was judiciously silent about particulars.

Soon after Armijo abandoned Apache Canyon his army disintegrated and scattered among the mountain valleys and pueblos from whence it had come. By now Kearny's "long-legged infantry" and jaded cavalry had ascended Raton Pass, and on August 15, 1846, they arrived at the new and unimportant village of Las Vegas. Here the General assured the local citizens that his men came as protectors, not as conquerors. The people were also told that they were now a part of the United States and that they would have a democratic form of government. There was neither rejoicing nor a show of despondency over the announcement.

On August 18, 1846, the "Army of the West" moved the

seventy miles from Las Vegas to Santa Fe. The city about which the soldiers had heard so much from the Missouri traders turned out to be a mud town of adobe hovels lying in a flat sandy valley near a stream. Too exhausted to care, the troops pitched camp on a nearby hill that was soon to become the site of Fort Marcy. The next day they sauntered into the plaza in semi-orderly fashion to listen to their commander address a large gathering in front of the Governor's Palace. Once again Kearny proclaimed that he and his men came in peace, that the New Mexicans were now a part of a powerful nation, and that a prosperous future awaited them. He then administered an oath of allegiance to those officials who wished to retain their former positions in the local government. At the conclusion of the ceremony the "Gringos" let loose with mighty yells before rushing forth to recoup their spirits at the grog shops, bawdy houses, and gambling establishments.

As long as the Americans paid good prices for merchandise, confined their amours to the pretty women of the streets, and did not approach the dark-eyed daughters of the wealthier families, prospects for a peaceful occupation were good. But the original dream of conquering the Pacific Coast empire for "glory, God, and country" was not diminished.

Before departing for California the American commander divided his army into three parts: one remained to occupy New Mexico and protect the civil government under Charles Bent, a former partner in the trading firm of Bent and St. Vrain; one was placed under command of Colonel A. W. Doniphan of the Missouri Volunteers and instructed to march southward to Chihuahua to join forces with General Wool from San Antonio; a third army composed of 300 dragoons was to follow Kearny westward.

Immediately after the two military forces left New Mexico, trouble developed between the New Mexicans and the occupation troops under Colonel Sterling Price. The belief that they had been cheated, the ease with which the province was conquered, and the actions of Armijo proved most humiliating to some of the prominent and influential citizens in the territory. Accordingly, Diego Archuleta and Tomas Ortiz conspired with the Pueblo In-

VIII · *The Mexican Cession*

dians, knowing that the townspeople were more interested in profits from trade than in evicting the foreigners. Price believed the Pueblos to be the last people in the Southwest from whom he could expect trouble; on the contrary, they were violently hostile to the Americans.

Taos was the best-known pueblo in New Mexico, partly because it was the largest and possessed several multi-storied structures and partly because it had been visited by so many American traders and mountain men. It contained an imposing church building, and missionaries exercised a major influence over the native residents; these co-operated with the conspirators. Soon plans were formulated and the local natives were inflamed to a frenzy, but the secret was betrayed by incompetence and procrastination. Colonel Price arrested some of the ringleaders, but Archuleta and Ortiz managed to escape to Mexico. On January 19, 1847, the Indians' inhibitions and capacities for violent action were loosened in one great orgy of destruction. A crowd formed in the town of Taos, three miles from the pueblo, and demanded the release of an Indian who had been arrested for thievery.

When the sheriff refused, he and the prefect were murdered by the angry mob. Now the cry of death for all Americans was raised, and a reign of terror quickly spread over the town. Charles Bent, appointed civil governor of the province by General Kearny, was besieged in his home. Despite his lifelong friendship with the Indians, he now appeared to them as a symbol of the hated foreigners. The mob broke into his home and killed him with arrows and bullets, but spared his family. The Governor of Taos Pueblo scalped Bent before he lost consciousness. Even this did not satisfy the half-crazed murderers. They cut off his head, stuck it on a pole, and paraded back to their village with the trophy.

All adult male Americans in Taos except two suffered torture and death before the holocaust ended. One was saved by the intercession of a friendly priest, while the other fled southward on a mule to inform the military commander at Fort Marcy. Before Colonel Price could rush a force of infantry, mountain men, and four cannon over the mountain trail from Santa Fe to Taos, the rebellion spread throughout the northern part of the province. Americans were slain in their homes, waylaid along the roads, and ambushed on the streets and scalped like the victims of the wild Comanches and Apaches on the plains.

The Indians' lust for blood cooled as the wrath of the American soldiers increased. By February 3, 1847, Colonel Price and Ceran St. Vrain, a long-time associate of the martyred Governor, reached Taos Pueblo with more than 350 men, some sixty of whom were civilian volunteers. The Mexican allies of the Indians deserted before the Americans arrived, but the Indians barricaded themselves in the principal building on the north side of the plaza and in the nearby eighteenth-century church. From the roofs they hurled insults at Price's men. After a few shots into the adobe walls of the church, the commander called his forces back and pitched camp near the pueblo.

By daylight on the following morning the Americans were ready to renew the attack. St. Vrain and his mountain men were assigned a position on the east side of the pueblo to prevent any escape to the nearby mountains. Price then hauled his cannon into position and opened fire on the church where most of the villagers had taken "sanctuary." Two hours of continuous firing left the edifice still standing although extremely battered. At eleven o'clock the cannons were silenced and a charge was ordered. As soldiers broke into the church, men, women, and children fled through shattered windows and gaping holes. Some ran toward the large building across the plaza, others toward the mountains. Within a few moments more than a hundred escapees were killed, and St. Vrain had the personal pleasure of running down the Indian who wore Bent's coat.

Some 150 defenders lay dead or severely wounded at the end of the fighting, a high price for the Indians' two weeks of "freedom." Eventually, every one of the leaders of the rebellion was found and tried. A public hanging in the Taos plaza on February 9, 1847, brought the grim episode to a close. The Indians returned to their pueblo to mourn their dead. In time the people of Taos accepted their inexorable fate of coexistence, but, although

VIII · *The Mexican Cession*

the white man had proved his military superiority, his culture would not penetrate the mud, dung, and straw walls of their homes for almost another century.

IN THE MEANTIME Kearny's dragoons proceeded toward California by way of southwestern New Mexico and southern Arizona, leaving Santa Fe on September 25, 1846. Somewhere along the Gila River they met a small American party led by Kit Carson, the famous mountain man and scout, who told Kearny that California was already in the possession of the American Navy and a small company of troops commanded by John Charles Frémont. Carson carried dispatches from both Frémont and Commodore R. F. Stockton which he intended to deliver to the President in Washington.

In view of subsequent developments, it is not difficult to believe that Kearny was disappointed to learn that the war on the Pacific Coast was over. But he did not turn back, for his orders from the War Department stipulated that he was to organize the government in California, just as he had done in New Mexico. After considerable resistance, he persuaded Carson to relinquish the honor of a personal audience with the President to one of Kearny's followers and to guide the General to California.

Kearny ordered most of his army to return to New Mexico. The remainder of the journey to the coast was made with only a hundred picked dragoons, a decision that almost proved fatal. When the skeleton force arrived in southern California it ran into some 200 ill-equipped Californians who had risen in rebellion against the Americans. Kearny defeated the revolutionists at San Pasquel before moving on to join Commodore Stockton at San Diego. The subsequent arrival of Frémont and 400 Californians, mountain men, and Indians enabled the American to mount a successful attack on Los Angeles. By mid-January 1847 southern California had been reconquered and the counterrevolution put down.

The Southwest: *Old and New*

Then began a squabble between Kearny and Frémont. When orders from Washington installed Kearny as governor of the new territory, the popular "Pathfinder of the West" was arrested for insubordination and summarily court-martialed.

WHILE THE dragoons pushed across the arid Southwest and entered California, Doniphan and his profane crew of frontiersmen prepared to move upon Chihuahua City, some 600 miles south of Santa Fe. Exactly how many men the part-time military leader and backwoods lawyer from Missouri had under his command is not known, but all authorities on the Mexican War agree that his nondescript army was the "cussingest" and most undisciplined collection of farmers that could be assembled. They established some sort of record for marching, as they covered almost 3,000 miles in little more than a year. Most of this long circular journey was through mountain passes, across deserts, and in heat and dust.

Leaving Price in command of the military forces at Santa Fe, Doniphan and "Los Goddammies" started for Chihuahua City before the end of 1846. The rendezvous with General Wool was never kept, and it eventually fell to the Missourians to take this important Mexican city alone. About midway on the Chihuahua Trail, as they approached El Paso, they encountered a considerable Mexican force. The so-called battle of El Brazito lasted for less than an hour, but these Mexicans showed more desire to fight than had the defenders of Santa Fe, and they outnumbered the Americans. But they tended to fire too high, their powder was mostly bad, and their small cannon was ineffective. The Americans merely waited until the defenders crept within range and then opened up, with devastating results.

At the end of the battle of El Brazito more than a hundred Mexicans had been slain and the remainder were in full and disorderly retreat. "Los Goddammies" seized the small two-pound can-

VIII · *The Mexican Cession*

non and the stores of wine and other delicacies. The occasion called for a celebration, for it was Christmas Day. Celebrate they did, and on the following morning many concluded that facing Mexican fire was a considerably less hazardous diversion.

The Mexican force retreated past El Paso to Chihuahua City, where its commander was arrested for cowardice. His warning to the authorities that the "Americanos do not fight as we do" went unheeded. The defenders of the city soon learned the truth of his statement. Meanwhile, Doniphan remained in El Paso for forty-two days awaiting the arrival of his heavy artillery from Santa Fe. The people living among the cluster of settlements that dotted the south bank of the Rio Grande were not unhappy to accept American rule, from which they hoped for order and prosperity. Like their neighbors to the north, many of the local residents had previously had cordial relations with American merchants. But the occupation soldiers did not prove to be good ambassadors, and their unlimited self-indulgence soon left its mark, both on the town and on themselves.

The arrival of six pieces of artillery from Santa Fe on February 1, 1847, brought out the entire population of El Paso. Another celebration was called for, and the two-pound cannon captured at El Brazito was hauled forth and made ready to fire a salute of welcome. The powder was poured in carelessly, and no wadding could be found to hold it in place. Finally an enthusiastic private peeled off his socks and rammed them down the barrel. Unfortunately, no one noticed that the cannon was pointed in the direction of the oncoming artillerymen. After the charge exploded and the smoke cleared, the cheers of the crowd turned to stunned silence when one of the new arrivals was seen rolling on the ground and giving out with loud cries of anguish.

It quickly became evident that no serious damage had been done, but the artilleryman continued to cry out as if he were dying. When asked why he persisted in such ridiculous behavior, he replied that he would rather be hit in the face with a cannon ball than receive the full force of a pair of socks that obviously had not been washed in eight months.

Many weeks passed before Doniphan's men had the opportunity for another laugh. They were soon on their way to Chihuahua City and some serious fighting. As already mentioned, they eventually turned eastward across northern Mexico and continued until they rendezvoused with Taylor's forces near Saltillo. It was at this time that their one-year enlistment expired, and they returned home before the battle of Buena Vista.

THE TREATY of Guadalupe Hidalgo ended the war in Mexico one year after the Pueblo uprising in New Mexico. All of the former Spanish and Mexican territory between the 42nd parallel and a line yet to be drawn from El Paso west to San Diego was quitclaimed to the United States. In return for undisputed possession of the Southwestern territory, the United States agreed to pay Mexico approximately fifteen million dollars.

The dispute that arose over the status of slavery in the newly acquired area was soon to be settled by the Great Compromise of 1850: California was admitted as a free state; New Mexico and Utah were to be created territories with the right to decide the status of slavery when they were reorganized as states; and Texas was to be financially compensated for the loss of her claim to New Mexico. Except for the Gadsden Purchase four years later, the southwestern boundaries of the United States were complete.

IX

THE IMPACT OF GOLD ON THE SOUTHWEST

ALTHOUGH the Spaniards and Mexicans wasted three centuries in a search for gold in the Southwest, the Anglo-Americans found it within a year after the conquest. By 1860 the quantity of precious metals removed from the mountains and streams of California alone compared favorably with the total production of the mines of Mexico and Peru. When mining activities along the Pacific Coast abated, the backwash of emigrants spilled into other areas. Soon every corner of the region beyond the Mississippi River, including heretofore unknown sections of the Southwest, was explored, exploited or settled.

The Southwest: *Old and New*

While gold and silver were not mined in the Southwest to the extent that they were elsewhere, the California rush was responsible for the settlement of large portions of this region a full generation or more earlier than might otherwise have been the case. And the mining boom resulted in the acquisition of another strip of territory from Mexico, southern Arizona. This caused an immediate increase in the permanent population of the Southwest and the opening up of the future state of Arizona. The excitement was generally known as "gold fever," and those who participated in the great drama were called "argonauts."

A small quantity of gold was mined in California, Arizona, and New Mexico long before James Wilson Marshall picked up some strange yellow flakes near Sutter's new sawmill on the American River in 1848. But this new discovery gave rise to a mania that seized the Pacific Coast and soon gripped the entire continent. People behaved as if their very lives depended on reaching the gold fields in the shortest possible time. By the end of 1848 the cry "On to California!" could be heard from New Orleans to St. Louis.

It would be difficult to find in world history a parallel to the events of 1849–50 when so many people traveled so far, so rapidly, and so hazardously. Some journeyed to California by sea, embarking from port cities along the Atlantic and Gulf coasts to sail around Cape Horn. Others took passage to Central America and crossed Nicaragua or Panama on foot or in primitive carts to wait for passage in one of the overcrowded boats of the Pacific Mail Steamship Company. But the great majority chose the cheaper and more dangerous overland journey, which could start almost anywhere but usually began at such cities as St. Louis, Memphis, New Orleans, Fort Smith, Dallas, San Antonio, and Houston.

The shortest and most popular overland route to California was the northern one that followed the Platte River through South Pass and continued along the Humboldt River to Sacramento and Stockton. By 1850, 30,000 argonauts passed over it, leaving approximately 4,000 graves as reminders of their suffering. And there were other trails to California, equally significant but far less

IX · *The Impact of Gold on the Southwest*

known, most of which passed through all or part of the Southwest.

News of the Indian attacks and epidemics of cholera associated with the overland route along the Platte River soon filtered to the East. This, together with the dangers of scurvy, the expense, and the length of time a sea voyage entailed, caused many would-be emigrants to consider a land route through the Great Southwest. Meanwhile, veterans of the Mexican War began to voice their opinions of the country, and thousands of prospective travelers learned of various roads from Texas through Mexico that could be traveled more safely than other routes. Even the respectable *New York Tribune,* which at first advised its readers to go by a water route, later suggested that various Southwestern trails were better. Other eastern newspapers soon advanced the same idea.

As attention shifted rapidly to the Southwest, the frontier states of Missouri, Arkansas, and Texas discovered that they were favorably situated. Missouri advocated the Santa Fe Trail as an alternative to the Platte River, although she stood to gain from either. Arkansas believed that a road from Fort Smith due west parallel with the Canadian River, or farther north along the Arkansas River, offered the best route to the travelers as far as Santa Fe. Texas energetically advertised the trail from San Antonio via Chihuahua City and the Gila River to southern California. As an alternative, some Texans suggested a direct route west from San Antonio to El Paso, thence through northern Mexico or southern New Mexico to the Gila River, and on west to the "promised land." Either road was open to winter travel, and the three essentials for western travel—water, wood, and grass—were in abundance all the way. All of these trails, as well as several others across the Southwest, were tried. None proved completely satisfactory, but each had its particular advantage.

The majority of the forty-niners proved to be a different breed from the hardy pioneers who had braved the hazards of the Oregon and Santa Fe trails in earlier years. Many of those who struck out in small parties with much useless equipment, inferior animals, and inadequate guides failed to reach California. The wiser emigrants followed experienced advice and remained at some point near the eastern edge of the plains until they could organize a large wagon company and employ a competent guide.

After officers were elected, regular duties were assigned to each man, and a set of rules and regulations was adopted, the caravan was ready to roll. Sometimes a company was fortunate enough to have a military escort; if not, it nevertheless proceeded in semi-military fashion and according to a predetermined routine.

The average party of argonauts traveled fourteen or fifteen miles each day before selecting a camp site near a stream and a cluster of trees. The captain usually rode ahead to locate the camp, and when the wagons joined him, he placed them close together in a huge circle. This arrangement served not only as a corral for the livestock but also as a stockade in the event of an Indian attack. Travelers along the Southwestern trails started at daybreak and stopped about noon in order to make repairs, graze the stock, and recuperate from dust and heat. Guards placed at outlying points kept the animals from straying and sounded the alarm when a band of Indians was sighted. Friendly tribes proved almost as bothersome as war parties, for they expected gifts from the travelers and the privilege of stealing everything in sight. Fortunately, the Southwestern Indians did not constitute a great danger during the early years of the California migration, a situation quite different from that farther north, where the Pawnee, Northern Cheyenne, and Sioux conducted periodic raids against the wagon trains.

As the end of each day on the trail approached, all cattle, mules, and horses were driven into the enclosure and hobbled. Meanwhile, each family prepared its tent or bedding for the night, laid in a supply of wood and water, and cooked the evening meal. Now began the most exciting part of the day. Guitars, fiddles, and jew's-harps were brought out, and groups gathered around campfires to dance, sing, and frolic. By nine o'clock the music and talk stopped and everyone except the guards went to bed, for the start next morning would be an early one.

IX · *The Impact of Gold on the Southwest*

A few minutes before sunrise a bugle call or the clang of a bell routed the travelers from their sleep. Fires were lighted, animals fed and watered, and breakfasts prepared and eaten quickly. Down came the tents in routine order and into the wagons they went once again, together with the sleeping equipment, water barrels, axes, pots, and pans. Another bugle sounded as a signal to drive the animals from the watering place. The captain now made a hurried inspection of the vehicles before ordering them to roll— each assuming a position in the line different from that of the previous day. Thus the bivouac ended and another arduous march through heat and dust was begun.

Once the caravans reached the great prairies of the Southwest, the emigrants faced the problem of finding sufficient wood and grass, not to mention water. Grass was generally plentiful during the early months of spring, particularly along the virgin trails. If wood was scarce, dry "buffalo chips" could be substituted. The inexperienced traveler generally had qualms about cooking over dry dung, but he was soon reconciled by necessity. Most companies followed the advice found in practically all of the current guidebooks and carried some dry wood along. One such publication even stipulated size and number of sticks and recommended that the camper dig a "hole in the ground about twelve inches in depth and of a size suitable for wood and cooking utensils. Thus the heat will be preserved and a very small amount of wood will cook a large meal." Travelers soon discovered that most of the other information in the guidebooks was both erroneous and useless.

In a study of the California migration published in 1925, Ralph Bieber observed that residents from every state in the union, with the possible exception of Delaware and Michigan, journeyed to California in 1849 over one of the well-advertised Southwestern trails.[1] Taking advantage of the mild January Texas climate, the first large parties of overland travelers departed from such towns as Brownsville, Corpus Christi, San Antonio, Fredericksburg, and

---

[1] Ralph P. Bieber: "The Southwestern Trails to California in 1849," *The Mississippi Valley Historical Review*, Vol. XII (December 1925), pp. 342–75.

Dallas. Local citizens took quick advantage of being on what they believed was the principal highway from East to West, and, indeed, each of these towns experienced a lively but short rush of business that exceeded that during the Mexican War.

When a group of gold seekers assembled at one of the debarkation points, some local settlers invariably succumbed to the fever and joined the wagon trains. The small village of Dallas, for example, which clustered in the vicinity of John Neely Bryan's ferry at the Trinity River crossing, quickly lost every adult male inhabitant except John C. McCoy. But within two years almost all local argonauts returned home rich in experience but not in California gold.

Although thousands started for the gold fields from various points in Texas, a severe epidemic of cholera which swept through the state during the spring of 1849 (in Brownsville, Laredo, and San Antonio it was particularly severe) caused many gold seekers to avoid the entire state. Some who had already arrived in Texas quickly retreated to Louisiana, Mexico, and elsewhere, but others stayed, survived the epidemic, and left for California in due course.

The ones who embarked from Brownsville in the first great overland migration crossed the Rio Grande near Mier and proceeded to Parras by way of Monterrey and Saltillo—the road taken earlier by General Taylor's army. Those who left from San Antonio generally followed the trail blazed by General Wool's forces, crossing the Rio Grande near Laredo. At Parras the emigrants had three choices. They could continue overland through Durango to the port city of Mazatlan and go by boat to San Francisco. An alternative route extended through the Mexican towns of Parral, Chihuahua City, and Janos to Guadalupe Pass near the common corner of the present Mexican and American states of Chihuahua, Sonora, New Mexico, and Arizona. The trail from this point paralleled Colonel Cooke's well-marked road across New Mexico and Arizona to San Diego, California. The third route from Parras followed a little-traveled trail northwest to Altar, Sonora, to the Pima Indian village near present-day Maricopa, Arizona, and west via the Gila

IX · *The Impact of Gold on the Southwest*

River to San Diego. Additional trails crossed the Rio Grande at various points and cut the northern corners of Chihuahua and Sonora, but only a few parties chose to follow them. On any of these routes it was possible to reach California in less than six months. Accordingly, those emigrants who departed from Texas and proceeded across the Southwest arrived in California long before the ones who took a more northern trail.

Several overland roads that ranged westward of San Antonio were also open to the eager gold seekers. One extended from San Antonio to Presidio del Norte (Del Rio) and thence along the Rio Grande to El Paso, but this was country that only pack mules and horses could travel. To make it more attractive, a number of enterprising merchants at San Antonio financed several explorations in the hope of discovering a more direct and practicable road to El Paso. Eventually they marked a wagon trail via Fredericksburg, slightly northwest across the Edwards Plateau country to Horsehead Crossing on the Pecos River, and thence due west to El Paso. There emigrants could turn southward through northern Chihuahua and Sonora or proceed northward to Dona Anna for a connection with Cooke's California road.

During the summer months all of these Southwestern routes proved unpleasant, due to heat, scarcity of water, dust, rocks, sand, desert plants, and the absence of settlements.

Merchants from Mexico and Missouri reaped a bonanza from the tired travelers who stopped at El Paso, the crossroads of the continent, to recoup their supplies, repair their wagons, replenish their stock, and quench their thirst. Prices were high, but emigrants had to pay what was demanded. Some exhausted their financial reserves quickly and either remained in the city and worked for wages or hired out to other emigrants. Some local citizens felt that the excesses of the travelers made the newfound prosperity more a curse than a blessing.

Although the San Antonio–El Paso roads became the most popular Southwestern trails, others experienced heavy traffic for short periods. Early in 1849 some 300 settlers in the region between Dallas and Preston, most of whom were members of the so-called "Kentucky Colony," departed for California. This group followed a course that extended across northern Texas and intersected the Trinity, Brazos, Colorado, and Pecos rivers before it eventually reached El Paso. Later in the same year Captain Randolph B. Marcy returned from southern New Mexico via a similar route, and, impressed with its advantages, he predicted that it would soon become a major highway. But, surprisingly, the Dallas–El Paso road failed to achieve its early promise.

Marcy also promoted another Southwestern trail. In the spring of 1849 he commanded a military escort that accompanied approximately 2,000 emigrants from Fort Smith to Sante Fe, following the course of the Canadian River most of the way. This route was laid out as a result of an intense promotion campaign on the part of the people of Arkansas. On September 23, 1848, a number of prominent citizens met at Fort Smith and adopted a resolution to request that state legislature to petition Congress for a military road between Arkansas and California. It was pointed out that emigrants could travel by steamboat up the Arkansas River and, by taking a land route due west from Fort Smith to Santa Fe, could reach California with ease and safety.

Citizens of western Arkansas were more interested in profiteering from the California emigrants than in providing them with a short route to the gold fields. Nevertheless, the Arkansas legislature quickly forwarded the Fort Smith request to Congress, where it was lost in the House Military Affairs Committee. Meanwhile, Senator Solom G. Borland requested that the War Department provide a military escort for emigrants who were preparing to depart from western Arkansas for California as soon as weather and grass permitted.

The War Department had already considered making various military surveys across the continent with a view to building a national highway that would link the Mississippi Valley with the Pacific Coast. It now decided to combine the surveys with military escorts for emigrant parties, and the Fort Smith proposal was accepted. Troops were to be drawn from the local forts. Accordingly, the commander at Fort Smith, General Matthew Arbuckle, se-

IX · *The Impact of Gold on the Southwest*

lected Captain Marcy, currently stationed at Fort Towson in the southeast corner of the Choctaw Nation, to lead the escort. Almost immediately the problem arose as to which was the best route west of Fort Smith—the one along the Arkansas River or the more direct course near the Canadian River. Both offered advantages. The Arkansas River route, pioneered by the Santa Fe trader Hugh Glenn several years before, was better known. But a road that followed the Canadian River would favor Fort Smith, whereas the more northern one would help Van Buren. As General Arbuckle resided at Fort Smith, he naturally succumbed to local pressure and selected the Canadian River route.

By the time Marcy arrived at Fort Smith on April 2, 1849, to take command of the two companies of infantry and dragoons which constituted the escort, some 2,000 emigrants from at least thirty-six states were assembled, organized into companies, and ready to roll. The largest group called itself the Fort Smith Company and included several prominent Arkansas residents, including Dr. John R. Conway, whose family had already furnished two governors to the state. Conway had filled several wagons with merchandise, which he later sold in California at a greater profit than most of the emigrants ever realized from the gold mines.

The various companies of civilians and military troops left Fort Smith during the first two weeks of April, expecting to reach Santa Fe in forty days. They made no attempt to stay together until all the groups had reached Edwards Trading Post on the south bank of the Canadian River. This historic establishment was approximately 125 miles west of Fort Smith near present-day Holdenville, Oklahoma, and its proprietor, James Edwards, had long enjoyed a flourishing business with Indian traders and Texas emigrants. As the Edwards store offered the last opportunity to purchase supplies and make major repairs before reaching the New Mexican settlements, the gold seekers camped for several days to take advantage of its facilities.

Before leaving Edwards on May 1, Marcy wrote to his wife that "the travelers are generally a very decent class of people, and some of them are intelligent and gentlemanly men." He also observed that they would soon reach the "broad prairies of the West."

The country near the center of what is now Oklahoma gradually leveled and the timber and brush lessened in density as it approached the eastern edge of the Cross Timbers. This geographic phenomenon was a belt of "shin oak" and chaparral extending north from the Brazos River in Texas across Oklahoma and into southern Kansas. Josiah Gregg, in his *Commerce of the Prairies*, had described it as varying in width from ten to thirty miles and constituting an effective barrier between the wild tribes of the plains and the civilized tribes of the Indian nations.

Marcy's party passed through the Cross Timbers near where Purcell, Oklahoma, now stands on United States Highway 77. He recorded in his journal: "We are now entering a 'tierra incognito' inhabited by the wild nomads of the plains," and he approached the region with mingled hope and awe. But the difficulties he encountered were relatively minor—the only trouble the Plains Indians caused was that their numerous visits to his camp delayed the expedition's progress. After eighty-five days the argonauts, "all in good health," reached Santa Fe, more than 800 miles from Fort Smith. This was the largest single party that traversed any of the Southwestern trails during the gold rush.

On the outskirts of the New Mexican capital the civilian members of the train were discharged to continue to California alone. Eventually the various companies divided, some proceeding down the Rio Grande to Dona Ana before veering west to Cooke's Road, while others turned back along the Santa Fe Trail through Las Vegas and Raton to follow the Front Range until they could find a pass through the mountains. From the Continental Divide the road extended to Salt Lake City and thence to the Humboldt River and on to northern California.

Marcy and his military command remained in Sante Fe for several weeks, during which time the Captain inquired about the possibilities of a more southern route that would by-pass the New Mexican capital and shorten the distance to California. He also interested himself in the local scene, for Santa Fe was experiencing

IX · *The Impact of Gold on the Southwest*

a bonanza in trade and excitement such as it had not known since the early months of the Mexican War when Kearny's forces first arrived. Emigrants reached the place almost daily, some to linger for a while for rest and relaxation. Others, unlucky and discouraged, abandoned hope of fortune and either turned back or stayed on as permanent residents. Many who decided to continue to the gold fields doubtless regretted their decision, for the hardest part of the journey lay across the Apache-infested desert of southern Arizona.

Marcy's return journey to Fort Smith probably was more significant than his trip to New Mexico, for he blazed a new and better trail that years later became part of a permanent route to the Far West. On August 14, 1849, he and his command of some fifty infantrymen, dragoons, and Indian guides left Santa Fe on the historic Chihuahua trail that extended along the Rio Grande. At Santa Anna, a small village north of El Paso, the commander decided to alter his course and turn eastward toward the Organ and Guadalupe Mountains, entering a region that was largely unknown. His route took him through Guadalupe Pass, where the Butterfield Overland Mail Company later established one of its better-known stage stations, the Pinery, halfway between St. Louis and San Francisco. The Pecos River was but a short distance beyond this point, and once the wagons were across they quickly emerged upon the *Llano Estacado*, or Staked Plains.

The great plateau at that latitude is only sixty miles wide, but the next three days were a virtual hell for men and beasts because of the shifting sand, the torrid sun, and the scarcity of water holes. When the party dropped down from its eastern rim on October 2, 1849, it chanced upon "a fine spring of water"—now Big Springs, Texas. From here to the crossing on Red River the travelers pursued a slightly northeast course which intersected the valleys of the upper Colorado and Brazos rivers. Most of the route extended a few miles north of and parallel to the present United States Highway 80 and the tracks of the Texas and Pacific Railroad. The long wearisome journey afforded Marcy an opportunity to examine the country for future military sites. Later he returned to this region and assisted in the location of a chain of posts that extended from Fort Worth to El Paso and also established the first reservation for various Comanche and Texas tribes.

At Preston, a town later flooded by sprawling Lake Texoma, the expedition continued along the well-marked Indian road via present-day Durant and Boggy Depot until it reached Fort Smith. In his report to the War Department, Marcy stated that both of the trails he had traversed were excellent for California emigrants. He was more enthusiastic about the more southerly route by which he had returned from New Mexico, however, for it shortened the distance to California by some 300 miles.

Professor Bieber estimates that approximately 3,000 traveled Marcy's Canadian River route before the end of 1849, but for several years there was less traffic along the southern route because it was publicized too late. There was some movement along both trails in 1850, but neither immediately became the great highway that the towns of western Arkansas had expected. Sections of the roads east of the Cross Timbers proved almost impassable for wagon traffic in wet weather, and many emigrants abandoned their equipment and continued by pack mules. Some wrote to friends that the Canadian road was the "worst in the world" and that the Fort Smith boosters were "a gang of liars." Also, outbreaks of cholera along the trails demoralized many and caused them to be wary of any trail that crossed the Southwest.

The total number who traveled along the various Southwestern trails during the gold-rush years is generally estimated at 60,000.[2]

---

[2] Some other Southwestern routes to California deserve mention. The Arkansas River route, pioneered by Dr. Josiah Gregg in 1839, began at Fort Gibson and extended to Santa Fe, thence north via Bent's Fort to South Pass before turning westward across Utah and Nevada to northern California. Also at Santa Fe the traveler could choose among three southern routes: the Philip St. George road, which passed through Guadalupe Pass to present-day Bisbee, Arizona, then westward to Tucson, Phoenix, and Yuma; General Phil Kearny's road, which paralleled the Gila River across Arizona to Yuma; and the road due west of Albuquerque to Los Angeles via Needles, Arizona, which later was officially surveyed by Lieutenant A. W. Whipple. All of these eventually served as routes for important railroads and highways to California.

IX · *The Impact of Gold on the Southwest*

AT THE TIME of the Treaty of Guadalupe Hidalgo the total Anglo-American population of our four Southwestern states approximated 100,000. Added to this were at least 150,000 inhabitants of various extraction—mostly Indians, Spaniards, Mexicans, and Negroes. Large areas throughout the region were uninhabited even by Indians, and present-day Arizona and Oklahoma had no towns worthy of the name.

Texas and New Mexico had gained in population as a result of the Mexican War, but the gold rush caused an even greater increase in population in the Southwest. By 1850 New Mexico (including what is now Arizona) had slightly more than 60,000 inhabitants. Anglo-Americans constituted less than ten per cent of this figure and resided chiefly in the areas around Taos, Santa Fe, and Albuquerque. The Oklahoma historian E. E. Dale estimates that the total population of Indian Territory (Oklahoma) at this same period was 65,000, practically all of whom lived east of the Cross Timbers within the Five Nations. This included only a handful of Anglo-Americans—missionaries, licensed traders, and sutlers at the military post. Also, the three principal military posts located among the Indian nations, Fort Towson, Fort Washita, and Fort Gibson, probably contained as many as 500 Anglo-American troops.

Since the Indian nations generally barred white men, the gold rush did little to increase the permanent population of what became Oklahoma. It did, however, bring many permanent settlers to other parts of the Southwest. Texas in 1848 had a total population of approximately 158,000, of whom 42,000 were Negro slaves. The census of 1850 shows 212,592 whites, 397 free Negroes, and 58,161 slaves. This dramatic increase within two years cannot be attributed solely to the gold rush, for many people moved to the new state because of the abundance of cheap land. But others stopped off en route or returned later to settle permanently. The same was true of other parts of the Southwest.

Except for a few Anglo-Americans who resided in the vicinity of present-day Yuma, at the mouth of the Gila River, modern Arizona in 1850 was populated by nomadic and sedentary Indians and an assortment of ranchers of Spanish and Mexican blood. The latter lived in the area south of the Gila River in what soon became the Gadsden Purchase; the northern two thirds of the region was populated entirely by Navajos, Apaches, and other Indian tribes. Within a short time this situation had changed and American settlers in Arizona were demanding a territorial government of their own. Most of these settlers, according to the late Rufus Kay Wyllys, Arizona historian, came in search of gold but later settled down as ranchers, farmers, and merchants.

The quest for gold in Arizona began as early as the sixteenth century, when Spanish explorers first crossed the region. By the following century some precious metals were being mined north of modern Prescott. From time to time, during periods when the Apaches were comparatively peaceful, Arizona mines were worked with Indian labor. H. H. Bancroft believes that the extent of these early operations has been greatly exaggerated, but the legend of rich Spanish gold mines continued into the nineteenth century. Occasionally wandering sheepherders or travelers made small discoveries of placer gold, but these events were all but forgotten during the early months of the California bonanza.

The thousands of emigrants who followed Cooke's Road across Arizona passed through the Mesilla Valley during their journey to the south bank of the Gila. In negotiating the Treaty of Guadalupe Hidalgo the American representative, Nicholas Trist, left most of this region in Mexican possession. He was criticized for this, but the fault was not all his. Even the Mexicans did not understand the geography of their northern provinces, and their maps proved extremely faulty. As more emigrants rolled over Cooke's Road and the belief spread that the lands south of the Gila contained valuable mineral deposits, the administration in Washington expressed interest in acquiring possession of the territory. There were other factors, including the importance of controlling the Indians in the

IX · *The Impact of Gold on the Southwest*

area and the desirability of building a railroad to California over the flat terrain.

Accordingly, James Gadsden traveled to Mexico City in 1853 as United States minister for the explicit purpose of obtaining from Mexico additional territory that would include Cooke's Road. He arrived at a fortunate time, for Antonio López de Santa Anna had just returned to power in desperate need of money. After much intrigue and delay the United States agreed to pay Mexico ten million dollars for the portions of present-day Arizona and New Mexico which extend below the Gila River.

The treaty did not give the Anglo-Americans control over all of the Mesilla Valley or a much coveted port on the Gulf of California. It was unpopular in both the United States and Mexico: it hurt Latin national pride and didn't satisfy the Anglos. The building of a railroad through the Gadsden territory was delayed a full generation. Meanwhile the new acquisition was thoroughly explored and partially settled.

Among the first Anglo-Americans to enter Arizona after the purchase treaty was Major William H. Emory, the United States commissioner in charge of surveying the new boundary line. Emory's counterpart on the Mexican boundary commission was José Salazar Ilarregui. The two men and their aides worked in perfect harmony, a marked contrast to the costly and incompetent activities of John Russell Bartlett and General Pedro García Conde a few years before.[3] In less than two years, or before the end of 1856, the various settlements in southern Arizona were transferred to the United States. These included Tucson and Tubac, but neither could boast of more than 400 inhabitants, and both were kept alive chiefly by the emigrants who traveled Cooke's Road to California.

The published reports of Emory and Bartlett contain excel-

---

[3] Bartlett and Conde were charged with surveying the boundary between El Paso and San Diego, following the signing of the Treaty of Guadalupe Hidalgo, but Bartlett was more interested in ethnology and other matters than in his survey work. He was removed before the completion of the project.

The Southwest: *Old and New*

lent descriptions of the country, as well as scientific appendixes of considerable value. These, together with narratives of other official exploring parties, soon publicized the whole region. In 1857-8 Edward F. Beale opened a wagon road from Zuñi Pueblo across the center of Arizona to the Colorado River, following a route similar to the one marked by Lieutenants A. W. Whipple and Lorenzo Sitgraves six years earlier. Incidentally, Beale carried out an experiment during the course of his expedition: he brought some of the army camels recently imported from the Middle East. The project proved interesting and romantic, but otherwise was of minor importance.

Another Southwestern experiment was conducted by Lieutenant Joseph C. Ives in 1857. Ives ascended the Colorado River in the small steamer *Explorer* and managed to get as far inland as the Virgin River. Here he shifted to land and eventually reached Fort Defiance in northeastern Arizona. His subsequent *Report upon the Colorado River, 1857-58* remains the most interesting and readable account of military exploration in this far corner of the Southwest published before the Civil War.

While the Arizona region was crossed by thousands of emigrants, surveyed by United States commissioners, and carefully explored by military parties, Anglo-Americans gradually came into possession of a few of the old Spanish-Mexican settlements. They first settled along the Gila River to search for gold, for many of the travelers, especially those in an official capacity, had noted signs of precious metals. Two individuals prominent in the early Anglo-American history of the state were Charles Poston and Herman Ehrenberg, who formed a company and began mining silver on a large scale near Tubac in 1856. Half a dozen other companies were in operation within another year, and copper-, gold-, and silver-mining developments quickly spread to the upper and lower Gila River, east to the present New Mexico [4] border, and even into the less-known regions of the north.

---

[4] Lead and silver were mined on a limited scale in the vicinity of Santa Fe as early as the seventeenth century. The Spaniards found veins of gold in the same region a century later. Again in 1833 a strike was made and a flurry

IX · *The Impact of Gold on the Southwest*

By 1858 the settlement of Tubac had a flourishing population of 800, almost a third of whom were Anglos, and supported the first weekly newspaper in the area. But the town still retained the atmosphere of a Mexican hacienda. "We had no law but love," Poston wrote, "and no occupation but labor; no government, no taxes, no public debt, no politics. It was a community in a perfect state of nature. As syndic under New Mexico, I opened a book of records, performed the marriage ceremony, baptized the children, and granted divorce. At first a saloon furnished the remaining 'necessities of life' and later a grocery store and a Chinese restaurant supplied the 'luxuries.' " [5]

Another "wild and wicked gold-rush town" mushroomed in 1858 when a number of Texas veterans of the Mexican War, led by Jacob Snively, settled about twenty miles above Fort Yuma on the Colorado River. The town took the name of Gila City, and by the time of the Civil War it had attracted more than a thousand miners, each able to make from $30 to $125 a day. The place had everything it needed except a church and a jail, but by 1864 the "pay dirt" was exhausted, part of the buildings had been destroyed by a flood, and the residents had drifted elsewhere. According to one observer, it was left with "nothing but three chimneys and a coyote." Meanwhile its nearby placer mines had produced more than two million dollars in gold.

Other mining settlements in Arizona flourished for a brief period before the Civil War and then disappeared. One was Arizona City—now Yuma—which was located on the east bank of the Colorado and was supplied by steamers. It is frequently referred to as a "thriving town." According to tradition, the first American settler in Arizona City was L. J. F. Jaeger, who established a ferry there in 1849 to transfer emigrants to the California side of the

---

of gold mining resulted. However, extensive mining of precious metals did not develop in New Mexico until after the Civil War and thus did not play so important a role in early Anglo-American settlement of the region as it did in Arizona.

[5] Tubac did not survive the occupation by American settlers for more than a few years. Exposed to the ravages of the Apaches, the depredations of the Mexicans, and the lawlessness of the Anglos, its population soon dwindled to less than 100.

river. Other ferries were established, one of which was operated by the Yumas. In 1850 the United States Army built a military post on the west bank to protect the crossing against the local Indians. Four years later the "Father of Arizona," Colonel Charles D. Poston, surveyed several lots for a new town on the east bank and called the place Colorado City. In 1857 it had only twenty permanent settlers, but after the arrival of the Overland stage that same year the population increased rapidly, and gambling houses and saloons soon dominated its landscape.[6]

The transfer of the Gadsden Purchase to the United States in 1856 added a sizable settlement to Arizona, the old Spanish town of Tucson. According to a Mexican census report, it had a population in 1848 of 760 inhabitants. Even though several adventurers and miners from various parts of the Southwest settled in the region, Father Joseph P. Machebeuf—Joseph in Willa Cather's *Death Comes for the Archbishop*—wrote in 1858 that it was "a village of about 800 souls, built around an ancient Mexican fortress."

Four companies of the First United States Dragoons were stationed in Tucson in 1856 and remained for several months before being transferred to Fort Buchanan, twenty-five miles east of Tubac. In 1857 Tucson was chosen as a major stop for the overland stage operating between San Antonio and San Diego. Only two stages arrived each month until the Butterfield line opened between St. Louis and San Francisco the next year. From then until the beginning of the Civil War, two eastbound and two westbound stages arrived each week, discharging and picking up the mail and an occasional passenger. One traveler described the accommodations at the Tucson station as far from adequate: the beds consisted of a board whereupon "one was forced to lie on his stomach and cover up with his back."

Another observer of Tucson at this period was even less flattering. He observed that the principal Anglo-Americans consisted of "traders, speculators, gamblers, horse thieves, murderers, and vagrant politicians. Men who were prevented from living in Califor-

---

[6] Considerable confusion exists regarding the name of this settlement. Its names included Arizona City, Colorado City, and Yuma, but after 1860 the name Yuma predominated.

IX · *The Impact of Gold on the Southwest*

nia found the Arizona climate congenial to their health. If the world were searched over, I suppose that there could not be found so degraded a set of villains as then formed the principal society of Tucson. Every man went armed to the teeth, and street fights and bloody affrays were of daily occurrence. It was literally a paradise of devils."

Besides the few Arizona settlements where Anglo-Americans resided before the Civil War, there were the military posts. The first such establishment, intended to control the Indians, was Fort Defiance, located just west of the New Mexico line on the edge of the present Navajo reservation in 1849. This post was far removed from the scattered white settlements on the Gila and Colorado rivers, but it was designed to protect the settlers of the upper Rio Grande Valley from the thieving Navajo. Late in 1858 Fort Mohave was built near Beale's crossing of the Colorado River and the next year Fort Breckenridge at the junction of the San Pedro and Arivaipa rivers.

The soldiers had several hard fights with the Arizona Indians, especially the fierce Apaches, although at no time did the military forces exceed 400, and frequently they dropped to as low as 120 men. When the Civil War came and the Arizona Indians increased their raiding, the War Department recognized the utter inadequacy of its military posts to protect so vast a region. Consequently, most federal military personnel were withdrawn from the Southwest, and the abandoned forts were destroyed by the Indians.

Meanwhile, a line of military posts protected the frontier extending across Oklahoma, Texas, and New Mexico. Many of these establishments were not reoccupied after the sectional conflict, but the soldiers played an important role in the post-war period and helped secure the Southwest for future development.

THE IMPACT of the California gold rush on various unsettled regions of the Southwest resulted in other activities besides mining. The most important of these was ranching. Just who were the first Americans to bring cattle into the desert regions of present-day Arizona is a matter of controversy. Very probably they included Texas and New Mexico cattlemen bent on driving their herds to California to supply the gold camps with beef. Some of them took advantage of the unclaimed ranch lands en route and settled down to increase their herds. Such a man was Peter Kitchen, who stopped on Potrero Creek near modern Nogales as early as 1854 and developed his herd into one of the largest to be found between El Paso and San Diego. Most of the ranchos, however, were in the Gila Valley, where, according to Bancroft, the Americans engaged in the cattle and sheep business before the Civil War far outnumbered those who lived in the towns.

The portion of the Southwest which is now Arizona experienced another flurry of activity that likewise was an indirect result of the gold rush. In 1857 a filibustering expedition led by Henry A. Crabb crossed Arizona from California and marched into Sonora. Crabb recruited a hundred followers to help overthrow the governor of Sonora and install Ignacio Pesquiera in his place. Crabb and his men were to be rewarded with a large strip of land near the Arizona boundary, but when they reached the borders of the Mexican state the usurper had already unseated his rival. Pesquiera now repudiated his agreement and besieged the Americans at Caborca.

Crabb fought for several days before reaching an agreement with the Mexicans which promised the filibusters safe transportation back across the Arizona line. No sooner did the Americans lay down their arms, however, than they were divided into parties and marched out and shot. According to legend, the leader's head was pickled in mescal and sent to Mexico City as proof of the new governor's incorruptible patriotism. Meanwhile, a party of twenty-nine citizens of Tucson rushed toward Caborca to rescue Crabb's party, but they reached the scene too late. The Mexicans had already disposed of the filibusters and came close to doing the same thing to the Arizonans.

One year before this bloody business, Anglo-Americans in the region below the Gila River took the first step to organize a civil gov-

IX · The Impact of Gold on the Southwest

ernment that would protect their lives and property against lawless emigrants, Apaches, and Mexicans. In late August 1856 most of the white settlers of the region assembled at Tucson and drew up a petition asking for separation from New Mexico and the organization of the Territory of Arizona. The petition stated that the population of the region, exclusive of Indians, was approximately 10,000, an estimate more than generous. Nathan P. Cook was elected to carry the memorial to Washington and to remain as delegate of the new territory, but Congress failed to act.

Other conventions were held and new petitions and pleas presented to Congress each year until 1860, but even President Buchanan's support of separate civil government for Arizona Territory could not overcome the Congressional deadlock. Buchanan pointed out on December 6, 1858, that the people in the western portion of New Mexico Territory [7] "are practically without a government, without laws, and without any regular administration of justice. Murder and other crimes are committed with impunity." But hopes for the creation of Arizona Territory were doomed in these years because Southern support of the plan alienated Northern Congressmen and Senators.

In April 1860 the people of Arizona finally established a temporary government "to operate until Congress shall organize a territorial government" for the region. But Congress ignored this move, and the temporary government for the proposed territory of Arizona, which was to consist of all the lands of New Mexico south of the 33° 40′ parallel, never functioned. Soon, however, the slavery controversy put the Arizonans in a most favorable position, as North and South vied for their support. Instead of being the pursuer, they became the pursued, with both the United States government and the Confederate government holding out the tempting bait of territorial status. Arizona's allegiance eventually would be decided on the basis of which side could bring the superior force of arms into the region.

---

[7] New Mexico Territory was organized under the Organic Act of September 9, 1850, as part of the great sectional compromise of that year. The territory originally included all of Arizona and part of Colorado.

X

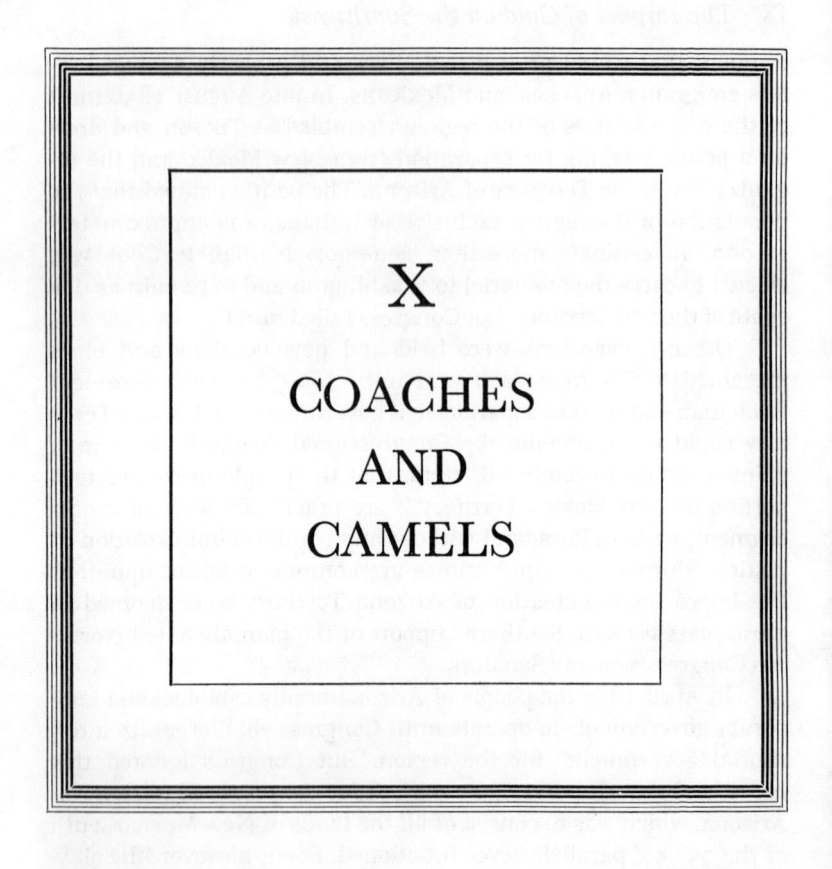

COACHES AND CAMELS

FOR TWO GENERATIONS after the Louisiana Purchase, ominous warnings were heard throughout the land that the United States was in danger of overextending itself. But the dramatic tide of events which swept Texas, California, and the Oregon country into the Union within two short years silenced the voices of gloom. By the middle of the nineteenth century the dream of Jefferson seemed to have been realized, the nation's manifest destiny had been fulfilled, and Americans turned their thoughts to new problems raised by their new acquisitions.

The most immediate of these was the status of slavery in the

X · Coaches and Camels

Southwestern territory recently acquired from Mexico, and almost equally important was the matter of transcontinental transportation. The Compromise of 1850 emerged as the unhappy solution to the first dilemma, and both major political parties eventually accepted it as final. Meanwhile, the California gold rush had compounded the second and demonstrated the urgent need for faster and safer communication between East and West. This problem appeared merely a physical one, and its obvious solution was the construction of a transcontinental railroad. The railroad age had arrived in America by 1830, and within two decades the speed of rail travel had increased from five to thirty miles per hour. A network of iron rails linked the Eastern cities and reached out to centers of population along the Mississippi Valley. By 1850 talk of a railroad to the Pacific was no longer dismissed as the babble of crackpots.

Yet, as the physical obstacles began to seem less formidable, others sprang up to replace them. Previous experience had revealed that the new type of transportation could survive financially only in densely populated areas. Obviously, a railroad link between the Far East and the Far West must wait until the great heartland received millions of new settlers. But Americans of the nineteenth century were not a patient people, and particularly those who had moved to the West and others who had a vested interest in the region were unwilling to wait. The alternative was a program of generous government subsidies.

The myth that only private capital could develop transportation facilities had long since tarnished; still, the traditional devotion to "free enterprise" could not easily be overcome. The only way to appease the opponents of government subsidy, therefore, was to build a railroad to the Pacific from sheer "military necessity." Opposition diminished with the coinage of the proper slogan. But the question of sectionalism entered this picture also. Southerners were determined that a transcontinental railroad would not bypass their section, while Northerners were equally anxious to reap the benefits of the route. The situation reached an impasse that was not resolved until the South left the Union.

The Southwest: *Old and New*

In the meantime, immigrants continued to pour into the Southwest and the Pacific Coast region. These people, whether they settled in Texas, New Mexico, California, or Oregon, soon felt their isolation from the rest of the country. It took one to three months for mail and supplies to reach them from the East. Their demands for better communication with friends and relatives back home were both vociferous and prolonged.

The federal government instituted regular mail service by stagecoach between Independence, Missouri, and Santa Fe, New Mexico, in 1849. A short time later another line was extended as far as Salt Lake City, but these points were long distances from Los Angeles and San Francisco.

In April 1854 a mail-and-passenger line using two-horse coaches was started between San Antonio and Santa Fe, a journey of over three weeks. Not until three years later did "The San Antonio Express" extend its route to southern California via El Paso. The schedule allowed a maximum of thirty days for the trip from San Antonio, the eastern terminus. Indian attacks were frequent, and the small coaches often broke down on the rugged roads of western Texas. A safer mail-and-passenger route, though still painfully slow and expensive, was the haphazard service offered by the Pacific Mail Steamship Company.[1]

Californians' pleas for a more adequate overland mail-and-passenger service during this period were joined by those of most of the states and cities along the Mississippi Valley, which expected to benefit by it. The subject was never allowed to die during the entire decade of the 1850's. Hopes for an early solution were encouraged when in March 1853 Congress set aside $150,000 of the Army's annual appropriation for "the purpose of conducting various surveys to determine the most feasible route for a transcontinental railroad." This action was the culmination of the aforementioned propaganda for a railroad as a "military necessity."

---

[1] The high costs of mail (twelve to eighty cents an ounce) and the thirty days required for the journey from New York to California via Panama only stimulated California's demand for overland service.

X · Coaches and Camels

The following day, March 4, the Democrats took the upper hand with the inauguration of Franklin Pierce as president. His new Secretary of War, Jefferson Davis, could be counted on to carry through the survey program quickly, for he had early advocated an iron link between East and West. All sections of the country awaited the results of the surveys, believing that construction of the first transcontinental railroad was near.

Davis was scrupulously careful not to give the appearance of favoring his native South over any other section. He was wise in this, because almost every town and city between the Canadian border and the Gulf of Mexico took an active interest in the routes and leaders of the various surveying parties. Citizens of Fort Smith, Arkansas, for example, sent the Secretary a huge petition urging him to appoint Captain Randolph B. Marcy as director of one of the Southwestern surveys. These people were not unmindful that Captain Marcy had previously pointed out the advantages of a railroad extending west of Fort Smith to California, following either the Canadian River or the Fort Smith–El Paso road that he had blazed in 1849–50. Davis ignored the petition.

Eventually the routes were determined and the commanders chosen for five separate expeditions. Two of the surveys extended across the Southwest, one to commence at Fort Smith and follow the 35th parallel as closely as possible to Los Angeles; the other, a far-southern route, was to extend along the 32nd parallel from El Paso to Yuma, Arizona. Lieutenant A. W. Whipple was appointed to conduct the 35th-parallel survey, while Captain John Pope, Lieutenant J. G. Parke, and others were assigned the more southern route.[2] Whipple left Fort Smith in June 1853, and ended his operations less than one year later. His work covered almost 2,000 miles, the greater portion of which became the route of the Atchison, Topeka, and Santa Fe Railroad across New Mexico and Ari-

---

[2] The other three surveys were carried out beyond the boundaries of the Southwest. The northernmost extended from St. Paul to the mouth of the Columbia River, between the 47th and 49th parallels. The second route followed the well-known immigrant trail to California, while the third pursued a course between the 38th and 39th parallels.

zona. Meanwhile, Pope and Parke laid out a trail that one day would be the roadbed of the Texas Pacific and Southern Pacific railroads.

All of the surveys were completed by 1855 and quickly published in copiously illustrated volumes. They proved conclusively that not one but several routes between the Mississippi Valley and the Pacific Coast were practicable. Besides contributing to the geographical, zoological, and botanical knowledge of the West and Southwest, the reports of the military commanders proved invaluable to future development of the various regions. The five great transcontinental railroads eventually built did not range far from the trails of these early surveyors.

After a careful study of the detailed information that poured into his office from the exploratory expeditions, Jefferson Davis announced his choice to Congress in 1855. To no one's great surprise, it favored the Southern states. Northern Congressmen immediately claimed that the Secretary had allowed sectional feelings to influence his decision, a charge not completely without foundation. However, there was much to be said for the Southwestern route. It was certainly the least costly because of the absence of great mountain barriers; it afforded the best year-round climate for construction and operational purposes; and the Southwestern Indians were relatively peaceful in the 1850's.

These points were countered with arguments that the arid stretches of western Texas, southern Arizona, and New Mexico would never support large populations; that most of the land was unfit for cultivation; and that the eastern extremities of the route were too far from the great industrial and commercial centers of the country. And overshadowing these obvious disadvantages was the great emotional issue of slavery. Everyone believed that any railroad that gave the slave states a direct link with the Pacific Coast would surely promote the spread of the "evil institution." Northerners determined that this should not happen, while Southerners preferred no railroad at all to one that did not link them to the adjoining region of the Southwest.

Thus, despite the carefully documented reports of feasible

X · Coaches and Camels

routes, the issue was quickly deadlocked. At the end of 1855 California was as remote from the world as ever, and if either of the great sections secured satisfaction in stifling the interests of the other, the people of the Pacific Coast were not impressed. They faced a condition and not a political or economic theory, and the need for better and faster communication continued to grow as more and more settlers arrived.

As there was to be no transcontinental railroad in the immediate future, Westerners searched for a temporary alternative. When the Thirty-fourth Congress convened in December 1855, Senator John B. Weller from California urged the construction of two wagon roads, one to extend from Independence, Missouri, through South Pass to northern California, the other from El Paso to Yuma and Los Angeles. Such roads, he pointed out, could be used by wagons for heavy freight and by fast stagecoaches for mail-and-passenger service until railroads were built. Congress failed to take any action on the proposal.

Again, in May 1856, Senator Weller introduced the subject of federal-constructed roads to the Pacific Coast.[3] This time he laid before his colleagues a petition, containing the names of 75,000 California constituents, which requested a single road along the South Pass–Humboldt River route. Weller pointed out that California's population numbered 500,000 people, that its mines had contributed $300,000,000 to the nation's economy, yet the state remained isolated from the rest of the Union.

With 1856 a presidential-election year, the persistent demands of the Western states and territories could not be completely ignored. Consequently, Congress responded with an appropriation of $600,000 "for improvement of overland transportation." In keeping with Senator Weller's original proposal, the

---

[3] Various overland trails and roads to California already existed, but travel over them was slow and difficult. In 1856 most of the freight between the Mississippi Valley and California was being hauled by the firm of Russell, Majors, and Waddell. This company employed 1,700 men and utilized 7,500 oxen and 500 wagons. The time between Independence and San Francisco was approximately two months, and the charge for a ton of freight was astronomical.

money was to be expended on rebuilding the so-called road through South Pass, as well as the one west of El Paso. Stipulations were also made for bridging streams, sinking water wells, and erecting freight depots along the way.[4] Thus, northern California would be linked more closely to the Midwest, while the South would be tied to the Southwest.

No sooner had construction work on the two roads begun than agitation was started for an overland stage line to provide Californians with semi-weekly mail-and-passenger service. But this talk once again raised the old "bugaboo" of sectionalism, and debate in Congress waxed hot and furious over which government-built road to utilize, for both sides feared that a railroad would eventually follow the stagecoach route. Another deadlock seemed imminent unless a formula could be found which would satisfy both the North and the South and at the same time placate California, the Midwest, and the Southwest. Soon a bill was devised which authorized the Post Office Department to call for bids "for carrying the entire letter mail from such points on the Mississippi River as the contractors may select, to San Francisco." The measure stipulated that the contract was to extend for six years at a government subsidy not to exceed $300,000 for semi-monthly, $450,000 for weekly, or $600,000 for semi-weekly mail service.[5]

Southern Congressmen managed to attach a rider to the measure which authorized the Postmaster General, and not Congress, to determine the route to be followed. As this gentleman, Aaron V. Brown, happened to be from Tennessee, the maneuver was not without ulterior purposes.

Brown immediately advertised for bids, making it clear that each bidder must designate his own route. Some nine or ten hastily formed companies responded, most of whom calculated their

---

[4] The bill, as approved and signed by President Pierce on February 17, 1857, allotted $300,000 for the South Pass road, $200,000 for the El Paso–Yuma road, and $50,000 for a construction of a short road from Fort Defiance across New Mexico to the Colorado River. W. Turrentine Jackson: *Wagon Roads West* (Berkeley: University of California Press; 1952), pp. 173–4.

[5] Signed by President Pierce on March 3, 1857.

X · Coaches and Camels

operational expenses on the shortest possible east-west line—namely, the road to California by way of South Pass and Salt Lake City. One syndicate organized by experienced New York expressmen, including John Butterfield and William G. Fargo, submitted a bid citing a route along the old Santa Fe trail and thence from Albuquerque to California on the 35th parallel, following most of the railroad survey made by Lieutenant Whipple in 1854. The route cut across part of the Southwest, but bypassed Texas and consequently isolated the South.

The Postmaster General refused to exclude his section of the country from any benefits of an overland stage. He therefore suggested to Butterfield that he and his associates might receive the contract if they agreed to operate their coaches from St. Louis to Memphis, thence by way of Springfield, Missouri, to Fort Smith, Arkansas, and across the corner of Indian Territory in a southwesterly line to El Paso. From this point they could use the newly constructed road to Yuma, then turn north to Los Angeles and San Francisco. Although the route measured 600 miles longer than that of Butterfield's original proposal, he accepted the alteration. On September 16, 1857, the New York syndicate signed a contract whereby it guaranteed semi-weekly mail delivery to California in twenty-five days or less in exchange for an annual subsidy of $600,000.

A howl of protest arose when terms of the contract were made public. Editors of various Northern papers called it "one of the greatest swindles ever perpetrated upon the country by the slaveholders." They immediately dubbed the 2,800-mile route the "oxbow," stating that it extended over impassable deserts, missed the few population centers that did exist in the West, notably Salt Lake City, and would prove too expensive to operate. Brown stood firm and withstood the storm that raged about him. He emphasized two facts that his critics, including the *Chicago Tribune,* conveniently overlooked: that St. Louis was still the eastern terminus of the stage line, and that a road extending across the heart of the Southwest was the only practicable one for year-round travel. Furthermore, he stated, grass and water were available for livestock along the entire semicircular trail, and the Southwestern Indians appeared less likely to give trouble than the more northern tribes of the Great Plains. Subsequent developments proved the Postmaster General more right than wrong.

Butterfield demonstrated enormous energy and ability in making his plans, and by the time the first transcontinental stage line opened he had quieted many of its Northern detractors. Born in Berne, New York, he had spent his youth with horses and acquired an abiding love for them. At eighteen he was already an experienced stage driver, and his booming voice, heavy eyebrows, dark hair, and prominent nose became well known in upper New York. He later formed his own business, the American Express Company. He left his mark in the field of men's fashions as well: his flat-crowned "wide-awake" hat, pantaloons tucked into high boots, and long yellow linen duster started a trend in Western garb which other men emulated. For several years stores throughout the area of his business activities were hard pressed to keep those "Butterfield items" in stock.

After receiving the contract John Butterfield made a rapid survey of the 2,800-mile route from St. Louis to San Francisco. Many of the existing roads needed repair and new ones had to be cut. In addition, hundreds of ferries, bridges, and stations had to be constructed. Meanwhile, orders were placed for 250 coaches, special mail wagons, water wagons, harness sets, and innumerable other items of equipment. Over 200 stations were established, 1,800 horses purchased, and 1,000 men employed—drivers, conductors, station keepers, blacksmiths, veterinarians, wheelwrights, mechanics, helpers, and herders. Within one year the preliminary work had to be completed, personnel and equipment distributed along the line, trial runs held, and time schedules worked out.

According to the conditions laid down by the Postmaster General, the coaches were allowed only twenty-five days between St. Louis and San Francisco, less than half the time taken by any previous stage. The $600,000 annual subsidy was not sufficient to es-

X · Coaches and Camels

tablish and operate such a vast enterprise, but the Butterfield syndicate expected to make its profit from carrying small express packages, newspapers, and passengers. A strict rule of the stockholders prevented shipment of gold or silver, thus minimizing the dangers from highwaymen. And during the brief period that the Overland stages rolled across the great Southwest, not a single coach was ever halted by a professional gunman, by weather, or by a mountain—a boast none of the other transcontinental lines could make. Except for one attack by outlaw Apaches in southern Arizona in 1859, the mails along the "oxbow" route were never seriously delayed.

On September 15, 1858, two new Concord coaches started on their lonely journeys, one from the little railhead of the Mississippi and Pacific Railroad at Tipton, Missouri, 160 miles west of St. Louis, the other from San Francisco. On the westbound coach traveled the president of the Overland Stage Company, accompanied by his son, who served as driver, and one or two passengers. Butterfield stopped at Springfield, and the stage rolled on across hilly country to Fayetteville and Fort Smith, where it entered the Indian Nations. From here to the Red River Crossing near present-day Sherman, Texas, lay "two hundred miles of the worst road that God ever built," with practically no settlement in between, unless one wanted to call a cluster of log houses and one store at Boggy Depot a town. This stretch proved to be one of the most difficult of the entire journey, and the driver was hard pressed to average more than four miles per hour.

Beyond Red River, where the coach was ferried across, the trail swung west through Grayson County toward the open Texas country and for the next 500 miles ran south and parallel to Marcy's old trail to El Paso. In 1858 there was not a human habitation between Sherman and El Paso other than those of Indians, company stations, and a few military posts, and little to see but dry rolling plains, rugged escarpments, cedar brakes, and prickly pear. Indeed, few towns were ever built on this part of the route when the western half of Texas was settled.

The Southwest: *Old and New*

Between Horsehead Crossing on the Pecos River and Yuma, Arizona, the country was open and barren. Now the stations were farther apart, or not yet built. Except for scattered military outposts that guarded this arid frontier and occasional glimpses of magnificent buttes and mesas, little broke the monotony of the journey. At Guadalupe Pass, several miles east of El Paso, stood one of the most important stations of the entire route, the Pinery. Its name is remembered today, not so much because of its situation at the base of the rugged El Capitan Mountain as because it was the halfway point between Missouri and California. Here, the eastbound and westbound coaches met—some ten or twelve days after the start of their long journeys.

At El Paso the Overland stage ran on toward Apache Pass in what is now southwestern Arizona and continued to Tucson, averaging ten or twelve miles per hour until it reached the Colorado River at Yuma. From this point to the end of the line was a matter of only four or five days. The first westbound coach approached San Francisco on the morning of October 10, 1858, twenty-four days from Tipton, Missouri. The words of its passenger, a tired correspondent for the *New York Herald*, have been frequently quoted: "Had I not just come out over the route, I would be perfectly willing to go back."

One day earlier, the eastbound stage rolled into Tipton, Missouri, a town surveyed but a few months previously. The mail sacks were quickly put aboard a special train of the Pacific Railroad and rushed to St. Louis, to Cincinnati, and eventually to New York. The full journey was completed in four weeks: the once fantastic dream of crossing the continent in less than thirty days had come true.

Needless to say, the event did not go unnoticed throughout the world. "It is a glorious triumph for civilization and the Union," stated President Buchanan. *Harper's Weekly* commented that "California is no longer a colony of the East." And *The Times* of London, some 3,000 miles away, described the success of the Overland Mail: "a matter of greatest importance to Europe, inasmuch as it will open up a vast country to European immigration,

X · *Coaches and Camels*

will be the precursor of the railroads, and will greatly facilitate intercourse with British Columbia." [6]

In the towns and settlements along the 2,800-mile "oxbow" route the first coaches were greeted with celebrations that, in the language of the day, were "real humdingers." Guns were fired, hats were tossed in the air, and bands played. When the stage pulled up for a brief stop before a flag-decked saloon, courthouse, hotel, or station, a welcoming committee shook hands with the driver and conductor and greeted the passengers with typical Western enthusiasm. Sometimes eloquent speeches by the town fathers preceded or followed the arrival. Perhaps the celebration ended with a giant barbecue, but, except at important stops, the coach did not tarry. A change of driver, horses, mail sacks, and it rolled away in a cloud of dust—leaving a settlement that, for better or worse, was changed forever.

The arrival of the first Overland coach stimulated the growth of many communities. Sherman, Texas, for example, "doubled in population, and without hesitation the residents built one of the finest new courthouses in their part of Texas." [7] Citizens of Tucson constructed a new hotel to accommodate passengers who wished to stay a few days. Its "private rooms" consisted of slab-board shelves behind a heavy duck curtain, but customers at least had a roof over their heads. At other important terminal points, including Springfield, Fort Smith, El Paso, Yuma, and Los Angeles, the population took a sudden turn upward after September 1858.

The coach that left San Francisco on September 15, 1858, carried six passengers, few of whom traveled the entire distance to Tipton, but one traveler accompanied the westbound all the way from Missouri to California. This was a young newspaperman, Waterman L. Ormsby, whose articles for the *New York Her-*

---

[6] Quoted in Ray Allen Billington's: *Western Frontier, 1830–1860* (New York: Harper & Brothers; 1956), p. 283, from 35th Congress, 2nd Session, Senate Executive Document No. 1, Pt. 4, pp. 739–44.

[7] J. W. Williams: "The Butterfield Overland Mail Road Across Texas," *The Southwestern Historical Quarterly*, Vol. LXI, No. 1 (1957), p. 7.

ald were later published in book form.[8] Ormsby's description of a transcontinental journey by stagecoach a century ago, although less humorous than Mark Twain's *Roughing It,* remains one of the most complete accounts available today. Perhaps it had a baneful effect on prospective travelers, for it was several months before the Overland Mail realized much revenue from passenger service. Even so, Ormsby's articles gave the Southwestern region of the United States wide publicity.

Three weeks of constant jolting over washboard roads and mud holes was not a pleasant experience, and one customer likened it to possible torture by a band of Comanches. Add to this the choking dust of the desert in summer, torrential rains and swollen streams in the spring, and bone-chilling winds during the late fall and winter months. Mark Twain described the food he encountered on a journey by an Overland Mail coach "something that would curdle a goat's stomach," and Ormsby admitted that "it could hardly be compared to the fare at the Astor."

From Tipton to San Francisco the fare was $200, while local or way fare ran to ten cents per mile traveled. Each passenger was allowed forty pounds of luggage—the same, incidentally, as on a modern airliner. The passenger paid extra for meals, and experienced travelers soon learned to carry their own staples.

There is an ancient tale that the Texas humorist and scholar J. Frank Dobie likes to tell about the New York "dude" who reached an Overland Mail outpost in western Texas in 1859 after a gruesome journey of ten days from St. Louis. The station keeper might well have been a fugitive from a dozen vigilante committees. He set a plate of rancid bacon floating in its own grease before the jaded traveler, who pushed it away and said he simply could not eat it. The burly proprietor then shoved a large sourdough biscuit, heavier than a good-sized rock, in the dude's direction. The New Yorker refused this also, whereupon his short-tempered host retorted: "Then help yourself to the mustard, dammit."

---

[8] Waterman L. Ormsby: *The Butterfield Overland Mail,* edited by Lyle H. Wright and Josephine M. Bynum (San Marino: The Huntington Library; 1955).

X · *Coaches and Camels*

It cost John Butterfield approximately one million dollars to put his line in operation. Much of this sum was used to purchase the best carriages and harness. The coaches were of two types: the Concord, named after the New Hampshire town where it was manufactured, and the "celerity wagon," made at Troy, New York. The first was a full-bodied vehicle weighing 3,000 pounds. It had a capacity of about two tons, cost $1,400, and could accommodate six to nine passengers inside and an additional number on top. Mail and express packages were carried in the "boot" at the rear. These coaches were manufactured from the finest white ash, oak, elm, and prime basswood grown in New England forests. Fashioned by the famous Abbott-Downing Company, makers of horse-drawn carriages throughout the nineteenth century, they proved to be light, elegant, and durable. Like the Colt revolver, another New England export to the frontier, they so permeated the Old West that no "horse opera" is complete without them.

Like all Abbott-Downing carriages, the Butterfield coaches were painted in bright colors, usually red, green, or canary yellow. Built for emergencies in soft sand and rough terrain, the heavy iron-tired wheels were set wide enough apart to keep the vehicle from toppling. The body was reinforced with iron and swung on huge leather straps called "thoroughbraces." As the coach bowled forward, pulled by four or six horses or mules, the cab rocked back and forth on the thoroughbraces, which took up part of the shock of the rough roads. The more elegant carriages were used only at each end of the line; the passengers shifted with the mail to the specially built celerity wagons for the thinly populated part of the route between Fort Smith and Los Angeles.

These latter coaches resembled the regular ones, although not so luxurious; the wheels were smaller, and the top was a frame structure covered with heavy duck. The seats inside could be adjusted to form beds for seasoned travelers who had reached a state of complete exhaustion—generally after three or four days on the road. Heavy leather or duck curtains helped keep out rain, dust, and cold. Like the fancier Concord, the celerity wagon was lined with russet leather and illuminated by candle lamps.

The Butterfield coaches rolled day and night, except for brief

The Southwest: *Old and New*

stops for meals, to change horses or drivers, or to pick up and discharge mail bags. Each driver worked a sixty-mile run, rested a few hours, and then took another coach back over the same stretch of road. Approximately every 250 miles constituted a district, presided over by a divisional superintendent. A conductor always rode with the driver and sometimes went from one end of the district to the other without sleep or rest. He had absolute charge of the mail, express matters, passengers, and equipment until he delivered them to the next conductor and took his receipt. When a coach was within two or three miles of a scheduled stop, the conductor sounded a bugle to announce its arrival and warn the station keeper and his helpers to go into action.

An agent and four or five assistants managed each of the 200 stations along the 2,800-mile route. They cared for the stock, changed relays, and prepared meals for the weary travelers. There were three types of stops, the most important of which was the "terminal station" such as Fort Smith, El Paso, Tucson, and Yuma. Here the Overland Mail stage made connections with one or more trunk or feeder lines. Sometimes the passengers could obtain a few hours sleep or even stay for a day or two before catching a subsequent stage.

For the "home station," like most of those in Missouri, Arkansas, northern Texas, and Indian Territory, a farmhouse usually served; here a quick meal of beans, beef, hoecake, onions, and what passed for coffee cost one dollar. Fortunate customers could sometimes obtain fresh milk, butter, and vegetables. And there are frequent references to a strange and mysterious concoction known as slumgullion. Mark Twain encountered this drink on the Overland line after it shifted from the Southwest to the South Pass route. "It really pretended to be tea," he wrote, "but there was too much dish-rag and sand, and old bacon-rind in it to deceive the intelligent traveler." [9]

The third and most common type of stop was the "swing station," a ten-minute stop for a new relay of horses or mules. These

---

[9] Samuel L. Clemens: *Roughing It* (New York: Harper & Brothers; 1871), I, 43.

X · Coaches and Camels

way-stations were maintained by no more than one or two people, who had to be on constant guard against marauding Indians. The latter were mostly interested in capturing the livestock, for they quickly discovered that the quality of the company's bacon and flour was not worth the effort.

In March 1861, just before the outbreak of the Civil War, the great days of the Butterfield Stage ended in the Southwest and the line was shifted north to the central route through South Pass and Salt Lake City. John Butterfield sold his interest in the enterprise to the more colorful Ben Holliday, who operated it for six years before releasing control to the Wells-Fargo syndicate.

In spite of earlier predictions by Northern detractors, the Butterfield Overland Mail proved a conspicuous success. The mails arrived on schedule, and all sections of the country were fused by the efficient operation of the durable coaches and employees. In 1860 the line carried more mail than went by sea, and after almost three years of operation the company earned approximately $100,000. In addition, several times that amount in passenger fees was collected.[1] And many new towns had been brought into existence, while others had been inadvertently saved from extinction.

Even though the Overland Mail operated briefly across the vast expanse of the Southwest, its activities constitute the greatest single chapter in the development of communication and transportation in this region before the Civil War. John Butterfield's work climaxed a generation of labor by explorers, mountain men, traders, forty-niners, freighters, and government surveyors and helped erase the label "terra incognita," long fixed on the Southwest.

EVEN MORE COLORFUL than the Overland Mail was another operation that took place at the same time: the experiment with

---

[1] Rupert N. Richardson: "Some Details of the Southwestern Overland Mail," *Southwestern Historical Quarterly*, Vol. XXIX (1925), pp. 6–8, 15.

camels. The idea of using these foreign animals as beasts of burden in America was an old one. Camels were tried in Virginia as early as 1701, the results proved far from satisfactory. Another century and a half elapsed before much thought was again given to the matter, for, in the public mind, camels were associated with arid and desert regions. But in 1850 the United States possessed such regions in large quantities, and it was natural, therefore, that the subject of camels should arise again as various plans for transportation in the Southwest were considered.

Several individuals became interested in the question about the same time, one of whom was George R. Glidden, an archaeologist who had lived in the Levant for twenty-eight years. In 1852 he wrote a lengthy essay pointing out that camels were superior to mules as beasts of burden in almost every way: they could transport heavier loads, cover more distance, subsist on less food, and go without water as long as four or five days. Such qualities should make them ideal for use in the Southwest.

During the same year, John Russell Bartlett returned to the East from his "misadventures" in the Southwest as director of the Mexican boundary survey. Bartlett's experience had convinced him of the feasibility of using camels for communication, transportation, and, particularly, for military purposes. The Secretary of War and the Senate Committee on Military Affairs took notice of these writings, and Jefferson Davis in his report to Congress early in 1853 suggested that camels might supply the remote forts scattered from Texas to California.

The Secretary argued that vast stretches of the Southwest would always remain isolated, even after construction of a transcontinental railroad. And he believed that the camel would give the military services more mobility, carry heavier expresses, make longer reconnaissances, and move troops and equipment across country. Congress appropriated $30,000 in 1855 for an experiment that modern historians refer to as "Operation Camel."

Major Henry C. Wayne was selected to initiate the project, and he proceeded at once to the Levant to purchase the necessary animals. Wayne's associate was Naval Lieutenant David D. Porter,

X · *Coaches and Camels*

later the celebrated Admiral Porter of the Civil War. This young naval officer took command of the *Supply*, a small steamship specially equipped to transport thirty or forty camels from the Middle East to a port on the Texas coast.

The expedition spent several months visiting various cities in the eastern Mediterranean and the Black Sea area. On February 15, 1856, it set sail from Smyrna with a complement of thirty-three camels, most of which were of the one-hump variety. The Atlantic voyage of almost three months resulted in the death of one of the adult animals and four calves, but six calves were born en route. When the thirty-four strange creatures were put ashore at Indianola, Texas, in May 1856, they created almost as much excitement as did the hurricane that destroyed the town a generation later.

While the *Supply* turned back to procure another herd, Major Wayne busied himself with learning more about his charges and preparing them for the overland trip to be made as soon as they could recuperate from the voyage. Wayne eventually selected a site for a permanent station at Camp Verde, eighty miles northwest of San Antonio, and consumed months in building living quarters for the men and stables and corrals for the camels.

Meanwhile, he conducted excursions between San Antonio and Camp Verde, using both camels and mules to haul supplies and equipment. For the first of these short journeys, in early September 1856, Wayne loaded each of six camels with approximately 600 pounds of oats, and two wagons with 3,600 pounds of supplies. The vehicles were pulled by six mules; thus a fair comparison between the American and foreign animals could be made. This test, like several others conducted during subsequent weeks, proved the camels far superior to the mules. The long-gaited creatures from the Middle East made the journey in two days, while the mules took more than four.

Wayne was now ready to test the camels in the desert country of the Southwest, but before a large-scale operation could be launched, the Major was transferred to Washington. John B. Floyd, who replaced Jefferson Davis as Secretary of War on

THE SOUTHWEST: *Old and New*

March 4, 1857, did not share his predecessor's enthusiasm for the camel experiment; nevertheless, he let it continue. Captain I. N. Palmer was put in charge of the corps and remained as commander of Camp Verde until its capture by the Confederates early in the Civil War.

Meanwhile, a naval officer, Lieutenant Edward Fitzgerald Beale, navigated a "flotilla" of twenty-five pack camels from Texas to California. Beale, a trail blazer of the Southwest, was selected in the spring of 1857 to survey a wagon road from Fort Defiance to the Colorado River,[2] and the project seemed ideal for the utilization of camels. Beale approached the assignment with considerable excitement, for he had followed the details of "Operation Camel" from its conception.

On June 25, 1857, the surveying party of Army engineers and their helpers left San Antonio for New Mexico. A train of several mule-drawn wagons and twenty-one camels brought from nearby Camp Verde carried supplies and equipment for a 2,000-mile journey. To Beale's utter disappointment and the complete disgust of the handlers, the camels lagged behind the caravan for the first few hundred miles. However, as soon as they became inured to the trail and fell in stride, the foreign animals actually throve on the mesquite bushes and thorny shrubs. "They are exceedingly docile, easily managed, and I see, so far, no reason to doubt the success of the experiment," Beale wrote to Secretary Floyd from Uvalde, Texas.[3]

The caravan pushed deeper into the barren region of southwestern Texas and across the heart of the Apache and Comanche country. After a brief rest at Fort Davis it moved on to El Paso. By now the camels were withstanding the many hardships "without the slightest distress or soreness." In places the road was covered with a fine, sharp, angular, flinty gravel that could not be crossed by the dogs that accompanied the expedition. But the ability of the camels to carry their 600-pound loads over this gravel, endure the

---

[2] See footnote 2, p. 34.
[3] House Executive Document No. 124, 35th Congress, 1st Session.

X · Coaches and Camels

torrid heat, and subsist without water and food for long periods captured the admiration of the entire party.

Beale and his fellows reached El Paso toward the end of July and were escorted through the streets by the "entire population," which doubtless thought that a circus had come to town. At nearby Fort Bliss they rested for several days before moving north to Albuquerque. At all the settlements along the Rio Grande, people could not at first believe what they saw; then they imagined that the strange caravan must be a circus, and expressed loud disappointment when a performance was not forthcoming.

In mid-August 1857 the expedition moved out of Albuquerque and took the 35th-parallel route surveyed by Lieutenant Whipple. As it passed the famous Inscription Rock (El Moro), some of the men paused long enough to carve their names near those of Spanish explorers, American explorers, and cowboys. The old pueblo of the Zuñi Indians which Coronado had visited three centuries before lay just a short distance away. But much of the journey passed among landmarks whose names, if any, were known only to the Indians. Almost every mile of what is today northern Arizona offered new challenges for the camels, which met them all with magnificent endurance.

Four months after leaving San Antonio the Beale party crossed the Colorado River and by October 26 it was en route to Los Angeles. "Without the aid of this noble and useful brute," the commander wrote to the Secretary of War, "many hardships which we have been spared would have fallen our lot. . . . I have subjected them to trails which no other animals could possibly endure. . . . They have been used on every reconnaisance [sic] whilst the mules were resting, and have gone down precipitous sides of rough volcanic mesas, which mules would not descend . . . they are perfectly content to eat anything, from the driest greasewood bush to a thorny prickly pear, and what is better, keep fat on it." [4]

---

[4] Beale to the Secretary of War, October 18, 1857. *Senate Executive Document*, 35th Congress, 1st Session (Serial No. 929), Document No. 43, pp. 3–4.

The Southwest: *Old and New*

The success of "Operation Camel" left little doubt that the use of camels in the Southwest offered a partial solution to the vexing problem of transportation. "The entire adaption of camels to military operation on the plains may now be taken as demonstrated," Secretary Floyd wrote in his report to Congress in December 1858. At the same time he requested funds for the purchase of a thousand additional animals, but Congress was either uninterested or else too involved with more pressing matters. The outbreak of the Civil War brought the official experiment to a close.

Meanwhile, the camels continued to be used in the Southwest. Other major reconnaissances were conducted from Camp Verde before 1861, with completely satisfactory results. The herd that Beale took to California never returned to Texas, however. Instead he quartered it at his own ranch near Fort Tejon and then turned it over to the Army for local transportation. Shortly before the outbreak of war the camels were sent to Los Angeles and sold at public auction. Most of them finally arrived in Nevada to carry salt to the silver mines, but the new owners were inexperienced in handling the sometimes recalcitrant beasts and eventually turned them loose on the desert of southern Arizona. Wandering tribes of Indians gradually killed the strange creatures, for food or for mere sport.

When the Confederates occupied Camp Verde during the early part of the war, what was left of the main herd of Army camels remained, but no use of them has been reported. And when the United States troops returned to the station in 1865, they showed little interest in the camels. Some were sold at public auction for express work between Laredo and Mexico City—a venture that soon failed—or to circuses. Some were abandoned on the desert. One or two of the stray beasts were seen in the Southwest as late as 1900.

Thus a unique experiment passed into history. Given a fair trial and succeeding in every test, camels never became an important adjunct to Southwestern transportation. Even without the Civil War, the railroads would have dealt them the same blow that

X · *Coaches and Camels*

inexorably came to the lumbering freight wagons and elegant stagecoaches.

THE AGE of the railroad was upon the West before the end of 1862, but another decade passed before the Southwest felt the full impact of interstate construction. By 1872 the Missouri, Kansas, and Texas Railroad had extended its tracks from Topeka across Indian Territory to Red River. There, on the Texas side, it joined the Houston and Texas Central Railroad to give the Southwest a through connection from the Gulf Coast to St. Louis. By the end of another decade the Santa Fe, Texas and Pacific and the Southern Pacific had tied the principal cities of the region together and given them access to all sections of the United States.

This network of railroads brought thousands of emigrants to the Southwest, hastened economic expansion, and developed great inland cities. Today such places as Dallas, Fort Worth, San Antonio, Phoenix, Tucson, El Paso, and Oklahoma City rank among America's largest metropolitan centers not on a navigable stream or coast. The freight wagons, camels, and coaches had developed primary patterns of local commerce and travel. But it was the railroads and, later, the airlines which ended the region's isolation.

XI
THE SOUTHWEST AND THE CIVIL WAR

NOT EVEN SUCH an embryonic section of the country as the Southwest escaped the impact of the Civil War. Thanks to its geographic location, it experienced few battles within its borders, and none comparable to the great slaughters on the Atlantic Coast, in the trans-Appalachian West, or in the Mississippi Valley. No grandiose strategy was drawn up in Washington for its conquest, no "anaconda plan" to capture its key cities, lay waste its countryside, and extinguish its way of life. Indeed, except for a few feeble thrusts at Texas and Indian Territory, the Union

XI · The Southwest and the Civil War

seemed little concerned with the Southwestern region of the United States between 1861 and 1865.

No common interests or unified purpose bound this region together, and it never thought of itself as a single area. Texas was tied to the South by bonds of slavery and by the fact that many of its people had migrated from there, but the memory of its independence as a republic remained fresh. And the Indians in present-day Oklahoma who had formerly lived within the borders of the "Deep South," even though many were slaveholders, could not be expected to entertain strong sympathies for their former neighbors, for those same Southerners had only recently harried them from their homes and lands. The Spanish-American settlers and Indians of remote New Mexico and Arizona had never had any contact with the Civilized Tribes of the extreme northeastern part of the region; and their traditional hatred of Texans was an obsession. And within New Mexico territory the people residing in the western half felt that they had little in common with those along the upper Rio Grande Valley; their chief concern at the time the war started was the organization of their own territorial government.

Before either North or South could succeed in controlling the Southwest, there were Indian problems to be faced. Among the Nation Indians of eastern Oklahoma, for example, the old pre-removal schisms were still far from healed. And the wild tribes that roamed the unsettled plains and desert regions of the Southwest were distrusted and feared by all; these nomadic peoples subsisted by hunting and raiding, paying deference to no one, and they considered it their natural right to prey upon white settlers, travelers, and peaceful Indians.

In Texas, support of the Southern cause was far from unanimous. At least one third of the 420,000 white settlers living west of the Sabine River opposed secession, and their spokesman was no less a giant than the venerable Sam Houston. In 1859 the old hero of San Jacinto resigned from the Senate of the United States to campaign for the governorship in an attempt to hold Texas in the Union. He won the election, but the diehard secessionists eventually forced him from office and carried the state into the Confederacy.

The dilemma of the Southwest in 1861 was further complicated by the fact that neighboring states and territories had extreme views. Louisiana and Arkansas on the eastern frontier joined the Confederacy without hesitation. After a slight wavering the border state of Missouri cast its lot with the North, while the Territory of Kansas was so strongly pro-Union that its loyalty was rewarded with statehood. And when a Confederate flag was run up on a Denver building on April 24, 1861, an angry mob quickly tore it down. The pro-slavery men of Colorado realized at once that they were in a minority. By the time Colorado's first territorial government was organized one month later all efforts toward Southern collaboration had vanished.

Just beyond the Colorado region lay the Mormon stronghold of Utah Territory. At first the "Desert Saints" appeared to take no interest in the sectional conflict. But they had not forgotten that the Republicans in the political campaign of 1856 had proclaimed that "polygamy and slavery remain the twin relics of barbarism." Also, the so-called "Mormon War of 1857" had created resentment toward the United States. Nevertheless, Utah entertained little sympathy for the South, and it remained loyal to the Union.

Nevada and northern California likewise turned their backs on the Confederacy, certainly no great surprise since most of their people had Northern origins. California in 1860 boasted a white population of more than 300,000, and eventually it contributed many volunteers to the Eastern campaigns. In addition, it equipped a column of troops in 1862 which routed the Confederates from western New Mexico Territory. Nevada, too thinly populated to be of much concern to either side, displayed so much enthusiasm for the North during the war that it, too, was rewarded with statehood by Congress.

Thus, the Southwest, surrounded by rabid and divergent views, split internally over the questions of slavery and secession, and removed from the centers of Southern and Northern fanaticism, naturally displayed confused and contradictory attitudes to-

XI · *The Southwest and the Civil War*

ward the war. Of the several engagements eventually fought within its present borders, most were local affairs—wars within wars, like those in Kansas and Missouri. In the end only Texas and part of the Five Civilized Tribes continued in the Confederate fold, while the present states of New Mexico and Arizona remained with the Union.

TEXAS'S ROLE in the Civil War far overshadowed that of the remainder of the region because more than three fourths of the Southwestern people were citizens of the former republic. The state constitution protected slavery, and most Texas leaders adhered to the principles of the states'-rights faction of the Old South, although a large segment of the population in 1860 had no direct interest in slavery. Most of the Negroes lived in the southeast, where the larger plantations flourished. The western half of the state was not settled, while the counties extending from north to south through the center of Texas were still thinly populated. Settlers scattered through the northeastern part of the state had come chiefly from Tennessee, Kentucky, and the Old Northwest and resided on relatively small farms. Of the state's substantial German population, some held a few slaves, but generally these recently arrived immigrants looked on the institution as even worse than serfdom, with which they were all too familiar.

Naturally the few Texas planters who had a vested interest in slavery were strongly vocal in its behalf, and as the "irrepressible conflict" drew closer their cause gained more support. Excitement reached a climax during the summer of 1859 with the election of sixty-six-year-old Sam Houston to the governorship. As Houston's views on secession were never in doubt, his victory was regarded by some as a final repudiation of the radicals. However, it proved to be no more than a tribute to his personal popularity.

The extreme "states'-righters" had lost a battle but not a campaign. John Brown's raid on Harper's Ferry gave them renewed determination. They were further strengthened when the 1860 Democratic National Convention ended in a deadlock. The Southern wing of the Democratic Party subsequently nominated John C. Breckinridge and adopted a strong states'-rights and pro-slavery platform. In spite of Houston's active opposition, Breckinridge later carried Texas as well as the rest of the "Deep South." This development and the election of Lincoln demoralized the conservatives and elated the radicals, who now demanded that the Governor call a secession convention. He refused, but the convention met anyway late in January 1861, in Austin, after six Southern states had already withdrawn from the Union.

Although some counties neglected to send representatives and Houston would not acknowledge the convention's legality, the delegates voted 168 to 8 in favor of separation. The question was put before the people for a final decision. Three weeks later they approved the action of the convention by a vote of three to one.[1]

Events unrelated to the slavery question had helped fan the flames of hysteria. The so-called "Cortina War," an outbreak of raids by Mexican banditti along the Texas border late in 1859, had aroused the people of the state and brought demands for systematic retaliation. Also, the Comanches on the western plains were conducting unrestricted raids against frontier settlers, killing and looting almost at will. These disturbances could scarcely be blamed on the federal government, yet they did not promote calm and judicial judgment on other problems at the moment.

Once Texas was a member in good standing of the Confederacy, it was in no mood to tolerate Old Sam's gloomy warnings about the consequences of a civil war. His refusal to take the oath of allegiance to the new government gave him no alternative but to retire to private life on March 18, 1861. Lieutenant Governor Edward Clark assumed the duties of the office of governor. Houston did not live to see the end of the war, but before his death a few weeks after the Battle of Gettysburg in July 1863, the truth of his

---

[1] Texas was the only state to submit the question of secession to a popular vote. The count was 46,129 to 14,697.

XI · *The Southwest and the Civil War*

prophecy that "the North will overwhelm the South" was all too evident.

AT THE TIME that Texas voted to secede from the Union some 2,700 federal troops were stationed at various posts within the state, all under the command of General D. E. Twiggs, a Georgian with strong Southern sympathies. A self-appointed "Committee of Public Safety" called on the General and demanded that he surrender all men and supplies. Twiggs was reluctant to violate his trust as an officer until an excuse could be found in some "show of force," and the Texans were quick to oblige him. Colonel Ben McCulloch rushed to San Antonio, Twiggs's headquarters, with approximately 300 state militia and took possession of the Alamo Plaza. Here, on February 17, he accepted on behalf of the Confederacy the surrender of all federal posts, supplies, and troops on Texas soil.[2] Soldiers who wished to return to their native states were permitted to do so, and the others were encouraged to join the Rebels. Twiggs's surrender resulted in a dishonorable discharge from the United States Army, but he quickly obtained a high rank in the Confederate Army.[3] McCulloch, incidentally, was destined to die a Confederate general at the Battle of Pea Ridge.

The over-all strategy of the Civil War obviously dictated that the principal areas of fighting would be east of the Appalachian and Allegheny mountains, with each side desperately seeking to capture the other's capital. Texas, therefore, felt relatively secure in 1861 from a Northern invasion and consequently could think primarily in terms of offensive maneuvering. Its geographic loca-

---

[2] The total value of military properties has been estimated at $1,500,000.
[3] Although Twiggs was charged with "treason to the flag of his country," he was not completely at fault. Weeks before his surrender he had appealed to his superiors in Washington for advice as to what he should do if Texas seceded. His dispatches went unanswered.

tion would enable the state to be of inestimable service in seizing and holding the entire Southwestern area of the United States for the Confederacy, which the Southern high command was quick to see. The vast New Mexico Territory loomed all-important, not only for future expansion of the Confederacy but also as a link with California. This former Spanish province on the Pacific possessed a large population, valuable seaports, and much-needed gold. If these were captured for the Confederacy, perhaps the northern states of Mexico could then be annexed as a step toward ultimate control of Central America.

The conquest of New Mexico was an assignment that the sons of the Lone Star State eagerly welcomed as a chance to avenge several decades of frustration. The "ungrateful" New Mexicans had spurned all offers to join the Republic of Texas, but in 1841 they had captured and cruelly mistreated the members of the "peaceful" Santa Fe trade mission. Furthermore, New Mexicans encouraged the Comanche traders, or *Comacheros*, to prey upon Texas settlements and carry off cattle, horses, and prisoners of war.[4] The hated *Comacheros* in turn enjoyed free intercourse with New Mexican merchants at Taos and Santa Fe.

When war was officially declared, conditions along the upper Rio Grande seemed more than favorable for an easy occupation of the former Mexican province. The government in Washington had always maintained a vacillating attitude toward the army in New Mexico; since 1848 federal troops had rarely exceeded 1,200, and not only were they inadequately supplied, but also their pay was usually several months in arrears. Furthermore, the local civilians were not excited about the issues that divided North and South. Some owned Negro slaves, and the archaic institution of peonage, in existence since the days of the Spanish conquest was little different from outright bondage. In addition, most of the Anglo-Americans residing in the territory had Southern backgrounds and prejudices, another fact which indicated that invasion of New Mexico would be a mere formality.

---

[4] The *Comacheros* did not necessarily engage in the raids themselves, but they eagerly bought the stolen goods from the Indians who did.

XI · The Southwest and the Civil War

Several weeks before the first Confederate forces departed from San Antonio to occupy New Mexico Territory still other developments combined to make their task easier. The colonel commanding the Military Department of New Mexico, a North Carolinian named W. W. Loring, joined the Confederacy. A short time later Major H. H. Sibley also accepted a commission in the Confederate Army, as did a third prominent officer, Alexander M. Jackson. The new commander, Colonel E. R. S. Canby, could obtain no instructions from Washington relative to the well-advertised invasion from Texas, while the continuing stream of resignations from some of his best officers and men complicated the problem of maintaining discipline and morale.

In the summer of 1861 Confederate Colonel John R. Baylor and a force of mounted rifles arrived from San Antonio without incident and occupied the former federal post of Fort Bliss near El Paso. Before the end of July he moved across the state line to the north and took possession of the small settlement of Mesilla. Again there was no opposition, for most of the Anglo-Americans residing in the area were former Texans. A short distance away, however, stood the federal garrison of Fort Fillmore, which was occupied by more than 400 troops. Its commander, Major Isaac Lynde, quickly advanced against the Confederates.

According to one account, the Federals first "captured" a saloon and "rescued" a substantial quantity of *tequila*. When they encountered the thirsty Texans a little later they were in poor condition to fight, and their subsequent retreat was said to be well marked by "dead soldiers"—empty bottles.[5] Lynde's entire force of men and officers, along with the depleted liquor supply, was captured. This left the road to Albuquerque and Santa Fe unprotected.

Colonel Baylor now proclaimed himself Governor and Mesilla the capital of the "Confederate Territory of Arizona." The bound-

---

[5] This anecdote is related by Paul Wellman in his narrative history of the Southwest, *Glory, God, and Gold* (Garden City: Doubleday and Company; 1954), p. 308. Wellman's writings are more colorful than exact; he does not vouch for the authenticity of the above account of the battle.

THE SOUTHWEST: *Old and New*

aries of his embryonic empire extended as far west as Tucson and included all of that portion of New Mexico lying south of the 34th parallel. The first land conquest by the Confederacy had been gained with a minimum of effort. The occupation of the remainder of New Mexico and all of California only awaited the arrival of additional forces that were being assembled by General H. H. Sibley at San Antonio.

This veteran of the Seminole Indian Wars and former commander of the New Mexico District did not depart for New Mexico until November 1861. His Confederates, many of whom were hard-bitten Texas Rangers with considerable experience in Indian campaigns, consisted of one brigade of two and one half regiments—approximately 1,750 men. They reached Baylor's headquarters at Mesilla in one month and began preparation to advance up the Rio Grande. But for various reasons the Rebels suffered painful delays, and the Federals had ample time to fortify Fort Craig, located farther north at Valverde on the west side of the Rio Grande.

Colonel Canby, Sibley's former comrade-in-arms, performed a near-miracle by augmenting a regular force of approximately 1,000 Federal troops with 3,000 militia volunteers. The great majority of these were peons with a mixture of Spanish and Indian blood. "Place no reliance on [them] . . . except for partisan operation," the Colonel warned his subordinates. The advice was sound, but at least the New Mexicans came forward to defend their territory. Perhaps their actions were not so much the result of loyalty to the Union as the fact that their homes were threatened by *Tejanos*.

As General Sibley and his Confederates approached Fort Craig, Canby waited just north of the Jornado del Muerto on the east bank of the Rio Grande. To reach the fort the Confederates must cross either at Pandero, seven miles below Fort Craig, or at Valverde, ten miles farther north. The latter crossing was the better of the two, and Canby concentrated the major portion of his defense there, expecting that Sibley would choose it. He guessed correctly. When an advance guard of Texas Rangers

XI · The Southwest and the Civil War

arrived at the Valverde crossing, a party of Federals was protecting the approach. A brief skirmish followed, and then both forces dug in for the night.

The main Confederate army extracted itself from the Jornado del Muerto the next day, February 21, 1862, but for the moment they showed little interest in capturing Fort Craig. Control of the crossing and replenishment of their water supply were their foremost objectives, but the Federals showered the thirsty Rebels with grape, canister, and musket balls. Both sides began to maneuver for position, and for the next few hours the fighting was desperate: the Texas cavalry charged the artillery like mad demons, "relying principally upon revolvers and bowie knives." Soon the defenders fell back, but the enemy troops were so busy quenching the fires in their throats that they did not pursue beyond the muddy waters of the river. The Confederate victory was decisive, even though the Federal losses were comparatively slight.[6]

After Sibley had rested his men and horses for a few days, he pushed north toward Albuquerque and Santa Fe, leaving Canby and his slightly battered troops still in possession of Fort Craig. The move was a dangerous one, but northern New Mexico lay undefended and the chances for its immediate conquest more than offset the risks of an enemy left in the rear.

Quickly Albuquerque and Santa Fe fell into Confederate hands. Sibley now learned of a concentration of Federal troops at Fort Union on the old Santa Fe Trail some ninety miles northeast of the New Mexican capital. Rumor said the fort contained food and equipment valued at more than $300,000, which the Federals were prepared to destroy as an alternative to letting them fall into enemy hands. Sibley needed supplies desperately and he knew that he must march to Fort Union by the shortest possible route. The principal danger to such a venture was the possibility of

---

[6] The rear guard of the Federals and the advance guard of the Confederates carried on most of the fighting at Valverde. There are many conflicting reports as to the number of men lost on both sides. Bancroft states that the Texans had approximately ninety killed and one hundred wounded, with the Federal losses slightly less.

ambush at nearby Apache Canyon, but the Confederates hoped they could leave before their plans were known. Once they were beyond the pass, they might be able to surprise the undermanned garrison at Fort Union before it could set the torch to the supplies.

Meanwhile, news of the invasion of New Mexico by Confederate troops from Texas had reached Colorado before the end of 1861. The governor of the newly created Territory of Colorado became genuinely alarmed and issued a call for volunteers. On February 22, 1862 an undisciplined crew of grizzly miners who called themselves the "Pikes Peakers" marched southward from Denver to defend New Mexico. They learned en route of the Confederate victory at Valverde, and that Fort Union was in danger of falling into the hands of the enemy. The principal officers in charge of the rescue expedition were Colonel J. P. Slough, Lieutenant Colonel S. F. Tappan, and Major J. M. Chivington. The last, a Bible-quoting Methodist minister, would win most of the laurels of the campaign, but his chief and lasting claim to "fame" would rest on the Sand Creek Massacre of the peaceful Cheyenne Indians in southeastern Colorado in 1864.

The nondescript, quarrelsome, and mutinous "Pikes Peakers" resembled anything but an army, but one great cohesive force bound them together—they hated all Texans. Their slight training was received during the trek to Fort Union, the last 172 miles of which were covered in five days. On March 22, 1862 they started toward Santa Fe, only to meet the Confederates unexpectedly at Apache Canyon.

Each force contained approximately 1,300 men. Considering the intensive fighting that quickly developed for control of the mountain pass, the casualties were not excessive: some 100 Confederates killed and Federal losses about the same. Each side subsequently claimed a victory, but the Texans withdrew first and thus furnished the Coloradans with considerable ammunition for future boasting. The skirmish, which is known as the Battle of Glorieta Pass, gathered momentous importance to the local citizens as time elapsed. Even today some avid Westerners refer

XI · *The Southwest and the Civil War*

to it as the "Gettysburg of the West" and proclaim it the most significant engagement ever fought west of the Mississippi. Most Texas historians, however, either do not mention Glorieta Pass in their writings or treat it with indifference.[7]

One fact is certain, however. The failure of the Confederates to attack Fort Union turned the tide overwhelmingly for the Northern cause and made the Confederate position in New Mexico extremely difficult to maintain. As Sibley retreated to Santa Fe, the Federals reinforced Fort Union. From here they dispatched harassing parties that captured Confederate supply trains and made life miserable for Rebels discovered outside the occupied towns. And soon Canby came to life in the southern part of the territory and threatened to recapture Albuquerque. The Confederates were cut off from their wagon trains bringing supplies from Texas, and the natives destroyed livestock and crops rather than let the Rebels confiscate them.

Other events developed which combined to doom the Confederate cause in this portion of the Southwest. While Sibley's forces occupied Albuquerque and Santa Fe and prepared to march on to Fort Union, Captain Sherod Hunter and a few hundred Texans were crossing the Mesilla Valley toward Tucson. They arrived there in February 1862, about the same time that the Colorado volunteers entered northern New Mexico. Occupying Tucson proved a simple matter, as all of the pro-Union men had fled southward to Sonora or westward to California. Thus, Hunter could settle in southern Arizona with supreme confidence that he would soon capture California with equal ease. But first he sent a small company of men westward to reconnoiter the country.

At Yuma the scouting party learned that a California column of 1,800 volunteers under Colonel James H. Carleton was poised to cross into Arizona and advance eastward via the Gila River to annihilate the Confederates. Quickly the Texans retreated across the torrid desert that they had so recently traversed, stopping

---

[7] See Rupert Norval Richardson and Carl Coke Rister: *The Greater Southwest* (Glendale: Arthur H. Clark; 1935), p. 267.

The Southwest: *Old and New*

long enough in Tucson to warn their commanding officer. Hunter lost no time in abandoning his position. Not only was he greatly outnumbered by the approaching Californians, but his occupation of Tucson had aroused the Apaches in the area.

The Texans retreated in fairly good shape before the advance guard of the pursuing Californians. A few insignificant skirmishes occurred, but by May 1862 they were encamped on the Rio Grande. The Arizona Apaches, in the meantime, had turned their attention to the Californians and kept them so busy that they could not enter New Mexico until the following August. Carleton eventually pursued the Rebels across the Texas line as far east as Fort Davis before he halted. His action brought about the Confederate abandonment of New Mexico. General Sibley returned to Texas with less than half of his original force, and most of his wagons, equipment, and supplies were captured, destroyed, or abandoned en route.

A short time after the exodus of the Texans, the New Mexican legislature at Santa Fe passed a resolution thanking "the brave California and Colorado troops for their timely aid in driving the traitors and rebels from our soil." Most of the honors belonged to the "hard-rock boys" under Colonel Chivington's command who had so systematically destroyed the enemy's supplies and wagons. When they returned to their homes early in 1863, they and the other Coloradans were received as conquering heroes. Some later rendered additional aid to the Union cause when they helped defeat a Confederate force estimated at 6,000 in Indian Territory.[8]

THE EXCITEMENT in New Mexico had just begun. In September 1862 the former commander of the California Column, Colonel Carleton, replaced General Canby as head of the Military Depart-

---

[8] This was the Battle of Honey Springs in mid-July 1863.

XI · *The Southwest and the Civil War*

ment. Carleton soon discovered that he had inherited a problem as serious as the one just eliminated: the wild Indians.

Most of the Territory of New Mexico remained under the domination of the Apaches, the Navajos, and some scattered untamed tribes. The exceptions, of course, were the few population centers along the banks of the principal rivers, including the Rio Grande and the Gila. During the Confederate invasion the non-Pueblo Indians of the arid deserts and basins had taken advantage of the turmoil to resume their age-old habit of plundering and murdering. Commander Carleton soon retaliated with all the force he was able to muster, boldly proclaiming his determination to kill every Apache man and imprison all members of the other wild tribes who could be found. For the next two years his troops carried on a relentless war until various Apache bands were brought under control—at least temporarily.

Meanwhile, Colonel Kit Carson marched against the Navajos. These Indians in the northern portion of the territory renewed their raids against the Pueblos at about the same time that the Apaches took the warpath in the south. Carson, now well past the prime of life, was the ideal man for the assignment against the Navajos, for he had spent most of his life in the region and knew the natives as few white men did. He was aware that the entire tribe wintered in the sacred Canyon de Chelly, a long, narrow, deep valley a few miles northeast of Fort Defiance. The canyon, where ancient cliff dwellers had once lived, could offer little protection against a surprise attack and modern weapons. With approximately 400 militia the former mountain man left Fort Defiance in January 1864 and reached the vicinity of the Navajo camp a few days later. Heavy snow blanketed the narrow valley hidden between the spectacular cliffs of the canyon. While some of the troops remained on the rim, others slipped down one end of the valley and caught the occupants by surprise. Then the soldiers moved forward, systematically destroying all livestock and food supplies that could be found. Several dozen warriors were killed and more than 200 women and children were captured within the first few minutes of fighting. The hapless Indians surrendered when they discovered that their escape was cut off by the troops along the rim of the canyon and that all their women, children, and property would surely be destroyed.

The terms of peace were explicit. The Navajos must forfeit all their lands and goods and be confined to a reservation as wards of the federal government. Eventually some 7,000 Indians were rounded up and moved to Bosque Redondo on the Pecos River in eastern New Mexico.[9] Here they remained until 1868, at which time they returned to their present reservation in Arizona. Their defeat by the New Mexican militia in 1864 and the four years of imprisonment which followed seem to have transformed them from a warlike to a docile people.

The Apaches did not surrender so easily or survive so well. Even though Carleton established formal peace with them in 1864, attacks and counterattacks continued, with the Apaches taking a life for each one given. White soldiers and civilians who ventured into their country did so at great risk. Gold seekers were "bushwhacked," stagecoaches and stations burned, and scouting parties ambushed. The war continued until 1885, by which time all the great Apache chiefs from Mangas Coloradas to Geronimo were either killed or imprisoned, while the members of their bands were confined to reservations.

As THE Civil War in the western half of the arid Southwest shifted from a struggle between Confederate and Union forces to a series of bitter clashes between the local militia and the Indians, the remainder of the region also experienced its share of excitement. Texas, of course, was most important to the Confederacy. At about the same time that she sent troops to the West, others prepared to move across Red River and occupy the Indian Na-

---

[9] The Navajos still refer to this event as the "long walk."

XI · *The Southwest and the Civil War*

tions. An alliance with the Five Civilized Tribes, as well as with the various nomadic bands beyond the Cross Timbers, meant the protection of the Southwest against possible invaders from Kansas and Missouri. Furthermore, the Nations were believed to possess enough cattle to feed Southern armies throughout a prolonged war. These factors, plus the possibility of using Indians as scouts and soldiers, prompted Jefferson Davis to appoint Albert Pike, a New Englander with Southern sympathies, to visit present-day Oklahoma in March 1861.

Pike arrived at Fort Smith at the time of a serious division among the red people. The majority preferred to remain neutral in the forthcoming struggle, but they knew this to be impossible. Those who favored the North as the lesser of two evils saw how difficult it would be to defend themselves against their powerful neighbors in Arkansas on the east and Texas on the south. Furthermore, by the time Pike reached Indian Territory, Confederate troops already occupied the former United States military establishments at Forts Smith, Gibson, Towson, Washita, Arbuckle, and Cobb. With Federal troops abandoning the territory, Pike was in an advantageous position to negotiate.

The Confederate agent remained at Fort Smith long enough to confer with Colonel Ben McCulloch, the new commander of the post. Pike then hastened to Tahlequah in advance of McCulloch and a few companies of his troops to meet the principal chief of the Cherokees, John Ross. But several days of discussion failed to persuade the Cherokees to align themselves with the Confederacy. Ross argued that such an action would mean exposure to Union attacks from Missouri and Kansas. Even the presence of McCulloch's troops had little effect on the stubborn chief. Pike then turned toward the south, where he expected a more favorable reception. At North Fork Village, near present-day Eufaula, Oklahoma, he met representatives of the Creeks, Choctaws, and Chickasaws and easily impressed them with dire warnings. In the words of one of the Indian delegates, the Confederate agent "told Indian that the Union people would come and take away property and take away land . . . all be dead . . . no more

U.S. no more Treaty . . . better make Treaty with the South."

The half-breeds believed him, and they convinced the more conservative full-bloods. Treaties were subsequently agreed upon by each of the three tribes represented.[1] Pike promised that the Confederate government would assume all of the obligations and responsibilities formerly assumed by the United States. Furthermore, the Indians were to receive arms and equipment, send delegates to the Confederate Congress, and eventually be incorporated into an Indian state on an equal basis with the other members of the Confederacy.

The Confederate orbit now included all but the Seminoles, Cherokees, and some of the smaller tribes in eastern Oklahoma, such as the Osage, Senecas, Shawnees, and Quapaws. Soon only the Cherokees remained outside, and they began to waver. Ross's rejection of the Confederate overtures meanwhile renewed a schism that had existed among his tribesmen since their removal to Oklahoma. His old enemies now demanded that he either agree to a treaty of alliance or resign as principal chief. The continuous pressure forced Ross to accept the fact that he could no longer maintain a neutral stand. Consequently, on Pike's return to Tahlequah in October 1861 from his visits to the other tribes, the climate in Cherokee country had altered greatly.

Approval by both parties of a treaty similar to those signed by the other tribes enabled the Confederate agent to return to Arkansas a few days later with his mission brought to a successful conclusion. After he presented his report to the Confederate government, Jefferson Davis appointed him a brigadier general and placed him in charge of the new Department of Indian Territory. But subsequent events proved him to be a far more able negotiator than a military leader. Before the end of the war he was removed from office.

---

[1] The Creeks delayed signing a treaty of alliance for several days until some of their principal chiefs returned from a hunting expedition. But this tribe, like the Cherokees, splintered over the question of supporting the Confederacy.

XI · *The Southwest and the Civil War*

When the treaties had been signed, McCulloch authorized the formation of a home guard in each Indian Nation, and the response was fairly enthusiastic. The Cherokees raised two regiments of volunteers, commanded by Colonels John Drew and Stand Watie. Both saw extensive service before the war ended. A regiment of Choctaws and Chickasaws and another of Creeks enlisted, and there were several smaller units from the various tribes. Undoubtedly the withdrawal of Federal troops from the forts in the area had convinced most of the Indians that the South would win the war. Some, however, did not approve the decision to join the Confederates, especially among the Cherokees and Creeks; more volunteers from these two tribes fought with the North than with the South.

The capitulation of John Ross stranded the Union Indians without strong leadership, but they turned immediately to the old Creek chief Opothle Yahola, who never wavered in his allegiance to the federal government. From his home near the confluence of the Deep Fork and North Fork of the Canadian River, he sent secret instructions to all known Union sympathizers to join him in a mass migration to Kansas. Some 7,000 people responded, including large numbers of Creeks, Cherokees, Seminoles, and even a few runaway Negro slaves. The Confederates heard of the Indians' plan and promptly dispatched a force of Texas cavalry and several companies of Indian troops under Douglas H. Cooper to stop the migration—peaceably if possible, forcibly if necessary. When Cooper arrived at the rendezvous point, the refugees had departed with their livestock and household belongings, but he had no difficulty in following the trail of discarded goods, wagon ruts, and the hoof prints of cattle, horses, and swine.

At a place in northeastern Oklahoma called Round Mountain the Confederate forces overtook the caravan, and the first engagement of the Civil War in Indian Territory followed. The date was November 19, 1861, seven months after Fort Sumter. The results were indecisive. The Union Indians continued their retreat and fought off the Confederates a second time on December 9 not far from present-day Tulsa. Neither side could claim a victory. Indeed, many of the Confederate Indians defected to the other side and joined the great exodus.

Cooper fell back toward Arkansas to obtain replacements and additional help, and soon three separate armies converged on the refugees. The day after Christmas, a few miles short of their destination, they were overtaken and almost annihilated. The surviving Indians fled on foot through the darkness in a raging blizzard. Most crossed the Kansas border and eventually arrived at the military camp of General David Hunter, where they received a small measure of relief. Facilities, however, were most inadequate for even the able-bodied, not to mention the sick and dying.

Many of the refugees were veterans of the Indian removals a generation earlier and consequently somewhat inured to hardships. Even so, hundreds of old people and children who crossed the border never recovered from the punishing journey. An Army surgeon who visited the Kansas camp in February 1862 found most of the refugees lying on the ground, helpless from frozen arms and legs. He counted more than a hundred who had already had one or more limbs amputated, and he estimated even more needed similar surgery.

The condition of the Indians continued to worsen until spring, with new refugees arriving in a steady stream to replace those who died. Undoubtedly the Union, hard pressed to supply its armies in the Eastern theaters of war, could give little attention to the plight of its loyal supporters in southern Kansas. Meanwhile, the price the Indians paid for their loyalty mounted with each passing day.

After the emigration, Confederate forces took complete control of Indian Territory, occupying all the military posts. In March 1862 Albert Pike received orders to assemble an army and move eastward into Arkansas to turn back a Union invasion. Among his forces rode the two Cherokee regiments under Stand Watie and John Drew, although he had originally promised them that they would never be forced to fight outside their home territory. The

XI · *The Southwest and the Civil War*

subsequent Battle of Pea Ridge in western Arkansas ended in a disastrous defeat for the South. The Cherokees, with other Southern regiments, were routed and demoralized, but Watie and Drew managed to retreat with most of their battered troops.

The most important battle fought in Indian Territory occurred at Honey Springs in the Creek Nation more than a year after Pea Ridge and approximately two weeks after Gettysburg and Vicksburg. Another defeat for the Confederates, it resulted in their further withdrawal toward the south. Choctaws and Chickasaws, now refugees, experienced the ravages of war as Union forces destroyed their homes, crops, and livestock. Many were eventually driven across Red River into Texas.

Indian Territory was now open to invasion from the north and east. Before the end of 1863 all Confederate white soldiers retreated, leaving their Indian allies to defend themselves against a vengeful enemy. Watie and Drew fought on, even though their troops were ragged, frequently hungry, and never properly armed or supplied. During the remaining months of the war various forces of Confederate and Union Indians continued to skirmish for possession of the red clay hills of Oklahoma, and many lives were lost. Stand Watie, eventually promoted to the rank of brigadier general, raided and harassed the Federals unceasingly, but never drove them back into Kansas.

When the South finally collapsed, the lands of the Five Civilized Tribes resembled parts of Georgia after Sherman's march to the sea. The Oklahoma historian Edwin C. McReynolds summarized the situation in his recent history of the Sooner State: "Probably no portion of the Unites States endured more hardships from civil war than the people of Indian Territory. The flight of the refugees, first Union families to the north and then Confederate families to the south, was a regular feature of the Indian campaigns; and before the fighting ended, a class of lawless raiders sprang up whose interest in the war was the opportunity it offered them to live by violence." [2]

---

[2] Edwin C. McReynolds: *Oklahoma: A History of the Sooner State* (Norman: University of Oklahoma Press; 1954), p. 208.

THE SOUTHWEST: *Old and New*

Immediately after the war the United States government nullified all existing treaties with the Nation Indians as the first step toward punishing those allied with the Confederacy. After much discussion, new treaties with the Nations were signed in 1866. By this time tempers had cooled somewhat and the results were less severe than the Indians had expected. The Civilized Tribes were forced to surrender their western lands as a home for the Plains Indians—the loss of territory represented more than fifty per cent of their original holdings. In addition, they agreed to grant the right-of-way for one north-south and one east-west railroad across their present domain [3] and to free all their slaves.

The Cherokees, Creeks, and Seminoles had owned more than two thirds of the land returned to the federal government. Ironically, these tribes had divided their loyalty almost evenly between the North and South, while the Choctaws and Chickasaws had given united support to the Confederacy. The latter did relinquish their claim to the "Leased District"—now the southwestern corner of Oklahoma—but this was a smaller area than the losses of the Cherokees alone. Furthermore, the suffering of the Choctaws and Chickasaws, although intense, was nothing compared to that of the northern tribes.

WHILE TEXAS contributed greatly to the disruption of other parts of the Southwest, there was little fighting on its own soil during the four years of the Civil War. Its over-all losses likewise were relatively small, for most of its men under arms did not leave the state's borders. A total of three regiments marched to New Mexico, and perhaps no more than 2,000 troops crossed Red River for the campaigns in Indian Territory. Texans who saw action on

---

[3] This paved the way for the eventual construction of the "Katy" and "Frisco" railroads.

XI · *The Southwest and the Civil War*

the Eastern fronts numbered only slightly more than 10,000. Casualties among these, however, were fairly high and included the state's outstanding soldier, General Albert Sidney Johnson, killed at the Battle of Shiloh.

One of the most famous Southwestern organizations, formed in September 1861, became known as Terry's Texas Rangers. It consisted of approximately a thousand men and was first assigned to Johnson's army in Kentucky, but eventually participated in the engagements at Shiloh, Bardstown, Perryville, Murfreesboro, Chickamauga, and Knoxville. When Terry's Rangers surrendered to General W. T. Sherman at Greensboro, North Carolina, late in April 1865, more than two thirds of the original volunteers had been killed. Another Texas outfit was Hood's Brigade in Lee's Army of Northern Virginia. It totaled approximately 4,000 men and participated in more than twenty-four battles, including Eltham's Landing, Gaines' Mill, Second Manassas, Antietam, Chickamauga, Chattanooga, and the Wilderness Campaign. Losses from these engagements amounted to more than 3,000.

For the most part, the remaining 40,000 Texas troops under arms at one time or another protected the several hundred miles of coastline and more than 2,000 miles of frontier from the Rio Grande to the Red. Most of these were merely home-guard militia, while the remainder enlisted as Texas Rangers. The latter campaigned chiefly against various Apache and Comanche bands along the western and northeastern borders, but they also captured large numbers of deserters, a task that proved as great a nuisance as the control of the Indians.

The home guard did a creditable job of defending the long Texas coastline from the mouth of the Rio Grande to the Sabine River. Late in 1862 a Federal force landed on Galveston Island, only to have General John B. Magruder recapture it on January 1, 1863, in an amphibious attack. Nine months later Commodore D. G. Farragut, fresh from his successes on the Mississippi, entered Sabine Pass with four gunboats and 5,000 men. A Texas garrison of only forty-seven men led by Lieutenant Richard Dowling and supported by two small gunboats forced his return. The

The Southwest: *Old and New*

victory was a remarkable feat against overwhelming odds, but the Federals determined to take possession of the coast and extend its blockade to all Confederate ports. Exactly one year after the Union force retreated from Galveston Island, another combined Navy and Army expedition took undisputed possession of Matagorda Island and soon controlled all shipping as far south as Brownsville, or more than one third of the Texas coastline.

The Federals' hold on the lower Gulf Coast was partly broken during the middle of August 1864, when a Texas army under Colonel John S. Ford retook Brownsville. From that date until the end of the war the invaders restricted their blockade activities to the vicinity of Brazos de Santiago.

A fourth Union attempt to cripple Texas was also made in 1864 when a fleet of gunboats and an army under General N. P. Banks proceeded up Red River as far as Mansfield in northwestern Louisiana. This represented almost the last serious threat to the Southwest. A minor exception occurred the same year when a Unionist refugee from Texas, Colonel E. J. Davis, and a party of 200 Texas Federalists tried to conquer the border city of Laredo. State militia gathered in time to thwart Davis's plans.

Lee's surrender at Appomattox ended all hope of Southern victory except in the minds and hearts of a few diehards. Six weeks after Appomattox, on May 13, 1865, Colonel John S. Ford made a futile attempt to prolong the Confederate occupation of Texas when he defeated a Union army of 800 men at Palmito Ranch, twelve miles east of Brownsville. By this time the small Rebel forces stationed at various points throughout the Southwest had dwindled. Some Texas leaders made desperate efforts to hold them intact for a retreat across the Mexican border, but desertions made this impossible. By June 1865 all organized resistance in Texas ceased.

Meanwhile, conditions throughout the region had deteriorated to chaos and confusion. The state was bankrupt. Its towns, countryside, and frontier were at the mercy of bands of carpetbaggers, ruffians, displaced Negroes, and rampaging Indians. In the words of the editor of the *Galveston News:* "We cease to be

XI · The Southwest and the Civil War

free men, and whatever of life, property, and personal security we can now claim are just such as our rulers may grant us, and no more."

MORE THAN ten years elapsed before the excesses of Reconstruction ended in the South, and their effects lingered for several decades. Meanwhile, that portion of the Southwest consisting of Texas and the present state of Oklahoma entered a new era of its colorful history. The Five Civilized Tribes continued to make slow but sure progress toward reclaiming their lands and property, for they knew from experience that little could be gained by dwelling on past misfortunes. The many small tribes that were moved in from the outside and settled on restricted reservations in the central and northeastern regions of Indian Territory as wards of the federal government prepared to accept whatever fate had to offer. But the various wild Indians who were gathered from all parts of the Southern Plains and restricted to reservations in the area west of the Cross Timbers were far from happy. The "white man's road" was not for them, and their refusal to accept it cost them dearly.

To Texas the post-war years brought sudden and dramatic changes. Not until 1870 was it reinstated in the Union, and another five or six years elapsed before it was rid of its Carpetbag regime. But Texas had something that the rest of the nation needed: cattle! And Texans were quick to capitalize on this fact as soon as the fighting ended.

XII

LONGHORNS AND WOOLLIES

No INSTITUTION stamped its mark more indelibly on the American Southwest than that of ranching. Within a span of twenty years following the Civil War it transformed the section's economy, revitalized its energy, reshaped its thinking, and altered the eating habits of the Anglo-Saxon world.

The rapid growth and spread of the livestock industry, especially the raising of cattle, was the result of many factors. These included the increased consumption of beef in preference to pork both here and abroad; the elimination of the Indian danger and the disappearance of the buffalo; the development of the great

XII · Longhorns and Woollies

packing centers and the invention of the refrigerator car; and the settlement of the High Plains and the extension of the railroads. And in southern Texas roamed the large herds upon which the industry could build. Large-scale ranching did not begin with the Civil War, but the war gave this industry the impetus for expansion, as it did to the steel, petroleum, and transportation industries. The boom began in 1865, reached its height about 1885, and then gradually adjusted to an environment that no longer included a frontier.

Cattle and sheep arrived in America with the early English colonists, and it was a poor settler indeed who could not boast of at least one milk cow and three or four sheep. But ranching as a business was first practiced in the New World by Spanish and Mexican cattlemen on the upland plains of northern Mexico and the low grasslands of southern Texas. From the first arrival of the Spanish conquistadors, cattle were part of the scene. In 1521 Gregory de Villalobos brought a tiny seed herd to New Spain, and almost every galleon that dropped anchor at a Spanish port during the next several decades carried animals as well as humans.

Coronado drove large herds, including horses, sheep, hogs, and cattle, into the Southwest during his memorable but fruitless journey in the 1540's. It is not known whether any of these animals remained to become the progenitors of the wild cattle and mustangs that later populated the region: the story is probably untrue, but the legend lives on. Even if Coronado did not introduce livestock permanently to the region, however, others soon did.

In 1598 Juan de Oñate drove cattle and sheep into New Mexico and planted a colony of Spanish settlers, while Father Kino encouraged the industry in southern Arizona a century later. Wherever the Spaniards dedicated missions they introduced livestock, so that the two supplemented each other to become permanent parts of Southwestern culture. When Stephen F. Austin's first Anglo-American colonists reached the Texas coast in 1821, they found the region swarming with more cattle than they had ever seen. The Mexicans developed the methods, tools, and terminology for ranching and the immigrants adopted them all, thus making the transition from farmer to stockman a quick and natural one. The Mexican government distributed 4,500 acres of free land to the new citizen who declared his intention to raise livestock, but only 177 acres if he came for the exclusive purpose of farming. Thus, by the time the Anglo-Saxon pioneers reached the Balcones Fault, ranching was an established institution.

The Texas cowboy appropriated the Mexican *vaquero*'s garb and modified it slightly to his own taste. Every item of wear had a practical use. The broad-brimmed sombrero shielded him from the broiling sun and shaded his eyes from glare; the kerchief could be pulled up over the mouth and nose to keep out choking dust; the leather chaps protected his legs from brambles and brush; the high-heeled, square-pointed boot fitted comfortably into the stirrup; the sharp-pronged spurs served as an accelerator for a quick burst of speed; and the long lasso was essential for roping and branding cattle. To this equipment the Texans later added the six-shooter, which had many uses besides ornamentation. Sometimes it was the only thing that would turn a stampeding herd or settle an argument; but more frequently it was used to kill snakes and coyotes, of one species or another.

From the *vaquero* the cowboy also acquired the language of ranching which he corrupted into his own vernacular: *rancho* became "ranch"; *lazo* was altered to "lasso"; *chaparreras* was shortened to "chaps"; *dar la vuelta* ("to give a turn") was distorted to "dolly welter" or "dally"; and *mesteño* was changed to "mustang." The Saxon also acquired the Latin custom of the round-up, branding, the art of "cutting" a steer from the herd, the skill of throwing a rope.

Cattle that the pioneer settlers found on the flat plains of southern Texas were a Moorish type, wild as deer and stubborn as buffalo. Gradually the settlers crossed their own oxen and milch cows with the native herds to produce a variety of strains. The most common, the so-called "Texas-Mexican," contained splashes of almost every color, mostly dull. These animals were tall and gaunt, with narrow hips, a coarse, thin head, and enormous horns that sometimes reached eight or nine feet from tip to tip. The

XII · Longhorns and Woollies

"Spanish" cattle were smaller and less fierce, while a third breed, the "Long-haired Texans," possessed rounder and fuller bodies, shorter horns, a brownish buffalo color, and extremely long legs. The fourth distinctive type was the "Wild Cattle" found in the interior—thin, brown, mealy-nosed "critters" with blue horns. All were tough, fast, and wiry—perfectly capable of defending themselves against a pack of wolves, subsisting on anything that grew, and surviving the cold "northers" of winter and hot droughts of summer.

Even though Texans discovered everything ready-made for ranching, including plenty of grass, cattle, and land, no market existed for their product. Deer, turkey, fish, ducks, and even bear meat were preferred to beef as long as game remained plentiful. Consequently, for many years cattle remained a source of hides and tallow, worth no more than two or three dollars a head. But by 1842 New Orleans provided a small outlet, and more and more ranchers rounded up their herds and drove them to Galveston for shipment. Later they discovered a small demand for Texas cattle in Cuba. In 1846 the first significant cattle drive occurred when Edward Piper drove a thousand steers from southern Texas to Cincinnati, Ohio.

Other herds were reported sold in the East before the Civil War, and, as already mentioned, several drives were made to California during the gold-rush period. A few of these drovers stopped in New Mexico and Arizona, staked out claims, expanded their herds, and sold their surplus stock to overland immigrants or drove them to San Diego and Los Angeles.

Gradually the demand for beef increased throughout the United States, and ranchers expanded their activities. But obstacles also appeared. Texas cattle carried a fever to which they were immune but domestic stocks were not, and intense opposition from out-of-state farmers developed as they saw their own animals die from contact with a trail herd. Furthermore, the northward drives soon caused an oversupply in the Eastern markets, so that by 1861 the average price of a Texas steer had dropped from twelve to six dollars—below the margin of profit.

The Southwest: *Old and New*

The Civil War brought a temporary halt to the ranching industry in the Southwest. Manpower was withdrawn for the Confederate armies, and cattle were left to their own devices. By 1865 they had multiplied so rapidly that the number in Texas alone was estimated at half a million, most of which were "mavericks" that carried no brand and later became the property of the man with the fastest horse and the longest rope. Meanwhile, Northern soldiers became accustomed to eating beef supplied to the Army by private contractors; and the great meat-packing centers and refrigerator cars soon gave the industry another stimulus.

The war emptied the East of its cattle, and as meat packers such as John Plankinton, P. D. Armour, and G. F. Swift located their stockyards in the railroad center of Chicago, they naturally looked to the Southwest as a source of supply. Word reached Texas, by way of the returning veterans, that cattle were selling for the unheard-of price of thirty to forty dollars a head on the Chicago market. The war-weary ex-Confederates required little arithmetic or imagination to realize that a tremendous profit could be made from a four-dollar steer.

Only a few soldiers reached Texas early enough in 1865 to participate in the first post-war drive, but others could at least make plans for the following year. Several enterprising veterans from Texas and various businessmen from Iowa and Kansas quietly hired cowboys, purchased ponies, rounded up herds, and collected camp equipment for the great adventure. By March 1866, with the grass already turning green on the prairies, numerous outfits moved out of southern Texas, each trailing a herd of 2,000 or 3,000 spike-horned steers in the general direction of Red River. Their destination was Sedalia, Missouri, the nearest railhead west of the Mississippi and some 750 miles northeast of San Antonio.

The technique of trail driving was already perfected by 1866, and most of the participants had obtained experience on drives into Louisiana or Missouri before the war. Six or eight cowboys, all adept in the use of the lasso and six-shooter, controlled each

XII · Longhorns and Woollies

band of cattle. During the first few days they pushed the herd to the point of exhaustion so as to lessen the danger of stampede. As soon as they were "trail broken," the pace slowed to ten or twelve miles per day, with stops early in the afternoon for the cattle to water and graze.

Usually the herd moved four to five abreast and extended a mile or more in serpentine fashion across the prairies. Two of the best men served as "points," riding on either side of the lead steers to keep them on a proper course. Back of the pointers rode the "wings," while bringing up the rear were the "drags." The cook drove the chuck wagon well ahead of the herd, carrying food and bed rolls. Not far behind him was the *remuda* of horses, managed by a wrangler, and the longhorns and their riders came last in the procession. In charge of the whole outfit was a trail boss, who selected the camp sites, located the water holes, and laid out the trail to be followed the next day. All "hands" received $25 to $40 per month, except the trail boss, who generally demanded $125 and perhaps a bonus.

With luck a good drover arrived with his herd at a northern shipping point in two or three months. By taking advantage of the spring grass all the way, picking up strays en route, and protecting the newborn calves, he could bring the stock to the end of the trail in better shape than when it departed. But few outfits reached their destination without encountering from one to half a dozen near-disasters.

All of the vicissitudes, adventures, and woes that could possibly come to a trail herd short of complete disintegration are recited in Andy Adams's *Log of a Cowboy*, the classic book on the subject, published in 1903. Adams describes the stampede of 3,000 terrified steers gone berserk; the bravery, skill, and endurance of the cowboys and their disregard for personal safety and comfort; thunderstorms, mud, rain, swollen streams, dry marches, encounters with Indians and Kansas "jayhawkers." All of these he pictures as common experiences during the course of a single drive. But in the end the "cow town" is reached, the herd is sold at a good profit, the Texans "let off plenty of steam" in the local saloon, and finally everyone returns home with green money and fresh memories. Of course, not all drives were so hazardous in the beginning nor so profitable in the end.

The first years of the great venture were among the least successful. Most of the drovers crossed Red River a few miles north of Denison and entered the eastern part of Indian Territory. Many pursued a course past Boggy Depot and Fort Gibson to the Kansas border just below Baxter Springs. A few veered farther east by way of Fort Smith and then swung north across the hilly wooded area of Arkansas toward Sedalia, while others turned straight north at Boggy Depot in an effort to avoid the principal Indian settlements. Few herds followed the same course across Oklahoma in 1866, but all trails were grouped together as the Texas Trail. In time they came to be more distinct and were appropriately designated as the East Shawnee and West Shawnee trails.

Regardless of the route, the drovers found their troubles multiplying as they moved farther north. Indian Territory contained many desperate characters who did not hesitate to stampede the herds at night or pick up stray animals by day. Some of the Indians demanded payment for allowing the cattle to trespass on their grazing lands; others, afraid that the fever would kill their own stock, tried to turn the Texans back. And conditions did not improve when the drovers reached the Kansas or Missouri border, where they encountered angry farmers with shotguns and rifles or outlaw bands ready to "bushwhack" the cowboys and drive off the cattle. Some men died, others received severe beatings, and many outfits simply disintegrated. Doubtless few drovers reacted as philosophically as George Duffield: "Have not got the Blues but am in Hel of a fix," he wrote on June 17, 1866, after reaching the Arkansas with what was left of his herd.[1]

Reliable estimates place the number of cattle that reached a

---

[1] Duffield was one of the few trail drivers to keep a daily journal of his experiences in 1866. His writings were published in the *Annals of Iowa* in 1924.

XII · Longhorns and Woollies

profitable market in 1866 at approximately 50,000—this out of more than a quarter-million longhorns that "pointed north" in the early spring. The situation discouraged many ranchers, but the thirty-five dollars per head at Sedalia tempted hundreds of determined Texans to try again. None of them knew when they started up the trail in the spring of 1867 that a Joseph G. McCoy was working on a solution for their problem. A prominent cattle feeder and dealer in Illinois, he studied a railroad map and saw that the Kansas Pacific Railroad then being built already reached as far as Salina, Kansas. An idea came at once: why not build loading pens at some point on this railroad far beyond the settlements, then urge the Texas drovers to swing their cattle west of the Indian Nations where they could be loaded on cars and shipped to Kansas City?

When McCoy learned that some herds had already headed north from Texas, he boarded a Kansas Pacific train and rode to the end of the line, where he found the one-saloon town of Abilene, Kansas, inhabited by a handful of people and several thousand prairie dogs. He quickly turned the sleepy hamlet into a beehive of activity. An employee was dispatched to Indian Territory to spread the word among trail drivers of the wonders of Abilene, while McCoy rushed to Hannibal, Missouri, for enough pine lumber to build stockyards, a hotel, and several other structures. The first of several Kansas cow towns was on its way to immortality.

With construction work under way, McCoy learned that a part-Cherokee trader named Jesse Chisholm was familiar with the country between Abilene and the Texas border, having spent many years in this area driving freight wagons to Fort Reno and Fort Supply. Chisholm reported that the country was generally open and had plenty of water and grass, confirming McCoy's theory that an ideal route for Texas cattlemen existed. However, it was too late in the year to change routes. Only a few drovers received word in time to alter their course and reach Abilene before the end of 1867. Some 35,000 steers were driven in that year over all or part of the route that soon became famous as the Chisholm Trail.[2]

The next year the number of cattle brought to Abilene doubled, and the volume continued to grow until the railroads reached other Kansas cow towns. When the Kansas Pacific was extended sixty miles farther west to Ellsworth, that town became an important shipping point. Later the Santa Fe Railroad connected with Newton, some distance south of Abilene, and for a while it too enjoyed a cattle boom. By 1875 Dodge City became a terminal point of the long drives and the Chisholm Trail gave way to Western Trail, which extended north from Vernon, Texas, and across the western edge of Oklahoma to the end of the railroad line in southwestern Kansas.

Life in the heyday of the cow towns was very much like that in the mining settlements of California a generation earlier and the oil boom towns of the Southwest two generations later. But it is doubtful if any place ever excelled them in pure, unadulterated wickedness. The Texas cowboys acquired such a bad reputation in Kansas that it is remembered to the present day. Many left more than their reputation behind and are now resting peacefully in the "boot hill" cemetery at Dodge City, in unmarked graves along the trail, or below the soil of Abilene, Ellsworth, Newton, or Wichita.

Dodge City was the last of the Kansas cow towns and probably the roughest while it lasted. A dusty, drab place whose streets were lined with dirty saloons, gambling dens, bawdy houses, and dance halls, Dodge City was from early spring until late fall a living hell for the few citizens who wanted peace and quiet. But to the swaggering cowboy it was the end of the trail,

---

[2] This trail was named after Jesse Chisholm the half-breed trader, not the well-known Texas rancher John Chisum. It entered Oklahoma near present Waurika and continued north along U.S. Highway 81 via Chickasha and El Reno. A group of livestock owners from Caldwell County, Texas, were the first to drive cattle the entire length of the Chisholm Trail in 1867. Green Peyton: *America's Heartland, the Southwest* (Norman: University of Oklahoma Press; 1948), p. 76.

XII · Longhorns and Woollies

the Fourth of July and New Year's Eve rolled into one. Debauchery came wholesale, but those who got too rowdy frequently landed in a dry well to cool off before receiving a "pass" out of town. Others, not so lucky, contracted "lead poisoning" and "died with their boots on."

After a while each cow town hired professional gun slingers who made a pretense of keeping law and order: Abilene had Wild Bill Hickok, who created almost as many disturbances as he settled; Dodge City had Bat Masterson and Wyatt Earp; Newton had Mike McCluskie and Jim Riley; and Ellsworth had Chauncey Whitney. The eventual departure of some of these worthies after the cow towns and the stockyards ceased to depend on each other was about as welcome to the Kansans as the exodus of the Texans.

Cattle raising was an important and obvious part of the Southwest's economy, and the cattleman is still an impressive figure. From Texas the industry spread to New Mexico, Arizona, and Oklahoma via the cattle trails and then dispersed in various directions. By 1890 Texas cattlemen, cowboys, ponies, and cattle could be found in every state or territory of the Great Plains, Rocky Mountains, and Pacific Coast. Wherever Texans acquired new lands and moved their herds, they introduced their own methods of ranching and peculiar customs—high-heeled boots, broad sombreros, jangling spurs, heavy saddles, pithy speech, hybrid Spanish. So thoroughly has Texas influenced the cattle industry that the general public is still inclined to think of the two as synonymous terms.

Between 1866 and 1886 some ten or twelve million cattle and horses were driven to Kansas railheads from below Red River. Various contradictory estimates have been made, but one authority states that at least six million head passed Doan's Crossing near Vernon for the Western Trail, five million at Red River Station farther east for the Chisholm Trail, and a million at other points near Preston Bend north of Denison. "The sale of these herds brought approximately $250,000,000—a tidy sum in the dollar of that day, bringing prosperity where there had been ruin in Texas."[3]

Gradually the cattle trails moved farther and farther west, and although the ones across Oklahoma are the most famous, there were others almost as important. As early as 1866 two Texas cattlemen, Charles Goodnight and Oliver Loving, drove a herd of steers from the vicinity of Fort Concho, near present-day San Angelo, Texas, to Horse Head Crossing on the Pecos River. Most of this route stretched across the torrid Staked Plains, sixty miles between watering places. From the Pecos River the trail turned north to enter New Mexico near Pope's Well and continued on to Fort Sumner in the Bosque Redondo Reservation, where 7,000 Navajos were confined. Here there was such a shortage of beef that the government paid the Texans eight cents per pound on the hoof, or approximately $13,000 for a herd of 1,700 steers.

Goodnight and Loving opened a new market, and their efforts were quickly duplicated by others. Eventually the Loving-Goodnight Trail divided at Pope's Well, the main branch extending past Fort Sumner, through Colorado, and on to Wyoming. The other turned west to El Paso, then up the Rio Grande River to Dona Anna, where it forked again. One branch continued along the river to Albuquerque, then west across New Mexico and Arizona via Whipple's old route to the Colorado River, through Walker's Pass in the Sierras to California. This route was sometimes dangerous because of hostile Apaches, but a few Texas cattlemen had the nerve to take it and the fortitude to succeed. The second branch across the Southwest followed the old Butterfield route from El Paso to Yuma, eventually reaching Los Angeles and northern California.

---

[3] Paul I. Wellman in his *Glory, God, and Gold*, p. 342, cites George W. Saunders, former president of the Texas Trail Drivers' Association, as the source for the figure of twelve million cattle and horses. Rupert N. Richardson and Carl Coke Rister in *The Greater Southwest*, p. 336, cite the same authority for the figure of eleven million livestock shipped to Kansas during a period of twenty-eight years.

XII · *Longhorns and Woollies*

In the meantime the Western Trail from Vernon to Dodge City was extended as far north as the Blackfoot Reservation in Montana. The flood of cattle which poured over these shifting trails established the Southwest as the great breeding ground for beef and gave the region a new phrase—"King Cattle."

Among the giants of the industry was Captain F. Lytle, who sold over 450,000 steers to Northern markets during his lifetime. And in a single season Colonel Ike T. Pryor drove 30,000 cattle beyond the Texas borders. Others who should be remembered are Shanghai Pierce, Captain Richard King, Mifflin Kenedy, Colonel D. H. Snyder, and Captain Charles Schreiner. The last great herd was driven from the fabulous XIT Ranch in the Texas Panhandle to Montana in 1896. By this time the cattle industry had entered a new era.

Many events conspired to bring an end to the most colorful aspect of the industry, for, romantic as it was, the trail drive could not survive the changes and difficulties it encountered. In the first place, it was a product of the open-range system of ranching, notoriously inefficient and possible only on an unsettled frontier.

During the decade that followed the Civil War, when stockmen first moved onto the High Plains of western Texas, they staked out several thousand acres of free land and took advantage of the lush grama grasses that had formerly supplied the gregarious buffalo. Two novel practices evolved from this situation: "line riding" and the "round-up." The rancher stationed cowboys in pairs some twenty miles apart. Each day they rode from their "dug-out" camps in opposite directions until they met the man riding from the next camp. In this way they attempted to hold the cattle on their home range and turn back intruders from the neighboring ranch.

Because of the vast territory that each cowboy surveyed, it was natural that many cattle strayed beyond immediate recovery. Hence the pooling of manpower from various outfits for the annual round-up. The men worked under an appointed "captain," who directed the far-flung operations, driving the cattle to a given area, separating those of similar brands, and marking the calves and "mavericks." The work was hard and the hours were long, but the excitement of the round-up was a rewarding experience. When the cattle in one region were "worked," the men shifted to another. But hundreds of steers remained lost, and the constant mixing of the herds on the open range contributed to a gradual deterioration of the stock which was reflected in the declining prices at Northern markets.

Before the end of the 1870's the ranching industry had spread from southern Texas and was firmly planted throughout the Great Plains and the entire Southwest. Meanwhile, farmers —"nesters"—moved in also to take advantage of the homestead law, which gave each qualified settler 160 acres of the public domain. But the open-range system and prairie farming were not compatible, and trouble soon developed. The ranchers began to fence off their holdings with barbed wire, and some nesters did likewise. Each resented the other's use of the new invention: it interfered with the movement of cattle, and it hampered the small farmer, who often discovered that he was excluded from a water supply and fenced in by a more powerful and greedy neighbor. Barbed wire had some blessings—it enabled a large outfit to keep its herds confined to a restricted area and to improve the stock by more selective breeding. But most Texans agreed that "it sure played hell with Texas in general."

The boom in the barbed-wire industry lasted from 1875 to 1883, although some land was still unfenced after that period. Among the more spectacular projects was the erection of a four-wire fence about the Frying Pan Ranch in the Texas Panhandle. The job, completed in 1882, cost approximately $40,000 and encompassed a quarter of a million acres. A short time later the King Ranch in southern Texas, which contained almost one million acres, was enclosed with 190,000 pounds of wire. And in 1886 the great XIT Ranch [4]—"Ten Counties in Texas"—erected

---

[4] The story of this fabulous empire is told by J. Evetts Haley: *The XIT Ranch of Texas and the Early Days of the Llano Estacado* (Chicago: The Lakeside Press; 1929).

XII · Longhorns and Woollies

800 miles of wire fencing at a cost of $181,000. Line riding now gave way to fence riding, the round-up was restricted to individual pastures, and trail herds were no longer free to move. The open range had disappeared.

Other factors had already made the long drive an outmoded institution. As the grass began to be eaten down by successive herds, cattle lost so much weight along the thousand-mile trail northward that they could not be sold to Eastern stock buyers at good prices. Most herds had to be held on the grasslands of the Indian reservations in Oklahoma or sent to Nebraska or Iowa to be fattened on corn. The Indians capitalized on the situation by charging ten cents a head for all steers driven through their reservation and much larger sums if they remained for a few months' grazing. By 1888, for example, the Cherokees extracted $200,000 annually from Texas and Kansas ranchers.

Added to these woes were the damages assessed by Kansas and Nebraska farmers and the "quarantee laws" enacted by various legislatures to prohibit cattle drives across state boundaries except during winter months when the fever abated. Also, an epidemic of "fence-cutters' wars" broke out all over the Southwest, involving ranchers, nesters, and sheepmen—these last just beginning to make their bid for what was left of the public domain.

Besides being economically unsound, the trail drive was no longer very necessary. The Missouri, Kansas, and Texas Railroad reached Denison, Texas, in 1872, and a short time later the Santa Fe extended its lines south of Wichita to connect with its southern branch at Fort Worth. Packing houses too moved closer to the great breeding grounds of Texas, first to Kansas City and eventually to Fort Worth, Dallas, San Antonio, and Houston. Except for a few spectacular drives from the Texas panhandle to western Indian reservations, the old-time cowboy reached the end of the trail before the close of the century.

While the beef bonanza lasted, it witnessed some interesting changes. The longhorn steer might be picturesque and good for speed and endurance, but "he wasn't much for meat." An extra-thick hide stretched tightly over enormous bones topped off by a

The Southwest: *Old and New*

set of awesome horns did not leave a great amount of marketable products. What meat remained in a 700-pound beast was tough and stringy, until the rancher began to change the animal's appearance and temperament by cross-breeding. Gradually a mixture of Hereford or Angus blood produced a heavier, more docile steer weighing approximately 1,400 pounds—with shorter legs and horns and rounder bodies.

It was at this period also that foreign investors became interested in the American cattle business. As more and more beef found its way to England, word reached there by 1880 that enormous sums could be made in Western ranching. Joint-stock companies, including the Prairie Cattle Company of Edinburgh, Scotland, the Francklyn Land and Cattle Company, the American Pastoral Company, the Matador Land and Cattle Company, and the Swan Land and Cattle Company, came into existence. English, Scottish, German, and French investors scrambled to buy shares and participate in the great barbecue. These companies acquired ranches too big for individuals to own and operate. Millions of dollars and hundreds of foreigners poured into Texas, New Mexico, Arizona, and the Great Plains area until soon the large outfit dominated the industry.

Meanwhile a group of Chicago investors laid out the three-million-acre XIT Ranch, which stretched over an area of the Texas Panhandle greater than the state of Connecticut, the largest single enterprise of its kind in the world. Another vast domain was the King Ranch in southern Texas, whose approximately one million acres are still intact and are operated today by the Kleberg family in much the same manner as a feudal barony.[5] In 1875 Charles Goodnight moved his herd of 1,600 longhorns from the headwaters of the Canadian River in New Mexico to the Palo Duro Canyon in the Texas Panhandle.

Palo Duro is at the headwaters of the main fork of Red River, some 1,200 feet below the surface of the plains in a spot ideally

---

[5] Much has been written about this century-old institution, but the definitive work on the subject is Tom Lea's *The King Ranch* (Boston: Little, Brown and Company; 1957).

XII · Longhorns and Woollies

situated for ranching. In 1875 it was a rich, green, well-watered valley of 600,000 acres, narrow at both ends, five miles wide at the center and thirty miles in length. Goodnight spent nine days driving out a vast herd of buffalo, then moved his cattle and equipment down the side of the canyon and built a ranch house on the floor of the valley. He formed a partnership with an Irishman named John Adair, acquired title to the area at fifty cents an acre, and named his new domain the JA Ranch. Soon after improving his herd with English Herefords and fencing in the land, Goodnight sold his interest to Adair and bought another holding some twenty miles away. The JA Ranch is still operated by members of the Adair family.

Few of the large operators profited from their investments of work and money, for nature combined with man to strike the ranching industry a staggering blow. The range quickly became overstocked, and there was no longer sufficient grass to feed the vastly increased herds. With few exceptions, stockmen did not read the signs in time, and when herd reduction started, the market was flooded and prices dropped alarmingly. Then in the winter of 1885–6 a great freeze killed thousands of cattle, followed by a drought the next summer that withered the grass and dried up the streams.

But the worst was yet to come. The winter of 1886–7 was undoubtedly the coldest one that the West had experienced since 1848. In late January the temperature on the northern plains dropped to more than sixty degrees below zero as a great blizzard swept down from Canada as far as Oklahoma, New Mexico, and southern Texas. In the past, cattle had withstood severe weather, but they had never experienced anything like this. As they drifted with the wind and blinding snow, thousands piled up against fences or were trapped in ravines, and when the ranchers dug out of their homes a few days later they found a sight unparalleled in the history of the West. Some had lost their entire herds, others were left with a few skeletons staggering about on frozen feet.

The great blizzard of 1887 dealt a death blow not only to the livestock industry, but to the whole Western boom. A few ranchers and farmers managed to survive and wait for better times, which came after the Populist movement in the following decade. The bitter lessons were not forgotten, and ranching emerged as a more scientific industry, with careful attention to conservation of grass and water, sheltering of beeves, selective breeding, and sensible marketing practices.

Nowhere have the changes been more apparent than in the individuals involved. The cattle baron is a man in a business suit, driving a fluid-drive car or piloting his own Cessna, calculating pounds of meat instead of heads, supporting several organizations for the advancement of business and his particular brand of politics, and sometimes using cattle as a tax exemption for more lucrative oil operations. He is likely to keep the old ranch house for week ends only and build a more lavish home in a nearby city so that his children can go to public schools and his wife can join bridge and music clubs. Some cattlemen turned to sheep raising, in spite of their traditional hatred of the ovine creatures. Two crops per year—lamb and wool—were found to be better than one—namely, beef. Besides, sheep thrived on land where cattle frequently starved. Other old-time ranchers turned to farming or started raising part of their stock feed.

The cowboy changed, too. By 1900 he was penned behind barbed wire, forced to dig post holes, repair windmills, and rack hay. He no longer knew the joys of the long drive, the danger of Indian attack, or the excitement of chasing cattle rustlers. In time the pickup truck or jeep supplemented or replaced his horse and saddle, and the six-shooter ceased to be necessary. Some turned cattleman or ranch employee, farmer or tradesman; others eventually prostituted themselves as "window dressing" for dude ranches.

The clownish posturing of film and TV heroes obscures the real cowboy, and indeed most fictional portraits of cowboys are distortions. Some serious writers insist that the cowboy was a cavalier, a nineteenth-century knight, reserved and courteous, with uncompromising courage. He is usually presented as a friend to small children and respectful to ladies. And of course he is alert,

XII · Longhorns and Woollies

enduring, and uncomplaining. His skill with gun and rope is uncanny, he is always kind to his horse, and he asks no better end than to die with his boots on. According to this viewpoint, he is indeed the finest of our frontier types.

But others have described him an an illiterate swaggering bully who fired upon Mexicans, Indians, and sheepherders without provocation. When not rustling cattle or horses, he spent his leisure time in saloons and whorehouses; he refused to do any work that could not be done on horseback. Although he could not hit the side of a barn with his six-shooter, he used it to settle minor arguments or to hold up banks and trains for his spending money.

The true cowboy is somewhere in between these extremes. In legends his faults are forgotten and his virtues exaggerated. Dime novelists first embalmed him, the movies resurrected him, and now television has distorted his image beyond recognition. For all practical purposes, this national hero could have lived on another planet, in another eon; but aside from the forgivable vice of bragging, he symbolized Southwestern characteristics of courage, generosity, and of friendliness as no other figure.

RANCHING is something more than the raising of cattle. In the Southwest it also entails the production of sheep and goats, especially in New Mexico, where sheep came before cattle. Indeed, every Spanish expedition brought sheep. The Navajos learned to weave blankets and woolen cloth for trade with New Spain long before the conquest was complete. Eventually some flocks were driven to California, Texas, and other points—thus making New Mexico the progenitor of the Southwestern sheep industry. Today sheep are more important than cattle in both New Mexico and Arizona, as well as large sections of southwestern Texas.

Throughout the Spanish period, sheep continued as the main staple product and New Mexico's principal article of export. Under Spanish laws grazing lands were free, and sheep barons (*ricos*) controlled them in much the same way that cattlemen later controlled other parts of the Southwest. In both cases the rich gained at the expense of the small operator. In New Mexico and Arizona this situation eventually brought about the *partido* system, whereby the poor man entered into a contract to care for the *rico*'s sheep. At the end of the year he returned a specified number of rams, wethers, ewes, and lambs, just as the Southern sharecropper turned over part of his cotton crop to the landowner. The net result was a continued increase in production with a minimum of capital, and some *ricos* counted their sheep on *partido* in hundreds of thousands.

At first the surplus stock were driven from New Mexico to markets below the Rio Grande and later across Arizona to California. Meanwhile the Indians systematically raided the *ranchos*, killed the Mexican sheepherders, and drove off sheep by the thousands. By this method the Navajos came into possession of large herds of sheep and goats and were said to boast that they preferred leaving a few behind each year for breeding purposes. And according to Josiah Gregg in his *Commerce of the Prairies*, their animals were of a better grade in the early nineteenth century than those of the Mexicans.

In spite of the perpetual raids by the Navajos and depredations by the Apaches, the sheep industry in New Mexico continued to expand. Sheep are the dumbest and most dependent of creatures, but nevertheless the reproduction process showed no signs of abating as long as rams retained their admiration for ewes. Between 1821 and 1846 more than 200,000 sheep were driven annually to Mexico, and a few *ricos* supplied as many as 75,000 to outside markets in a single year.[6] After the discovery of gold in California, herds were diverted to that region, and Anglo-Americans soon dominated the industry on the Pacific Coast. But in New Mexico it remained in the hands of Spanish-Americans,

---

[6] Richardson and Rister: *The Greater Southwest*, p. 365.

XII · Longhorns and Woollies

and even as late as 1900 two dozen native New Mexican families owned four fifths of the sheep in the territory.

The Indians of Oklahoma preferred not to raise sheep except on a small scale, and even today the Sooner State produces less wool and mutton than almost any of the major sheep-producing counties throughout the remainder of the Southwest.

"Woollies," as Southwesterners call sheep today, arrived in Arizona in the early part of the nineteenth century by way of New Mexico, although Father Kino introduced a few head in the region south of the Gila River in the previous century. Because of climatic conditions the industry at first was largely confined to the Hopi and Navajo Indians of the north. The drives between New Mexico and California and later between the Mormons of Utah and northern Mexico gave the business a new impetus, and it developed more rapidly when the Apache raids stopped. According to Hamilton's *Statistics,* Arizona sheep numbered 700,000 by 1883, or more than seventeen for each person. The Bureau of Agricultural Economics estimated slightly more than 800,000 in 1938, a little less than the number today.[7]

Approximately half the sheep in Arizona continue to be raised on the Navajo Reservation in the northeastern section of the state. Another twenty-five per cent are grazed on the northern forests in summer and driven south during winter, while the remainder are pastured in the Salt River Valley, Casa Grande Valley, and Yuma Valley. The northern herds produce an average of four pounds of wool each year, while those in the south yield almost twice as much. The lambs grow fat and the mild climate enables the ranchers to market them early and thus capture the top spring prices.

The first colonists who settled near the missions of San Lorenzo and Ysleta in the vicinity of present-day El Paso brought sheep to Texas in 1681. Thirty-seven years later, when Martin de Alarcón established San Antonio, he made livestock raising, prin-

---

[7] Ibid., p. 332.

cipally sheep and goats, the basis of the local economy. Soon the sheep and goats owned by other Spanish missions on the Rio Grande and in eastern Texas far outnumbered the settlers in the area. But the animals, like the settlements themselves, deteriorated. When the first Anglo-Americans arrived in the 1820's, they found a scrubby stock that had degenerated from inbreeding and neglect—like the wild horses and cattle that also occupied the country.

Although the Anglo-American settlers raised sheep and goats along with cattle, they made little attempt to improve the quality of their livestock until forced by circumstances. The coarse, short wool brought such low prices that it discouraged Texans from trying to market it. And as for meat, they preferred almost any kind to mutton.

The scrubby Spanish sheep had one outstanding quality, however: they were hardy animals, able to resist disease, survive on almost any plant that grew, and withstand extreme variations of climate. By 1850 they had been crossed with the American Merino, and the results were a heavier animal capable of producing four pounds of wool each year and lambs that brought fair prices as mutton on the eastern markets. By 1860 the production of wool and mutton had become a major industry in parts of southern and southwestern Texas, but, like other local businesses, it fell into neglect between 1861 and 1865 and many of the herds become depleted.

After the Civil War Texas sheepmen did not enjoy an equivalent of the high prices that cattlemen achieved by the long drives. Furthermore, hostile Indians made expansion into the region best suited for sheep raising, the southwestern hill country of Texas, a hazardous undertaking. Meanwhile, twenty-five or thirty million acres of grazing land between San Antonio and El Paso remained virtually unoccupied until after 1880, supporting less than 400,000 sheep that year, as compared to approximately seven million two generations later. Not until the end of the Indian wars did farmers and stock raisers move into the unsettled regions west of the 98th meridian.

XII · Longhorns and Woollies

It soon became obvious that the hill country of southwestern Texas, the area of the great Edwards Plateau, was better suited to ranching than farming and particularly favored the raising of sheep and goats. Farmers gravitated elsewhere, leaving the country to the ranchers. Today this is one of the largest wool-, mohair-, and mutton-producing regions in the world: twenty-five per cent of the sheep in the United States are found here and over fifty per cent of the goats. Most of the wool is marketed through San Angelo, where various Boston and New York firms maintain branch offices, while Kerrville has long claimed to be the "Mohair Center of the World."

Early ranchers in the Edwards Plateau first ran cattle, but they quickly discovered that there was not enough rainfall for sufficient grass and that cattle would not eat the semi-desert plants that grew on the thin, rocky soil. But if cattle failed to thrive here, sheep could, and where sheep could not subsist, goats could. Consequently, stock growers gradually adjusted to the type of soil and plant growth which their land offered, in many cases running cattle, sheep, and goats on the same holding. Today a typical outfit in Crockett County, Texas, for example, may graze 2,000 head of sheep, 500 or 600 goats, and 100 Hereford cattle on thirty sections. In a good year the owner markets 1,500 lambs, 16,000 pounds of wool, and 1,500 pounds of mohair, from which he realizes a profit of $25,000 to $50,000, depending on the amount of rainfall and the market prices.

One of the reasons that wool growing on a large scale developed rather late in Texas was the manner in which the fleece was prepared for marketing. Ranchers originally baled all of their clip together, and buyers based their bids on the poorest grade in each bale. The Texans soon learned to separate the better fleece from the poorer grades and to demand bids accordingly. Also they organized their own Wool Growers Association to market their wool and lambs, and by selling in larger quantities to a single buyer they obtained a better price.

By the time sheep ranchers reached the western part of the Edwards Plateau and Big Bend Country of Texas, barbed wire was already in common use throughout the West. Most of the ranchers had originally been cattle raisers, and they naturally applied this experience to sheep and goats. Except in the very early days, the flocks in Texas were never tended by a "herder," as in New Mexico and Arizona. The employee on a Texas sheep ranch is still basically a cowboy who rides fences, rounds up the sheep two or three times each year, marks the lambs, brands cattle, repairs windmills, puts out salt, and feeds and doctors the stock. During the season when ewes are lambing he stays out of the pastures altogether, for the least intermingling of the flock will cause a newborn lamb to get separated from its mother and it will be unable to find her again.

Unlike the Spanish-American sheepherder of New Mexico who depends on his dog to guard and control the herd, the Texas sheepherder—or cowboy—uses only a horse or a pickup truck. If the pastures are enclosed by fences—and all of them are on Texas ranches—the "woollies" generally are able to take care of themselves unless they become entangled in wire or infected by cuts. And the many canyons of the Edwards Plateau afford protection to the flock in winter so that they do not have to be driven into sheds at night. A dog therefore is not only unnecessary but is even considered a nuisance—to be shot on sight, as wolves and coyotes are. The heavy, awkward Rambouillett sheep, the predominant breed in Texas today, will die if forced to run for even a few minutes on a hot day, and it is commonly believed in southwestern Texas that a dog can do more damage to a herd in one hour than a mountain lion in a full month.

A sheep ranch does not require many "hands," except during certain seasons. When spring lambs are six or eight weeks old, they are rounded up for "marking" or castrating.[8] The doctored animals are then set free to put on weight and later to be sold as mutton, while some of the females are kept for breeding and wool pro-

---

[8] Until a few years ago this operation was performed with a sharp knife, used to cut off the end of the bag. The testicles were then jerked out by the teeth so as not to cause permanent "damage" to the animal. Strangers to the sheep country have to see this performance in order to believe it, but it was the custom for several generations and is sometimes practiced today, although a special instrument is more frequently used.

XII · *Longhorns and Woollies*

ducing for at least five or six years more. Usually during the spring round-up the winter wool is clipped from the many ewes and a handful of rams. The work was formerly done with old-fashioned hand shears, but now it is done with mechanical equipment by professional shearers who travel in crews. The clippers look very much like those used by barbers, although larger, and a good worker can shear a hundred sheep in one day. The wool is tramped down in sacks by a man muffled against the dust in a large kerchief, while the peeled animal, streaked with blood and bleating piteously, runs to find her lamb and return to the range to grow more wool. Only the female lamb escapes major torture of one kind or another at this time; but, like all the others, she must undergo a minor alteration of one or two ears, which designates the owner's brand.

During the late summer or early fall the flock is rounded up again and the six-month-old wethers are shipped off to market. If the range offers natural or artificial protection during the winter months, they are clipped a second time. But on the "flats" or "divide" country they will need a full coat to protect them until spring against "northers" and occasional snows.

Extra crews are hired to help with the round-up and marking. Almost invariably these itinerants are Mexican workers in Texas and Spanish-Americans in New Mexico and Arizona. Before World War II additional hands could be employed for two or three dollars a day and board. But continual demands for higher wages have led more and more ranchers of the Southwest to depend on "wetbacks"—Mexicans who have entered the United States illegally. In Texas, wetbacks are also used to clear brush and, during periods of drought, to knock over sotol plants so that the stock may eat the kernel which grows at the base.

Wetbacks are willing to work for a few dollars per month, stay on a ranch for three or four months at a time, then return to Mexico without demanding much more than their *dinero* each month and their *frijoles* and *cabrito* each day. Their illegal status is frequently exploited by ranchers, who hold them as virtual prisoners during the period for which the wetbacks have contracted to work. This system operates to the detriment of the local Mexican residents, who cannot compete with the low wages and therefore migrate elsewhere.

Sheep ranching in parts of New Mexico and Arizona is carried on much as in Texas where the ranches are divided into separate pastures by a network of fences. Yet in large sections of this region, particularly where sheep are grazed on government lands or on the Indian reservations, herders and dogs are still used as in ancient times. The flock must be watched constantly and moved from valley to mountain slope and back again, wherever there is grass. The winters, particularly in the northern regions, are often severe; shelter pens are constructed, and the stock is closely guarded against predatory animals.

Sheep are generally driven in bands of from 1,500 to 2,500 by a herder and his assistant, the *campero*, who moves the camp, takes care of the supplies, and does the cooking. Each camp is visited frequently by the owner or his overseer, the *caporal*, who travels by horseback or jeep. As the herder never leaves his sheep, the *caporal* must scout the range for better grass and order the herds moved as conditions dictate. He also keeps a tally of his herds, searches for strays, supervises medication of diseased stock, and watches for signs of wolves, coyotes, and bears.

The work goes on unceasingly, and few men are willing to accept the long hours and living conditions that are the lot of the lonely sheepherder. Ranchers throughout the Southwest still long for "the good old days" when they could hire a sheepherder for thirty dollars a month, and they naturally complain that "help is not what it used to be."

In the Southwest the term "sheepherder" is one of scorn, and no self-respecting Anglo-American allows himself to be called by it. In the first place, a sheepherder has the reputation of being a little loco—a helpful qualification, incidentally, for enduring complete isolation from the world for months at a time. Even the present wages of $125 to $150 a month are not enough to attract individuals who can do anything else, and those who do sign up rarely last the period of their contract. Consequently, New Mexican and

XII · *Longhorns and Woollies*

Arizona ranchers, like those in Texas, are turning more and more to the "wetbacks," who work for less, take orders, do not grumble out loud, and, above all, have a feeling for the sheep. "Where else can you entrust twenty thousand dollars of perishable property to an illiterate and be sure that he will care for it with intelligence and devotion?" a New Mexican sheep rancher recently remarked.[9]

Unlike the beef growers, sheep ranchers cannot supply the domestic demand for their product, and they are subject to stiff competition from foreign imports, particularly from Australia and New Zealand. In New Mexico and Arizona they continue to use both state and federal lands; in Texas only state lands, as federal grazing lands are not available. Hence, the growers of cattle and sheep are vitally interested in politics insofar as they concern lease fees, tariffs, income taxes, and price supports. They will co-operate with government agencies as long as they derive immediate benefits, but they hate so-called "dictation from Washington."

As long as one avoids the subject of the "New Deal," the Southwestern rancher is a pleasant individual to know. He is sometimes generous to a fault, possesses a sardonic sense of humor, is not troubled with ulcers or anxious to impress anyone with intellectual conversation. Most ranchers are only one or two generations removed from pioneers to whom "rugged individualism" was a sacred term that commanded the same reverence as a church benediction. Perhaps this partly explains their ultraconservative political philosophy, which might be illustrated by a remark made to the author a few years ago by a Texas ranch wife: "Roosevelt did not raise our standard of living," she fumed. "He only succeeded in raising others up to our level. And you and I both know that God never intended for everyone to be equal."

---

[9] Quoted in Erna Fergusson's: *New Mexico: A Pageant of Three Peoples* (New York: Alfred A. Knopf; 1951), p. 319.

XIII

COMPLETION OF STATEHOOD

ALL FOUR Southwestern states joined the Union under anomalous circumstances. Texas was an independent republic at the time of admission and was recognized as such by various foreign powers. Oklahoma was set aside in the 1830's as a permanent homeland for the Indian Nations. These so-called Nations existed as free domains under the protection of the United States throughout the next half-century. White men were forbidden by federal law to trespass on their land.

New Mexico was among the first of the present fifty states to receive a permanent white population—only Florida and Virginia

XIII · *Completion of Statehood*

preceded her. Yet she and her offspring, Arizona, were among the last to be admitted into the Union. They entered in 1912, five years after Oklahoma and sixty-seven years after Texas. Both possessed a highly indigenous Indian society that the Spaniards had failed to destroy and the Anglo-Americans had altered only slightly.

Unlike the rest of the region, Oklahoma had no stable Indian culture and no settled Spanish civilization on which to build. Considered the youngest of the four Southwestern states, it is also the smallest. Its neighbors, particularly Texans, are inclined to look on it as a poor and backward relative. Of course, a fraternal feeling has always existed among the oil millionaires of the two states bordering Red River, but Texans in general, traditionally prejudiced against the Indian and intensely proud of their own great heritage, are apt to dismiss their northern neighbor as a young upstart without a past. Few of them are aware that the story of the Sooner State is as singular and complex as that of Texas. Indeed, Oklahoma's past hundred years are more colorful, for when political developments in the larger state approached a climax in 1845, they were just beginning in the smaller one.

Oklahoma became a part of the United States in 1803 with the Louisiana Purchase, but it did not begin to take its present shape until 1819.[1] In that year the Adams-Onís Treaty set the Red River and the 100th meridian as the boundaries between United States and Spanish territories in the Southwest. These lines eventually marked the extent of Oklahoma on the south and part of the west. By 1828 the threefold bend in the present eastern boundary took form as a result of the creation of Missouri and separate land transactions with the Cherokees and Choctaws. In the Compromise of 1850 Texas gave up her claim to what is now the Oklahoma Panhandle; and the Kansas-Nebraska Bill four years later, setting

---

[1] The name "Oklahoma" was derived from two Choctaw words—*okla*, meaning "people," and *humma*, meaning "red"—and literally means "Red People." The Reverend Allen Wright, Governor of the Choctaws, is supposed to have proposed this name in 1866, but it was not officially used by Congress until 1890, when the Organic Act providing territorial government for the land was passed.

the 37th parallel as the southern boundary of Kansas, completed the outline of the future forty-sixth state.

Long before the establishment of these boundaries Oklahoma received its first permanent citizens: the principal tribes who formerly lived in the Southeastern section of the United States. These Indians were civilized in every sense of the word, more so than some of the restless white men who seized their land and forced them to migrate westward. For many years the Cherokees, Creeks, Choctaws, Seminoles, and Chickasaws lived in Tennessee, Georgia, Mississippi, Alabama, Florida, and North Carolina as farmers, ranchers, craftsmen, and traders. Some rose to the status of rich planters, occupied large colonial houses, and owned African slaves. Their governments were patterned after that of the United States, with written constitutions and legislative, judicial, and executive departments. They maintained their own schools and attended Christian churches.

Indian immigration to Oklahoma began soon after the federal government created the Arkansas Territory, of which it was a part, in 1819. Two years before a group of Cherokees from Tennessee and Georgia had sold their farms and moved to what is now the northwest corner of Arkansas. Among them was Sequoyah, an illiterate Indian who later invented an alphabet for his people and taught them to read and write. Consequently, the Cherokees were able to develop the highest Indian civilization in the United States and to remain at peace.

Meanwhile, southwestern Arkansas was occupied by an advance guard of the Choctaws, who had likewise been forced from their traditional homes when their Mississippi holding gained in value as cotton and tobacco land. By the time Andrew Jackson became president in 1829 the racial problem had become intense and white settlers were demanding that all Indians be removed from the region east of the Mississippi. As present-day Oklahoma remained virtually unoccupied except for a few white traders and scattered tribes of Indians, it appeared to furnish an ideal solution.

On May 28, 1830, the Indian Removal Act put the federal

9a (above) Roundup on the open range, northwestern Oklahoma-Texas Panhandle, 1892.
9b (below) Waiting for the Cherokee Strip opening, 1893.

10a (above) Early settler in the Cherokee Strip, present Garfield County, Oklahoma. Justice of the Peace and Law Office.
10b (below) Arapaho Indian camp in western Oklahoma, approximate date, 1870.

11 Mule train ascending the south rim of the Grand Canyon.

12a (above) Giant Saguaros of southwestern Arizona.
12b (below) Cliff-dwelling ruins—Montezuma Castle National Monument near Flagstaff.

13 San Xavier del Bac Mission near Tucson.

14 The Enchanted Mesa in western New Mexico, as seen from the top of nearby Acoma Mesa.

15a (above) Petrified Forest in eastern Arizona.
15b (below) Canyon de Chelly in northeastern Arizona.

16a (above) In the heart of the Dust Bowl, Texas Panhandle, 1938.
16b (below) Oil derrick and pump near McCamey, Texas.

XIII · *Completion of Statehood*

government on record as favoring a policy of "complete" removal and gave the president power to negotiate an exchange of lands with any and all tribes. This meant that the Indians of Tennessee, Georgia, Mississippi, Alabama, and Florida—the Five Civilized Tribes—were to be ejected from their homes and transported beyond the Mississippi. They were told that they could live on their new lands in peace and happiness "as long as grass shall grow and water run." [2]

The great migration of the Five Civilized Tribes began in earnest in 1831 and continued intermittently until 1846. Most of the Indians were forced from their homes at bayonet point, and the suffering and heartbreak they endured form one of the blackest chapters in the history of the United States. Of the 13,000 Cherokees driven along the "Trail of Tears," at least 4,000 died of privation and exposure. And out of one group of a thousand Choctaw immigrants "only eighty-eight survived." [3] The Creek removal was almost as grim, while many of the Seminoles, the least advanced of the five tribes, chose to fight and die rather than evacuate their Florida land. Two full-scale campaigns were directed against them by the United States Army before they surrendered, and a few of their descendants remain in Florida today. Only the Chickasaws escaped major disaster or partial annihilation.

The lands assigned to the Cherokees as a permanent home consisted of seven million acres in the northeastern corner of Oklahoma. In addition, the Indians were given a perpetual outlet as far as the limit of the old Louisiana Territory, the 100th meridian. The shape of their domain resembled a derringer pointing west toward the Rockies; the rectangular area that formed the barrel was known as the "Cherokee Outlet." Tahlequah, the capital of the new nation, was located in the stock of the gun, Some twenty-five

---

[2] This time-worn phrase appears in all of the removal treaties the federal government made with the various tribes. If it had been literally interpreted, the Indians could have been dispossessed of their lands many times, for during the periodic droughts in the Southwest the grass does not grow and the water does not run.

[3] James D. Horan: "Thus the Frontier Vanished," *Collier's*, November 9, 1956, p. 100.

The Southwest: *Old and New*

miles south of the trading post built at Salina in 1802 by the French-American trader Jean Pierre Chouteau.

The Canadian River, running from west to east, divided the Indians' new home into two almost equal parts. The Creeks and Seminoles moved into the area between this stream and the southern boundaries of the Cherokee Nation; the southern half, between the Canadian and Red rivers, was allotted to the Choctaw and Chickasaw. Each nation contained enough acreage for every Indian family to claim all the land it could possibly use and more. But the settlers invariably clustered along their eastern boundaries. This portion of Oklahoma is a region of red clay hills, fresh streams, dense woods, and fertile valleys, while the western half of Indian Territory was part of the Great Plains and was not intended for permanent settlement by the Five Civilized Tribes. Instead, it was to be shared with the nomadic tribes for hunting purposes.

During the decade and a half prior to the Civil War the Nation Indians were unmolested by white men and thus able to develop their governments, improve their farms and livestock, and even educate their children at mission schools established by Eastern church groups. Although each of the five nations lived under its own constitution and laws and was legally independent, the federal government posted garrisons at Fort Gibson, Fort Washita, and five or six other points inside Indian Territory. The purpose of these posts was to protect the civilized Indians from the Plains Indians who haunted the western portion of present-day Oklahoma, the region beyond the Cross Timbers.

The financial, political, and social progress of the Indians abruptly halted in 1861. As previously noted, the Five Civilized Tribes cast their lot with the Confederacy, but a large segment in each nation sympathized with the Union and another group tried to remain neutral. All suffered. Thousands were killed or died of starvation, and many more were left destitute—their governments torn by strife and dissension, their homes burned, cattle stolen, and their lands reverting to weeds and grass.

When the fighting ceased, it was obvious to the Indians that

XIII · Completion of Statehood

further punishment was forthcoming. On September 8, 1865, their representatives met with commissioners from Washington at Fort Smith, Arkansas, to receive the terms of peace. Although the Indians were in no better bargaining position than the German representatives at Versailles in 1919, the conditions imposed on the Five Civilized Tribes were not so severe as expected. The terms required them to make peace with the United States and with one another, free their slaves and provide suitable arrangements for their welfare, and surrender their public lands for other tribes that were to be moved to Oklahoma. On the other hand, they retained sufficient land for agriculture and received the promise that white persons would be forbidden to dwell in their country except by consent of their tribal councils.[4]

Within one year after the Fort Smith Council, treaties were signed between the United States government and all of the separate nations. In 1867, at Medicine Lodge, Kansas, the government opened negotiations with representatives of the Indians of the South Plains. All of these nomads, Southern Cheyenne, Arapaho, Kiowa, Comanche, Apache, Wichita, and Caddo, were eventually given large reservations in the former hunting ground of the Five Civilized Tribes. And a short time later the Osage settled in a sizable area in the Outlet, immediately west of the Cherokee.

As the wild tribes shifted to Oklahoma, the federal government found it necessary to move its line of forts farther west and garrison them heavily. Even so, it proved difficult to keep the Plains Indians under control, and intermittent wars occurred. But by 1875 the Southern Cheyenne, Arapaho, Kiowa, and Comanche warriors were so thoroughly chastised and so reduced in number that they agreed to remain on the reservation and "follow the white man's road." Meanwhile a systematic program of locating additional tribes in Oklahoma was under way. Sixteen small reser-

---

[4] In fairness to the United States government it should be pointed out that provisions were made later to reimburse loyal Indians for losses sustained during the war and that each of the Five Civilized Tribes was compensated for lands surrendered. Edward Everett Dale and Morris L. Wardell: *History of Oklahoma* (Englewood Cliffs: Prentice-Hall; 1948), pp. 184–7.

THE SOUTHWEST: *Old and New*

vations were opened: seven in the extreme northeast corner of the Cherokee Nation, five more in the Old Cherokee Outlet immediately west of the Osage, and four in the lands between the Arkansas and Canadian rivers which had formerly belonged to the Creek and Seminole nations.

Into these small reservations were moved such minor groups as the Kickapoo, Sac and Fox, Kaw, Seneca, and Wyandotte from various parts of the United States. By 1885 representatives from some fifty Indian tribes had settled on the lands once promised to the Cherokees and others for "as long as grass grows and water runs." With the exception of a heart-shaped district between the Canadian River and the southern boundary of the Cherokee Outlet, all of Oklahoma was allocated. The western half of the Outlet, still claimed by the Cherokees, was also unoccupied, although ranchers from Texas and Kansas pastured their cattle on its lush grass for several years.

For a full generation after the close of the Civil War the Five Civilized Tribes maintained governments that were independent in name only. From time to time they tried to draw up a union of the various nations, excluding the federal government, but no such plan was ever accepted by Congress.[5] The Indians realized why. "Boomers" from Kansas, Texas, and Arkansas were casting covetous eyes on the fertile unoccupied heartland, while cattlemen moved their herds into the empty ranges, sometimes paying lease money and sometimes not.

This was also the period of railroad construction across Indian Territory. The Missouri, Kansas, and Texas extended south from Kansas and reached Sherman, Texas, in 1872, and, incidentally, the hands of the receivers the next year. The Atlantic and Pacific, later known as the "Frisco," was built from east to west a short time later; and in 1887 the Atchison, Topeka, and Santa Fe came south from Wichita, crossed the center of the unassigned lands, and extended to Forth Worth and beyond. There were other

---

[5] The most famous of these schemes of government was known as the Okmulgee Constitution," drawn up by the Intertribal Council of the Five Civilized Tribes in 1870.

XIII · Completion of Statehood

railroads, but their names have disappeared. Each brought in thousands of workers, hundreds of unpainted section houses, and dozens of dingy depots that remained a permanent part of the landscape.

Some of the Indians realized that the old ways were gone forever and joined the tide of events. Ranching now appeared more profitable than farming, and a few carved out large holdings and ran their own herds. Others leased farm land to white tenants or grazing land to Texas and Kansas cattlemen. Still others sold their timber rights to sawmill operators from Arkansas and Louisiana. But the largest transaction was made by the Cherokee Council when it leased 6,500,000 acres in the Outlet to a syndicate calling itself the Cherokee Strip Livestock Association. Some smaller outfits obtained grazing rights in the name of a silent Indian partner for whom they claimed to be working. One of these in the Osage country later became the famous 101 Ranch, whose Wild West Show played before millions of people on two or three continents.

By 1890, 110,000 white ranchers, farmers, and railroad workers lived in the territory—more than twice the number of Indians. The overwhelming majority of each tribe bitterly resented the intruders, but was powerless to stop them. The whites were neither subject to laws of the Indian Nations nor protected by those of the United States. Legally they could not obtain title to the land, but they settled on it anyway. Some ostensibly worked for the railroads, but these transportation lines did only a small business with the Indians and complained severely that there was little to buy and less to sell. Other white men "bootlegged" whisky from nearby states in defiance of the Indian police. And no small number of outlaws used the territory as a place to hide between cattle-rustling and horse-stealing forays.

But the Americans whom the Indians worried most was the group called "boomers" because they "boomed" the Unassigned Lands for white settlement. These men were the last of a restless breed that had opened up one frontier after another since 1607. For almost three centuries such men had moved along wilderness traces or rutted trails, stopping to build log cabins in the forest or

The Southwest: *Old and New*

sod houses on the prairie before pushing on for one last stake. Suddenly the pioneer days were gone and the frontier had vanished. Cattle and sheep had already replaced the buffalo; the soft underbelly of the ancient prairie sod lay exposed to the ravages of the sun, wind, and rain; and the once unbroken horizon of the Great Plains was now disfigured by dirty railroad towns, sordid houses of ranchers and nesters, miles of ugly barbed-wire fences, and thousands of grotesque windmills. An era had ended, but it was to have one brief revival, one final outburst, in Oklahoma.

IT IS DIFFICULT to pinpoint the exact beginning of the "boomer" movement, but February 17, 1879, serves well enough. On that day a long article appeared in the *Chicago Times* declaring that the several million acres of unoccupied public land in Indian Territory should be turned over to white homesteaders. The author of the piece was Elias Cornelius Boudinot, a part-Cherokee lawyer then living in Arkansas and believed to be a silent spokesman for the Missouri, Kansas, and Texas Railroad. Boudinot promised to send applicants additional information, including maps and a detailed description of the land and the best route to it. He pointed particularly to the Unassigned Lands in the heart of the Indian Territory. He also regarded the Cheyenne-Arapaho, the Kiowa-Comanche, and the Wichita-Caddo reservations as public domain, as well as Greer County, then a part of Texas. The beauty and fertility of these lands, he said, was unsurpassed—a slight exaggeration, but no more so than the claim that they did not belong to the Plains Indians.

Almost overnight he was swamped with thousands of requests from every section of the country. Meanwhile the original article, reprinted by other papers, fanned the flames of hope in men who had believed that all of the free land was gone. Every letter that reached his office was answered promptly and courte-

XIII · Completion of Statehood

ously, an indication that vast financial resources supported him.

Needless to say, the propaganda emanating from Boudinot's Arkansas headquarters caused plenty of excitement among the diverse interests that favored opening Oklahoma to white settlement and the forces the opposed it. "It is difficult to imagine more incongruous groups than were to be found in each of these rival camps," writes E. E. Dale, the Oklahoma historian. "On the one hand were wealthy railroad officials making common cause with needy farmers or with tiny border towns that were aligned in turn with the great cities interested in a larger wholesale business. On the other side were powerful cattle barons joining hands with poor full-blood Indians and Eastern philanthropists, missionaries, and church groups, and joining their strength to that of whiskey peddlers and outlaws. The struggle was to prove a long and bitter one, but the end must have been apparent quite early even to those determined to fight to the last ditch the influx of whites." [6]

White settlers made their first concerted move to cross the borders of Kansas into the Unassigned Lands in 1879. In April a considerable company of men and women gathered at Chetopa, their covered wagons pointed southward, their leader a man named C. C. Carpenter who had attempted a similar invasion of Indian land in the Black Hills of Dakota the previous year. News of Carpenter's well-advertised venture soon reached Washington D.C., and President Hayes telegraphed General Philip H. Sheridan, commander of the Department of Missouri, to send a military force to the scene immediately. Sheridan complied, and the presence of his troops discouraged the would-be settlers. The "boomers" turned back to their homes, and their leader disappeared.

One observer of the border happenings was not so easily frightened or discouraged, however. David L. Payne, a Union veteran and a former member of the Kansas legislature, assumed the mantle of leadership which Carpenter had abandoned.

On April 26, 1880, Payne and twenty-one followers evaded the troops stationed near Arkansas City, crossed the Kansas border

---

[6] Dale and Wardell: *History of Oklahoma*, p. 231.

into the old Cherokee Outlet, and continued into the Unassigned Lands as far south as the Canadian River. At a site not far from present-day Oklahoma City this advance guard built a stockade and surveyed a town. The leader then sent word back to the remaining members of his colony that "a city of 720 blocks" awaited their arrival. But federal troops arrived instead, and Payne and his small band were escorted back to Kansas.

Payne was later taken to Fort Smith for trial before the United States District Court on a charge of trespassing on Indian lands. Found guilty, he was ordered to pay a fine of $1,000 but never did so. Within a few weeks he was back in Kansas organizing another boomer invasion. Again and again he crossed into the forbidden territory, only to be escorted back by federal troops. In 1884 he was indicted for "conspiracy against the United States," but this only increased his determination. In the midst of preparing for his ninth journey into the Unassigned Lands, now generally referred to as "the District," Payne died of a heart attack on November 28, 1884. But the movement did not collapse. William L. Couch, one of Payne's lieutenants, stepped forward as the new leader.

Within a very few days after Payne's death Couch and a sizable group of boomers camped on Stillwater Creek in the northeastern corner of the District. All of the men were heavily armed and were soon entrenched behind earthworks. Colonel Edward Hatch and a company of troops arrived to dislodge them on January 7, 1885, but Hatch knew that this time it was no routine matter. Rather than attack the boomers and make martyrs of them, he merely surrounded their camp and cut off their supplies from Kansas. At last, with starvation a certainty, Couch abandoned the cause, and the boomer movement temporarily collapsed.

The press throughout the country reported the activities of Carpenter, Payne, and Couch, and this publicity and increasingly exaggerated descriptions of the Oklahoma district as a veritable Garden of Eden added fuel to the fire. Gradually the opposition to opening the lands to white settlement disappeared, except for a rear-guard struggle by the cattle barons, who wanted to retain them for grazing. Realizing that another promise would inevitably

XIII · *Completion of Statehood*

be broken, the Five Civilized Tribes attempted to obtain some concessions before the blow fell.

In January 1885 the principal chiefs of the Creek tribe sent a letter to the Secretary of the Interior protesting the opening of the District but stating that they were entitled to compensation in such an event. Consequently, during the next three years several bills were introduced in Congress to authorize purchase of the Indians' shadowy claims to the unoccupied lands. Each time the powerful ranch lobby prevented passage. Finally, in January 1889 the Secretary of the Interior negotiated agreements with delegations of chiefs who traveled to Washington. The Creeks gave up all their claims to the Unassigned Lands for $2,280,857, a rate of $1.25 an acre. Two million of this amount was to be invested in United States Treasury notes at five-per-cent interest, while the remainder was to be given to the tribe in cash.

The Seminoles sold their holdings at the same rate, receiving $1,912,942, most of which remained in the Treasury at interest. The final barriers to opening the virgin lands were now removed, and America's last continental frontier literally disappeared in a cloud of dust.

On March 2, 1889, Congress rushed through a homestead act that opened almost two million acres of land for white settlement. The land constituted a strip thirty miles wide and approximately fifty miles long from north to south. It was to be distributed on a "first-come-first-served" basis as soon as the President issued the appropriate proclamation. In the meantime the region had to be surveyed into tracts of 160 acres and town sites laid out to receive the rush of anxious homesteaders, merchants, doctors, lawyers, and adventurers already assembled on the north, west, and south sides of the District. The day set for the "run" was April 22, 1889, and as it approached, excitement grew to such intensity that the air seemed charged with electricity.

On April 19 an endless train of canvas-topped wagons, carriages, buggies, and carts moved out of Arkansas City, ambled across the sixty-mile strip of the Cherokee Outlet, and began to line up on the northern border of the Oklahoma District. There were men, women, and children from almost every state: some in the slow-moving vehicles, others on horseback or bicycles, some pushing household belongings in wheelbarrows, and a few carrying fifty- or sixty-pound loads on their backs.

A similar scene was enacted fifty miles farther south, where thousands of people assembled at various fords along the Canadian River, all anxiously awaiting the shot to be fired at high noon on April 22, and turn semi-order into utter confusion. Others jostled for position at various starting points along the western line in the Arapaho Reservation. Some slipped across to hide in ravines and caves until the signal was given, then dash forth and claim choice sites. Although cavalry troops flushed many of these "Sooners" from their places of concealment, a few were able to achieve an unfair advantage.

The mobs gathered on the three sides of the District [7] represented every good and bad class that America had ever produced: honest "sodbusters," "tinhorn" gamblers, Eastern "tenderfeet," painted ladies, and the inevitable "crackpots." They came from everywhere, including the worn-out sand hills of eastern Texas and western Arkansas, the slums of St. Louis and Chicago, the burned-out ranches of New Mexico and Colorado, and the small towns and villages in the North, East, South, and West. There was a farmer from Garden City riding a buffalo, four circus midgets mounted on one horse, a bearded Russian recently escaped from a prison camp in Siberia, a former professor from Heidelberg, a barefooted preacher from Missouri. It was the great American melting pot.

April in Oklahoma is beautiful. It was especially so on April 22, 1889, with the trees in foliage, prairie flowers so thick that there was not a clear space large enough to spread a quilt, the air clean and crisp and moving slightly from south to north. Fifty thousand people waited, with muscles taut and nerves on edge. At the northern border of the District some fifteen passenger trains of

---

[7] The eastern boundary of the District, which joined the frontier of the Indian Nations, was closed to the run.

XIII · Completion of Statehood

the Santa Fe Railroad waited on a single track, all space inside, on top, and between cars filled with human cargo. Fifty miles to the south at Purcell other trains waited. The trains were not to proceed faster than fifteen miles per hour, in fairness to those in wagons and on horseback. But, once the line was crossed, there was no way for the military guards to keep them in check, and people fortunate enough to be aboard grabbed all the town lots in Norman, Oklahoma City, Edmond, and Guthrie before the others could arrive.

At each starting point a mounted Army officer fired a pistol to signal the great opening. People rushed pell-mell across the line and fanned out in all directions. Every eligible homesteader carried a stake with his name or initials carved near the top. He drove it into the ground near the center of a 160-acre plot, then rushed to the nearest land office to pay the fifteen-dollar fee for recording his claim. Disputes were inevitable, and some men were killed; others sold one claim to jump another, but, on the whole, the new homesteaders conducted themselves like participants in an exciting game played according to rules. Within twenty-four hours every farm in the District was taken and half a dozen new towns had sprung into existence.

Where only a slab-board land office and a small forest of wooden stakes designated business sites at eleven o'clock on the morning of April 22, a city of 15,000 people mushroomed into existence by nightfall. This was Guthrie, the capital of the new territory. Here people who had known each other only a few hours came together in a mass meeting, organized a government, wrote a charter, elected officials, and enacted laws. They levied a tax of twenty-five cents a head, but many could not pay it.

"The people were young and enthusiastic," one of the participants explained many years later, "and it was an example of real democracy in action. But we did not have enough money to operate our new city government, so we rounded up a dozen or so prostitutes every night and assessed them a fine of five dollars. We did not have a jail, and the girls would be back in business a short time later. I guess you can say that those tired women kept us solvent for the first few months, until things got better organized."[8]

Scenes similar to the one in Guthrie, but on a smaller scale, took place at Oklahoma City, Norman, Edmond, Kingfisher, El Reno, and Pond Creek. Doctors and lawyers raised flimsy tents and put out their shingles, ready for business. Fly-by-night bankers opened their strongboxes and started receiving deposits. False-front buildings made from pre-cut lumber rose from the prairie sod; livery stables, blacksmith shops, and lumberyards sprang into existence. Muddy water was sold from buckets by the dipper. Wash-tub gin or freshly distilled corn liquor was dispensed at the "open" saloons for twenty-five cents a tin cup. And red dust was everywhere.

THERE WERE other runs after 1889. The largest occurred four years later when the Cherokee Outlet was opened and some 100,000 men, women, and children gave a repeat performance. As Indian titles to Oklahoma lands were extinguished, white settlers moved in. Between 1889 and 1906 there were some ten separate openings, the first five by runs and the remainder by other methods. A lottery distributed a total of 13,000 tracts of 160 acres each in the Kiowa-Comanche and Wichita-Caddo reservations; qualified homesteaders placed their names in a giant box to be drawn out one at a time. Later farms were sold at public auctions.

Acquiring title to the Unassigned Lands proved fairly simple: the federal government merely compensated the Creek and Seminole for their dubious claim to the territory. Meanwhile Congress passed the Dawes Severalty Act in 1887, providing for the

---

[8] The name of this venerable gentleman, interviewed by the author in Guthrie in August 1948, has long since been forgotten, but the memory of his exact words remains fresh. Proof of his statement can be found in the records of Guthrie's first city government.

XIII · Completion of Statehood

eventual dissolution of the Indian tribes as legal entities and the division of their land among individual members. Two years later the Jerome Commission was created to treat with the Western tribes for a cession of their surplus lands, and ultimately the Dawes Commission was set up for the Five Civilized Tribes.

Enormous complications were involved in the work of the two commissions, particularly in seeing that each qualified Indian received a fair share of land. Some individuals received as little as eighty acres and others, notably members of the Osage tribe, 500. This discrepancy was based on the fertility of the soil and its known mineral reserves.[9]

In 1890 "No Man's Land," the strip between the Texas Panhandle and the southern boundaries of Kansas and Colorado, was added to Oklahoma Territory. And six years later, after a prolonged and bitter dispute, the land between the principal forks of Red River—Greer County—was awarded to Oklahoma by the Supreme Court of the United States. As the commissioners cleared various tracts of all titles, they were opened immediately to white settlement. With rare exceptions, each distribution of land added new counties to Oklahoma Territory,[1] until there were twenty-six in 1907, the year of statehood.

The two commissions completed their work by June 30, 1905. With a total Indian and white population in excess of one million, the region of Oklahoma was ready for statehood. At first the members of the Five Civilized Tribes hoped to organize a state of their own, separate from the twenty-six counties constituting

---

[9] Allotment in severalty was made only of the surface soil; the subsurface rights were retained by the tribe as a whole. With the subsequent discovery of oil in the Osage country, all members of the tribe became wealthy, at least for a time.

. . .

[1] The terms "Oklahoma Territory" and "Indian Territory" are confusing and sometimes used wrongly. Official territorial government was not provided for any part of present-day Oklahoma until the so-called Organic Act of 1890. Oklahoma Territory at first included the former Unassigned Lands, or District, and the region of the Panhandle. Eventually it applied to all the territory outside the Five Civilized Tribes. "Indian Territory," therefore, refers to the latter, although it was not a territory in a strict sense, for it did not have a governor appointed by the president or an effective legislature elected by local residents.

Oklahoma Territory, and many of the whites also thought in terms of two states rather than one. From time to time both groups held conventions and sent petitions to Congress, but these aroused little interest. It became evident to the majority of the people in the Twin Territories that single statehood was the only plan that had a chance of success.

In 1906 an enabling act permitting Oklahoma and Indian territories to form a single state government finally passed the Senate and House. This measure also stipulated that New Mexico and Arizona could form a single state, but both rejected the offer, and the measure signed by President Roosevelt on June 16 applied only to the Twin Territories. The people of Oklahoma responded quickly. A constitutional convention of 112 delegates—fifty-five from Oklahoma Territory, fifty-five from Indian Territory, and two from the Osage country—was called at Guthrie.

The president of the convention was William H. ("Alfalfa Bill") Murray, a white citizen of the Chickasaw Nation with an Indian wife and who played a prominent role in shaping the type of government which Oklahoma would have. For more than a generation Murray remained a dominant figure in state politics, even considering himself a serious candidate for the Presidency of the United States on various occasions.

The document that resulted from the convention's effort and was approved by an overwhelming vote of the people in the Twin Territories was a product of the Progressive Era in which it was written. It borrowed heavily from the constitutions of South Dakota and other Midwestern states then under the control of various "farm blocs." Except for its prohibition clause, it was very liberal, providing for a lengthy bill of rights and the initiative and referendum from the outset, as well as regulation of trusts and protection of labor and agricultural interests.

On the morning of November 16, 1907, thousands of people from all over the region poured into Guthrie to witness a symbolic marriage service between "Mr. Oklahoma" and "Miss Indian Territory," the former a tall youth in cowboy garb, the latter a beautiful Indian girl in native costume. The event represented the union of

XIII · Completion of Statehood

the Twin Territories and was climaxed by the swearing in of new officials—all Democrats—and a tremendous barbecue.

To most citizens inauguration day marked the millennium, but to some, especially the full-bloods, it was a day of tragedy. "It broke my heart," one old woman explained. "I went to bed but cried all night long. It seemed more than I could bear that the old Cherokee Nation—my country and my people's country—was no more." [2]

Soon after statehood a major tragedy struck Guthrie. As most of the Republican territorial officials had settled there, the Democratic state government moved the capital to the more friendly climate of Oklahoma City. A half-century later Guthrie's population is only half what it was on April 22, 1889.

November 16, 1907, was both an end and a beginning for Oklahoma, and now only two continental territories remained outside the union of states: New Mexico and Arizona.

THE STRUGGLE for statehood by the former Spanish provinces began early and ended late. They were joined as a single United States territory in the Great Compromise of 1850 and remained united for thirteen years. On February 24, 1863, New Mexico Territory, as the whole region was called, was divided: the western half became Arizona.

Population growth in the Southwestern territories was exceedingly slow. As late as 1890 New Mexico had little more than 150,000 people, while Arizona had less than 90,000, including Indians. The failure of the two regions to keep pace with the rest of the country after the Civil War was partly due to the fierce battles waged between federal troops and the untamed Apache. Both territories were heavily garrisoned, Arizona alone having approxi-

---

[2] Dale and Wardell: *History of Oklahoma*, p. 318.

THE SOUTHWEST: *Old and New*

mately fifteen army posts and 5,000 troops at one period. In April 1879 Chief Victorio and his outlaw band left the Mescalero Reservation and terrorized southern New Mexico and Arizona. Driven south into Chihuahua by American forces, Victorio was attacked and killed by Mexican troops in 1883. A short time later a second band, under Geronimo, left the San Carlos Reservation to spread an even bloodier path of destruction. When Geronimo finally surrendered on September 3, 1886, the Indian wars on the Southwestern frontier came to an end.

Meanwhile New Mexico suffered from another kind of war which thwarted its growth and political development—the Lincoln County War. This bloody feud began in 1876 and involved many prominent cattlemen and rival politicians. Its most famous participant, William H. Bonney, better known as "Billy the Kid," killed a score of men before he was shot by Sheriff Pat F. Garrett on July 14, 1881. Territorial officials took no effective measures to stop the bloodshed in Lincoln County and southwestern New Mexico until President Rutherford B. Hayes appointed General Lew Wallace governor in 1878. At the same time federal troops were ordered to the scene, but a truce was reached before they saw action.

With few exceptions, the appointed officials of New Mexico and Arizona were political hacks who served without distinction. General Wallace, the best known, devoted most of his time at Santa Fe to writing his monumental book *Ben-Hur*. The outstanding feature of Governor William A. Pile's administration, 1869–71, was his alleged sale of the Spanish Santa Fe Archives as waste paper.[3] Throughout most of its territorial days New Mexico remained under the control of a political group known as the "Santa Fe Ring," while ranchers and silver and copper barons constituted the real powers in Arizona Territory. Their influence continued after the two regions became states in 1912.

---

[3] Only one fourth of these valuable records was subsequently recovered. *New Mexico: A Guide to a Colorful State* (New York: Hastings House; 1940), p. 77.

XIII · Completion of Statehood

Transportation remained a chronic problem in New Mexico and Arizona until the coming of the Santa Fe and Southern Pacific railroads, and even then large areas remained comparatively isolated. More than half of the people were Spanish-Americans and Indians living on haciendas, ranches, and reservations in a status similar to that of medieval serfs. A few prosperous ranchers operated vast "spreads" scattered over far-flung areas; and small irrigated farms in the river valleys yielded lush crops. A few valuable mines were producing silver, copper, and coal, but most such properties were absentee-owned and never extensive enough to attract a large population from the outside.

Various movements for statehood for the territories were inaugurated from time to time. Sparsity of population was the explanation Congress gave for rejecting them, and this excuse had some validity. Arizona in 1900, for example, still had no more than 120,000 people, most of whom were concentrated in the four towns of Tucson, Prescott, Phoenix, and Yuma. New Mexico's population did not extend much beyond the Rio Grande Valley or outside the cities of Albuquerque, Santa Fe, and San Fernando de Taos. But perhaps the real reason for the long delay in granting statehood was political: the belief that Arizona would be Democratic and New Mexico Republican.

As early as 1892 a bill providing for the admission of Arizona as a state passed the House of Representatives, but it was killed in a Republican-dominated Senate. Similar bills were introduced for New Mexico from time to time, but not until the Spanish-American War in 1898 did either territory win widespread support. Arizona supplied three full troops and New Mexico 340 volunteers to the Rough Riders, a would-be cavalry unit organized by Colonel Leonard Wood and Lieutenant Colonel Theodore Roosevelt. This small but colorful outfit landed near Santiago on June 22 and went into action two days later. Although not mounted, as the public generally believed, and not even very rough—as some of Roosevelt's critics subsequently charged—they nevertheless gained no small degree of fame for themselves and their commander, as well as for the Southwest.

When Roosevelt became president in 1901, New Mexico and Arizona felt certain that they would soon be rewarded with statehood. Governor Miguel A. Otero of New Mexico launched an all-out campaign for admittance the next year, and a short time later Senator Albert J. Beveridge and his subcommittee on statehood made a tour of inspection of the three Southwestern territories, Arizona, New Mexico, and Oklahoma. The committee returned to Washington unimpressed by what it had seen. It reported that Arizona did not have enough people to support a state government, but recommended that it be admitted into the Union as part of New Mexico. A bill embodying this proposal was rejected by Congress.

Again in 1905 Beveridge's subcommittee presented a bill providing for single statehood, subject to approval of the people in the two territories. New Mexicans were willing, but Arizonans voted against the measure overwhelmingly. They argued that all but 25,000 of their 150,000 people were Anglo-Americans, whereas the New Mexicans were predominantly Spanish-American and would outvote them in legislative matters. Consequently, the question was dropped and only Oklahoma was admitted at this time.

Finally on June 10, 1910, Congress passed the enabling act that authorized Arizona and New Mexico to frame state constitutions. Both territories called constitutional conventions and set to work. The two documents were ready for federal consideration early in 1911, but President Taft felt that the proposed constitutions were too radical. He especially objected to the clauses providing for the recall of judges, and the initiative and referendum were not looked upon with great favor either. Accordingly, Arizona and New Mexico modified their handiwork and Taft reluctantly approved. Most of the so-called radical features were promptly reinstated as soon as the state governments began to function. Even so, the constitutions of New Mexico and Arizona basically are conservative documents, for their provisions for the initiative and referendum are practically unenforceable.

The Enabling Act for New Mexico became effective with the President's signature on January 6, 1912, and the forty-seventh

XIII · *Completion of Statehood*

state joined the Union. Five weeks later, on February 14, Arizona added the forty-eighth star to the flag. All of the Southwest, America's so-called last frontier, was now a part of the contiguous system of states: equal, separate, sovereign, dependent.

XIV

THE CHANGING INDIAN

AT MID-CENTURY the American Indian population is variously estimated from 400,000 to 800,000, depending on one's definition. The maximum figure includes all those with one quarter or more Indian blood, while the minimum indicates only those with more than half. A large proportion of these Indians lives in the Southwest. Oklahoma claims 120,000, New Mexico 44,000, and Arizona about 70,000. Texas, where probably more Indians lived at the time of the Spanish conquest than in any of the other Southwestern states, had only 300 or 400 when the census of 1950 was taken, and they lived on one small reservation.

XIV · *The Changing Indian*

The Indians increased in some parts of the Southwest after the arrival of Anglo-Americans. In others they were expelled or almost exterminated as the result of war, disease, disappearance of the buffalo, and loss of land. Where a particular group managed to remain stable or gain population, it was owing principally to geographical and cultural isolation. Outstanding examples are the Pueblos of New Mexico, whose population has remained static for almost four centuries, and the Navajos, who have increased more than a thousand per cent since 1868.

The reservation system inaugurated for most Southwestern Indians soon after the Civil War proved to be both good and bad for the Indian. Tribes such as the Navajo, Hopi, and Apache have retained their identities, customs, and traditions. But it contributed to their impoverishment and degradation by isolating them from scientific and technical developments. And whether the full-blood lives on or off a tribal reserve, he knows that he must "follow the white man's road" if he wishes to survive.

When the federal government abolished the reservation system in Oklahoma in 1898, it inadvertently encouraged intermarriage between the red and white races. The process of course diluted Indian blood, but the resulting individuals fared better financially than their full-blooded Indian forebears. The Oklahoma Indians undoubtedly would have preferred to remain members of a sovereign tribe or independent nation. However, a weak nation surrounded by powerful neighbors usually leads an insecure existence.

Indians in Oklahoma are fully integrated into the community, a situation that surprises many visitors. John Gunther wrote in *Inside U.S.A.* about a visit to Oklahoma City: "Perhaps I had been in the South too long. I was thinking about the Indian 'problem,' and I had the uncomfortable premonition that I would now have to confront another race almost totally excluded from social affairs, as well as politically downtrodden and economically submerged."[1] But his fears disappeared quickly. A prominent insur-

---

[1] *Inside U.S.A.* (1946), p. 870.

The Southwest: *Old and New*

ance man and governor of the Chickasaw "nation" told him: "My folks started marrying white people, until they damn well married all the Indian blood out." And subsequent observations and comments proved this to be the general rule rather than an exception.

Some old-time "blanket Indians" live in remote parts of the state, but there is no prejudice against them or against Anglo-Saxons with Indian blood. In fact, a touch of Indian blood is usually a source of pride and prestige and can afford a candidate for political office considerable advantage. Some of the richest people in Oklahoma are part Indian—thanks largely to tribal mineral rights granted at the time of the abolition of reservations and the allotment of the land in severalty. The people classified as Indians represent less than six per cent of the state's total population, yet they exercise an influence far out of proportion to their numbers.

In Texas, Arizona, and New Mexico the Indian has not fared so well as in Oklahoma. Many have retained their tribal customs, language, land, religion, and dress, but they have been—until very recently—the most impoverished, illiterate, and disease-ridden people in the United States. They resisted the white man's civilization and religion so persistently that they failed to improve their health and living standards. Their history would seem to condemn the whole idea of the reservation.

Happily, however, there is another side of the story, and today it appears unlikely that the principal reservations remaining in the Southwest will ever be abolished. During recent years the federal government, private associations friendly to the Indians, and the various tribal councils have been working to raise living standards for the people on the reservations. Some of the changes have been revolutionary, particularly in schools, roads, health, and opportunities for employment. Some have proved too drastic and too sudden for immediate acceptance by the conservative members of the tribes. Clearly, however, a traditional way of life is disappearing.

To understand the Southwestern Indians today, some knowledge of the reservation system is necessary. Although the idea of confining various tribes to large specific tracts of land was

XIV · *The Changing Indian*

introduced soon after the American Revolution, it was not tried in the Southwest until a few years before the Civil War.[2] In 1854 Texas set aside twelve leagues of land in three separate districts for various Indian tribes. The land was to be approved, surveyed, and supervised by the United States government, but was to revert to state jurisdiction when no longer used by the Indians.

Captain Randolph B. Marcy, representing the War Department, and Robert S. Neighbors, Indian Agent for the State of Texas, selected and surveyed the reserves. After conferring with representatives of the Comanche, Waco, Wichita, and Caddo tribes, they decided on two sites of four leagues each—18,576 acres—near the headwaters of the Brazos and Clear Fork rivers in northwestern Texas. A third tract in the same area was eventually set aside for the Mescalero and Lipan Apaches living west of the Pecos River, but these tribes refused the offer.

A few scattered bands of Indians eventually settled on the Brazos and Clear Fork reservations, but they hated the new arrangement. The reservation was abandoned because of distrust between the Indians and the white settlers. The whites complained that the Indians stole their livestock, and some of these charges were true. In 1859 a settler accused Neighbors of showing more concern for the Indians than for the whites and killed him. Threats, attacks, and reprisals kept the frontier of Texas in continuous turmoil until the Indians abandoned the reservations and moved across Red River.

Meanwhile, except for a small band of Alabama-Coushatta, most of the Texas Indians moved into the far western part of the state. Even so implacable a foe of the red man as Mirabeau B. Lamar, second president of the Republic of Texas, adopted a peaceful policy toward this tribe as early as 1839. Fifteen years later the Alabama-Coushatta obtained a permanent home when the state gave them 1,200 acres of land near Houston. In 1928 the federal

---

[2] Removal of the Five Civilized Tribes to Oklahoma was begun a full generation before the Civil War, as previously noted. Their new holdings were called "nations," rather than reservations, and technically the members of each tribe were not wards of the federal government.

government purchased an additional league (4,428.4 acres) for their reservation, and today the Alabama-Coushatta Reservation remains the only one in Texas.

With the exception of some of the older people, the approximately 400 Alabama-Coushatta are bilingual; they learn the Indian tongue first, and then English. There is little intermarriage with whites, but adoption of the white man's way of life is reflected in the Indians' housing, clothing, food, education, newspapers, transportation, and medical care. Many of the younger generation attend colleges in Texas and Oklahoma, and others secure jobs in nearby towns and cities. All members still consider the reservation as home, however, and return there for traditional ceremonies and festivals.

The departure of the Indians from the Brazos and Clear Fork reservations by no means ended the problem in that region. In Texas, as in other parts of the Southwest, the red men took advantage of the distractions caused by the Civil War to harass white settlements. Repeated raids by Comanches, Kiowas, and Apaches forced the abandonment of millions of acres of farm and ranch land in the western half of the state. For four years several companies of Texas Rangers and Confederate troops were occupied with efforts to counter these forays, and Colonel Kit Carson of the U.S. Army led the New Mexico militia in a campaign against a large encampment of Comanches and Kiowas of Texas soil in 1864.[3]

When the Civil War ended, the federal government undertook to settle the frontier Indian problem once and for all. In 1867 representatives of the government met with chiefs of the Kiowa, Southern Cheyenne, Arapaho, Wichita, Apache, and Comanche bands at Medicine Lodge, Kansas. The Indians agreed to accept restricted reservations between the Arkansas and Canadian rivers, but the ink was hardly dry on the treaty before the Southwestern

---

[3] Carson's campaign culminated in the first Battle of Adobe Walls in what is now Hutchinson County, Texas, November 26, 1864. Carson's force consisted of 400 mounted troops with two howitzers. The Indians' overwhelming numbers forced Carson to retreat, but the battle convinced them that they would stand little chance in the future against well-armed whites.

XIV · *The Changing Indian*

frontier erupted in a war that continued intermittently until 1875.

The causes were many, but the most fundamental was the Indians' unwillingness to be confined to a reservation. "We have tried the white man's road, and found it hard," explained Satanta, leading chief of the Kiowas in 1869. "We find it nothing but a little corn which hurts our teeth; no sugar; no coffee. We want to have guns, breech-loading carbines, ammunition and caps. These are part of the white man's road, and yet you want us to go back to making arrow-heads, which are used by bad, foolish Indians. . . ."[4]

The Plains Indians depended on the buffalo for food, clothing, and shelter. By 1873 these gregarious beasts were practically gone except for a few thousand that grazed on the tall prairie grass of western Oklahoma and the Texas Panhandle. With hides bringing top prices in the 1870's, unscrupulous white men poached on reservation land to slaughter the buffalo. The Indians naturally retaliated.

Government policies for controlling the Indians and protecting the whites changed from year to year. The Indian was caught between the activities of the War and Interior departments, each jealous of the other's authority. Added to this was the confusion caused by conflicting reports of agents, military commanders, and well-meaning missionaries. Whenever a tribe received a tract of land, it also accepted the promise that this was its permanent home. But soon the bewildered tribe was shifted to another, and usually a smaller, reservation. This and the constant pressure of white settlers to obtain or destroy the red men's possessions resulted in a fight to the death.

The reservation Indians easily slipped past the line of forts protecting the Texas and New Mexico frontiers. For years they carried out moonlight raids along the border, destroyed homes, bushwhacked travelers, stole or killed livestock, kidnapped women

---

[4] Quoted from "Report of Commissioner of Indian Affairs made to the Secretary of the Interior for the year 1869," p. 62, in Carl Coke Rister's *Southern Plainsman* (Norman: University of Oklahoma Press; 1938), p. 93.

THE SOUTHWEST: *Old and New*

and children. Federal troops occasionally surprised them in their winter camps. The most famous incident of this kind occurred in November 1868 when General George Custer killed more than a hundred Cheyenne, Kiowa, and Arapaho in the Washita Valley of western Oklahoma. At other times Indians were held as hostages and captured chiefs were forced to stand trial for the crimes committed by their young braves. In 1871 the three principal chiefs of the Kiowas—Satank, Big Tree, and Satanta—were imprisoned by General W. T. Sherman at the Fort Sill agency. Later Satanta was killed while trying to escape, and Satank and Big Tree were confined to the Texas state prison at Huntsville for several months.

Each atrocity by Indian or white man brought retaliation, with innocent people the most frequent victims. Throughout 1874 the whole frontier of northwestern Texas and southwestern Oklahoma remained in turmoil. Forty-six companies of cavalry and infantry constantly searched for outlaw bands of Indians, and the reservation system in western Oklahoma hardly existed except in name. Toward the end of the next year the last of the Plains Indians, the Kwahari Comanche, under their chief Quanah Parker, rode in to the Wichita agency at Anadarko and asked to settle in peace. The agency eventually assigned Parker and his band a tract of land near present-day Lawton, Oklahoma.

How many were killed in the decade of fighting is not known, but the once powerful bands of Comanche, Kiowa, Southern Cheyenne, and Arapaho were reduced to about 7,500—less than half their original numbers. Probably more died of disease and hunger than from bayonets and bullets, and the surviving members of the various tribes were too weak to offer further resistance.

The reservations in western Oklahoma stayed intact for only a few years after 1875. They comprised about eight million acres, or more than a thousand acres for each Indian.[5] This seemed more than enough to support the Indians decently, but few knew how to farm, nor were they disposed to learn. They preferred to

---

[5] The Kiowa-Comanche-Apache reservation was situated between the Red and Washita rivers in the southwestern corner of present-day Oklahoma. The Cheyenne-Arapaho and Wichita-Caddo reservations were located in the west-central part of the state.

XIV · *The Changing Indian*

live on the paltry annuities issued in monthly installments at agency headquarters at Fort Sill, Anadarko, and Darlington, plus the fees they extracted from Texas trail drovers and ranchers who crossed their lands or leased them for grazing purposes.

In 1892 the Cheyenne-Arapaho reservation was opened to white settlement after each member of the tribe, regardless of age, had received an allotment of 160 acres. Nine years later the Kiowa-Comanche-Apache and Wichita reservations likewise were divided between tribal members and white settlers. Thus, the reservation system established in Oklahoma and Texas during the last half of the nineteenth century disappeared in 1901, except for the small Alabama-Coushatta tract in the southeastern corner of Texas. The Indians still faced many difficulties in adjusting their lives and cultures to a new environment, but they no longer constituted a severe problem to the white man.

Pleasant Porter, one of the Indians' most able spokesmen, probably summed up the feelings of his people when in 1906, just before several thousand of them became citizens of the new state of Oklahoma, he said: "The vitality of our race still persists. We have not lived for naught. We are the original discoverers of this continent and the conquerors of it from the animal kingdom. . . . We have given the European people on this continent our thought forces—the best blood of our ancestors has intermingled with [that of] their best statesmen and leading citizens. We have made ourselves an indestructible element in their national history. . . . We have led the vanguard of civilization in our conflicts with them for tribal existence from ocean to ocean. The race that rendered this service to other nations of mankind cannot utterly perish." [6]

THE INDIAN civilizations in New Mexico, older than those of Oklahoma and Texas, were less violently affected by the arrival of

---

[6] Creek Tribal Records, 35644; 59 Cong., 2 sess., Sen. Rep. No. 5013. I, pp. 627 ff. Quoted in Angie Debo: *The Road to Disappearance* (Norman: University of Oklahoma Press; 1941), p. 377.

The Southwest: *Old and New*

white settlers from the East. Their arid lands did not attract the vast populations that crowded into Oklahoma and Texas.

The Spaniards had largely subdued the New Mexico Indians before the arrival of the Anglo-Americans. By the sixteenth century most of the Indians dwelt in some thirty pueblos along the banks of the Rio Grande. Today more than half of these settlements are occupied exclusively by Indians. These 20,000 people live in picturesque adobe houses that look much like the ones Coronado found in 1540. They are civilized Indians in every sense of the word. They grow their own food on communal farms close to their villages, make pottery, clothes, and ornaments for sale, and occasionally work at odd jobs in the nearby cities of Taos, Santa Fe, Gallup, Los Alamos, and Albuquerque. Except for the uprisings of some of the pueblos against the Spanish in 1680 and 1696 and against the Anglo-Americans in 1847, these Indians have remained at peace with the whites.

By the Treaty of Guadalupe Hidalgo in 1848 the United States recognized the Spanish Crown's ancient land grants to the Pueblos. Their eighteen reservations now occupy a total of almost 700,000 acres, scattered from Taos in the north to Isleta in the extreme south and as far west as Zuñi, near the Arizona–New Mexico line. For more than a century their interests have been protected by federal agents at Santa Fe, who perhaps have experienced less difficulty with their charges than any similar officials in the Indian service. Accustomed to a self-sufficient economy and social life, the Pueblos ask little from the government.

From time to time they faced minor problems caused by white encroachment, for some of the boundary lines of their reservations are vague. Lack of water for irrigation and the scarcity of land suitable for farming also plagued them. Before the 1930's the federal government did little to improve irrigation facilities, and the Pueblos did not always help themselves in this regard.

The largest of the pueblos, Laguna, lies about forty miles west of Albuquerque on United States Highway 66 and contains approximately 4,000 inhabitants. A few years ago the Lagunas leased part of their reservation lands to the Anaconda Copper Com-

XIV · The Changing Indian

pany for uranium mining. The company pays the tribal council approximately two million dollars in fees each year. "Although the Lagunas need a water supply badly, and they are eager to have a public junior high school on their land," the Secretary of the New Mexico Indian Association told this writer in August 1957, "they have been poor so long that they can't resist the temptation to divide the money among themselves." Some other Southwestern tribes that have acquired large sums of money in recent years are using their trust funds more judiciously.

Since the end of World War II, Pueblo Indian children have attended schools in Oklahoma, Colorado, and New Mexico in appreciable numbers. Day schools were established and partly supported by the federal government soon after the conquest of New Mexico, but for religious reasons the people were reluctant to send their children to them. As late as 1885 there were only three such institutions, and little more than ten per cent of the children attended. Gradually new buildings were added, and after 1900 enrollment showed a steady increase. The current trend, both on and off the reservation, is toward attendance of public rather than parochial schools.

In 1956 more than 5,500 Indian children were enrolled in New Mexican public schools. This figure represents between eighty-five and ninety per cent of all children of school age in the eighteen pueblos and on the Jicarilla and Mescalero Apache and Navajo reservations.[7] The federal government pays sixty-five per cent of the school cost of each child, including noon meals, transportation, and supplies, plus the construction cost of school buildings on the basis of a thousand dollars a pupil.

The percentage that graduates from high school is comparatively small, but the number of boys and girls who attend colleges and universities is increasing. Most of these study engineering, nursing, law, or education at the University of New Mexico, and

---

[7] This total showed an increase of more than 1,500 over the previous year, which undoubtedly was due to New Mexico's recent compulsory-school-attendance law. *Newsletter* (Santa Fe: New Mexico Association on Indian Affairs), October 1956.

then return to their reservations to help their own people. This new generation of college students is very conscious of the transitional problems its race is facing and of the fact that the reservations cannot support the expanded Indian population. They are also aware that a landless Indian more often than not goes on relief.

Every year since January 1955 delegates from the various pueblos and reservations in New Mexico have attended an Indian Youth Council at the state university at Albuquerque. There is an unwritten rule that anyone who wishes to speak will be heard, however long the meeting. In the course of a typical convention some twelve or fifteen papers are read by Indian students, most of whom are members of the Kiva Club, a University of New Mexico student organization.

The quality of these papers and speeches would do credit to almost any professional academic group, and they give a strong indication that the younger generation of Southwestern Indians is determined to join the twentieth century. Speakers admonish their young listeners, many of whom are of high-school age, "to compromise with the white civilization." They point out that indifference and withdrawal are no longer effective responses to the powerful pressures and changes about them. Indian youths are urged to take advantage of the many scholarships that are available, to exercise their right to vote when they come of age, to combat the evils of alcohol and *peyote* that plague their people, to seek regular employment, to hold their jobs in spite of conflicting tribal ceremonies on fixed dates, and, above all, "not forever take and not return." [8]

Another sign of the Pueblos' "awakening" is their recent interest in state politics. In 1947 a federal judge ruled that Southwestern Indians were entitled to the franchise, even though their reservation lands were not subject to state taxes. By 1957 the people at all but four of the New Mexico pueblos—Taos, Santa Ana, San Fe-

---

[8] Ibid., February 1957.

XIV · *The Changing Indian*

lipe, and Santo Domingo—were registered and qualified to vote in state and national elections.

Farming is still the mainstay of the eighteen New Mexican pueblos, although pottery making is also an important source of income. Perhaps the most famous pottery comes from San Ildefonso. However, the women of Isleta, Tesuque, Jemez, Picuris, Santa Clara, Acoma, Cochiti, Zia, and Santo Domingo sell products of various degrees of quality. Zuñi Pueblo is known for its turquoise-and-silver jewelry and shell mosaics, and Santo Domingo and Cochiti likewise manufacture handsome jewelry. Although Laguna Pueblo is richer today, Taos is considered the most prosperous, for it is surrounded by fertile agricultural land at the foot of the Sangre de Cristo Mountains and has plenty of water for irrigation.

Pueblo lands generally are not fertile enough to support rising standards of living and the increased population. As a consequence, the men seek part-time jobs on ranches or in the nearby cities, while their women and children sell pottery and jewelry along the highways and in town plazas.

During World War II more than a thousand Pueblo Indians served in the armed forces, and hundreds more took jobs in factories. At the war's end practically all returned to their villages without much money. Not everyone came back with a desire to take up the old ways: some wanted the white man's gadgets such as cookstoves, iceboxes, plumbing, even cars; and today both the exterior and interior of almost every adobe home show evidence that they have such items.

Each pueblo has an autonomous government. Laws are enacted by a local council of ex-governors of the pueblo, and if these conflict with laws passed by the legislature of New Mexico, the pueblo's laws take precedence. The lands are held in common, and they are inalienable, but the federal government reserves the right to supervise their management. This means that the Pueblo Indian residing on the reservation finds himself in a peculiar position: he is not a ward of the government, but he must obey regulations governing the use of his land.

The Southwest: *Old and New*

The young Pueblo Indian is also torn between the old life and new ideas. He is taught from childhood to respect the authority of the local council, and several veterans of the armed forces who violated rules against drinking have been publicly whipped. Children are obliged to make decisions that would test an adult, for in the public schools they are told by teachers that the secret rituals of the Kiva are only fit for savages. Breaking with the past is a struggle that continues into adulthood and becomes ever more complex.

The results of this transition can be foreseen. The extent to which the younger generation has absorbed the white man's religion, education, economy, and gadgetry makes it clear that the ancient ceremonies, rituals, secret societies, and traditions cannot be preserved in an unadulterated form forever. The Indians will not be the only losers, for the white man has yet to learn how to live with his neighbor in peace and settle his arguments by the "long talk."

More numerous than the Pueblo Indians in the modern Southwest are the Apaches and Navajos—and their histories are more bloody and tragic. At the same time their transition to the white man's way of life was more revolutionary. When the United States acquired what is now Arizona at the end of the Mexican War, the region was inhabited by several bands of Indians which no one had completely subdued. The Yumas, Washos, Paiutes, Miwoks, and Havasupis were few in number, but the Apaches and Navajos presented a major problem.

In 1848 the Apaches resided in southern Arizona, New Mexico, and southwestern Texas and included various groups—Jicarilla, Mescalero, Haulapai, Mogollon, Mimbreno, and Chiricahua. Their kinsmen the Navajo, Ute, and a few Shoshone occupied northern Arizona and a small portion of New Mexico. The Apaches

XIV · *The Changing Indian*

probably numbered 12,000 and were almost completely nomadic, living by hunting and plundering.

The Navajos—an Athapascan word meaning "people"—were slightly more numerous than the Apaches and roamed over an enormous territory—northern Arizona, northwestern New Mexico, southeastern Utah, and southwestern Colorado. Except for raids against the Spanish, these nomads had little contact with white civilization before 1848. Bands of them roamed the land seeking pasturage for their sheep, cattle, goats, and horses; others cultivated small fields of corn, melons, and vegetables in Canyon de Chelly.

The United States first attempted to exercise control over these wild bands through local Indian commissioners appointed to work with the military commanders at various strategic forts. The Navajos took to the warpath in 1858, followed by the Apaches a short time later. The problem of managing them was made more difficult when the Civil War caused the transfer of many federal troops east of the Mississippi. Raids by Apaches and Navajos and counterraids by federal troops and state militia continued for several years.

In 1869 approximately 20,000 Indians lived in New Mexico and 30,000 in Arizona: the Navajos, Pueblos, Hopis, and Pimas. But the several bands of Apaches remained virtually at large, roaming and plundering the entire Southwest and northern Mexico. Federal troops stationed at more than half a dozen frontier posts, plus thousands of militia and white settlers carried on unrelenting war against them for another decade, but did not entirely subdue them. President Ulysses S. Grant attempted to make peace by appointing agents recommended by various church groups, but this plan failed as miserably as earlier ones. The Apaches merely used the agents' headquarters as feeding stations where they came from time to time for food and issues of blankets and clothing between raids.

Atrocities increased until 1871. Then the federal government decided to confine them to reservations that unlicensed white men would be forbidden to enter. Rounding up the Indians took fifteen or sixteen years, but by 1887 all the tribes in Arizona and New Mexico were settled, more or less permanently. The Apaches were assigned two large reservations in New Mexico—the Jicarilla, a 1,165-square-mile tract in the northwest, and the Mescalero, a 741-square-mile reservation in the south. They turned to farming, cutting timber, and raising livestock, and since 1887 have given little trouble to their white neighbors.

Each reservation now has approximately a thousand inhabitants. The Mescaleros are well known in the Southwest for the high quality of their livestock and enjoy some degree of prosperity as a result. During recent years the Jicarillas have accumulated a substantial tribal trust fund from mining and oil leases.

The more primitive and wilder Apache bands, such as the Mimbreno, Mogollon, Coyotero, and Chiricahua, proved more difficult to bring under control. Between 1871 and 1886 these groups shifted from reservation to reservation throughout the Southwest. No matter what the military or civilian policy, or where their lands were located, they refused to stay confined to a restricted area. Small bands under the leadership of such irreconcilables as Cochise, Choto, Natchez, Loco, Geronimo, and Victorio periodically fled the reservation, only to be hunted down and harassed until they sought permission to return to the agency. By 1886 all of the outlaw Apache leaders were either dead or imprisoned.

There are fifteen Indian reservations in Arizona today, and twenty-five in New Mexico. According to the 1950 census, approximately half of all the Indians in Arizona, or more than 33,000, reside on the Navajo reservation.[9] Some 6,000 live on the reservations of Fort Apache and San Carlos, which total about 5,000 square miles along the Gila River in southern Arizona. After 1890 these Indians leased much of their acreage to cattle companies and lived on the meager proceeds and government annuities. But the cattlemen abused their privileges and pastured some 12,000 head

---

[9] About two thirds of the Navajo reservation are in Arizona, and the rest is in Utah and New Mexico. The total Navajo population, on and off the reservation, is estimated at 88,000. The reservation contains almost sixteen million acres of land.

XIV · *The Changing Indian*

where there should have been no more than 2,000. Meanwhile the Indians learned the cattle business from the white ranchers and by 1936 got them dispossessed from Indian land entirely. Livestock raising and truck farming now support a fair standard of living for the Indians.

In addition to the Apache and Navajo, there are several smaller tribes on a dozen reservations in Arizona. The largest of these are the Papago (4,500) and the Hopi (4,000) whose thousand-square-mile reservation lies within the boundaries of the Navajo holdings—a reservation within a reservation. The Havasupi, Haulapai, Yavapai, Maricopa, Pima, Kaibab, and other groups vary in number from two or three dozen to 300 or 400.

As the Navajos are the largest single body of full-blooded Indians remaining in the United States and occupy an area in the Southwest greater than all of New England, they deserve special attention. With the possible exception of the Pueblos, the Navajos have changed less during the past four centuries than any other Indians in North America. Within two decades, however, they undoubtedly experienced a greater transformation than in their entire previous existence.

When the Navajos left Fort Sumner on the Bosque Redondo reservation in 1867 and returned to their traditional home in the Four Corners, the tribe had grown to almost 9,000. To help rehabilitate them the federal government set aside land sufficient to give 160 acres to each family and eighty to individuals. Furthermore, it was agreed that they would receive a total of 15,000 sheep, plus rations of clothing, seed, food, and farming equipment for a period of five years. Had the People understood what an acre was, they might have refused these seemingly generous terms. For, even in the nineteenth century, a whole section (640 acres) of this barren mesa country could barely feed a handful of goats; and as for farming, the Navajos had neither skill nor desire—not to mention water.

The promised sheep arrived two years after the Navajos returned. Meanwhile, the People lived on government rations grudgingly handed out by the military officials at Fort Wingate and what-

The Southwest: *Old and New*

ever rabbits, rats, and other small game they could capture. But the sheep and goats multiplied rapidly after 1870, and so did the Navajos. The job of herding, shearing, and weaving was transferred to the women and children, while the men sought part-time jobs on farms and ranches near the reservation. It was during these hard years of reconstruction that they began their work in silver which has become so famous. Also, where irrigation was possible, they produced small crops.

Perhaps the Navajo was happy in his old surroundings, but it soon became obvious that the government had not given the tribe enough land. The original grant was only half a million acres, but between 1878 and 1934 additional tracts were added by the federal government until the reservation approximated sixteen million acres. By the latter date the tribal population of 40,000 owned herds numbering more than 880,000 animals. Even so, the situation was desperate. Crops suffered from periodic droughts; the quality of sheep had degenerated because of unselective breeding; the wool clip had dropped from an average of four pounds per animal to little more than one and a half pounds; and grass had almost disappeared from the land. Alcoholism and illiteracy were increasing rapidly; tuberculosis and trachoma, or "sore eyes," were widespread; and because of the great depression odd jobs could no longer be found.

Friends of the People had seen the crisis approaching a decade earlier and taken feeble steps to help. Already many Americans knew that overgrazing and destruction of the soil in one part of the country meant floods and trouble in other parts. Government officials tried to persuade the Navajo to adopt sounder methods of husbandry, and they pointed out that the herding methods borrowed from the Spaniards were unscientific. But the Indian only smiled at the idea of keeping rams and ewes apart so that lambs would be born at convenient times, or dipping sheep to avoid ticks and diseases. And the suggestion that they reduce their herds by half and sell or destroy "hammerheaded" horses in order to give the grass a chance to come back was greeted with contempt. All of this was "crazy talk" from "Washington." Every hogan kept its

XIV · *The Changing Indian*

sheep and nearly every man his horse. Traditional ceremonies continued to hold the People together and preserve the old customs as the general level of prosperity dropped alarmingly.[1]

A depression and a new administration suddenly brought the Navajo problem into focus. With the New Deal came a fresh program for the reservation Indian.

The Navajo now obtained relief work just as the unemployed white man did, except that forty dollars per month meant mere existence to one and wealth to the other. The Indian was put to work conserving the soil and building irrigation projects on his reservation; men and boys came from remote corners of the mesa country to dig ditches, wells, and reservoirs and to construct dams. Some learned to drive tractors and operate drag lines. In the evening they could attend trade classes or study English. "It was a healthy start towards a new life, but it could not fail to mean injury to the old." The Navajo with money in his pockets was not the same person who a few months before had had little food and a small flock. He now began to act and think more like the white man whom he traditionally despised.

Millions of dollars in federal funds were spent on the Navajo reservation during the remainder of the thirties. In addition, experts arrived to improve the health of the People and their flocks, introduce fertilizer and new crops, and improve the quality of silverwork. A Navajo capital was built at Window Rock, near Fort Defiance. New school buildings went up, as well as a new hospital and an animal-research laboratory. Later the reservation was divided into districts, and the number of sheep which each could support on the available grass was determined. The Navajo was told to slaughter the "extra" livestock, but was paid for doing so.

Instead of welcoming government help, the Navajo—like many other groups during those years—resented the intrusion. He

---

[1] The so-called "Meriam Report" in 1927 revealed that the annual income of some Navajo families was as low as $31, that schools stood empty and government hospital beds unused in spite of the alarming increase in tuberculosis. Ruth M. Underhill: *The Navajo* (Norman: University of Oklahoma Press; 1956), pp. 233–4.

was being hurried into a new way of life overnight, and he could not make the transition without feeling that he was losing more than he gained.

World War II did the most to bridge the gap between his Middle Ages and the modern world. Young men volunteered for the armed services faster than they could be drafted. Some 3,600 men and a few dozen women served in the United States Army, Navy, and Marine Corps. They received the same compensation as other Americans, and their families the same allotments. Those too old or too young to enlist could make "fortunes" at the big ordnance plants and airplane factories constructed in the desert country. Money poured in from various directions and poured out in even more. Liquor and sweet wines took a lot of cash, but some families, for the first time in their lives, acquired dishes, stoves, factory-made blankets, furniture, and secondhand cars.

When the four-year bonanza ended, soldiers and war workers drifted back to the reservation. The great "barbecue" ended as suddenly as it began, but the Navajo would never again be exactly the same. Once he had become accustomed to money, three meals a day, a comfortable bed and clothing, he could not relish the idea of giving them up. Some Navajos even wanted an education.

The post-war period proved the most difficult that the Navajo ever faced. Suddenly there were not enough schools, hospitals, adequate houses. The reservation could not provide employment for everyone, and the government was no longer in the large-scale relief business. Not even the old ceremonies gave the young men and women comfort, yet they were not ready for the white man's world. Some sought refuge from their frustrations in the use of *peyote*, a narcotic plant that produces hallucinations, and others escaped from reality with "firewater." Many moved from the reservation to Los Angeles, San Francisco, Denver, Chicago, and other cities, only to find themselves more miserable.

Only a few years before, the Navajos had appeared ready to venture forth with new wings, but now they were fast slipping back to hopeless poverty and decadence. By 1947 various national magazines and metropolitan newspapers were featuring stories

XIV · *The Changing Indian*

about their plight and about other reservation Indians in the Southwest. Readers were exposed to article after article about the starving Navajos, illustrated with photographs of skeleton-like babies and wrinkled old men and women dying in filthy hogans. The entire nation was shocked by the death of Ira Hayes, one of the six marines who raised the American flag on Iwo Jima—a scene memorialized in a ten-ton statue in the national capital at a cost of $850,000.

"The whole nation did not mourn Ira Hayes," wrote Dorothy Van de Mark in *Harper's* (March 1956), "but many people did and felt, with their grief, a sense of guilt. For the toughest battle Ira Hayes fought was not on Iwo Jima, which he won. It was the fight for survival in his homeland. He was found dead on the Pima Reservation 'due to exposure'—common Bureau parlance for drink."

As Americans began to understand the Indian problem, they donated tons of clothing and truckloads of food and medical supplies. The Red Cross went into action, and the federal government appropriated emergency funds to better the lot of the Indians. But these efforts fell short of a permanent solution, for not all the Navajos and other Southwestern tribes could live on their reservations. At least half the tribe had to find employment elsewhere. Thus, eighty years after the reservation was set aside, the nation's provisions for its Indians were in need of a drastic overhauling.

The federal government sought the advice of experts on Indians and in 1950 appropriated $88,570,000 for the rehabilitation of the Navajos and Hopis. This long-range approach to an age-old dilemma involved extended irrigation and conservation projects, more and better schools, hospitals, roads, houses, communication facilities, encouragement of small business and handicraft trades, social-security assistance, relocation, and off-reservation employment.

By 1958 more than half the original appropriation was spent, and the effects had brought new life to the Navajos and Hopis. As early as 1955 approximately ninety-two per cent of Navajo children of school age attended classes regularly in new or renovated buildings scattered among the fifty-one boarding and eight day schools in the area.[2] Twenty-two new deep wells and 352 stockwater wells had greatly increased the domestic and range water supply. Hundreds of retention dams had been constructed; irrigable lands on the reservation had been increased from 33,000 acres to more than 60,000, with 122,000 acres as the eventual goal. A new medical center was under construction at Fort Defiance, as well as five field hospitals, one tuberculosis hospital, and dozens of field clinics with public-health nurses already in operation. Modern homes were being constructed, also 636 miles of primary roads and 635 miles of secondary roads.[3]

Resettlement, or relocation, is a project that has received considerable publicity. By December 1955 almost a million dollars had been spent on this phase of rehabilitation alone, but the results are questionable. Only 109 Navajo and 36 Hopi families had been resettled on a 75,000-acre tract acquired from the Mohaves and Chemeheuvis, but the work continues gradually. The Indian Bureau announced at the end of 1955 that 3,500 Southwestern Indians had been transferred to the four relocation centers in California, Colorado, and Illinois. It did not release complete reports on the rate at which some returned to the reservation.[4]

Perhaps the most radical change in the reservation Indians' way of life is the result of the tremendous sums of money which have come to them. Some tribes have won lawsuits against the federal government for broken treaties and loss of land. Dozens of such suits are still pending, and some observers believe the federal government is deliberately trying to lose these cases so that, having paid off past obligations, it can leave the Indian business completely. Mineral resources have brought wealth to several tribes—notably the Jicarilla Apaches, Laguna Pueblos, and Navajos; oil,

---

[2] Robert W. Young, ed.: *The Navajo Yearbook of Planning in Action* (Window Rock, Arizona: Navajo Agency; 1955), p. 172.

   . . .

[3] Underhill: *The Navajo*, pp. 260–3.

   . . .

[4] Dorothy Van de Mark points out in her aforementioned article, "The Raid on the Reservations" (*Harper's*, March 1956), that relocation is a subterfuge for the old gimmick "allotment," and that it is not primarily intended to benefit the Indian, but rather to let greedy special interests obtain the land, minerals, timber, grass, and water of the Indian reservations.

XIV · *The Changing Indian*

gas, and mining companies pay several million dollars in royalties each year to their respective tribal councils.

In 1956 the Navajos' oil income alone amounted to thirty-five million dollars. Divided among 86,000 members, this would have meant $400 apiece, but the tribal system that enabled them to survive the years of poverty has thus far saved them from such imprudence. Instead, the Navajos hold their new wealth in trust, and by 1958 it amounted to approximately sixty million dollars. The seventy-four well-dressed members of the Navajo Council had met in their new octagonal headquarters building in Window Rock, Arizona, the previous year and planned a twelve-million-dollar budget for fiscal 1958: five million dollars to be invested in bonds, interest from which would provide 400 college scholarships; three million for reservoirs and other irrigation projects; half a million for clothing for school children; and the remainder for new school buildings, a model farm for teaching irrigation techniques, and a ranch for breeding high-grade rams to improve the herds.

Time (June 3, 1957) summed up the future of the Navajos with a quote from a member of their tribal council: "We are growing. Indian tribes may be declining in some places, but the Southwest will have to deal with the Navajo forever."

Not only the Navajos are growing, but other Southwestern tribes as well, and their future looks brighter than at any time since the white man arrived. Transition is creating new problems and responsibilities as fast as old ones are solved. One thing is certain, however: the Indian is changing. And his newfound wealth, energy, and outlook suggest that the time may not be far distant when the white men in Arizona and New Mexico will boast of their Indian blood—as white men in Oklahoma have done for a generation or more.

XV

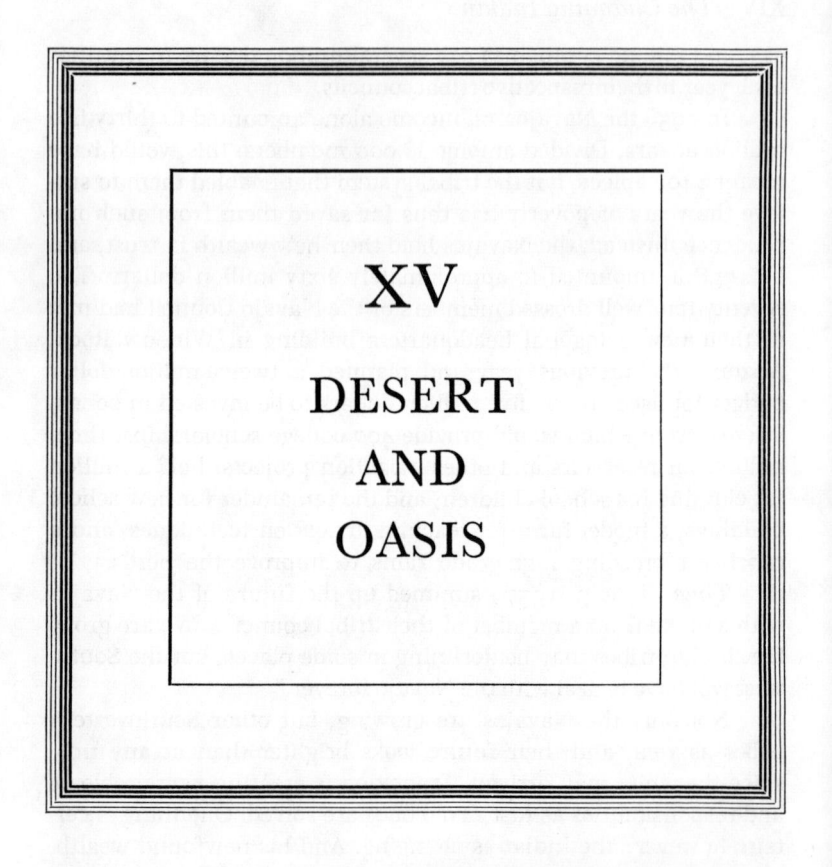

DESERT AND OASIS

IT IS DOUBTFUL whether any subject is discussed more frequently in the Southwest—day in, day out, year in, year out—than its climate. And since World War II the topic has seriously concerned people outside the region, especially since the Southwest suffered one of the worst droughts in its history. Unfortunately, the latest cycle of dry years, which began around 1950, came when this section of the country was in the midst of a great industrial boom. Some companies that were considering building factories here were frightened away by the sudden shortage of water.

From earliest times water has been a precious commodity in

XV · Desert and Oasis

the Southwest, and periodic droughts have caused the abandonment of entire regions. The United States Weather Bureau has kept precipitation records for the Southwest only since 1886, but studies of tree-ring growths reveal that the problem is centuries old. Several hundred years ago the cliff dwellers on Mesa Verde abandoned their homes and migrated toward the Rio Grande and Gila river valleys. The exact reason for the mass exodus is not known, but tree rings show conclusively that there was little rainfall in this section for twenty-five years or more. Three hundred years later the Indians living along the Gila River in southern Arizona moved, leaving dry irrigation canals and adobe buildings as mute reminders of a once thriving community.

It seems fairly certain that other communities were abandoned because of a disastrous lack of water. During periods of adequate rainfall the ancient Southwest produced great oases that supported sizable populations, but most of the oases reverted to desert when a dry cycle succeeded a wet one. The droughts of the 1930's and 1950's, however, affected millions of people instead of thousands.

The annual growth rings of trees in the southern part of the Great Plains indicate that the region has experienced fourteen drought periods since 1539, each lasting five years or more. The longest dry cycle began that year and ended a quarter of a century later. Others occurred in 1587–1605, 1688–1707, 1761–73, 1822–32, 1880–9.[1] The most recent cycles were in 1931–9 and 1950–8. These droughts and others of shorter duration total slightly more than 160 years out of the past 400.

In parts of New Mexico and Arizona one can still hear secondhand accounts of the great drought of the 1850's, when no rain fell in most of the area for more than two years and "the air was so still and hot the birds could not fly."[2] And there are people living in Oklahoma and Texas who remember the disaster of 1886–7. For-

---

[1] Carl Frederick Kraenzel: *The Great Plains in Transition* (Norman: University of Oklahoma Press; 1959), p. 21.

[2] Oliver La Farge: "A Drought Is Slow Lightning," *The New York Times Magazine*, August 13, 1954, p. 50.

tunately, the population was thin and cities practically nonexistent. But two torrid summers that bore a close resemblance to conditions in hell and two severe winters not unlike those associated with the polar regions brought death to thousands of cattle and livestock and bankruptcy to dozens of ranching companies.

The annual-precipitation charts kept by the United States Weather Bureau show that droughts have arrived in the four Southwestern states in fairly regular cycles since 1886. Arizona and New Mexico, for example, have endured six periods eight to ten years apart when less than ten inches of rain fell in twelve months. And less than ten inches of annual rainfall signifies a true desert.

Because of the heavy rainfall in the eastern portions of Texas and Oklahoma, average-precipitation statistics for these states are deceiving, and their so-called "dry spells" do not always correspond with those in New Mexico and Arizona. Nevertheless, the droughts in the western portions of Texas and Oklahoma are just as regular and acute. Invariably, one cycle of six or seven years is followed by another of similar length in which the capriciousness of nature is reversed. The extremely dry years for modern Oklahoma and Texas were 1886, 1901, 1910, 1917, 1936, and 1953. During each of these years the average rainfall for the entire region approximated twenty inches. Meanwhile forty inches fell in some areas in the eastern sections, and less than ten in others.

These conditions are frequently denied or minimized by local boosters—especially in Oklahoma and Texas, where any mention of "desert" is disapproved by the chambers of commerce and service clubs. Residents of New Mexico and Arizona, however, could no more deny the existence of deserts than Alaskans could deny the presence of snow, and state agencies convert their small deserts here and there into assets by "selling" them as tourist and real-estate attractions.

In an article entitled "American West: Perpetual Mirage," published in *Harper's* in May 1957, Walter P. Webb observed that the Rocky Mountain region consists of eight "desert states," including New Mexico and Arizona, while those along the edges—Texas

XV · *Desert and Oasis*

and Oklahoma among them—he classified as "desert-rim states." Webb pointed out that the mountain region barely exceeds the true desert mark of ten inches of annual rainfall, and that the states along the rim are semi-arid and receive approximately twenty inches. He was denounced by practically every governor, senator, congressman, and chamber-of-commerce secretary in each of these states. They regarded the noted historian's remarks as insulting, but few undertook to refute him.

Early travelers across the West and Southwest recognized a desert when they saw it. Coronado, the first white man to enter all four Southwestern states, referred to "these deserts" in his report to the king of Spain in 1542. This designation, plus the fact that he found no gold, was sufficient to discourage other Spanish explorers from visiting the Southwest for several decades. When they did venture from Mexico during the following two centuries, they invariably brought walking commissaries in the form of cattle, sheep, and swine, for they knew that they could not live off the land.

Zebulon Montgomery Pike, who crossed the Southwest in 1806–7, was the first Anglo-American to return to the United States and report his experiences. To Pike it seemed possible that the Southwest might someday "become as celebrated as the sandy deserts of Africa." "I saw in my route in various places," he continued, "tracts of many leagues where the wind had thrown up the sand in all the fanciful form of the ocean's rolling wave, and of which not a speck of vegetable matter existed."[3]

The term "Great American Desert" was coined by Major Stephen H. Long after he led a military and civilian party of twenty men into the Great Plains in 1819–20, via the Missouri and Platte rivers, down the Front Range into New Mexico, and across Oklahoma by way of the Arkansas and Canadian rivers. Long prepared a map of the area on which he set down "the Great American Desert" and thus fixed the idea in the public mind. Most geography and history books of the next three or four decades referred to the

---

[3] Elliott Coues, ed.: *The Expeditions of Zebulon Montgomery Pike* (New York: Francis P. Harper; 1895), II, 523.

region between the 98th meridian on the east, the Rocky Mountains on the west, and the Canadian and Mexican borders to the north and south as a vast desert. So thoroughly was this idea implanted that parts of the West and Southwest were the last frontiers to be thoroughly explored and settled by American pioneers. Had the earliest explorers arrived during a wet cycle, the Southwest might have become famous as a great oasis.

Walter P. Webb has written that the American desert was "abolished" after the Civil War. "It has hardly been mentioned in polite Western society since, and never by a Chamber of Commerce. . . . The desert did not know that it had been abolished; it waited patiently as puny men moved in from all sides to conquer it."[4]

The men whom Webb calls "puny" had moved into the Southwest in force by 1886 and carved great ranches out of the vast reaches of western Oklahoma, western Texas, eastern New Mexico, and southern Arizona. By then the Indians had been subdued and cattle, sheep, goats, and horses had replaced the buffalo and other game. Gone too was the balance of nature whereby the quantity and quality of grass determined the amount of animal life. More than normal rainfall during 1880–6 and the increasing demands for beef, wool, and mohair on the world markets led ranchers to overstock. Soon the ancient sod that gave natural coverage to the land and prevented it from blowing away had been cropped down to its roots. And livestock, restricted by barbed-wire fences, were no longer free to wander in search of greener pastures.

Thus, the stage was set for catastrophe. Rains did not fall during the spring of 1886, and when the normal winds blew from the south, the soil rose in great clouds of red dust. For two seasons it moved back and forth with the shifting winds, and man was given a severe object lesson. Many ranchers departed never to return, but a few persisted with depleted herds through the cycle of dry summers and cold winters. Never again would the survivors of

---

[4] Walter Prescott Webb: "The American West: Perpetual Mirage," *Harper's Magazine* (May 1957), p. 27.

XV · Desert and Oasis

the great drought of 1886–8 act so foolishly in such wholesale fashion. But later generations had to learn for themselves that the thin coverage of the Southwestern plains and deserts had a specific purpose.

Even after the disaster of the 1880's the Southwest remained basically a ranching country except for the humid regions of the east and the irrigated valleys of New Mexico and Arizona. Dry and wet cycles alternated with regularity, and ranchers suffered and prospered accordingly. As long as men kept in mind that dry years would follow periods of heavy moisture, they managed to adapt to nature's moods. Eventually they believed that the region west of the 98th meridian was destined to remain a land of picturesque cowboys, cattle, sheep, grama grass, sagebrush, cactus, mesquite, and great open spaces. This was no country for farms, large cities, or great factories.

World War I dispelled these ideas about the arid regions of the Southwest. Unprecedented demands caused ranchers to turn into wheat farmers. And when the federal government guaranteed a minimum price of $2.20 per bushel, grass coverage seemed very unimportant. "Suitcase" farmers rushed into the Great Plains and Southwest to buy cheap land and put it into cultivation. Millions of acres of sod were turned under in favor of wheat.

A long wet cycle began in 1918, and Oklahoma experienced approximately six inches of rainfall above normal. Texas had an increase of more than twelve inches that same year and a further gain of twenty-nine inches in 1919. Rainfall in New Mexico in 1917 totaled nine and a half inches, in 1918 almost fifteen, and in 1919 approximately twenty. Even Arizona, although it still did not produce much wheat, had similar experiences.

Some old-time residents remained cautious at first, but when they saw the profits of their neighbors, they succumbed to temptation, for it looked as if the wet years would continue indefinitely.

All through the 1920's and the early 1930's the Southwest—except in isolated spots—experienced heavy moisture. Meanwhile, nature's bountiful supply was supplemented in certain areas of Texas, Oklahoma, New Mexico, and southern Arizona with irriga-

THE SOUTHWEST: *Old and New*

tion. Cotton, wheat, and corn reached record production figures each year. Eventually prices dropped as a result of overproduction and declining demands, but farmers attempted to maintain their abnormal profits by digging more and deeper water wells and plowing up more grassland. The Great Depression arrived about the time of another dry cycle, and the combination of the two proved a double-barreled disaster to the Southwest.

The drought began in Arizona and Texas in 1933. It reached New Mexico and Oklahoma the next year. At this time the Southwest contained almost ten million people—five times as many as in 1886. Amarillo and Lubbock, cities located in the heart of the Texas Panhandle, had barely existed fifty years earlier. Surrounded by cotton and wheat fields that stretched from horizon to horizon, they were also in the heart of a newly created desert that spread rapidly in all directions and quickly became known as the Dust Bowl.

The scenes of desolation and human suffering throughout most of the Southwest during the "dirty thirties" were almost unprecedented in American history. As one who saw hundreds of families fleeing the blighted area in worn-out jalopies during those terrible years, I can testify that John Steinbeck's account of the wretched and pathetic victims of man's crime against nature in *The Grapes of Wrath* was not exaggerated. The book shocked thousands of readers by its realistic language and four-letter words, but the stupidity of the people who helped create the Dust Bowl was even more shocking. The effects of the unfavorable publicity that Steinbeck's book brought to regions of the Southwest had not altogether disappeared a quarter of a century later.[5]

On May 12, 1934, a great "duster" rolled across the country, blotted out the sun over the nation's capital, and deposited red soil

---

[5] Oklahomans bitterly resent being called "Okies." When the University of California student body chanted "Kill the dirty Okies" in 1954 during a football game with the University of Oklahoma, the Oklahoma fans and players were deeply offended—not by the words "kill" and "dirty" so much as by the word "Okies."

XV · Desert and Oasis

from the plains of Oklahoma, Texas, and New Mexico on the decks of ships hundreds of miles off the Atlantic Coast. Doubtless it was the first such experience of white men in the New World, but it was not the last. Within a few months the drought spread from Canada deep into Texas, from the 98th meridian to the slopes of the Rocky Mountains. If there was ever a desert, this was it. Even the alluvial soils of river bottoms turned into dry, hard bricks. Wells and creeks stopped flowing, and springs disappeared.

During spring and summer months the wind blew sand with enough force to strip the paint from houses and barns. Two or three feet of sand covered whole farms, while highways, outbuildings, cultivators, and fences were completely buried. There were stories of crows that built nests with bits of wire picked up from barren farmsteads in the absence of enough plant material for the purpose. Even rabbits, which can exist almost without water, died of thirst and starvation, as did cattle, horses, and sheep. Plants succumbed to the drought more quickly than animals, and Russian thistle, which has great tolerance for arid conditions, was used for hay. Finally, this too died.

The owner of a large sheep ranch on the Edwards Plateau informed me in 1940 that all that had saved his cattle, sheep, and goats from starvation was the Spanish dagger and cactus, which grew in abundance. Both are desert plants that nature has provided with sharp-pointed leaves and needles. Crews of Mexican workers, "sotol knockers," were employed to overturn the dagger plants and expose the edible part at the base, while others set fire to the thorns of the cactus with specially built flame throwers. Neither plant offers a very well-balanced diet, but each contains moisture as well as food.

Farmers generally were less able to withstand the drought than ranchers, and many of them deserted their lands and moved in waves of migration to California and other distant states. Some died of "dust pneumonia," malnutrition, or sheer exhaustion before their worn-out trucks and broken-down Model T's moved beyond the rim of the Dust Bowl. Everyone who saw the motion-picture

The Southwest: *Old and New*

version of *The Grapes of Wrath* sensed the hopelessness these people felt when Tom Joad "spoke" over his grandpa's grave alongside the dusty highway: "We'll put his name in this 'ere bottle and bury it with him so they will know he just died and weren't killed. Sometimes the government is a lot more interested in a dead man than a live one."

On April 27, 1935, the federal government created the Soil Conservation Service and assigned it the task of preventing future dust bowls. Every proved measure of controlling soil erosion was utilized, and many new ones were developed through trial and error. The Service placed great emphasis on contour plowing and planting and warned against overgrazing. It put millions of acres in grass and discouraged the planting of crops on land not suited to them. Rows of trees were planted to check the wind and break up dust storms, and thousands of tanks and reservoirs were constructed to hold future run-off of surface water. In addition, the Soil Conservation Service paid farmers and ranchers to reduce the number of their livestock, take submarginal lands out of cultivation or grazing, and even plant weeds in order to hold the soil.

At last, near the end of the decade, rains returned and people trickled back to the Dust Bowl. The cycle had run its course, and once again the desert became a succession of oases. To a considerable degree, wind erosion had been halted and the great sand dunes had been leveled and controlled by contour planting. Thanks to government price supports and the increased demand for wool, lamb, cotton, wheat, and feed resulting from the decline of depression at home and the outbreak of war abroad, Southwesterners experienced a taste of renewed prosperity.

Fortunately, rainfall continued at a normal pace in Texas, Oklahoma, and New Mexico throughout World War II and well

XV · *Desert and Oasis*

into the post-war period. Hard pressed to meet military and civilian needs, fulfill commitments to allied countries under "lend lease" and later to much of the world under the Truman Doctrine and the Marshall Plan, the government maintained record price levels on cotton, wheat, beef, and wool.

Ten years of prosperity caused many ranchers and farmers to forget the lessons of the Dust Bowl days. They chafed under government regulation of land usage and succumbed to the temptation to put grass land into wheat. The federal government's price support of two dollars a bushel once again encouraged "suitcase farmers" to buy up cheap range land. In a single wet year they could harvest thirty-five bushels of wheat an acre, pay for the land in full, and perhaps show some profit—and they little cared what happened to the soil after that. Even if the crop failed completely, one could recover as much as eight dollars an acre from the Federal Crop Insurance Corporation, created in 1938.

Bountiful crops and high prices continued for six consecutive years after the war ended. Buicks and Cadillacs far outnumbered Fords and Chevrolets in some wheat areas of the Southwest and Great Plains. Many farmers and ranchers who had never been in an airplane acquired planes of their own.

Meanwhile a handful of Southwesterners took a long-range view of their situation. They made less money, but they followed sound practices of conservation. They put their worst land in grass and left it that way; they took great care to keep some type of vegetable cover on the ground at all times. These people did not suffer so severely as their neighbors when dust storms returned in the early 1950's, and their farms stood like blooming islands when the Southwest succumbed again to the desert. But those who remembered that dry years always follow wet ones were far too few.

The second major drought in this area during the twentieth century started in Arizona in the early 1940's, a full decade before it spread in cancerous fashion to the rest of the region.

Except for an occasional freak year (such as 1905, when rainfall in Arizona exceeded twenty-seven inches), this section of the Southwest rarely receives more than fifteen inches. Therefore, it was never considered to have great agricultural possibilities until the federal government constructed a series of great reservoirs following the Reclamation Act of 1902. With plenty of water the desert could produce two or three crops a year. And projects such as the Roosevelt Dam near Phoenix quickly converted millions of acres of once barren land into man-made oases.

Where surface moisture could not be trapped, underground water could. Sometimes it was found only fourteen feet below the surface. Dry land was worth three or four dollars an acre, but when irrigated it was worth several hundred. Almost overnight desert lands were converted into verdant islands of alfalfa, truck, and Pima cotton. This was especially true in the region around Phoenix and Tucson and along most of the Salt River Valley, which extends across southern Arizona. The underground water supply, plus a few wet years just before 1940, gave Arizonans false hopes. Unfortunately, they used their water faster than it could be replaced. In places water levels dropped from a few feet below the surface to several hundred.

Around 1941 Arizona entered a cycle of below-average snow and rainfall. To offset the deficiency, farmers bought more powerful pumps and drove wells deeper and deeper—in spite of warning by experts that the subsurface reserves would be depleted. Warnings were ignored as the desert was pushed back farther and farther in all directions. In 1950 the average rainfall for the entire state reached an all-time low of seven and a half inches. Practically all rivers and lakes dried up. Cities and towns were forced to sink wells to 600 feet or more, considerably below the range of all but the largest irrigation pumps.

Once the drought started, it had the vicious capacity to perpetuate itself, both vertically and horizontally. Pumps worked day and night to save crops, causing the water level in some sections to drop thirty-seven times faster than it could be replenished. Additional equipment and electricity, plus the abandonment of some previously cultivated land, cost farmers in the Gila Valley more than twenty-five million dollars in 1950 alone. The water level in

XV · *Desert and Oasis*

Horseshoe Dam, fifty miles northeast of Phoenix, dropped 150 feet, leaving little more than a mud pond to quench the city's mighty thirst.[6]

A drought has many results besides abandoned fields, depleted reservoirs, dried-up wells, and thirsty cities. When midsummer showers do come, they fall on dehydrated soil packed too hard to absorb the precious moisture, causing flash floods that endanger cities and towns, wash out bridges and highways, and destroy crops and human lives. The water rushes over the surface of the land without really wetting it, and two days later winds can whip the soil into rolling clouds of dust and sand. Grasshoppers, bugs, and other insects invariably move in with a drought to attack plants and animals. Worse yet are the forest fires, which destroyed 56,000 acres of valuable Arizona timber during a nightmarish two months in 1951.

In 1952, as conditions improved in Arizona and reservoirs experienced a slow build-up, the drought reached its peak in Texas, Oklahoma, and parts of New Mexico. As this region uses more water than Arizona and supports larger populations, the devastation was greater. Oklahoma and Texas normally average thirty inches of rain, the eastern sections having much more. But from 1951 to 1958 the annual precipitation approximated barely half that amount. Much of this frequently came in a single day or night, doing as much harm as good. The little Texas town of Ozona in the heart of the Edwards Plateau, for example, considers fifteen inches of rain a year as normal; in the summer of 1955 it received twelve inches in one four-hour period.

The great drought spread from the Southwest to more than half the nation's 1,700,000 square miles and into twenty-six states by 1956. But it was most harsh and most prolonged in some 500,000 square miles of the Southwest. All of Oklahoma, most of Texas, and a large part of New Mexico were classified that year as "critical" by the United States Department of Agriculture. The most severe damage, however, was confined to an area of twelve

---

[6] "A Decade of Drought Cracks Arizona," *Life*, August 31, 1951, p. 21.

THE SOUTHWEST: *Old and New*

million acres, the approximate size of Massachusetts and Vermont. The old Dust Bowl of the thirties returned with a vengeance.

This time, however, there was no mass exodus in overloaded flivvers with boiling radiators and protruding mattresses and springs. Except in isolated counties there were no idle and silent men, gaunt and shabbily dressed women, or hungry children. Even the heavy dust clouds were less frequent than twenty years earlier. This time the booming national economy made it possible for farmers and ranchers to obtain jobs in nearby industrial plants. And the more intelligent use of cover crops, deeper plowing, and new reclamation projects helped. Also, the Eisenhower administration's soil-bank program and drought-relief payments to farmers averted bankruptcy for thousands.

Still, the loss of agricultural revenue was tremendous and the suffering prolonged. In parts of New Mexico and Colorado drifting sand covered fences and blocked roads, and buried tracks derailed trains. Some people swept up as much as ten or twelve bushels of dust that had sifted into their houses through cracks and around doors and windows during a twenty-four-hour storm. In Clovis, New Mexico, in the summer of 1954 a woman smothered to death under a drift of Colorado topsoil. During the first five years of this drought Texas farmers and ranchers sustained losses of three billion dollars.

Among those who suffered most were tenant farmers in Oklahoma and Texas, some of whom did not produce a single bale of cotton in four consecutive years. And most of the small stockmen of New Mexico and Arizona were forced to sell their breeding stock because they could not afford to buy feed and haul water for them.

I drove through every section of the drought-stricken area in the four Southwestern states during the summers between 1952 and 1957. At Brownsville, Texas, I saw people walking across the dry bed of the Rio Grande to the Mexican city of Matamoras, the first time in modern history that this was possible. In July 1953 the once great stream did not contain a drop of water in some stretches of fifty to a hundred miles.

When I stopped at Rio Grande City for a drink of water in Au-

XV · Desert and Oasis

gust 1953, I was bluntly told that there was none. Finally, a geologist agreed to sell me a glass for ten cents. He explained that it was hauled from Laredo, one hundred miles away, at a cost of fifty cents a gallon.

During the summer of 1955 I visited Ozona, approximately ninety miles southwest of San Angelo, Texas. This place was famous for its "silk-stocking row" of ten or twelve millionaire families and its tremendous production of wool and mohair. Children of most ranchers in the area customarily became part-owners of the land and owned their flocks of sheep by the time they finished high school. Before their twenty-fifth birthday many young men had annual incomes in five figures. But three or four years of continuous drought had brought unbelievable changes.

Regardless of how extensive the family ranch was, no one had "broken even" in three or four years. Ranchers who had looked forward to an early retirement now tried desperately to stave off bankruptcy. Their sons, few of whom had bothered to go to college, were obliged to work in filling stations, feed stores, tourist courts, or for oil and gas companies. It was quite a comedown for proud Texans who since childhood had worn fifty-dollar hand-tooled boots and expensive Stetson hats.

One could drive hundreds of miles over parts of the Southwest during most of the 1950's and not see a green blade of grass beyond the reach of an irrigation ditch. Yet the people never lost their sense of humor. Always Southwesterners have made a game of meeting bad luck and frustration with grim humor. It was said that water was so scarce that even the churches were affected: the Baptists were forced to sprinkle, the Methodists to use a damp cloth, and the Presbyterians to pass out rain checks.

But beneath the humor lurked one of the most prolonged and agonizing tragedies ever experienced in the United States. The damage to land, homes, animals, forests, crops, and cities slowly increased from one day to the next. It was not dramatically sudden, hence people outside the drought-stricken area were slow to understand what was happening. First the crops disappeared, then the soil, then the livestock. One rancher in Menard County in the

THE SOUTHWEST: *Old and New*

Edwards Plateau region, who normally cleared $15,000 or $20,000 a year on his small four-section sheep ranch, operated at an annual loss of from $1,000 to $1,500 from 1951 to 1956. Another ran between 6,000 to 7,000 sheep and 350 cattle in 1950 and had a bank balance of $90,000. Four years later his herd had dwindled to half and his bank account had vanished.[7]

In many small towns in Texas and Oklahoma the population dwindled by fifty per cent as young people moved to the aircraft plants at Dallas and Fort Worth, the oil fields at Odessa, Texas, and Hobbs, New Mexico, or the great Tinker Airfield Depot at Oklahoma City. I counted more than fifty abandoned farmhouses twenty-five miles east of Dallas in 1956. This is one of the richest black-land farming belts in the Southwest, but most of the countryside was deserted and along the main streets of the small towns there were more empty buildings than occupied ones.

One heard various theories advanced in the early fifties as to the cause of the prolonged dry spell. Along the Arkansas and Louisiana borders in eastern Texas and eastern Oklahoma, "brush-arbor" and "radio" evangelists interpreted the drought as God's vengeance on His wicked people: "I say to you all, we've done sinned, that's what we've done, and God is ah-punishin' us for it." A retired farmer near Austin explained it this way: "It's this 'ere damn pavin'. They've paved up this whole country with seement and blacktop. Blocks the seepage! And there's thousands of cars a-suckin' the moisture out of the air."

For every theory as to the cause, another was proposed for inducing rain. The mayors of Laredo, San Antonio, and a dozen other Southwestern towns from time to time proclaimed "prayer days." Preachers of practically every fundamentalist sect devoted entire revival meetings to attempts to convince the Lord of the need for His personal attention to the matter. Others hung snakes on barbed-wire fences, belly up, to make it rain or followed the advice of various "old Indian chiefs." Some city councils hired cloud seeders with fleets of special airplanes or hundreds of smudge

---

[7] "Texas, the Unhappy Land," *Time*, April 23, 1956, p. 32.

XV · Desert and Oasis

pots. But, as one observer pointed out, the devices that work best are those tried during wet cycles.

By 1956 the drought had affected thirty million acres of topsoil, practically all of which was left parched, feverish, and barren of vegetation. In some isolated Southwestern counties there were more people on relief rolls than during the days of the Dust Bowl and Great Depression of the thirties. *The Texas Observer*, a small weekly newspaper published in Austin, stated in December of that year that "nearly 100,000 Texans . . . are eating federal relief food." In Karnes County in the southeastern part of the state as many as 10,000 people out of a total population of 16,000 received government rations. Practically all of these were victims of the drought. Relief rolls also bulged in the Texas Panhandle, the Blackland–Grand Prairie region of central Texas, the upper Wichita and Brazos river area of northern Texas, the Piney Woods of eastern Texas, and even in Dallas—the home of the *nouveaux riches*.

Torrance County, in central New Mexico, lost fifty per cent of its farmers by 1957. And in Melrose, New Mexico, twenty-five children withdrew from the tiny school in a two-week period as their families fled the blighted area. A sales representative of a leading pen maker remarked that year that his company had stock on the shelves in western Oklahoma which was five years old.

Northern New Mexico near Bandelier National Monument and Los Alamos had been one of the most beautiful spots on the continent and boasted a great natural forest. In 1956 this region received less than five inches of rain, with the result that millions of acres of yellow pine, spruce, and cedar died outright. Trees hundreds of years old were so weakened by lack of moisture that they became easy prey to the armies of beetles that moved in. More than 100,000 visitors and campers visited Bandelier National Monument during the 1955 season, but fewer than 30,000 registered the following year. By 1958 this area looked from the air as if it had been seared by an atomic explosion.

An example of how the drought spreads underground as well as above is found in the once beautiful Comal Springs area, headwaters of the Guadalupe River in southern Texas. In midsummer 1956 the springs went dry for the first time in history. Instead of the normal two hundred million gallons of cool clear water per day, they flowed not a drop. This situation forced eleven electrical power plants downstream to drill deep and expensive wells to obtain condensing water. In eastern Texas, where the average normal rainfall is forty inches per year, water tables dropped from twenty to one hundred feet in a single season. Geologists estimated in 1957 that underground supplies currently in use were more than four centuries old.

Even in ordinary times less than half of Texas receives enough rainfall to meet the needs of farmers, city dwellers, and industrial plants. But some counties near San Antonio where a rainfall of twenty inches was normal had less than one inch during the first six months of 1956. Most reservoirs and dams in the area dropped to less than half of capacity as rivers and springs continued to dry up. In June the huge Falcon Dam on the Rio Grande between Laredo and Brownsville ceased operation—no power was produced, no water released for irrigation or domestic consumption. Fairly heavy rains came that fall, but were too late to save crops.

It was during this period that a strange sight was created by the water shortage at the Falcon Dam. The submerged towns of Zapata, Falcon, and Lopeno reappeared on the bed of the lake, the debris-covered Zapata County courthouse emerging from the mud like a tremendous monster from another world.

Few cities in the entire Southwest escaped the rationing of water during the fifties. In more than one city local residents were forbidden to wash their cars or water their lawns for periods of more than six months. In the summer of 1956 Dallas obtained water from the Red River, seventy miles distant, while pure spring water was trucked in and sold at fifty cents a gallon. A glass of ordinary drinking water gathered a saline scum on the surface if left to stand for a few hours, and salt cones formed like tiny icicles on leaky hydrants. The damage to human stomachs, however, was slight in comparison to what happened to household plumbing and

XV · Desert and Oasis

car radiators. More than half the water heaters in certain areas of Dallas County were replaced within one year, while November 1956 was the biggest month in history for radiator repairmen.

Other Southwestern cities experienced unique problems. El Paso originally obtained its water from the Rio Grande. When this proved insufficient, it tapped its underground supply until that too ran nearly dry. The federal government eventually built Elephant Butte Dam several miles upstream to catch the flood water, but the river quickly dried up. The city then acquired dam sites a hundred miles to the east, but until they are developed El Paso is forced to pump water from the University of Texas lands in Hudspeth County forty or fifty miles away.

For more than three centuries San Antonio depended on the great San Pedro Spring, which flowed into the San Antonio River. As the city grew, it tapped powerful artesian wells, but these dwindled during the drought of the 1950's. At the time of this writing the city fathers are desperately pleading with the state for the right to acquire water from the Guadalupe basin fifty miles distant to avoid another crisis.

Ironically, during a dry spell the demand for water becomes all the greater. Dallas, for instance, used 175 million gallons during the hot days of August 1956, as compared to less than half that amount the same month the previous year. The spread of industry likewise increases demands, particularly the petrochemical factories that are being built along the Gulf Coast area. And irrigation of cotton and other crops, which is fast becoming the rule rather than the exception in most of the region west of the 98th meridian, consumed in 1956 six times as much water as all the combined cities and industries. A farmer in western Texas reported recently that he originally obtained water at eighteen feet, but now must drill 150 feet or more. "Then, in some cases the water comes up salty, damaging the crop." [8]

Texas uses three million acre feet of water for its homes and industries, and it expects an urban demand of eight million acre

---

[8] "Why Texas Is Thriving," *U.S. News and World Report*, November 23, 1956, pp. 70 ff.

feet by the year 2000. In New Mexico, Arizona, and Nevada the problem is less pressing because these states are not swarming with people. But water is the key to their growth. In California the water issue has dominated state politics for years.

During the recent disaster, there was much loud talk about all kinds of solutions to the water shortage, particularly in Texas, where the situation was most critical. But the accomplishments were very small. Governor Allan Shivers, Chief Executive since the year the drought began, left office in January 1957. Throughout his tenure he refused to sponsor any kind of state drought or water-conservation plan. An ardent "states' righter" and advocate of "free enterprise," he had also impeded the flow of emergency federal aid. Shivers's successor, the almost equally conservative Price Daniel, announced that he would keep the legislature in session "until it solves the drought."

Bountiful rains rescued the legislature from this embarrassing situation in the spring of 1957. They continued throughout the following year until reservoirs were filled to ninety per cent of capacity—a mark they had not reached since 1950. Rains fell all over the Southwest except in parts of northern New Mexico and Arizona. Oklahoma City, for example, received less than seventeen inches in 1956, but more than forty-six in 1957. Green pastures, sleek cattle, fat lambs, and fuller reservoirs and lakes across the Southwest proved a welcome change from previous years. The Texas legislature, like those of Oklahoma, New Mexico, and Arizona, promptly dropped the subject of water shortage, and none of them passed any new laws governing the conservation of underground supplies.

In each of the Southwestern states during the spring of 1959 I was struck by the public's apathy toward the subject of water. It was a wet year, and most people acted as if the problem no longer existed. Texas, for example, has not agreed upon a master plan, although its board of water engineers is preparing one with a 1963 deadline. Even so, the 1959 legislature cut its 1960–1 budget by $800,000. Several Southwestern cities are designing long-range wa-

XV · *Desert and Oasis*

ter plans of their own, but often they are stymied by fights between politicians and special interests.

ALL OF THE Southwestern states except Oklahoma have experienced tremendous population increases since 1940, but a continuation of this is improbable. New dams are under construction in each state, but surface water supplies alone will not suffice. Unless underground water is conserved, as Oklahoma and Texas have conserved their oil since the early thirties, many of the oases created from the deserts and prairies may disappear. "It is not a question of whether the whole underground will be dewatered," warns Professor Webb, "it is only a question of when. At the present acceleration of water usage, the crisis will come to some region [of the Southwest] in ten or fifteen years, and it will spread to the entire region within less than a century." [9]

Webb does not stop with this gloomy prediction, but offers a bold and imaginative long-range plan to solve the water problem in the Southwest. Between 1953 and 1957 he wrote several articles on the subject and one book, which were partly based on an enormously detailed Department of Interior study prompted by Senator Lyndon Johnson. His thesis is both simple and blunt: part of the Southwest will never have enough water, unless the climate changes drastically; water that is available year in and year out should be captured and made to work for industry and agriculture.

"Water is today the most valuable asset in Texas—more valuable than oil, or cattle, or cotton, or any other commodity. The demand for water is increasing at a tremendous rate, but the total supply is not increasing at all. As a result, the demand is outlast-

---

[9] Walter P. Webb: "Billion-Dollar Cure of Texas' Drought," *Harper's Magazine*, December 23, 1953, p. 77.

ing the supply—running far ahead of it in many sections of the state."

Webb believes that the obvious solution to Texas's problem lies in its twelve important rivers, ten of which cut across the state and flow into the Gulf. Two others—the Red and Canadian—run into the Gulf also, but not directly from Texas. An average of sixty-three million acre feet of water flows down these rivers each year. Texas captures only nine million acre feet; the rest is wasted. "Let us," Webb continues, "corral—by act of state or federal government, or both—all these many streams by connecting them—from the Sabine on the east to the Rio Grande on the southwest—with a continuous canal inland from the Gulf." The cost of such a project would exceed a billion dollars, but it is estimated that it could increase the region's income by five billion dollars a year. And it is the last easy water project of really big size in the United States.

This plan calls for putting most of Texas's industrial eggs in the Gulf Coast basket. It also asks Dallas, Fort Worth, Austin, San Antonio, Waco, Wichita Falls, and hundreds of other cities and towns to slow down or even abandon their boosters' dreams—a demand not likely to be considered seriously until a drought even more terrible than the most recent one again dehydrates the Southwest into a giant desert.

Unless the Southwestern cities find a solution to their water problem, their present industrial and population booms will not continue indefinitely. All four states contain many sites for dams, but it is questionable if much of the arid portions will ever support large populations. Southwestern rivers constantly change their courses and their banks wander in all directions. Damming them is difficult, and some water engineers argue that dams on such streams as the Canadian and Arkansas rivers would become mere silt traps.

It is entirely possible that sections of Texas, Oklahoma, New Mexico, and other Western states may someday bring water to their arid lands through large pipelines from the Mississippi or Missouri rivers. Arizona has not fully utilized the waters of the

XV · *Desert and Oasis*

Colorado, but her situation will be greatly improved when the Glen Canyon Dam is completed. Perhaps this state, as well as New Mexico, will eventually pipe water from Utah and Colorado.

The conversion of sea water for irrigation and industrial purposes may offer a solution. Arizona and New Mexico are not beyond reach of the Gulf of California, while Texas has several hundred miles of coastline. Someday Southwesterners may lift water from these great bodies and transport it to dry counties hundreds of miles inland. Most experts believe that sea-water conversion is possible only with the use of atomic energy. The federal government announced plans early in 1959 to build a plant at Point Loma near San Diego, California, for experiments along these lines. But Harvey O. Banks, California's director of water resources, warns that conversion and transportation of sea water to desert areas by pipeline is still a dream.[1]

Oklahoma City depends for part of its water supply on Lake Canton, 150 miles to the northwest on the North Canadian River. For several years its city government has studied plans to pipe fresh water from the rivers and lakes in the humid section of the state, more than a hundred miles to the southeast. Lubbock and Amarillo talk of a large dam on the Canadian River in the Texas Panhandle, but they have been unable to agree on water rates and other details. Other cities west of the 98th meridian are searching for solutions to their water problems. One thing is certain: the cost for all or any of these proposed projects will be staggering.

But the alternative is equally obvious: the Southwest can continue to change from desert to oasis, oasis to desert, until the desert gradually encompasses most of the land. This will never happen unless Southwesterners suddenly lose their pioneer traits of optimism, ingenuity, and determination. Major decisions about plans for the future, and not just complaisance, are required of the citizens, the states, and the federal government if the problem of adequate supply is to be solved.

---

[1] John R. Morganthaler: "Drought Peril Is Real," *Oklahoma City Times*, November 16, 1959.

XVI
THE BIG INDUSTRIAL BOOM

THE DUST BOWL and the depression dominated the Southwestern scene throughout most of the thirties, but World War II touched off an industrial boom of major proportions as the decade ended. Its momentum, accelerated by the Korean War and the Cold War, continues after two decades. The region that resembled a great desert has become an industrial giant—based mainly on local natural resources and nourished by large government contracts.

When the Spaniards arrived in the Southwest four centuries ago, they found the Indians in what is now New Mexico and Ari-

XVI · *The Big Industrial Boom*

zona raising beans, squash, and corn in small irrigated fields along the riverbanks. The conquerors introduced cattle, sheep, goats, and swine to the economy, but they soon learned that mere survival in this hard land was a major achievement. Expansion beyond an agrarian or pastoral society appeared impossible. And for three centuries or more the entire Southwest remained in a state of arrested development, a place that travelers passed through as quickly as possible en route to more agreeable surroundings.

Texas appeared even less attractive than New Mexico and Arizona, and Europeans deliberately avoided it. The Spaniards thought it so worthless that they parceled it out in generous grants to Anglo-American settlers in the early nineteenth century, a policy that Mexico continued for another decade after it achieved independence of Spain. As for Oklahoma, even the aggressive Anglo-Americans showed little interest in the future Sooner State until almost three generations after the United States acquired it from France in the Louisiana Purchase. There was more attractive land elsewhere, and Oklahoma acquired a reputation as a place fit only for Indians.

Thus, except for a few pioneer ranchers and farmers, most of the region now known as the Southwest seemed to offer little to the white man. Eventually Anglo-Americans discovered that the river bottoms east of the Balcones Fault grew excellent cotton, and within a generation after they first arrived in Texas in 1821 they put most of the better soil into cultivation. At the same time the Indians of the Five Civilized Tribes in Oklahoma expanded their fields and herds as far west as the Cross Timbers. Following the Civil War the cattle kingdom spread to the rolling plains of Texas and Oklahoma and beyond the mesas and deserts of New Mexico as far as the Salt River Valley of southern Arizona. Within a brief span it appeared a permanent fixture on the arid reaches of the Southwest, never to be supplanted by industry and large centers of population.

During the post-Civil War period the northeastern portion of the United States experienced an industrial revolution, but only one section of the Southwest could claim any factories worthy of

THE SOUTHWEST: *Old and New*

the name: a few cottonseed-oil mills, small ironworks, flour and grist mills, packing houses, and tanneries located in eastern Texas. Some mining was carried on in other parts of the Southwest, but it played a small role in the region's total economy. Most of the country west of the 98th meridian remained thinly peopled; few settlements existed other than scattered army posts and sleepy hamlets such as El Paso, Santa Fe, Albuquerque, Tucson, and Phoenix. The rest of the land belonged to cattle, sheep, sagebrush, cedar, cactus, and Indians.

Even the dawn of the twentieth century revealed little promise for the Southwest beyond its agricultural heritage. In 1900 Arizona counted 123,000 people, New Mexico 195,000, Oklahoma 790,000, and Texas 3,000,000; eighty-five per cent of the total in all four states lived in rural communities. Fifty years later Arizona's population had increased to nearly 750,000, forty-five per cent of whom were rural, while New Mexico's approached 700,000, about equally divided between town and country. By 1950 Oklahoma had leveled off at approximately 2,250,000, half in cities and half on farms or in rural communities. Texas, meanwhile, more than doubled its population during the same period; of its 7,700,000, sixty-five per cent lived in cities.

The Lone Star State was the only one of the four which approximated the national average of urban population at mid-century. But the trend from an agricultural to an industrial economy throughout the Southwest had begun, and its pace grew faster during the decade of the fifties. In all but Arizona the average number of farm operators decreased by forty per cent.[1] Because of larger farm units and various irrigation and reclamation projects, more acreage was in cultivation in 1954 than in 1920, and agricultural production figures showed steady increases.

Nevertheless, compared with the importance of industry to the total economy, agriculture's importance declined rapidly. Arizona is the single exception in the Southwest, for along with its

---

[1] Statistics and percentages in reference to population, agriculture, and industry are based on *The Statistical Abstract of the United States* (Washington: Department of Commerce; various years) unless otherwise cited.

XVI · *The Big Industrial Boom*

dramatic industrial expansion went an eightfold increase in its irrigated lands.

AT THE TURN of the century about 3,500 Oklahoma residents were employed in manufacturing. Some 900 establishments, large and small, produced goods whose value was in excess of seven million dollars annually—such items as cheese, flour, brooms, and lumber. But agriculture engaged at least ninety per cent of the 400,000 Indians and whites. Tulsa, presently the state's second largest city, was only a tent town, while Oklahoma City was still a collection of clapboard buildings. Oil had been discovered in a number of shallow fields, and refineries produced more than 6,000 barrels of kerosene each year. The automobile soon brought a demand for other petroleum products and gave Oklahoma an important role in the nation's economy, at least for a while.

Mining employed the largest percentage of people in New Mexico and Arizona in 1900, and the total value of refined gold, silver, lead, zinc, copper, and coal produced each year exceeded that of agriculture and livestock. Commercial manufacturing—leather goods, Indian silverwork, and a few domestic items—supported only a handful of people in each territory. Even statehood in 1912 failed to generate a boom in industry or population. And as late as 1932 a former prominent official in the federal government referred to New Mexico and Arizona as "little Western boroughs" so thinly populated that they should not be dignified with the status of states.[2]

The story of Texas is somewhat different, for Texas had a sizable population and had emerged from complete dependence on

---

[2] Harry M. Daugherty: *The Inside Story of the Harding Tragedy* (New York: The Churchill Company; 1932), p. 206. Daugherty, the battle-scarred Attorney General under President Harding, is hardly a good source for political theory. Nevertheless, his views in respect to the Southwest probably represented the opinions of many people living east of the Mississippi in the 1930's.

agriculture before other parts of the Southwest advanced beyond territorial governments. In 1870 the state was ninety-five-per-cent rural, and the value of its manufactured goods, such as cottonseed oil, flour, sugar, pottery, saddles, boots, harness, and furniture—equaled only one fourth the value of all farm products. Thirty years later the value of the industrial output was half that of agricultural products, but the state could not be considered industrialized. The per-capita average of manufactured goods in Texas in 1900 was only $39, compared to the national average of $171.[3]

It was during the three decades between 1870 and 1900 that farmers, sheepmen, and cattlemen moved out of eastern Texas and onto the grassy plains and prairies farther west. There they transformed an unoccupied area of a hundred million acres into a great agricultural and livestock empire. The drama of this transformation overshadowed events elsewhere in Texas, leaving most natives unprepared for the twentieth century. Indeed, agriculture seemed to dominate the economic and political life of the region so firmly that the growing superstructure of industry could barely be recognized.

Eighty per cent of the population of Texas lived on farms or in rural communities in 1900, and cotton alone exceeded the value of all manufactured goods. With rare exceptions, the few men of great wealth obtained their fortunes from cotton, cattle, or lumber. Suddenly, almost within the span of a few minutes, the doom of agricultural predominance was sealed. At ten thirty on the morning of January 10, 1901, the great oil well named Spindletop erupted near Beaumont. In the next nine days it sprayed the flat countryside with an estimated 75,000 barrels of "black gold" and veered Texas and the Southwest sharply toward an industrial economy.

Spindletop, hailed as the greatest discovery of its kind, was only the beginning for the Southwest. Oil continued to flow in increasing amounts from tremendous underground deposits in various parts of Texas and Oklahoma for four or five decades. It be-

---

[3] John S. Spratt: *The Road to Spindletop: Economic Changes in Texas, 1875–1901* (Dallas: Southern Methodist University Press; 1955), p. 251.

XVI · *The Big Industrial Boom*

came the undisputed titan of the region, the basis of thousands of personal fortunes and the progenitor of hundreds of petroleum refineries and dozens of allied industries. Cotton and cattle remained important but no longer predominant.

Even before Spindletop, petroleum had been found in Oklahoma. By 1905 the territory ranked next to Texas with twenty-five per cent of the region's known reserves, and the opening of the great Glenn Pool field the next year elevated it to first place in production—fifty per cent of the total for the Southwest. This position remained unchanged for two decades. In 1931 the eastern Texas development pushed the Lone Star State so far ahead that its rank as the greatest oil-producing state in the nation has never again been challenged.

Texas produced more than a billion barrels of crude oil annually throughout the fifties—approximately half of the nation's output. (Because of Middle East competition and strict conservation and price-regulation practices, its wells operated only twelve to fifteen days per month; otherwise this production average would be even more impressive.) Oklahoma dropped to fourth position by 1958 with 215,000,000 barrels, while New Mexico rose to eighth. Arizona, the other Southwestern state, only recently entered the contest, and its oil industry hardly rates a statistic in the region's economy. Since statehood, however, Arizona has ranked near the top in nonferrous-mineral production.

In spite of the great natural-resource deposits, much of the Southwest remained a *terra incognita* as recently as 1940. The oil boom had brought new people and wealth and a shift from agriculture to manufacturing, but the effects were not much felt outside scattered population centers in Texas and Oklahoma. Suddenly the whole Southwest found itself in the midst of unprecedented changes and growth. The industrial pace quickened and developed into an economic explosion, and new people poured in from all parts of the United States.

Fortune estimated in March 1958 that six million Americans moved across the nation after World War II looking "for elbowroom and the sun-drenched life." Most of these settled on the Pacific

	Southwest	U.S.
FARMING	248	234
MINING	484	230
MANUFACTURING	977	492

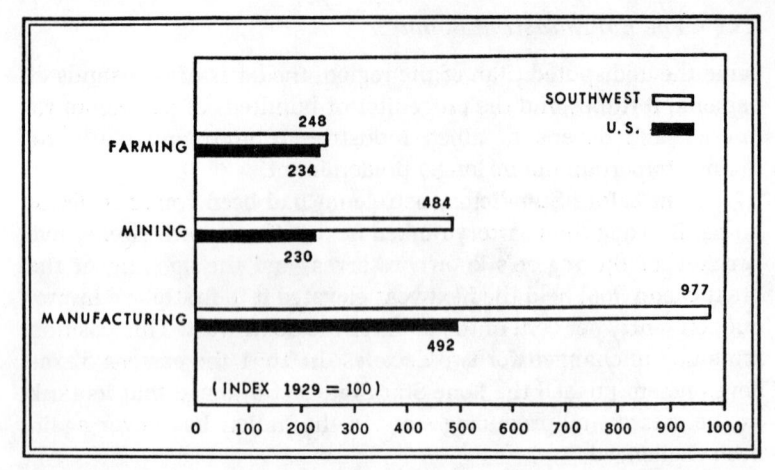

(INDEX 1929 = 100)

CHART I Percentage Change in Civilian Income in Farming, Mining, and Manufacturing in the Southwest and in the United States, 1929–1958. *Source:* Data for 1929 computed from data in U.S. Department of Commerce: *Personal Income by States since 1929* (Washington, D.C.; 1956), Table 64, p. 207. Data for 1958 from *Survey of Current Business,* August 1929, Table 70, p. 24.
Note: Data refers to income received by persons for participation in current production.

Coast, but many stopped in Texas, New Mexico, or Arizona. As a result, some cities acquired almost more residents than they could absorb. "Our immediate problem," said the Secretary of the Phoenix Chamber of Commerce in an April 1959 interview, "is to take care of those we now have. We don't want any more people—at least for a while—because we are hard pressed to find jobs for the thousands of new families that are already here."

Before the start of World War II the Southwest had three and a quarter million more cattle than people. In New Mexico and Arizona the ratio stood 2:1, while in Texas and Oklahoma it approximated 1:1. During the next eighteen years cattle increased from eleven to twenty million, but the population grew from eight to ap-

XVI · The Big Industrial Boom

proximately fourteen million.[4] But these statistical changes tell only a small part of the story.

If a visitor returned to the Southwest in 1959 after an absence of twenty years, he would not recognize it. There are long-staple cotton fields near Yuma, Arizona, electronic plants at Phoenix and Tucson, oil, gas, and uranium mines in the Four Corners, the atomic city of Los Alamos in New Mexico. Armed-forces installations dot the area—the proving grounds of Fort Huachuca, the Sandia Base near Albuquerque, the guided-missile development at El Paso, the great Air Force Depot at Tinker Field near Oklahoma City. Hundreds of giant factories ring Fort Worth, Dallas, Waco, Austin, and San Antonio.

Yet, the greatest change has occurred between Brownsville and Beaumont in Texas. Along this 370 miles of the Gulf Coast, which various writers have labeled the "Golden Crescent," is a procession of gleaming chemical plants, giant refineries, and manufacturing plants of a dozen other varieties. Like most others between the Sabine River on the eastern boundary of Texas and the Colorado River on the western boundary of Arizona, the factories along the Gulf coast are relatively new. And they have altered the region so drastically that the image of cattle, cotton, and cactus fades beyond recognition. The Old Southwest is now the New Southwest, and the traditional high-heeled boots and broad-brimmed hat are far less common than formerly.

What caused the sudden evolution whereby an industrial, urban society supplanted an agrarian, rural economy? The answer is found in the development of latent natural resources and the growth of local markets and capital, and in the obvious fact that

---

[4] *U.S. News and World Report* (November 9, 1959) estimated the population of the four Southwestern states for 1960 as follows: Texas, 9,585,000; Oklahoma, 2,311,000; Arizona, 1,198,000; and New Mexico, 869,000. It also estimated that within the next ten years Arizona will increase its population by 49.6 per cent, New Mexico by 28.9 per cent, and Texas by 21.1 per cent. Oklahoma, which has not gained in population for the past twenty years, is expected to remain static for another decade. However, the editors of *U.S. News and World Report* failed to consider the effects of the multibillion-dollar water and power projects now under construction in eastern Oklahoma.

the whole country has experienced unprecedented changes and developments since the end of World War II. These processes began before the nineteenth century, but the Southwest has only recently joined the trend away from agricultural employment and small towns toward factories and large urban communities.

Much of the recent manufacturing in the Southwest is the result of huge defense spending and the desire of the federal government to scatter its plants, air bases, military installations, and research facilities over a wide area to lessen the effect of possible enemy attack. And as farm units grow larger and more mechanized, fewer workers are needed and marginal farmers go out of business. Their obvious course is to move into nearby cities and obtain employment in the new industrial plants. Newcomers are welcomed by merchants and realtors seeking additional customers; a growing population attracts still more industries, which in turn draw more people. Once the action starts, it is sustained by its own momentum.

Not to be minimized in the rapid growth of Southwestern industry is the willingness of state boosters and legislatures to meet prospective manufacturers beyond the halfway mark. Frequently, a hint that a company may build a new plant or relocate an old one is enough to start aggressive cities bidding against one another. Sometimes they offer free building sites, guarantee an adequate supply of water, construct additional schools, annex new subdivisions, expand airport facilities, and promise adequate housing and recreational facilities for employees. Real-estate men, Chamber of Commerce representatives, bank executives, building contractors, school superintendents, and merchants join in. And usually it is the city that can offer the most, do the best selling job, or work most quickly which wins.

Co-operating with the local government is a state planning-and-resources department that studies trends, compiles data, and directs a national advertising campaign. Arizona sponsors an attractive magazine called *Arizona Highways* which has a national circulation of over 150,000, and Oklahoma and New Mexico publish similar magazines, *Oklahoma Today* and the *New Mexico*

XVI · *The Big Industrial Boom*

Magazine. All three feature colorful photographs of local scenery and happenings, and none fails to extol the industrial advantages of particular cities or sections in the state.

At times governors, legislative bodies, and local citizens' committees are capable of acting quickly and boldly. Soon after World War II the Sperry Rand Corporation let it be known that Phoenix was under consideration as a site for two separate plants that would employ a total of three thousand people. But the company expressed some misgivings about a state tax on sales to the federal government, as much of its output would go to the Defense Department. Governor McFarland called a special session of the legislature, which repealed the tax. Sperry Rand was ready to start construction, but could not find an adequate factory site or a large enough airport runway. Phoenix businessmen promptly organized an industrial-development corporation and raised $650,-000 within seventy-two hours. The amount was enough to purchase the site and lengthen the runway at the local airport. Sperry Rand built its factories, and Phoenix captured a large payroll and several hundred highly skilled and well-salaried new residents.

This story is not unique: it has been repeated many times in cities such as Dallas, Fort Worth, Houston, El Paso, Albuquerque, Oklahoma City, and Tulsa. After World War II when it appeared that the great Chance-Vought Aircraft plant would not be built in Dallas, a small group of Dallas citizens settled the matter in exactly three hours and forty minutes. Following a telephone conversation with a Chance-Vought official, the city council, called into emergency session, voted to condemn ten blocks of residential property and appropriate $250,000 to lengthen an airport runway. And on the same day the group informed a contracting firm that it had less than one week to start the project.

In record time the plant was moved "lock, stock, and barrel" from Bridgeport, Connecticut, and with it came the families of 1,500 key employees. During 1958 the Chance-Vought Aircraft factory constituted the second largest single industry in northern Texas, employed thousands of people, and poured millions of dollars each month into the local economy.

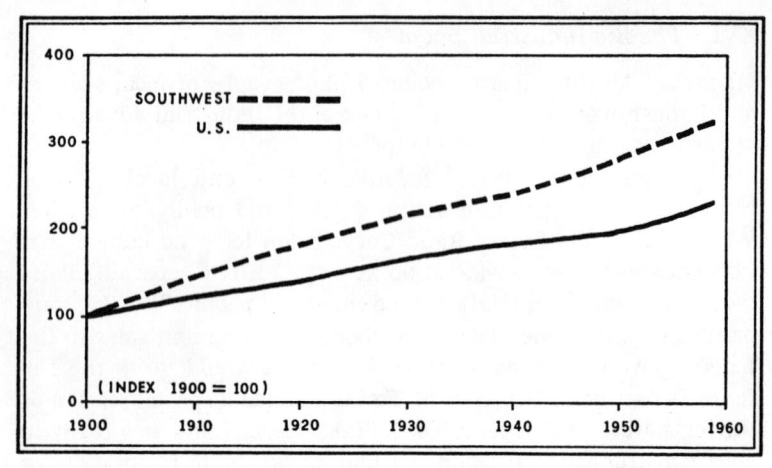

CHART II Indexes of Population Growth in the United States and the Southwest 1900–1958. *Source:* Data for 1900–1950 from U.S. Bureau of Census: *Statistical Abstract of the United States* (Washington, D.C., 1959), Table 9, p. 12. Data for 1958 from *Survey of Current Business,* August 1959, Table 3, p. 15.

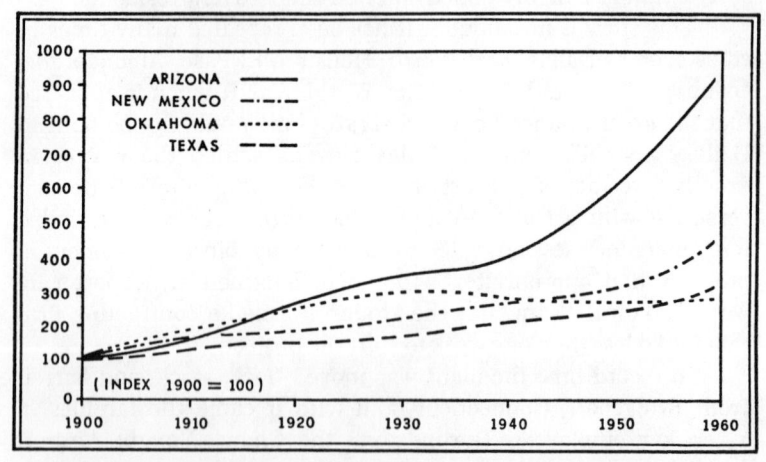

CHART III Indexes of Population Growth in Arizona, New Mexico, Oklahoma, and Texas 1900–1958. To compute index numbers for each state in the Southwest, divide the number for 1900 into the number for that state in 1910, 1920, etc., and multiply by 100. For example, Oklahoma's population in 1900 was 790,000. Divide this into 1910 population of 1,657,000; the index for 1910 is thus 197. The index for 1920 is 269, etc.

XVI · *The Big Industrial Boom*

Action such as the above is one of the principal reasons that Arizona, New Mexico, and Texas ranked among the first eight states in growth of manufacturing employment between 1947 and 1957. During the decade factory workers in Arizona increased from 14,700 to 39,500—a gain of 168.7 per cent, the highest gain in the nation. New Mexico ranked second with an increase of 131 per cent, though the 1957 total was still small: 20,800, as compared to 9,000 ten years earlier. During the same period Texas advanced from approximately 325,000 manufacturing workers to more than half a million, a gain of approximately fifty per cent. Oklahoma ranked below the first ten states with a forty-per-cent increase, but its shift from 62,000 to 87,000 is nevertheless impressive.[5]

Although Oklahoma gained steadily in manufacturing employment, it fell far behind the rest of the region in rate of population growth. Between 1930 and 1940 depression and the "black dusters" drove approximately 60,000 people out of the state and forced a reduction from eight to seven congressmen. The 1950 census revealed a further loss of 103,000—reducing the state's population to 2,233,000 and its representation in Congress to six. This last exodus occurred in a period of peak birth rates and high prosperity during which the other three Southwestern states increased by more than two million and the United States as a whole by seventeen million people. The tide shifted in the other direction in the early fifties, but unless the change continues upward at a more rapid pace, the Sooners may still suffer further reductions in its congressional delegation.

For the most part, the white settlers of Oklahoma were young, vigorous, and enthusiastic pioneers who looked on the red hills and rolling prairies as a land of opportunity. Few territories moved so rapidly into maturity, yet few states settled so quickly into inactivity. Even before 1950 Oklahoma had more permanent

---

[5] During the same period Arizona led the nation in rate of income growth, with 165.4 per cent; New Mexico ranked fourth, with 143 per cent; and Texas tenth, with 96.4 per cent. *Arizona Statistical Review* (Phoenix: Valley National Bank), October 1958, p. 2.

residents past twenty-five years of age than under, and, unlike the rest of the Southwest, it attracted as permanent residents a mere handful of the thousands of veterans who had received training at its military bases during the war years. Worse yet, a steady stream of graduates from the state university's engineering, geology, and other schools migrated southward across Red River to accept employment at Houston, Beaumont, Corpus Christi, Dallas, Odessa, Midland, or any one of a dozen other Texas towns. Schoolteachers too moved to New Mexico and surrounding states in such numbers that many systems could claim more Sooners on their staffs than natives.

It did not take much imagination to determine the main cause of Oklahoma's decline: there were not enough well-paid jobs, especially for the younger generation. Traditionally, the state's major manufacturing enterprise was petroleum refining, but the depletion of oil reserves, plus the trend toward automation, gradually reduced the number of workers needed. Meanwhile, other factors led new industries to bypass the state. The local road system acquired the reputation of being the poorest in the nation, and the per-capita tax exceeded the national average by twenty dollars or more. Added to this was a four-per-cent corporation tax that neighboring states did not exact. Also, income tax, stiff excises, dry laws, and outmoded constitutional restrictions on cities and towns kept many industrialists from even considering Oklahoma.

During the early fifties various leaders launched campaigns to attract industry. Politicians consistently held the line against increased taxation for fear it might discourage prospective clients. Governor Raymond Gary touched off an extensive highway-construction program in 1955 which eventually pushed the state within closer reach of the national standard. And the Oklahoma Development Council sponsored "industrial tours" throughout the country in an effort to induce manufacturers to move to the state.

Since 1951 these tours have been an annual event to which fifty or more business and professional men donate two weeks of their time, paying their own expenses. Teams of two or three in-

XVI · The Big Industrial Boom

dividuals call on executives in industrial cities and attempt to convince them that they need Oklahoma as much as Oklahoma needs them. They do not offer free taxes, free sites, free buildings, or free machinery to lure factories from long-established industrial areas. Neither do they promise low wages, "right-to-work laws," or restriction of union activities. Instead, they concentrate on new branch plants, warehouses, industries that must move to keep pace with a migrating market, and small operators anxious to survive outside the shadow of overpowering competitors. And they are prepared to help finance plant construction at reasonable rates, offer sites at modern prices, and lease-purchase new buildings.

This low-key industrial recruiting is slower to achieve results than the methods practiced in other Southwestern states. Texas, for example, added 4,400 new business enterprises during 1953—large and small—while Oklahoma attracted only 600. By 1957 some 573,000 Oklahomans were engaged in non-agricultural employment, almost 87,000 of whom worked in petroleum-refining, glass, steel-fabrication, chemical, and rubber industries. In the same year the number of farm operators barely exceeded 100,000, only half the number of a generation earlier. Another 25,000 were employed at Tinker Air Force Base near Oklahoma City, the state's largest single enterprise, while a lesser number of civilians worked at the military bases at Norman, McAlester, Enid, and Fort Sill. Small businessmen, construction workers, and professional people dominated the remainder of the non-agricultural employment field.

Oklahoma also has moved forward in the tourist business in an effort to attract new people and money and create employment for the displaced farm population. A unique effort is the construction at state expense of attractive lodges at strategic places along the chain of lakes in the eastern portion of the state. Not only is this region rapidly being discovered by thousands of vacationers and sportsmen from surrounding areas, but because of several large multi-purpose dams currently being completed it is evolving into a small TVA that will furnish power for industrial growth.

And if the long-range plans to develop navigation on the Canadian and Arkansas rivers ever become reality, Oklahoma may emerge as one of the most densely populated and highly industrialized centers of the Southwest.

National advertising of the dozens of lakes, state parks, Gilcrease and Philbrook art museums at Tulsa, Woolaroc Museum at Bartlesville, and the Will Rogers Memorial at Claremore has made the Sooner State known throughout the country. Thousands visit the Plains Indians' villages at Anadarko, Frontier City near Oklahoma City, and the annual Easter Sunrise Service near Lawton. All of these combined do not attract so many tourists as a Grand Canyon or a Yellowstone National Park, but their contribution to the state's economy cannot be overlooked.

The repeal of prohibition in the spring of 1959, after fifty-one years of hypocrisy and failure, opened a new business outlet and furnished some evidence of a progressive awakening in Oklahoma. But many additional reforms and changes will have to come before the Sooners can compete with their Southwestern neighbors. Even so, Oklahoma's future certainly looked brighter at the end of the fifties than at the beginning.

IF PROGRESS TOWARD an industrial economy is slow and steady in Oklahoma, it is rapid and prodigious in Texas. In fact, if the Lone Star State added no new manufacturing plants and business enterprises for twenty years while the rest of the Southwest continued expansion at its present rate, it would still be far ahead of Oklahoma, Arizona, and New Mexico combined. The former republic still has a lot of land where the "distance between watering places is a far piece." But mushrooming cities and hundreds of new plants manufacturing chemicals, "miracle fabrics," dyes, synthetic rubber, gasoline, magnesium, paper, steel, tools, machinery, automobiles, and airplanes are transforming it into the new powerhouse of the United States.

XVI · *The Big Industrial Boom*

Almost everything in Texas is booming. Oil and gas continue to be pumped out of the ground. More new industry is taking root. Cattle, sheep, cotton, corn, wheat, rice, sugar, and peanuts appear in plenty. Wide ribbons of concrete and asphalt tie various sections of the state together. Quiet towns are transformed into large cities and metropolitan centers are overlapping county lines. Giant aircraft factories sprawl over inland prairies, and new oil refineries and chemical plants fill in the coastal marshes. Lonesome cowboys may still sing beneath Texas stars, but they are not typical of the new breed of Texans. The state has become an industrial complex as its oil industry has reached maturity and its manufacturing potential is twelve times greater than that of Pittsburgh.

The most important factors contributing to this tremendous growth have been natural resources and agricultural production. Texas has half the oil in the United States and most of the known sulphur in the world. In 1955 the value of its petrochemical production approximated three billion dollars—eighty per cent of the nation's output. In that same year wells pumped more than a billion barrels of oil from the subsurface, and pipelines transported more than four trillion cubic feet of natural gas.

In 1958 Texas contributed fifty-five per cent of the carbon black and fifty-nine per cent of the helium produced in the United States. It led all other states in production of cotton (twenty-seven per cent), beef cattle (twelve per cent), wool (nineteen per cent), mohair (ninety-seven per cent), and rice (twenty-eight per cent). Since 1948 Texas has continued to rank first in the quantity and value of magnesium production in the United States, most of which is made from sea water. Production of steel and aluminum also is advancing rapidly, and the lumber industry approximates half a billion dollars annually.[6]

Oil remains the parent of Texas industry, but other types of manufacturing are overtaking it rapidly. It is chiefly in these non-

---

[6] "Why Texas Is Thriving": *U.S. News and World Report*, November 23, 1956, pp. 74–5.

THE SOUTHWEST: *Old and New*

petroleum fields that the former republic hopes for continued prosperity and growth, especially since imports from the Middle East have cut heavily into demands for Southwestern crude. A noticeable trend toward non-petroleum manufacturing began during the early months of World War II when aircraft plants around Dallas and Fort Worth started building bombers and fighters. The trend became a surge as influential Texans such as Jesse Jones, Sam Rayburn, Tom Connally, and Lyndon Johnson secured for their state a generous share of new military bases and a variety of war plants. When the war ended, the surge was redirected to meet the needs of a prosperous civilian market. Northern industrialists moved to Texas en masse, and by 1960 the migration still showed few signs of abating.

During the fifties the aircraft industry in Texas alone employed more workers than all types of manufacturing in the entire state of Arizona. But aircraft construction is only a minor part of the over-all picture. Soon after World War II the Dow Chemical Company constructed two plants near Freeport at a cost of more than one and a half billion dollars. Other post-war developments are the Du Pont nylon salt plant at Orange, the General Motors plant at Fort Worth, the Celanese Corporation chemical plant at Bishop, the General Tire and Owen Glass Company factories at Waco. These, together with hundreds of new firms, enabled Texas's industrial products to double in value between 1948 and 1955.[7]

During the first nine months of 1958 more manufacturing plants were built in Dallas—fifty-seven—than in any other city in the United States or in twenty-five combined states. The total of 218 for the state for this period was second only to California's 244.[8] Though agriculture continues strong,[9] new factories draw people from the rural areas and small towns into the cities like

---

[7] *The Texas Observer* (Austin), April 4, 1955, p. 8.
[8] *The Dallas News*, April 19, 1959.
[9] *Changing Times* (Washington), April 1956, p. 25. The cash income from Texas agriculture in 1955, a drought year, came to almost two billion dollars—four times the figure for 1939.

XVI · *The Big Industrial Boom*

giant magnets. In 1959 only one out of every eight Texans lived on a farm, as compared to one out of two in 1920.

Texas tempts prospective industrialists in many ways. In 1958 it had no personal income tax and no general sales tax, and its average state-tax collection of $70.36 was lower than that of all but a dozen other states. Oil and gas are the principal reasons, for they pay about a third of governmental costs.

The Lone Star State likewise has a fairly abundant supply of labor, although there is a shortage of personnel in certain professions such as engineering, mechanics, and medicine. Unions are not so strong as in Northern industrial centers, including only twenty per cent of the non-agricultural labor force, whereas the national average is thirty per cent. The state's "right-to-work" law is, with the possible exception of Arizona's, the strongest one in existence. Its labor code bans the closed shop, union shop, dues check-off, mass picketing, and secondary strikes.[1] Also, it is one of the few states where contract labor is still a legal practice and where the company union, especially in the oil industries, frequently predominates.

Weather and geography are other assets in luring industry to Texas. Year-round flying and plenty of space for plant expansion are strong inducements for some manufacturers. Except for occasional "northers," the former republic has relatively mild winters, but its summers can be, and frequently are, brutal. Air-conditioning, however, is so universal that more than a dozen firms turn out equipment to meet local demands alone. Some 40,000 Texas homes had air-conditioning by 1956—ten per cent of the national total—and since that date much new construction has included it as standard equipment. Office buildings, hotels, tourist courts, and places of business are air-conditioned, as well as many drive-in restaurants and theaters, dairy barns, public schools, and even some animal cages in municipal zoos. One

---

[1] Dr. Nelson Peach, Professor of Economics at the University of Oklahoma, maintains that anti-labor laws and low taxes are not necessarily important factors in attracting industry. He believes that good schools, availability of natural resources, parks, recreational facilities, and progressive governments are far more significant.

The Southwest: *Old and New*

Houston automobile dealer in 1957 estimated that seventy-five per cent of his customers specified air-conditioning in the new cars they bought.

The editors of *U.S. News and World Report,* after completing a study of business and industrial developments of Texas late in 1956, observed: "Texas no doubt still needs the rest of the United States. But the United States is finding, more and more, it cannot get along without Texas." They added that "the state's power yet to be derived from its vast geography and resources could scarcely be calculated."

Though the Texas picture overshadows other regions of the Southwest, the transformation of Arizona and New Mexico in many ways is even more spectacular. In 1947 the sun-baked deserts, high mesas, and raw, harsh lands of these states were thought by most Americans to be inhabited only by picturesque Indians, asthmatic and tubercular refugees from the East, and a few weather-beaten and hard-bitten natives. By 1959 one could question fifteen or twenty people in Albuquerque, Tucson, or Phoenix before finding a native-born resident or even one who had lived in the locality more than ten years. The thousands of new citizens have acted as a blood transfusion. New ideas, enthusiasm, and energy that they brought from the outside overwhelmed the traditionally easy-going Arizonans and New Mexicans. And, rather than resenting the newcomers, the natives soon joined in the rush to move forward.

Since 1952 I have made a dozen or more trips into or across New Mexico and Arizona, and each time the changes since the last visit appeared almost beyond belief. Both states are large and scenic, and a lot of landscape, but not much plant or animal life, separates the few urban centers. Viewing it from a glass-domed railroad car, an airplane, or an automobile, one feels that all the publicity about the big boom is a myth created by state and local boosters. But this illusion disappears as soon as Albuquerque, Tucson, or Phoenix moves into sight. Always one finds that new industrial plants, residential areas, motels, and small businesses have driven the city limits a few miles farther into the desert or

XVI · *The Big Industrial Boom*

up the mountain slopes. The reality of the boom quickly becomes evident.

Amazement at the changes since one's last visit is followed by skepticism, as one recalls the Florida "boom and bust" of the 1920's. This attitude meets opposition from bankers, lawyers, realtors, and other local citizens who believe that their economy has a solid base for maturity, barring a national calamity. But taxi drivers, store clerks, waiters, and small motel operators are generally less optimistic. They point out that they are forced to hold two or three jobs simultaneously to support their families; wages are low, they say, living costs high, and the threat of a "lay-off" ever present. Yet, no matter from which end of the spectrum one views the situation, these desert states have made an amazing transformation within a remarkably brief period.

Most of the growth and changes in Arizona center on Phoenix and Tucson, while Albuquerque is the focal point in New Mexico. In 1945 Greater Phoenix had 156,000 people, but by 1959 it claimed 465,000. During the same period Tucson increased from 85,000 to 225,000 and Albuquerque expanded from 50,000 to 225,000. Back in 1940 Ernie Pyle used to write about the jack rabbits around his home on the outskirts of Albuquerque. In 1960 his former residence was just about in the center of the city.

The annual rush to Albuquerque and other Southwestern cities is expected to double the population of Arizona and New Mexico by 1975, according to projections based on Census Bureau methods. But such Western population experts as Herbert Leggett, of the Valley National Bank in Phoenix, and Ralph L. Edgel, director of the Bureau of Business Research at the University of New Mexico, believe that such estimates are far too conservative. They predict that by 1975 their respective states will top three million.

Since the time of the Spanish padres the economy of Arizona and New Mexico has rested on two enterprises: mining and agriculture. More than fifty per cent of the nation's lead, zinc, and copper is found here, while New Mexico leads all other states in the production of potash. And, according to Atomic Energy Commission officials, it possesses nearly seventy per cent of the nation's proved uranium. Farming and mining in 1945 accounted for seventy-five per cent of the income for both states. A decade and a half later these enterprises produced approximately half the local income, in spite of the development of large irrigation projects, tremendous discoveries in uranium, and the opening of several oil and gas fields.

At the beginning of World War II, industry contributed fifty million dollars a year to Arizona's economy. The establishment and expansion of some 500 new manufacturing plants brought this to almost half a billion in 1957. Typical is the AiResearch Manufacturing Company, which began operation in Phoenix in 1950 with ten employees. In 1958 it had over 3,700 workers and claimed to be the world's largest production center of small gas turbine engines. During the decade following 1948 the Phoenix area alone acquired 280 new manufacturers, who created more than 15,000 jobs and boosted the annual payroll by approximately seventy-five million dollars.[2]

Most of the new plants are similar to AiResearch in that they are light water-users. And for obvious reasons Arizona boosters do not encourage enterprises other than the so-called "dry and smokeless" varieties. Also, because of freight costs and remoteness from Eastern markets, the new companies must turn out products of high value and low weight. A good example is the small transistor: a million dollars' worth of these electronic items can be shipped in a single truck from Phoenix to Los Angeles within a few hours.

The state's biggest industry, Hughes Aircraft, near Tucson, manufactures Falcon missiles and employs 5,000 people, many of whom are scientists or highly skilled technicians. The nearby Douglas plant is similar in the quality of its employees, though its payroll is considerably smaller. Other companies in the Tucson and

---

[2] During the same period Tucson in Pima County acquired more than 125 industries. "Arizona: Sun, Room, and Low Taxes," *Fortune*, March 1958, pp. 247 ff.

XVI · The Big Industrial Boom

Phoenix areas are General Electric, which produces electronic components and computers, and Goodyear Aircraft Corporation, which fabricates parts for airships. Kaiser Aircraft and Electronic Corporation makes electronic systems, while Motorola has three Arizona plants turning out transistors and electronic military devices. In addition, Sperry Gyroscope Company makes aircraft instruments and the Reynolds Metals Company in Phoenix operates the world's largest extrusion plant. Others are National Malleable and Steel Casting, Allison Steel Manufacturing, Babb Aircraft, and General Electric's computer division.

Yuma also is growing. In 1946 this ugly border city of 5,000 people had the distinction of having the lowest annual rainfall average in the United States, three to five inches, and the hottest climate, with frequent temperatures of 120°. In 1960 it was still an ugly border city and its climate had not changed, but its population exceeded 30,000. Yuma's location gives it two advantages for an industrial future: it is near the largest Pima-cotton area in the United States and it can obtain water from both the Gila and Colorado rivers. Observers predict that this Arizona outpost will develop into one of the great manufacturing centers in the West.

Closer to the middle of the state, the sleepy little town of Casa Grande has a garment factory employing 150 people, which is more than the total population of the place in 1940. Benson has the Apache Powder Plant, where 300 workers make high explosives for industrial use, and Fort Huachuca, an old cavalry post on the Mexican border, is the site of the Army Signal Corps's electronic proving ground for space equipment.

Flagstaff, in northern Arizona, is the railhead for the $420,000,000 Glen Canyon Dam on the Colorado. When completed, about 1968, this project will be second in size to Hoover Dam and will hold back a lake stretching 186 miles up the Colorado River. Until then Flagstaff should continue its unprecedented prosperity, and once the lake is formed it could well become the center of a vast new playground.

Perhaps the stage was set for the present boom in this corner of the Southwest during World War II when the United States gov-

THE SOUTHWEST: *Old and New*

ernment began training pilots by the thousands and GI's by the tens of thousands at bases near Phoenix, Tucson, and other Arizona cities. Many returned when the war ended to a region that outsiders had formerly regarded as offering little except scenery and sunshine. Neither Arizona nor New Mexico possessed a seaport, adequate railroads, or much capital, and their vast resources in land, metals, asbestos, coal, silica sand, and limestone remained largely untapped. A few copper barons were very rich, while the status of Indians, sheepherders, miners, cowboys, and farmhands varied from extreme to moderate poverty. The middle class remained relatively inconspicuous until the veterans brought a social revolution to the existing order.

Suddenly thousands of other Americans discovered Arizona and learned to appreciate the beauty and solitude of its desert. No small number of these came as tourists and remained permanently or returned at a later date. Others settled in Arizona to take advantage of cheap government land or to escape the urban areas of the East and West coasts.

During April 1959 I spent several days in Tucson and Phoenix talking to political, civic, and business leaders, and the topic of the new interest in Arizona invariably arose. "This used to be a place one passed through going somewhere else. Few dared to stop longer than it took to stretch their legs and let the car radiator cool off before tackling the desert again," explained Orme Lewis, a prominent Phoenix attorney. "But two developments in recent years have helped immeasurably to put us on the map—air-conditioning and the airplane. It's as simple as that."

The nearly perfect year-round flying weather makes the problem of transportation from Phoenix to Los Angeles or New York a minor one. And Mr. Lewis added that his city is a crossroads for "visiting firemen" anxious to escape the cold weather elsewhere. "Naturally we are glad to see them, but now we look forward to the return of summer when all our relatives, friends, and friends' friends have gone home and we can get back to work."

The boom in Arizona is only slightly more spectacular than the one in New Mexico, where farming and ranching also re-

XVI · *The Big Industrial Boom*

mained the major occupations until the end of World War II. These are tough businesses in a region where the rainfall is so scarce that few crops can be raised without irrigation and most of the land is held by the federal government.

Unlike Arizona's, the boom in New Mexico can be dated from a single event. In the misty dawn of July 16, 1945, the world's first atomic bomb exploded on the White Sands Desert near Alamogordo. Since that moment the state that calls itself the "Land of Enchantment" has remained the nation's center for nuclear research and the production of atomic weapons. Most of the local manufacturing is geared to this development.

A large portion of the new industry is located in the vicinity of Albuquerque, where lives one fourth of the state's population. Indians and cowboys still roam the streets, but they are outnumbered by crew-cut scientists, smartly dressed lawyers, bronzed-faced geologists, and important-looking federal men with brief cases.

More than a hundred motels line Highway 66 as it cuts a swath twenty miles long through the heart of this sprawling metropolis. From the eastern edge of the city to its western fringe the din of traffic rarely ceases during any twenty-four-hour period. Massed on the Albuquerque perimeter is an endless complex of research laboratories, military bases, machine shops, and industrial plants. Among these are the Atomic Energy Commission Operation's Office, the $40,000,000 Sandia Laboratory, the Armed Forces Special Weapons Project at Sandia Base, and the Air Force Special Weapons Center at Kirkland Air Force Base. These installations employ more than 21,000 people and have an annual payroll of approximately $93,000,000. The AEC office spent $388,000,000 during the 1956–7 fiscal year, mostly in New Mexico. During the same period the Armed Forces spent $71,000,000 at Sandia Base and White Sands Proving Ground and the Air Force $19,000,000 at Sandia Base.

The Sandia Base houses the site of the Sandia Corporation plant where such items as bomb casings, fusing, and firing mechanisms for nuclear weapons are made. The federal government also

THE SOUTHWEST: *Old and New*

has invested more than $250,000,000 at Los Alamos, a hundred miles straight north in the Jemez Mountains. This city of 13,000 did not exist in 1940, and few Americans were aware of its creation until after the end of World War II. It is now an open city and known throughout the world as the nation's nuclear-weapons center, but its heavily guarded laboratories are still shrouded in mystery. Approximately 3,000 well-paid employees work there, many of them physicists or highly skilled technicians.

Farmington, in the Four Corners, is frequently called the "boomingest town in the Southwest." A mere hamlet on the edge of the Navajo Reservation before World War II, it was primarily a trading area for Indians, farmers, and ranchers. In 1945 uranium prospectors and oil and gas men swarmed into the area from all directions. Within a decade it boasted more than 1,500 natural-gas and 150 producing oil wells. The population increased to approximately 3,500 by 1950 and to 15,000 eight years later. When I visited the place in 1956, more than 1,200 trailer houses cluttered the city from end to end, while construction of new homes was two years behind the demand.

Discovery of oil and gas in the San Juan Basin around Farmington has created a network of pipelines that reach out in all directions. One that extends almost 1,500 miles carries gas to the Pacific Northwest, while a larger, sixteen-inch line transports crude oil 600 miles due west to Los Angeles. The El Paso Natural Gas Company has a new refinery at Ciniza, a few miles east of Gallup, which eventually will process 13,000 barrels daily. The other principal oil and gas production center is in the opposite corner of New Mexico, around Roswell, Hobbs, Carlsbad, and Jal. In 1958 all of New Mexico's fields together produced oil valued at approximately $300,000,000 and more than $77,000,000 worth of natural gas.[3]

Another boom area is near the town of Grants, halfway between Albuquerque and the Arizona line on Highway 66 and the Santa Fe Railroad tracks. Its population in 1956 was over 6,500,

[3] *1958 Annual Summary Issue of New Mexico Business* (Bureau of Business Research, University of New Mexico), pp. 16–17.

XVI · The Big Industrial Boom

as compared to one third that number the previous year. The gain resulted from the discovery of the largest uranium deposit in the United States under the dry bed of nearby Ambrosia Lake. AEC officials estimated that in 1958 six uranium mills in the vicinity of Grants processed ore worth $115,000,000.

Because of New Mexico's military bases and abundant natural resources, its economic boom may outlast Arizona's, but some New Mexicans are frankly worried about the state's "having so many eggs in the federal basket." "This place could be in a hell'va mess if the cold war ended and peace broke out," is a remark heard often throughout the region.

Most natives, however, believe that atomic energy is here to stay and that its industrial uses have not been scratched. Ralph L. Edgel states emphatically that "high type non-military manufacturing has already secured such a foothold that the industrial expansion would continue even if defense spending stopped." Even so, New Mexico—like its sister states of the Southwest—would suffer a crippling blow if the nation's military program experienced a sudden and drastic cutback. The transition to other activities could be painful. The region's economy cannot be considered a healthily balanced one when so much of the local income depends on military bases, aircraft factories, supply depots, and government research projects. But for the first time in New Mexico's long slow history an almost complete dependence on farming and ranching is of the past.

PERHAPS the mid-twentieth-century boom in the Southwest has its closest precedent in the California gold rush a hundred years before. Both gained by the prosperity that followed a major war and increased the nation's wealth, attracted thousands of new residents from other regions, and inexorably altered the local landscape, people, traditions, and politics.

XVII
POLITICS AND POLITICIANS: TEXAS AND OKLAHOMA

THERE IS no single interest, individual, or political machine that controls the Southwest—nor has there ever been. The region possesses too varied a geography, climate, economy, tradition, and people. But there are enough common political features to support a few generalizations.

Traditionally, the Southwest is a Democratic stronghold. All four states followed the national trend toward Republicanism in the presidential elections of 1952 and 1956, but in the five previous elections Roosevelt and Truman carried the region by sub-

XVII · Politics and Politicians: Texas and Oklahoma

stantial margins. The Hoover landslide in 1928 marks the only other time Texas supported a Republican. In twelve presidential elections between 1912 and 1956, Oklahoma voted Democratic eight times and Arizona and New Mexico seven. Neither Texas nor Oklahoma has ever elected a Republican governor during the twentieth century, though the Sooners have chosen two Republican senators and a dozen congressmen. And in Arizona and New Mexico, Democrats consistently outnumber Republicans, but they frequently lose control of state governments because of interparty strife.

In 1957 the Eighty-fifth Congress contained seven Southwestern Democratic senators and one Republican, Barry Goldwater of Arizona. Goldwater, one of the most conservative men in Washington, won a second term in 1958 in a close contest with Ernest W. McFarland, Arizona's Democratic governor. His election was considered a triumph of personality rather than an endorsement of "old-guard" conservatism. Goldwater's senior colleague, Carl Hayden, and the six other Southwestern senators are generally recognized as moderate-liberals. If this group or the states it represents has a spokesman, it could only be Lyndon Johnson; yet the powerful Senate majority leader is associated with the South as frequently as with the Southwest.

The Southwest possesses a liberal tradition and eagerly embraced most reforms advocated by Populists, Progressives, and New Dealers. World War II and the return of prosperity, rapid industrialization, and the accumulation of great personal fortunes brought an abrupt turn to the political right, marked by a violent reaction against the New Deal and increased conservatism on the part of metropolitan newspapers. Opposition to various liberal ideas came chiefly from farmers and ranchers who desired government handouts without federal controls, manufacturers who objected to the forty-hour week and so-called "coddling of labor unions," exploiters of natural resources who opposed federal conservation practices, racial bigots who considered Mrs. Roosevelt a "nigger lover," anti-intellectuals who distrusted government experts, and the *nouveaux riches* who complained with increasing bitterness as they moved into higher income-tax brackets.

At the same time, the Southwest never gave much support to isolationism. It advocated preparedness and intervention in both world wars earlier than most sections of the country. Later it produced a host of vociferous opponents to the League of Nations, the United Nations, and foreign aid, but their following remained limited. Though parts of Texas share the Deep South's attitude toward the racial question, most Southwesterners accepted the Supreme Court's decision in 1954 on school integration. Large minorities—Indians, Mexicans, Negroes—reside throughout the region, and at various times each group has been the victim of discrimination. But within a decade after World War II they enjoyed most of the political and civil rights of other citizens and the attention of politicians who desired their votes.

Pressure groups abound in the Southwestern states. Farmers demand rigid parity and larger crop-acreage allotments; ranchers watch carefully the importation of foreign beef; sheep raisers support a high tariff on Australian wool; oil producers and mine operators fight to retain mineral-depletion allowance and limitations on foreign imports; and gas producers clamor for removal of federal price controls on natural gas shipped in interstate commerce. Cities likewise make active and often successful efforts to ensure the continuation of military bases, most of which date from the early days of World War II and still play an important role in local economy.[1]

If a single subject attracts more political attention in the region than any other, it is water. All governors and state legislators pretend to be interested in its conservation and use. Each Southwestern state has at least one senator who specializes in this general area: Robert S. Kerr of Oklahoma, Lyndon Johnson of

---

[1] The number of military bases, depots, airfields, and other defense installations in the United States is not public information. It is common knowledge, however, that the Southwest has a generous share of the Navy, Air Force, and Army bases. In 1959 there were thirty-three Air Force bases still activated in the four Southwestern states: twenty-one in Texas, four in New Mexico, and three each in Arizona and Oklahoma.

XVII · Politics and Politicians: Texas and Oklahoma

Texas, Clinton Anderson of New Mexico, and Carl Hayden of Arizona. In 1957, while the Southwest still suffered from a severe drought, I queried the region's eight United States senators on the subject of political pressures which they experience from their constituents. Each of the seven who replied listed reclamation aid, public power in the form of REA, flood control, and various other aspects of the water problem as "must" legislation.

Indeed, Southwesterners constantly demand more dams and lakes to supply thirsty cities, new water recreational facilities, more water for industrial usage, cheap hydroelectricity, flood control projects, and irrigation water for agricultural expansion. There is often disagreement as to what type of dam is needed and what its functions should be, but virtually all Southwesterners are convinced that such projects should be financed by federal appropriations. In this respect the attitude of Southwesterners is more than a little paradoxical: they wail long and loud about federal spending, waste, and unnecessary taxes, but they are not timid in asking for, nor unsuccessful in obtaining, generous appropriations from Washington.

According to the Bureau of Reclamation, there was a total of eighty-three federal-built reservoirs in the United States in 1957, each with a capacity in excess of 300 billion gallons. One fourth were located in the Southwest, where lived less than ten per cent of the nation's population: Oklahoma contained eight, Texas seven, and Arizona six. Concrete dams in the United States numbered 160, ten of which were found in Arizona and five in both Texas and Oklahoma.[2] By 1959 several others were under construction, had already been approved, or were in the advanced planning stage. The Glen Canyon Dam on the Colorado River in Arizona is notable among these; others are the Eufaula, Keystone, Oologah, and Fort Gibson projects in eastern Oklahoma, the proposed $1,170,000,000 Arkansas River navigation project sponsored by Senator Kerr for Oklahoma, and the even more expensive con-

---

[2] These figures refer to dams more than 200 feet in height. Smaller ones in the Southwest number several dozen and are especially numerous in Oklahoma and New Mexico.

servation and navigation scheme for various rivers in Texas backed by Senator Johnson.

Until 1940, as we have already noted, the entire Southwest was more rural than urban, more oriented toward agriculture than industry. Almost two decades later the region still led the nation in livestock production and remained among the top producers of cotton, wheat, peanuts, and other crops. But industry now surpassed agriculture in economic importance and more people lived in cities than in rural communities. These changes brought shifts in political thinking also. The pattern evolved similarly in the four states, yet local traditions, racial groups, diversity of natural resources, geography, and climate were factors that contributed to sectional differences. Thus, it is difficult to trace recent political developments in the Southwest without separating Texas and Oklahoma from New Mexico and Arizona, for each state is more like its sectional partner than like the region as a whole.

Since 1900 Texas and Oklahoma have exchanged several hundred thousand residents. Both states are predominantly Anglo-Saxon, Protestant, and Democratic; and they have the additional common denominators of cotton, oil, wheat, and cattle. They are economically oriented to the Midwest and East rather than to the West Coast; they are more populous and industrialized than New Mexico and Arizona; their state governments are almost identical in the matter of concentrating appointive power in the hands of the governor and giving control of the legislature to thinly populated rural counties.

By 1960 approximately two thirds of all Texans and Oklahomans lived in cities, but because neither state had reapportioned its legislature in more than a generation, urbanites were denied fair representation. In both Texas and Oklahoma no county

XVII · *Politics and Politicians: Texas and Oklahoma*

can elect more than one senator or seven representatives. This enables the rural areas to control the legislature and their representatives to cater to the demands of farmers for special tax exemptions, county roads, state aid to rural education, and prohibition.[3] Frequently they co-operate with conservative business interests who advocate fair-trade laws, restriction of labor unions, and careful protection of corporations. Often the demands of liberals and urban residents are ignored.

But the center of political gravity is shifting, albeit slowly, toward more progressive points of view in Texas and Oklahoma. Demagogues such as Jim Ferguson and "Alfalfa Bill" Murray, whose powers depended on the votes of the "boys from the forks of the creek" have disappeared, and the old "labor baiter" W. Lee O'Daniel no longer attracts crowds or arouses enthusiasm.

These three men were among the nation's best-known demagogic governors during the twentieth century, and they warrant special attention in any political history of the section. They achieved power at a time when sharecroppers outnumbered wage earners, when bigotry held a wide edge over tolerance, and when poverty was more general than prosperity. In the early part of the century few Texans and Oklahomans possessed indoor plumbing; the evangelistic church and the rural consolidated school remained the centers of most community life; large segments of the population had never voted; most highways and country roads resembled frontier conditions; and few men of wealth had yet accepted the responsibility that goes with it. The setting was ideal for politicians who could "promise the moon and only deliver the cheese."

Such a politician was Jim Ferguson of Texas, the section's

---

[3] Oklahomans repealed prohibition in April 1959 by a majority of more than 80,000. Most of the rural counties voted dry, but the cities went wet. The legislature, still controlled by rural constituents, then drafted a liquor law that could dry up the state more effectively than prohibition. The liquor-tax revenue, however, is distributed disproportionately among the dry counties. In Texas, meanwhile, local option exists whereby most of the cities are legally wet and the rural communities legally dry. This enables the "drys" to have their law and the "wets" their liquor.

first demagogue of importance. No man—not even Sam Houston —played a longer and stronger role in the state's history, and few contributed less to its prestige and welfare. For a generation the eyes of Texas and those of the nation were upon "Pa" Ferguson and his wife, "Ma." This gubernatorial team was an issue in every Texas election from 1914 to 1940. Two decades later, memories of the Fergusons are still fresh.

Jim Ferguson was born in the hamlet of Salado Creek, Texas, in 1871, the son of a poor Methodist minister and farmer. His schooling came spasmodically "between the crops," and he left home at sixteen. After a few years of odd jobs Jim returned to Bell County to study law. In 1897 he gained admittance to the Texas bar and two years later married the daughter of a wealthy farmer. He and his bride settled in Temple, where the young lawyer founded his own bank and joined all the local fraternal lodges and business organizations. He also adopted the traditional trademarks of a Southern politician—dark suit, heavy gold watch chain with masonic emblem attached, broadcloth vest, moderately broad-brimmed hat, and thin black tie.

In 1912 the forty-one-year-old Ferguson confided to his wife, Miriam Amanda, that Texas "should have a governor who has been a successful farmer, stock raiser, and business man." Obviously, he meant himself. A short time later he entered the Democratic gubernatorial primary, which in "one-party" Texas is the real election. In the 1914 campaign he directed his attention to the great mass of sharecroppers or tenant famers who paid the landholders bonuses in addition to a percentage of their crops. Although he hired men to work on his own farm, Ferguson presented himself as "a real dirt farmer" who knew at first hand the plight of the "boys from the forks of the creek."

"Farmer Jim" concluded that the 200,000 tenant farmers held the balance of power in state elections, and he constructed a platform designed to win their votes. He proposed to limit the amount of crop rent a landlord could charge to one fourth of the cotton and one third of the grain, provide cheaper credit for

17 Laying an 18-inch pipeline across the Llano River in Texas.

18a (above) One of the large refineries at Baytown, Texas.
18b (below) Open-pit Jackpile uranium mine on the Laguna Indian Reservation in New Mexico.

19 Roosevelt Dam, the first of Arizona's great irrigation projects.

20a (above) Navajo Indian sand painters at work.
20b (below) Navajo Indian rug weaver.

21a (above) Cattle-branding methods have changed little in Texas during the past century. Spring roundup on the Rocker B Ranch, 1958.
21b (below) Sheep ranch near White Mountains in eastern Arizona.

22 *Downtown business section of modern Phoenix.*

23a (above) Houston—the Southwest's largest city.
23b (below) Dallas. Most of the office buildings in the foreground have been built since World War II.

24 Oil derricks on Oklahoma's State Capitol grounds.

XVII · *Politics and Politicians: Texas and Oklahoma*

farmers, and increase financial aid for the "little schoolhouse on the country road." Not only his program but also his appearance and mannerisms as a "suspender-snapping tobacco-chewing son of the soil" appealed to rustic audiences, and he used language that they understood and appreciated. Ferguson's land proposal could be interpreted to please both landlord and tenant, but actually offered little to either. He pictured his opponent, Colonel Thomas H. Ball, as a "durned high-toned educated city slicker" and made Ball's membership in the Houston Club a major issue. "Since Ball claims that he neither drinks nor gambles, then why don't he resign?" Farmer Jim demanded.

Ball replied that he belonged to the club for literary reasons. Jim then produced a statement of the organization's yearly expenses which showed $112 expended for books and magazines $361.48 for cards and poker chips, and $10,483.15 for hard liquor. Ball struck back by charging his opponent with accepting financial support from the whisky industry. Prohibition was a raging issue, so Ferguson vehemently claimed that he was a "personal dry." Almost in the same breath he promised to "veto any bill that has to do with the liquor business no matter from what source it comes."

When the ballot boxes at the crossroads and in the piney woods of eastern Texas were opened, they showed an overwhelming vote for Ferguson. The Governor-elect accepted victory as a great triumph of plain people and told them that "when you call at my office, just come right in, sit right down, and make yourself at home."[4] A few weeks later he took the oath of office before thousands of bronzed-faced farmers who had ridden to Austin with their wives and children in wagons and buggies from all over Texas. The scene resembled that in the national capital almost a century earlier when 30,000 people witnessed the inauguration of

---

[4] Most of the quotes relating to Jim Ferguson's career and speeches are taken from Reinhard H. Luthin: *American Demagogues, Twentieth Century* (Boston: The Beacon Press; 1954), unless otherwise indicated. Some undocumented quotes are based on my personal recollections.

THE SOUTHWEST: *Old and New*

the "champion of the common man," Andrew Jackson. Farmer Jim evidently felt even closer to the people than "Old Hickory," for he concluded his address in an emotionally choked voice:

> "If you love me as I love you,
> No knife can cut our love in two."

The new Governor co-operated fully with the legislature during his first term and secured the passage of his promised farm-rental bill. Never rigidly enforced, the law was declared unconstitutional by the Supreme Court. But the sharecroppers were grateful just the same. By repeating his threat to veto any liquor legislation that might be passed, he prevented any from being offered. Thus he kept the brewers and their money behind him. And his vigorous promotion of state aid to rural education endeared him to the country people.

The "common people" elected Ferguson again in 1916 by a greater majority than for his first term. By now his opponents knew the power of the farm vote, and at least one of them tried to outdo Jim in demagogic appeal. "My wife won't have one of them social secretaries," he told the farm women of Texas, "and if you want to see her just come on around to the back yard of the governor's mansion in Austin. Likely as not you will find her out ther' making lye soap in an arn pot." Even the master himself could not top this statement.

Trouble began not long after Ferguson's second inauguration. State monies were deposited in his Temple bank and other banks throughout the state in which he owned stock. These banks naturally paid no interest on the state funds, but they invariably took care of the Governor's personal "overdrafts." Ugly rumors of "borrowed" sums from men Ferguson appointed to office and a $156,000 "loan" from Texas brewers refused to die. Then he turned his anger on the University of Texas. The Board of Regents failed to check with the State House before selecting a new president. Furthermore, some of the faculty members openly opposed Ferguson's re-election. The Governor denounced them as "snobs,"

XVII · *Politics and Politicians: Texas and Oklahoma*

"educated fools," "butterfly chasers," and "two-bit thieves." He later asserted that the "high-toned" rich fraternity boys lived in stately mansions while less fortunate students existed in crowded boarding houses.

The situation became more serious when Jim vetoed the university-appropriation bill. Now the faculty, student body, and well-organized alumni association demanded that the Governor's charges be investigated and that, if they were proved false, he should be impeached. Ferguson counterattacked in his customary manner until a Travis county grand jury met late in July 1917 and indicted him on various counts of misapplication of public funds and acceptance of bribes. The impeachment trial that followed in the House of Representatives lasted three weeks. Jim refused to answer questions about the $156,000 loan from the brewing interest or about other charged irregularities. The state legislature dismissed him from the governorship on September 25, 1917, and disqualified him from holding any future "office of honor, trust, or profit under the State of Texas."

When he returned to his old home in Temple, he was prepared for martyrdom. Thousands of letters from the plain people of Texas—those who lived in the "tank towns," along creek banks, and deep in the piney woods—arrived every day. They assured him that he had been wronged by political tricksters and that they would elect him governor once again. In November 1917 the former Governor started a weekly journal, *The Ferguson Forum,* as a means of attracting financial contributions and striking back at the "highbrow University of Texas clique and their controlled newspapers." He soon announced his candidacy for re-election to the governorship and declared that it was a contest between "the so-called educated few and the great democratic many."

Despite superhuman efforts and a speaking tour that carried him to every town and crossroads in the Lone Star State, Ferguson suffered defeat in 1918 by more than 200,000 votes. Two years later he formed the "American Party" and accepted his own nomination for President of the United States, but, though he missed few county fairs and farmers' meetings, he won only 50,000 votes. Even so, he kept the Ferguson movement alive and the hard-core nucleus of his followers intact.

In 1922 Farmer Jim ran unsuccessfully as a Democratic candidate for the United States Senate on a slogan of "Kill the Rent Hog and the Interest Hog." Most men would have renounced politics after three consecutive defeats, but Ferguson was no ordinary man. To finance further campaigns, he moved his *Forum* to Dallas in the hope of attracting advertisements from local merchants. When these did not materialize, he blamed the Jews, who, he said, had organized a boycott of his paper. "Between the Dallas Jew and the Dallas Ku Klux," he declared, "I want to say that the Ku Klux is the better of the two."

At the time of Ferguson's impeachment in 1917 one of his friends had predicted that he would be an issue in Texas politics until he died. The prophecy was vindicated by each subsequent election, for Jim announced his candidacy for the governor's office again in 1924. When Democratic leaders obtained a court order ruling him out of the party primary election, he entered his wife's name. The campaign that followed must rank among the great circus performances in Texas history. Poets composed verses about home, motherhood, children, and Mrs. Ferguson. "Me for 'ma'" and "I Ain't Got a Durn Thing Against 'Pa'" became popular slogans.

The Fergusons' opponent, Judge Felix Robertson, received support from the revived Ku Klux Klan. Though Jim's private prejudices against Catholics, Jews, and Negroes did not conflict greatly with those of the Klan, he attacked the hooded order with devastating effect. A signed editorial in the *Forum* accused the Klan's Imperial Wizard, Hiram Evans, of riding around the country in his private Pullman car with a "big buck Nigger" as his bodyguard. "Don't forget that Evans is a Nigger lover," he warned. Obviously this made Judge Robertson a "Nigger lover" too, for Ma won an overwhelming victory and gave Texas the distinction of having "two governors for the price of one."

Within a period of twenty months Mrs. Ferguson conferred

XVII · *Politics and Politicians: Texas and Oklahoma*

more than 2,000 pardons on state prisoners—certainly an effective means of replenishing one's bank account and building popularity at the same time. The *Forum* likewise experienced prosperity, as it printed all of the advertisements from highway contracting companies that desired state contracts.

In 1926 Texans turned Ma and Pa out of the State House in favor of the young Attorney General, Dan Moody. Jim ran a handpicked candidate against Moody in 1928 and lost, and many felt confident that "Fergusonism in Texas is now dead." Ross Sterling defeated Ma for the governorship in 1930 by 100,000 votes, but two years later the depression and other factors favored the Fergusons. They depicted Governor Sterling as a fat greedy "monster" who owned a house with twenty bathtubs and charged that he had created a $100,000,000 deficit in the highway department. Sterling produced an auditor's report to show that the highway books balanced, but Jim retorted: "Any crooked bookkeeper's books are balanced."

For the fourth and last time the Fergusons captured the State House in 1932, but two years later the gubernatorial team declined to run again. The decision did not mean that Farmer Jim had retired from the political scene; he supported a hand-picked candidate that year and another in 1936. Both failed to defeat the young and able James V. Allred, the only liberal governor Texas has elected to office during the twentieth century. The Fergusons tried once again in 1940 for the governorship, but they could do no better in the primary than fourth. They had finally lost their appeal, and four years later Jim died of a stroke.

By 1938 another of what John Gunther characterized in *Inside U.S.A.* as "self-seeking old buffoons" came forward to wave the "ballyhoo" banner. This new champion of the common people was a former flour salesman named W. Lee ("Pappy") O'Daniel, and he proved a greater master of the technique of demagoguery than Pa Ferguson himself.

Texas, in 1938, had almost recovered from the depression, but its politics had grown less liberal without acquiring sophistication. Money from oil and industry drew farm boys away from the country, but they retained the habits, speech, and tastes of their former life. The state remained rural at heart, even though most of its citizens now lived in cities and urban communities. It was in a condition of "completely contradictory pandemonium," according to Owen P. White in his *Texas: An Informal Biography.* "It was both drunk and sober, wicked and virtuous, rich and poor, honest and dishonest."

A full year of celebrating its centennial in 1936 had also imbued Texas with still another characteristic. Texans believed that they lived in the largest, greatest, and most glorious state in the Union, and every Texan knew the words and tune of the local hit song, "Beautiful Texas."

> Oh beautiful, beautiful Texas,
> The land where the bluebonnets grow.
> We're proud of our forefathers,
> Who fought at the Alamo.
> Oh you can live on the plains or the mountains,
> Or down where the seabreezes blow,
> And still be in beautiful Texas,
> The most beautiful place that we know.

Words and music were written by the poet laureate of the Texas flour industry, Pappy O'Daniel. Born on the Kansas plains, he moved to Texas while its cities were still young and full of country-boy spirit. By the time he reached middle age he had mastered the technique of selling flour—aided by a radio microphone and the lilting tones of a fiddle, a guitar, and a few other instruments. He organized the "Light Crust Doughboys" and sent their simple melodies and his melodious voice into almost every Texas home two or three times daily. His folksy music and homespun philosophy pleased the cultural palates of most of his listeners. Besides extolling the virtues of "Light Crust Flour," he led a crusade to induce children to walk on the left-hand side of the road facing the oncoming traffic. He frequently denounced sin. He advised childless couples to adopt babies, fathers to quit drinking, families to

XVII · *Politics and Politicians: Texas and Oklahoma*

love their neighbors, and everyone to lead a Christian life while seeking to better his economic condition.

This self-styled friend of humanity and philosopher startled his radio audience on Palm Sunday, 1938, with the announcement that hundreds of friends and admirers had urged him to become a candidate for governor. He asked his audience to tell him what they thought of his entering the race. According to his own statement a few weeks later, exactly 54,499 responded with letters and telegrams.

On June 10, 1938, a red circus wagon rolled into Waco bearing "the friend of common people," his three teen-aged children, Pat, Mike, and Molly, a hillbilly band, and a young ballad singer named "Texas Rose." O'Daniel started his campaign speech with a song and ended it two hours later with a prayer. He likened himself to David facing Goliath, the latter having assumed the form of the "professional politican" who robbed the state, ignored the underprivileged, and neglected the old and infirm. He declared that he had borrowed his platform from Moses: the Ten Commandments.

The campaign that followed attracted national attention. "Like the camp-meeting preachers of the previous generation, O'Daniel cut across all lines of local authority. . . . Also, like the camp-meetings of old, the flour salesman's rallies were out in the open, under God's sky, in the bare light of the heavenly bodies."[5] Pappy's hillbilly show attracted crowds of 30,000 and 40,000 from urban communities and rural regions. Not only did he win a majority over eleven opponents in the first primary, but his campaign contributions exceeded expenses by $800. The balance went to charity.

In addition to supporting all good things and opposing all bad ones, O'Daniel promised to give every aged Texan a $30-per-month pension, bring industry to the state, reduce taxes, abolish the poll tax, pay off the debt, and remove restrictions on business-

---

[5] Frank Goodwyn: *Lone-Star Land: Twentieth-Century Texas in Perspective* (New York: Alfred A. Knopf; 1955), p. 258.

men. How he planned to do all this remained a closely guarded secret, but hundreds of thousands of his devoted followers believed that he could perform these miracles.

When the new Governor brought the Ten Commandments and the Golden Rule to Austin in January 1939, he soon found that it was easier to make promises than to keep them. Though he had declared that he opposed sales taxes to finance his old-age pension program, he nevertheless sent to the legislature a bill providing for a "transaction tax." This body rejected the scheme, but O'Daniel's popularity with the masses did not suffer. The rapid development of natural resources and consequent industrial boom caused Texans to forget the depression, and though Pappy had little to do with the wealth that flowed from beneath the Texas surface and the new jobs created by the return of prosperity, he graciously accepted all the credit. In time he boldly denounced the New Deal, an action that caused many businessmen to believe that he possessed more wisdom than they had previously suspected. In 1940 he received some 70,000 votes above the record majority of two years earlier. This time his opponents were not "professional politicians," but the "labor-union leader racketeers" who posed an ever greater danger to peace and happiness.

Even two overwhelming victories failed to win the open support of Texas newspapers for O'Daniel, but, like Pa Ferguson, he kept his loyal supporters informed through a publication of his own, *The W. Lee O'Daniel News*. He had never belonged to a church before he announced his candidacy for the governorship in 1938, but he had captured the church vote nevertheless, and religion played an important role in his political career. His Sunday-morning radio broadcasts were not unlike those of numerous Southwestern evangelistic preachers. In between denunciations of professional politicians and "wild-eyed labor racketeers" he rendered a mixture of "the old-time religion," news bulletins about dying babies, the virtues of hard work, and the need for honesty and economy in government. He closed each broadcast by announcing which rural church he would attend that morning.

O'Daniel's decision to attack labor-union leaders was care-

XVII · *Politics and Politicians: Texas and Oklahoma*

fully attuned to the times. World War II had begun in Europe, and in the United States defense spending took the place of relief. Organized labor had expanded under the protection of the New Deal, but many Texas businessmen and much of the general public believed that labor's new power was too often abused. In 1941, soon after his second inauguration, the Governor launched a full-scale crusade against the "wild-eyed labor leaders drifting into Texas from other places." He threatened to send them to the cotton patches on the Texas prison farms if they violated local laws, and he asked the legislature for additional restrictions on their activities. The resulting anti-labor laws were the first of a series enacted during the next decade. By 1951 it was unlawful in Texas for a union to maintain a closed shop or union shop, engage in secondary boycotts, contribute money to political campaigns, establish pickets closer than fifty feet to the entrance of a plant, operate hiring halls, or secure collective bargaining for public employees.[6]

The anti-labor "reforms" introduced by O'Daniel pleased the big business interests, and he further ingratiated himself with this group by appointing university and college boards of regents from the most reactionary and wealthy elements of the population. This short-sighted policy had lasting effects on many of the state educational institutions, especially the University of Texas. Regents who distrusted academic freedom attempted to cleanse the University of all forms of "radicalism." Ultimately they discharged the liberal president, Homer P. Rainey, and many of the better scholars on the teaching staff migrated to other states. The American Association of University Professors "blacklisted" the University, the faculty divided over the various issues, and the institution's prestige suffered greatly.

A few days after Pappy O'Daniel inaugurated his "labor-reform program" in 1941, Texas's senior United States senator, Morris Sheppard, died in Washington. The Governor faced a dilemma. Under the state constitution, he could not appoint him-

---

[6] Ibid., pp. 268–71.

The Southwest: *Old and New*

self to an ad-interim term. Whoever received the appointment would be in an excellent position to win the special election a few months later. Pappy solved the problem masterfully: on April 21, 1941, he appointed eighty-six-year-old Andrew Jackson Houston, senile son of the Hero of San Jacinto.

Senator Houston barely survived the trip to Washington. He appeared on the floor of the Senate three times before he died on June 26, twenty-four days after taking the oath of office. Meanwhile, Governor O'Daniel had already hinted that he might be a candidate for the office—provided the people wanted him. They quickly responded with thousands of letters and telegrams, and he bowed to the inevitable. "I have twisted the politicians' tails in Austin," he proclaimed in his campaign speeches, "and I can twist their tails in Washington."

His strategy worked, but his audiences dwindled to a small fraction of the thousands he had attracted in 1938 and 1940. He won in a close race against his Roosevelt-backed opponent, Lyndon Johnson. In Washington his million-dollar smile and demagogic maneuvers were of no value. His campaign charges of corruption at the national level did not enhance his popularity with his new colleagues, most of whom gave him a cool reception. Continued criticisms of the wartime President and agitation for the repeal of Roosevelt's Fair Labor Standards Act, which required employers to pay time-and-a-half for work done in excess of forty hours per week, deprived him of any chance of federal patronage. Party leaders in the Senate barred him from important committees, so that his political effectiveness became almost nil.

The Senator struck back at the administration with bitter and reckless charges. In practically every speech and public appearance he linked the New Dealers, Communists, and labor racketeers in one group. He lent his name and support to organizations such as "America First" and "Christian Americans" which were dedicated to the preservation of America from assorted isms. He opposed such wartime measures as price controls and rationing; yet, in spite of everything, the former Governor won a full Senate term in 1942.

XVII · *Politics and Politicians: Texas and Oklahoma*

In the seven and a half years that O'Daniel served in Washington he failed to secure a single appointment or important piece of legislation. According to Dr. V. O. Key in *Southern Politics,* the junior Senator from Texas ranked as the most Republican of all Southern Democrats—more Republican even than most Republicans from the Midwest. In 1944 he joined forces with a few disgruntled Texas businessmen to pack the state Democratic convention with anti-Roosevelt delegates and place "uninstructed" electors on the national ballot. He stumped the state that year in behalf of these electors, but by now the people of Texas showed disgust with their "carpetbag senator." When he appeared at the City Auditorium in Houston on November 2, 1944, they greeted him with a shower of eggs and vegetables and a chorus of boos. His so-called Texas Regulars received approximately thirteen per cent of the votes cast, while Roosevelt electors carried the state by a larger majority than in 1940.

Few events brightened Pappy's last four years in the Senate. Drew Pearson revealed, near the end of his term, that the Senator's older son had been given three chances to graduate from Officer Training School, though less-favored soldiers seldom received a second opportunity. O'Daniel's other son threatened to evict from his Dallas apartment house a young war veteran who objected to a hundred-per-cent increase in rent. Worse publicity yet came from Pappy's eviction of fourteen tenants from a large apartment house in Washington during the critical post-war housing shortage.

Long before 1948 O'Daniel realized that a try for a third term would surely end in defeat.[7] Perhaps Texas voters had become more sophisticated and realized that the Senator had outlived his usefulness; certainly most of them were embarrassed by the publicity he received. John Gunther states that both of Texas's well-known demagogues of this period, O'Daniel and Martin Dies, were beaten by a single development—industrialization. Perhaps

---

[7] O'Daniel emerged from retirement a few years later to run for the governorship as an Independent. He suffered disastrous defeats in 1956 and 1958.

THE SOUTHWEST: *Old and New*

so, but the trend toward political conservatism which began with Pappy did not end with his return to private life. Since 1941 all of his successors in the State House—Coke R. Stevenson, Beauford H. Jester, Allan Shivers, and Price Daniel—have been extreme conservatives and have given the state a strongly pro-business government.

Indeed, with rare exceptions, businessmen, industrialists, and individuals of great wealth have commanded the government of Texas for more than half a century. Lynn Landrum, political writer for the *Dallas News*, wrote in 1956: "It [Texas] is basically distrustful of the intelligentsia in matters of government."[8] In spite of the exposure of political graft, particularly during the Shivers administration (1949–1957), and strong protests from within and without, the conservative element continues to deny the intellectual and liberal element much voice in the affairs of state.

Self-made and informally "educated" millionaires such as Roy Cullen, Clint Murchison, and H. L. Hunt have tried to extend conservative control beyond Texas boundaries by pouring money into campaign funds of favored congressional candidates in other states. It is common knowledge, too, that Senator Joseph McCarthy obtained his largest contributions for his various projects from Texas supporters. General Douglas MacArthur received consistent support from Texas millionaires who were determined to have him nominated for the presidency. And Gerald L. K. Smith, John O. Beaty, and other racial bigots could always count on wealthy Texans to finance their propaganda campaigns against Negroes, Jews, and Catholics.

ON THE national political scene Texas presents a slightly different picture from the rest of the nation. The two most power-

[8] Quoted from George Fuermann: *Reluctant Empire: The Mind of Texas* (Garden City: Doubleday and Company; 1957), p. 62.

XVII · *Politics and Politicians: Texas and Oklahoma*

ful men in Congress during the decade of the fifties were both Texans, Lyndon Johnson and Sam Rayburn. Though neither is considered an outright liberal, both are far more progressive than the last half-dozen Texas governors.

Meanwhile the liberals have moved doggedly uphill until their voice is gradually being heard. In 1956 they elected Ralph Yarborough to the United States Senate and Mrs. R. D. Randolph to the National Democratic Committee. Yarborough suffered three defeats for the governorship of Texas against the ultra-conservative Shivers before winning a Senate seat in a special election. A lifelong liberal, he has made a voting record since entering the Senate which approximates those of Senators Humphrey and Douglas. Mrs. Randolph, a wealthy Houston matron, supported Adlai Stevenson in 1952 and 1956; her leadership, courage, and financial contributions to the cause of Texas liberalism have won recognition throughout the state.

On the other hand, many liberals have paid for their convictions. Notable among these are Dr. Byron R. Abernethy, a professor at Texas Technological College, and Herbert M. Greenberg, a blind assistant professor at the same institution. Shivers-appointed regents discharged both men in 1957. Abernethy's crime was his keynote speech before a convention of Liberal Democrats earlier that year, while Greenberg publically advocated racial integration in the schools.

Texas's legislature has generally been as conservative as its governors. A political writer once described it as an organization controlled by the three B's—Bourbon, Beefsteaks, and Blondes— and one of its members in the 1959 session summarized the situation as follows: "In Austin, the climate is very corporate, cloudy, and full of oil." [9]

Both statements contain as much truth as metaphor. Well-financed lobbyists consistently exercise more influence over legislation than the people do, blocking more bills than they advocate. This will remain possible as long as rural Texas and conservative

---

[9] *Texas Observer* (Austin), July 25, 1959.

urban elements combine to resist political transformations in a rapidly changing state. But as cities continue to attract an even greater majority of voters, a more balanced political picture seems inevitable. Texas has not completed the 180-degree turn from conservatism to liberalism, but it has grown weary of demagogues and clowns; it has outgrown the Solid South; it is outgrowing Bourbon democracy; and many Texans no longer believe that mere "bigness" is everything.

THE POLITICAL HISTORY of Oklahoma, like Texas's, has included some colorful episodes. When Oklahoma's lands were opened to white settlement, two states made the heaviest population contribution—Kansas on the north and Texas on the south. These population streams met near the center of the new state, each bringing the political attachments of its parent. The results are still evident after more than half a century of statehood: the northern sections remain predominantly Republican and the southern counties Democratic.

Unlike Texas, Republicans in Oklahoma more generally register and vote as Republicans, so that the two-party system exists in fact as well as name. They have never won the governorship, but the Republicans poll a substantial vote and on at least one occasion (1920) elected a majority of state legislators. Otherwise, the politics of the two Southwestern states during the twentieth century have been much alike. Both have been individualistic; both have been basically conservative; both have impeached one or more governors and threatened to impeach several others; both have sent better men to Washington than to the State House; and both have produced unique political characters.

In the same year that Jim Ferguson launched his maiden political campaign in Texas as a friend of the "boys from the forks of the creek," a former train robber, Al Jennings, ran for governor of

XVII · *Politics and Politicians: Texas and Oklahoma*

Oklahoma as a friend of reformed outlaws. He collected more than 21,000 votes and finished third in the race. But his performance was a side show in comparison to the antics of a professional by the unforgettable name of "Alfalfa Bill" Murray, the "Sage of Tishomingo."

Murray resembled Ferguson and O'Daniel in more ways than one. He posed as a friend of "the common man," a term synonymous with "sharecropper" in the early part of the century, and he fought the special interests in behalf of the many. Alfalfa Bill made impossible promises to obtain votes and later used his office to harangue, insult, and bludgeon the opposition, to the delight of his rustic supporters. Like O'Daniel and Ferguson, he operated his own newspaper, *The Blue Valley Farmer,* in lieu of support from city editors. "I will be governor by the people," he promised in his first campaign for governor in 1930. "I will continue *The Blue Valley Farmer,* my official organ, after I am given the office of governor. I shall keep the common people in my confidence."

Companies soon discovered that advertisement in Murray's newspaper was important if they wanted to do business with the state. And state employees quickly learned that a subscription to *The Blue Valley Farmer* counted for more than experience in qualifying for a job.

If Alfalfa Bill's actions as governor of Oklahoma (1931-5) were comical to outsiders, his looks were even more so, resembling the proverbial hick in a burlesque show: large hawk nose, protruding Adam's apple, and tobacco-stained walrus mustache. His black shiny suit was always rumpled and speckled with cigar ashes. His white cotton shirt, with collar attached and one layer of cloth worn through, was usually dirty. White cotton socks showed above his high-top black shoes. Sometimes he failed to wear a tie, but he rarely removed his wide-brimmed black felt hat even while working at his desk.

The Sage of Tishomingo was "a man of the people"—even more so than Ferguson and O'Daniels. "I learned my politics out there in the country," he proclaimed at his inauguration in 1931. "Don't know as I'm much of a politician, but I do know people, and

The Southwest: *Old and New*

people make a government."[1] That evening the "people" appeared to greet him. They came to his inaugural ball from the red hills of eastern Oklahoma, the main streets of dusty towns, and the back alleys of the cities. Farmers in overalls and cowboys in high-heeled boots mingled with "blanket Indians," oil-field workers, country preachers, professional gamblers, wealthy oilmen, painted prostitutes, and farm women with squalling babies. Although Murray professed to be a "dry," there was plenty of corn liquor and homebrew to add zest to the festivities.

The ninth governor of Oklahoma was born at Toadsuck, Texas, in 1869 and did not settle in the future state of Oklahoma until 1898. After a varied career as farmhand, rural schoolteacher, politician, and lawyer, he decided to move to Tishomingo, capital of the Chickasaw Indian Nation. Eventually he married the daughter of the tribal governor and settled down to practice law in the Indian courts, raise alfalfa hay, and beget a family of five children. When the territories of Oklahoma and Indian Territory were united into the State of Oklahoma, Murray presided over the constitutional convention and acquired the title of "Father of the Oklahoma constitution."

Later he served as speaker of the state House of Representatives and ran unsuccessfully for governor in 1910. From 1912 to 1916 he represented southeastern Oklahoma in the United States Congress. Defeated for re-election in 1916 and again for the governorship in 1918, he became increasingly bitter and left Oklahoma to begin a colonizing project in Bolivia. This venture failed miserably, and in 1929 "Alfalfa Bill"—who meanwhile had picked up the additional nicknames of "Cockleburr Bill" and "Bolivia Bill"—returned to Tishomingo. Oklahoma newspapers carried only brief notices of his arrival for fear he would re-enter politics.

Murray waited less than a week before he began a series of political speeches that carried him to all parts of the state. A few weeks after the stock market collapsed in October 1929, he announced that he was a candidate for the governorship and de-

---

[1] Wayne Gard: "Alfalfa Bill," *The New Republic*, February 17, 1932, pp. 11–12.

XVII · *Politics and Politicians: Texas and Oklahoma*

clared war on millionaires, courts, and public-utility companies. Two of the previous chief executives in Oklahoma had been impeached, and it took courage on anyone's part to run for the office in those days. But Alfalfa Bill told his audience that the legislature would have about as much chance against him as "a pack of jack rabbits against a wildcat."

At first most of the state newspapers treated Murray's candidacy as a joke, but the tenant farmers in the rural areas looked on him as a "second Lincoln," or as a Moses destined to lead them out of the valley of two-bit wheat and five-cent cotton. They flocked to hear him berate the "tools of the corporate interest," and they applauded his promises to reduce ad-valorem taxes fifty per cent, boost the taxes on high incomes, and "throw a bombshell" into the state colleges and universities. He also promised to abolish half the jobs in the state capital, to live in the garage of the governor's mansion in order to rent out the main house, and to plant the six-acre lawn in potatoes for the poor.

As many of Murray's opponents were men newly rich from oil, the Sage of Tishomingo dramatized himself as a champion of the poor. He had to hitchhike from town to town, he told his audiences, while the millionaire candidates traveled in chauffeur-driven Cadillacs. And while they ate steaks and fine foods, he subsisted on eggs, onions, buttermilk, and cheese. Alfalfa Bill wore the same unpressed suit during the entire campaign and rarely shaved oftener than once a week. His friends might have wondered how he could afford to mail thousands of copies of *The Blue Valley Farmer* to the rural areas each week, but most of them were too busy singing:

> At the forks of the creek every day in the week
> You can hear the people say,
> Just wait and see how it will be
> On Election Day.

As election day drew nearer, many Oklahomans became upset at the thought that the rural rustic from Tishomingo might become the next governor of the state. An Oklahoma city paper assigned a woman columnist the task of exposing him to the public in a series of special articles. She told, among other things, that Alfalfa Bill lived in a house with a sod roof, a dirt floor, and no bathroom, that he ate hot cakes with his fingers and wore a dirty undershirt. She forgot, or did not know, that seventy-five per cent of Oklahomans in 1930 had "outdoor plumbing," that most of them were proud of having lived in sod houses, and that many could not afford a change of clothing. To their delight, Murray asked how the lady knew that his underwear was unclean. She did not answer, but the voters did; they gave him a majority of sixty-four of the state's seventy-seven counties.

As governor, Alfalfa Bill always made good "news copy," but he carried out few campaign promises other than planting the lawn of the governor's mansion in potatoes and "throwing a bomb" into higher education. When visitors stepped into his office, they were frequently greeted with a roar of "What the hell do you want?" or dismissed with a crude "Get on out—I'm busy." If they did get an opportunity to say a few words—though "Alfalfa Bill" rarely listened to anyone but himself—they discovered that the chairs in the room were chained to the radiator against the wall. "I don't like folks to put their damn faces plumb into mine," he explained. On busy days he ate his lunch from a paper sack in his lap while conducting state business. He relaxed by pulling off his shoes and socks, tilting back his chair, and resting his unwashed feet on the desk. Those who annoyed him by pushing closer than their chairs allowed were sometimes overwhelmed by a blast of onion breath.

The Sage of Tishomingo constantly held himself up as an authority on constitutional law, but he frequently ruled by executive order, called out the state troops on numerous occasions, and ignored the legislative and judicial branches of the government. He packed the state payroll with relatives and assorted political hacks and campaign workers, granted double the number of pardons given by his successor, purchased several hundred additional state automobiles, and denounced all criticism as a "pack of damn lies." His demagogic denunciations of those who opposed him, the "un-

XVII · *Politics and Politicians: Texas and Oklahoma*

declared war" against Texas over a bridge across Red River, the military shutdown of the Oklahoma oil fields during a price war, and his colorful language and personality attracted national attention.

During his first year in office Murray instituted what was little less than a reign of terror among the colleges in the state and at the state university at Norman. He dismissed members of the boards of regents and at least one college president. He called for legislation to prevent the institutions from graduating "hightoned bums who refuse to return to overalls," and he demanded "a full eight-hour day for college professors" and elimination of sabbatical leaves. "As a result of the Governor's activities, no member of the faculty of any state educational institution dares to draw a free breath," *The New Republic* editorialized on May 18, 1932. "Like the famous Bilbo of Mississippi, Governor Murray never heard of freedom of speech in the classroom, wouldn't understand it if he did hear of it, and obviously would not respect it even if he ever discovered what it is all about."

Murray was as shrewd as he was crude, for he knew that the people from the "red-neck" districts of the state applauded his antics. One observer remarked that he was as versatile as a chameleon; when addressing a select audience outside the state, he could speak the language of a cultivated gentlemen. "His cutaway fits him perfectly. His linen is immaculate. His pearly gray trousers are creased impeccably." On the other hand, he could put on a show before a jam-packed audience at Chicago or Kansas City "better than the heavyweight wrestling match in the evening."

The Governor's invectives against the wealthy classes "who seek to scalp the common people of Oklahoma" lost none of their venom with time. He constantly compared "these craven wolves of plutocracy" with "varmints" and "polecats" and promised to destroy them even if he had to use grapeshot, shrapnel, bombing planes, and submarines (his deployment of these last weapons in dry Oklahoma would have been interesting to see).

Even while the Governor continued to break campaign promises and to fail miserably in securing passage of his legislative program, he considered himself presidential timber. Publicity from critics within the state and from without inadvertently established him as a national figure. And at a time when rival demagogues such as Huey Long, Father Charles E. Coughlin, and Dr. Francis E. Townsend were putting forward various "share-the-wealth" schemes, the Sage of Tishomingo came out for "Bread, Butter, Bacon, and Beans." His support at the 1932 Democratic convention did not extend far beyond his own hand-picked Oklahoma delegation, but his efforts to obtain the nomination afforded delegates some comic relief from the Chicago heat.

Back home, Murray renewed his circus performance, but the act was growing stale. Additional firings, waste, and general inefficiency proved more than the people would tolerate. When President Roosevelt withdrew federal relief distribution from the Governor's control, his political future dimmed. On January 14, 1935, he took his feet off the State House desk for the last time. Again and again he tried to re-enter Oklahoma politics, as governor, as United States senator, as congressman, but each time he drew fewer votes. By the late 1940's the face of Oklahoma had changed from rural to urban and Alfalfa Bill Murray had become a relic of another age.

LIKE TEXAS, the Sooner State produced few outstanding governors during the first half of the twentieth century. Most were conservative businessmen who shunned liberal ideas. The four Oklahoma governors who served between 1935 and 1951 were millionaire oil- and businessmen closely associated with the urban industrial elements of the state. Robert S. Kerr (1943–7) and Roy J. Turner (1947–51) were able administrators who gave the state eight years of efficient leadership. But in 1950 the Murray name still held magnetism for Oklahoma voters. Johnston Murray,

XVII · *Politics and Politicians: Texas and Oklahoma*

son of "Alfalfa Bill," won the gubernatorial election with a campaign slogan of "Just Plain Folks." His administration was undistinguished, but he did not resort to the demagogic techniques of his father. In 1954 his then current wife failed in an effort to succeed her husband as governor.

Mrs. Murray's defeat did not prove that Oklahoma had completely shaken off the power of the rural voters. Thousands of farm families now living in towns and cities remained country people at heart, and most of them supported Raymond Gary, a former schoolteacher from the "Little Dixie" section of the state. Gary defeated a city candidate in the Democratic run-off, chiefly because he had fewer political enemies. A small-town background, membership in the Baptist Church, and strong advocation of prohibition laws stamped him as another man of the people.

By 1958 Oklahoma was weary of rural-oriented politicians and showed it by electing a young Tulsa attorney, J. Howard Edmondson, to the office of governor by the largest majority in the state's history. Edmondson promised to abolish prohibition, increase appropriations for higher education and common schools, inaugurate a state merit system, and reapportion the legislature on a more equitable basis. His program appealed to all classes of Oklahoma society, but especially to urban dwellers, boosters of industry, and professional people. Several of his reforms passed the 1959 Oklahoma legislature, but he failed to obtain reapportionment or to curtail the power of the state's 231 county commissioners.

IT IS MORE difficult at the end of the fifties to identify the forces that dominate state politics in Oklahoma than in Texas. In both states the oil interests are strong. Oklahoma has more independents than Texas, and its major companies are absentee-

The Southwest: *Old and New*

owned. Several oilmen have served as governor, but none was subservient to the petroleum industry, as various Texas politicians have been.

In both states the Baptists and other fundamentalist denominations wield enormous political power. Everything in Oklahoma and Texas seems to open with a prayer—meetings of bankers' associations, conventions, football games, rodeos, even bathing-beauty contests. Parts of each state still hold the convictions that characterize the Bible Belt—strangely, when one considers the robust and bawdy character of the Southwest as a whole. Few states have as many "blue laws" and restrictions against sin. The Texas Baptist General Convention effectively opposed the conferring of an honorary degree by Baylor University on President Truman in 1945 because he drank bourbon and played poker. And when Oklahoma abolished prohibition in 1959, the Oklahoma Baptist General Convention announced that it would expel any member who operated a legal liquor store.

Another political factor in this section of the Southwest is the education lobby. Texas and Oklahoma lead all the other states in the number of teachers' colleges. The Oklahoma Education Association and the Texas State Teachers Association maintain full-time lobbyists at their respective state capitals.

Old-age pensioners are especially well organized in Oklahoma and, to a lesser extent, in Texas. Unions were weak before World War II, but labor has since become an important voting bloc. Perhaps there are few states where the metropolitan newspapers are more reactionary in their political outlook, or where the courthouse politicians exercise so much power. The "County Rings" are built around the county commissioners, and because they administer considerable state funds—especially in Oklahoma—their power is so great that few politicians will oppose their wishes. Other political forces in Oklahoma and Texas are the building and road contractors, trucking companies, manufacturers, and college and university boards.

On the national political scene the Southwestern states of Oklahoma and Texas are represented by several influential and

XVII · *Politics and Politicians: Texas and Oklahoma*

useful men. Speaker Rayburn, Senator Johnson, and Senator Yarborough have already been mentioned. In 1946 Congressmen Mike Monroney, currently Oklahoma's junior senator, won the first *Collier's* award for distinguished service. And few men in the Senate dare clash with Robert S. Kerr in a rough-and-tumble debate or challenge his statements about a project in which he has a special interest.

The political future of Oklahoma and Texas naturally cannot be projected with certainty. But as both become more industrialized and urbanized, the *status quo* inevitably will change. A more equitable representation in the legislature must be accorded to the larger counties in these states if the principles of democratic state government are to survive. There are welcome signs that Oklahoma and Texas are outgrowing the domination of rural and agricultural interests. It is a development toward which the other two Southwestern states, New Mexico and Arizona, are also moving.

XVIII

POLITICS AND POLITICIANS: NEW MEXICO AND ARIZONA

NEITHER New Mexico nor Arizona has produced a political demagogue who achieved such national notoriety as Murray, Ferguson, or O'Daniel. This is not to suggest, however, that the newer states in the Southwest have shown greater political maturity than Oklahoma and Texas, or that their citizens have consistently seemed more enlightened. This section of the Southwest is often described as a land where comic-opera politics flourish, party labels mean little or nothing, and issues are subordinated to personalities. And the early years of New Mexico's statehood saw

XVIII · *Politics and Politicians: New Mexico and Arizona*

the development of "the most gorgeously corrupt political systems imaginable."

Republicans dominated New Mexico politics during territorial days. Thus, at the time of its admission to statehood in 1912 they determined the membership of the constitutional convention. Among other failings, the convention neglected to provide primary-election laws,[1] and for a full generation all candidates obtained nominations through the convention system. This meant that the man with the most money possessed an overwhelming advantage, for party organizations were scarcely more than bargain counters where votes were sold to the highest bidder. Such conditions produced Albert B. Fall, Republican Senator from the new state from 1912 to 1921; the story of his oil operations as President Warren G. Harding's Secretary of Interior is well known.

Because New Mexico politics are always close to the individual, almost everyone is interested in them. Before the great population boom in the early forties, most candidates for state offices knew the majority of voters personally. A democratic society hardly existed, for a large portion of the population consisted of illiterate sheepherders, *vaqueros,* and peons. Unable to read or write and uninterested in affairs beyond the home range, they voted according to the orders of the "Big Boss."

This was known as the *patrón* system, and it endured until the beginning of World War II. Many *patrónes* owned original Spanish land grants larger than the state of Rhode Island and employed hundreds of workers over whom they exercised feudal powers. Individuals voted as they were told, considering it a part of their job. The Big Boss in turn expected political "plums" for his hacienda and henchmen when he delivered the vote. There is a legend in New Mexico that the *patrónes* even voted their sheep, and the one with the largest flock consequently had the greatest advantage. A prominent sheep rancher from one of the northern

---

[1] The first New Mexico primary-election law was enacted in 1938.

counties once phoned the capital at Santa Fe to ask how the election was going.

"How has your county gone?" headquarters asked him.

"How many votes do you need?"

"About two thousand."

"All right," the *patrón* promised, "I'll send them up to you in the ballot box tomorrow." [2]

Before World War II most of the large land grants were divided and the system withered away in its social and economic aspect. But the *patrón* in the guise of the *politico* remains after a half-century of statehood. The average voter tends to give his allegiance to the individual leader rather than the party. The leader, if he is successful, rewards his supporters by means of patronage. Most of the jobs are petty, but they are tempting to a group that has been, as a whole, underprivileged. "It is a thin mess of pottage to accept in place of favorable laws or wages, health, welfare, taxation, etc., but it is the pottage that they have demanded and both major parties have found that they could get more votes by delivering jobs to shrewdly selected leaders than by a direct appeal based on issues." [3]

Until the post-World War II period, voting places in New Mexico were a disgrace and the secret ballot a farce. Electric voting machines were unknown and unwanted, and the laws actually encouraged irregularities that even Tammany Hall could not match. One law allowed the blind and illiterate to receive help in marking their ballots, which were printed on long sheets in Spanish and English. At every election place there were plenty of ward workers eager to assist. When an individual stepped up on a box at the schoolhouse window and called out his name, two or three men inside inspected the books to see if he had registered. As he received the ballot, he found one or two helpers at his elbow. The

---

[2] Ruth Laughlin Baker: "Where Americans Are 'Anglos,'" *The North American Review*, Vol. 228 (1929) p. 570.

[3] Charles Judah and Frederick C. Iron: *The 47th State: An Appraisal of Its Government* (Albuquerque: Division of Government Research, University of New Mexico; 1956), pp. 10–11.

XVIII · *Politics and Politicians: New Mexico and Arizona*

small group then retired to the privacy of an open booth and proceeded to select the candidate of the "voter's choice." The folded ballot went back through the window, for no ballot boxes were in sight. If the individual was not cowed sufficiently by the ward workers, his ballot could easily be identified by the inky thumb marks of the man behind the window and later altered or suppressed. The system is less crude today, but tampering with ballots is not completely unknown.

Broadly speaking, New Mexico's population consists of three distinct groups: the Indians who live on the reservations and who have only recently begun to play an effective role in politics; the natives of Spanish descent; and the citizens of Anglo-American descent. The latter groups have held each other in mutual contempt since the days of the Santa Fe Trail when the swaggering Anglos found New Mexico a Mexican state. They dubbed the natives "greasers" and in turn received the name of *gringos salados*, from the fact that strange freckles appeared to have been salted freely on their white faces. The Texans who moved into the area after it became a part of the United States used "Mexicans" as a term of insult and ridicule, and the natives with equal scorn referred to them as "gringos."

By the time New Mexico became a state in 1912 its Spanish-Americans resented being called "Mexicans," while the Anglos objected just as strongly to the term "gringo." Thus, one group eventually became "Spanish-Americans" and the other "Anglos." Politicians quickly learned to use both terms skillfully. Meanwhile Spanish-Americans continued to follow their leaders, and the Anglos held to frontier traditions of survival of rugged individualism and rapid exploitation of natural resources. The two groups eventually combined and gave vested interests the right to direct basic public policy and political leaders a free hand with patronage.

Both Democrats and Republicans have found it more profitable to support these conditions than to reform them. Except for their names, the two parties remain as difficult to distinguish as Tweedledum and Tweedledee. Both are conservative; they stand for the same things, serve the same interests, and employ the same political techniques. Organized pressure groups find it unnecessary to distinguish between them to obtain their goals. Democrats and Republicans alike construct platforms to please the Cattlemen's Association, the Taxpayers' Association, the New Mexico Educational Association, liquor interests, trucking interests, mining companies, oil and gas producers, and other business and professional groups seeking favorable legislation. On the other hand, labor, the consumer, and low-income groups generally receive scant consideration from either party.

The late Senator Bronson Cutting is a notable example of the chameleonic character of New Mexico politics and politicians. Like many others in the state's political history, Cutting came from the "outside," a victim of tuberculosis. A native New Yorker, son of a wealthy family, this shy young Harvard graduate arrived in New Mexico in 1910 on a stretcher. But he soon recovered, bought a newspaper, and became extremely interested in politics. Old-guard Republicans, who had controlled local politics since the Civil War, laughed at his cultivated accent, ridiculed his radical ideas, and ignored his attempts to win political preferment.

Young Cutting was willing to bide his time—to wait, listen, and learn. Soon he owned three newspapers, *The Santa Fe New Mexican*, *The New Mexican Review*, and *El Nuevo Mexicano*, all of which reflected his personal political views. He knew that the Spanish-Americans outnumbered the Anglo element two to one, and it was to them that he turned. He gave jobs to young Mexicans in preference to young Americans. And he assiduously cultivated leaders who might be useful to him later. A Spanish-American major-domo could always borrow a few dollars from the good "Don of Santa Fe" to tide him over until he sold his sheep or cattle or harvested his crop.

Cutting attacked the vested interests and the machine politicians of New Mexico. He favored a government that represented and served all the people equally, and stated that such a government could be achieved only by perfecting the machinery of politics and using such instruments as initiative, referendum, recall, and corrupt-practice acts. These sentiments were shared by all

XVIII · *Politics and Politicians: New Mexico and Arizona*

progressives of the period, but Cutting did not include a demand for political morality on the part of the voters. Though he hated machines and political bosses, he put together and directed one of the tightest-knit, most effective political machines New Mexico has known. It is doubtful if any Spanish *patrón* or Anglo boss in the state's history ever controlled more votes than Bronson Cutting.[4] By shifting thousands of Spanish-American votes from one candidate to the other, he determined the outcome of state elections for almost two decades.

The former New Yorker could not win an office for himself, but his fellow Republicans soon discovered that it was almost impossible to win without his backing. In 1922 he helped elect a Democrat, James F. Hinkle, to the governorship. Two years later he joined the opposition party officially and supported another successful Democratic candidate, Arthur T. Hannet. Governor Hannet managed to get some twenty progressive laws passed, but he lost Cutting's support within six months after he took office. In 1926 the unpredictable "Don of Santa Fe" teamed with Republicans in a smear campaign that elected a former shoeshine boy turned businessman, Richard C. Dillon. It marked only the second time since statehood that the Republicans had captured the office. Dillon carried both branches of the legislature with him and gave the state a businessman's administration. He is referred to as the most popular governor in New Mexico's history.

Cutting contributed his own money, time, and newspapers in support of Dillon's cause, and he was amply rewarded. In December 1927 a ten-year veteran of the United States Senate, A. A. Jones, died. Dillon appointed Cutting to fill the Democrat's seat. His fellow Republicans raised a storm of protest, but to no avail. Within a few months Cutting proved his capabilities in the Senate and established a reputation as a progressive. He remained unpredictable, however. In 1928 he demanded the Republican nomination for a full term in the Senate and received it.

---

[4] Charles B. Judah: *Governor Richard C. Dillon: A Study in New Mexico Politics* (Albuquerque: Division of Government Research, University of New Mexico; 1948), pp. 11–12.

Although the regular Republicans did not like the idea of supporting him, they had no alternative.

A few months later Senator Cutting led a scathing attack against Governor Dillon and other Republicans in New Mexico when they objected to the establishment of the post of State Labor Commissioner. Cutting's followers in the state Senate backed the proposal one hundred per cent, but Dillon and the conservative faction fought bitterly and succeeded in blocking it. At last the United States Senator handed in his resignation and demanded that the Governor do likewise. No action was taken on either resignation, but the split between the two political leaders shattered the Republican Party so completely that even as late as 1952 not all the damage had been repaired.

When Senator Cutting supported a Democrat, Arthur Seligman, for governor in 1930, the Republicans "steamrollered" him out of the party, but his candidate was elected. He repeated the performance in 1932 with even greater success, this time supporting the Democratic candidate A. W. Hockenhull. Twenty years elapsed before the Republicans again captured the governorship. The Democrats were not pleased at having to win their victories by following Cutting, but they, like the Republicans, knew that the Senator represented an unbeatable combination of forces. He was the *patrón grande* who could elect or defeat any candidate—regardless of party affiliation.

While Cutting continued to create political turmoil in New Mexico, from time to time he also shocked his fellow senators in Washington. He had barely taken office when he attacked the infallibility of the "Holy American Constitution," declaring that it had gone "sour" and that the people would be better off if Congress "pitched a lot of that ancient and venerable document into the trash can."[5] In 1930 he visited Russia, and on his return to the United States he advocated the adoption of various communistic practices. He also advocated recognition of the Russian Soviet government, a suggestion that so upset some of his ultra-conserva-

---

[5] Owen P. White: "Cutting Free," *Collier's*, October 27, 1934, p. 24.

XVIII · *Politics and Politicians: New Mexico and Arizona*

tive political adversaries that they started a secret investigation of possible ties between Cutting and the Reds. Later he denounced both major parties for their subservience to Big Business and stated that a new liberal-conservative organization was necessary to intelligent voting.

The irony of Cutting's position as a progressive senator lay in the fact that he did not represent a progressive political organization. The great bulk of his enthusiastic supporters, the Spanish-Americans, were removed by at least two centuries from most of the principles he advocated in Washington. This, of course, made his course easy. As he received no mandate from his constituents, he felt perfectly free to air his views on all subjects, including huge government building programs, unemployment insurance, anti-injunction laws, and federal labor exchanges. President Herbert Hoover branded him a dangerous radical, a man who would overthrow the government if given the power. His rejoinder to Hoover, over a national radio network, was so devastating, concise, and convincing that President-elect Franklin D. Roosevelt later offered him the position of Secretary of the Interior. Cutting might have accepted and thus affiliated himself with the national Democratic organization if another New Mexican, Albert B. Fall, had not already brought the Department of the Interior under a black cloud of suspicion.

When Cutting ran for re-election to the Senate in 1934, his opponent was Dennis Chavez, a former clerk in the United States Senate who had made a notable record in the House of Representatives from 1930 to 1934. Chavez had been developed by the Democrats to wean the Spanish-American voters from the Republicans.[6] In spite of his racial origin and his ability to remind his Spanish-American audiences in fluent Spanish that *"Soy de ustedes"* ("I am one of you"), he found the Cutting machine invincible. Also, Roosevelt's refusal to support the Democratic

---

[6] Everett Grantham in a personal interview at Albuquerque, New Mexico, April 21, 1959. Mr. Grantham has been a leader in the Democratic Party in New Mexico for several years. In 1952 he was defeated for the governorship by Republican Edwin L. Mechem.

nominee that year amounted to a virtual endorsement of Chavez's opponent.

Senator Cutting died in 1935. Clyde Tingley, the Democratic Governor, appointed Dennis Chavez to fill the position until a special election could be held. Chavez had no difficulty in defeating another Spanish-American, Miguel Otero, for the remaining four years of the long term. At the same time Carl A. Hatch defeated ex-Governor Dillon for the other Senate seat. Thus, the Democrats captured solid control of all major New Mexico offices for the first time since statehood. Also, they were free of Bronson Cutting. Both Hatch and Chavez established records as progressive liberals in the Senate, and with John J. Dempsey, Congressman-at-large, they gave New Mexico an effective Congressional delegation. Meanwhile the colorful Governor Tingley (1935–39) preserved the state's political reputation with his oft-quoted remark, "I ain't goin' to stop saying ain't in no public speech, I ain't." [7]

In spite of WPA scandals during Tingley's second term which revealed that relief workers had been pressured into making contributions to the party, Democrats captured the State House again in 1938 and in each successive election until 1950. In that year Edwin L. Mechem won the governorship, breaking the long string of Democratic victories. Whether this was an example of New Mexico's ability to anticipate a change in the national trend, or the result of overconfidence in the Democratic Party, the fact remains that the Republican nominee won by an overwhelming majority. Even so, New Mexico reserved the remainder of State offices for Democrats.

Meanwhile, in 1946 another "outsider" had entered New Mexico's political battles and attracted national attention. He was Patrick J. Hurley, a native Oklahoman who had served as Hoover's Secretary of War and later as Ambassador to China. A man who invited controversy, Hurley made his bid for the senatorship against the veteran Dennis Chavez. Racial ties and language

---

[7] John Gunther: *Inside U.S.A.* (New York: Harper & Brothers; 1947), p. 891.

XVIII · *Politics and Politicians: New Mexico and Arizona*

parallels again spelled the difference between victory and defeat. Two years later Hurley ran against Clinton P. Anderson, the former Secretary of Agriculture, to fill the vacancy created by the retirement of Senator Carl A. Hatch. This time he was inundated by a flood of Anderson votes.

The national trend toward Republicanism in 1952 was reflected in New Mexico. Eisenhower carried the state, keeping intact its record of always voting for the presidential winner. Governor Mechem defeated Everett Grantham by a sizable margin, while Hurley almost unseated Chavez from the United States Senate. When he lost by approximately 5,000 votes, Hurley charged that more than 30,000 of the 240,000 ballots cast were illegal. A United States Senate committee investigated the charges and deliberated for ten weeks before announcing its findings: evidence of errors and irregularities but no proof of fraud. Even though the seating of Hurley could have given the Republicans a majority of one vote in the Senate, the Republican Governor of New Mexico showed little enthusiasm for accusations against the Chavez Democratic machine—another paradox in the turbulent politics of the Southwestern state.

In 1954 the Democrats captured the governorship, and many political observers predicted that the state Republican Party was dead. As the presidential election of 1956 approached, Democrats were confident that they could carry the state. Both Adali Stevenson and Estes Kefauver campaigned there, while neither Dwight Eisenhower nor Richard Nixon made an appearance. However, by the middle of October 1956 it was clear that the Eisenhower-Nixon ticket would win. And win it did—by almost 40,000 votes. Even the Democratic Governor, John F. Simms, Jr., lost his office to ex-Governor Edwin L. Mechem, who had failed two years before to replace Clinton P. Anderson in the United States Senate. Simms's defeat was attributed in part to the fact that Senator Dennis Chavez refused to support him.

The pendulum swung back in 1958 when Democrat John Burroughs defeated Governor Mechem in a contest that observers had predicted might go either way.

THE SOUTHWEST: *Old and New*

Though Eisenhower and Nixon carried New Mexico in 1952 and 1956 and Mechem won the governorship three times during the decade of the fifties, the state is generally still considered Democratic. No Republican has been able to win a seat in Congress during the past quarter-century, and, with rare exceptions, the Democrats controlled the state offices throughout the same period. The gradual decline in Republican strength is due to several things: the loss of Spanish-American support since the death of Bronson Cutting; the rise of the popular and capable Dennis Chavez in Democratic circles; the factional warfare among Republicans; the influx of *tejanos* [8] into eastern New Mexico; and, finally, the Pueblo Indians' recent participation in politics.[9]

Perhaps the most important of these is the arrival of the *tejanos,* who have come in great numbers since World War II. Many are oil-field workers and others have purchased ranches and farms. There is some apprehension that these newcomers may refashion the state in their own image of Texas. The fear is not altogether groundless, for Texans are noted for their openly anti-Mexican, anti-Negro sentiments, and some of the "East Side" counties of "Little Texas" have seen many instances of discrimination and attempts at segregation. Recently anti-discrimination ordinances were passed in Albuquerque and other cities to prevent "outsiders" from foisting their prejudices on the unwilling natives.

The expanding number of *tejanos* in the state has brought an increase in Democratic registration and has forced both major parties to consider whether a prospective candidate will be acceptable to the East Side. If his name is Martinez, Sandoval, or Romero, he will almost certainly be rejected for high office. This

---

[8] The word *tejano* literally means "Texan," but more recently it has also come to mean any prejudiced person—Southerner, Westerner, or even Yankee. It is the Texans, of course, who are most numerous in the eastern counties of New Mexico.

[9] Since they began to vote in the early fifties, the Pueblo Indians have usually supported Democratic candidates. On the other hand, the Navajos vote Republican.

XVIII · *Politics and Politicians: New Mexico and Arizona*

factor works in favor of Senator Anderson and against Senator Chavez. It enabled the Anderson group to seize control of the Democratic Party in New Mexico and reduce the Chavez faction to a minority. Yet the Spanish-American Senator himself remains unbeatable.

Despite the unpredictableness of New Mexican political behavior, the situation as a whole is much healthier than a generation ago. A sizable proportion of the new residents since World War II are well-educated people, and they are difficult to deceive. They enjoy comedy by professional comedians, not by politicians. More important, the legislature is reapportioned according to population regularly—and cities such as Albuquerque and Santa Fe are adequately represented. "Second-floor governors" are no longer in vogue, and the practice of counting the sheep and dead men is declining. Inevitably the state will have to elect its congressmen from districts rather than at-large. This will mean that Republican Albuquerque will control one of the two seats, for a third of New Mexico's population lives in this metropolitan area. It will also mean a stronger two-party system.

Like other Southwestern states, New Mexico generally has sent more able men to Washington than to the State House. Its present United States Senators, Clinton P. Anderson and Dennis Chavez, have accumulated considerable seniority and hold important committee assignments.[1] The rejection of Lewis Strauss as Secretary of Commerce in June 1959 not only marked the first time in thirty-four years that a presidential appointment to the Cabinet had been turned down, but also demonstrated the ability of Senator Anderson to muster the necessary negative votes almost single-handedly.

Even Strauss admits that his "implacable enemy is a good Senator,"[2] and the record of the Southwesterner bears him out.

---

[1] Senator Anderson is chairman of the important Joint Committee on Atomic Energy and a member of five other committees, including Finance and Interior and Insular Affairs. Senator Chavez is chairman of the Public Works Committee and a member of the powerful Appropriations Committee.

. . .

[2] *Time*, June 15, 1959, p. 22.

THE SOUTHWEST: *Old and New*

In 1917 young Anderson moved from South Dakota to New Mexico, where he spent nine months in a tuberculosis sanatorium. (He has since suffered from diabetes, shingles, and a coronary condition.) Eventually he entered the newspaper business, opened an insurance agency, and served five years in the United States House of Representatives. President Harry Truman named him Secretary of Agriculture in 1945, succeeding Henry A. Wallace. A decade and a half later he remained one of the few Democrats who supported Ezra Taft Benson's stand against high rigid price supports.

Elected to the Senate in 1948, Anderson stands in the front rank of Democratic liberals who work for civil-rights legislation. He took part in setting up the first foreign-aid program—the Marshall Plan—though he has criticized it often as having outlived its original intent. He is an articulate and effective partisan of reclamation and is the author of Public Law 485 of the Eighty-fourth Congress, which authorizes the Upper Colorado River Storage Project, a billion-dollar undertaking that will affect a five-state region. "The Senator also favors public power in the form of REA and is an avid supporter of federal aid to education." [3]

New Mexico's other Senator, Dennis Chavez, hews more closely to the liberal, or New Deal, philosophy. Frequently the two colleagues oppose each other on controversial issues. For example, Chavez was the only Southwestern senator who voted against the Kerr Bill in 1950 to remove federal price fixing on natural gas. Anderson was quoted as saying that there would have to be a "showdown" between them for power in the state. It came a few months later when he helped defeat Judge David Chavez, the Senator's brother, for the governorship of New Mexico. Observers estimated that $300,000 was spent to elect the Democrat John Miles, much of the money coming from oil and gas interests.[4]

Senator Chavez is a consistent champion of civil rights,

---

[3] Letter from Doyle Kline, Secretary to Senator Clinton P. Anderson, Washington, D.C., to W. Eugene Hollon, October 11, 1957.

[4] *The New Republic,* June 19, 1950, p. 7.

XVIII · *Politics and Politicians: New Mexico and Arizona*

foreign aid to underdeveloped countries, particularly Latin America, fair employment practices, drought and disaster relief in time of need, federal aid to education, and rehabilitation of the arid lands of the Southwest. Those who criticize his exploitation of the racial question during political campaigns in New Mexico concede that he sometimes displays outstanding courage in the Senate. He spoke out at an early date against McCarthyism and deplored the use of "professional witnesses" to pin the Communist label on various individuals.

When the Senator rose to attack former Communist Louis Budenz in 1950 for misusing his standing as a Catholic convert, he observed: "This country has embarked upon a course which breeds hysteria and confusion—a course so dangerous that few dare to oppose the drift lest they be marked for destruction." [5] When he finished, he was so marked. Various elements of his church, including the Jesuit Fathers of Fordham University and the Archbishop of Santa Fe, rebuked him severely. One Catholic spokesman even asked the "good people of New Mexico" to refrain from stealing votes or tampering with ballot boxes. He reminded them that associates of Chavez had frequently been suspected of this.

Arizona bears a political resemblance to New Mexico in that it is traditionally a one-party Democratic state that has been carried by every successful Republican presidential candidate since its admission to the Union. Also, Republican-appointed officials governed it during the long territorial years, except in Cleveland's two terms. Most of the early Anglo-Saxon settlers came from Texas, and the Texas influence asserted itself soon after statehood. Arizona likewise has a large Indian population and a sizable number of Spanish-Americans.

The so-called "Baby State" originally belonged to New Mexico Territory and has similar climate, geography, racial groups, and Spanish heritages, but twentieth-century political developments in the two states present a study in contrast. New Mexico's politi-

---

[5] Ibid.

cal behavior traditionally has been stormy, machine-ridden, and unpredictable. Arizona's has been tranquil, colorless, and stable. In New Mexico elections the crucial voting bloc is the East Side; in Arizona it is the South Side. In one state Texans are disliked and distrusted; in the other they are liked and influential. Indians and Spanish-Americans are important political groups in New Mexico, but in Arizona they are practically ignored by politicians.

New Mexico office holders, with rare exceptions, find re-election difficult, but the same candidates win term after term in Arizona—often without opposition. Only eleven men have sat in the governor's seat in Arizona during a half-century of statehood, as compared to more than twice that number in New Mexico. Governor George W. P. Hunt served seven terms in the State House at Phoenix, and Sidney P. Osborn won the governorship four times. Carl Hayden, present dean of the United States Congress, was elected the first congressman-at-large in 1912, switched to the Senate in 1927, and has never left.

Arizona has a long-standing Democratic tradition of conservatism similar to that of Southern cotton-planters and Texas-ranchers—bolstered by the mining interest. In the days when free silver ranked as a national issue, the territory's economic welfare depended on federal price supports. When the Democrats staked their future on "free and unlimited coinage of silver" in the nineties, they won the grateful support of the silver barons. No other issue mattered in Arizona as long as silver was king.

Since World War II this traditional conservatism has been strongly spiced with Midwestern Republicanism. Party labels mean comparatively little, and party registration figures are easily misconstrued. In 1940 the Democrats outnumbered Republicans eight to one; by 1958 the figure was two and a half to one. This change does not reflect a swing from left to right, but rather the fact that being an avowed Republican is no longer a political liability. It has long been a practice of Arizona conservatives to register as Democrats in order to have an effective voice in state and local affairs. A large proportion of these are called "pinto" Democrats by those who consider themselves "real" Demo-

XVIII · *Politics and Politicians: New Mexico and Arizona*

crats, for the "pintos" are indistinguishable from conservative Republicans. Since the war thousands of bona fide Republicans have arrived in the state, about one third of whom do not need to earn a living.[6] These newcomers have been less hesitant to register according to their true affiliation. And under the enthusiastic leadership of Republican Party workers additional thousands of so-called Democrats have been persuaded to do likewise. Many realistic "pintos," however, particularly those in the urban centers of Phoenix and Tucson, are reluctant to surrender a strategic advantage: by retaining their Democratic registration they succeed in obtaining desired results as members, candidates, and manipulators of the dominant party.

The situation is clearly demonstrated in the legislature, where the terms "majority" and "minority" are substituted for Republican and Democrat. In nearly every legislature since statehood the "majority" has meant the conservative Democrats and the "minority" has been the liberal Democrats. The "majority" is always responsive to the views of the "big interests"—mines, railroads, utilities, banks, investors, and large ranchers and farmers. The "minority" claims to represent the people—union members, unskilled workers, pensioners, small businessmen, Indians, and Spanish-Americans. Only rarely have the liberals been able to organize and control either house in the state legislature. In both 1956 and 1958 the conservatives won such overwhelming victories that they organized the legislature without help from the official Republican members.

Nor does the future offer much encouragement to Arizona liberals. All-out support from the AFL-CIO Political Action Committee is the "kiss of death," and any candidate who has it will be attacked by the local Republican press. Reapportionment of the legislature every four years also operates against the liberals. Conservative strength is concentrated in the heavily populated Maricopa and Pima counties. These counties gain representation

---

[6] N. D. Hougton: "The 1956 Election in Arizona," *Western Politics and the 1956 Election* (Salt Lake City: University of Utah Institute of Government; 1957), p. 24.

THE SOUTHWEST: *Old and New*

at the expense of the remainder of the state as the population shifts to the urban centers of Phoenix and Tucson. (The situation is almost the reverse in Oklahoma and Texas.)

Between 1912 and 1950 Arizona elected only two Republican governors, Thomas E. Campbell (1917–21) and John C. Phillips (1929–31) and one United States senator, Ralph H. Cameron (1921–7). In 1950 Republican Howard Pyle won the governorship and repeated his victory in 1952. When Ernest W. McFarland vacated his United States Senate seat in 1952, Republican Barry Goldwater replaced him in Washington. Eisenhower and Nixon carried the state that year by a large majority, and they did even better in 1956. Two years later things went badly for the Republicans throughout most of the nation—but not in Arizona. Goldwater defeated McFarland for the Senate in a contest that attracted national attention. Two other conservative Republicans also won high Arizona offices: Paul Fannin took the governorship and John J. Rhodes captured one of the two congressional seats.

John C. Waugh, in the *Christian Science Monitor* on March 11, 1959, summarized the situation as follows: "Arizona Republicans are well organized, united, and weighted with young, attractive talent. They have vigorous leadership in such men as Messrs. Goldwater, Fannin, and Rhodes and the youthful Richard Kleindierst, who at 35, is the youngest Republican state chairman in the United States. . . . By contrast, the Democratic Party in the state appears strife-ridden, unorganized, and short of fresh new candidates and strong leadership."

About the same time the *Arizona Daily Sun*, a Democratic daily at Flagstaff, suggested that revitalization of the Democratic Party might well begin with "cleaning house on [sic] the 10th-rate hacks who have worked their way into high places in the party organization in this state." Before this happens, the Republicans are likely to be the dominant party throughout the state in name as well as fact.

Considering its robust and not always sober history, Arizona's calm indifference to politics seems strange. In each election since statehood the voters have elected candidates of one party to some

XVIII · *Politics and Politicians: New Mexico and Arizona*

offices and candidates of the opposing party to others. Before the senatorial campaign of 1958 few contests created much excitement; candidates did not conduct vigorous campaigns, and a relatively small percentage of the total population bothered to vote. Seldom has a defeated candidate made charges of fraud. There has been little evidence of racial bigotry, and no blind following of political bosses.

Yet the political climate in Arizona is not completely healthy. With the election of a new governor everybody loses his job, even members of the state highway patrol. Legislators are generally undistinguished, and conservatives dominate the House so thoroughly that sometimes they can elect the speaker by acclamation. This body, like the Senate, spends most of its time during a typical sixty-day session in squabbles with the governor. The upper chamber is so small that fifteen members constitute a majority and whoever controls them frequently can control state legislation.

The question naturally arises as to who or what actually runs Arizona. I asked numerous residents during a week's visit to Phoenix and Tucson in April 1959, and the answers were in general agreement. "Nobody runs the state," explained Orme Lewis, a prominent Phoenix attorney. "But there is a powerful veto power in the Senate representing mining, utilities, cattle, big farmers, big ranchers. They don't initiate much, but they can and do check expensive bills. It used to be that copper ran things by itself, but not so much any more."

A question about political pressures and pressure groups brought a variety of observations. Some Arizonans pointed to the public schoolteachers' demands for higher salaries, others mentioned the large property holders who desired an increased sales tax in lieu of other forms of state revenue measures. Several people emphasized the pressure to obtain land. "The majority of voters do not understand reclamation per se," one Phoenix resident explained, "but they obviously know that there is a great scarceness of available land. Farmers can purchase land from the state, provided they can get the state to sell. Or they can deal

The Southwest: *Old and New*

with the federal government in areas where underground water is available. In either case, they put constant pressure on the politicians to intercede in their behalf."

Other questions on Arizona politics dealt with unions and "right-to-work" laws. I observed that the state had the reputation of being unfriendly to organized labor, which appears relatively weak and uninfluential in Arizona. The explanations I got were more general than specific. "In the first place," one Arizonan replied, "no candidate—Democrat or Republican—who comes out against 'right to work' in this state stands a chance of being elected to anything." Even the liberal Mayor of Tucson, Don Hummel, admitted to me that he favored "right to work," though his philosophical reasons were not clear.

Arizonans have remained suspicious of unions since World War I, when the International Workers of the World called strikes in the mining towns of Bisbee, Globe, Miami, and Jerome. Violence broke out in several camps, property was destroyed, and lives were lost. Mine operators appear to have been as much at fault as the unions, but they succeeded in branding the strikers as anarchists, traitors, and German sympathizers. Sheriffs' posses were formed in a number of towns to "escort" strikers across the state line. Though these events belong to the past, local politicians still use them to discredit labor leaders throughout the state.

Union membership in Arizona in 1958 totaled less than 33,000 out of a population of 1,070,000. It included most of the miners, some construction workers, and a few factory employees. Reliable observers believe that unions seldom rally more than forty to sixty per cent of their members in state elections, yet the general public resents their political efforts. "We were run from the outside so long and so recently that we don't like the idea," a Phoenix businessman explained. "Unions are national. They usually send men in to tell their people how to do things. They oppose 'right-to-work' laws, but only succeed in establishing them more firmly."

Arizona was the second of eighteen states to have a so-called "right-to-work" law, passed by popular referendum in 1947. It has

XVIII · *Politics and Politicians: New Mexico and Arizona*

since put teeth in the law and made it an issue in every subsequent election. No politician has capitalized on the subject to more advantage than fifty-year-old Barry Goldwater, Republican Senator from Arizona and handsome scion of a pioneer family. In 1952 he promised to sponsor a measure that would prevent compulsory unionism throughout the nation. After his election to the United States Senate he became the outspoken champion of "right to work," but he made few converts among his colleagues. In his campaign for re-election in 1958 against Governor McFarland he made it appear that he was running against Walter Reuther. He also branded his slow-spoken, conservative Democratic opponent as a foe of "right to work." The results gave the republicans one of their few excuses to cheer in November 1958 and enhanced Goldwater's leadership of the GOP's conservative wing.

The junior Senator from Arizona infuriates the liberals, both within the state and without, and his name is almost a term of profanity in many labor-union circles. Paul F. Healy described him in a *Saturday Evening Post* article, June 7, 1958, as "the most aggressive, articulate, colorful, and possibly the most conservative conservative in the United States Senate. At a time when conservatives are retiring or subsiding and dullness is settling over the Senate generally, Goldwater stands out like a spitball expert at a caucus of deacons."

Because of the controversy he arouses and the publicity given to his verbal bouts with Walter Reuther, Goldwater is the best-known living Arizonan. Some of his friends consider him the most outstanding all-round citizen the state has produced, while others call him a disgrace to the nation. At least he enlivens Arizona politics and, for the first time in several decades, furnishes both Democrats and Republicans with some excitement.

As the overwhelming majority of Arizona politicians favor "right to work" and labor unions have as much influence in the state's politics as the Indians on the small Havasupai Reservation, Goldwater's success is puzzling to an outsider. "How can he make so much noise with so little ammunition?" I asked a Goldwater supporter. The answer:

THE SOUTHWEST: *Old and New*

"When Barry went to the Senate in 1953, he found himself in a position similar to all new men: no good committee assignments. He wanted on the Interior Committee, and was disappointed at first when he got on Labor. But he goes at anything with determination to become an expert—photography, swimming, flying. Well, he became an expert on labor. He found things that upset him and he spoke out at every opportunity. He is not always the wisest, but he is courageous and to-hell-with-the-consequence. . . . Besides, what else is there to talk about out here?"[7]

When asked what Goldwater did for Arizona during his first six years in Washington, a Phoenix banker admitted that much of the Senator's "crusade" against unionism was mere shadowboxing. However, he insisted that Goldwater had forced Senator Carl Hayden to stronger action in behalf of Arizona. "Hayden was resting upon his laurels until Barry built a fire under him," he said. "Now he is pushing harder and more effectively for federal projects for this state. Hayden gets the credit, but Goldwater is frequently responsible."[8]

Not every business or professional man in Phoenix admires the "glittering Mr. Goldwater." A member of a prominent law firm expressed his feelings without equivocation: "Goldwater is the most useless man in Washington. He is nothing more than a clever demagogue operating on borrowed time. He flies all over the state exuding glamour, displaying his handsome profile, performing oratorical acrobatics, and bamboozling audiences of frightened reactionaries. He makes the voters believe that he is getting things done and that the state is really going places. He has succeeded in nothing except making us the laughingstock of the nation."

Goldwater hurt himself through his association with the late Senator Joseph R. McCarthy, but he makes no attempt to apologize for his actions. The two had been friends since McCarthy started visiting the state for his health in the early 1940's. Goldwater

---

[7] Interview with Orme Lewis, Phoenix, Arizona, April 20, 1959.

[8] Interview with Herbert Leggett, Valley National Bank, Phoenix, Arizona, April 20, 1959.

XVIII · *Politics and Politicians: New Mexico and Arizona*

gave him warm support at the time of the senate censure in 1954. He still maintains that McCarthy was a greater patriot than those who condemned him. In a speech before the Wisconsin Republican State Convention on June 8, 1958, he paid the following tribute to his late friend:

"Joe McCarthy, your Senator, was my good friend, and a man of whom all Republicans can be justly proud. . . . He was a faithful, tireless, and conscientious American. He fought just as hard for the things he believed were right as he did against the things he knew were wrong.

"Joe McCarthy gave himself—his life—to the service of God and his country. He did a job that no other man could, or would, do. He was completely selfless and his single motive was the preservation of those principles which make it possible for the Republican Party to proclaim now its fulfillment of the confidence of all Americans.

"Because Joe McCarthy lived, we are a safer, freer, more vigilant nation today. That fact, even though he no longer dwells among us, will never perish. And I know you will join with me in thanking God that while Joe lived he made a contribution to his country that will forever redound to the credit of the people of Wisconsin and to your Republican organization."

Senator Goldwater was pro-Eisenhower at the 1952 GOP convention in Arizona, though he is now the most outspoken critic of so-called "modern Republicanism." When it seems expedient, he claims to retain his admiration for the President and blames the administration's liberal pronouncements on Eisenhower's advisers. He is opposed to foreign aid and the welfare state. He is in favor of states' rights, drastic government economy, and lower taxes. Naturally, he supports free enterprise, but remains vague in defining it. In these principles he reflects the conservative views of most Arizonans.

It is curious that millions of Americans know of Arizona's junior Senator, a man who never held public office before 1952 and has never successfully sponsored an important piece of legislation. But few outside the state and the District of Columbia recognize the name of Carl Hayden. The senior Senator seldom makes the headlines, for he avoids publicity with as much fervor as Goldwater seeks it. He has made few Congressional speeches since he arrived at the national capital in 1912. He prefers to work quietly behind the scenes, avoid controversy, and enjoy the respect of members of both parties. The only active Arizona politician whose career reaches back to territorial days, he is neither liberal nor conservative, neither colorful nor controversial. He belongs to the "old school" in a state that is rapidly breaking with the past in more ways than political. And as chairman of the Senate Appropriations Committee, he is invaluable to Arizona.

XIX

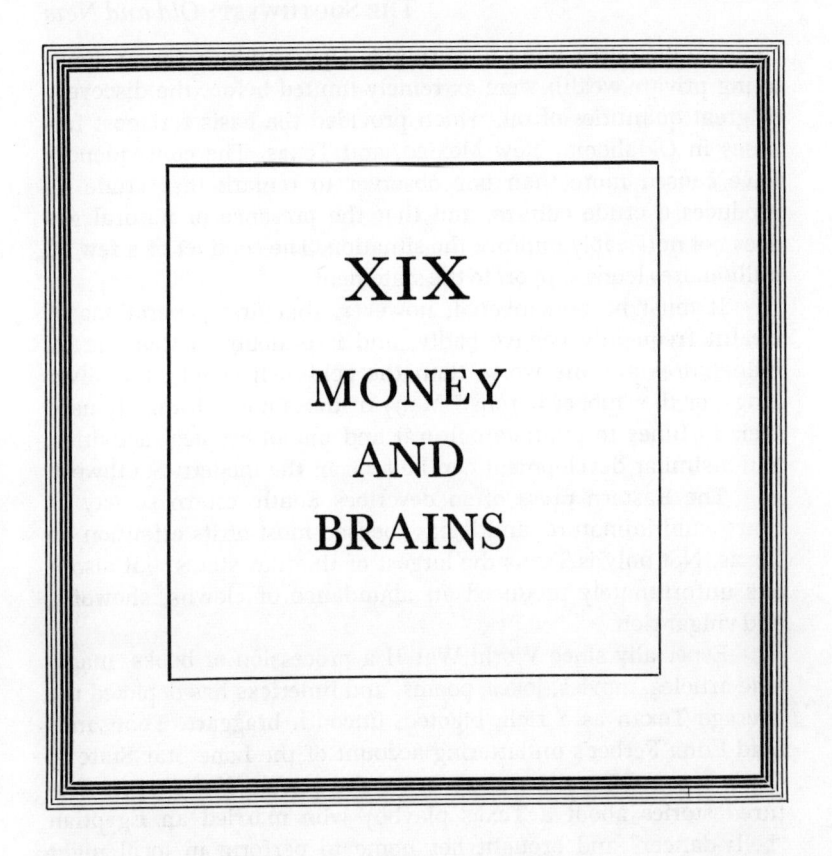

MONEY AND BRAINS

A REGION'S CULTURE is reflected in the behavior and attitudes of its people and in their respect for and appreciation of intellectual and artistic achievement. It may also be gauged by the quality of public schools, universities, libraries, and newspapers. The Southwest ranges from high to low in these various categories, and evidence can be assembled to support almost any conclusion about the level of its culture. In truth, the region contains some areas that are culturally barren and others that stand out like lighthouses.

At mid-century it is still possible for Southwesterners to become millionaires almost overnight. Opportunities for accumulating private wealth were extremely limited before the discovery of great quantities of oil, which provided the basis for most fortunes in Oklahoma, New Mexico, and Texas. The consequences have caused more than one observer to remark that crude oil produces a crude culture, and that the presence of natural gas does not noticeably improve the situation. The conduct of a few oil millionaires lends support to the statement.

It must be remembered, however, that first generations of wealth frequently behave badly, and it is doubtful that the oil millionaires are any worse than the gold-rush people, the silver kings, or the "robber barons." Many of those men ultimately used their fortunes to promote cultural and philanthropical activities, and a similar development can be seen in the modern Southwest.

The Eastern press often describes Southwestern society as coarse and immature, and it has focused most of its attention on Texas. Not only is Texas the largest of the four states, but also it has unfortunately produced an abundance of clowns, showoffs, and vulgar rich.

Especially since World War II a procession of books, magazine articles, movies, jokes, poems, and limericks has depicted the average Texan as a rich, bigoted, uncouth braggart. Thousands read Edna Ferber's unflattering account of the Lone Star State in *Giant* and millions more saw it on the screen. Newspapers featured stories about a Texas playboy who married an Egyptian "belly-dancer" and brought her home to perform in local night clubs, a Houston oilman who regularly tossed silver dollars out of hotel windows and tipped hat-check girls with hundred-dollar bills, and a philanthropist who sent a check for $2,350,000 to Houston University when it defeated Baylor University in a football game.

Most "poetry" about Texas follows along the lines of:

> My grandfather lived in Texas,
>   He couldn't write his name.
> He signed his checks with x's,
>   But they were worth a helluvalot just the same.

XIX · *Money and Brains*

New York columnists welcome doggerel of this sort because it makes good copy, as do such anecdotes as the one about the Texan who rose to his feet during a charity benefit and announced: "Mah name is James R. Robinson, and my nickname is Jimmy. I like this 'ere charity and ah wants to donate ten thousand dollars—ah-nony-mously!" By printing them constantly, the Eastern press perpetuates the idea that Texas is an intellectual desert, a colony of "perpetual Philistines, provincials, and materialists."

Most jokes about Texas suggest that the state is inhabited chiefly by millionaires. This picture is, of course, more than a little exaggerated. Texas has a full share of the nation's poor people, and, according to a prominent Houston banker, its "real" millionaires number just over one hundred. (This figure did not include the oilmen who make a million dollars one week and lose it the next.[1]) Texas does not buy as many Cadillacs per capita as New York or Illinois. A few Texans, however, are *rich*. One writer observed in 1957 that five of the ten wealthiest men in the United States are Texans, and that the proportion would be even higher if persons of inherited wealth were omitted.[2]

Who are these Texas multimillionaires and how have they amassed such tremendous fortunes in an age of astronomical income taxes? Of the group, H. L. Hunt of Dallas is undoubtedly the most prosperous—indeed, he is one of the richest men in the world. Born in Vandalia, Illinois, this onetime barber and professional gambler entered the oil business in Texas in 1920, and ten years later struck it rich in the great oil boom in eastern Texas. By 1950 his income was estimated at a million dollars per week. Though Hunt is seldom photographed and avoids the limelight, he has done much to create a national antipathy to oil-rich Texans. Personally shy and a man of simple tastes, he was not asked to submit his biography for *Who's Who in America* until 1956; the resulting entry was only six lines long and included no birth date.

The only evidence of an interest in civic works and philan-

---

[1] "Why Texas Is Thriving," *U.S. News and World Report*, November 23, 1956, p. 70.

[2] Cleveland Amory: "The Oil Folks at Home," *Holiday*, February 1957, p. 52.

thropy on Hunt's part was his now defunct Facts Forum. This organization sponsored radio and television programs and published a journal entitled *Facts Forum News*. According to Hunt, it was non-profit, non-partisan, and devoted to the promotion of political science, soil and water conservation, and the art of living. Actually, it promoted Hunt's own brand of fascism, which included a strong tinge of McCarthyism. The organization obtained several million dollars' worth of free time on radio and television networks before a national clamor caused a sudden suspension of operation in 1956. Three years later Hunt inaugurated a daily nation-wide radio program called "Lifeline" which is devoted to promoting patriotism, along with various Hunt products, and denouncing foreign aid and the United Nations.

Second to Hunt in Texas oiligarchy until his death in 1957 was Hugh Roy Cullen of Houston, who considered the federal government the source of all evil. His crusading activities in behalf of Americanism exceeded his reputation for philanthropy. Cullen, along with H. L. Hunt, Clint Murchison of Dallas, the late Sid Richardson of Fort Worth, and several others among the "big rich" of Texas, avoided a college education. Their support of conservative candidates in states other than Texas is well known; Cullen and Murchison were among the most avid and generous contributors to the activities of the late Senator McCarthy.

When an important Southwestern collection of books and manuscripts was sold to Yale University in 1956, a prominent Texas writer observed that Texans were "too poor to purchase the collection and keep it at home." "And our oil millionaires," he continued, "are too busy making money to be interested in history or culture."

Not all Texas oilmen have a one-track mind, and a remarkable exception was the late Everette Lee DeGolyer. Internationally recognized as the father of petroleum geology, DeGolyer was a scholar and a man of humility and refinement. He worked his way through the University of Oklahoma and studied under the great scholar Vernon Lewis Parrington. While still an undergraduate he discovered the world's largest oil well in Mexico, an event

XIX · Money and Brains

which naturally made him a millionaire. Later he established a firm of petroleum engineers in Dallas which kept maps and records of every oil field in the world and soon became the equivalent of Dun and Bradstreet among credit ratings in the oil business.

DeGolyer believed that a talent for making money often implies a lack of talent for leading a useful life, yet he was successful at both. His large Spanish-style house on Dallas's White Rock Lake directly opposite the home of H. L. Hunt contained 11,000 books. It included one of the largest private collections in existence on the history of the Southwest, plus a valuable collection of books relating to the history of science. The latter eventually became the nucleus of the DeGolyer Collection in the History of Science and Technology at the University of Oklahoma. Before his death in 1956 the donor purchased more than a thousand additional volumes to make the collection one of the most complete of its kind in the United States. Throughout his long life, historians, writers, and statesmen visited DeGolyer's home and worked in his library. With all his world-wide interests, he found time to write frequent book reviews and conduct historical research; and for several years he gave financial support to the *Saturday Review of Literature*.

Many Americans are convinced that Texas oilmen have money to throw away because of special concessions denied to others, particularly the 27½-per-cent depletion allowance.[3] The clownish behavior of Texas millionaires who flaunt their wealth bolsters this argument. But not all criticism of Texas comes from outside the Lone Star State.

---

[3] The depletion allowable permits a man to deduct a percentage of his gross income in figuring his taxes. In the case of oil the percentage seems unusually high, and bills were proposed in every session of Congress between 1946 and 1959 to reduce the amount, usually to 15 per cent. Opponents argue that the present 27½ per cent was instituted in 1926, before the astronomical rise of private income taxes. Oilmen claim that the allowance is a necessary incentive to risk the cost of drilling an oil well, and they do not seem in danger of losing it, especially as thirty-seven men in Congress come from Texas, Oklahoma, and New Mexico, and twenty or more representatives and senators from other oil-producing states. Meanwhile, oil explorations continue to become more expensive, but the "big rich" somehow manage to get richer.

The Southwest: *Old and New*

Three recent books by Texas writers exemplify the spirit of self-analysis found in Texas: Green Peyton's *America's Heartland* (1948), Frank Goodwyn's *Lone-Star Land: Twentieth-Century Texas in Perspective* (1955), and George Fuermann's *Reluctant Empire: The Mind of Texas* (1957). It is doubtful if a non-Texas writer has ever presented a more critical and objective picture of the state than any one of the above. Each deplores the monkey-shines of the oil millionaires, the irrational contempt for pure learning, and the emphasis on material possessions. But each recognizes that a cultural awakening is in process beneath the crude exterior.

The crusading weekly *Texas Observer* reports regularly on happenings and shenanigans of local politicians and oil millionaires which are seldom mentioned in the local metropolitan press. Some of its editorial comments, such as the following, are devastating: "Texas, a state. Inhabited principally by three racial stocks, of which the largest is Anglo-Saxon, a fattening but still aggressive breed given to absurd boasting. Major crops, politicians, oil, cattle, and cotton. Land area, biggest. Egghead dimension, thin. Universities, yes, freedom, no. Topography, some. Cultural highlights, symphony orchestras, little theaters, and Bank of the Southwest. Characteristic slang, hell, shucks, and bird bait. Most popular housepets, dogs, cats, Negroes, and Mexicans. State motto: Ye shall know the truth if the truth shall make ye rich."

Hugh Russell Fraser, a historian now living in San Antonio, wrote in *Harper's* (May 1956) that Texas constitutes "a journalistic Sahara" and that its daily newspapers are "the worst in America." The author admitted that his statement could not be proved, but he furnished facts and figures to show that Texas papers carry less news of the nation and the world than those of any other state. *The Dallas News,* for example, is an enormously prosperous newspaper that boasts of its coverage of sports, theater, books and oil. It is often cited as a model in Texas journalism classes. In typical week-day editions it carries an average of only five and a half columns of out-of-state news in a total of

XIX · Money and Brains

twenty-eight columns. The scores for the large Houston *Chronicle,* the Houston *Post,* and the Fort Worth *Star Telegram* are only slightly better.

A display of independence by fledgling Texas journalists sometimes brings swift repercussions. In 1956 the student newspaper at the state university, the *Daily Texan,* published a series of editorials about land and insurance scandals, gas regulation, state tax policies, segregation, and political immorality. The board of regents, whom Fraser describes "as distinguished a collection of intellectual fossils as you can find anywhere above the Permian strata," demanded that the editor resign. At first he refused to step down but a tight censorship of the newspaper was inaugurated which left him with no alternative. Across the journalism building, where the campus newspaper is edited, falls the shadow of the University of Texas Library building. Carved in stone on the front of this magnificent structure of more than twenty stories are the words: *Ye Shall Know the Truth and the Truth Shall Make You Free.*

This was not the first time that the conservative ranchers, industrialists, and oil millionaires who constitute the University of Texas Board of Regents had got excited. In 1944 the board dismissed a distinguished liberal educator, Dr. Homer Price Rainey, because of his unyielding defense of academic freedom. Among other charges, the university president was blamed for allowing John Dos Passos's *U.S.A.* to remain on the library shelves. The book contains some "four-letter words" and assorted passages about socialism for which the regents held Dr. Rainey responsible.

A decade and a half later repercussions from the Rainey affair are still evident on the University of Texas campus. Though members of the present Board of Regents are an improvement over those who once governed, the academic air is not so bracing as it could be and the university has not fully regained the prestige it once enjoyed. Great universities throughout the United States harbor refugees from the University of Texas, and most of its present faculty are extremely cautious in their criticism of the administration, regents, or state officials. Meanwhile the conservative rich keep a close watch on "subversive" activities on the campus.

Dr. Logan Wilson, President of the University of Texas, is an able man who understands that his position is a vulnerable one. When a state legislator protested because the lead in a university opera had been assigned to a young Negro student, the production was canceled. Pressure from the regents also caused an invitation to Mrs. Franklin D. Roosevelt to be withdrawn. Mrs. Roosevelt had been invited by a Great Issues student committee to speak on the campus in 1955, but Regent Tom Sealy, a banker from Midland, lost no time in informing President Wilson that she was too liberal to be permitted to appear. Adlai Stevenson and J. Robert Oppenheimer were other distinguished Americans rejected for the same reason.[4]

So dismal has been the cultural past in Texas that outsiders are reluctant to acknowledge any progress for fear of ridicule. Many native sons, in their reaction against sectional vanity, have decided that if something is Texan, it must be tainted. But Texans have much for which they can be proud, among other things its more than 140 foundations, trusts, and benevolent institutions. According to the latest edition of *American Foundations and Their Fields* (1955), Texas ranked fifth among the states in the assets of its foundations, seventh in their expenditures, and seventh in their grants. The majority of these foundations have been created since 1950. Most are based on oil holdings and will continue to grow richer. George Fuermann, an authority on Texas philanthropy, estimates that by 1970 his state will have a richness of foundation resources exceeded only by New York. One of the newest, the William L. Moody, Jr. Foundation, has assets estimated at $400,000,000 and ranks among the three or four largest in the world.

Activities of Texas foundations so far have been directed chiefly toward education, religion, medicine, and agriculture. Dr.

---

[4] *Texas Observer* (Austin), May 16, 1955.

XIX · *Money and Brains*

Robert L. Southerland of the Hogg Foundation at the University of Texas brings officers of all the foundations together for an annual conference. Thus each foundation finds out about the work of others and tries not to duplicate their efforts. With rare exceptions, Texas philanthropy is concerned with local projects and institutions, though the Le Tourneau Foundation directs private Point Four programs in faraway Peru and Liberia. A few support mental hygiene, cancer research, and similar humanitarian projects that transcend geographic boundaries. The ones whose sole purpose is influencing legislation or promoting racial bigotry have won little support in Texas.

Texas also ranks high in the quantity of its public schools and higher educational institutions: 4,000 elementary schools, 1,788 high schools, and 132 universities and colleges (including 29 junior colleges). The University of Texas is the largest educational institution in the Southwest (approximately 19,000 students), and, according to the 1959 *World Almanac*, its endowment exceeds $287,000,000. Before the ousting of Rainey in 1944 it was recognized as one of the nation's outstanding state universities in the fields of humanities, science, and engineering.

Attempts to restore the university to its former position have progressed slowly. It is no longer blacklisted by accrediting associations, and it is making valiant efforts, particularly in the field of science, to rebuild its once great faculty. In 1950 it created a university press that, under the direction of Frank Wardlaw, is making a national reputation as a publisher of scholarly books. Its library contains more than 1,200,000 volumes and ranks seventeenth in size among university libraries in the nation. Talk of making Texas "a university of the first class" is heard more and more often amid renewed emphasis on producing a winning football team. The two ideas are not so incompatible as they sound, for many Southwesterners will support culture if they can associate it with success.

Like the University of Texas, Southern Methodist University at Dallas and Rice Institute at Houston are important regional institutions. Southern Methodist is a church school, but it pursues

The Southwest: *Old and New*

a liberal policy and is the academic nucleus around which Dallas builds its claim of being "the cultural center of the Southwest." When one of its English professors, Dr. John O. Beaty, wrote the notorious anti-Semitic *Iron Curtain over America* in the early 1950's, he was repudiated by the administration, faculty, and student body.

Southern Methodist supports the oldest university press in Texas, and also sponsors a regional quarterly, *The Southwest Review*. The journal's primary field is literary criticism, but it also investigates the social troubles of the time, and its scope and influence extend beyond the region. Sometimes it incurs the wrath of the Dallas Minute Women and other local patriotic groups, but it continues to speak with authority, restrain its temper, and retain its integrity.

Of the more than 150 colleges and universities in the four Southwestern states, only five have Phi Beta Kappa chapters: University of Oklahoma, University of Arizona, Southern Methodist University, University of Texas, and Rice Institute. The last institution is unique for the Southwest in that its student body is highly selected and limited to 1,600; and it charges no tuition fee. It emphasizes engineering and science and attracts graduates from Eastern universities for postgraduate work in these fields, but no one receives a degree from Rice without a broad exposure to the humanities. It also manages to produce its share of All-American football players and once dismissed eight members of the team for violating the honor code on an English examination.

Texas has produced few painters, poets, or novelists of outstanding reputation, and little architecture of distinction. Its painters did not surpass regional interests until the 1940's, and its composers rarely won recognition beyond the state's boundaries until the fifties. Among its outstanding painters is Tom Lea of El Paso, while young Van Cliburn from Kilgore won international acclaim as a concert pianist in 1958.

There has been no lack of Texas writers since the days of the Republic. Most of their work is in the form of memoirs, biog-

XIX · Money and Brains

raphy, history, and folklore, and their subjects are largely confined to cowboys, Indians, badmen, and Texas Rangers. The list of Texas books and writers is prodigious, but J. Frank Dobie's *Guide to Life and Literature of the Southwest* and Walter Campbell's *The Book Lover's Southwest* contain more than adequate cross-sections.

Among the Texas fiction writers active in the 1950's were Tom Lea (*The Brave Bulls* and *The Wonderful Country*), Horton Foote (*The Chase*), William Goyen (*House of Breath* and *Ghost and Flesh*), Fred Gipson (*Hound-Dog Man, Old Yeller*, and *The Home Place*), John Howard Griffin (*The Devil Rides Outside*), George Williams (*The Blind Bull*), John W. Wilson (*High John the Conqueror*), J. R. Williams (*Tame the Wild Stallion*), Dillon Anderson (*I and Claudie* and *Claudie's Kinfolks*), and the late George Sessions Perry (*Hold Autumn in Your Hand* and *The Walls Rise Up*). Most of these writers drew on their Texas background. Some wrote about life in a small town. Some dealt with tragic themes and others wrote about humorous characters. None has affected the nation so profoundly as Faulkner has with his novels of the Deep South.

John Gunther nominated J. Frank Dobie in 1947 as "my candidate for being the most distinguished living Texan" and described him as the conscience of his state. Various Texas conservatives have often nominated him for less distinguished positions, but even they concede that Dobie is the "Dean of Texas Letters." His classes in Life and Literature of the Southwest attracted hundreds of students each semester at the University of Texas. In 1943 Dobie served as visiting professor of American History at Cambridge University; on returning to his home campus, he found the academic climate created by reactionary politicians so unbearable that he ultimately resigned.

Among his historical writings *The Mustangs* and *The Longhorns* are considered classics in their field. But perhaps his greatest work has been the promotion of writing by others and the encouragement and help he has given to hundreds of fledgling authors. He and Walter Prescott Webb, more than any other Texas literary figures, refute the common charge that Texas is void of culture.

Dobie towers above all other Texas writers in the field of folklore. He has written at least a dozen volumes that fall within this classification, among which are *Coronado's Children, Tongues of the Monte,* and *Apache Gold and Yaqui Silver.* Second is Moody Boatright (*From Hell to Breakfast, Tall Tales from Texas Cow Camps,* and *Folk Laughter on the American Frontier*). Another Texas folklorist, now living in Maryland, is Frank Goodwyn (*The Magic of Limping John* and *The Devil in Texas*). The late John A. Lomax spent a lifetime collecting ballads and folklore in Texas and other parts of the world and should not be omitted from any list of cultured Texans. Associated with the same interest is J. Mason Brewer, the state's only Negro writer of importance.

In a category of his own is Roy Bedechek, who died in 1958. For more than forty years he combined a job of supervising Texas interschool sports with observing nature. At the age of seventy he produced the award-winning *Adventures of a Texas Naturalist* and followed it three years later (1950) with *Karánkaway County.* Both books have been compared to Thoreau's *Walden,* for they have much to say not only about birds and animals but also humanity.

Most Texas historical writers have hewed close to facts and footnotes and have steered away from interpretation and ideas. An outstanding exception is Walter Prescott Webb, a historian who gives both interpretation and ideas plenty of free play. "If any Texan has created a universal of culture, if any has altered the mind of man, he is Walter Prescott Webb," George Fuermann declares.[5] Now retired from active teaching at the University of Texas, Webb is the only man born west of the Mississippi River to have served as president of the American Historical Association. In 1938 he was Harkness Lecturer in American History at London

---

[5] George Fuermann: *Reluctant Empire: The Mind of Texas* (New York: Doubleday & Company; 1957), pp. 248–9.

XIX · *Money and Brains*

University and in 1943 was Harmsworth Professor of American History at Oxford University.

A man of kindness and humility, the Texas historian has nevertheless aroused controversy with almost every book and article. His *Great Plains* (1931), dismissed by some early reviewers as a pedestrian work, has since been acclaimed as one of the great books of the twentieth century and continues to sell steadily. In it the author explains the presence of man on the plains, the institutions and adjustments that enabled him to live there, and the effects of climate and geography on the culture he developed. *The Texas Rangers* (1935) is a history of one of the most famous police forces in the world. In *Divided We Stand* (1939) Webb compares the economic supremacy of the North over the South and the giant corporations with feudal institutions. *The Great Frontier* (1952) attempts to explain the rise of democracy and capitalism in relation to physical frontiers; as the frontiers disappear, Webb believes, democracy and capitalism are inexorably altered—perhaps doomed.

VARIOUS INDIVIDUALS have benefited from the fact that some Southwestern universities are publishing sponsors. Even better known than the Southern Methodist University Press and the University of Texas Press is the University of Oklahoma Press. This organization published its first book in 1929, and thirty years later its list had grown to 426 titles. They range in subject matter from the influential *Plowman's Folly*, which has sold over 340,000 copies, to *Athens in the Age of Pericles*.

Most University of Oklahoma Press books relate to Southwestern themes and deal with Indians, cattle, the oil industry, travel, or general history. During the twenty years that Savoie Lottinville has served as director he has broadened the list to include literary criticism, natural science, and art. *Time* (October 12, 1959) observed that its music books make the University of Oklahoma Press better known in Milan and Bonn than many a famed name on publishers' row in Manhattan.

For more than thirty years the university has sponsored *Books Abroad,* a quarterly devoted to publications in languages other than English. Ironically, this magazine has a larger circulation and greater influence in Europe and South America than in the United States. Thousands of Sooners, including more than half the 11,000 students at the University of Oklahoma, are unaware that it exists.

Unlike the University of Texas, the University of Oklahoma has remained relatively free of political interference in recent decades. A flurry of excitement about radicals on the campus followed World War II, and the state legislature passed an "oath law," similar to California's, designed to "weed out the subversives." After the faculty carried the fight to the United States Supreme Court and the law was declared unconstitutional, the legislature quieted down.

Green Peyton once described the University of Oklahoma as "a broadly democratic seminary in a new and uninhibited land where attention is focused on the liberal arts." Its president, George L. Cross, understands the meaning of academic freedom and faculty government in university affairs. His democratic philosophy has prevented many staff members from accepting better-paying positions elsewhere.

Oklahoma supports eighteen colleges and universities, more than any other state of comparable size and resources, and almost three times as many as New Mexico. In addition there are five or six denominational institutions of importance. The Oklahoma State University at Stillwater is equal to the University of Oklahoma in the size of its campus and student body, but it emphasizes science, agriculture, and technical subjects more than the humanities. It, like the state university at Norman, stands out in a region where culture often seems a sideshow to the more interesting business of oil.

XIX · *Money and Brains*

Interest in the work of Oklahoma Indian artists has grown in recent decades. In the early 1930's Susan Peters of Anadarko and Dr. Oscar Brousse Jacobson of the University of Oklahoma began to encourage Indian students to preserve their tribal traditions and culture on canvas. Some became internationally famous, especially Woodrow "Woodie" Crumbo and Acee Blue Eagle. Indian art always appears two-dimensional; its designs are bold and its colors bright. It can be seen in post offices, schools, museums, and buildings all over Arizona, New Mexico, and Oklahoma.

The undisputed Athens of Indian art in the United States is Tulsa, Oklahoma. Located here are two handsomely endowed art museums, Gilcrease and Philbrook, while fifty miles north near Bartlesville is Woolaroc Museum. The most remarkable of the three institutions is the one established by Thomas Gilcrease, a part-Creek Indian who struck it rich in oil. Much of Gilcrease's wealth and energy has gone into the collection of documents, rare books, artifacts, paintings, and sculptures. In 1940 he established the Gilcrease Foundation and turned over to it his unique collection and his Tulsa estate. Now owned by the city of Tulsa and valued at more than $12,000,000, it contains the best record of the American Indian in the world. The library has more than 65,000 rare books and manuscripts and most of the original paintings of Frederick Remington and Charles M. Russell. Also, the work of every important Indian artist in the United States is represented here.

In 1938 Waite Phillips, one of the founders of the Phillips Petroleum Company, converted his sixteenth-century Italian villa in Tulsa into the Philbrook Art Center. The structure dominates a twenty-three-acre formal garden and houses an important collection of American, English, and European paintings of the eighteenth and nineteenth centuries. It includes paintings by Sir Joshua Reynolds, Sir Peter Lely, Thomas Moran, Thomas Gainsborough, Benjamin West, and Sir Thomas Lawrence, and works by Oklahoma sculptors Bernard Frazier, Lawrence Terry Stevens, and Joseph R. Taylor.

Frank Phillips, Waite's older brother, made his ranch home

The Southwest: *Old and New*

near Bartlesville into Woolaroc Museum ten years before Philbrook was established. Woolaroc is noted for its collections of archaeological materials and Western paintings and sculptures. It also has the most valuable collection of Indian blankets in the world. The Frank Phillips Foundation, which owns and operates Woolaroc, has also endowed the Phillips Collection of Southwestern History and Literature at the University of Oklahoma.

Oklahoma has not had many fiction writers comparable to the ones who call New Mexico their home. (It required a Steinbeck to tell the dismal story of the Dust Bowl in *The Grapes of Wrath* and a Ferber to capture the excitement of the opening of the Cherokee Strip in *Cimarron*.) Though many graduates of the Professional School of Writing at the University of Oklahoma have achieved commercial success with novels and short stories, few have produced outstanding literature. Among the most successful post-World War II group are William Brinkley (*Don't Go Near the Water*), Ennen R. Hall (*Reluctant Angel* and *A Saint and Seven Sinners*), Fred Grove (*Flame of the Osage*), Harold Keith (*Rifles for Watie*), and Marjorie McIntire (*River Witch*).

Some of the best fiction by Oklahomans has been about Indians. In 1934 John Joseph Mathews recounted in *Sundown* the failure of an intelligent Osage youth to learn the white man's ways. The author wrote with dignity and honesty, and without romanticizing, of the maladjustments and human waste among prosperous Oklahoma Indians. His earlier novel *Wah' Kon-Tah* was a Book-of-the-Month Club selection and established him as an authentic interpreter of his people. Unfortunately, he has done little literary work since the late thirties.

Other Oklahoma fiction writers who won recognition in the late twenties and the thirties were Donald Joseph (*October Child*), Stanley Vestal (*'Dobie Walls*), George Milburn (*Oklahoma Town*), and John Oskison (*Brothers Three*). Milburn's disillusioned account of Oklahoma small-town life is especially brilliant, and his work has not been equaled by the present group of Sooner writers.

The writing of history appears more congenial to Oklahomans

XIX · *Money and Brains*

than fiction or poetry, though their work in this field has frequently been clouded with smoke from the guns of cowboys and desperados. Best known among Oklahoma historians is Edward Everett Dale, Research Professor Emeritus at the University of Oklahoma. His range of interest is wide, but his special fields are the cattle industry (*The Range Cattle Industry*) and Indians (*Indians of the Southwest*). Professor Dale's writings are spiced with humor and anecdotes drawn from more than eighty years of life in the Southwest, and he is widely known as a raconteur and lecturer. His influence on Oklahoma historians has been enormous. One of his former students is Angie Debo, whose command of the English language and thorough research give her various works on the Five Civilized Tribes a distinguished quality. Another is Dr. Edwin C. McReynolds, who did not begin writing until he was almost sixty. His *Oklahoma: A History of the Sooner State* is generally considered the best single-volume interpretative work on the subject.

Some other important Oklahoma historical writers are the late Carl Coke Rister (*Robert E. Lee in Texas, Oil: Titan of the Southwest,* and *The Greater Southwest*); the late Grant Foreman, a thorough documentarian; Muriel Wright (*The Indians of Oklahoma*); Alice Marriott (*The Ten Grandmothers, Maria, the Potter of San Ildefonso,* and *The Valley Below*); Gilbert C. Fite (*George N. Peek and the Fight for Farm Parity, Mount Rushmore,* and *An Economic History of the United States*); and Walter Campbell, Oklahoma's first Rhodes Scholar, whose fiction, published under the pen name Stanley Vestal, has already been mentioned. Before his death in 1958 Professor Campbell produced more than twenty books. Among his best known non-fiction works are *Kit Carson, Jim Bridger,* and *Joe Meek,* biographies of the three most famous mountain men of the early nineteenth century, and *The Missouri* in the Rivers of America Series.

Professor Campbell maintained that writing skill can be taught to anyone who has intelligence and determination. In the late thirties he established a professional school of writing at the University of Oklahoma and made it one of the most successful in

THE SOUTHWEST: *Old and New*

the United States. Today the work he began is continued by Foster-Harris and Dwight Swain, able writers and excellent teachers whose seminars and special conferences attract hundreds of mature students to the Norman campus each year.

No Oklahoma writer has won a Pulitzer Prize, and only a few have produced non-fiction books that approached the best-seller list. But perhaps quantity in literature must always precede quality. The first already exists in Oklahoma, and the second is inevitable.

UNTIL RECENTLY the people of New Mexico and Arizona have been too engrossed in the frequently bitter task of making a living to devote much time to aesthetic matters. New Mexico has produced or attracted some of the nation's best writers of fiction and artists, but in other cultural areas it has progressed slowly. Arizona has influenced many well-known novelists, including Owen Wister, Harold Bell Wright, Zane Grey, Stewart Edward White, and Alfred Henry Lewis. It is currently attracting outstanding artists, sculptors, and playwrights, but few of them have had time to sink roots deep in the state.

The music of New Mexico and Arizona shows little originality. As in Texas and Oklahoma, ballads, cowboy songs, Mexican music, and Indian chants predominate. Both Albuquerque and Phoenix support symphony orchestras, but neither compares with those of Houston, Dallas, and Oklahoma City. In 1957 Santa Fe launched an opera festival that features outstanding artists from the Metropolitan Opera in New York and from other Eastern cities during the summer months. With the modern trend toward bringing classical music outdoors, the mountains of New Mexico and Arizona, as well as eastern Oklahoma, are proving increasingly attractive to concert artists. And their "long-hair mountain music" is equally attractive to thousands of Southwesterners.

XIX · Money and Brains

Probably the strongest architectural influence in the two Southwestern states is the Spanish by way of the Mexican. The greatest single triumph is San Xavier del Bac, a mission built on the desert near Tucson in 1700 by the Jesuits. The influence of Frank Lloyd Wright, who maintained a winter home near Phoenix during the latter years of his life, is also much in evidence in the Southwest.

New Mexico and Arizona rank among the top ten states in per-capita expenditure for public education, and their schoolteachers are among the highest paid in the nation. Neither has so large a number of colleges and universities in proportion to size as Texas and Oklahoma, however, and the burden of financing education is not so great. Also, because of Indian children and military installations, the desert states receive generous grants-in-aid from the federal government.

The leading institution of higher learning in New Mexico is the state university at Albuquerque. One of its outstanding assets is its press, which has published ten or twelve books annually for more than three decades. Originally it leaned towards the "shoot-'em-up" variety and also offered occasional books for young readers. But under the direction of Ronald Dickey the University of New Mexico Press has become an important cultural force in the Southwest.

The *New Mexico Quarterly*, another University of New Mexico Press publication, is similar to *The Southwest Review* in that it has a general literary interest. Other publications in the state are the *New Mexico Historical Review*, edited by Frank Reeve of the University of New Mexico History Department, and *El Palacio*, a monthly news bulletin and commentary on archaeological activities. The Quivira Society at Santa Fe specializes in publishing translations of original Spanish narratives.

Before World War II the University of New Mexico's reputation as a "play school" attracted students from all over the nation who were more interested in skiing and sunshine than in scholarship and learning. Like the University of Texas, it has suffered from political interference. Prior to 1942 the governor had the power to appoint all members of the board of regents. This meant that higher education was involved in politics, as the terms of various educational boards ran concurrently with the governor's term. One state college had three presidents and two acting presidents in six years, a record that caused it to be blacklisted by the Central Accrediting Association. A constitutional amendment in 1942 making the terms of the members of the boards staggered corrected much of the political evil.

The University of New Mexico has traditionally emphasized archaeology, anthropology, law, and Southwestern history. But Los Alamos and various rocket-research activities attracted thousands of government scientists to the state, and the university's interest is shifting toward science. Generous appropriations by the legislature enabled this and other state institutions to attract outstanding physicists, purchase expensive research equipment, and obtain large federal grants-in-aid. Dr. Joseph Kaplan of UCLA predicts that New Mexico will be a key center of the next revolution in physics and that the university at Albuquerque will become one of the nation's leading institutions in this field.[6]

NEW MEXICAN writers gained prominence in the fiction field before those of the other Southwestern states. Most of the state's early authors were born elsewhere, but their lives have been associated with New Mexico too long for others to claim them. Their work began to attract attention as early as the 1920's and made some internationally famous.

Probably the most admired and best-known Southwestern novel is Willa Cather's *Death Comes for the Archbishop* (1927). This is a beautiful, quiet story about an austere French priest, and like so many other books written in New Mexico, it is drawn from

---

[6] Albert Rosenfield: "New Mexico Cashes In," *Harper's*, January 1954, p. 29.

XIX · *Money and Brains*

native materials. Mary Austin, in whose home Miss Cather lived in Santa Fe while writing her masterpiece, was even better known at the time. Her books are no longer read, but the simple tales she relates in *One-Smoke Stories* have qualities that do not fade with time.

In 1929 Oliver LaFarge produced *Laughing Boy*, a story of the modern Navajo, which received the Pulitzer Prize. In the thirty years since, LaFarge has written a dozen books [7] and hundreds of magazine articles. He does not invent his characters or plots, but takes them from his New Mexico environment.

Harvey Fergusson of Albuquerque wrote a series of realistic novels about the early days of the Upper Rio Grande Valley (*The Blood of the Conqueror, Wolf-Song,* and *In These Days*). His sister, Erna Fergusson, began writing in the following decade and since 1931 has produced more than ten fictional and interpretive works on the Southwest. Her *Dancing Gods, Our Southwest,* and *New Mexico* established her as one of the state's best-known writers.

Conrad Richter's *The Sea of Grass* is a saga of the passing cattle kings and is a literary achievement almost the equal of *Death Comes for the Archbishop*. Frank Water's *The Man Who Killed the Deer* portrays the mysticism of the Indian religion as fiction, while his *Masked Gods* gives a factual account of Pueblo and Navajo religious beliefs and practices. D. H. Lawrence lived for a while in New Mexico. In *The Woman Who Rode Away* and *Mornings in Mexico* he describes a Pueblo dance as an ancient Aztec rite. Both books are Southwestern masterpieces, though they are far less famous than Lawrence's *Lady Chatterley's Lover*.

Another New Mexico writer is Paul Horgan, a New York–born Yankee who has spent most of his life in the Southwest. His earliest works were satirical (*No Quarter Given*, 1935), but later he turned to portrayals of the landscape, and finally to history. *The Great River*, a two-volume history of the Rio Grande won the

---

[7] His latest is *The Story of Santa Fe,* published by the University of Oklahoma Press in August 1959.

Texas Institute of Letters Award and also the Pulitzer Prize in 1954.

A comprehensive history of New Mexico which includes the political, industrial, and sociological developments since statehood is yet to be written. Perhaps this void will be filled when Professor Frank Reeve of Albuquerque completes his three-volume work now in progress.

NORTHERN NEW MEXICO, particularly the area around Santa Fe and Taos, has long had a peculiar attraction for artists. For many years the only serious painters of the region were Ernest Blumenschein, Bert Phillips, and Joseph Sharp. Each was drawn to Taos from the East and remained to paint the landscape, Indian life, and portraits. Others followed in the early part of the twentieth century, including Oscar Berninghaus, Walter Ufer, and Irving Couse, and by 1914 they had founded the Taos Society of Artists, followed in 1923 by the Society of New Mexico Painters. The list of notables is long, but among the most successful members active at the beginning of World War II were Andrew Dasbury, Victory Higgins, Kenneth Adams, George Bellows, John Marin, Maurice Sterne, Randall Davey, B. J. O. Nordfeldt, and Yasuo Kuniyoshi. Like the writers, they drew on the overpowering landscapes of New Mexico, the "blanket Indians," and adobe houses for their materials.

At the Art Museum in Santa Fe, founded in 1917 by artist Robert Henri and the archaeologist Dr. Edgar Lee Hewett, free space is available to any painter in New Mexico who wishes to exhibit. Among the group of outstanding New Mexico artists are Peter Hurd, Georgia O'Keeffe, and Van Soelen. There are also some good Indian painters: Fra Angelico Chavez, Awa Tsireh, Fred Kabotie, and Velino Sheje.

XIX · *Money and Brains*

ARIZONA HAS lagged behind the other sections of the Southwest in cultural interest and achievement. In its small towns, as in those of Texas and Oklahoma, aesthetic tastes are usually satisfied by listening to the high-school band at football games, but both Tucson and Phoenix support symphony orchestras. In 1957 there were only fourteen daily newspapers and forty-five weeklies in the entire state, plus eighteen periodicals. Like most Southwestern newspapers, Arizona's are extremely conservative. However, the Arizona *Daily Star* enjoys a reputation as the best newspaper in the four-state region. The state-published magazine, *Arizona Highways*, features some of the best photographic art in America, and a new historical and literary quarterly, *Arizona and the West*, shows promise of becoming an important scholarly journal.[8]

There are only three state-supported colleges and universities in Arizona: the University of Arizona at Tucson, Arizona State College at Flagstaff, and Arizona State University at Tempe. All offer graduate work, but only the Tucson institution confers the Ph.D. In addition, there are two junior colleges and two parochial colleges.

Because of the climate, the University of Arizona attracts a cosmopolitan student body from every state in the Union and from many foreign countries. Its enrollment (8,600) exceeds that of the University of New Mexico by approximately 3,000, and, like its sister Southwestern institution, it is trying to live down a reputation as a "play school." Its Agricultural Experimental Station is superior, while the Laboratory of Tree-Ring Research is the first of its kind in the world. Recently the academic emphasis at Tucson has shifted to science and mathematics because of various govern-

---

[8] This magazine is published by the University of Arizona and is edited by Pulitzer Prize winner John Alexander Carroll, a native of Wyoming. Its first issue appeared in June 1959.

ment research and experimental projects scattered throughout the state.

The Tucson Community Playhouse is producing first-rate plays and attracting outstanding actors. Though not so well established as the Pasadena Playhouse in California, it is fast gaining a comparable reputation. Arizona also supports three or four museums, notably at Flagstaff and Phoenix, which emphasize pioneer artifacts, prehistoric culture, and modern Indian crafts. But so much of the landscape offers breath-taking beauty that formal collections in man-made buildings seem almost superfluous.

Much has been written about Arizona, but the state has produced few native-born writers whose reputations extend beyond local boundaries. Stories of Indians, Indian life, cowboys, and badmen make up a large part of the literature. Ross Santee is the best-known writer, and though he was born elsewhere he must rank as a native, for he spent many years in the saddle in Arizona before he became known as an artist and author. His *Cowboy* is an authentic story of life on the open range, and, like most of Santee's other books, it is as distinctive for its black-and-white illustrations as for its content and style.

Most Arizona writers in the past treated the state either realistically or with romantic simplification. Earle Forrest in *Arizona's Dark and Bloody Ground* tells the story of tragic feuds between Indian clans. William H. Robinson in *Thirsty Earth* describes the struggle of early settlers for water, and Jack Weadock in *Dust of the Desert* gives an authentic picture of life on the border. Adolph Bandelier's *The Delight Makers* is a fictional account of prehistoric Arizona and one of the best novels of ancient life in America. The state's outstanding poet is Sharlot Hall, whose collected poems appear under the title *Cactus and Pine*.

Since World War II writers' clubs have sprung up in various Arizona communities, one of which, Arizona Professional Authors, has a membership of more than 150. Among the contemporary writers are Nora Laing (*Desert Ships*), Mary Kidder Rak (*Cowman's Wife*), Jack O'Connor (*Conquest*), Stuart Engstrand (*The Invaders*), Frances Gillmore (*Windsinger*), Laura Adams Armer

XIX · *Money and Brains*

(*Waterless Mountain*), and Charles G. Finney (*The Circus of Dr. Lao*).

Interest in art is growing in Arizona. R. Ferrington Elwell, who lives in Phoenix, is an outstanding cowboy artist and Max Ernst is a prime mover in the school of surrealism. He and his surrealist-painter wife, Dorothea Tanning, commute between Paris and their home in Sedona, Arizona. Other prominent members of local art colonies are Ted de Grazia, Jay Datus, and Paul Coze, winner of the French Academy of Arts medal for outstanding interpretation of Indian folklore.

UNTIL THE twentieth century was well under way, the Southwest had little time for intellectual achievements. Its people were too occupied with conquest, survival, and the accumulation of material things. The average frontiersman cared little for culture—indeed, he was likely to sneer at it. Culture starts with maturity, a stage of development which the Southwest is only now reaching. More time and historical perspective are needed before it can achieve equality with older regions.

But culture in the United States is no longer concentrated in New York and San Francisco. The "hicks" are vanishing, and ideas are emerging in regions far removed from the great cities on the East or West Coast. In the Southwest this development is shifting emphasis from cattle, cotton, and oil to things of more enduring value.

XX

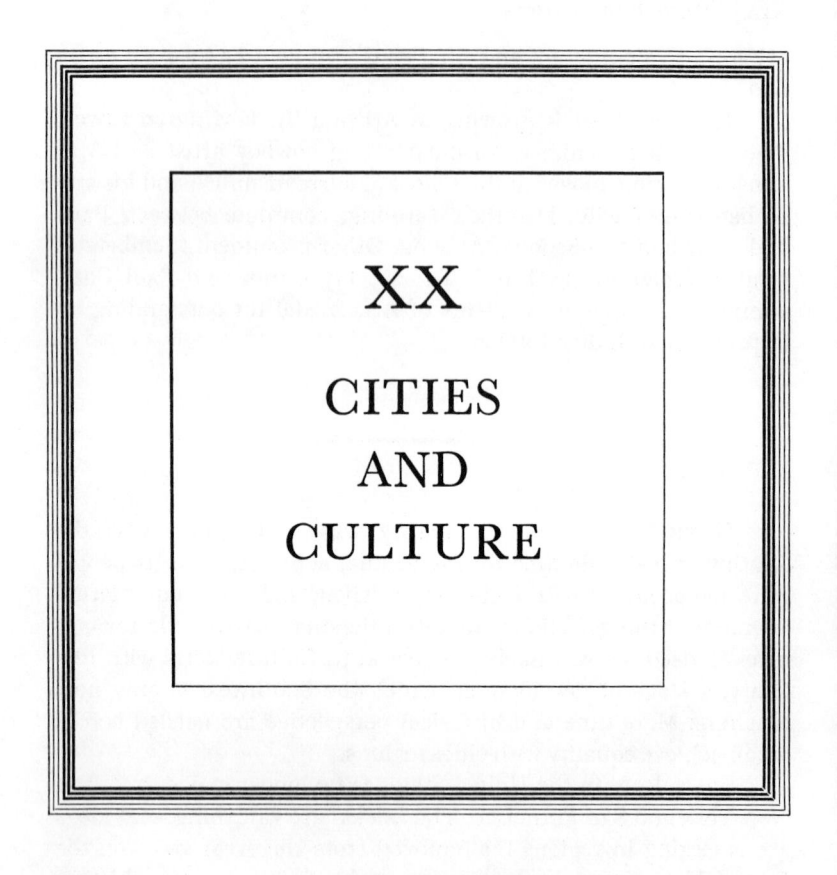

CITIES AND CULTURE

IRREFUTABLE PROOF that Southwestern cities flourished and died long before the first white man set foot in the New World is furnished by the ruins at Mesa Verde, Canyon de Chelly, Casa Grande, Bandelier, and elsewhere. Perhaps the term "cities" is misleading, for none could have supported more than 5,000 or 6,000 inhabitants at a time, but they pooled their resources by forming loose confederations or states. However, by the time the legend of the Seven Cities of Cibola and their fabulous wealth led Coronado into the region, most of them had disappeared. He found

XX · Cities and Culture

several city sites still inhabited, but these had declined from the peak of their civilization.

Others followed Coronado into the Southwest, but sixty-five years passed before the establishment of Santa Fe in 1610. It remained the largest of a handful of Southwestern cities built by the Spaniards, and after two and a half centuries it contained a population no larger than 5,000. Meanwhile, New York, Boston, Philadelphia, and Baltimore had become great metropolitan centers. Even after Americanization, Southwestern cities developed slowly, for there were few navigable streams on which industries could be based.

Before the close of the nineteenth century the railroads minimized this handicap, and the automobile, paved highways, and eventually the airplane further reduced dependence on water transportation. Development of natural resources, the mechanization of agriculture, industrialization, and the twentieth-century population boom made the rapid growth of cities inevitable. The pace quickened around 1940, and the 1960 census will show that fully two thirds of the thirteen million Americans in the four Southwestern states are urban dwellers. Most of these reside in a dozen cities.

Without the highway markers a traveler would have difficulty in recognizing the boundary lines separating the various Southwestern states. Traveling the more than 300-mile stretch of U.S. Highway 66 between Amarillo and Albuquerque, one is gradually aware of higher altitude and dryer atmosphere. But not until the Sandia Mountains that shield Albuquerque on the northeast come into sight is a change in the flat terrain noticeable. Immediately beyond these mountains, in a valley along the banks of the Rio Grande, lies the city in which one out of every four New Mexican citizens resides. Albuquerque's wide streets, nearby mesas, and rolling hills remind the visitor of El Paso, a city to which it bears more than a physical resemblance.

Erna Fergusson, perhaps Albuquerque's best-known writer, made this observation about the city in her study of the Southwest in 1940: "Albuquerque has never struck a bonanza nor known a

The Southwest: *Old and New*

boom. Little gold has been discovered in its hills, no oil nor artesian water in its subsoil. The fertile Rio Grande Valley produces less nowadays than it did before the building of the modern town. . . . Cut off from the rest of the country, Albuquerque literally would not have enough to eat." [1] The last sentence remains true two decades later, but a boom has come to Albuquerque in the intervening years. The 1930 census gave Albuquerque a population of 26,000, but it has more than doubled in every decade since. By 1959 the rate of increase averaged 1,500 people per month, and the Albuquerque Chamber of Commerce expects the 1960 census to show a population in the metropolitan area in excess of 300,000.

The Villa de Albuquerque was founded in 1706 and named for the Viceroy of New Spain, the Duke of Albuquerque. When the American explorer Zebulon Montgomery Pike visited the place a century later, he found it a village of no more than a thousand people. The network of canals that led from the river to irrigated fields reminded him of his boyhood and his readings about the Nile Valley of Egypt. But it must have been a peaceful spot, for Pike reserved some of his warmest compliments for Albuquerque and "the beautiful girls who converted our wine into nectar."

A few years after Pike's visit, American merchants engaged in the Santa Fe trade discovered Albuquerque. They, and the soldiers who came with Kearny and Doniphan during the Mexican War, followed by the California gold seekers and the military personnel, steadily altered the town's Spanish character. No longer was it a sleepy village like dozens of others that dotted the Rio Grande Valley from Santa Fe to El Paso. When the Santa Fe Railroad reached it in 1881 and built its shops a mile east of the Villa de Albuquerque, most of the townspeople moved to a new site near the tracks. Old Albuquerque and its plaza were left alone by the river until new Albuquerque grew back to it. The two places have long since merged into one bustling city, scarcely distinguishable from many others of comparable size.

---

[1] Fergusson: *Our Southwest*, p. 227.

XX · Cities and Culture

Except for a few old Spanish landmarks and modern Pueblo architecture, Albuquerque is not typical of New Mexico's way of life. Developments in electronic and atomic-energy fields as a result of nearby Kirkland Air Force Base, Sandia Corporation, White Sands Proving Ground, and Los Alamos scientific laboratories have brought numerous manufacturing, machine, and service industries. The pace of urban expansion and industrial growth has been too rapid for problems to be solved as they arose. City facilities are hard pressed to keep up with the population growth, and schools, highways, and street construction already are several years behind the needs. In 1940 the cost of city government barely exceeded $800,000; the municipal budget for 1959–60 was more than $16,000,000. If expectations that the population will number between 500,000 and 750,000 by 1970 are realized, the problems of tax revenue and city services will be compounded.

Some 350 manufacturing plants in the Albuquerque area employ more than 10,000 people. But tourism is the largest single industry, supporting 138 modern motels and bringing in a revenue of approximately $25,000,000 annually. The Chamber of Commerce estimated that in 1959 4,000 out-of-state cars entered Albuquerque every day via the coast-to-coast U.S. Highway 66, the "main street" of America, and U.S. 85, the Pan American Highway, which runs from Alaska to Mexico City. In addition to tourists, the high, dry climate of Albuquerque has attracted "health seekers" ever since it became an American city more than a century ago.

The Albuquerque Civic Symphony Orchestra, under the baton of Maurice Bonney, is one of the better concert groups in the Southwest. The Summerhouse Theater, Light Opera Company, and University of New Mexico Summer Lecture Series also contribute to Albuquerque's reputation as a cultural center.

Santa Fe and Taos, northeast of Albuquerque, reflect more of the traditions of New Mexico. Neither can be considered a city by modern standards, for Santa Fe claimed less than 40,000 people in 1960 and Taos considerably less. But Santa Fe is so well known and remains so faithful to the past that it can hardly be omitted from the group of Southwestern cities. In 1960 Santa Fe celebrated its 350th birthday, and its people are well aware that it is something "different" and "special."

Santa Fe has little industry, and has made no determined effort to attract any. The Plaza remains the hub of the city, and its streets are as narrow and crooked as when Spanish conquistadores traveled them. Most of its ancient houses and churches are intact, and new structures, too, are invariably built of adobe. Santa Fe is inundated by a flood of tourists each summer, and the downtown traffic congestion becomes a nightmare. But the natives take over again in September and for eight or nine months resume a more leisurely pace. Except for travelers who make brief stops at the luxurious hotels and fancy bars, or those who come to ski, Santa Fe once again belongs to the Indians, the artists and writers, the local merchants, and the capital politicians.

Santa Fe has no university on which to anchor its culture, but it has five or six museums that feature archaeological and historic artifacts, international folk art, and both Indian and modern art. No other American city of comparable size supports as many museums. Perhaps they flourish here because of a dogged determination that the past will not be left behind. If Santa Fe should succumb to progress and urbanization as other Southwestern cities have done, the perpetual search by Americans for something different will be made more difficult.

Just as western Texas blends into eastern New Mexico, with only man-made signs to designate the difference, so western New Mexico indistinguishably becomes eastern Arizona. The first metropolitan center one approaches in crossing the desert west of El Paso or Albuquerque is the oasis city of Tucson. It too is encircled by mountains, though from the plains they look more bare and rugged than those which guard Albuquerque or El Paso. And Tuc-

XX · Cities and Culture

son is similar in other ways—in its past history as a Spanish settlement and its modern growth from a city of 58,000 in 1940 to a metropolitan center of more than 250,000 by 1960.

Tucson is one of the oldest communities in America, for excavations indicate that it was occupied by people before the time of Christ. The present settlement dates from 1776, when the Spaniards moved the presidio and mission from Tubac, on the Santa Cruz River, to the site. By this time the region had been thoroughly explored by Padre Eusebio Francisco Kino, who built or laid the foundation for nine missions in southern Arizona. The northernmost mission was San Xavier del Bac, which remains Tucson's outstanding landmark and is generally accepted as the most beautiful Spanish architectural structure in the Southwest. Spain maintained a handful of troops at the presidio of Tucson, but the combination of desert heat, extreme isolation, and fierce Apaches did not attract many settlers.

A few mountain men passed through Tucson in search of beaver along the Gila River as early as the 1820's, and a generation later several thousand California gold seekers gave it new life. Almost overnight Tucson became a bustling town of blacksmith shops, wagonyards, merchandising establishments, saloons, and brothels. The Gadsden Purchase in 1854 made it a part of the United States, and when the first Butterfield stage arrived four years later the town was no longer cut off from the rest of the world. During the Civil War Confederate troops occupied it for several months before Union forces arrived from California. For another twenty-five years Tucson remained an American outpost against the Apaches, and the military garrison played the principal role in the town's post-war economy. Even today the local military installations contribute more than $50,000,000 annually and provide Tucson's third-largest source of income.

Meanwhile Texas cattlemen made Tucson headquarters for feudal baronies, and cowboys, outlaws, and miners turned it into almost as gaudy and lawless a town as the neighboring outpost of Tombstone. Local peace officers and territorial rangers eventually tamed southern Arizona, and many who started as outlaws be-

The Southwest: *Old and New*

came law-abiding citizens. A few large corporations soon controlled the mines, and the cattle business settled into respectability and smaller "outfits." Railroads, paved highways, and airlines transformed the old Spanish settlement into a metropolis. Irrigated farming became more profitable than ranching and "dudes" more numerous than cattle. Modern office buildings, smart hotels, restaurants, bars, and curio shops replaced the original false-front buildings and adobe structures. Instead of dusty streets, long straight thoroughfares now extend from the center of town for miles into the desert. And instead of two-story clapboard or adobe houses, there are mansions of brick, stone, or stucco—air-conditioned against the desert heat.

Before World War II, Tucson depended more on the tourist trade than any other city in the Southwest. The post-war boom brought 200,000 new residents and hundreds of large and small factories. By 1960 manufacturing and processing contributed $60,000,000 annually to the local economy. But the luxurious "dude ranches" that dot the surrounding area, together with motels, convention hotels, and boarding houses, provide another $58,000,000 each year. Tucson's blistering sunshine, desert isolation, and gaudy reputation have been turned into assets. Though agriculture, mining, and cattle are still important industries, they rank eighth, ninth, and tenth to other occupations.

The zeal to acquire culture along with added wealth and population is characteristic of all expanding cities in the Southwest—and especially of Tucson. The University of Arizona, with its ten colleges and 8,600 students, ranks among the four or five largest educational institutions in the Southwest. The Chamber of Commerce points with pride to four public-supported music organizations: the Tucson Symphony Orchestra, Civic Chorus, Boys Chorus, and Boys Band. Also there are the Sunday Evening Forum, the Community Theater, a Fine Arts Center, and three museums.

Of the four largest oasis cities of the Southwest—El Paso, Albuquerque, Tucson, and Phoenix—the most spectacular example of post-war growth is Phoenix. Though its site supported an ancient civilization that disappeared centuries before Coronado

XX · *Cities and Culture*

reached the Southwest, present-day Phoenix did not have a single inhabitant until 1867. In that year a trader named John Y. T. Smith secured a contract to supply hay for the cavalry horses of Fort McDowell, Arizona Territory. Thirty miles down the Salt River from the fort Smith discovered a network of prehistoric Indian irrigation ditches and established his first "hay camp" there. A few months later about a dozen men from the mining settlement of Wickenburg joined him and soon cleared out miles of old irrigation ditches, built new ones, and planted crops. The next year they named their small settlement Phoenix, for the mythical fire bird that was destroyed by fire every 500 years and sprang up again in youthful vigor.

Early visitors to Phoenix were not impressed by the small agricultural community and its dry climate, dreary location, and tremendous number of tarantulas and rattlesnakes. But by 1870 it claimed about 300 people and by the next year a school, a hotel, a brewery, a bakery, butcher shops, and the inevitable saloon and jail. That year it was dignified by being named the county seat of the newly created Maricopa County. The first railroad, the Maricopa Phoenix, reached Phoenix in 1887, and the second, the Santa Fe, in 1895. The population now approached 2,000, enough for the town to supplant Prescott as the territorial capital.

The 1940 census showed 65,000 people in Phoenix, with farming and tourism the region's principal industries. But the war changed this drastically as the federal government took advantage of Arizona weather to establish six military air bases in the vicinity of Phoenix. Along with the bases came several major war industries, the result of the government's dispersal strategy. Thousands of people followed the factories and air bases, and the population boom began. Old-time residents of Phoenix expected that after the war they could return to raising vegetables, cotton, and fruit, and to the tourist business.

But when the war bases and war plants closed, most of the new population remained. Not only that, more arrived. Phoenix could either industrialize and provide jobs for its expanding population or face a real depression. The Korean War reopened the

THE SOUTHWEST: *Old and New*

bases and war factories, and the Cold War kept them going. Meanwhile, more than 280 manufacturing enterprises were established in Phoenix between 1948 and 1960. The 1960 census will show a metropolitan population (which includes most of Maricopa County) of approximately 500,000. And the Chamber of Commerce anticipates double that number by 1975.

Tourism is still important, but it is not vital to Phoenix's economy. In 1959 it amounted to $80,000,000, as compared to $250,000,000 from manufacturing and $180,000,000 from agriculture and livestock. The city is no longer dependent on faraway El Paso and Los Angeles, but has become its own trade center for a $715,000,000 annual retail sales business.

Phoenix resembles southern California more than the surrounding Southwest, and though it still has a large Spanish-American population, it has effaced much of its Spanish influence. In the absence of a major educational institution, its cultural advancement has not kept up with its phenomenal growth. Chamber of Commerce brochures emphasize its industrial and recreational facilities in superlative language, but carry only brief mention of the city's Little Theater, Civic Opera Company, Art Museum, and the Phoenix Symphony.

THE PATTERN of the post-war boom witnessed in most Southwestern cities is also evident in Oklahoma City and Tulsa. Here the growth has been steady, but less spectacular than in Houston, Phoenix, Albuquerque, Amarillo, or a dozen others. Oklahoma City, for example, claimed 204,000 people in 1940 and 236,000 a decade later. The 1960 census will probably show a population of 360,000 for greater Oklahoma City, or a substantial increase of approximately 120,000 for the previous decade.

However, Oklahoma City has altered in seventy years from a

tent-and-clapboard town on the Santa Fe Railroad to an important oil, transportation, military, industrial, and airline center. Few cities in the world started so suddenly and dramatically. On April 21, 1889, it was only a name on a railroad map, but twenty-four hours later it boasted 10,000 residents, all of whom had arrived by train, wagon, or horseback in Oklahoma's first "run."

Within five days the city had a few "permanent" buildings, banks, a newspaper, a post office, several stores, and an organized government. Most of the people were young, hopeful, and excited, though there were the inevitable gamblers, shyster lawyers, and prostitutes. "We ate sand and we slept sand," one of the original settlers observed fifty years later. "Practically all were living in tents, and with the sand constantly stirred up and constantly borne by the wind, cooking was a joke and sleeping a nightmare. But while we remembered this, we did not mind it greatly. Every man was pushing to a goal, and we did not stand on trifles." [2]

The enthusiasm of Oklahoma City's early months diminished rapidly, and the census of 1890 showed that the population had shrunk to approximately 4,000. A decade later it had attained its original size of 10,000, and the next thirty years were ones of accelerated growth. The continued expansion of agriculture, plus the opening of the Oklahoma City oil field in 1928, brought the population to 185,000 in the 1930 census. Agriculture is no longer all-important, and most of the present residents are engaged in oil leasing, state government, insurance, banking, construction, merchandising, or employed at Tinker Air Force Depot or the Civil Aeronautics Center at nearby Will Rogers Field. Because of its location, Oklahoma City is also the center of a vast trade area that extends north, south, and west to the state boundaries.

The capital city of Oklahoma has much to recommend it as a place to live and work. Its growth since World War II has been gradual enough to enable the city council to keep abreast in school construction, traffic and parking facilities, and the extension of municipal services. Its skyline rises sharply from the rolling plains,

---

[2] Angelo C. Scott: *The Story of Oklahoma City* (Oklahoma City: Times Journal Publishing Co.; 1939), p. 26.

and its oil derricks and checkerboard squares present a pleasing picture from the air. Like all Southwestern cities, where natural gas is abundant and cheap for homes and industry, it has a fresh, clean look. And despite a preponderance of fundamentalist churches and religious sects (this region is in the center of the "Bible Belt") and an extremely conservative press, Oklahoma City offers a remarkably sophisticated and tranquil atmosphere.

It does not pretend to be a great cultural mecca like Dallas, yet it supports one of the best symphony orchestras in the Southwest, has a reasonably good Art Center, the Mummers Theater, and a historical museum. The Metropolitan Opera's annual appearance at the Municipal Auditorium attracts a capacity audience of more than 6,000 to each performance. Oklahoma City University and proximity to the University of Oklahoma at Norman offer additional cultural advantages to the city that claims the largest percentage of American-born white residents in the nation.

A ninety-mile turnpike connects Oklahoma City with its nearest rival to the northeast, Tulsa. Oklahoma City is larger by approximately 100,000 people, and it is not particularly jealous of its neighbor. But Tulsans are apt to be jealous of Oklahoma City, and believe that eventually their city will become the state's largest metropolitan center. It is located on the Arkansas River, which someday may be made a navigable stream; it is close to Oklahoma's oil, coal, and other mineral reserves; and it will soon have an abundance of water storage and hydroelectricity for industrial expansion. Its anticipations of growth—from 265,000 in 1960 to 500,000 by 1975—are not so optimistic as Oklahoma City's, but may be more realistic.

Tulsa is located where the transcontinental highways from Canada and the eastern seaboard cross the Arkansas River. "It is small, as cities go, but it has a startling skyline—so compact, so symmetrical, so high and clean that it seems to float in the air." [3] Tulsa lives on the oil and gas service industry, which is diversified in itself, and it has long boasted of being the "Oil Capital of the

---

[3] Angie Debo: *Tulsa: From Creek Town to Oil Capital* (Norman: University of Oklahoma Press; 1943), p. 3.

XX · *Cities and Culture*

World." It is still headquarters for many major and independent companies, though several have moved to Houston and elsewhere since World War II. Tulsa has other distinctions: it is the home of the American Airlines fleet, and it has a greater square footage of office space per capita than any other city in the United States; it is more Eastern than Southwestern, with little of the rural provincialism found in smaller cities of Oklahoma; and it is predominantly Republican.

Tulsa was founded a few years before the Civil War (the exact date is in dispute) by Creek Indians, who named it for their former Alabama capital, Tallasi. For many years it consisted of a trading post and a few dozen Creek families; for a brief period after the Civil War it became an important camp site and river crossing for Texas trail drovers. When the St. Louis and San Francisco Railroad built through the settlement in 1882, some of the workers remained in Tulsa with their families. It quickly became a "wide-open" town, for the "iron horse" brought more outlaws than decent settlers. Members of gangs such as the Doolin, Cook, Buck, and Glass were familiar on Tulsa streets, and some of them committed crimes against both Indian and white citizens. But Tulsa reached a sort of gentlemen's agreement with the outlaws by which the town furnished them asylum in exchange for immunity.

As the Indian Nations began to disappear, Tulsa became an incorporated town in 1896 where whites outnumbered Indians. In 1900 its population approximated 1,400, but the discovery of oil in 1905 started a boom that eventually made "Old Tulsey Town" one of the most beautiful and prosperous cities in America. Its oil millionaires built mansions, a few of which cost a million dollars, its businessmen raised skyscrapers, and its city planners laid out wide boulevards, planted trees, and landscaped parks.

Noted for its beauty and its wealth, Tulsa also enjoys a reputation as a cultural center. Though Tulsa University is a Presbyterian school, it sometimes has to turn to downtown businessmen for financial support. In addition, the city has two outstanding museums—Philbrook Art Center and the Thomas Gilcrease Institute

THE SOUTHWEST: *Old and New*

of American History and Art—the Tulsa Philharmonic Orchestra, Tulsa Opera, Broadway Theater League, Tulsa Little Theater, and the Civic Music Association.

THE LARGEST and most important Southwestern city is Houston, where one out of every eight Texans lives. It was founded in 1836 by two New York real-estate promoters, A. C. and John K. Allen. The town was laid out on Buffalo Bayou, a few miles from the battlefield of San Jacinto, where Sam Houston won his victory over Santa Anna six months earlier.[4]

Houston was only one of many towns surveyed during the early months of the Republic of Texas. None showed less promise, for it was located on a mud bank that rose barely forty feet above sea level and was fifty miles inland from the Gulf. But the Allens proved able promoters. In May 1837, before the town was finished, they persuaded the Texas Congress to move the capital to Houston. They soon had the first railroad and one of the first newspapers in the Republic. When the capital moved to Austin a few years later, Houston's future looked bleak, and for the next several decades it lived under the shadow of nearby Galveston, the largest city in the state and the leading port.

When a hurricane demolished Galveston in 1900, much of its surviving population and business moved to Houston. In 1914 the city completed a fifty-eight-mile deep-sea channel to the Gulf, which ultimately made it one of the largest port cities in the United States. Six years later it was the third city in Texas, following San Antonio and Dallas. By 1930 Houston had become the largest city in the state. Its population that year exceeded 290,000

---

[4] One of the town surveyors employed by the Allen brothers was Gail Borden, who later invented a process for condensing milk and founded the Borden Milk Company.

XX · Cities and Culture

people, and by 1960 numbered more than 1,200,000.[5] It is now the eighth-largest city in the United States and the third-largest port. According to United States census projections, the metropolitan area will double in population by 1975.

Houston owes its phenomenal growth to natural resources and the industries built on them, notably the chemical industry based on hydrocarbons and salt, sulphur, and lime. It is also headquarters for the area's $125,000,000 annual cotton crop, $60,000,000 rice crop, $50,000,000 cattle business and equally vast dairy and truck-farming business. Houston's banking and insurance and much of its business growth has come with the development of other prosperous Gulf Coast cities, notably Beaumont, Port Arthur, Galveston, Texas City, Brownsville, and Corpus Christi.

Like other exploding American cities, its phenomenal growth has brought problems that seem almost insurmountable. With a metropolitan area of more than 1,700 square miles, the task of building new streets, repairing old ones, laying new sewer and water lines, and erecting new school buildings increased annual expenditures from less than $10,000,000 in 1939 to more than $70,000,000 in 1959. Meanwhile Houston has never settled the question of where its downtown is, and its transportation is a scramble. To go from one of the larger buildings to another, one has to drive for miles. During the 1960's an ambitious express program to facilitate rapid transit will be completed, but an anticipated tripling of registered vehicles by 1975 will make it obsolete.

Houston possesses one of the most gracious residential suburbs in America. In addition to three universities—Rice Institute, the University of St. Thomas, and the University of Houston—it has an excellent symphony orchestra under the baton of Leopold Stokowski, four museums, including the lavishly endowed Museum of Fine Arts, several good bookstores, three professional the-

---

[5] At the time of this writing the 1960 census reports are not complete, and statistics relating to populations and business of various Southwestern cities are based on questionnaires I sent to various Chambers of Commerce in December 1959. All population citations for 1960, therefore, are estimates, and perhaps optimistic ones. Also, they include the people living in the incorporated metropolitan area.

aters, three or four passable hotels and restaurants, and 674 churches. Yet it is still so new and is expanding so rapidly that one visitor in 1958 observed that its business center looked as if some superbillionaire had mail-ordered a dozen blocks of Manhattan C.O.D. and dumped them along the ship channel.

In December 1959 the Houston City Council announced plans to construct a $100,000,000 downtown center. Named after the late oil tycoon Hugh Roy Cullen, this proposed twelve-acre center will be privately financed and have a 500-room hotel and three office buildings with a total of 1,650,000 square feet of office space. The entire unit will be connected by air-conditioned pedestrian malls at second-story level.

Houston has had a difficult time overcoming its reputation as one of the most reactionary communities in the United States. Activities of such organizations as the Houston Minute Women and the Committee for Sound American Education made it a national spectacle throughout the decade that followed World War II. And its proclivity for unfavorable publicity reached a new summit in 1956 when India's Ambassador to the United States, G. L. Mehta, charged that he had been discriminated against in a Houston public dining room. The incident took on some of the aspects of an international event as interested parties denied, affirmed, or apologized for what transpired.

Another embarrassment to Houston's pride is the highest percapita murder rate in the whole country—about fifteen per 100,000, or a total of 136 during 1957. Since then a group of local citizens have organized a "Murdertown Committee" and are at work on various crime-prevention methods. Other signs of the city's growing awareness of the twentieth century are seen in its gradual acceptance of its Negro residents as American citizens. Segregation is declining, without violence, and in 1958 the first Negro was elected to the Houston School Board. In 1956 the city completed the first phase of its merge with political liberalism when it gave fifty-one per cent of its vote to Ralph Yarborough in the gubernatorial run-off against the conservative United States Senator Price Daniel.

XX · Cities and Culture

Two hundred miles of superhighway separate Houston from its nearest rival, Dallas, a city that is a few years younger but tries to act much older. Other than the fact that the two cities are located in the same state, they have little in common. Dallas has no port, no oil resources, no rice fields, and no wealth of cattle. It has no Intercoastal Canal or ship channel, though it has long dreamed of making the Trinity River navigable for 294 miles to the Gulf of Mexico. But it centers a trade area in north-central Texas which covers parts of four states, and its estimated population of 700,000 in January 1959 made it the largest American city not on a water route. It is gradually merging with nearby Fort Worth, which until a few years ago was its hated rival. Together the cities contain a larger concentration of people, industry, and wealth than any other area of comparable size in the entire Southwest.

Dallas was born in 1841 when John Neely Bryan, a Tennessean, came from Arkansas to investigate the possibilities of a trading post. He was so impressed with the area near the headwaters of the little Trinity River that he returned to Arkansas determined to sell his holdings and make his home in the new land. Having spent most of his mature life among the Indians, Bryan believed that he could establish a trading post here that would lure the Indian trade from a vast territory. But when he returned to the site of Dallas in November 1841, he discovered that most of the Indians had left the region because white men had moved in on them.

He constructed a shelter of cedar boughs on the banks of the Trinity River and was soon operating a ferry across the stream for Texas immigrants. Eventually a few families settled nearby and the place became known as Dallas. Bryan supplemented his ferry business by selling powder, lead, and whisky to the settlers; later he engaged in farming. The city that he founded continued to grow until it had more than 260,000 people by 1930 and was second in size only to Houston among Southwestern cities. It passed the 400,000 mark in 1950 and anticipates that by 1975 its population will be 1,300,000.

Modern Dallas is less typically Texan or Southwestern than

The Southwest: *Old and New*

any other city in the Lone Star State, for it maintains close contact with the sophisticated East and wears with pride its reputation as a cultural center. The Dallas Symphony Orchestra began its sixtieth season in the fall of 1960, and, under the direction of Paul Kletski, scheduled a series of sixteen concerts between November and April. Recent guest artists and conductors have included Yehudi Menuhin, Artur Rubinstein, Isaac Stern, and José Iturbi. At the same time the Margo Jones Theater closed its sixteenth season; it was the first professional community theater-in-the-round and among the few professional repertory theaters in the nation until the recent death of its founder Margo Jones.

Dallas is also the city of museums, supporting a total of seven. Six of these are located on the State Fair Grounds, which are visited by approximately three million people each year. The Dallas Museum of Fine Arts displays a permanent collection covering all media and periods of art, with emphasis on prints and on American and especially Southwestern paintings and sculptures. The Dallas Museum for Contemporary Arts exhibits contemporary collections on loan.

The bases of Dallas's economy are banking, insurance, aviation, and mercantilism. It has three municipally owned airports, including one of the largest and most modern in the United States, Love Field. The Federal Reserve Bank was established in Dallas in 1914, and its more than 625 members are spread through the Southwestern states and parts of Louisiana. Bank clearings for the six national banks and eighteen state banks in Dallas in 1958 approached $25,000,000. And 218 insurance companies have home executive offices here—more than in any other American city. Dallas has one of the world's most famous fashion shops, Neiman-Marcus, one of the nation's biggest bookstores, and the Southwest's tallest skyscrapers. It is the home of Southern Methodist University, the Medical College of the University of Texas, and Baylor Dental School.

By the end of World War II the downtown section of Dallas contained many blocks of rundown buildings, its streets were cluttered with neon signs, and its traffic was a nightmare for motor-

XX · Cities and Culture

ists. A decade and a half later large areas of dilapidated buildings had been replaced with modern structures,[6] hundreds of overhead advertising signs along the principal downtown streets had been removed, and parking facilities to accommodate 40,000 automobiles had been constructed. A new expressway system and one-way traffic patterns had solved the major congestion—at least temporarily. If and when the $125,000,000 Exchange Park, an 120-acre business center planned for the 1960's, is completed, it will contain modern buildings, air-conditioned streets covered with glass, and beautiful malls.

Politically, Dallas is one of the most conservative cities in the Southwest, and its two great newspapers, the *Dallas News* and the *Dallas Times Herald,* vie with each other in support of reactionary ideas. In spite of its go-getting spirit, it also contains scattered slum areas, a high crime rate, and no medium through which issues of public concern can be argued. Major decisions of city planning are made by a junta of city bosses without public participation. This group of 175 members was chartered in 1937 as the Citizens Council; though it has performed outstanding services, its critics object that it constitutes an almost complete oligarchy and is not responsible to the public for its decisions. Its work frequently results in civic projects that cost $20,000,000 or more.

Although Dallas and Fort Worth are only thirty miles apart, they too could be in different states. Sophisticated Dallas speaks of itself as "the gateway to the East," while Fort Worth people call their city "the gateway to the West." Indeed, Fort Worth is one of the few cities in the Southwest where cattlemen in cowboy boots and hats are still common sights. Whereas Dallas is the mecca for bankers and merchants, Fort Worth serves the same purpose for cattlemen and oilmen. Dallas is larger, but Fort Worth is expanding rapidly. Its metropolitan population grew from 225,000 in 1940 to an estimated 600,000 in 1960, while the number of manufacturing plants increased from 300 to approximately 1,000.

---

[6] Since World War II Dallas has built more square feet of office space than any other city except New York—approximately seven million square feet, doubling what was available before.

The Southwest: *Old and New*

Dallas talks of itself as a financial and cultural center, but Fort Worth is equally proud of its reputation as "Cowtown, U.S.A." By 1955 it was the only city of major importance in the Southwest which did not support a symphony orchestra, though its Civic Opera Association now brings stars from the Metropolitan and other opera groups each fall for a three-month season. Most of the supporting roles are filled by local talent. Brochures published by the Fort Worth Chamber of Commerce devote no more than a few words to cultural advantages, but they emphasize the opportunities for entertainment, especially the new theater-in-the-round, Casa Mañana. During the three summer months this institution presents "spectacular stage productions which feature the prettiest dancers and showgirls." But Fort Worth's Southwestern Exposition and Fat Stock Show is the highlight of the year and attracts a larger audience than any rodeo in the United States except the annual performance at New York's Madison Square Garden.

Fort Worth people are proud also of their four small colleges and Texas Christian University. In addition, the city has an excellent municipal library that extends its services to remote sections by "bookmobiles," an Art Center, and a new Children's Museum.

Like its neighbor Dallas, Fort Worth has few natural resources at hand and is not located on a navigable stream. These facts alone are enough to dismay economic geographers, who predict that its population will exceed one million by 1975. The explanation of its spectacular growth can be found in cattle, grain, oil, and aircraft. The first of these has been important almost from the beginning, in 1849, when Fort Worth was a tiny outpost on the lonely frontier of northern Texas. Named after General William J. Worth, the commander of the Eighth and Ninth United States Military Department with headquarters in San Antonio, Fort Worth was established to protect settlers against the Indians.

Its location on a bluff overlooking the Trinity River became an important point on the old Chisholm Trail, along which Texans drove their herds to the Kansas railheads before the railroads

XX · Cities and Culture

reached the Lone Star State. From that beginning it grew to be one of the largest cattle centers in the United States. Its stockyards cover more than eighty acres and in 1958 handled approximately 600,000 cattle, 225,000 hogs, and more than 900,000 sheep. The nearby Swift and Armour packing plants are the largest in the Southwest.

The city whose motto is "Where the West Begins" also is the most important grain storage and milling center in the region and receives approximately 50,000 carloads of wheat annually from the wheatfields of western Texas. Though there is not a single producing oil well in the county where Fort Worth is situated, it is the center for the important oil fields of central Texas, the Panhandle, and western Texas, and it supports several major refineries and pipeline companies. But perhaps the major reason that the total number of people employed in manufacturing in Fort Worth increased from 80,000 in 1940 to 200,000 in 1960 is the presence of a General Dynamics plant where the B-58 supersonic Convair bombers are produced. Bell Helicopter Corporation is also located nearby.

Rivalry between Fort Worth and Dallas has been well advertised in the past, but urbanization is forcing them to work together on common problems. And Fort Worth has enough problems of its own without seeking further publicity from its historic feud with Dallas. Its most pressing problems as it enters the 1960's are modernizing its downtown section and untangling its traffic scramble.

In dealing with traffic Dallas began first, but Fort Worth is working on plans that perhaps will outdo its neighbor's. In addition to a network of freeways and bypasses currently under construction, Fort Worth expects to renovate its business district completely by 1965. The project, known as the "Gruen Plan," will eliminate traffic altogether in the downtown section—setting up instead a six-lane highway belt and parking space around the 370-acre business district. Inside this area, rundown buildings will be demolished and replaced by modern office structures, a cultural center, and tree-lined malls. These will be covered with glass and air-conditioned for the comfort of workers and shoppers as they go to and fro in electric carts.

Almost 300 miles south of the Dallas–Fort Worth area is the historic city of San Antonio, which in 1950 was the third-largest city in the Southwest with approximately 400,000 people. A decade later it had grown to 600,000, but its rank was being challenged by Fort Worth. Founded by the Spaniards the same year that the French laid out New Orleans (1718),[7] San Antonio has remained the most Spanish city in the United States and is mentioned along with San Francisco and New Orleans on any list of the most colorful and cosmopolitan cities. Its buildings are spread over hundreds of rolling acres, its streets are cramped and crooked, and many of its gracious old houses are hidden by skyscrapers and filling stations.

The main streets and plazas of San Antonio swarm with people of many races and cultures: Mexican peons in straw hats and rags, Army officers, privates, and Air Force Cadets, Spaniards of aristocratic backgrounds, millionaires, laborers, businessmen, beggars, marihuana peddlers, and prostitutes. Before World War II one out of every six San Antonio citizens was of German birth or descent and one out of four was Mexican. And almost from the time Texas entered the Union in 1845 San Antonio has been an Army town. The diversity of people, interests, and viewpoints has made the Alamo City the scene of many bitter battles. After the struggle with knives, swords, pistols, muskets, and cannon ended in the nineteenth century, the political wars continued. Few cities in America can match San Antonio's history of political corruption, turbulence, and feuds between the "outs" and the "ins," though recently it is showing signs of mellowness and maturity.

San Antonio has an attractive atmosphere, and several things contribute to its $40,000,000 annual tourist business. It has the

---

[7] San Antonio was named twenty-seven years earlier by the Spanish explorer Domingo Ramón because he arrived at the site on the Saint's Day of San Antonio de Padua, en route to the eastern boundary of the Texas province.

XX · Cities and Culture

Alamo, where the early heroes died for Texas independence, Spanish missions that have been in continuous use for more than two centuries, Brackenridge Park, a major zoological garden created from the bed of an abandoned rock quarry, the palace occupied by Spanish governors, and the winding San Antonio River and La Villita.

Perhaps none of these has been of more importance in saving the town from conformity to the usual American city plan than the little San Antonio River, which meanders through the heart of the business district. The stream passes under more than forty bridges and is a haven of calmness in spite of the din of traffic above. Mexican restaurants with outdoor tables and art and craft shops line both banks, while here and there are terraced spots where people gather for plays and operettas, listen to orations, or admire works of local artists. Some take leisurely rides along the stream in Spanish gondolas; others lie on the grassy slopes and enjoy the "perpetual" sunshine or stroll along the river walks below street level. The stream itself is illuminated at night by colored lights set beneath the water.

Near the southern edge of the San Antonio River is La Villita, originally a native Indian village and later one of San Antonio's worst slums. With the help of NYA and Carnegie money Mayor Maury Maverick cleaned out the slums prior to World War II and restored the old buildings. The place eventually emerged as a cultural center where Latin American youths are taught crafts and trades and Spanish and Mexican arts and customs are preserved. La Villita is more than a tourist attraction—it is an authentic part of the past which flourishes in the present-day world.

Higher education in San Antonio is entirely church-endowed, with two Protestant and four Roman Catholic colleges. And because of its large Latin and Irish population the city has more Catholic churches—forty-three—than any other Southwestern metropolitan area. There are two or three good museums, ten public libraries, the McNay Art Institute, and the San Antonio Opera, Symphony, and Little Theater.

San Antonio is a leading center of Latin American trade, as well as meat-packing, agriculture, oil, tourism, and manufacturing. It is also advancing rapidly as one of the nation's leading medical centers. But its military bases constitute the principal source of local income. These have a total military personnel exceeding 50,000, a civilian employment in excess of 36,000, and an annual payroll of $300,000,000.

More than 500 miles due west of San Antonio is El Paso, another Southwestern center of Spanish origin. Few other large cities in the nation are so far removed from every other populous area, but El Paso is less isolated than it appears, for it is a business and industrial center for the vast reach of barren land around it. Until the recent growth of Albuquerque it remained the great market place for all New Mexico, western Texas, and northern Mexico. In 1960 the population of this crossroads of the Southwest approached 300,000—three times its size in 1940. It is a modern city with the businesslike air of a miniature Chicago, and it makes no particular point of its romantic past.

Various Spanish travelers passed the site of El Paso during the seventeenth century en route to Santa Fe and other northern outposts. In 1659 Father García de San Francisco and Juan de Salazar settled ten families of Christianized Indians on the south bank of the Rio Grande and erected the mission Nuestra Señora de Guadalupe del Paso. Three hamlets grew up in the vicinity, and by the end of the century they counted approximately 200 settlers. As traffic between Chihuahua and Santa Fe increased in the eighteenth century, the settlements merged into El Paso del Norte (modern Juárez) and became a thriving community of 2,000 merchants, ranchers, and peons. Missouri traders were soon passing through en route to Chihuahua with wagonloads of goods, some of which they traded to local residents.

Colonel A. W. Doniphan and his Missouri Volunteers captured the place during the Mexican War in 1847, before moving on to northern Mexico. By 1850 an American merchant, James Wiley Magoffin, had established himself on the United States side of the river and given the name of Magoffinville to the post office

XX · *Cities and Culture*

and store he operated. About the same time another American, Franklin Coons, acquired a ranch in the vicinity which covered most of the downtown district of modern El Paso. Eventually the region became known as Franklin, and by 1858 as El Paso. Meanwhile the California gold rush and the Butterfield Overland coaches gave impetus to the town's growth. By the 1880's it was tied to faraway Los Angeles, Denver, Fort Worth, and New Orleans by four railroads and was the crossroads of the continent. Its destiny still lies in its location.

The early years of El Paso's history were notable for lawlessness and disorder, raids by Mescalero Apaches and Mexican banditti, and the many saloons and gambling houses in the town. Lawlessness, Apaches, and banditti soon passed, and the saloons and gambling houses confined their operation to El Paso's twin city, Juárez, across the river. The once predominant Mexican population has been reduced to a minority by the Anglo-Americans who have arrived since World War II to work in the air bases, guided-missile developments, electronic-device manufacturing, and textile factories.

Unlike many Texas cities, El Paso values people of Mexican blood—for business reasons if for no other. Its bilingual heritage has kept it more tolerant than most Southwestern cities, and it was one of the first to oppose the power of the Ku Klux Klan in Texas politics in 1921. El Pasoans also rejected the demagoguery of W. Lee O'Daniel, and they gave a solid majority to their liberal native son Ralph Yarborough on the three occasions when he was defeated for the governorship. On the other hand, it is doubtful whether any other newspaper—even in Texas—can match the conservative philosophy frequently expressed on the editorial pages of the *El Paso Times*.

El Paso has long depended on cotton, cattle, copper, and tourism. With irrigation it has grown into one of the great cotton markets of the country, and its ore smelters vie in importance with those of Montana. Manufacturing has long since replaced cattle as the most important business, but it still provides flavor for the city's character. Like San Antonio, it is an Army town and, like most Southwestern cities, it has become culture conscious. The local symphony conducts "under-the-stars" concerts during the summer months, and the Community Playhouse offers stage productions the year round. El Paso has some outstanding writers and artists, the most famous of whom are Tom Lea and C. L. Sonnichsen, and Carl Hertzog, a member of the faculty of El Paso's Texas Western College, is one of the best-known typographers in the United States.

There are other Texas cities whose growth has been phenomenal since 1940 and which are expected to become great metropolitan centers by 1975. Among these are Amarillo, Lubbock, Waco, Austin, Corpus Christi, Midland, Beaumont, and Wichita Falls.[8] The populations of these cities ranged from 30,000 to 80,000 before the United States entered World War II. Austin, Waco, and Beaumont doubled in population during the next twenty years, Amarillo, Corpus Christi, and Wichita Falls experienced a threefold increase, and Lubbock expanded fivefold.

ALL OF THE major Southwestern cities have followed similar patterns in their development and experienced common problems that accompany rapid growth. All are hard pressed to finance new schools, find adequate parking space, extend city facilities to new subdivisions, and route through traffic around town while solving the problem of local transportation.

Until World War II it was easy to maintain that the Southwest remained detached, provincial, and different from the rest

---

[8] Another Texas city that ranked among this group in 1940 is Galveston. Its population that year stood at 60,000, and in 1960 at 74,000. Its failure to expand with others of comparable size is attributed to several factors: it is located on an island and has limited room to expand; nearby Houston has taken most of its port trade; it is not a desirable location for military bases; and its climate and frequent hurricanes discourage industrial development.

XX · Cities and Culture

of the United States. But this is no longer true. The pattern by which American society changed from pioneer to urban civilization is clearly visible in the modern Southwest. Though its cities are newer, cleaner, and more dispersed than those in most regions of the country, they are chiefly remarkable for the rapidity with which they have grown into large islands of business, industry, and culture. As each city acquires more factories, annexes more land, builds newer expressways, supports more cultural institutions, and raises more revenue, it tends to become more like other metropolitan centers. If the present trend continues, the Southwest someday may offer few distinctive characteristics—other than climate and geography.

BIBLIOGRAPHICAL NOTES

I · LAND OF CONTRAST

Rupert Norval Richardson and Carl Coke Rister: *The Greater Southwest* (Glendale, California: Arthur H. Clark; 1935) provides an adequate description of the geography and climate of the Southwest. More detailed geographic information is found in C. Langdon White and Edwin J. Foscue: *Regional Geography of Anglo-America* (Second Edition, New York: Prentice-Hall; 1954), though the Southwest is treated as parts of several regions rather than as a separate one. Walter P. Webb: *The Great Plains* (Boston: Ginn and Company; 1931) analyzes the climate, the flora and fauna, and the resulting culture of the Great Plains area, including the Southwestern states of Oklahoma, Texas, and New Mexico.

Definitions, descriptions, and interpretations of the Southwest are found in Erna Fergusson: *Our Southwest* (New York: Alfred A. Knopf; 1952); Walter Campbell: *The Book Lover's Southwest* (Norman: University of Oklahoma Press; 1955); Green Peyton: *America's Heartland: The Southwest* (Norman: University of Oklahoma Press; 1948); and The Editors of *Look: Look at America: The Southwest* (Boston: Houghton Mifflin; 1946), II.

Difficulties of defining the Southwest as a cultural region are discussed by John Caughey: "The Spanish Southwest," in Merrill Jensen (ed.): *Regionalism in America* (Madison: University of

Wisconsin Press; 1952), and by J. Frank Dobie: *Guide to Life and Literature of the Southwest* (Dallas: Southern Methodist University Press; 1952). And among the best descriptions of the Southwest is Walter P. Webb: "The American West: Perpetual Mirage," *Harper's*, May 1957.

II · BEFORE THE WHITE MAN

Much has been written about the ancient civilizations of the Southwest. Among the most readable accounts are Fergusson: *Our Southwest;* Adolph Bandelier and Edgar L. Hewett: *Indians of the Rio Grande Valley* (Albuquerque: University of New Mexico Press; 1937); Edgar L. Hewett: *Ancient Life in the American Southwest* (Indianapolis: The Bobbs-Merrill Company; 1930). In Hewett's later work: *The Chaco Canyon and Its Monuments* (Albuquerque: University of New Mexico Press; 1936) he describes the ruins of the great communal houses and ceremonial chambers in Chaco Canyon, New Mexico, as the greatest on the continent north of the Aztec empire.

Walter P. Webb discusses the Plains Indians of the Southwest before the white man arrived in *The Great Plains*. Frederick Webb Hodge: *The Early Navajo and Apache* (Washington: Judd & Detweiler; 1895) remains the most authoritative study of American ethnology in the Southwest. A serious study of the Comanches is Ernest Wallace and E. Adamson Hoebel: *The Comanches: Lords of the South Plains* (Norman: University of Oklahoma Press; 1952). Muriel H. Wright: *A Guide to the Indian Tribes of Oklahoma* (Norman: University of Oklahoma Press; 1951), an encyclopedic treatment of the sixty-seven Indian tribes in Oklahoma, presents most of those who inhabited the Southwest at various times. Minor tribes such as the Pima, Hopi, and Yuma are treated in Frederick Webb Hodge: *Handbook of American Indians North of Mexico. Bureau of American Ethnology, Bulletin* 30 (2 vols., Washington; 1907–12).

Edward E. Dale: *The Indians of the Southwest* (Norman: University of Oklahoma Press: 1949) deals with developments

Bibliographical Notes

among major New Mexico and Arizona tribes in the past century. Interesting observations about the smaller tribes of Arizona at the beginning of the Anglo-Saxon period are found in Edward S. Wallace: *The Great Reconnaissance* (Boston: Little, Brown and Company; 1955). Another secondary source on Southwestern Indians during the nineteenth century is my own work: *Beyond the Cross Timbers: The Travels of Randolph B. Marcy* (Norman: University of Oklahoma Press; 1955).

III · FIRST CAME THE SPANIARDS

One of the most readable sources, in English translation, on the first white men in the Southwest is Herbert Eugene Bolton (ed.): *Spanish Explorations in the Southwest* (New York: Charles Scribner's Sons; 1916). Another Bolton work based on original manuscripts is *Kino's Historical Memoir of Pimería Alta* (Berkeley: University of California Press; 1948). The best account of Coronado's journey through the Southwest is one by Pedro Castañeda de Nagera, translated and edited by George Parker Winship: *The Journey of Francisco Vásquez de Coronado, 1540–1542* (New York: A. S. Barnes; 1904). Another excellent translation is George P. Hammond and Agapito Rey (eds.): *Narratives of Coronado Expedition 1540–1542* (Albuquerque: University of New Mexico Press; 1940).

Several accounts of Cabeza de Vaca's adventures in Texas have been published. One of the easiest to read is Morris Bishop: *Odyssey of Cabeza de Vaca* (New York: Century; 1933). *The Journey of Fray Marcos de Niza*, by Cleve Hallenbeck, tells in English the story of Cabeza de Vaca's Negro companion and his association with the Coronado expedition (Dallas: Southern Methodist University Press; 1949). The original documents of Oñate's colonizing efforts in New Mexico have been translated by George P. Hammond: *Don Juan de Oñate, Colonizer of New Mexico, 1596–1628* (Albuquerque: University of New Mexico Press; 1953). Practically all of the significant Spanish explorers and colonizers of the Southwest are discussed in Paul Horgan:

THE SOUTHWEST: *Old and New*

Great River: The Rio Grande in North American History (2 vols.: New York: Rinehart and Company; 1954). Horgan re-creates the ebb and flow of human destiny up and down the Rio Grande, from the time of the Basket Makers to that of the Bomb Builders.

IV · APPROACH AND RETREAT OF THE FRENCH

Accounts of the French intrusion in the Southwest are far scarcer than those of the Spaniards because the French barely penetrated the area, had little lasting effect on its culture, and left few records. Activities of French colonizers, explorers, and traders are interestingly synthesized in Herbert Eugene Bolton and Thomas Maitland Marshall: *The Colonization of North America, 1492–1783* (New York: The Macmillan Company; 1920). Francis Parkman: *La Salle and the Discovery of the Great West* (Boston: Little, Brown and Company; 1869) contains several chapters on La Salle's ill-fated ventures in Texas. Single chapters dealing with the French in the Southwest are contained in John Bartlet Brebner: *The Explorers of North America* (New York: The Macmillan Company; 1933); LeRoy R. Hafen and Carl Coke Rister: *Western America* (New York; Prentice-Hall; 1941); and Green Peyton: *America's Heartland: The Southwest* (Norman: University of Oklahoma Press; 1948).

The Franco-Spanish conflicts for control of the Southwest are described in scholarly articles by Isaac J. Cox: "The Significance of the Louisiana-Texas Frontier," *Mississippi Valley Historical Association Proceedings*, III (1909–10); William E. Dunn: "Spanish Reaction against the French Advance towards New Mexico, 1717–1727," *Mississippi Valley Historical Review*, II (December 1915); Louise P. Kellogg: "France and the Mississippi Valley: A Résumé," *Mississippi Valley Historical Review*, XVIII (June 1931); William E. Dunn: "French and Spanish Rivalry in the Gulf Region of the United States, 1678–1702," University of Texas *Bulletin* (Austin, 1917); and Frederick Webb Hodge: "French Intrusion toward New Mexico in 1695," *New Mexico Historical Review*, IV (January 1929).

Bibliographical Notes

A significant study of French traders in Oklahoma is Elizabeth Ann Harper: "The Trade and Diplomacy of the Taovayas Indians on the Northern Frontier of New Spain, 1719–1835," M.A. thesis, University of Oklahoma (1951).

V · ANGLO-AMERICANS COME TO STAY

The most complete and original study of the Anglo-American filibusters in the Southwest during the early nineteenth century is J. Villasana Haggard: "The Neutral Ground between Louisiana and Texas, 1806–1821," Ph.D. dissertation, University of Texas (1942). Several Texas histories contain chapters on the era of the Texas filibusters, notably: Rupert N. Richardson: *Texas: The Lone Star State* (New York: Prentice-Hall; 1943); Henderson Yoakum: *History of Texas from Its First Settlement in 1685 to Its Annexation to the United States in 1846* (2 vols., New York: Redfield; 1856); and G. P. Garrison: *Texas: A Contest of Civilizations* (Boston: Houghton Mifflin Company; 1903).

The interesting adventures of one of the first Anglo-Americans in the Southwest are told in W. P. Yoakum (ed.): *Memoirs of Colonel Ellis P. Bean* (Houston: The Book Club of Texas; 1930). Several editions of the journals of Zebulon Montgomery Pike, the first official Anglo-American explorer in the Southwest, are in print; the most useful for my purposes has been Stephen H. Hart and Archer B. Hulbert (eds.): *Zebulon Montgomery Pike's Arkansaw Journal* (Denver: Denver Public Library; 1932).

The activities of Sir William Dunbar and Dr. George Hunter on the Southwestern frontier are adequately covered in I. J. Cox: *The Early Exploration of Louisiana* (Cincinnati: University of Cincinnati Press; 1906). Major Stephen H. Long's sojourn in New Mexico and Oklahoma is described in Edwin James (ed.): *Account of an Expedition from Pittsburg to the Rocky Mountains in the Years 1819, 1820* (Glendale: Arthur H. Clark; 1905). Harrison Clifford Dale: *The Ashley-Smith Exploration and the Discovery of a Central Route to the Pacific, 1822–1829* (Glendale: Arthur H. Clark; 1918) covers the fur-trading adventures of

THE SOUTHWEST: *Old and New*

Jedediah S. Smith in Arizona in 1826. The Pattie party crossed the Southwest en route to California before 1830, and its adventures are told in Timothy Flint (ed.): *The Personal Narrative of James O. Pattie* (Chicago: R. R. Donnelley & Sons; 1930). Dozens of books on the Santa Fe trade have appeared; among the more recent popular histories is R. L. Duffus: *The Santa Fé Trail* (New York: Longmans, Green; 1930).

The leading authority on the American colonization of Texas is Eugene C. Barker, whose *Life of Stephen F. Austin* (Nashville and Dallas: Cokesbury Press; 1925) is the standard work on the subject. Activities of white traders in Oklahoma in the early nineteenth century are covered briefly in Edwin C. McReynolds: *Oklahoma: A History of the Sooner State* (Norman: University of Oklahoma Press; 1954). The concentration of the Five Civilized Tribes in Oklahoma is given a thorough treatment in Grant Foreman: *A History of Oklahoma* (Norman: University of Oklahoma Press; 1942).

VI · THE CLASH OF CIVILIZATIONS

At least a hundred articles on the Texas Revolution may be found in the files of the *Quarterly of the Texas State Historical Association*, I-XV, and *The Southwestern Historical Quarterly*, vols. XVI-LXII, published at Austin. Among the general works on the Texas revolution are G. P. Garrison: *Texas: A Contest of Civilizations* (Boston: Houghton Mifflin Company; 1903); Richardson: *The Lone Star State;* Richardson and Rister: *The Greater Southwest;* Yoakum: *History of Texas;* Louis J. Wortham: *A History of Texas: From Wilderness to Commonwealth*, I-V (Fort Worth: Molyneaux; 1924).

Political developments during the period of the Texas Republic (1836–46) are treated in Marquis James: *The Raven: A Biography of Sam Houston* (Indianapolis: The Bobbs-Merrill Company; 1929); G. P. Garrison (ed.): *Texan Diplomatic Correspondence*, American Historical Association *Annual Report for 1907 and 1908*, I-III (Washington; 1908–11); Herbert Gambrell:

Bibliographical Notes

Anson Jones: The Last President of Texas (Garden City: Doubleday and Company; 1948); Gambrell: *Mirabeau Bounaparte Lamar: Troubadour and Crusader* (Dallas: Southwest Press; 1934); Stanley Siegel: *A Political History of the Texas Republic, 1836–1845* (Austin: University of Texas Press; 1956); Donald Day (ed.): *The Autobiography of Sam Houston* (Norman: University of Oklahoma Press; 1954); Llerena Friend: *Sam Houston: The Great Designer* (Austin: University of Texas Press; 1954); W. Eugene Hollon (ed.): *William Bollaert's Texas* (Norman: University of Oklahoma Press; 1956).

The standard work on annexation of Texas to the Union is Justin Smith: *Annexation of Texas* (New York: Baker and Taylor; 1911).

VII · LIFE AND CULTURE IN THE TEXAS REPUBLIC

Most of the above-mentioned books on Texas contain sidelights on the cultural and social developments of the infant republic. The most complete single volume is William R. Hogan: *The Texas Republic: A Social and Economic History* (Norman: University of Oklahoma Press; 1946). Among the standard works by contemporary observers are William Kennedy: *Texas: The Rise, Progress and Prospects of the Republic of Texas,* I-II (London: R. Haskins; 1841); Nicholas Doran P. Maillard: *A History of the Republic of Texas* (London: Smith-Elder; 1842); Mary Austin Holley: *Letters of an Early American Traveller, Mary Austin Holley: Her Life and Works, 1786–1846,* edited by Mattie Austin Hatcher (Dallas: Southwest Press; 1933); and Francis Cynric Sheridan: *Galveston Island, 1839–1840,* edited by Willis W. Pratt (Austin: University of Texas Press; 1954).

Hundreds of personal memoirs and scholarly articles relating to education, literature, social conditions, and pioneer life in the Texas Republic have been published in the *Quarterly of the Texas State Historical Association* and the *Southwest Historical Quarterly*. The two-volume *Handbook of Texas,* edited by Walter Prescott Webb (Austin: The Texas Historical Association; 1952),

THE SOUTHWEST: *Old and New*

contains thousands of brief articles relating to various facets of life in the Republic.

VIII · THE MEXICAN CESSION

The most thorough study of relations between the United States and Mexico preceding the outbreak of the war is George L. Rives: *The United States and Mexico, 1821–1848* (2 vols., New York: Charles Scribner's Sons; 1913). Individual chapters on the same subject are found in the general diplomatic histories of the United States, two of the best-known of which are Thomas A. Bailey: *A Diplomatic History of the American People* (New York: F. S. Croft; 1958) and Samuel Flagg Bemis: *A Diplomatic History of the United States* (New York: Henry Holt; 1955).

The definitive work on the campaigns and individual battles of the Mexican War is Justin H. Smith: *The War with Mexico* (2 vols., New York: The Macmillan Company; 1919). Excellent summaries of the principal campaigns are found in Ray Allen Billington's extensive *Westward Expansion* (New York: The Macmillan Company; 1949) and his more recent *The Far Western Frontier, 1830–1860* (New York: Harper & Brothers; 1956). The best analysis of the expansionism that resulted in the acquisition of the Southwest by the United States is Albert K. Weinberg: *Manifest Destiny: A Study of Nationalist Expansionism in American History* (Baltimore: Johns Hopkins Press; 1935).

A popular account of the war, with special emphasis on events in Texas, New Mexico, and Arizona, is Paul I. Wellman: *Glory, God, and Gold* (Garden City: Doubleday and Company; 1954). Even more fascinating is the *Mexican War Memoirs of Samuel E. Chamberlain,* published in three installments in *Life* in 1956 (July 23, July 30, August 6). Important memoirs of soldiers attached to the romantic Doniphan and Kearny expeditions have been edited by Ralph P. Bieber: *Journal of a Soldier under Kearny and Doniphan, 1846–1847* (Glendale: Arthur H. Clark; 1935).

Bibliographical Notes

IX · THE IMPACT OF GOLD ON THE SOUTHWEST

A brief account of mining in the Southwest is discussed in Richardson and Rister: *The Greater Southwest*. Less scholarly but more interesting reading is Wellman: *Glory, God, and Gold*. H. H. Bancroft: *History of Arizona and New Mexico, 1530–1888* (San Francisco: The History Company; 1889) is still the best work on early mining activities in the Southwest. Many diaries and memoirs of gold seekers who crossed the Southwest to California gold fields have been published; one that describes life during the rush in especially vivid terms is Clement Eaton (ed.): "Frontier Life in Southern Arizona, 1858–1861," *Southwestern Historical Quarterly*, XXXVI (January 1933).

In Ralph P. Bieber (ed.): *Southern Trails to California in 1849* (Glendale: Arthur H. Clark; 1937) and "The Southwestern Trails to California in 1849," *The Mississippi Valley Historical Review*, XII (December 1925), the gold trails across Oklahoma, Texas, New Mexico, and Arizona are described in considerable detail. Grant Foreman: *Marcy and the Gold Seekers* (Norman: University of Oklahoma Press; 1939) identifies the geographic place names along Marcy's Canadian River route between Fort Smith and Santa Fe and the return journey across southeastern New Mexico, western Texas, and southeastern Oklahoma, *1849–50*. Descriptions of these two trails, along with stories of hardships experienced by gold seekers in the Southwest, are found in my own work: *Beyond the Cross Timbers: The Travels of Randolph B. Marcy* (Norman: University of Oklahoma Press; 1955).

The significance of the Gadsden Purchase to Southwestern routes is found in Paul N. Garber: *The Gadsden Treaty* (Philadelphia: Press of the University of Pennsylvania; 1924). And three articles by J. Fred Rippy pertinent to the subject are: "The Boundary of New Mexico and the Gadsden Treaty," *Hispanic American Historical Review*, IV (November 1921); "Anglo-American Filibusters and the Gadsden Treaty," *Hispanic American Historical Review*, V (May 1922); and "The Negotiation of the

THE SOUTHWEST: *Old and New*

Gadsden Treaty," *Southwestern Historical Quarterly*, XXVII (July 1923). Activities of official surveyors, explorers, and boundary commissioners in southern Arizona and New Mexico during the middle of the nineteenth century are interestingly summarized in Edwin S. Wallace: *The Great Reconnaissance, 1848–1861* (Boston: Little, Brown and Company; 1955).

Establishment of military posts throughout the Southwest in the wake of the gold seekers is discussed in Billington: *Westward Expansion* and *The Far Western Frontier, 1830–1860*. Rufus Kay Wyllys: *Arizona: The History of a Frontier State* (Phoenix: Hobson & Herr; 1950) describes the arrival of the first Anglo-American settlers in Arizona and early attempts to organize a government.

X · COACHES AND CAMELS

Historical developments in transportation in the Southwest are covered in Billington: *Westward Expansion;* Richardson and Rister: *The Greater Southwest;* W. Turrentine Jackson: *Wagon Roads West* (Berkeley: University of California Press; 1952); Samuel L. Clemens: *Roughing It* (New York: Harper & Brothers; 1871); Robert E. Riegel: *The Story of Western Railroads* (New York: The Macmillan Company; 1926); Wallace: *The Great Reconnaissance, 1848–1861;* Wyllys: *Arizona: The History of a Frontier State;* and in various general histories of the West.

The sectional struggle over subsidies for an overland mail service is treated in Curtis Nettels: "The Overland Mail Issue in the Fifties," *Mississippi Valley Review*, XVIII (July 1924). LeRoy R. Hafen: *The Overland Mail, 1849–1869* (Cleveland: Arthur H. Clark; 1926) is one of the most scholarly works on the whole subject of Western mail routes.

Two books have been published on the Butterfield Overland Mail route across the Southwest. A contemporary account by Waterman L. Ormsby, which appeared as a series of newspaper articles, has recently been issued in book form, edited by Lyle H. Wright and Josephine M. Bynum: *The Butterfield Overland Mail*

Bibliographical Notes

(San Marino: The Huntington Library; 1955). The subject is treated more authoritatively in Roscoe Conkling and Margaret B. Conkling: *The Butterfield Overland Mail, 1858–1869* (Glendale: Arthur H. Clark; 1946). There are several articles on the subject, including Rupert N. Richardson: "Some Details of the Southern Overland Mail," *Southwestern Historical Quarterly*, XXIX (July 1925), and J. W. Williams: "The Butterfield Overland Mail Road across Texas," *The Southwestern Historical Quarterly*, LXI (July 1957). A popular account of the episode is my own: "Great Days of the Overland Stage," *American Heritage*, VIII (June 1957).

The story of the camel experiment in the Southwest is told in Cris Emmett: *Texas Camel Tales* (San Antonio: The Naylor Company; 1933); Senate Executive Document No. 43, 35th Congress, 1st Session; and House Executive Document No. 124, 35th Congress, 1st Session. Also in Frank Bishop Lammons: "Operation Camel: An Experiment in Animal Transportation in Texas, 1857–1860," *Southwestern Historical Quarterly*, XLI (July 1957).

XI · THE SOUTHWEST AND THE CIVIL WAR

The Civil War in the Southwest has received scant attention from historians, though single chapters on the subject appear in various general and state histories. Richardson and Rister in *The Greater Southwest* confine their discussion to fighting in Texas and the Confederate invasion of New Mexico. And Bancroft: *History of Arizona and New Mexico, 1530–1888* is less comprehensive in covering the Civil War than in dealing with most other subjects.

The war in Oklahoma is given adequate coverage in Edward Everett Dale and Morris L. Wardell: *History of Oklahoma* (New York: Prentice-Hall; 1948) and Edwin C. McReynolds: *Oklahoma: A History of the Sooner State* (Norman: University of Oklahoma Press; 1954). The wartime activities of the Five Civilized Tribes are described by Annie H. Abel: "The Indians in the Civil War," *American Historical Review*, XV (March 1910).

All of the general histories of Texas contain one or more chap-

THE SOUTHWEST: *Old and New*

ters on the Civil War in this region, but the most complete accounts are in Yoakum: *History of Texas* and Wortham: *A History of Texas: From Wilderness to Commonwealth*. A record of most of the campaigns in Texas is contained in Joseph P. Blessington: *The Campaigns of Walker's Texas Division* (New York: privately printed; 1875). Good brief accounts are found in the following articles: W. C. Holden: "Frontier Defense in Texas during the Civil War," West Texas Historical Association *Yearbook*, IV (Abilene; 1928), and C. W. Ramsdell: "The Frontier and Secession," Columbia University *Studies in Southern History and Politics* (1914).

Frank C. Lockwood: *Pioneer Days in Arizona* (New York: The Macmillan Company; 1932) gives brief coverage to the war in Arizona, while Wyllys is only slightly more detailed in his *Arizona: The History of a Frontier State*. The best account of fighting in New Mexico to be found among the state-published histories is in Ralph Emerson Twitchell: *The Leading Facts of New Mexico History* (Cedar Rapids: The Torch Press; 1912).

Paul Wellman: *Glory, God, and Gold* is colorful and entertaining but superficial on the Civil War fighting in Texas, New Mexico, and Arizona. On the other hand, Ray C. Colton: *Civil War in the Western Territories* (Norman: University of Oklahoma Press; 1959) is a scholarly and detailed study of the major campaigns in New Mexico and Arizona.

XII · LONGHORNS AND WOOLLIES

One of the best single chapters on the cattle industry in the Southwest is in Billington's *Westward Expansion*, while adequate coverage is found in Richardson and Rister: *The Greater Southwest*; Webb: *The Great Plains*; Peyton: *America's Heartland: The Southwest*; Wellman: *Glory, God, and Gold*; and, indeed, in practically every scholarly and popular history of the West. Three standard books that tell the story thoroughly are: Ernest S. Osgood: *The Day of the Cattleman* (Minneapolis: University of Minnesota Press; 1929); Edward E. Dale: *The Range Cattle In-*

Bibliographical Notes

dustry (Norman: University of Oklahoma Press; 1930); and Louis Pelzer: *The Cattleman's Frontier* (Glendale: Arthur H. Clark; 1936).

A thorough but old study on the origins of Texas ranching is Clara M. Love: "History of the Cattle Industry in the Southwest," *Southwestern Historical Quarterly*, XIX (April 1916) and XX (July 1916). J. Frank Dobie: *A Vaquero of the Brush Country* (Dallas: The Southwest Press; 1929) gives a colorful description of wild-cattle roundups along the Rio Grande. Helpful biographies of leading Southwestern ranchers are J. Evetts Haley: *Charles Goodnight, Cowman and Plainsman* (Norman: University of Oklahoma Press; 1949), and *George W. Littlefield, Texan* (Norman: University of Oklahoma Press; 1943). Good histories of the two largest Southwestern ranches are Haley: *The XIT Ranch and the Early Days of the Llano Estacado* (Chicago: The Lakeside Press; 1929) and Tom Lea: *The King Ranch* (Boston: Little, Brown and Company; 1957).

The classic book on the cattle drives is a plotless narrative based on factual events by Andy Adams: *The Log of a Cowboy* (New York: Houghton Mifflin Company; 1903). A more recent and well-documented study is Wayne Gard: *The Chisholm Trail* (Norman: University of Oklahoma Press; 1954). But the definitive work on the subject is John Marvin Hunter (ed.): *The Trail Drivers of Texas* (2 vols., San Antonio: Jackson Printing Company; 1920).

The standard work on the history of the sheep industry is Charles W. Towne and Edward N. Wentworth: *Shepherd's Empire* (Norman: University of Oklahoma Press; 1945). A description of cattle and sheep raising in New Mexico as practiced in both the past and the present is contained in Erna Fergusson: *New Mexico: A Pageant of Three Peoples* (New York: Alfred A. Knopf; 1951). Here, as in Arizona, the industry still retains some of the flavor of the days of the open range.

XIII · COMPLETION OF STATEHOOD

Several good histories of Oklahoma trace developments from the first white settlement to territorial status and finally to statehood. The most complete work is Joseph B. Thoburn and Muriel H. Wright: *Oklahoma: A History of the State and Its People* (4 vols., New York: Lewis Historical Publishing Company; 1929). An older but more scholarly study is Roy Gittinger: *The Formation of the State of Oklahoma, 1803–1906* (Norman: University of Oklahoma Press; 1939), yet it concentrates on the Five Civilized Tribes and stops on the eve of statehood. Grant Foreman: *A History of Oklahoma* (Norman: University of Oklahoma Press; 1942) represents solid scholarship and offers a reliable chronology of historical events.

The story of the "boomers" in Oklahoma is told in Carl Coke Rister: *Land Hunger: David L. Payne and the Oklahoma Boomers* (Norman: University of Oklahoma Press; 1942). One of the most exciting accounts of the first "run" into Oklahoma is James D. Horan: "Thus the Frontier Vanished," *Collier's*, November 9, 1956. And the two standard textbooks that cover Oklahoma from earliest times to the present are Dale and Wardell: *History of Oklahoma* and McReynolds: *Oklahoma: A History of the Sooner State*.

An adequate history of political developments in New Mexico from the end of the Spanish period to the present does not exist. Twitchell: *Leading Facts of New Mexico History* contains valuable material on the territorial period, as does Cleve Hallenbeck: *Land of the Conquistadores* (Caldwell, Idaho: The Caxton Printers; 1950). Brief syntheses of political developments leading to statehood for New Mexico and Arizona are found in *New Mexico: A Guide to a Colorful State* (New York: Hastings House; 1940) and *Arizona: A State Guide* (New York: Hastings House; 1940).

Two recent general histories of Arizona that contain chapters on territorial and state politics are Wyllys: *Arizona: The History*

Bibliographical Notes

of a Frontier State and Edward Haddock Peplow: *History of Arizona* (New York: Lewis Historical Publishing Company; 1958).

XIV · THE CHANGING INDIAN

No comprehensive history of the various Indian tribes during the twentieth century exists. The most comprehensive reference work on the subject before 1912 is Frederick Webb Hodge: *Handbook of American Indians North of Mexico* (Bureau of American Ethnology, *Bulletin* No. 30, 2 vols., Washington, D.C.; 1907–12). Muriel H. Wright has done a similar encyclopedic treatment of the sixty-seven Indian tribes in Oklahoma which describes their contemporary life and culture: *A Guide to the Indian Tribes of Oklahoma* (Norman: University of Oklahoma Press; 1951). Edward E. Dale: *The Indians of the Southwest* (Norman: University of Oklahoma Press; 1949) deals with the reservation Indians of New Mexico and Arizona during the past century and excludes entirely the Oklahoma and Texas tribes.

Angie Debo: *The Road to Disappearance* (Norman: University of Oklahoma Press; 1941) describes the changing Indians in Oklahoma since their removal, with particular emphasis on the Choctaws. Peyton: *America's Heartland: The Southwest* has an excellent interpretative chapter or two on the same subject, as does John Gunther: *Inside U.S.A.* (New York: Harper & Brothers; 1947). The small Alabama-Coushatta Indian reservation in Texas is adequately discussed in various articles in Walter P. Webb (ed.): *The Handbook of Texas* (Austin: The Texas State Historical Association; 1952). The establishment and failure of the reservation system for the wild tribes of Texas is discussed in Carl Coke Rister: *Southern Plainsman* (Norman: University of Oklahoma Press; 1938).

Writings and interpretative studies on the Pueblo Indians are legion. Among the works I have consulted on the subject of the changing Indian are Adolph Bandelier and Edgar L. Hewett: *Indians of the Rio Grande Valley* (Albuquerque: University of New

Mexico Press; 1937); Adolph Bandelier: *Final Report of the Investigations among the Indians of the Southwestern United States* (2 vols., Cambridge: J. Wilson & Sons; 1890–2); Erna Fergusson: *New Mexico: A Pageant of Three Peoples* and *Our Southwest* (New York: Alfred A. Knopf; 1940). Also, Oliver LaFarge (ed.): *The Changing Indian* (Norman: University of Oklahoma Press; 1942).

The social, political, and economic history of the largest Southwestern reservation tribe has been covered expertly in Ruth M. Underhill: *The Navajos* (Norman: University of Oklahoma Press; 1956). Additional information on the problems, progress, and education of the Navajo is found in Robert W. Young (ed.): *The Navajo Yearbook of Planning in Action* (Window Rock, Arizona: Navajo Agency; 1955). Similar works on other important reservation tribes are Walter Collins O'Kane: *The Hopis: Portrait of a Desert People* (Norman: University of Oklahoma Press; 1953) and C. L. Sonnichsen: *The Mescalero Apaches* (Norman: University of Oklahoma Press; 1958).

Recent articles about the reservation tribes have appeared in various popular magazines; one of the most significant is Dorothy Van de Mark: "The Raid on the Reservations," *Harper's*, March 1956.

XV · DESERT AND OASIS

References to droughts and desert conditions in the Southwest are found in the published journals of early American explorers and travelers, but none contains extensive information on the subject. Webb: *The Great Plains* contains a chapter on climate in the plains area of the Southwest in which desert conditions are discussed. Carl Frederick Kraenzel: *The Great Plains in Transition* (Norman: University of Oklahoma Press; 1959) explains by analysis of tree-ring growth that droughts were common in the Southwest long before the white man arrived.

Hundreds of articles on the Dust Bowl of the 1930's have appeared in newspapers and magazines, but the only scholarly and

Bibliographical Notes

thorough treatment of the subject is Fred Floyd: "A History of the Dust Bowl," Ph.D. dissertation, University of Oklahoma (1950).

A listing of the newspaper and magazine articles on the most recent drought in the Southwest and the accompanying problems of water, relief, conservation, and future planning would require several pages. The article that stirred up the most controversy, because it described the region as a collection of oasis cities in the midst of an expanding and contracting desert, is Walter Prescott Webb: "The American West: Perpetual Mirage," *Harper's*, May 1957. *Time, Life, Newsweek, U.S. News and World Report, Reader's Digest, The Saturday Evening Post, The New York Times Magazine, Fortune,* and other popular periodicals reported regularly the problems of water and climate in the Southwest between 1950 and 1958. Also, local newspapers throughout the area have given the subject more than adequate coverage.

XVI · THE BIG INDUSTRIAL BOOM

Statistics relating to population changes, transformation in agriculture, and growth of manufacturing in the four Southwestern states during the twentieth century are based on the official United States census reports and *The Statistical Abstract of the United States,* published annually by the Department of Commerce, Washington, D.C.

Summary accounts of manufacturing and mining enterprises in the Southwest during the nineteenth and early twentieth centuries are found in most of the previously mentioned state histories. A comprehensive history of the petroleum industry is Carl Coke Rister: *Oil! Titan of the Southwest* (Norman: University of Oklahoma Press; 1949), with special emphasis on discoveries and developments in Texas and Oklahoma. John S. Spratt: *The Road to Spindletop: Economic Changes in Texas, 1875–1901* (Dallas: Southern Methodist University Press; 1955) traces the gradual shift from agriculture and manufacturing prior to 1901.

THE SOUTHWEST: *Old and New*

Bulletins published regularly by the business-research bureaus at the state universities of Oklahoma, Texas, New Mexico, and Arizona contain detailed information on industrial, agricultural, and mining developments of the post-World War II period. Much information of this type is consolidated for easy reference in the *Arizona Statistical Review* (Phoenix: Valley National Bank; October 1958). Innumerable articles on Southwestern industrialization are found in the files of the official state magazines *Arizona Highways, Oklahoma Today,* and *New Mexico.* Many of these are promotional articles, but they contain information about new industries not available elsewhere.

Since World War II magazines such as *Fortune, Newsweek, U.S. News and World Report,* and *Business Week* have often emphasized industrial developments in various sections and cities of the Southwest. Also, the leading metropolitan newspapers of the area, the local chambers of commerce, and the state industrial commissions have produced a steady flow of material dealing with Southwestern industrialization. These bulletins, brochures, statistical tables, and articles supply valuable information on the subject, but the accuracy of some of the information is subject to doubt.

XVII · POLITICS AND POLITICIANS: TEXAS AND OKLAHOMA

Most of my general observations about political pressure groups and political philosophy of Texans and Oklahomans are based on informal interviews and on my own experiences during more than forty years as a resident of the two states.

John Gunther's *Inside U.S.A.* was written more than fifteen years ago and is, of course, somewhat dated; nevertheless, many of the pressure groups Gunther discusses, as well as some of the politicians such as Kerr, Rayburn, and Johnson, are still active and influential.

More recent scholarly studies are three works by V. O. Key: *Politics, Parties, and Pressure* (New York: Thomas Y. Crowell

Bibliographical Notes

Company; 1958), *Southern Politics in State and Nation* (New York: Alfred A. Knopf; 1949); and *American State Politics: An Introduction* (New York: Alfred A. Knopf; 1956). Some recent articles dealing with political scandals in Texas are: Ronnie Dugger: "What Corrupted Texas," *Harper's*, March 1957; Graig Thompson: "Those Texas Scandals," *The Saturday Evening Post*, November 12, 1955; "Keep the Rascals In," *Time*, July 2, 1956; Ronnie Dugger: "Texas Liberals Revolt," *The Nation*, June 2, 1956; "It's War among Texas Democrats," *U.S. News and World Report*, April 27, 1956; and D. B. Hardeman: "Shivers of Texas: A Tragedy in Three Acts," *Harper's*, November 1956.

Information regarding state officials and legislative developments in each state is kept up to date in *The Book of the States*, published annually by The Council of State Governments, Chicago, Illinois. Statistics relating to the distribution of people in rural and urban communities in Texas for various periods since 1900 are taken from *The Statistical Abstract of the United States*, while information relative to dams and irrigation projects is found in the 1960 *World Almanac*.

Each of the Southwestern political demagogues discussed in this chapter has rated full-length biographies. Seth Shepard McKay: *W. Lee O'Daniel and Texas Politics, 1938–1942* (Lubbock: Texas Technological College Research Fund; 1944) comes close to being objective. Gordon Hines: *Alfalfa Bill: An Intimate Biography* (Oklahoma City: Oklahoma Press; 1932) and Ouida Ferguson Nalle: *The Fergusons of Texas* (San Antonio: The Naylor Company; 1946) are extremely partisan. Ferguson, Murray, and O'Daniel are treated objectively in separate chapters in Reinhard H. Luthin: *American Demagogues, Twentieth Century* (Boston: The Beacon Press; 1954).

Three recent studies that cover the political scene and leading politicians in Texas during the twentieth century are Frank Goodwyn: *Lone-Star Land: Twentieth Century Texas in Perspective* (New York: Alfred A. Knopf; 1955); George Fuermann: *Reluctant Empire: The Mind of Texas* (Garden City: Doubleday and Company; 1957); and Green Peyton: *America's Heartland:*

THE SOUTHWEST: *Old and New*

The Southwest (Norman: University of Oklahoma Press; 1948).

Wayne Gard: "Alfalfa Bill," *The New Republic*, February 17, 1932; "Alfalfa Bill and Academic Freedom," *The New Republic*, May 18, 1932; and "Alfalfa Bill in War, Peace, and Politics," *The Literary Digest*, September 19, 1931, make entertaining reading, as do dozens of articles that appeared in magazines at the height of William Murray's notoriety in the early 1930's. Recent articles especially critical of Oklahoma politics are Johnston Murray: "Oklahoma Is in a Mess!," *The Saturday Evening Post*, April 30, 1955, and "How Wet Is Wet," *Newsweek*, September 8, 1958. Texas politicians, particularly the two Fergusons, Congressman Martin Dies, Allan Shivers, and the still active congressional leaders Sam Rayburn and Lyndon Johnson, have furnished subject material for newspaper stories and magazine articles too numerous to list. The best critical coverage of Texas politics and politicians since 1952 is found in the liberal weekly *Texas Observer* (Austin, Texas).

XVIII · POLITICS AND POLITICIANS: NEW MEXICO AND ARIZONA

General works dealing with twentieth-century New Mexico and Arizona politics are yet to be written. Uncritical treatments appear in separate chapters of the previously mentioned state histories, while critical treatments are found in the above-mentioned studies by V. O. Key. Much of my information on this topic, therefore, is based on personal interviews and correspondence. The most important of these are identified in footnotes. (It is significant to note that almost 400 books on "Billy the Kid" have been published, but not a single definitive biography of a New Mexican governor or United States senator.) John Gunther's chapter on politics in the "Desert States" of New Mexico and Arizona in *Inside U.S.A.* still makes interesting reading.

Several excellent monographs on New Mexican politicians and politics have been published by the Division of Government Research at the University of New Mexico. Among those I found

Bibliographical Notes

most helpful are Charles B. Judah and Frederick C. Iron: *The 47th State: An Appraisal of Its Government* (1956) and Charles B. Judah: *Governor Richard C. Dillon: A Study in New Mexico Politics* (1948). The man who had a greater impact on twentieth-century politics in New Mexico than any other individual, Senator Bronson Cutting, is analyzed in Owen P. White: "Cutting Free," *Collier's*, October 27, 1934. Another article that helps explain the peculiar traditions of New Mexican politics is Ruth Laughlin Baker: "Where Americans Are Anglos," *The North American Review*, CCXXVIII (1929).

Also, Albert Rosenfield: "New Mexico Cashes In," *Harper's*, January 1954; "New Mexico Politics," *Newsweek*, October 4, 1948; "The Catholic Church in New Mexico Politics," *New Republic*, June 19, 1950; "Dead Men Tell Tales," *Newsweek*, May 11, 1953; and "Feudalism and Senator Cutting," *American Mercury*, XXXIII (November 1934). The disputed contest between Senator Chavez and Patrick J. Hurley for the United States Senate in New Mexico in 1952 is reported fully in Senate Document No. 44,021, 82nd Congress, 2nd Session.

Arizona politics have not attracted much national attention. Three recent articles that deserve mention, however, are N. D. Hougton: "The 1956 Election in Arizona," *Western Politics and the 1956 Election* (Salt Lake City: University of Utah Institute of Government; 1957); Paul F. Healy: "The Glittering Mr. Goldwater," *Saturday Evening Post*, June 7, 1958; and John C. Waugh: "Arizona Politics," *Christian Science Monitor*, March 11, 1959.

XIX · MONEY AND BRAINS

No book devoted exclusively to the culture of the Southwest has appeared, though Green Peyton's *America's Heartland: The Southwest* (which includes Arkansas and Louisiana in the Southwest) comes close to a definitive interpretation of the arts and artists. Unfortunately, it is dated (1948). Frank Goodwyn: *Lone-Star Land: Twentieth Century Texas in Perspective* has some excellent sections on the changing cultural pattern in Texas, as

THE SOUTHWEST: *Old and New*

does George Fuermann: *Reluctant Empire: The Mind of Texas.* Walter S. Campbell: *The Book Lover's Southwest: A Guide to Good Reading* and J. Frank Dobie: *Guide to Life and Literature of the Southwest* not only list and discuss the several thousand books on the Southwest published during the past century, but also devote considerable discussion to the region's cultural growth and attempt to explain its past, present, and future. Erna Fergusson: *Our Southwest* surveys and evaluates the leading Southwestern artists and writers active during the first half of the twentieth century.

Additional bibliographies of Southwestern books include Jesse L. Rader: *South of Forty, From the Mississippi to the Rio Grande: A Bibliography* (Norman: University of Oklahoma Press; 1947); Mabel Major, Rebecca W. Smith, and T. M. Pearce: *Southwest Heritage: A Literary History* (Albuquerque: The University of New Mexico Press; 1948); Lawrence Clark Powell: *A Southwestern Century: A Bibliography of One Hundred Books of Non Fiction about the Southwest* (Van Nuys, California: J. E. Reynolds; 1958); and *Books West Southwest* (Los Angeles: The Ward Ritchie Press; 1957).

The Saturday Review of Literature devoted an entire issue (May 16, 1942) to a cultural inventory of the Southwest. Seventeen articles by recognized authorities, most of them highly laudatory, discussed various types of cultural achievement.

Unfavorable comments on Southwestern culture, especially the Texas brand, appear frequently on the editorial pages of *The Texas Observer*. Current magazine articles both condemn and praise Texas culture. Some recent ones are: Cleveland Amory: "The Oil Folks at Home," *Holiday*, February 1957; Lewis Nordyke: "The Truth about Texas," *The Rotarian*, February 1958; and Sean O'Faolain: "Texas," *Holiday*, October 1958.

The state magazines published by Oklahoma, New Mexico, and Arizona contain excellent illustrations and laudatory articles on the work of local artists, writers, musicians, sculptors, museums, and book and art collectors.

Bibliographical Notes

XX · CITIES AND CULTURE

Some of the important cities of the Southwest have been the subject of one or more historical books, not to mention fiction. Among those recommended are: Claude M. Aniol: *San Antonio: City of Missions* (New York: Hastings House; 1942); Mary Austin: *Taos Pueblo* (San Francisco: Grabhorn; 1930); Erna Fergusson: *Albuquerque* (Caldwell, Idaho: The Caxton Printers; 1947); George Fuermann: *Houston: Land of the Big Rich* (Garden City: Doubleday and Company; 1951); Ernest Knee: *Santa Fe, New Mexico* (New York: Whittlesey House; 1942); Oliver Knight: *Fort Worth: Outpost on the Trinity* (Norman: University of Oklahoma Press; 1953); John Rogers: *The Lusty Texans of Dallas* (New York: E. P. Dutton; 1951); Angie Debo: *Tulsa: From Creek Town to Oil Capital* (Norman: University of Oklahoma Press; 1943); Gil Proctor: *Tucson, Tubac, Tumacacori, Tohell* (Tucson: Arizona Silhouettes; 1956).

Articles originally published in the *Saturday Evening Post* have been collected in an entertaining and informative book by George Sessions Perry: *Cities of America* (New York: McGraw-Hill; 1947), and portraits of all the important Southwestern cities are included.

Brief histories of all Texas cities are found in *The Handbook of Texas*, while historical material for the remaining regional cities is contained in various state histories of Oklahoma, New Mexico, and Arizona. In addition, the chambers of commerce of Southwestern cities generously supplied me with brochures containing information about population expansion, cultural advantages, industrial expansion, recreational facilities, civic problems, and plans for future development.

INDEX

Abbott-Downing Company, makers of stages, 209
Abernethy, Byron R., 379
Abilene, Kansas, as shipping point, 249–50
aborigines, 4; see also Indians
Acee Blue Eagle, 427
Acoma, N.M. ("Sky City"), 27, 56, 60
Adair, John, 257
Adams, Andy, description of trail drive, 247
Adams, John Quincy, 98, 113
Adams-Oñis Treaty: boundary settled with, 89; signed, 98; encouraged liberal land laws, 99; set south boundary of Oklahoma, 269
adobe, 442, 444
Adobe Walls, Battle of, 294 n
agriculture: of cliff dwellers, 25; in Texas, 87, 349; early, 335; trend from, 336–8; in New Mexico, 359; before 1940, 364; mechanization of, 439; near Tucson, 444; near Phoenix, 445; near San Antonio, 460; see also farmers
Aguayo, San Miguel de, Marquis de, 73–5, 78
ague, treatment of, 149
Air Force Special Weapons Center, 357
Alabama-Coushatta Indians, 293–4, 297
Alamo, the, 120–2, 150, 458, 459
Alamogordo, N.M., 357
Alamo Plaza, 223
Alarcón, Martin de, 261–2
Albuquerque, N.M.: 6, 9, 16, 27, 63, 442; conquered by Confederates, 227; population of, 353, 439, 440, 441; new industry at, 357; symphony orchestra, 430; university at, 431–2; early history of, 440; industry and culture of, 441; oasis city, 444; growth, 446, 460
Allen, A. C. and John K., founders of Houston, 450
Allred, Gov. James V. (Texas), 371
Alvarado, Capt. Hernando de, 56–7
Alvarez de Pineda, Capt. Alonso, 45–6
Amarillo, Texas: 15, 439; water supply of, 333; growth of, 318, 446, 462

American Pastoral Company, 256
American River, gold at, 176
Amiable (ship), 69
Amichel, described by Pineda, 45; see also Texas
Anahuac, Mexico, 114, 115, 118
Anasazi ("Old People"), 23, 28
Anderson, Clinton P.: and water conservation, 363; political activities of, 399–403; policies of, 402
Anderson, Dillon (Texas author), 423
Anglo-Americans: in Southwest, 5, 8; and Pueblos, 28; unable to control Apaches, 33; penetration of Southwest, 86–106; importance of forests to, 87; early explorers, 88–92; early traders and trappers, 93–5; in conquest of Texas, 96–9; and colonization of Texas, 99–102; in Oklahoma, 102–3, 105–6; and racial conflict in Texas, 107–8; and slavery, 108–9; and religious freedom, 109–10; convention of on grievances, 115–16; in Indian Territory, 187; settlers raise sheep, 262; as voters in New Mexico, 393
"Antelopes," see Kwahari Indians
antilabor laws, 375
Anza, Juan Bautista de, 65–6
Apache Canyon, 167, 228
Apache Indians: raids of, 27, 30, 294, 304; description of, 30, 32–4; bands of, 32; near Santa Fe, 77; in Gadsden Purchase, 188; in Arizona, 193; uprising of near Tucson, 230; war against, 231–2; hostile to cattle drives, 252; raids on sheep, 260, 261; in Oklahoma, 273; and reservations, 291, 304–5; sites of, 302; numbers of, 303; near Tucson, 443
Apache Powder Plant, 355
Apalachee Bay, 45
Appalachen, rumor of gold at, 48
Arapaho Indians: alliances with French, 76; in Oklahoma, 273; "run" starts at reservation of, 280; Custer attacks, 296; numbers of, 296
Arbuckle, Gen. Matthew, 182–3
Archuleta, Diego, conspiracy of, 168–9

Index

argonauts, 176, 177–9; *see also* gold, gold rush
Aricara Indian, guide to Santa Fe, 80–1
Arista, Gen. Mariano: in Battle of Palo Alto, 157–9; at Resaca de la Palma, 159–60
Arizona: as part of Southwest, 4, 5, 6, 7, 9, 18, 19, 20; artifacts in, 23; cliff dwellers migrate to, 25; Indians in, 28–35; reached by Spaniards, 54–62; ranching introduced in, 65; exploration in, 65, 92–3; early interest in, 92; trappers and traders in, 94; "Army of the West" marches through, 166; acquisition of territory, 176; gold in, 176, 188, 190; population of, 188, 285, 290, 336, 340–1, 344, 345, 353; and Gadsden Purchase, 189; petition to separate from New Mexico, 195, 285; sheep industry in, 261; statehood of, 269, 284, 287–9; cities in, 287, 442–6; reservations in, 304–5; climate of, 313–33 *passim;* agriculture in, 336–7, 354; mining in, 337, 353–4; oil in, 339; industry in, 352–7; newcomers to, 352–3; tourists in, 356; politics in, 361, 364, 390, 403–12, 407; novelists and music of, 430; universities in, 435–6; authors, 436–7; art, 437
Arizona and the West, 435
Arizona Daily Star, 435
Arizona Daily Sun, 406
Arizona Highways, 342, 435
Arizona Professional Authors, 436
Arkansas, 4, 9, 12
Arkansas City, Kan., 68, 279
Arkansas River: 68, 71, 448; exploration of, 89, 90, 91; fur trappers on, 93, 95; on trail west, 183
Arkansas Territory, 103, 270
Armed Forces Special Weapons Project, 357
Armer, Laura Adams, 436
Armíjo, Gov. Manuel, 127, 166–7
Armour, P. D., 246
Army of the North, conquest of Texas, 96–7
"Army of the West": organized, 165; marches, 166–8; divided, 168
Arroyo Hondo, 83, 87, 96
art: in Texas, 422; in Oklahoma, 427–8; in New Mexico, 434
Artesia, N.M., wells at, 20
artifacts: aid study of history, 23; in Pueblo Bonito, 25; of Hopi, 28
Asinai Indians, 64
Atchison, Topeka, and Santa Fe Railroad: route of, 199; in Oklahoma, 274; *see also* Santa Fe Railroad
Athapascan Indians, 29, 30
Atkinson, Col. David, 91
Atlantic and Pacific Railroad, 274
Atomic Energy Commission Operations Office, 357

Austin, Mary, 433
Austin, Moses, 99
Austin, Stephen F.: and colonization of Texas, 99–102; land grant to, 101; secures slavery law, 109; his colonies preferred, 110; appeases Santa Anna, 115; goes to Mexico City, 116; arrest and return to Texas, 117; characterized, 118; takes command, 119; defeated for president, 124; as subject of poetry, 150; finds livestock, 243
Austin, Texas: and Balcones Fault, 9; in Texas Republic, 131; Bollaert's description of, 137; stage service, 140; theaters and churches in, 144; factories at, 341; growth of, 462
authors: Texas, 422–5; Oklahoma, 428–30; New Mexico, 430, 432–4; Arizona, 430, 436–7
Aztec, N.M., people of, 25, 26
Aztec Indians, 29
Aztec National Monument, 23

Baird, James, 94
Balcones Fault, 9, 12, 14, 89–90, 244, 335
Ball, Thomas H., 367
Bancroft, Hubert Howe: on Yuma Indians, 34; on Spanish gold mines, 188; on ranching business, 194; on fight at Valverde, 227 *n*
Bandelier, Adolph, 436
Bandelier National Monument: description of, 18 *n;* ruins at, 26; effect of drought on, 327; ruins furnish proof, 438
Banks, Harvey O., 333
Banks, Gen. N. P., 240
Baptists, 388
barbed wire, 254–5, 263–4
Barr, William, 87
Bartlett, John Russell, 189, 212
Basin and Range Province: in Southwest, 9; boundaries of, 18; geography of, 18–20; climate of, 19–20; Hollywood look of, 21
Bastrop, Baron de, 99
battles, *see under names of individual battles*
Baylor, Col. John R., 225
Baylor University, 146–7
Beale, Edward Fitzgerald: on Mohaves, 34; opens road, 190; in charge of camels, 214–15
Bean, Ellis P., 88, 96
Bean, Roy, 88
Beaty, John O., 378, 422
Beaumont, Texas: industry at, 341; development of, 451; growth of, 462
beaver, trapping of, 93, 94; *see also* fur trade
Becknell, William, 93, 94
Bedechek, Roy, 424
beef: increased preference for, 242, 245, 246; list of men dealing in, 253; *see also* cattle

Index

Bemis, Samuel Flagg, *quoted*, 152
Benson, Arizona, factory at, 355
Benson, Ezra Taft, 402
Bent, Charles: builds Bent's Fort, 95; to protect government of New Mexico, 168; killed, 169; his murderer killed, 170
Bent, William, 95
Bent's Fort: early trading post, 95; "Army of the West" camps at, 166, 167
Bernalillo, N.M., 57
Bernardino, Fray, 60
Beveridge, Sen. Albert J., 288
"Bible Belt," 388, 448
Bieber, Ralph P., 179, 186
Bienville, Jean le Moyne, Sieur de, 71, 73, 81
bigotry, 361, 365
Billington, Ray, *quoted*, 153, 207 *n*
Biloxi, Miss., 71
"blanket Indians," 292
blizzards, effect on cattle, 257
Blue Valley Farmer, The, 381
Blumenschein, Ernest, 434
Boatright, Moody, 424
Boggy Depot, 186, 248
Bollaert, William: travels in Texas, 134–5; on Texas houses, 137; on roads, 139; on religion, 144
Bolton, Herbert E., 32
Bonney, Maurice, 441
Bonney, William H. (Billy the Kid), 286
Boomers: covet Indian land, 274, 275–6; movement, 276–8
"boot hill," 250
Borden, Gail, 450 *n*
Borland, Sen. Solom G., 182
Bosque Redondo: Indians moved to, 232; cattle for, 252; Navajos leave, 305
Boudinot, Elias Cornelius, 276–7
Bourgmond, Étienne Venyard, Sieur de, 76, 79–80
Bowie, James, 120, 121
Brackenridge Park (San Antonio), 459
Bradburn, Col. John Davis, 114–15
Brazos River, 9, 10, 14, 57, 88
Brazos River Reservation, 42
Breckinridge, John C., 222
Brewer, J. Mason, 424
Brinkley, William, 428
Brown, Postmaster General Aaron V., 202–3
Brown, Maj. Jacob, 158
Brownsville, Texas: origin of, 158 *n*; army camped at, 161; industry at, 341; development of, 451
Bruyère, Fabry de la, 81
Bryan, John Neeley, 453
Buchanan, President James, 195, 206
Budenz, Louis, 403
Buena Vista, Battle of, 162, 164, 174
buffalo: and prairie sky, 15; staple of Comanches, 37; Cabeza de Vaca's

buffalo (*continued*)
 quote on, 50; disappearance of, 242; Indians and, 291, 295; replaced, 316
Buffalo Bayou, 450
buffalo chips, 179
"Buffalo-eaters," *see* Katsoteka Indians
Bureau of Indian Affairs, 106
Burnet, David G., 101, 121, 127
Burr, Aaron, 89, 90, 96
Burroughs, Gov. John (New Mexico), 399
Butterfield, John: submits bid, 203; description of, 204; expenses of, 209; sells interest, 211
Butterfield Overland Mail Co., 185, 211
Butterfield Overland Stage: in Texas, 141; given contract, 203; preparations made, 204–5; first run of, 205–6; importance of, 206–7; fares of, 208; coaches used by, 209; method of travel, 209–11; arrives at Tucson, 443; influence on El Paso, 461

Cabeza de Vaca, Álvar Núñez: hardships of, 49; explorations of, 50–1; mentioned, 69, 72
Caddo Indians: tribes listed, 40, 41; description of, 41–2; villages reached by Moscoso, 52; in Oklahoma, 273
Calhoun, John C.: proposes removal of Indians, 103; on annexation and slavery, 129–30, 153
California: as part of Southwest, 4; Spanish missions in, 66; stages from Texas to, 141; negotiations for purchase of, 155–6; admitted as free state, 174; gold rush to, 175–86, 192, 359; routes to, 176–86; method of travel to, 177–9; transportation to, 197–206; population of, 201; time to get to, 201 *n*, 204, 206; *see also* Pacific Coast
Camargo, Diego de, 46–7
camels: imported to West, 190; use of on California route, 211–17
Camino del Diablo, 66
Camino Real, 72
Campbell, Gov. Thomas E. (Arizona), 406
Campbell, Walter S., 4, 423, 429; *see also* Vestal, Stanley
camp meetings, in early Texas, 143–4
Camp Verde, 213, 215, 216
Canadian River: 14, 76; route of, 17; too shallow for boats, 81; mistaken for Red, 91; on trail west, 183; divides Indian Territory, 272; "run" from, 280; dams on, 332
Canary Islanders, settle in Texas, 75
Canby, Col. E. R. S., 225, 226–30
Canyon de Chelly, 31, 231, 438
caravans, to California, 177–9
Carleton, Col. James H.: leads Californians to Arizona, 229–30; replaces Canby, 230; fights Indians, 231–2

Index

Carlsbad, N.M., 20, 358
Carpenter, C. C., leads Boomers, 277
Carson, Col. Christopher (Kit): 94; carries dispatches, 171; marches against Navajos, 231–2; fights Indians, 294
Casa Grande: castle-like structure, 29; visited by Kino, 65; ruins furnish proof, 438
Castillo, Alonso de, 49
Cather, Willa, 192, 432, 433
cattle: types in Texas, 244–5; fever, 245; drives, 246–53; numbers driven, 251–2; ranches, 253–7; foreign interest in, 256; disasters to, 257–8; barons, 258; ranges in Indian territory, 274; effects of drought on, 314, 319; writings on, 429; at Tucson, 443–4; business near Houston, 451; at Fort Worth, 455; at El Paso, 461
Caughey, John, 5
Cerro Gordo, Battle of, 164
Chaco Canyon National Monument, 23
Chamberlain, Samuel E., *quoted,* 162
Champlain, Samuel de, 68
chaparral, in Coastal Plains, 11
Chapultepec, Battle of, 164
Chavez, Judge David, 402
Chavez, Sen. Dennis (New Mexico), 397–403
Cherokee Indians: removal to Oklahoma, 42, 270; move to Arkansas Territory, 103; develop alphabet, 104, 270; in Civil War, 233–8; charge for cattle, 255; land granted to, 271, 272; rent land to cattlemen, 274, 275; end of nation, 285
Cherokee Outlet, 271, 282
Cherokee Strip, 428
Cherokee Strip Live Stock Association, 275
Cheyenne-Arapaho Reservation: regarded as public domain, 276; site of, 296; opened to whites, 297
Cheyenne Indians: in Oklahoma, 273; Custer attacks, 296; numbers of, 296
Chicago, stockyards at, 246
Chicago Times, article on Indian Territory land, 276
Chichitecalli, castle-like structure, 29
Chickasaw Indians: come to Oklahoma, 42, 270; in Civil War, 233, 235, 237, 238; lands of, 272
Chihuahua, Mexico: prisoners taken to, 88; fighting around, 172–4; on road to California, 180, 181; traders to, 460
Chihuahua Trail, 172, 185
Chiricahua Indians, 32–3, 302, 304
Chisholm, Jesse, 249, 250 n
Chisholm Trail: route of, 250 n, 251; through Fort Worth, 456
Chisum, John, 250 n
Chivington, J. M., 228, 230
Choctaw Indians: come to Oklahoma, 42, 270; removal of, 103–5; in Civil War, 233, 235, 238; lands of, 272

Chouteau, Auguste Pierre, 102–3
Chouteau, Jean Pierre, 272
Christian Science Monitor, 406
churches, 144–6, 325
Churubusco, Battle of, 164
Cibola, Seven Cities of, *see* Seven Cities of Cibola
Cimarron, 428
civil rights, 362, 402
Civil War: importance of in Southwest, 218–21; Texas role in, 219, 221–41; conquest of New Mexico, 224–30; in Indian Territory, 232–8; Reconstruction, 241; influence on cattle industry, 242, 243, 246; and sheep, 262; Indians, 272–3; Indian depredations during, 294; Confederates occupy Tucson, 443
Clark, Gov. Edward (Texas), 222
Clay, Henry, 130
Cliburn, Van, 422
cliff dwellings, 23–6, 28, 313
climate: of Southwest, 6, 7, 8, 312–33; of Coastal Plains, 10–11; of Interior Highlands, 12; of Rolling Plains, 13–14; of Southern Rockies, 17–18; of Basin and Range, 19–20; known by tree rings, 22–3; as inducement in Texas, 351
clothing, of early Texans, 141–2
Coahuila, Mexico, 73, 75
Coastal Plains, 8–12
Cochise (Apache chief), 33, 304
Cocpah Indians, 34 n
Cole, E. W., 70 n
Colorado: as part of Southwest, 4; volunteers to New Mexico, 228–30
Colorado Plateau, 18–19
Colorado River: 10, 14, 19, 65; Yuma Indians along, 34; Anglo-Americans explore, 93; explored by boat, 190
Comal Springs, effect of drought on, 328
Comanche Indians: language of, 27; description of, 36–8; near Santa Fe, 77; French alliance with, 79–80; friendly to French, 82; and removal Indians, 105; outbreaks in Texas, 222; in Oklahoma, 273; raids of, 294; numbers of, 296
Committee for Sound American Education, 452
Compromise of 1850: and slavery in the Southwest, 174, 197; gives Oklahoma the Panhandle, 269; on New Mexico Territory, 285
Concord coaches, 205, 209; *see also* stage coaches
Confederacy: and neighboring states of Southwest, 220; Texas member of, 222
Connally, Tom, 350
conservatism: in Texas, 415–22 *passim;* J. F. Dobie and, 423; of press, 448, 455
constitutional convention: Oklahoma, 284; New Mexico and Arizona, 288

iv

Index

Contreras, Battle of, 164
Conway, Dr. John R., 183
Cooke, Col. Philip St. George, 166, 167, 180
Cooke's Road, and Gadsden Purchase, 188, 189
Coons, Franklin, 461
Cooper, Douglas H., 235-6
Coronado, Francisco Vásquez de: explorations of, 14-15, 51-3; visits Hopi, 28; meets Wichitas, 40; in search of Quivira, 57-8; abandons search, 58-9; brings livestock, 243; refers to desert, 315; finds cities, 438, 439; mentioned, 444
Corpus Christi, Texas, 451, 462
Cortés, Hernán, 44-7
"Cortina War," 222
cotton: center at Lubbock, 15; in Texas Republic, 132-3; in Texas, 338, 349; at Phoenix, 445; crop headquarters, 451; at El Paso, 461
Couch, William L., leads Boomers, 278
Coughlin, Father Charles E., 386
Coushatta Indians, 42
cowboy: description of, 244; on trail, 246-53; on ranch, 253-4; changes in, 258; as hero, 258-9; as heel, 259; in Tucson, 443
cow towns: 249-53; sheriffs of, 251
"Cowtown, U.S.A.," see Fort Worth
Coyotero Indians, 32
Coze, Paul, 437
Crabb, Henry A., 194
Creek Indians: come to Oklahoma, 42, 270; in Civil War, 233, 234 n, 235, 237, 238; lands of, 272, 279; found Tulsa, 449
Crockett, David, 121, 150
Crook, Gen. George, *quoted*, 32
Cross, George L., 426
Cross Timbers, 5, 9, 14, 184, 186, 272, 335
Crumbo, Woodrow ("Woodie"), 427
Cullen, Hugh Roy, 378, 416, 452
culture: of Navajos, 31; in Texas Republic, 142-51; in Southwest, 413-37; Texas, 413-25; Oklahoma, 425-30; New Mexico, 430-4; Arizona, 430, 435-7; Albuquerque, 441; Santa Fe, 442; Tucson, 444; Phoenix, 446; Oklahoma City, 448; Tulsa, 449-50; Houston, 451-2; Dallas, 453-4; Fort Worth, 456; San Antonio, 459; El Paso, 462
Custer, Gen. George Armstrong, 296
Cutting, Bronson: lays political groundwork, 394; power of, 394-5; as senator, 395-8; mentioned, 400

Daily Texan, 419
Dale, Edward Everett: concept of Southwest, 4; on population of Indian Territory, 187; on Indians in Civil War, 273 n; on Boomer movement, 277; as historian, 429

Dallas, Texas: in Republic, 131; gold seekers join caravan, 180; water supply of, 329, 332; factories at, 341, 343, 350; population of, 450, 453; early history of, 453; culture and industry of, 453-4, 448; improvement of, 454-5; and Fort Worth, 453, 455-6, 457, 458
Dallas Minute Women, 422
Dallas News, The, 419, 455
Dallas Times Herald, 455
dams, for water conservation, 363-4
Daniel, Gov. Price (Texas), 330, 378, 452
Datus, Jay, 437
Davenport, Samuel, 87
Davis, Col. E. J., 240
Davis, Jefferson: and railroad routes, 199, 200; and use of camels, 212; replaced as Sec. of War, 213; sends Pike to Indian Territory, 233, 234
Dawes Commission, 283
Dawes Severalty Act, 282-3
"Dean of Texas Letters," *see* Dobie, J. Frank
Death Comes for the Archbishop, 432
Debo Angie, 297 n, 429
De Garay, Gov. Francisco (Jamaica), 45-7
DeGolyer, Everette Lee, 416-17
De Grazia, Ted, 437
Delaware Indians, 42
demagogues, 365, 371-8
Demmit's Point, 70 n
Democratic Party: in Southwest, 360-1; in Oklahoma, 380; in New Mexico, 393-4, 396, 399, 400, 401; in Arizona, 403, 404, 406; "pintos," 405
depletion allowance, 417 n
desert, 314-16, 333
De Soto, Hernando, 51-2, 58-9, 68, 69
De Voto, Bernard, *quoted*, 156
Dickey, Ronald, 431
Dies, Martin, 377
Dillon, Gov. Richard C. (New Mexico), 395-6
disease: in Texas army camp, 156, 161; in Wool's army, 163; along route to California, 177, 180
Dobie, J. Frank, 4, 208, 423-4
doctors, in Texas Republic, 148-9
Dodge City, Kan., 250-1
Doniphan, Col. A. W.: march of, 162, 168, 172-4; soldiers of, 440; captures El Paso, 460
Dorantes, Andrés, 49
Dos Passos, John, book banned, 419
Douglas, A. E., study of tree rings, 22-3
Dowling, Lt. Richard, 239
Drew, Col. John, 235, 236, 237
drought: cycle of, 312, 313, 317; effects of, 313-16, 323; ranchers and, 316-17; wheat farms and, 317, 321; forms dust bowl, 318-20; in Arizona, 321-3; interpretations of, 326; and water supply, 326-31

Index

dude ranches, 258, 444
Duffield, George (trail driver), 248
Dunbar, Sir William, 90–1
"dust bowl": 13, 334; formation of, 318; extent of, 319; lessons of, 320–1; return of, 324; story of, 428
"dust pneumonia," 319
dust storms, 318–20, 324
dwellings: of Anasazi, 23–4; development of, 24, 25, 26; of Hopi, 28; of Hohokans, 29; of Pimas, 30; of Navajos, 31; of Chiricahuas, 33; of Mohaves, 34; of Wichitas, 40; in Texas Republic, 135–8; *see also* kivas, pit houses, sod houses

Earp, Wyatt, 251
"Eastern Apache," *see* Lipans, Mescaleros
Edgel, Ralph L., 353, 359
Edmondson, Gov. J. Howard (Oklahoma), 387
education: in Texas Republic, 144–7; University of Texas, 419–20, 421; Texas public schools, 421–2; Southern Methodist U., 421–2; Rice, 421, 422; Oklahoma schools, 425–6, 431; in Arizona, 431, 435–6; in New Mexico, 431–2
Edwards, Benjamin, 112
Edwards, Haden, 111–12
Edwards, James, 183
Edwards Plateau: as boundary of Rolling Plains, 12; description of, 15–16; ranching on, 16; sheep raising on, 263, 264; drought on, 319, 326; rainfall of, 323
Edwards Trading Post, 183
Ehrenberg, Herman, 190
Eisenhower, Dwight D., 399, 400, 406, 411
El Brazito, Battle of, 172
elections: presidential, 360–1, 369–70, 377; gubernatorial, 366–7, 368–71
Elephant Butte Dam, 329
Ellsworth, Kan., as cow town, 250
El Moro, *see* Inscription Rock
El Palacio, 431
El Paso, Texas: 63, 442; tourists in, 20; stage service to, 141; Doniphan waits in, 173; wagon trail to, 181, 182; camels arrive, 214, 215; water supply of, 329; industry of, 358, 461; resemblance to Albuquerque, 439; oasis city, 444; population of, 460; history of, 460–1; culture of, 462
El Paso del Norte, 460
El Paso Times, 461
Elwell, R. Ferrington, 437
Emory, Maj. William H., surveys Gadsden Purchase, 189
empresarios: in Texas, 108, 110, 111; system revived, 125
Enchanted Desert, 28
England, part of in annexation of Texas, 129
Engstrand, Stuart, 436

Ernst, Max, 437
erosion: on Rolling Plains, 14; of Colorado Plateau, 20; control of, 320
Espejo, Antonio de, 60–1
Espíritu Santo River, 45; *see also* Mississippi River
Estevanico: and Cabeza de Vaca, 49; and Fray Marcos, 53–4
Eufaula Dam, 363
Evans, Hiram, 370
Explorer (steamer), 190
explorers, Spanish, 44–66; *see also under individuals*

Facts Forum News, 416
Falcon Dam, 328
Fall, Sen. Albert B. (New Mexico), 397
Fannin, James W., Jr., 121
Fannin, Gov. Paul (Arizona), 406
Fargo, William G., 203
farmers: effect of drought on, 319; suffering of, 324; as pressure group, 362, 365; in politics, 365
Farmington, N.M., 358
Farragut, Commodore D. G., 239
"fence-cutters' wars," 255
Ferber, Edna, 414, 428
Ferguson, Jim ("Pa"): 365, 390; reign in Texas, 365–71; impeached, 369; runs for president, 369–70; backs "Ma," 370–1
Ferguson, Miriam Amanda ("Ma"): 366–71; as governor, 370–71
Ferguson Forum, The, 369, 370, 371
Fergusson, Erna: concept of Southwest, 4–5; on hazards of Southwest, 7–8; quoted, 267 *n;* in New Mexico, 433; on Albuquerque, 439–40
Fergusson, Harvey, 433
filibusters, 96–9, 194
Finney, Charles G., 437
First Missouri Mounted Volunteers, 165
Fite, Gilbert C., 429
Five Civilized Tribes: listed, 35 *n;* forced to migrate, 43; removal of, 103–5, 270–2; in Civil War, 232–8, 272–3; and Reconstruction, 241; suffering of, 271; lands granted to, 272; concessions to, 279; and Dawes Commission, 283; and statehood, 283–5; and reservations, 293 *n;* expand fields and herds, 335; *see also under individual tribes*
Flagstaff, Ariz., 355, 436
floods: flash, cause of, 323; control of, 363
Florida, 44, 45, 104
Floyd, Sec. of War John B., 213, 216
food: of Anasazi, 23; development of, 24, 25, 26; of Hohokans, 29; of Pimas, 30; of Chiricahuas, 33; of Mohaves, 34; of Spanish explorers, 50; in early Texas, 133–4; on stage route, 208
Foote, Horton, 423

vi

Index

Ford, Col. John S., 240
Foreman, Grant, 429
Forrest, Earle, 436
Fort Arbuckle, 233
Fort Breckenridge, 193
Fort Brown, 158 n
Fort Buchanan, 192
Fort Cobb, 42, 233
Fort Craig, 226, 227
Fort Defiance, 193, 231, 310
Fort Fillmore, 225
Fort Gibson: built, 105; in Indian Territory, 187, 272; in Civil War, 233
Fort Gibson Dam, 363
Fort Huachuca, 341, 355
Fort McDowell, 445
Fort Marcy, 168, 169
Fort Mohave, 193
Fort Orléans, 79, 80
Fort Pickens, 33
Fort St. Louis, 70
Fort Smith: built, 105; military road from, 182; and railroad surveys, 199; in Civil War, 233; Indians receive peace terms at, 273
Fort Towson: built, 105; Marcy at, 183; in Indian Territory, 187; in Civil War, 233
Fort Union, 227-30
Fort Washita: in Indian Territory, 187, 272; in Civil War, 233
Fort Worth: as eastern limit of Southwest, 5; factories at, 341; and Dallas, 453, 455, 456, 457, 458; population of, 455; culture, 456; history of, 456-7; industry of, 457
Fort Worth *Star Telegram*, 419
Fort Yuma, 191
Fortune, on migration to West, 339-40
forty-niners, 177; *see also* argonauts, gold
Foster-Harris, 430
Four Corners (New Mexico, Colorado, Arizona, Utah), 18, 23
Fowler, Jacob, 93, 94
Francklyn Land and Cattle Company, 256
Frank Phillips Foundation, 427
Fraser, Hugh Russell, *quoted*, 418
Frazier, Bernard, 427
"Fredonian Rebellion," 112-13
freedom of speech, under Gov. Murray, 385
free enterprise, and railroads, 197
Freeman, Thomas, explorer, 91
Frémont, John Charles, 171, 172
French: arrival of in Southwest, 67-8; explorations of Mississippi River, 68-71; in Louisiana, 71-2; compete with Spaniards in Texas, 72-5, 82; interest in New Mexico, 75-82; rivalry ends, 84
Frontenac, Louis de Buade, Comte de, 68
frontier, first and last, 7, 21
Frying Pan Ranch, 254

Fuermann, George: Texas writer, 418; on philanthropy, 420; on W. P. Webb, 424
fur trade, 68, 72, 93

Gadsden, James, 189
Gadsden Purchase: mentioned, 174; population, 188; consummated, 189; adds Tucson, 192, 443
Galisteo, N.M., 29
Galveston, Texas: houses in early, 137, 138; churches in, 144; music in, 150; disaster strikes, 450; failure to expand, 462 n
Galveston Bay, 115
Galveston Island: landing of Cabeza de Vaca at, 49; Long's headquarters, 98; government flees to, 121-2; importance in early Texas, 131; in Civil War, 239, 240
Garcés, Fray Francisco, 65-6
García Conde, Gen. Pedro, 189
Garrett, Pat F., 286
Gary, Gov. Raymond (Oklahoma), 346, 387
geography, of Southwest, 8-19
Geronimo (Apache chief), 33, 232, 286, 304
"Gettysburg of the West," 229
Gila River: 19, 65, 66, 443; Anglo-Americans explore, 93; silver on, 190
Gila Valley, 30, 34
Gilcrease Art Museum (Tulsa), 348, 427
Gillmore, Frances, 436
Gipson, Fred, 423
Glen Canyon Dam, 333, 355, 363
Glenn, Col. Hugh, 93, 94
Glenn Pool, Okla., 339
Glidden, George R., 212
Glorieta Pass, Battle of, 228-9
goats, *see* sheep and goats
"Goddammies, Los," 162, 172-4
gold: Indians wore, 46, 48; search for by explorers, 51; stories of at Quivira, 57; found in Arizona, 60-1; Oñate searches for, 62; search for by Spaniards, 175, 191 n; by Anglo-Americans, 175-95; "fever," 176; influence of on Southwest, 187-95; in Arizona, 188-93
gold rush: to California, 179-82; and transportation, 187; influence of on El Paso, 461
"Golden Crescent" (Texas), 341
Goldwater, Sen. Barry (Arizona): mentioned, 361; elected, 406; political activities, 409-12
Goliad, Texas, 121, 137
Gonzales, Texas: fight at, 119; Houston trains army at, 120, 121
Goodnight, Charles, 252, 256-7
Goodwyn, Frank, 418, 424
Goyen, William, 423
Grand Canyon, 18, 35, 56, 93
Grant, Ulysses S., 159, 303

Index

Grantham, Everett, 397 *n*, 399
Grants, N.M., boom at, 358
Grapes of Wrath, The, 318, 320, 428
grass: of Rolling Plains, 13; on Staked Plains, 15; on road to California, 179; in quote on Indian lands, 271; as cover crop, 321, 324
"greasers," 393
Great American Desert, 103, 315
Great Bend, Kan., 58
Great Plains: and geography of Southwest, 4, 8, 9, 12; Indians of, 40; Spaniards approach, 50
Greenberg, Herbert M., 379
Greer County, Okla., 276, 383
Gregg, Josiah: describes Cross Timbers, 184; on sheep and goats, 260 goats, 260
Grey, Zane, 430
Griffin, John Howard, 423
gringos salados, 393
Grove, Fred, 428
"Gruen Plan," 457
Guadalupe Pass, 185
Gulf of Mexico: mentioned, 9; exploration of, 45; route to via Gulf of St. Lawrence, 68; and Texas Coast cities, 451
Gulf of St. Lawrence, route to Gulf of Mexico, 68
Gunther, John: on Indians in Oklahoma, 291–2; on Texas politicians, 371; on demagogues, 377; on J. Frank Dobie, 423
Guthrie, Okla.: as capital, 281, 282; constitutional convention at, 284; tragedy strikes, 285
Gutiérrez de Lara, 96, 97
Guzmán, Gov. Nuño de (New Galicia), 53

Hainai Indians, 41
Haley J. Evetts, 254 *n*
Hall, Ennen R., 428
Hall, Sharlot, 436
Hannet, Gov. Arthur T. (New Mexico), 395
Harper's Weekly, quoted on stage run, 206
Hatch, Sen. Carl A. (New Mexico), 399
Hatch, Col. Edward, 278
Haulapai Indians, 302, 305
Havasupai Indians, 34 *n*, 35, 302, 305, 409
Hawikuh (one of Seven Cities), 54, 56
Hayden, Sen. Carl (Arizona), 361, 363, 404, 410, 412
Hayes, Ira, 309
Hayes, Pres. Rutherford B., 277, 286
Hays, Jack, 161–2
"health seekers," 441
Healy, Paul F., *quoted*, 409
Henri, Robert, 434
Herrera, Gen. José J. (Mexico), 155
Hertzog, Carl, 462
Hewitt, Edgar L., 26, 434

Hickok, Wild Bill, 251
hidalgo, 61
High Plains: 10, 11; geography of, 12; description of, 14; *see also* Great Plains
highways: 439, 441; transform Tucson, 444; Dallas and Fort Worth, 457
Hinkle, Gov. James F. (New Mexico), 395
historians: Texas, 423, 424–5; Oklahoma, 428–30; New Mexico, 434; Arizona, 436
Hobbs, N.M., 358
Hockenhull, Gov. A. W. (New Mexico), 396
Hogan, William R., 149, 150, 151 *n*
hogan, of Navajos, 31
Hogg Foundation (Texas), 421
Hohokam Indians, 29, 34
Holliday, Ben, operates stage, 211
Homestead Act, 279
"Honey-eaters," *see* Penatekas
Honey Springs, Battle of, 230 *n*, 237
Hood's Brigade, 239
Hoover, Pres. Herbert, 361, 397, 398
Hopi Indians: language of, 27; description of, 28; numbers of, 29, 303, 305; raising sheep, 261; and reservations, 291; rehabilitation of, 309–11
Horgan, Paul, 433
horses: as wealth of Comanches, 36, 37–8; hides made into boats, 48; Plains Indians acquire, 84; trading in wild, 87–8, 93; racing in early Texas, 142
Horseshoe Dam, 323
Houston, Andrew Jackson, 376
Houston, Sam: arrives in Texas, 114; accepts command of forces, 120; leads army, 120–3; policy of watchful waiting, 124; policies of as president, 124–5; on annexation, 125–6; second term, 127–30; works for annexation, as lawyer, 148; as subject of poetry, 150; opposes secession, 219, 221, 222; mentioned, 366, 450
Houston, Texas: houses in, 138; stage service, 140; theaters in early, 144; early schools in, 145; music in, 150, 430; growth of, 446; population of, 450–1; early history of, 450; industry of, 451; culture of, 451–2; reputation of, 452
Houston and Texas Central Railroad, 217
Houston *Chronicle*, 419
Houston Club, 367
Houston Minute Women, 452
Houston *Post*, 419
Houston University, 414, 451
Hualpai Indians, 35
Humboldt River, 176, 184
Hummel, Mayor Don (Tucson), 408
Hunt, Gov. George W. P. (Arizona), 404

viii

Index

Hunt, H. L., 378, 415–16, 417
Hunter, Gen. David, 236
Hunter, George, 90–1
Hunter, Capt. Sherod, 229–30
Hurley, Patrick J., 398–9

Iberville, Pierre le Moyne, Sieur de, 71
Ilarrequi, José Salazar, 189
Independence, Mo., trade with Santa Fe, 94
Indian Intercourse Act, 106
Indianola, Texas, 213
Indians: numbers in Southwest, 6; early tribes in Arizona and New Mexico, 23–35; early population, 27; language families of, 29–35; in Texas and Oklahoma, 35–43; with gold ornaments, 46, 48; encounters of with early Spaniards, 46–66 passim; coastal, 49; French alliances with, 76–7; moved to Arkansas Territory, 103; Five Civilized Tribes moved, 103–5; struggle to adjust, 106; and travelers in Texas, 139; on route to California, 178; in Gadsden Purchase, 188; in Arizona, 193; uprisings in New Mexico, 231–2; in Civil War, 232–8; tribes in early Oklahoma, 270; move to Oklahoma, 273–4; ranching of, 275; population of, 290–1; reservation system for, 291–7; intermarriage of, 291; raids of, 295; reduction of, 296–7; New Mexico and Arizona, 297–311; as minority group, 362; in politics, 393; fiction about, 428; writer on, 429; artists, 434; stories of, 436; prehistoric irrigation of, 445; see also under individual tribes
Indian Territory: civilized tribes in, 43; population of, 187; Civil War in, 232–8; on cattle trail, 248, 252; charge for cattle on, 255; as opposed to Oklahoma Territory, 283 n
industry: comes to Southwest, 334–59; dispersal of, 342; Oklahoma, 337, 345–8; advertising for, 342–3; Texas, 348–52; Arizona, 352–7; New Mexico, 357–8; surpasses agriculture, 364; and growth of cities, 439; in Albuquerque, 441; Tucson, 444; Phoenix, 445–6; Oklahoma City, 448–9; Tulsa, 451; Houston, 454; Fort Worth, 457; San Antonio, 460; El Paso, 461
Inscription Rock, on California route, 215
integration, of schools, 362
Interior Highlands Province, 9, 11–12
Interior Plains, see South Plains
intermarriage, of Indians and whites, 35
Intermontaine Province, see Basin and Range Province
International Workers of the World, 408

irrigation: on the Staked Plains, 15; of early Indians, 28, 445; of Pimas, 30; ditches built by Spaniards, 61; and underground water, 322
Isleta Pueblo, N.M.: as early village, 27; Santa María killed at, 59–60
isolationism, 362
Ives, Lt. Joseph Christmas: impressions of Havasupai Indians, 35; explores Colorado River, 190

Jackson, Alexander M., 225
Jackson, Pres. Andrew: tries to buy Texas, 113; myth of, 124; on annexation of Texas, 126, 129
Jacobson, Oscar Brousse, 427
Jaeger, L. J. F., 191
Jal, N.M., 358
James, Marquis, 123
JA Ranch, 257
Jefferson, Pres. Thomas, 90–1
Jemez Mountains, 17, 26
Jennings, Al, 380–1
Jerome Commission, 283
"Jersey" wagon, 135
Jester, Gov. Beauford H. (Texas), 378
Jesuits, mission of, 431
Jicarilla Apaches, 32, 302, 304, 310
Johnson, Gen. Albert Sidney, killed, 239
Johnson, Lyndon B.: study of water shortage, 331; in state politics, 350, 361, 379; and water conservation, 362–3; defeated, 376; mentioned, 389
Jolliet, Louis, 68–9
Jones, Sen. A. A. (New Mexico), 395
Jones, Anson, 130, 148
Jones, Jesse, 350
Jones, Commodore Thomas A. C., 153
Jornado del Muerto, 226, 227
Joseph, Donald, 428
Juárez, Mexico, 460, 461
Juchereau, see St. Denis, Louis Juchereau de

Kadodacho Indians, see Caddo Indians
Kaibab Indians, 305
Kansas: as part of Southwest, 4; and cattle trails, 248–55 passim; influence of on Oklahoma, 380
Kansas Indians, 79, 80
Kansas-Nebraska Bill, 269–70
Kansas Pacific Railroad, cattle shipping via, 249
Kaplan, Joseph, 432
Karankawa Indians, 42
Karnes County, Texas, effect of drought on, 327
Kaw Indians, in Oklahoma, 274
Kearny, Gen. Stephen W.: march to California, 154, 165–8, 171–2; soldiers of, 443
Kefauver, Estes, 399
Keith, Harold, 428
Keller, Father Ignacio, 65
Kemper, Samuel, 97

ix

Index

Kendall, George Wilkins, 126–7
Kenedy, Mifflin (cattleman), 253
Keres, language of Pueblos, 27
Kerr, Robert S.: and water conservation, 362, 363; as governor, 386; as senator, 389
Kerrville, Texas, 16
Key, V. O., 377
Keystone Dam, 363
Kichai Indians, 40
Kickapoo Indians, 42, 274
King, Capt. Richard, 154, 253
King Ranch, 11, 254, 256
Kino, Father Eusebio Francisco: visits Casa Grande, 29; explorations of, 65; and livestock, 243, 261; builds missions, 443
Kiowa Indians: territory of, 36; description of, 38–40; and removal Indians, 105; in Oklahoma, 273; raids of, 294; Custer attacks, 296; numbers of, 296
Kiowa-Comanche Reservation, 276, 296 n, 297
Kirkland Air Force Base (New Mexico), 357, 441
Kitchen, Peter, 194
kivas, 24, 26
Kleindierst, Richard, 406
Kletski, Paul, 454
Kotsoteka Indians, 37
Kraenzel, Carl Frederick, on dry cycles, 313 n
Ku Klux Klan, 370, 461
Kwahari Indians, 37, 296

La Bahía Presidio: Ramón takes, 73; rebuilt, 74–75; siege of, 97; attacked by Long, 98
labor: and politics, 374, 375, 388; in Arizona, 408–9
LaFarge, Oliver, 313, 433
Lafitte, Jean, 98
Laguna, N.M., 27
Laguna Pueblos, 310
La Harpe, Bernard de, 76
Lake Texoma, 186
Lamar, Mirabeau B.: policies of, 126–7; and public schools, 145; as lawyer, 148; policy on Indians, 293
land: grants to Texas settlers, 99, 100; grants to Stephen F. Austin, 101; demand for Indian, 103–5; titles to in Texas, 111–12; asset of Republic of Texas, 125
Landrum, Lynn, *quoted*, 378
language: of Southwest, 6; of Pueblo Indians, 27; Shoshoni dialect, 38; Caddoan, 40–1; of cowboy, 244
L'Archeveque, Jean de, 78
La Salle, Robert Cavelier, Sieur de: meets Caddos, 41; meets Karankawas, 42; explores Mississippi River, 68–9; bad luck of, 69–70
Lawrence, D. H., 433
lawyers, in Texas Republic, 148

Lea, Tom: on King Ranch, 256 n; Texas painter, 422; author, 423; mentioned, 462
lead, near Santa Fe, 190 n
League of Nations, 362
Leger, Dr. Theodore, 148–9
Leggett, Herbert, 353, 410 n
León, Alonso de, 70
Le Tourneau Foundation (Texas), 421
Lewis, Alfred Henry, 430
Lewis, Orme, 356, 407, 410 n
Lewis-and-Clark expedition, 89–90
Lincoln County War, 286
line riding, 253
Lipan Indians, 32
livestock: brought by Spaniards, 315; and balance of nature, 316–7; effects of drought on, 325–6; *see also* cattle, sheep and goats
Llano Estacado: as boundary of Rolling Plains, 12; description of, 14–15; Coronado reaches, 57; Marcy on, 185; *see also* Staked Plains
lobbyists, on education, 388
lodging, in Texas Republic, 134–5
Lomax, John A., 424
Long, Huey, 386
Long, Dr. James, 98–9
Long, Maj. Stephen H., 91–2, 315
longhorns, 256; *see also* cattle
Longstreet, James, in Battle of Palo Alto, 159
López, Fray Francisco, 59–60
Loring, Col. W. W., 225
Los Alamos, N.M.: atomic city, 341; and University of New Mexico, 432; mentioned, 358, 441
Los Angeles, California, 5, 18, 66, 171
Lottinville, Savoie, 425–6
Louisiana: added to Southwest, 4; proposed colonies for, 69; French settlements in, 71–2; French influence in, 84
Louisiana Purchase: influence on Caddos, 41; condition after, 196; includes Oklahoma, 269
Louisiana Territory, 3–4, 84
Love Field (Dallas), 454
Loving, Oliver, 252
Loving-Goodnight Trail, route of, 252
Low Plains, *see* Rolling Plains
Lubbock, Texas: growth of, 318, 462; water supply of, 333
Luttin, Reinhard H., 367 n
Lynde, Maj. Isaac, 225
Lytle, Capt. F., 253

MacArthur, Gen. Douglas, 378
McCarthy, Sen. Joseph R. (Wis.): support of in Texas, 378, 416; association with Goldwater, 410–11
McCluskie, Mike, 251
McCoy, John C., 180
McCoy, Joseph G., 249
McCullock, Col. Ben: 161–2; takes over Alamo Plaza, 223; in Indian Territory, 233

x

Index

McFarland, Gov. Ernest W. (Arizona), 343, 361, 406, 409
Machebeuf, Father Joseph P., 192
McIntire, Marjorie, 428
McNay Art Institute (San Antonio), 459
McReynolds, Edwin C., 237, 429
Magee, Augustus, 96–7
Magoffin, James Wiley, 167, 460
Magoffinville, Texas, 460–1
Magruder, Gen. John B., 239
mail: to Pacific Coast, 198, 202–3; cost of, 198 n; success of Butterfield, 211
Maillard, Nicholas Doran P., quoted, 138
Malhado ("Misfortune"), see Galveston Island
Mallet, Paul and Pierre, 80–1
Mangus Colorado (Apache chief), 232
"manifest destiny," 106, 123
manufacturing, 441, 446
Manzano Range, 16
Marcy, Randolph B.: description of prairie, 13; story of Kiowa, 39; as escort to emigrants, 182–4; in Santa Fe, 184–5; explores on return journey, 185–6; petitioned as director of survey, 199; trail to El Paso, 205; surveys reservations, 293
Marcy, Mrs. Randolph B., and proposal of Kiowa chief, 39
Margo Jones Theater, 454
Maricopa Indians, 34 n, 305
Maricopa Phoenix (railroad), 445
Marin, John, 434
Marquette, Father Jacques, 68–9
Marriott, Alice, 429
Marshall, James Wilson, discovers gold, 176
Massanet, Father Domian, 64
Masterson, Bat, 251
Matador Land and Cattle Co., 256
Matagorda Bay, 69, 70
Matamoras, Mexico: Arista stationed at, 157; Taylor occupies, 161
Mathews, John Joseph, 428
Maverick, Mayor Maury (San Antonio), 459
mavericks, 246, 254
Maya Indians, 29
Meade, George Gordon, in Battle of Palo Alto, 159
meat packing: 246; in Fort Worth, 457; in San Antonio, 460
Mechem, Gov. Edwin L. (New Mexico), 397 n, 399, 400
Medicine Lodge, Kan., treaty with Indians at, 273, 294–5
medicines, in Texas Republic, 148–9
Medina River, 16
Mehta, G. L. (India's ambassador), 452
Mendoza, Viceroy Antonio de, 51, 53–9
Mesa Verde: cliff dwellings in, 23, 24; deserted, 26; cliff dwellers abandon, 313; ruins furnish proof, 438

Mescalero Indians, 32, 36, 302, 304, 461
Mexican Cession, changes Southwest, 4, 152–65
Mexicans: and racial conflict in Texas, 107–8; alarmed at rush to Texas, 111–13; garrison troops, 114; fight for Texas, 114–23; border clashes, 127–8; search for gold, 175; as minority group, 362; in San Antonio, 458; banditti at El Paso, 461
Mexico: Karankawa Indians flee to, 42; tribes driven to, 43; cession of Texas, 152–65; scope of war with, 153–4; other battles with, 165–74; Treaty of Guadalupe Hidalgo with, 174
Mier y Terán, Gen. Manuel de, 113
Milburn, George, 428
Miles, Gov. John (New Mexico), 402
military bases: in New Mexico, 357–8; important in economy, 362; near Phoenix, 445
millionaires: in Ozona, Texas, 325; others in Texas, 415–19; in Tulsa, 449
Mimbreno Indians, 302, 304
Mimbres, band of Apaches, 32
mining: in New Mexico and Arizona, 337; near Tucson, 444
missionaries: Alvarado, 57; trip of to New Mexico, 59–60
Mission of Dolores (Sonora), 65
Mission San Juan Bautista, 64, 73
Mission San Xavier del Bac, 65, 66, 431
missions: among Caddos, 41; in New Mexico, 63; founded by Spain, 64; in Texas listed, 64 n; established by Fray Garcés, 66; livestock to, 243, 261–2; schools in Oklahoma, 272; Tubac moved, 443; in San Antonio, 459
Mississippi River: as boundary, 3; Pineda sees, 45; explorers reach, 48; Moscoso at, 52; De Soto at, 52; French explorations of, 67–71
Missouri, Kansas, and Texas Railroad: in Oklahoma, 217, 274; and Boomer movement, 276
Missouri Indians, 79
Missouri River, 68
Missouri Volunteers, 460
Miwok Indians, 302
Mobile, Ala., 71
Mogollon Indians, 32, 302, 304
Mohave Indians, 34
Molino del Rey, Battle of, 164
Monclova, Mexico, 162, 163
money, in Texas Republic, 147–8
Monroney, Sen. Mike, 389
Monterey, California, 153
Montero, Bernardino, 96
Monterrey, Mexico, 162, 180
Montezuma's Castle, 28
Moody, Gov. Dan (Texas), 371

xi

Index

Mormons: Apache raid on, 33; march to California, 166; in Civil War, 220; raise sheep, 261
Moscoso de Alvarado, Luís de, 41, 52
Murchison, Clint, 378, 416
Murphy, Edward, 87
Murray, Gov. Johnston (Oklahoma), 386–7
Murray, William H. ("Alfalfa Bill"): part in Oklahoma statehood, 284; popularity declining, 365; politics of, 381–6; campaign promises, 382–3; mentioned, 390
museums: Tulsa, 348, 427, 449; Flagstaff and Phoenix, 436; Santa Fe, 442; Tucson, 444; Houston, 451; Dallas, 454; Fort Worth, 456; San Antonio, 459
music: Mexican, 149–50; in Texas, 149–50, 422; in Southwest, 430
mustangs: broken by Texas army, 156–7; progenitors of, 243; origin of term, 244; *see also* horses

Nacogdoches, Texas: missions at, 72; Anglo-American settlement near, 87; conquest of, 96; "Fredonian Rebellion" at, 112–13; in Republic, 131, 137
Nacogdoche Indians, 41
Narváez, Pánfilo de, 48
Nasoni Indians, 41
Natchez Indians, 80
Natchitoches, La.: post founded at, 64; French outpost, 72; traders in, 80; post at, 82–3; Anglo-American settlement near, 87
Navajo Indians: 19, 23; raids of, 27; description of, 30–2; in Gadsden Purchase, 188; war against, 231–2; weaving, 259; and sheep, 260–1; and reservations, 291, 305; numbers and activities of, 303; hardships of, 305–8; rehabilitation, 305–7, 308–11; oil income of, 311; religious beliefs of, 433
Nebedache Indians, 41
Neches River, 74
Negroes: in Texas, 187, 221; as minority group, 362; discrimination against, 420; in Houston, 452
Neighbors, Robert S., 293
"nesters," 254
Neutral Ground, in Texas, 96
Nevada, as part of Southwest, 4
New Deal: and sheep growers, 267; jobs for Navajos, 307; reaction against, 361; denounced by O'Daniel, 374; mentioned, 402
New Mexico: as part of Southwest, 4–7, 9, 14, 16–20; people of, 6; artifacts in, 23, 25; settlements in, 23–29; Indians of, 28–35; attempts to colonize, 61; claimed for Spain, 61; French activities in, 75–82; Pike's travels through, 89; early interest in, 92; early Anglo-American explorers

New Mexico (*continued*)
in, 93; traders and trappers in, 94–95; negotiations for purchase of, 156; "Army of the West" marches through, 166; gold in, 176; Gadsden Purchase, 189; Arizona separation, 195, 285; population of, 187, 285, 335–6, 340–1, 344, 345, 353; role of in Civil War, 224–30; Indian uprising in, 231–2; cattle driven to, 252; sheep brought in, 259; expansion of sheep industry, 260–2; ranching in, 266–7; statehood of, 268–9, 284, 287–9; Lincoln County War, 286; cities in, 287, 438–42; population of Indians in, 290–1; Pueblos, 297–302; reservations in, 303–5; Navajos, 303–11; climate of, 313–33 *passim;* early agriculture in, 335–6; mining in, 337, 353–4; oil in, 339; newcomers to, 352–3; industry in, 357–8; economy of, 359; politics in, 361, 364, 390–403; voters, 391–3; music, 430; University, 431–2; authors, 432–4; art and artists, 434
New Mexico Historical Review, 431
New Mexico Magazine, 342–3
New Mexico Quarterly, 431
New Orleans, La., 4, 71, 458
New Orleans Picayune, 126
New Republic, The, quoted on Murray, 385
newspapers: Texas, 418–19; Arizona, 435
Newton, Kansas, as cow town, 250
New York Tribune, recommends trails, 177
Nicollet, Jean, 67
Nixon, Richard M., 399, 400, 406
Niza, Fray Marcos de, 53–6
Nolan, Philip, 88, 96
"No Man's Land," added to Oklahoma, 283
Norman, Okla.: in "run" of 1889, 281, 282; military base at, 347; University at, 426; proximity to Oklahoma City, 448
"northers," 13–14
Nueces-Rio Grande strip, 154, 155
Nueces River: 11, 16; Taylor's army on, 154, 156
Nuestra Señora de Guadalupe del Paso (mission), 460
Nuestra Señora del Pilar de los Adaes (mission), 72
Nuevo Mexicano, El, 394

oases: 313–33 *passim;* man-made, 322
O'Connor, Jack, 436
O'Daniel, W. Lee ("Pappy"): popularity declines, 365; in politics, 371–8; writes song, 372; philosophy of, 372–3; campaign of, 373–4; as governor, 374–5; as senator, 375–7; defeats of, 377; in El Paso, 461
O'Daniel News, The W. Lee, 374

xii

Index

oil: discovery of, 338; in Southwest states, 338–9, 346; in Texas, 338–9, 349; Arizona, 338; New Mexico, 358; wealth from, 414–17, 418, 419; in Mexico, 416; importance to Oklahoma City, 447; importance to Tulsa, 448–9; near San Antonio, 460
"Okies," resentment of term, 318 n
Oklahoma: as part of Southwest, 4–12, 16, 21; people of, 6; Indians in, 35–43, 270–6; French in, 76; early exploration in, 91–2; nature of, 102; Chouteau settles in, 102–3; Indians removed to, 103–5; Indians adjust in, 106; on western trail, 184; sheep industry in, 261; becomes part of U.S., 269; meaning of name, 269 n; boundaries, 269–70; population of, 275, 290–1, 336, 340–1, 344, 345; Boomers in, 276–8; opened to whites, 279–82; statehood, 283–5; intermarriage with Indians in, 291; integration of Indians, 291–2; reservation system, 291–7; climate of, 313–33 passim; unattractive to Spaniards, 335; industry in, 337, 345–8; oil in, 339; highways in, 346; tourist attractions, 347–8; politics in, 361, 364, 380–6, 388; reapportionment in, 364–5; repeal of prohibition, 365 n; "Alfalfa Bill" Murray, 381–6; other governors, 386–8; universities, 425–6; art, 427–8; authors, 428–30; cities of, 446–50
Oklahoma City: Boomers arrive, 278; lots grabbed, 281; capital moved to, 285; water supply of, 330, 333; Tinker Field near, 341, 347; symphony orchestra, 430; population of, 446, 447; early history of, 446–7; industry of, 447; culture of, 448; University, 448
Oklahoma Territory, 283 n, 284
Oklahoma Today, 342
old-age pensioners, 388
"Old Ones," see Anasazi
Old San Antonio Road, 72, 73; see also Camino Real
Oñate, Juan de: exploration of, 61–2; brings livestock, 243
101 Ranch, 275
Oñis, Luis de, signs treaty, 98
Oologah Dam, 363
Opothle Yahola (Creek chief), 235
Oppenheimer, J. Robert, 420
Oraibi (Hopi town), 66
Organic Act of 1890, 283 n
Ormsby, Waterman L., 207
Ortiz, Tomas, 168–9
Osage Indians: alliances with French, 76; to Kansas, 79; and removal Indians, 105; in Civil War, 234; in Oklahoma, 273; story of, 428
Osborn, Gov. Sidney P. (Arizona), 404
Oskison, John, 428

Otero, Gov. Miguel A. (New Mexico), 288
Otoe Indians, 79
Ouachita Mountains, 11
"oxbow" route, 207
Ozona, Texas, effect of drought in, 325

Pacific Coast: Mexico step to, 153; gold rush to, 175–93; transportation to, 197–217; proposed railroads to, 199–200; Overland stages to, 203–11; camels to, 211–17; proposed wagon roads to, 220–3
Pacific Mail Steamship Company, 176, 198
Paiute Indians, 30, 302
Pajanto Plateau, 26
Palmer, Capt. I. N., 214
Palo Alto, Battle of, 158–9, 165
Palo Duro Canyon, 15, 256–7
Pan American Highway, 441
Panhandle (Texas), 15
Pánuco River, 47, 52
Papago Indians, 30, 305
Parke, Lt. J. G., 199–200
Parras, Mexico, 180
Parrington, Vernon Lewis, 416
Parrot, William S., 155
patrones, and voting, 391–2
Pattie, James Ohio, 93
Pattie, Sylvester, 93
Pawnee Indians: alliances with French, 76, 77; attack Spaniards, 78; make peace, 80
Payne, David L., leads Boomers, 277–8
Peace of Paris, 83
"Peaceful Ones," see Hopi Indians
Peach, Nelson, on attracting industry, 351 n
Pea Ridge, Battle of, 223, 237
Pearson, Drew, on "Pappy" O'Daniel, 377
Pecos River, 12, 14, 16–20, 32
Penateka Indians, 37
Peralta, Pedro de, 62, 63
Perry, George Sessions, 423
Pesquiera, Ignacio, 194
Peters, Susan, 427
peyote, 300, 308
Peyton, Green: on Chisholm Trail, 250 n; as Texas writer, 418; quoted, 84–5, 426
Phi Beta Kappa, chapters in Southwest, 422
philanthropy, 414–16, 420–1
Philbrook Art Center (Tulsa), 348, 427, 449
Phillips, Bert, 434
Phillips, Frank and Waite, 427–8
Phillips, Gov. John C. (Arizona), 406
Phillips Collection of Southwestern History and Literature, 428
Phoenix, New Mexico: people in, 6; irrigation at, 20, 322, 323; migration to, 340; electronics plants at, 341;

xiii

Index

Phoenix (*continued*)
Sperry-Rand Corp. at, 343; population of, 353, 445–6; AiResearch Mfg. Co. at, 354; other industries at, 355; symphony orchestra, 430; museum, 436; early history of, 444–5; industry and culture at, 446; growth of, 446
Pierce, Franklin, 199
Pierce, Shanghai, 253
Pike, Albert, 233–4, 236
Pike, Zebulon Montgomery: travels of in Southwest, 88–90; statement about prairies, 89; quoted on desert, 315; visit to Albuquerque, 440
"Pikes Peakers," 228
Pile, Gov. William A. (New Mexico), 286
Pima Indians: 29, 303, 305; description of, 30; missionaries among, 65
"Pine Tree Folk," *see* Hualpai tribe
Piper, Edward, 245
pit houses (Hopi), 28
Plains Indians: 27; importance of, 35–6; tribes of, 36; acquire horse, 84; treaties with Five Civilized Tribes, 105
Plankinton, John, 246
Platte River: post planned near, 78; on route to gold, 176, 177
Plowman's Folly, 425
Point Isabel, 157, 158, 161
politicians: Ferguson, 365–71; O'Daniel, 371–8; liberals, 379–80; Murray, 381–6; Okla. governors, 386–8; Cutting, 394–8; Chavez, 397–403; Hurley, 398; Anderson, 399–403; Hayden, 404, 410, 412; Goldwater, 406–12
politics: Texas, 361, 364–80; Oklahoma, 361, 364, 380–8; New Mexico, 361, 364, 390–403; Arizona, 361, 364, 390, 403–12; contrast in, 403–4; "majority" and "minority," 405
Polk, Pres. James K.: on annexation of Texas, 130; sends troops to Texas, 154; attempts to buy territory, 154–6; transfers soldiers from Taylor, 163–4; and annexation of Mexico, 165 n
Ponce de León, Juan, 44
population: of Southwestern states, 187; of California, 201; census figures, 451 n; *see also individual states and cities*
Port Arthur, Texas, 451
Porter, David D., 212–13
Porter, Pleasant, *quoted*, 297
Poston, Charles, 190, 192; *quoted*, 191
prairie: description of, 13; Pike's views on, 89–90; Long's statement on, 92
Prairie Cattle Company, 256
Prairie du Chien, Wis., 68
Prescott, Ariz., 60, 445
Presidio, Texas, 59
Presidio Tubac, 66

pressure groups: farmers, 362, 365; in New Mexico, 394; in Arizona, 407–8
Price, Col. Sterling, 166, 168–71
prohibition: repeal in Oklahoma, 348, 365 n, 387; in Texas, 367; and Baptists, 388
prostitutes, 34, 281–2
Pryor, Ike T., 253
Puaray, N.M., 60
Pueblo Bonito, N.M., 25
Pueblo de los Muertos, 29
Pueblo Indians: early settlers, 7; numbers of, 27; language of, 27; description of, 27–8; in Arizona, 29; blamed by Oñate, 62; on scouting expedition, 78; revolt of in New Mexico, 168–71; population of, 291; land of, 298; education of, 299–300; interest in politics, 300, 400; industries and government of, 301; religion of, 433
Pulitzer prize, 433, 434
Pyle, Ernie, 353
Pyle, Gov. Howard (Arizona), 406

Quapaw Indians, 42, 234
"quarantee laws," 255
Quivira: search for, 14, 28; described to Spaniards, 57; Oñate explores for gold, 62
Quivira Society, 431

railroads: in early Texas, 140; proposed construction, 197; army survey for, 198; routes of, 199–201; and development of Southwest, 217; extension of for beef, 243, 249–51, 255; across Indian Territory, 244–51, and industry, 439; influence Tucson, 444; reach Phoenix, 445; to Houston, 450; influence El Paso, 461; *see also individual railroad lines*
Rainey, Homer Price, 375, 419
rainfall: in Coastal Plains, 10, 11; in Interior Highlands, 12; in Sangre de Cristo Mountains, 18
rain makers, 326–7
Rak, Mary Kidder, 436
Ramón, Capt. Domingo, 72, 73, 458 n
ranching: in Arizona, 65, 193–4; in Texas, 244–6; after trail driving, 253–6; round-ups, 253–4; spread of, 254, 256–7; foreign interest in, 256; effect of drought on, 319; pressure group, 362; *see also* cattle, sheep and goats
Randolph, Mrs. R. D., 379
Rayburn, Sam, 350, 379, 389
reaportionment: in Oklahoma and Texas, 364–5; in Arizona, 405–6
Reclamation Act of 1902, 322
Reconstruction, 241
Red River: 9–11, 13, 14; exploration of, 90, 91; as boundary of Oklahoma, 269; dams on, 332
Reeve, Frank, 431, 434

xiv

Index

Religion: source of friction in Texas, 109–10; in early Texas, 142–4; in politics, 374
Remington, Frederick, 427
remuda, 247
Republican Party: in Southwest, 360–1; Oklahoma, 380; New Mexico, 391, 393–6, 399, 400; Arizona, 403, 404, 406
Resaca de la Guerrero, 159–60
Resaca de la Palma, Battle of, 160, 165
reservations: Oklahoma system, 273–4, 291–7; considered public domain, 276; in New Mexico and Arizona, 297–311
Reynolds Metals Co., 355
Rhodes, John J., 406
rice, crop headquarters, 451
Rice Institute, 421, 422, 451
Richardson, Rupert N., 211 *n*, 252 *n*
Richardson, Sid, 416
Richter, Conrad, 433
Riley, Jim, 251
Río de las Palmas, 45; *see also* Rio Grande
Río del Norte, 61
Río de Nuestra Señora, 56; *see also* Rio Grande
Rio Grande: and coastal plains, 10, 12; route of, 16–17; floods on, 18; landings at mouth of, 45–7; report of cities and gold on, 52–3; Oñate reaches, 61; exploration of, 91; fur trappers on, 93; fixed as boundary, 123; Mexican army on, 154; Taylor's army shifted to, 157; Taylor crosses, 161; on road to California, 180, 181; dry, 324; and Albuquerque, 439, 440
Rio Grande Valley: rainfall in, 10; temperature in, 10–11; migrants to, 26, 27; Spanish population increases, 63
Rister, Carl Coke, 4, 252 *n*, 295 *n*, 429
Rito de los Frijoles, ruins at, 26
roads, in early Texas, 138–9; *see also* highways
"robber barons," 414
Robertson, Judge Felix, 370
Robinson, William H., 436
"Robson's Castle," 136
Rodríguez, Fray Agustín, 59–60
Rolling Plains, 12–14
Roosevelt, Franklin D.: Texan's view on, 267; election of, 360–1; electors in Texas, 377; and W. H. Murray, 386; and Bronson Cutting, 397
Roosevelt, Mrs. Franklin D., 361, 420
Roosevelt, Theodore, 284, 287
Roosevelt Dam, 322
"Root-eaters," *see* Yamparikas
Ross, John (Cherokee chief), 233–5
Roswell, N.M., 20, 358
Round Mountain, fight at, 235–6
round-up, 253–4
"run": of 1889, 279–82; others, 282; and Oklahoma City, 447

Rusk, Thomas J., 124, 148
Russell, Charles M., 427
Russell, Majors and Waddell, 201 *n*
Rutersville College, 146, 149

Sabine River: in Coastal Plains, 11; as boundary of Texas, 72 *n*, 83; as international boundary, 91, 95; and Adams-Oñis Treaty, 98
Sac and Fox Indians, 274
St. Denis, Louis Juchereau de: exploration of, 64; founds settlement, 71–2; compromises with Spaniards, 72–3
St. Louis, Mo., 93, 94
St. Louis and San Francisco Railroad, 449
St. Vrain, Ceran, 95, 170
Salado Creek, Texas, 366
Salado River, battle at, 97
Salazar, Juan de, 460
Saltillo, Mexico, 162, 174, 180
Salt River, 65; Valley 28; Reservation, 30
salt water, conversion of, 333
San Agustín del Tucson, 66
San Angelo, Texas, 16, 325
San Antonio, Texas: at edge of Southwest, 4–5; and Balcones Fault, 9; Mexicans to, 73; settlers moved in 75; and conquest of Texas, 97; captured, 98; surrendered by Mexicans, 119; fight at Alamo, 120–2; houses in early, 137; in Texas Republic, 141; stage service from, 141, 198; churches in, 144; lawyers in, 148; road from to California, 181; water supply of, 329, 332; factories at, 341; population of, 450, 458; atmosphere of, 458–9; culture of, 459; industry of, 460
San Antonio de Bejar, 64
"San Antonio Express, The," 198
San Antonio River, 459
San Augustine, Texas, 138
Sandia Base (New Mexico), 357–8
Sandia Mountains, 16, 439
San Diego, Calif., 171
San Felipe, 119
San Francisco, Father García de, 460
San Francisco, Calif., 205–8
San Gabriel, Calif., 61, 92
Sangre de Cristo Mountains, 17, 18
San Ildefonso, N.M., 301
San Jacinto: battle of, 122–3; treaty signed after battle, 155; mentioned, 450
San Luis Potosí, Mexico, 88
San Pasquel, Calif., 171
Santa Anna, Antonio López de: assumes control, 115; grants audience to Austin, 116–17; proclaims self dictator, 117; military exploits of, 118–23; defeated, 123; warns U.S. on annexation, 153; and Treaty of Velasco, 155; at Buena Vista, 164;

XV

Index

Santa Anna (*continued*)
  sells territory to U.S., 189; mentioned, 450
Santa Barbara, Mexico, 59
Santa Catalina Mission, 93
Santa Cruz River, 63, 65, 443
Santa Fe, New Mexico: people in, 6; founded, 63, 439; French interest in, 75–82; Pike arrives in, 88; becomes center of trade, 93; fur trade at, 93–5; Texan expedition to, 126–7; "Army of the West" arrives at, 166–7; on route to California, 177; Marcy to, 182–4; stage service to, 198; conquered by Rebels, 227; opera festival, 430; Quivira Society, 431; as art center, 434; trade with Albuquerque, 440; population of, 441; industry and culture of, 442
Sante Fe New Mexican, The, 394
Santa Fe Railroad: and cattle, 250; in "run" of 1889, 281; in New Mexico and Arizona, 287; reaches Albuquerque, 440; and Oklahoma City, 447; reaches Phoenix, 445; *see also* Atchison, Topeka, and Santa Fe Railroad
"Santa Fe Ring," 286
Santa Fe, Texas and Pacific Railroad, 217
Santa Fe Trail: beginning of, 93; "Army of the West" on, 166; on route to California, 177, 203
Santa María, Fray Juan de, 59–60
Santee, Ross, 436
Santo Domingo, Costa Rica, 48
Santo Domingo Pueblo, 61
San Xavier del Bac Mission, 431, 443
San Xavier Reservation, 30
Saturday Evening Post, quoted, 409
Saunders, George W., 252 *n*
schools: in Texas Republic, 144–7; present county system, 145 *n*; numbers of in Texas, 421; Albuquerque, 441; Tucson, 444; Houston, 451; Fort Worth, 456; San Antonio, 459
Schreiner, Capt. Charles, 253
Scott, Gen. Winfield, 154, 164
Sealy, Tom, 420
secession, 219–20, 222
Sedalia, Mo., railhead for cattle, 246, 249
Sedlmayr, Father Jacob, 65
Seligman, Gov. Arthur (New Mexico), 396
Seminole Indians: war in Florida, 104; in Civil War, 234, 235, 238; removal to Oklahoma, 270; lands of, 272; sell lands, 279
Seneca Indians: in Civil War, 234; in Oklahoma, 274
Seven Cities of Cibola, 53, 55, 438
sharecroppers, 365, 366, 368, 381
Sharp, Joseph, 434
Shawnee Indians, 42, 234
sheep and goats: industry, 259–67; barons, 260; numbers of, 260–61; characteristics of Spanish, 262; cas-

sheep and goats (*continued*)
  trating of, 264 *n*; shearing of, 264–5; herders of, 264–7; politics and, 267; for Navajos, 305; effect of drought on, 319
sheepherders: killed by Indians, 260; duties of, 264–7; and voting, 391
Sheppard, Sen. Morris, 375
Sheridan, Gen. Philip H., 277
Sherman, Gen. William T., 296
Sherman, Texas, importance of stage to, 141, 207
Shivers, Gov. Allan (Texas), 330, 378
Sibley, H. H., 225, 226–30
Sibley, John, 41
silver: Navajo work in, 31; discovery of in Arizona, 65, 190–1; near Santa Fe, 190 *n*; mentioned, 404
Simms, Gov. John F., Jr. (New Mexico), 399
Sitgraves, Lorenzo, 190
slavery: as source of friction in Texas, 108–9; question of in new territory, 174; in territory acquired from Mexico, 197; in Texas, 221; in New Mexico, 224
Slidell, John, 155–6
Slough, Col. J. P., 228
"slumgullion," 210
Smith, Ashbel, 148
Smith, Gerald L. K., 378
Smith, Henry, 120
Smith, Jedediah S., 92
Smith, John Y. T., 445
Smith, Luther, 87
Snively, Jacob, 191
Snyder, Col. D. H., 253
Society of New Mexico Painters, 434
soil: in Coastal Plains, 10; of the Llano Estacado, 15; of Colorado Plateau, 19
Soil Conservation Service, 320
Sonora, Mexico, 65, 66
Sonnichsen, C. L., 462
"Sooners," 280
"sotol knockers," 319
Southerland, Robert L., 421
Southern Methodist University, 421–2, 454
Southern Pacific Railroad: route of, 200; importance of, 217; in New Mexico and Arizona, 287
Southern Rockies Province, 16–18
South Pass–Humboldt River route, to California, 201
South Plains, 12–16
Southwest, distinctive features of, 3–21, 462–3
Southwest Review, The, 422, 431
Spaniards: in Basin and Range Province, 21; unable to control Apaches, 33; influence on Yumas, 34; and Plains Indians, 36; build missions, 41, 72; efforts to convert Karankawas, 42; infiltration of in Indian land, 43; come to Southwest, 44–66; seek route to India, 45; Pineda, 45–

Index

Spaniards (*continued*)
  6; Garay, 46, 47; Fray Marcos, 53–6; missionaries, 53–6, 59–66 *passim*; search for Quivira, 57–8; capture ship, 69; compete with French in Texas, 72–5; in New Mexico, 76–80; rivalry ends, 84; capture Anglo-Americans, 88–9; thwart explorers, 91; in conquest of Texas, 96–8; search for gold, 175; bring in livestock, 243, 259, 335; discouraged by desert, 315; in Tucson, 443; found San Antonio, 458
Spanish-Americans: in Southwest, 5–7; as voters, 393, 395, 400, 403–4, 497
Spindletop (oil well), 338, 339
stage coaches: in early Texas, 140; at Tucson, 192; to Pacific, 198, 202–3; route chosen, 203; time limit, 204; gold and silver banned on, 205; first run of, 205–6; types of, 209; methods of travel, 209–11
stage stations: established, 204; on California route, 205, 206; food at, 208, 210; description of, 210–11
Staked Plains: Marcy on, 185; on cattle trail, 252; *see also* Llano Estacado
stampedes, 247, 248
statehood: Texas, 125–30, 268; New Mexico, 268–9, 284, 287–9; Arizona, 268–9, 284, 287–9; Oklahoma, 283–5
steamboats, in Texas, 140
Steinbeck, John, 318, 428
Sterling, Gov. Ross (Texas), 371
Stevens, Lawrence Terry, 427
Stevenson, Adlai, 379, 420
Stevenson, Gov. Coke R. (Texas), 378
Stockton, Commodore R. F., 171
stockyards, in Fort Worth, 457
streets, in early Texas towns, 138
"suitcase" farmers, 317
"Sun People," *see* Yavapai Indians
Supply (steamship for camels), 213
surrealism, 437
Sutter's sawmill, gold at, 176
Swain, Dwight, 430
Swan Land and Cattle Co., 256
Swift, G. F., 246
symphony orchestras: in Southwest, 430; Albuquerque, 441; Tucson, 444; Phoenix, 446; Oklahoma City, 448; Houston, 451; Dallas, 454; San Antonio, 459; El Paso, 462

Tampa Bay, 48
Tanning, Dorothea, 437
Taos, New Mexico: people in, 6; granaries at, 58; early trading center, 93, 94; revolt at, 169–71; as art center, 434; population of, 441
Taos Society of Artists, 434
Taovaya Indians, 40
Tappan, Lt. Col. S. F., 228
tariffs, on cotton, 132, 133
Tawakoni Indians, 40
Taylor, Joseph R., 427

Taylor, Gen. Zachary, 154–62, 180
tenjano, 400
Tejas Indians, 41
Tempe, Ariz., 65
Temple, Texas, 366, 368, 369
Tewa, language of Pueblos, 27
Texarkana, trading post at, 76
Texas: as part of Southwest, 4–12, 14, 15, 18, 19, 21; climate and people, 6; Indians of, 32, 35–43; derivation of name, 41; Spanish interest in, 63–4; settlements listed, 64 n; French and Spaniards compete in, 72–5; colonization in, 75, 99–102, 110–14; migration of Anglo-Americans to, 87; wild horses in, 87–8; early explorers in, 88–9, 95; conquest of, 96–9; racial conflict in, 107–8; slavery in, 108–9; religious toleration in, 109–10; advertisements of, 110, 111; Mexico's fears for, 111–14; war with Mexico, 114–23; annexation of, 125–30, 152–65; Republic of, 131–51, 450; population of, 187; role of in Civil War, 219, 221–41; conquest of New Mexico, 224–30; in Indian Territory, 232–8; post-war years in, 241; cattle industry, 243–59; sheep industry, 262–5, 267; attitude toward Oklahoma, 269; population of Indians in, 290; reservations in, 293–4, 296, 297; climate of, 313–33 *passim*; unattractive to Spaniards, 335; population in, 336, 340–1, 344, 345; growth of industry, 338, 348–52; oil in, 338–9, 349; taxes in, 351; politics in, 361, 364, 365–80; reapportionment in, 364–5; picture of people, 414–15; millionaires in, 415–17; books, 418; newspapers, 418–19; University, 419–20; foundations, 420–1; schools, 421–2; artists and writers, 422–5; cities of, 450–62
Texas Christian University, 456
Texas City, Texas, 451
Texas Observer, The, 147 n, 327, 418
Texas Pacific Railroad, route of, 200
Texas Rangers: in Wool's army, 163; skirmishes of, 226–7; surrender of, 239; and Indians, 294; subjects for books, 423
"Texas Rose," 373
Texas Technological College, 379
Texas Trail, 248
Texas Western College, 462
theater: in early Texas, 144, 150; Albuquerque, 441; Tucson, 444; Phoenix, 446; Mummers in Oklahoma City, 448; Tulsa, 450; Houston, 451; Margot Jones in Dallas, 454; Casa Mañana in Fort Worth, 456; San Antonio, 459; El Paso, 462
Thomas Gilcrease Institute of American History and Art, 449–50
Thornton, Capt. S. B., 158
"Those Who Have Vanished," *see* Hohokan Indians

Index

Tiguex, N.M., 57, 58
Tingley, Gov. Clyde (New Mexico), 398
Tinker Air Force Depot (Oklahoma City), 341, 347, 447
Tipton, Mo., 205-8
Tlascaltecan Indians, 75
Tombstone, Arizona, 443
tornadoes, of Rolling Plains, 13
Torrance County, N.M., effect of drought on, 327
tourists: in Arizona and New Mexico, 20; in Oklahoma, 347-8; in Arizona, 356; in Albuquerque, 441; in Santa Fe, 442; in Tucson, 444; in Phoenix, 445, 446; in San Antonio, 458, 460; at El Paso, 461
towns: cattle shipping points, 248-51; rise on lake bed, 328; *see also individual towns and cities*
Townsend, Francis E., 386
traders, French to Santa Fe, 80-1; *see also* fur traders
trail driving: technique of, 246-7; troubles of, 247-9, 255; cow towns, 249-51; end of, 253, 255
"Trail of Tears," 271
trails: Santa Fe, 177; Oregon, 177; cattle, 248-53
transportation: in Texas Republic, 139-41; to Pacific Coast, 197-217; proposed railroads, 199-200; proposed wagon roads, 200-3; Overland stages, 203-11; camels, 211-17; railroads, 217
Travis, William Barrett, 117-18, 120, 121
treaties, with Indians after Civil War, 238
Treaty of Guadalupe Hidalgo: 165, 174, 187, 188-9, 298
Treaty of Velasco, 123, 155
tree rings: study of, 22-3; and history, 25; and climate, 26; show cycles, 313
Tree-Ring Research, Laboratory of, 435
trees: in Coastal Plains, 11; die from drought, 327
Trinity River, 10, 453, 456
Trist, Nicholas, 188
Truman, Harry S, 360-1, 388, 402
Tubac, Arizona: silver mined near, 190; description of, 191; end of, 191 *n;* mission moved, 443
Tucson, Arizona: missionaries to, 65; added to Arizona, 192; description of, 192-3; importance of stage to, 207; in Civil War, 229-30; effects of irrigation on, 322; electronics plant at, 341; other industries at, 354-5; new interest in, 356; mission near, 431; Community Playhouse, 436; population of, 443, 444; early history of, 443-4; industry and culture of, 444
Tule Canyon, erosion, 15

Tulsa, Oklahoma: as art center, 427; population of, 448, 449; industry of, 448-9; early history of, 449; University, 449; culture of, 449-50; Philharmonic Orchestra, 450
Turk, the (El Turko), 57, 58
Turner, Gov. Roy J. (Oklahoma), 386
Twain, Mark, 208, 210
Twiggs, Gen. D. E., 223
Twin Territories, 284, 285
Tyler, Pres. John, 128-9

Ugartechea, Domingo de, 119
Unassigned Lands, 276-9, 282-3
Underhill, Ruth M., on Navajos, 307 *n*
United Nations, 362
United States Weather Bureau, 313, 314
universities, in Texas Republic, 146-7
University of Arizona, 422, 435-6, 444
University of New Mexico: and Indians, 299, 300; Summer Lecture Series, 441; reputation of, 431-2
University of Oklahoma: under Murray, 385; DeGolyer at, 416; DeGolyer Collection at, 417; Phi Beta Kappa at, 422; University Press, 425-6; academic freedom, 426; artists, 427-8; Phillips Collection, 428; Professional School of Writing, 428, 429-30; historians, 429-30; proximity to Oklahoma City, 448
University of St. Thomas, 451
University of Texas: and Gov. Ferguson, 368-9; in reign of O'Daniel, 375; newspaper, 419; academic standing, 419-20, 421; Phi Beta Kappa at, 422; Dobie at, 423
University Presses: Texas, 421; Southern Methodist, 422; Oklahoma, 425-6; New Mexico, 431
Upshur, Abel, 129
uranium, 19, 341, 354, 358, 359
Utah, as part of Southwest, 4
Ute Indians, 19, 77
Uto-Aztecan Indians, 29

Valverde, Gov. Antonio de (New Mexico), 76-9
Valverde, battle at, 226, 227
Van Buren, Pres. Martin, on annexation of Texas, 126
Van de Mark, Dorothy, *quoted,* 309
Van Zandt, Isaac, 129
vaquero, 244, 391
Vargas, Gov. Diego de, 63
vegetation: in Coastal Plains, 11; of Rolling Plains, 13; on Edwards Plateau, 16; of Southern Rockies Province, 17; of Colorado Plateau, 19
Vehlein, Joseph, 101
Vera Cruz, Mexico, 45
Vestal, Stanley, 428; *see also* Campbell, Walter S.
Victorio (Apache chief), 33, 286, 304
Villa de Albuquerque, 440

xviii

Index

Villalobos, Gregory de, 243
Villasur, Capt. Pedro, 78
Villita, La (San Antonio), 459
Virgin River, 92
voyageurs, 69, 76, 80

Waco, Texas: Balcones Fault at, 9; factories at, 341; growth of, 462
Waco Indians, 40
wagon roads, 201
wagon trains, to Santa Fe, 94
Wah'Kon-Tah, 428
Wallace, Henry A., 402
Wallace, Gov. Lew (New Mexico), 286
Wallace, William Alexander ("Big Foot"), 162
Walter, Paul A. F., 27
Wardell, Morris L., on Indian losses in Civil War, 273 *n*
Wardlaw, Frank, 421
War of 1812, influence on expansion, 42
Washington-on-the-Brazos, convention at, 121
water: underground supply, 15, 322, 328, 331; in Basin and Range, 20; on road to California, 179; in quote, 271; shortage of, 312–33; rationing, 328; supply for cities, 328–31; plans for shortage, 331–3; legislation on, 362–4
Watie, Stand, 235–7
Waugh, John C., quoted, 406
Wayne, Maj. Henry C., 212–13
Weadock, Jack, 436
wealth, in Texas, 414–17, 420
weapons: of Anasazi, 23; development of, 24; of Lipans and Mescaleros, 32; of Chiricahuas, 33; of Garay's men, 47; of Coronado's party, 55; sale of to Indians, 82
Webb, Walter Prescott: on climate and geography of Southwest, 8; on influence of Plains Indians, 35–6; on deserts, 314–16; on water supply, 331–2; Texas historian, 424–5
Weller, Sen. John B., 201
Wellman, Paul, 225 *n*, 252 *n*
Wells-Fargo, 211
Western Trail (cattle), 250, 251, 253
"wetbacks," 265–6, 267
Wharton, William H., 125–6
wheat: center at Amarillo, 15; and drought, 217–18; prices of, 317, 321; in Texas and Oklahoma, 364; at Fort Worth, 457
Wheeler Peak, 17
Whipple, Lt. A. W.: route of, 186 *n*, 190, 203; and railroad survey, 199
White, Owen P., 372

White, Stewart Edward, 430
White Sands Desert, 357
White Sands Proving Ground, 441
Whitney, Chauncey, 251
Wichita-Caddo Reservation, 276, 296, 297
Wichita Falls, Texas, 462
Wichita Indians: territory of, 36; description of, 40; alliance with French, 76; friendly to French, 82; and removal Indians, 105; in Oklahoma, 273
Wild Horse Desert, 154
Wilkinson, James, 89, 90, 92 *n*
Williams, George, 423
Williams, J. R., 423
Williams, J. W., 207 *n*
Will Rogers Memorial, 348
Wilson, John W., 423
Wilson, Logan, 420
Wise, Henry, 128
Wister, Owen, 430
Wood, Leonard, 287
Wool, Gen. John E.: advance of from San Antonio to Parras, 154, 162–3, 168, 172; trail blazed by, 180
wool, production of, 262–5
Woolaroc Museum, 348, 427, 428
Wool Growers Association, 263
"woollies," *see* sheep and goats
Worth, Gen. William J., 456
Wright, Rev. Allen, 269 *n*
Wright, Frank Lloyd, 6, 431
Wright, Harold Bell, 430
Wright, Muriel, 429
Wyandotte Indians, 274
Wyllys, Rufus Kay, 188

XIT Ranch, 253–6

Yale University, buys Texas manuscripts, 416
Yamparika Indians, 36–7
Yarborough, Ralph, 379, 389, 452, 461
Yavapai Indians, 34 *n*, 66, 305
Young, Brigham, 166
Yscani Indians, 40
Yucatán, 45
Yuma, Arizona: rainfall at, 20; mining town, 191–2; confusion in name, 192 *n*; cotton fields near, 341; growth of, 355
Yuma Indians: 29, 34 *n*, 302; description of, 34–5; met by Garcés, 65; kill settlers, 66

Zavala, Lorenzo de, 101
Zuñi Indians: 19, 27; language of, 27; visited by Spaniards, 60; silver work of, 301

A Note About the Author

W. Eugene Hollon, *a professor of history at the University of Oklahoma, was born in Commerce, Texas, 1913. He was educated at East Texas State Teachers College and at the University of Texas. After several years of teaching school in Texas, he joined the faculty of the University of Oklahoma in 1945. He is the author of* The Lost Pathfinder, Zebulon Montgomery Pike (*1949*) *and* Beyond the Cross Timbers, The Travels of Randolph B. Marcy (*1955*), *and* William Bollaert's Texas (*1956*).

March 1961

A NOTE ON THE TYPE

THE TEXT OF THIS BOOK was set on the Linotype in a new face called PRIMER, designed by RUDOLPH RUZICKA, earlier responsible for the design of Fairfield and Fairfield Medium, Linotype faces whose virtues have for some time now been accorded wide recognition.

The complete range of sizes of Primer was first made available in 1954, although the pilot size of 12 point was ready as early as 1951. The design of the face makes general reference to Linotype Century (long a serviceable type, totally lacking in manner or frills of any kind) but brilliantly corrects the characterless quality of that face.

Composed, printed, and bound by KINGSPORT PRESS, INC., Kingsport, Tenn. Paper manufactured by S. D. WARREN CO., Boston. Typography and binding design by WARREN CHAPPELL.